AIDA Europe Research Series on Insurance Law and Regulation

Volume 3

The AIDA Europe Research Series on Insurance Law and Regulation is the first book series of its kind and area of specialization. It comprises volumes on topics researched and written with an international, comparative or European perspective.

The regulatory response to the financial crisis in 2008 has pushed towards the adoption of transnational principles and rules also in the field of insurance by encouraging the convergence of national regulations to common regulatory framework. The need for a common legal language emerges to fully understand the process of transnational convergence in place and its impact on national legislation. On the other hand, persisting national peculiarities must be examined in the light of the transnational convergence of rules and concepts. Moreover, new risks, business practices and customers' issues are emerging worldwide, so requiring increasingly global responses.

The scope of the series is to bring together academics, practitioners and policy makers in order to exchange views and approaches to the topics concerned, which are based on the new transnational dimension of insurance law, business and regulation. All contributions are peer reviewed.

More information about this series at http://www.springer.com/series/16331

Pierpaolo Marano • Kyriaki Noussia
Editors

Insurance Distribution Directive

A Legal Analysis

Springer

Editors
Pierpaolo Marano
Department of Legal Studies
Catholic University of the Sacred Heart
Milan, Italy

Kyriaki Noussia
School of Law
University of Exeter
Exeter, UK

ISSN 2662-1770 ISSN 2662-1789 (electronic)
AIDA Europe Research Series on Insurance Law and Regulation
ISBN 978-3-030-52737-2 ISBN 978-3-030-52738-9 (eBook)
https://doi.org/10.1007/978-3-030-52738-9

This Springer imprint is published by the registered company Springer Nature Switzerland AG.
The registered company address is: Gewerbestrasse 11, 6330 Cham, Switzerland

Preface

The Insurance Distribution Directive (IDD) constitutes a piece of the European Union's primary legislation. This book analyses the impact that the IDD has on insurance distributors, that is, insurance intermediaries and insurance undertakings, as well as the market. The main changes introduced by the IDD are examined and thoroughly discussed. This is the first book approaching in a detailed manner the analysis and interpretation of the IDD. It forms a comprehensive legal and regulatory analysis of the changes introduced by the IDD and draws on interrelations between the rules of the Directive and other disciplines that are relevant to the distribution of insurance products. This book discusses various topics related to the interpretation of the IDD in relation to (a) the harmonization achieved under it, (b) the role of the IDD as a benchmark for national legislators, (c) the interplay of the IDD with other regulations and sciences and (d) an empirical analysis of the standardized pre-contractual information document.

One of the key objectives of the IDD was to further facilitate cross-border activities of insurance intermediaries. The new rules on the freedom to provide services and freedom of establishment are analysed with the aim to understand whether the IDD has led or will lead to more market integration. The principle of proportionality is examined. Whilst the presumption is that all the measures adopted in the IDD are proportional to the aim of enhanced customer protection, in reality proportionality in the IDD is put in doubts, as the information duties go beyond what is necessary to achieve the objectives. Product oversight and governance (POG), which forms one of the major innovations introduced by the IDD, is addressed together with the way that POG fits into the overall EU insurance regulation. The impact of the IDD on life insurance and its effect in the insurance industry are also examined. The international character of the life insurance sector and its impact on the implementation of the IDD, which aims at the so-called minimum harmonization, are also addressed. The EU regulatory framework with regard to insurance-based investment products (IBIPs) is analysed as many provisions on IBIPs under the IDD are based on the corresponding rules under MiFID II, even though differences remain.

This book also discusses (a) the principle of ensuring the best interest of customers, (b) the impact of the IDD on insurance companies, because of the fact that distributors are also assessed together and (c) the lessons to be learned from the IDD by other legal regimes. In relation to the latter, the sanctions and other pecuniary measures in other legal regimes, including a comparison with the US law and the micro-insurance regulation of South Africa, are also examined and discussed. Moreover, the impact of the General Data Protection Regulation (GDPR) and the IDD on the EU data protection and insurance distribution laws, as well as data-driven innovations and applications such as 'Telematics' insurance, is examined. Also, the role of IDD as the new EU legal framework for enforcing consumer ADR system in the insurance sector is addressed. In addition, the implications of the introduction of the IDD on distribution risk management and on firm's entire value chain are discussed together with the influence of the new rules on the product management to the insurance undertakings, intermediaries and the insurance market. This book also contains a thorough analysis of the rules regarding the Insurance Product Information Documents mandated in Article 20 of the IDD by making an empirical analysis of several IPIDs.

Academics, regulators, practitioners and students who are interested in the issues of insurance distribution can draw useful insights from the legal and regulatory analysis provided by this book.

Milan, Italy
Exeter, UK
April 2020

Pierpaolo Marano
Kyriaki Noussia

AIDA Europe

AIDA Europe was established in 2007 with the aim of promoting, either directly or through its members, the development of insurance and related laws. It attempts to achieve this, mainly through:

- furtherance of the study and knowledge of international and national insurance law and of related matters;
- proposition of measures aiming at the harmonization of insurance law or the means for resolution of insurance disputes;
- facilitation of exchange of academic know-how between its Members or any other European organizations dealing with insurance-related matters, similar to those of AIDA Europe;
- support of academic work in the field of insurance, e.g. through cooperation with universities or the sponsoring of academic research and papers.

AIDA Europe organizes conferences mainly geared to the European-based jurisdictions, offering to all interested stakeholders a platform for an open and solution-minded scientific and practice-related dialogue on key developments in the area of insurance, reinsurance and related law and thus supporting its members in their respective endeavours. Conferences are open to all stakeholders and regularly attract representatives from the insurance sector, academia, private practice, regulatory authorities or law-making bodies.

AIDA Europe also maintains a keen focus on supporting the development of young academic talents by sponsoring academic work and by inviting young academics to its conferences. AIDA Europe's Scientific Committee, which supports AIDA Europe through the scientific agenda setting, also manages AIDA Europe's Calls for Papers.

AIDA Europe is a non-profit organization, pursuing altruistic goals, and has its seat in Zurich, Switzerland. Its events are open to all interested parties. For further information, please see https://aidainsurance.org/regional-groupings/aida-europe.

Contents

Abbreviations

CEIOPS	Committee of European Insurance and Occupational Pensions Supervisors
EIOPA	European Insurance and Occupational Pensions Authority
ESAs	European Supervisory Authorities
EU	European Union
FAIS	Financial Advisory and Intermediary Services Act
FOE	Freedom of establishment
FOS	Freedom to provide services/Freedom of services
IA	Insurance Act
IAIS	International Association of Insurance Supervisors
IDD	Directive (EU) 2016/97 of the European Parliament and of the Council of 20 January 2016 on insurance distribution (recast)
IDD	Insurance Distribution Directive
IMD	Directive 2002/92/EC of the European Parliament and of the Council of 9 December 2002 on insurance mediation
IMD	Insurance Mediation Directive
Implementing Regulation	Commission Implementing Regulation (EU) 2017/1469 of 11 August 2017 laying down a standardised presentation format for the insurance product information document
IPID	Insurance Product Information Document
NCA	National Credit Act
PPRs	Policyholder Protection Rules

Part I
The Harmonization Achieved under the Insurance Distribution Directive

Insurance Distribution Directive and Cross-Border Activities by Insurance Intermediaries in the EU

Isabelle Audigier

1 Introduction

The Insurance Distribution Directive (IDD[1]) came into force on 22 February 2016 and repealed the Insurance Mediation Directive (IMD[2]). EU Member States were required to implement it into their national laws by 1 July 2018 and had to apply their national rules from 1 October 2018.

Despite the European passport granted to insurance intermediaries by the IMD in 2002, the single market for insurance distribution remained very limited and fragmented. One of the key objectives of the IDD was therefore to further facilitate cross-border activities of insurance intermediaries, thus promoting the emergence of a genuine Single Market in insurance services.[3]

This Chapter will present the new rules on the freedom to provide services (FOS) and freedom of establishment (FOE) introduced by Chapter III of the IDD and by EIOPA[4] measures that apply to insurance intermediaries and ancillary intermediaries and will explain how they have partly simplified and clarified the procedure to

[1]Directive 2016/97 of the European Parliament and of the Council of 20 January 2016 on insurance distribution.

[2]Directive 2002/92/EC of the European Parliament and of the Council of 9 December 2002 on insurance mediation.

[3]The text is based on Article 53 (1) and Article 62 of the Treaty on the functioning of the European Union (TFEU), that is to say, mutual recognition of diplomas in case of freedom of establishment and restrictions to freedom to provide services.

[4]European Insurance and occupational pensions authority.

I. Audigier (✉)
BIPAR (The European Federation of Insurance and Investment Intermediaries), Brussels, Belgium
e-mail: ia@bipar.eu

P. Marano, K. Noussia (eds.), *Insurance Distribution Directive*, AIDA Europe Research Series on Insurance Law and Regulation 3,
https://doi.org/10.1007/978-3-030-52738-9_1

operate cross-borders. The restrictions by the general good provisions of EU Member States will be explained, on the basis of recent reports provided by the Commission and EIOPA.

It will also detail the new division of competence between the home and host Member State competent authorities for ensuring intermediaries' compliance with the IDD requirements (in particular in the context of the new concept of primary place of business and in other exceptional situations) and will explain how this new balance could impact intermediaries' passporting rights. It will also focus on residual host Member States powers in some exceptional situations.

Finally, it will explore whether the IDD has led or will lead to more market integration. Part III will also briefly analyse the impact of 'Brexit', that is, the leaving of the EU by the United Kingdom, on cross-border activities of insurance intermediaries.

2 Simpler and Clearer Rules for Cross Border Activities by Insurance Intermediaries?

2.1 Some Background

In 2002, the European legislature explained that a first step to facilitate the exercise of freedom of establishment and freedom to provide services[5] for insurance agents and brokers had been made by the 1976 Directive,[6] followed by the 1991 Commission Recommendation[7,8] that largely harmonised national provisions on professional requirements and registration of insurance intermediaries. However, barriers to the taking up and pursuit of the activities of insurance and reinsurance intermediaries in the internal market remained, and the inability for the latter to operate freely

[5]The freedom to provide services (FOS) and the freedom of establishment (FOE) are two of the fundamental freedoms existing between EU Member States, the others being the free movement of goods, persons and capital. Pursuant to Articles 56 to 62 of the Treaty on the Functioning of the European Union (TFEU), restrictions on the freedom to provide services within the Union are prohibited in respect of nationals of Member States who are established in a Member State other than that of the person for whom the services are intended. Likewise, pursuant to Articles 49 to 55 of TFEU, restrictions on the freedom of establishment of nationals of a Member State in the territory of another Member State are prohibited. The European Court of Justice has over the years extensively interpreted the two notions of FOS and FOE, establishing several principles interpreting the basic EU concepts.

[6]Council Directive 77/92/EEC of 13 December 1976 on measures to facilitate the effective exercise of freedom of establishment and freedom to provide services in respect of the activities of insurance agents and brokers.

[7]Commission Recommendation 92/48/EEC of 18 December 1991 on insurance intermediaries.

[8]Recitals 2 and 4, IMD.

throughout the Community hindered the proper functioning of the single market in insurance.[9]

In practice, an insurance intermediary who was not a member of an international network and who wanted to operate cross-border had to get several documents to make himself known in all concerned host EU member States and in some cases comply sometimes with their whole national legislation. It was a "dive in troubled waters".[10]

The IMD took a second step and introduced a single passport for insurance intermediaries[11]: it provided a registration system for all insurance intermediaries based on a whole range of binding professional requirements aimed at enhancing consumer protection in insurance matters but also at facilitating intermediaries' cross-border activities. Registered insurance intermediaries were to be allowed to take up and pursue the activity of insurance mediation within the EU by means of both freedom of establishment and of services[12] after going through a notification procedure.[13]

With the IMD, insurance intermediaries were at last given the legal framework to play their role as the essential accompanying factor to the single licence scheme for insurance companies, which was introduced in July 1994.

It is interesting to recall that the IMD was the outcome of a very difficult compromise between the EU Member States due to the significant disparities that existed between the national legislations, some very developed (France and Spain for example) and some virtually non existent (for example, Germany).

The IMD provisions on cross-border notifications were further clarified in 2006 by the CEIOPS (now EIOPA) Luxembourg Protocol[14] and then in 2008 by its revised version. The revised Protocol introduced an important "common understanding of freedom to provide services" by intermediaries. The protocol bound the existing CEIOPS members.

The Commission systematically plans evaluations of all adopted European legislation. In 2005 the Commission services initiated an implementation check of the

[9]Recitals 5 and 7, IMD.

[10]B. Debuisson, *La distribution transfrontalière des produits d'assurance. Plongée en eaux troubles*, Université Catholique de Louvain, 1996 - Doc 96/26.

[11]As defined by Article 2.5, IMD.

[12]Article 3, IMD.

[13]Article 6, IMD.

[14]On 28 April 2006 the Committee of European Insurance and Occupational Pensions Supervisors (CEIOPS) published the Luxembourg Protocol relating to the cooperation of national supervisors in particular concerning the Insurance Mediation Directive (*2002/92/EC*). The Protocol developed the procedure for the exchange of information and co-operation in the supervision of insurance intermediaries' cross-border activities. It also promoted a consistent implementation of the registration and notification procedures by the presentation in its annex with special templates or standardised forms for those procedures. Its annexes also included a list of competent authorities for making and receiving notifications and a list of national bodies for out-of-court settlement of complaints.

IMD and in May 2007, in its Green Paper on Retail Financial Services in the Single Market, the Commission explained that it was planning a complete review of the IMD in 2008/2009: "*the IMD will be reviewed to ensure it is achieving its objectives of protecting consumers while promoting the Single insurance market*". Also, Recital 139 of Solvency II Directive[15] required the European Commission to put forward "*as soon as possible and in any event by the end of 2010*", a proposal for the revision of the IMD, "*taking into account the consequences of the Directive for policyholders*". As a first step the Commission asked CEIOPS to examine how the IMD had been implemented. This report was used as a basis for the revision of the IMD.

In July 2012, the Commission adopted a proposal for a Directive amending the IMD. One of the objectives of the proposal was to make it "*easier for intermediaries to operate cross-border, thus promoting the emergence of a real internal market in insurance services*".[16] It proposed introducing a simpler notification process for intermediaries and ancillary intermediaries going cross-border as well as a centralized registration system and to clarify the application of the Treaty principles regarding the FOE and the FOS. We will see that the final text of the IDD that was adopted on 20 January 2016, after a four-year process by the two EU legislators, appears however to offer less clarity than intended.

The IDD has a wider scope than the IMD and applies to all insurance distributors, including insurance undertakings. However, the latter do not have to register[17] under

[15]Directive 2009/138/EC of the European Parliament and of the Council of 25 November 2009 on the taking-up and pursuit of the business of Insurance and Reinsurance (Solvency II). Recital 139 provides: "*Adoption of this Directive changes the risk profile of the insurance company vis-à-vis the policy holder. The Commission should as soon as possible and in any event by the end of 2010 put forward a proposal for the revision of Directive 2002/92/EC of the European Parliament and of the Council of 9 December 2002 on insurance mediation, taking into account the consequences of this Directive for policy holders*".

[16]In the impact assessment accompanying the proposal, the Commission explained that "*The market for cross-border insurance services in general, irrespective of the means of marketing, is still very limited in the retail insurance sector. Evidence suggests that only global and multinational business insurance intermediaries, serving major and multinational and domestic firms, and providing a wide range of services in addition to traditional brokerage, establish themselves in several Member States. When an intermediary wants to sell insurance products cross border under the freedom to provide services (FOS), it must notify its intention to the competent authority of its home member State (which must notify the host Member State) and go through a notification procedure. Several respondents to the public consultation from the insurance industry and insurance intermediaries, as well as EIOPA, acknowledged that there is room for improvement, modernization and increased transparency in this area. There are different approaches to the FOS problem in current EU legislation, all of which appear more favorable than that under IMD 1.*

There is no single EU register for insurance intermediaries where a consumer can easily find information about registered sellers of different insurance products. As a consequence, sellers of insurance products lack easy access to information about how to go cross-border and this has a negative impact on competition in the EU insurance market".

[17]Article 3.1 (2) of the IDD.

the IDD and their passporting rights remain governed by the relevant domestic provisions implementing the Solvency II Directive.

The IDD applies to ancillary intermediaries.[18] Registered ancillary insurance intermediaries under the IDD will be allowed to operate under FOS and FOE. This is the first time this category of intermediaries has been granted a single licence. Under the IDD, ancillary insurance intermediaries are service providers and distributors of goods who distribute insurance products on an ancillary basis. The insurance products they distribute must be complementary to the good or the services they are selling. And they must not cover life assurance or liability risks, unless that cover complements the product or service which the intermediary provides as its principal professional activity.[19] This chapter focuses mainly of the cross-border activities of insurance intermediaries.[20]

2.2 A Simplified and Clearer Notification Procedure?

Under the IMD, once the intermediary had informed its home Member State of its intention to operate cross-border in one or more Member States under FOS or FOE for the first time, the home Member State authority was required, within 1 month of receiving the information, to notify the competent authorities of the relevant host Member States. It had also to advise the applicant intermediary that it had done this. The intermediary could only commence its activities 1 month after the date of notification. The IMD allowed an exemption for the host Member State to be notified.

In practice, in cases where Member States chose to be notified—and they were a majority – this meant that an intermediary had to wait up to 2 months before being allowed to operate across borders. The approach of other Directives was more favourable: under MiFID, for example, an investment firm could go cross-border immediately upon notification by home to host Member States of the firm's intention

[18]Ancillary intermediaries are defined under Article 2(4) of the IDD.

[19]Article 1.3 of the IDD: Ancillary intermediaries are excluded from the IDD where: the insurance they sell covers the risk of breakdown, loss of or damage to the goods or non-use of the service, OR covers damage to or loss of baggage and other risks linked to travel booked with that provider; and where the amount of the premium for the insurance product does not exceed €600. In circumstances where the insurance is complementary to the good or service and the duration of that service is equal to or less than 3 months, the amount of the premium paid per person should not exceed €200.

[20]The notification procedure for ancillary intermediaries is similar to the one for insurance intermediaries. It is however important to note that the IDD requirements ancillary intermediaries need to comply with to be registered under the IDD (when not exempted by Article 1) differ slightly from the one of insurance intermediaries: Adapted appropriate knowledge and ability/CPD (can be proven by certificate), Good repute/clean record, PI cover (level established by MS according to nature of product and activity/Financial capacity, to act in the best interests of customers, no remuneration that conflicts with the duty to act in the best interests of customers, disclosure of nature and basis of remuneration, IPID to customer (non-life).

to passport under FOS. This waiting period was sometimes problematic in a FOS context in particular, where intermediaries need to act sometimes quickly to cover their clients with establishment and exposure in other Member States.

In 2006—and again in 2008—this notification procedure was further clarified by the CEIOPS Luxembourg Protocol, and documents used to make the necessary notifications were harmonised.[21] Building on the Protocol and the outcome of various consultations of the industry and Member States by the Commission, the IDD, in two separate articles (Articles 4 and 6), details different notification requirements for FOS and FOE activities.

Before starting business under FOS in another EU Member State for the first time, an intermediary must notify its home Member State competent authority of its intention to do so. It must communicate the following information[22] to its home Member State: its name, address, registration number, the host Member State where it intends to operate, the category of intermediary (and name of insurer represented if appropriate) and the relevant classes of insurance. The home Member State communicates this within 1 month to the host member state competent authority concerned (which must acknowledge receipt without delay) and informs the intermediary about it. The home Member States must also inform the intermediary that, provided it complies with the general good provisions of the host Member States that are available on EIOPA and the host Member State websites, it can start its business. Any changes will have to be communicated by the intermediary to its home Member State that will communicate it to the host Member State.

In addition to the above requirements, EIOPA, in its 2018 Decision on the cooperation of the competent authorities with regard to the IDD (updated Luxembourg Protocol),[23] states that the notification shall also specify the name of the

[21]Information such as for example the precise name of the intermediary, its address, the category it belongs to, the name of the insurer the intermediary is authorised to work for (if applicable), the classes of insurance for which the intermediary is authorised or the address of the online register in which details about the intermediary may be found, had to be included in the notification form transmitted by the home MS to the host MS. It was further clarified that all the documents had to be written in English or in another language agreed upon by the authorities concerned and that the authority of the host Member State must acknowledge receipt of the documents without undue delay by letter.

[22]Article 4(1), IDD.

[23]28 September 2018 EIOPA Decision of the Board of Supervisors on the cooperation of the competent authorities of the Member States of the European Economic Area with regard to Directive (EU) 2016/97 of the European Parliament and of the Council of 20 January 2016 on insurance distribution—EIOPA-BoS/18-340—The revision was needed to align CEIOPS (EIOPA)'s Luxembourg Protocol with the new IDD provisions (broader scope than the IMD, new chapter Freedom to Provide Services (FOS) and Freedom of Establishment (FOE), enhancement of exchange of information and cooperation between national competent authorities in registration and notification procedures etc.).

According to Article 2 of the Decision, it applies to all national authorities competent for the supervision of insurance and reinsurance distributors, which are Members of EIOPA and to the EEA EFTA Members of the Board of Supervisors of EIOPA to the extent to which the IDD is binding on them.

current home competent authority, if different from the registration authority, the address of the online register in which details about the intermediary may be found and where available, the nature of the risks and commitments which will be covered by the insurance contracts which the intermediary intends to distribute in the host Member State.

Where the intermediary intends to operate, entirely or principally, in other Member State(s) on a FOS basis, the home competent authority shall consider communicating any other available information to allow the host competent authority to have a deeper knowledge of the FOS activity and facilitate awareness for ongoing supervision. An example of additional information that could be provided by the home competent authority to the host competent authority could be the provision of any available information resulting from discussions with intermediary about its business strategy and how its FOS activity fits into that strategy. While such information can be useful from a supervisory perspective, they may however, not always be available at the time they are being requested.

Any changes also have to be communicated by the intermediary to its home Member State that will communicate it to the host Member State. In its Decision, EIOPA explains that this could for example include the change of intention to provide insurance distribution activities by FOS in a specific host Member State in the future or the intermediary's removal from the register in its home Member State.

The removal of the "waiting period" of 1 month after the date of notification as well as the exemption for Member States not to be informed, are clearly improvements compared to the IMD approach. They facilitate procedure for activities under FOS and are in line with the objectives of the IDD. These two provisions had given rise to two problems: the timing for commencement of operations under FOS that was driven by the position of the host member State (not all Member States agreed to be notified) and the wait itself for an intermediary needing to insure its client's activities in a host Member State, for another month before able to do so.

It is important to note that the EIOPA Decision explains that the intermediary has to notify its intention to do business under FOS only in the Member State where the policyholder is established or has his residence, also in the case where the policyholder acts on behalf of different insureds and/or risks established or situated in one or more other Member States.[24] This key explanatory narrative was included in the 2008 revised version of the CEIOPS Luxembourg Protocol and one can but regret that it was not transposed (at least into recitals) in the IMD. The clarity and legal certainty it brings are essential for cross-border activities.

As far as the IDD notification procedure to operate under FOE is concerned, the intermediary has to provide the same information as for the FOS notification, with in addition the address in the host member State from which documents may obtained and the name of any person responsible for the management of the branch or permanent presence. It still needs to wait up to 2 months before starting its activities in the concerned host Member States. During the second month, the host Member

[24]Section 2.2.1 of the EIOPA Decision, page 14.

State must communicate the general good provisions that are applicable in its territory to the home Member State of the intermediary and that latter authority must then inform the intermediary about it and that it can commence business in the host Member State territory, provided it complies with those legal provisions.

Any changes will have to be communicated by the intermediary to its home member state that will communicate it to the host member state. In its Decision, EIOPA explains that this could include the change of intention to provide insurance distribution activities on the territory of the host Member State through a branch or permanent presence or the intermediary's removal from the register in its home Member State.

The differentiation between the notification procedure for FOS and FOE activities, the harmonisation of information to be provided to the home Member State by intermediaries bring more clarity for all parties concerned. The information was already contained in the CEIOPS Luxembourg Protocol but that was less binding on the Member States. Also, the IDD addresses the changes made to notifications—this was only addressed in the CEIOPS Luxembourg Protocol—to ensure records are fully up to date. This is in line with better consumer protection which is one of the objectives of the IDD. One could regret that the passport notifications do not require the intermediary, who has applied for a passport to operate cross-border, to inform the concerned competent authorities whether it really does so. From a consumer protection and supervision point of view, it would be useful to know who is actually using the passport, and who is not. It is interesting to note that under the Solvency II Directive, insurance undertakings are required to report to their supervisory authority the amount of transactions carried out under the right of establishment and those carried out under the freedom to provide services, in host Member States.[25]

As mentioned earlier, the single passport under the IMD and now under the IDD is derived from the intermediary's registration in its home Member State. Like the IMD, the IDD requires the national registers to indicate the Member States in which "their" intermediaries conduct business under FOE or FOS. The IDD[26] also requires EIOPA to establish, publish on its website and keep up to date a single electronic register containing records of insurance intermediaries which have notified to carry on cross-border business under FOE or FOS. The register must contain links to, and be accessible from, the website of each of the Member States' competent authorities.

Such a register, when available, will allow private but also commercial clients to quickly and easily find information about registered intermediaries operating cross-border in their respective countries. This is a positive improvement. For the time being EIOPA has established on its website a page with hyperlinks to national registers or single information points.[27] EIOPA explains that its website serves as a provisional database of hyperlinks to national registers and that "it is assessing the

[25] Article 159, Solvency II Directive.

[26] Article 3(4), IDD.

[27] https://eiopa.europa.eu/Pages/Consumer-Protection/Single-electronic-register-for-cross-border-business.aspx.

most adequate long-term approach towards an online register by analogy to existing EIOPA registers to further enhance transparency and facilitate cross-border trade".

If it appears that the IDD has brought some much-needed and useful changes to the notification procedures, it has however missed an important opportunity that was "to clarify intermediaries' FOS/FOE activities", despite the fact that was one of the main objectives of the EU text.

2.3 *No Clarification Regarding the Triggering Element of Cross Border Activities*

The general objectives of the revision of the IMD were consumer protection, undistorted competition and market integration.

In the impact assessment accompanying the proposal for revision of the IMD, the Commission explained that one of the following preferred option would help addressing these objectives as "*they involve slight costs and may trigger more cross-border trade*": "*option 2 would incorporate definitions already existing in the Luxembourg Protocol in the IMD (...). This option would clarify the application of Treaty principles regarding the FOE and the FOS and introduce some enforcement rules linked to those freedoms, based on the MIFID II.*" It further explained that "*clarification of the definitions of FOE and FOS would render the cross-border process more effective*".

However, there is no recital or article in the IMD II proposal, nor later in the adopted IDD, that defines these activities. This a matter of regret. For the sake of legal certainty it is necessary to have a clear description of the triggering element of the FOS activities of an intermediary (is it the location of the intermediary? of the client? of the risk? both?) because general good rules and stricter information requirements of the host Member State may have to be complied with by intermediaries when they are considered to be carrying out FOS activities in that Member State.

In addition, because of the new distribution of powers between host and home supervisors in the IDD, Member States can in certain cases impose national requirements upon intermediaries working on a FOS basis (for example, in the case of advice being mandatory for the sale of any insurance products in Member States like France[28]). Therefore, it is necessary for the intermediary, but also for the supervisory authority and the consumer or client to know when intermediaries' activities are considered as FOS activities.

It is equally important for the same reasons to clearly describe the triggering element of the FOE activities of an intermediary.

Even if the draft text of the IDD included at one point during the trilogue phase, the useful EIOPA decision's (updated Luxembourg Protocol) definition of the

[28]Article 22.2, IDD.

triggering element of an intermediary's FOS activity (see below), unfortunately no agreement could be reached to keep the definition in the final text of the Directive. The Commission Legal Services advised against it explaining that an EU Directive—that is secondary legislation—could not contain such a definition and that freedom of services can only be defined in the Treaty. This was a surprising position as clarity on territorial criteria was for example introduced by the Solvency II Directive regarding FOS business of insurers.[29]

2.4 EIOPA Clarifications

FOS and FOE need to be distinguished, for it makes a difference whether an insurance intermediary is acting under one or the other concept with respect to, for example, notification requirements (see above) or possible restrictions for the general good (see below).

In the absence of a judicial or regulatory definition of when an intermediary is likely to be pursuing cross-border activities under FOS, reference has been made since 2006 to the common understanding of "freedom to provide services"[30] of the CEIOPS Luxembourg Protocol that was replaced in September 2018 by the EIOPA Decision. The clarifications contained in the CEIOPS Luxembourg Protocol on the triggering element of insurance intermediaries' cross-border activities under FOS remained in the Decision of EIOPA, slightly adapted to include ancillary intermediaries.

EIOPA understands freedom to provide services in the case of intermediary to mean:

> An Intermediary or Ancillary Intermediary is operating under freedom to provide services ("FOS") if it intends to provide a policyholder, who is established in a Member State different from the one where the Intermediary or Ancillary Intermediary is registered, with an insurance contract relating to a risk situated in a Member State different from the Member State where the Intermediary or Ancillary Intermediary is registered.[31]

[29]Under Article 13(9) the host Member State, i.e. the Member State of the provision of services, is the Member State of the commitment (life insurance) or the Member State in which the risk is situated (non-life insurance). In other words, an insurer is providing services under FOS if the risk/commitment is situated in another Member State.

[30]This common understanding was presented in the revised CEIOPS Luxembourg Protocol as *"the most workable definition in line with the objectives of the IMD regarding the intention of the intermediary, the creation of the Single Market and consumer protection"* – See footnote 6 to point 2.2.3 of the Protocol.

[31]EIOPA decision provides a non-exhaustive list of examples regarding activity carried on under FoS:

- An Intermediary or Ancillary Intermediary is actively marketing, providing insurance distribution services or seeking business from a customer resident or established in another Member State.

In practice, this means for example that an intermediary having its office in Antwerp and intending to procure property insurance to a Belgian client with regard to the client's holiday house in the Netherlands, would not provide cross-border mediation services in the Netherlands as only the risk to be covered is situated in another Member State, whereas the client has his habitual residence in Belgium.

However, an intermediary with its office in Karlsruhe (Germany) and intending to procure fire insurance to a French client in Strasbourg (France), would be providing cross-border mediation services in France. It would have to notify his intention to carry out cross-border business into France under FOS.

Even though such definition is not binding upon the courts, it can be expected to be adhered to by the Competent Authorities provided no overruling definition has been adopted by legislation or a Community Court. Depending on national legislation implementing the IDD, local courts could also rule that the location of the client is the only criteria as to when national general good rules apply to a foreign insurance intermediary providing insurance distribution services to a local client.[32] Article 22 of the IDD on information exemptions and flexibility clause also seems to refer to that unique criteria.

In their July 2019 report on cross-border supervision of retail financial services,[33] the European Supervisory Authorities (ESAs) admit that they "*have noticed that the legislation reviewed lacks clear criteria for determining the location where the*

- An Intermediary or Ancillary Intermediary asks for and organises on its own initiative meetings with customers established in another Member State.
- Regarding advertisement: an Intermediary or Ancillary Intermediary gives/sends information on specific products, conditions etc. to selected groups of customers established in a given country/ in specific languages of some Member States etc. Here the advertisement has an active character, the intention of the Intermediary or Ancillary Intermediary to contact customers in another Member State is clear.
- Regarding electronic distance or distance marketing activities: If the content of the website of an Intermediary or Ancillary Intermediary is general and only in the language of the Member State of the Intermediary or Ancillary Intermediary, if it is not addressed to a specific group of customers or customers in specific Member States and when the customer is not able to directly or indirectly conclude an insurance contract using a website or other media, then the Intermediary or Ancillary Intermediary cannot be considered as actively seeking these customers and therefore cannot be considered as having the intention to do FoS in the Member State, where those customers are established. If an Intermediary or Ancillary Intermediary is contacted by those customers, it will not be considered as an intention to write business under FoS in the Member State of residence or of establishment of these customers.
- Where an Intermediary or Ancillary Intermediary opens a branch in another host Member State under freedom of establishment and where this branch sells insurance contracts to residents of the Intermediary's or Ancillary Intermediary's home Member State, it shall not be deemed as being an activity provided under FoS.

[32]BIPAR/Steptoe: The insurance Distribution Directive: A handbook on cross-border insurance distribution by insurance intermediaries—January 2019.

[33]ESAs report on cross-border supervision of retail financial services, 9 July 2019, JC/2019-22—In this report the ESAs carried out a general mapping of the main Level 1 provisions for the different financial institutions operating across borders. The EU directives and regulations that the ESAs have reviewed include amongst others, the IDD, the SII and the MiFID 2.

services is provided, which is key to determining whether there is cross-border provision of services and whether it falls under the FOS and the FOE, and as a consequence, which Competent Authority is responsible for its supervision. This lack of clear criteria is even more problematic when services and products are provided through digital means".

In their conclusions and suggestions for EU co-legislators, the ESAs further explained that they *"are of the view that more clarity on this issue cannot be provided through Level 3 work and that such clarity should be provided by the EU -co-legislators, especially in the light of the growing phenomenon of the digitalization of financial services".*

Although late, the recognition by the ESAs of this key issue is welcome. It is however, quite frustrating to read such a statement when market's associations have been drawing the attention to this lack of clarity for years before the adoption of the IDD and when it seems that action is now required only because it is problematic to services being provided via digital means It is also surprising to see that the ESAs do not believe that clarity on the issue could be brought by level 3 work when EIOPA itself introduced such clarity in its 2018 Decision.

It has always been less challenging to determine whether an intermediary is operating in another EU Member State on a FOE basis, since a FOE activity has a clearer cross-border element. The IDD has also slightly clarified the concept of FOE for IDD purposes: an intermediary is operating under FOE in another Member States if the intermediary establishes a branch—defined in the IDD as "*an agency or a branch of an intermediary located in the territory of a Member State other than the home Member State*"[34]—or a permanent presence that is equivalent to a branch unless the intermediary lawfully sets up such a permanent presence in another legal form.[35]

In its Decision, EIOPA simply states that it understands freedom of establishment, in the case of intermediaries and ancillary intermediaries, as meaning if they intend to carry out of insurance distribution activities through a branch or permanent presence established in a different Member State according to Article 6(1) of the IDD.

Even if under EU law the notion of "establishment" includes branches, it is surprising and somehow confusing that the IDD definition of the "host Member State" does not expressly mention a branch—as the Solvency II Directive does, for example—but only refers to a permanent presence or establishment.

[34]Article 2.1 (12), IDD.

[35]Recital 25, Article 6.1, IDD.

2.5 General Good Rules: Will More Transparency Be Enough to Avoid Their Possible Detrimental Impact on the Single Market?

As explained above, the principle under the IDD—like under the IMD—is that the single registration in the home Member State triggers the provision of the EU passport to the insurance intermediaries subject to the appropriate notification procedure. However, as recalled in the EIOPA 2019 report analysing national general good rules,[36] "*the basic principle underlying the general good in the insurance sector is that (...) insurance intermediary operating under the (..) arrangements laid down by the IDD, is obliged to adapt its activities to the host Member States' rules if the measures enforced against it serve the general good, irrespective of whether it carries on those activities*" through FOS or FOS.

Despite increased clarity and transparency introduced by the IDD and a greater role given to EIOPA, the effect of some of these general good rules can be challenging for intermediaries operating cross-border and be detrimental to the proper functioning of the IDD and the Single Market for insurance distribution.

Under the IMD, the competent authorities of the host Member State could decide "*to take the necessary steps to ensure appropriate publication of the conditions under which, in the interest of the general good, intermediaries' business under FOS or FOE must be carried on in their territories*".[37] The IDD makes the publication mandatory and introduced more requirements as well as an additional criterion as explained below.

Member States competent authorities must publish on their websites the general good rules that apply in their respective territory and update them regularly.[38] Links to the websites of each Member State competent authorities must be available on the EIOPA's website "with all national general good rules categorised into different areas of law". Each Member State must also designate a single point of contact for providing information on its general good rules.

There is no real definition of what constitutes a general good rule in the IDD or in another EU text or in the CJEU case law. However in its Interpretative Communication,[39] the Commission lists a number of cumulative (but not definitive) conditions for a general good rule to be valid under the EU law and that have been developed by the CJEU over the years: it must govern a matter which has not been harmonised at the EU level; the rule must pursue an objective of the general good; it must be non-discriminatory; objectively necessary and proportionate to the objective pursued

[36]EIOPA: Insurance Distribution Directive—Report analysing national general good rules – 22/07/2019.

[37]Article 6.3, IMD.

[38]Article 11, IDD.

[39]OJ of the EC, C43/5 – 16-2 -2000—Commission interpretative communication on the freedom to provide services and the general good in the insurance sector.

and the general good objective is not safeguarded by the rules of the provider's home Member States.

As rightly noted by EIOPA in its report,[40] the IDD provides an additional criterion[41] regarding how "general good' rules should be applied by Member States for insurance distribution, namely "*the administration burden stemming from general good provisions should be proportionate with regard to consumer protection*". One could wonder whether this criterion could be interpreted as a limitation of the IDD general good rules, meaning that these rules can only aim at protecting consumer and therefore can't applied to professional clients/SMES or in relation to large risks.

Under the IDD, a minimum harmonisation text, the national general good rules may relate to stricter rules in areas expressly mentioned in the Directive and stricter rules relating to other matters covered by the Directive. The IDD includes 11 options which allow Member States exercising them to introduce general good rules in their context.[42] The EIOPA report provides a quite comprehensive though not exhaustive overview of those rules that Member States have introduced so far in the context of their national implementation of the IDD. It seems for example that a majority of Member States have used the options provided in Article 22 of the IDD to introduce stricter information requirements, mandatory advice for the sale of any insurance products and limitation or prohibition of remuneration paid to insurance intermediaries in relation to the distribution of insurance products.

More time and hindsight are needed to have a correct understanding on how these national general good rules can have an adverse effect on intermediaries' cross-border activities. However, it appears already that some national legislations that implement the IMD could be an obstacle to the proper functioning of the IDD Single Passport.

One example is the Romanian secondary legislation implementing the IDD. It states that the cooperation of foreign insurance distributors, including insurers carrying out activity in Romania on the basis of FOS with local intermediaries, must be based on reverse solicitation and the duration of that cooperation cannot be more than 3 years.[43] It seems that this legislation is aimed at protecting consumers from "dubious" EU insurers operating under FOS in Romania and at preventing intermediaries from working with them and to ensure that consumers are not left without cover. However, if after 3 years the insurer operating under FOS in Romania is no longer able to collaborate with the same intermediary, it can still operate in Romania under FOS with different intermediaries.

These rules do not appear to meet the objective of consumer protection and have significant consequences for local Romanian insurance brokers as they are no longer

---

40 See footnote 19.

41 Article 11 (2).

42 Annex 1 of EIOPA report analysing national general good rules.

43 EIOPA—Country-by-country analysis of national general good rules—Annex III to the Insurance Distribution Directive: Report analysing national general good rules, - Romania, page 82.

able to put in place long-term partnerships with EU insurers authorised to work on a FOS basis in Romania, thus hindering their ability to fully serve their clients' interests. In such a context, the introduction of Insurance Guarantee Schemes at EU level—to protect private policyholders by compensating for their claims in the event an insurance company becomes insolvent (in particular in the framework of cross-border activities and failures)—and more supervisory control on cross-border insurers would perhaps be more appropriate. This would also support a drive towards a single market.

It is interesting to note that in October 2019, the European Commission sent a letter of formal notice to Romania regarding the conditions for the sale of insurance products by insurance distributors from other Member States: "*The Commission urges Romania to adjust national rules setting restrictive conditions insurance distributors from abroad who want to sell products to Romanians. (...) These conditions prevent insurance distributors from making effective use of their basic freedom to provide services within the internal market*".[44]

The reaction of the Romanian supervisor to "protect" its market from insurers operating under FOS or FOE in their market is not an isolated case. Over recent years there have been failures of insurers operating in some Member States under FOS or FOE, and Member States are starting to think of solutions to protect their respective markets and consumers. In France, for example, the FFA (the French Federation of Insurers) published in May 2019 a position paper on "Strengthening the Internal Market by tackling failures of insurance companies operating under FOS". It explains that since November 2016, the French insurance market has been experiencing numerous run-offs, or failures of insurers authorised in the EU and operating in France under FOS. The FFA has advanced concrete proposals aimed at preventing default by operators operating in the EU under FOS.[45]

These failures have an important disruptive impact on local markets and might lead the public to wonder about the efficiency and effectiveness of supervision within the Single Market. However, this should not bring into question passporting rights for insurers and intermediaries. There is obviously a need for a review of the supervision system of insurers operating cross-border and for a better cooperation amongst supervisors in the EU. It is expected that the current review by the European Commission of the Solvency II Framework, and in particular its part on the supervision of cross-border activities of insurers and the possible need of minimum harmonised rules on Insurance Guarantee Schemes (IGS), will suggest solutions to this serious issue.

The Directive amending Solvency II in the context of the ESAs review[46] has already introduced some positive changes in this respect: the cooperation between

---

[44]European Commission's website, press corner, 10-10-2019.

[45]https://www.ffa-assurance.fr/ - Document de position: Renforcer le marché intérieur en luttant contre les défaillances d'entreprises d'assurance qui opèrent par voie de LPS.

[46]Art. 2 of Directive (EU) 2019/2177 of the European Parliament and of the Council of 18 December 2019 amending Directive 2009/138/EC on the taking-up and pursuit of the business

the NCAs and also between EIOPA and the NCAs is strengthened in relation to cross-border activities carried out by insurance undertakings. For example, the supervisory authority of the home Member State will have to notify EIOPA and the supervisory authority of the relevant host Member State where it identifies deteriorating financial conditions or other emerging risks posed by an insurance or reinsurance undertaking carrying out activities based on the freedom to provide services or the freedom of establishment that may have a cross-border effect. In its opinion on the 2020 review of Solvency II, EIOPA[47] also advises to amend Article 36 of the Solvency II Directive by adding a new paragraph 7 as follows:

> 7. In case of material cross-border insurance business under the right of establishment or the freedom to provide services, the supervisory authority of the home Member State shall actively cooperate with the supervisory authority of the host Member State to assess whether the insurance undertaking has a clear understanding of the risks that it faces, or may face, in the host Member State.
>
> This cooperation shall cover at least the following areas:
>
> (a) system of governance including the ability of the head office management to understand the cross-border market specificities, risk management tools, internal controls in place and compliance procedures for the cross-border business;
> (b) outsourcing arrangements and distributions partners;
> (c) business strategy and claims handling;
> (d) consumer protection.
>
> 8. Where appropriate, the supervisory authority of the home Member State shall inform in a timely manner the supervisory authority of the host Member State about the outcome of its supervisory review process which concerns the cross-border activity, in particular where the supervisory authority of the host Member State has already raised concerns.

Lastly, it is also interesting to note, that amongst EIOPA's follow-up actions to address the issues identified in its report on the general good, is the analysis from a legal and supervisory perspective of general good rules imposed on incoming insurance intermediaries in areas of the home Member State competence such as registration requirements. As this is clearly a matter for home Member State competence and the IDD single licence for intermediaries is based on the single registration in the home Member State, it is hoped that follow-up actions will indeed be taken in this area.

---

of Insurance and Reinsurance (Solvency II), Directive 2014/65/EU on markets in financial instruments and Directive (EU) 2015/849/ on the prevention of the use of the financial system for the purposes of money-laundering or terrorist financing, OJ L 334, 27.12.2019, p. 155.

[47] https://eiopa.europa.eu/Pages/Consultation-Paper-on-the-Opinion-on-the-2020-review-of-Solvency-II.aspx.

3 New Division of Competence Between Home and Host Member State Authorities and the Possible Impact on Intermediaries' Passporting Rights

Under the IMD, the only power clearly given to host Member States over insurance intermediaries operating under FOS or FOE in their markets, was the one to adopt specific legal provisions to protect the general good. They could ensure the appropriate publication of the conditions under which, in the interest of the general good, the business concerned must be carried on in their territories and take appropriate measures to prevent or to penalise those irregularities committed in their territories which are contrary to their general good measures.[48]

The IMD did not, however, clearly divide competences between home and host member State competent authorities. This led some EU regulators, such as the UK's Financial Conduct Authority (FCA), to claim authority to take enforcement action against all EU intermediaries passporting into the UK and claim jurisdiction over all activities of UK firms passporting into other EU states.

The IDD brought an important change to the framework established by the IMD: it clearly divides the oversight powers between the home and host Member States competent authorities over insurance intermediaries who are passporting in the EU. Although this division of competence aims to ensure the compliance of intermediaries with the IDD requirements, one could wonder whether the powers given by the IDD to the host Member States, in addition to an (excessive) use of the general good rules could not weaken or go against the concept of the IDD Single Licence.

3.1 Powers Given to Host Member States Over Intermediaries Operating Under FOS in Their Territories

The IDD does introduce new powers as far as FOS activities of insurance intermediaries are concerned. Like under the IMD, when operating under FOS, an insurance intermediary must comply with the minimum requirements of the IDD as implemented in its home member State and the general good rules of the host Member State.

At the time of the trilogue, the Council of the EU had explained that the intention was here to strike a proper balance, taking inspiration from relevant legislative texts such as the Solvency II Directive and the Mortgage Credit Directive: "*We considered that a proper solution aimed at enhancing consumer protection, while preserving a smooth functioning of the passport, might come from graduating competences and powers differently in the cases of freedom to provide services and freedom of*

[48] Article 6.3 and article 8.4, IMD.

establishment and introducing appropriate safeguards in order to clarify supervisors' powers and to avoid regulatory arbitrage".

The IDD makes clear that in case of intermediaries' FOS activities, the home Member State competent authority will be responsible for ensuring compliance with all IDD requirements (such as good repute, professional knowledge and competence, and conduct of business obligations) with regard to all business activities of the intermediary within the internal market.[49] And—as under the IMD—the host Member State competent authority can take appropriate and non-discriminatory measures to penalise any failure of the intermediary to comply with its general good rules and prevent it from carrying out new business.

If the host Member State competent authority considers that the intermediary operating under FOS is in breach of any IDD requirements[50] (for example, breach of the rules on good repute), it will inform the home Member State competent authority which should then take appropriate measures against the intermediary to remedy the breach. Further clarity is also introduced by the EIOPA Decision.[51]

In exceptional situations,[52] the competent authority of the host Member State is entitled to intervene and take measures against the incoming intermediary if it continues acting in a way that is clearly detrimental to the interests of consumers of the host Member State on a large scale, or to the orderly functioning of the host Member State (re)insurance market, despite the measures taken by the home Member State or where it fails to take any. The host Member State can also intervene in urgent cases[53] to prevent or penalise breaches by the intermediary in the host Member State, where it is necessary to protect the rights of the consumers in the host Member State. In such cases the competent authorities of the host Member State have the right to prevent the intermediary from carrying out new business within the territory of the host Member State. EIOPA is also granted with some powers in this context. The home or host Member States may request its assistance to settle disagreements between them in such cross-border situations.[54]

These enhanced powers of the host Member States in a FOS context clearly reinforce some safeguards for the consumers. Time will tell however whether these new powers given to the host Member States and EIOPA will hinder or not intermediaries' cross-border activities.

The IDD goes even further and introduces new powers for host Member States to help them preventing the circumvention of their rules by insurance intermediaries.[55] The competent authorities of the host member States have the right to prevent a foreign intermediary from carrying out business in its Member State if the

[49]Recital 21, IDD.

[50]Article 5.1, IDD.

[51]Section 3.2 of EIOPA Decision.

[52]Article 5.1 (3).

[53]Article 5.2, IDD.

[54]Article 5.1, IDD that refers to Article 19 of Regulation No 1094/2010.

[55]Article 9, IDD.

intermediary's activities are entirely or principally directed towards its territory with the sole purpose of avoiding the legal rules which apply to local intermediaries of the host Member State. They have equivalent powers in cases where the intermediary's activity seriously endangers the proper functioning of the (re)insurance market in the host Member State in terms of consumer protection.

This crystalized in the IDD the ECJ case-law concerning freedom to provide services, clarifying that the host authority is entitled to take appropriate measures to prevent forum shopping aimed at avoiding falling within the competence of a specific legal framework.

3.2 Powers Given to Host Member States Over Intermediaries Operating Under FOE in their Territories

In the case of the establishment of a branch or a permanent presence in another Member State, the IDD distributes new responsibility for enforcement between home and host Member States and introduces the new concept of a "primary place of business[56]".

The home Member State remains responsible for ensuring that the intermediary, including its establishments in host Member States, complies with its IDD obligations affecting the business of the intermediaries as a whole: rules on good repute, professional knowledge and competence.[57] As with the provision of services regime, if the competent authority of the host Member State suspects any breaches of these requirements, it must inform the competent authorities of the home member State. The competent authority of the host Member State is entitled to intervene if the home Member State fails to take appropriate measures or if such measures are insufficient.[58] EIOPA is also granted with some powers in this context. The home or host Member States may request its assistance to settle disagreements between them in such cross-border situations.

The competent authorities of host Member States are responsible for ensuring that the intermediaries' branches that provide services in their territories comply with the IDD conduct of business and information requirements as implemented by them. The host Member State can take measures if the branch breaches these requirements. More powers are given to the host Member States in this context, as they are entitled to examine the establishment arrangements of an intermediary in their territories and request changes to enable them to correctly enforce the obligations of the intermediary.[59]

---

[56]Article 7, IDD.

[57]Article 8, IDD Section 3.2.2 of EIOPA Decision.

[58]Recital 22, IDD.

[59]Article 7(2) and 8(1), IDD.

It is clear here that the EU legislators perceived the need to enhance consumer/ client protection as a priority, even if at the cost of some possible limitations to the functioning of the IDD passport.

The IDD introduces a new concept of the "*primary place of business*" into the insurance distribution sector. This is "*the location from where the main business of an intermediary is managed*".[60] If the intermediary's primary place of business is in a Member State other than its home Member State, the relevant competent authority may then agree that the competent authority of the Member State of the primary place of business will act as if it were that of the home Member State. In such a situation, the competent authority of the primary place of business will oversee the intermediary's compliance with professional and organisational requirements, and information and conduct of business rules. This competent authority will also have the right to impose sanctions against the intermediary in the case of non-compliance.

It is very likely that the new concept of the "primary place of business" will have to be further clarified by EIOPA in order to ensure that Member States have the same understanding of it and that the division of competence is clearly organised between the competent authorities when needed. It is surprising that EIOPA decision[61] is silent on the new concept (for example, what does the word "managed" mean in this context).

Together with the power given to Member State competent authorities to prevent the circumvention of the host Member States rules, this new concept empowers host Member States to better protect their consumers and markets. It encourages them to better cooperate to ensure better supervision of the distributors operating in their market. Without such a provision, the Member State where the intermediary is established but not that where its primary place of business is located, would have little incentive to supervise the conduct of the intermediary's activities. Equally the Member State where the primary place of business of the intermediary is located would have little power to properly supervise the activities of the intermediary.

The risk of prioritising the supervision of domestic markets was one of the issues mentioned in the ESAs report on cross-border supervision of retail financial services, and one that the competent authorities must face. However, in the report, the ESAs note that some of the most recent legislation reviewed, such as the IDD, will be helpful for tackling such an issue.

---

[60] Article 2.1 (14), IDD.

[61] The notification procedure for ancillary intermediaries is similar to the one for insurance intermediaries. It is however important to note that the IDD requirements ancillary intermediaries need to comply with to be registered under the IDD (when not exempted by Article 1) differ slightly from the one of insurance intermediaries: Adapted appropriate knowledge and ability /CPD (can be proven by certificate), Good repute/clean record, PI cover (level established by MS according to nature of product and activity/Financial capacity, to act in the best interests of customers, no remuneration that conflicts with the duty to act in the best interests of customers, disclosure of nature and basis of remuneration, IPID to customer (non-life).

4 Towards More Cross-Border Activities of Insurance Intermediaries?

As mentioned earlier, one of the objectives of the IDD was to make it easier for insurance intermediaries to carry out cross-border activities using IDD passports, ensuring more market integration and more consumer protection. As explained in the ESAs report on cross -border supervision of retail financial services: *"The increase in the cross-border provision of financial services has benefits for consumers, as it fosters competition and expands the offer available to consumers, who then have a broader number of financial institutions among which to choose"*.[62]

According to the European Commission impact assessment on the IMD proposal, *'the total cross-border life insurance business was roughly 5% in 2007. In non-life segment, the cross-border business accounts for 8% of total non-life business"*[63] Cross-border activities of insurance intermediaries could at that time considered a nearly inexistent.

Most of the EU Member States implemented the IDD only at the end of 2018: it is therefore too early to clearly assess the impact of the new provisions of the IDD Chapter III on the cross-border activities of insurance intermediaries. More time is needed to have a clear perspective of the extent to which the IDD passport will actually be used, including by new market participants such as digital intermediaries.

Some interesting and positive trends have been observed in this respect in some recent reports of the EIOPA and of the ESAs. Can it be reasonably expected that these trends will be accelerated by the IDD?

In its 2018 report on *"Insurance distribution Directive: Evaluation of the structure of insurance intermediaries' markets in Europe"*, EIOPA has noted an steady increase of the evolution of passport notifications for insurance intermediaries and an increase in cross-border notifications by insurance intermediaries between 2013 and 2017, both on a FOE and FOS basis, hence mainly under the IMD framework.

However, as EIOPA explained, this increase has to be interpreted carefully. First there is a lack of useful data available and secondly, notifying an intention to provide services under FOS or FOE does not mean actually providing services in a host Member State. As mentioned before, intermediaries did not have the obligation to report their actual business under the IMD, i.e. the volume and products/lines of business they really mediate across borders. And this situation has not changed with the IDD. After the implementation of the IMD, thousands of Czech intermediaries, for example, had notified their intention to do business in most of the EU Member States. As it turned out, they never actually carried out any cross-border business

[62]ESAs report on cross-border supervision of retail financial services, 9 July 2019, JC/2019-22.

[63]Commission staff working document, Impact assessment, accompanying the document Proposal for a Directive of the European Parliament and of the Council on Insurance Mediation, Strasbourg, 3.7.2012, SWD (2012) 191 final.

except in Slovakia. As explained in the ORIAS[64] annual reports, the body that registers French intermediaries in France, since 2011 "*the notifications of some 2000 Czech intermediaries operating in France must be analysed with care. In fact, the body holding the Register of Intermediaries in the Czech Republic sent a notification of operation in France for all its registered intermediaries*".

It is also interesting to note that, according to the 2018 EIOPA report, a significant portion of intermediaries' notifications mainly relate to "neighbouring" Member States. For example, in France, it is predominantly insurance intermediaries from the UK, Spain, Italy, Luxembourg, and Belgium who have notified their intention to operate under FOS in France. French intermediaries, meanwhile, have similarly notified their intention to operate in these countries under FOS. This situation has been in a slow and constant evolution since 2008.

4.1 IDD Passport, Digitalisation and Consumers

The 2019 ESAs report on cross-border supervisions confirms this evolution. They explained that "*in monitoring consumer protection developments and financial innovations, the ESAs have noted the continued increase in the cross-border provision of financial services to consumers across of the EU. This increase is both the development of the single market in financial services and the digitalisation of financial services across the banking, insurance and securities sectors, which further enables financial institutions to provide their services across borders*".

The IDD is an activity-based text: it applies to every person who is undertaking the activity of insurance distribution, whether via traditional or digital means. An increasing number of insurance intermediation business models are today partially or entirely digitised,[65] providing services to customers established in other Member States. It is very likely that these intermediaries operating through digital means will make increased use of the IDD passport, making its supervision even more challenging for national and EU supervisors if key issues are not solved rapidly, such as the lack of clear criteria for determining the location where services are provided.

Because the digitalisation of financial services is seen by EU regulators as a means to further integrate the single market, they are encouraging its development via regulatory 'sandboxes'.[66]

[64]Registre unique des intermédiaires en assurance, banque et finance - https://www.orias.fr/welcome.

[65]On legal and regulatory issues arising from these models, see Marano (2019), pp. 294–315.

[66]The ESAs define in their joint report on regulatory sandboxes and innovation hubs as "*scheme set up by a competent authority that provides regulated and unregulated entities with the opportunity to test, pursuant to a testing plan agreed and monitored by a dedicated function of the relevant authority, innovative products or services, business models, or delivery mechanisms, related to the carrying out of financial services*".

Competent authorities are however concerned about the impact on the level playing field if material divergences were to emerge between the approaches of the national competent authorities to the design and operation of such 'sandboxes', such as regulatory arbitrage. It is therefore interesting to note the ESAs believe that "*regulatory sandboxes may not be used as a mechanism to dispense with requirements under EU law, such as the requirement to obtain a licence before carrying out certain financial services, such as payments services, insurance services etc. Levers for proportionality embedded into law, for instance with regard to systems and controls requirements, may be applied in the context of firms participating in a regulatory sandbox in the same way as to firms outside the sandbox*". This is a key principle to ensure that sandboxes remain 'channels of distribution'—neutral.

Are clients and consumers ready to benefit from these products offered by intermediaries not established in their countries?

It is a common practice for commercial clients to employ the services of intermediaries established in other EU Member States—a diverse range of European companies rely for example on insurance coverage provided by the specialised intermediaries of the London insurance market. It is interesting to note that according to the Commission Special Eurobarometer 446 on financial products and services,[67] the attitude of private customers towards purchasing financial products or services on a cross-border basis is also changing, albeit very slowly. More and more are eager to buy financial products or services from a provider in another EU Member State, the proportion increasing from 5% in 2011 to 7% in 2016. However, there are some large differences between countries, consumers for example in Romania, Luxembourg, Cyprus and Ireland being more likely to have purchased at least one financial product or service in another EU country. However, some consumers believe that there are fewer consumer protection rules in other EU member State or simply do not know their rights if there are problems. These are clear barriers to cross-border purchases of financial products and services.

And there are other barriers that, despite the simplification of the IDD notification rules and despite the fact that insurance contracts are legal and intangible products which make them particularly suitable for cross-border sale, may make the IDD single passport still difficult to use. At a consumer level, language and cultural differences, consumer preferences and national consumer protection rules, often still act as entry barriers. At the intermediary level, the need for local risk knowledge, business and distribution characteristics as well as the occasionally abusive use of general good provisions by the host Member State as mentioned earlier, can make cross-border selling difficult. It will be interesting to study whether the need to identify a target market under POG rules as introduced by the IDD will help cross borders activities of intermediaries or, on the contrary, will create another obstacle to them.

Finally, it seems worth dedicating a final paragraph to the impact of Brexit on cross-border activities of insurance intermediaries.

---

[67]Special Eurobarometer446, Report, financial products and services, July 2016.

4.2 *The Impact of Brexit on Cross-Border Activities of Insurance Intermediaries*

On 23 June 2016, the UK voted to leave the European Union. The UK had been due to leave the EU on 29 March 2019, but the departure date was revised and the UK in fact left the EU on 31 January 2020 with a Withdrawal Agreement. The UK has entered a transitional period, which is due to operate until 31 December 2020. During the transition period, EU law continues to apply in the UK.

Once the UK becomes a "third country" under EU legislation, the IDD will no longer apply to UK intermediaries (only the UK requirements will continue to apply) and UK intermediaries will be no longer treated as EU intermediaries. UK intermediaries will lose the IDD passporting rights they currently enjoy and similarly, EU intermediaries will lose the IDD passporting rights in relation to the UK.

In most EU Member States, governments have adopted legislative acts on the UK's withdrawal from the EU providing for contingency measures should there be a 'hard Brexit' (i.e., UK withdrawal with limited alignment). This will ensure that policyholders with existing life and non-life insurance policies with UK insurers undertakings, operating in their respective countries in FOE or FOS under the Solvency II single licence, will not be affected by these insurers losing their passport rights. Most of these national acts of the EU Member States provide for a temporary run-off regime which, subject to a number of conditions, will enable UK insurers to continue to fulfil their obligations, contracted to their EU customers prior to Brexit, for a transitional period after the date of the UK's withdrawal from the EU. However, it is unfortunate that in many countries, UK insurance intermediaries are not included in the relevant local legislations, as during this transitional period they could help their EU 27 clients, for example to resolve claims problems on multiple insurers' London policies.

In the UK, European insurance intermediaries currently operating in the UK can continue to carry out insurance business, including writing new contracts as well as servicing existing contracts, for a temporary period after even a 'no-deal' Brexit (i.e., UK withdrawal without agreement). In order to do so, they must submit applications for UK authorisation and complete any necessary restructuring.

The interpretation of Articles 1 and 16 of the IDD in a Brexit context is a complex issue. According to Article 16 of the IDD on the restriction on use of intermediaries,[68] EU intermediaries are permitted to use only the insurance distribution services of other EU registered intermediaries.

When reading Article 1 on the scope of the IDD in parallel with Article 16, one can wonder about the possible unintended consequences of Article 16 in a Brexit context. The IDD does not apply to insurance distribution activities in relation to

[68]"Member States shall ensure that, when using the services of the insurance, reinsurance or ancillary insurance intermediaries, insurance or reinsurance undertakings and intermediaries use the insurance and reinsurance distribution services only of registered insurance and reinsurance intermediaries or ancillary insurance intermediaries including those referred to in Article 1(3)."

risks **and** commitments **located** outside the Union[69] or insurance distribution activities **carried out** in third countries.[70] Further, the IDD does not affect a Member State's law in respect of insurance or reinsurance distribution activities pursued by intermediaries established in a third country and operating on its territory under FOS.[71]

It is however not clear which activities are exactly covered by Article 1, as no definition is given in the IDD of the EU Member States in which the risk or the commitment are situated (unlike the Solvency II Directive). Therefore, Member States have differing interpretation of where activities of intermediaries take place.

Although it is known that it was not the intention of the IDD, Article 16 could mean that EU intermediaries are not permitted, even if their national law so provides, to accept/place risks located in the EU, with third country intermediaries, i.e. who are not registered in the EU, such as UK intermediaries post-Brexit.

This of course would significantly restrict choice and competition for insurance products to the detriment of EU clients. Insurance intermediaries very often work in collaboration with colleagues in other non-EU markets. This ensures that the client, via the intermediaries' cooperation, has access to local expertise in the respective markets which are part of the insurance contract or related risk services. The ability to access third countries' capacity also widens the pool of available products for their EU consumers and can allow them to obtain vital coverage that might not be available in EU.

Effectively shutting the EU off from global markets was clearly not the intention of the EU regulators. During the adoption process of the IDD, the EU co-legislators had agreed that clarity was needed to ensure that intermediaries registered within the EU could still work with those outside of the EU, that the IDD did not aim to exclude international activities of the European intermediaries.[72] Article 16 was even deleted for a while.[73] However, no such clarity was introduced in the final version of Article 16 and it is unfortunate that it leaves the door open to possible restrictive interpretations.

---

[69]Insurance Distribution Directive, Article 1(6) subparagraph 1.

[70]Insurance Distribution Directive, Article 1(6) subparagraph 3.

[71]Insurance Distribution Directive, Article 1(6) subparagraph 2.

[72]A draft Article 16 read as follows: *"Member States shall ensure that, when using the services of the insurance or reinsurance intermediaries established in the EU, insurance and reinsurance undertakings and intermediaries use the insurance and reinsurance mediation services only of registered insurance and reinsurance intermediaries or of the persons referred to in Article 1(2) or of the persons who have fulfilled the declaration procedure referred to in Article 4."*

[73]The Council, until the very last trilogue meetings, had deleted Article 16 as "it was considered superfluous. The scope of the Directive is already laid down in Article 1". Then it seems that in the end Article 16 was reintroduced because of Article 33.1 b) on Sanctions. However, it is clear that Article 33.1 b) refers to intermediaries or insurers using the insurance or reinsurance distribution services of persons referred to in Article 3 that covers intermediaries registered with the competent authority in an EU Member State.

In its February 2019 Recommendations[74] for the insurance sector, in light of the UK withdrawing from the EU without a withdrawal agreement, and in particular in its Recommendation 9 on insurance distribution, EIOPA confirms that the IDD applies only to distribution activities to EU27 policyholders **and** for EU27 risks:

> Competent authorities should ensure that UK intermediaries and entities which intend to continue or commence distribution activities to EU27 policyholders **and** for EU27 risks after the UK's withdrawal are established and registered in the EU27 in line with the relevant provisions of the IDD. (. . .). When assessing whether a specific UK intermediary or entity is providing distribution activities in the EU, competent authorities should take into account that only the consistent and uniform application of the IDD can guarantee the same level of protection for consumers and ensure a level playing field in the Union. Competent authorities should ensure that all intermediaries carrying out distribution activities which target EU27 policyholders and EU27 risks fall under the scope of the IDD. For this purpose, competent authorities should assess any distribution model against the definition of distribution activity as provided for in the IDD.

The activities outlined above will be subject to local Member State regulations or supervisory requirements and therefore there is potential for divergent approaches and practices in each of the EU Member States. UK and European intermediaries will need to consider carefully whether their arrangements leave them exposed to potential legal and regulatory risk through acting without regulatory permission.

5 Final Remarks

The IDD's main objective to further facilitate the cross-border activities of insurance intermediaries, thus promoting the emergence of a genuine internal market in insurance services, was bold and audacious.

But an EU legislative text is always the product of compromises. Despite the improvements introduced by the IDD such as a real simplification and clarification of the FOS and FOE notification procedures or more transparency on general good rules, the opportunity was missed to clarify the badly-needed criteria for determining when an intermediary is deemed to be transacting business on a FOS basis in a host Member State, thus having to comply with the general good rules of that State. This clarity was also key for national supervisors given the increasing powers given by the IDD to competent authorities of host Member States.

Even if businesses can currently rely on EIOPA common understanding of FOS, it does not originate from EU secondary legislation and has its potential limitations.

[74]The Recommendations provide guidance on the treatment of UK insurance undertakings and distributors with regard to cross-border services in the EU after the withdrawal of the UK from the EU without a withdrawal agreement. EIOPA explains that the objective of its Recommendations is to minimise the detriment to policyholders with cross-border insurance contracts. The Recommendations addressed to National Competent Authorities are to foster supervisory convergence and to ensure consistent supervisory practices.

Time will soon tell whether the new exceptional powers given to host Member States over intermediaries operating in their territories, combined with an excessive use of general good rules—in particular in areas of the home Member State competence such as registration requirements—will emerge as being serious obstacles in practice to the IDD single licence. This could well happen, in particular given the current context where recent failures of insurers operating in some Member States under FOS or FOE have led Member States to start revising the access to their respective markets.

The current review by the European Commission of the Solvency II Framework will need to bring solutions to this serious issue.

Finally, the IDD single licence is not used in isolation. There remain important obstacles to the cross-border activities of insurance intermediaries: they relate for example to areas like taxation or labour law, languages and culture, including expectations of the local policyholder. And these obstacles will never be addressed by the IDD.

Acknowledgements The author would like to thank Rebekka de Nie, EU Policy Manager at BIPAR, and Stella Mitta, legal assistant at BIPAR, for their generous assistance.

References

BIPAR/Steptoe: The insurance Distribution Directive: A handbook on cross-border insurance distribution by insurance intermediaries – January 2019

Debuisson B. La distribution transfrontalière des produits d'assurance. Plongée en eaux troubles, Université Catholique de Louvain, 1996 - Doc 96/26

Marano P (2019) Navigating Insurtech: the digital intermediaries of insurance products and customer protection in the EU. Maastricht J Eur Comp Law pp 294–315

Legislation

Commission Recommendation 92/48/EEC of 18 December 1991 on insurance intermediaries

EIOPA Decision of the Board of Supervisors on the cooperation of the competent authorities of the Member States of the European Economic Area with regard to Directive (EU) 2016/97 of the European Parliament and of the Council of 20 January 2016 on insurance distribution - EIOPA-BoS/18-340

EIOPA: Insurance Distribution Directive – Report analysing national general good rules – 22/07/2019

EIOPA – Country-by-country analysis of national general good rules - Annex III to the Insurance Distribution Directive: Report analysing national general good rules, - Romania, page 82

ESAs report on cross-border supervision of retail financial services, 9 July 2019, JC/2019-22

OJ of the EC, C43/5 – 16-2 -2000 – Commission interpretative communication on the freedom to provide services and the general good in the insurance sector

Documents

Document de position: Renforcer le marché intérieur en luttant contre les défaillances d'entreprises d'assurance qui opèrent par voie de LPS. https://www.ffa-assurance.fr/
Registre unique des intermédiaires en assurance, banque et finance - https://www.orias.fr/welcome
Special Eurobarometer 446, Report, financial products and services, July 2016

Information Duties Stemming from the Insurance Distribution Directive as an Example of Faulty Application of the Principle of Proportionality

Marta Ostrowska

1 Introduction

1.1 The Argument

IDD Directive has given rise to a number of difficult challenges for its implementation, among which numerous information duties imposed on all insurance distributors. Over the recent years, it can be observed that information duties became to the EU legislator a default 'regulatory technique' employed wherever the customer protection must have been strengthened. It is believed that they aspire to improve decisions customers make in their economic relationships and particularly to protect the inexperienced and marginally—literate from the industry professionals. Basically, the technique requires the insurance distributor to give the customer information which he may use to make better decisions and to keep the insurance distributor from abusing its superior position. Thanks to different information duties the customer is supposed to receive information for analyzing his choices critically and to choose optimally. Thus informed, he understands his choices well enough to make an intelligent decision about the insurance product he wants to purchase. This is a general reason justifying the need for transparency and information disclosures.

Information duties are ubiquitous. Not only are they introduced by IDD Directive, but they are also broadly employed by Solvency II Directive, PRIIPs Regulation, Distance Marketing Directive, MiFID, E-commerce Directive, General Data Protection Regulation to name just the major regulations governing the financial market.

M. Ostrowska (✉)
Insurance Law Institute, Faculty of Law and Administration – Warsaw University, Warsaw, Poland
e-mail: m.ostrowska@wpia.uw.edu.pl

P. Marano, K. Noussia (eds.), *Insurance Distribution Directive*, AIDA Europe Research Series on Insurance Law and Regulation 3,
https://doi.org/10.1007/978-3-030-52738-9_2

Undoubtedly, information duties address modern problem of customers who must face financial choices of many kinds while they are often not experienced enough to understand them. Eventually the customers conclude contracts they do not understand and cannot evaluate under terms they do not know. The reason why the EU legislator chose information duties as a technique that suits best to tackle the problem rests on a plausible assumption that when it comes to decision making, more information is better than less.[1]

Although indeed information duties seem to be the right measure to tackle the problem, the academics and industry participants have for some time now been doubting that they accomplish their purpose.[2] To make things worse, it has been raised that not only do not they accomplish the purpose, but also create unnecessary negative effect. Such effect is called 'information overload' which might be as harmful as lack of information,[3] to say the least. All these concerns give rise to specific questions: Is more information indeed better than less? If so, is there any limit to the amount of information where 'more' becomes 'too much'? How does information affect customers' choices in the financial market? How best to assess the utility of the information disclosed?

As the assumption—more information is better than less—does sound plausible but the reality does not seem to prove this assumption, the aim of this study is to demonstrate that the information duties, which the EU chose as a measure to tackle the problem of customer protection with is likely to be incompliant with the general principle of the EU law—principle of proportionality. Simultaneously, it should be underlined that the aim of this study is not to propose an alternative to the measure under scrutiny. The author believes that the information duties are necessary to maintain high level of customer protection, however, the following analysis raises doubts as to the way they are employed and therefore, it aspires to encourage legislators to take further steps to eventually tailor solutions to problems.

1.2 The Method

The study consists of three steps. The first one is to present the concept of the principle of proportionality which will facilitate to understand the rules of EU legislation and, most importantly, will give background for the core analysis of whether or not the information duties are proportional.

The second is to show the subject of analysis—an overview of the information duties introduced by IDD Directive, which will also serve to demonstrate how extensive and intensive the information to be provided is. The analysis is limited

[1]Ben-Shahar and Schneider (2011), p. 650.

[2]E.g. Maśniak (2015), pp. 221–233; Jiang (2018), pp. 487–526; Kielholz and Nebel (2005), p. 36.

[3]Fung et al. (2008), p. 90.

to the information duties relevant for non-life insurance only. Moreover, the purpose of information disclosures will be addressed.

The last and the most important step is to address a question of whether the discussed information duties satisfy the requirements of proportionality principle and, consequently, whether they comply with the rules of high-quality legislation. To this end, so-called 'proportionality test' will be applied. As the verification of proportionality involves a variety of interdisciplinary knowledge, the author surveys the relevant literature.

This study joins the broad literature on the information in the insurance law and on the phenomenon of the 'information overload'. Furthermore, it extends this literature by examining the problem from very different perspective—the EU legislation standards and policy efficiency.

2 Principle of Proportionality: What Does It Mean and How Do We Know It Is Respected?

The principle of proportionality is one of the general principles of the EU law which basically has two different scopes of application and meanings. The first one is partially stipulated in the Article 5(4) of TEU:[4] 'Under the principle of proportionality, the content and form of Union action shall not exceed what is necessary to achieve the objectives of the Treaties'. It directly refers to the actions undertaken by the EU institutions which are verified in terms of their proportionality *ex ante* by the Regulatory Scrutiny Board and could be evaluated *ex post* by the European Court of Justice ('ECJ') within the judicial control of the validity of the EU measures. Besides the EU actions, proportionality is also applied to the legislative measures adopted at the national levels by the EU Member States. For the purposes of this study and further analysis, specific focus will be given only to the first approach, i.e. proportionality as an important requirement of EU legislation.

In order to prove that the information duties introduced by IDD Directive do not satisfy the requirements of the proportionality principle, the meaning of proportionality should be deciphered in the first place. Besides the above cited TEU provision, there is no other binding legal act which would provide for a clear definition of the principle of proportionality. Therefore, the modern understanding of proportionality mostly derives from the ECJ case law which was once summarized in famous case of National Farmer Union: 'the principle of proportionality (...) requires that measures adopted by Community institutions do not exceed the limits of what is appropriate and necessary in order to attain the objectives legitimately pursued by the legislation in question; when there is a choice between several appropriate measures recourse must be had to the least onerous, and the disadvantages caused must not be

[4]Treaty on European Union (OJ C 326, 26.10.2012, p. 13–390).

disproportionate to the aims pursued[5]'. In other words, to safely claim that EU measure is proportional, the three requirements must be jointly met:

i. EU measure is **suitable** (appropriate) to attain the desired objective;
ii. EU measure is **necessary** to attain the desired objective;
iii. disadvantages caused by adopting EU measure are acceptable compared to the benefits of the objective achieved (**proportionality *sensu stricto***).

Now, to consider the measure **suitable**, a causal link between that measure and the objective sought should be identified. The measure under review must be useful to attain properly the regulatory objective and it must not be out of proportion to that aim, which is well illustrated by the famous saying 'one must not use a steamhammer to crack a nut'.[6] The measure is **necessary** to attain the objective if the objective will not come about by itself and if the objective cannot be attained by other measures which are as useful and, at the same time, less harmful for other interests. Finally, in relation to **proportionality *sensu stricto***, proportionality requires that the measure—although it is recognized suitable and necessary, as compared with other possible measures—must nonetheless be abandoned, or replaced by another less appropriate measure, because of a substantial adverse impact on other interests, so much so that the advantages for which it is preferred over other measures are out of proportion to the harm caused to those other interests.[7] Thus, it should be emphasized that proportionality *sensu stricto* is verified only if the measure was recognized both 'suitable and necessary' but the burden caused by that measure is more onerous than the benefits which are the added value of the regulatory measure.[8]

Interestingly, proportionality principle becomes of more and more interest within the insurance regulation. EIOPA has issued a report on the principle of proportionality[9] in an insurtech context in which proportionality is indeed recognized as a principle applied throughout the EU law, including EU insurance law, both at the regulatory and supervisory level. However, a closer analysis of the report leads to the conclusion that proportionality addressed by EIOPA ('insurance proportionality') differs from proportionality principle discussed above ('general proportionality'). The substantial difference regards appropriateness criterion (proportionality *sensu stricto*). Based on EIOPA report, appropriateness requires that the drawbacks of a measure are not totally disproportionate to the benefits it reaps in light of the nature,

[5]Judgement of the Court of 5 May 1998 In Case C-157/96, The Queen v Ministry of Agriculture, Fisheries and Food, Commissioners of Customs & Excise, ex parte National Farmers' Union, David Burnett and Sons Ltd, R.S. and E. Wright Ltd, Anglo Beef Processors Ltd, United Kingdom Genetics, Wyjac Calves Ltd, International Traders Ferry Ltd, MFP International Ltd, Interstate Truck Rental Ltd, and Vian Exports Ltd, ECR 1998, ECLI:EU:C:1998:191.

[6]See R v. Goldstein [1983] 1 WLR 151, p. 155.

[7]van Gerven (1999), p. 61.

[8]Craig (2012), p. 602.

[9]EIOPA, Report on best practices on licensing requirements, peer-to-peer insurance and the principle of proportionality in an insurtech context, Luxembourg: Publications Office of the European Union, 2019, p. 20.

scale and complexity of an undertaking's risk profile. In other words, a certain requirement is applied in a proportional manner if it is too burdensome for an undertaking to apply this requirement without relief. At the same time, while applying proportionality, the same level of customer protection has to be ensured.[10] It seems thus that **insurance proportionality complements general proportionality** principle stipulated in the Article 5(4) of TEU and does not substitutes it nor constitutes a different type of general proportionality. The author claims that complementary nature of insurance proportionality results from the fact that it is applicable when, as a result of balancing the benefits and damages of a certain measure, a significant burden for the undertaken has been identified but nevertheless accepted (i.e. balance is appropriate and therefore the measure is proportional within the meaning of general proportionality). Consequently, insurance proportionality serves to reduce the burden which has to be taken on in order to achieve the objective. While applying the insurance proportionality, it is assumed that a measure is proportional within the meaning of general proportionality. However, since this study focuses on the general proportionality, insurance proportionality will not be subject to further analysis.

Obviously, proportionality of a measure should be first analyzed at the stage of drafting legislation where, in fact, proportionality is applied as such. Results of such analysis should be included in the impact assessment report. The said report is subsequently verified by the Regulatory Scrutiny Board within the process of *ex ante* control which aims at doublechecking whether or not legislative proposals put by the European Commission comply with the principle of proportionality.[11] The so-called 'test of proportionality' has been developed by ECJ while dealing with disputes relating to incorrect application of proportionality. Longstanding application of the abovementioned test as well as its contribution to clarify the meaning of proportionality makes it reasonable to use this test for the purposes of this study.

3 Information Duties Set Out in the IDD

3.1 What Stands Behind the Information Duties? Reasons for Implementation

The policy of strengthening consumer protection on the insurance market being implemented over the recent years in the EU clearly refers to the works undertaken in

[10] Van Hulle (2019), p. 171.

[11] Better regulation guidelines, Chapter III – Guidelines on impact assessment, available at: https://ec.europa.eu/info/law/law-making-process/planning-and-proposing-law/better-regulation-why-and-how/better-regulation-guidelines-and-toolbox_en.

this area by G20 group[12] and is broadly consistent with its adopted model of protection. Obviously, what directly triggered taking radical steps towards improving consumer position on the financial markets in general was financial crisis of 2007–2010 which called into question an old belief in rationality of markets and financial institutions. It revealed that 'no interference' approach was not the best and the faith that the markets are effective enough when left to their own protection mechanisms has been completely destroyed. Also, since the consequences of financial crisis took its toll directly on the consumers, it has been noted that the paradigm of consumer's rational choice[13] simply did not work. The reasons are twofold. First, rational choice theory assumes an economic reality where disclosed information is transparent and understandable, while it is now clear that it is not always such.[14] Second, making the market more transparent and giving the customers access to the market information is not enough to prevent them from irrational decisions often taken on the basis of e.g. their personal attitude, emotions,[15] life circumstances, way of the product's presentation[16] or time of a day,[17] instead of the given market information. In respect of insurance specifically, the behaviour of consumers is also based on subjective preferences. The decision of whether or not to take out insurance is closely related to the individual's attitude towards the risk.[18] Empirical studies proved that the average customer does not make a full use of all the received information[19] as he does not have technical background[20] to understand modern financial products which often involve complex legal and economics mechanisms. High level financial and legal knowledge is actually required to make a sound choice.[21]

In the light of the above conclusions, it has been decided that the current customer protection regime focused mainly on **providing customer with information** should

[12]See e.g. G20 The Seoul Summit Document, G20 High Level Principles on Financial Consumer Protection, OECD, October 2011.

[13]According to the theory of rational choice it was assumed that, in principle, all the market participants are rational, and therefore are able to assess all the possible options by weighting their costs and benefits to eventually take economically justified decision which reflects best their preferences.

[14]Schwarcz (2011), p. 98.

[15]On the influence of the emotions on the insurance choice see Kunreuther and Pauly (2018), pp. 335–355.

[16]On the influence of the insurance product's presentation see Richter et al. (2019), p. 186.

[17]For more information on how decision making is differentiated depending on circumstances under which the decision is taken and on the individual itself see REP 632 A joint report from the Australian Securities and Investments Commission (ASIC) and the Dutch Authority for the Financial Markets (AFM): Disclosure: Why it shouldn't be default. 14 October 2019, available at: https://asic.gov.au/regulatory-resources/find-a-document/reports/rep-632-disclosure-why-it-shouldn-t-be-the-default/.

[18]Loacker (2015), p. 20.

[19]Ben-Shahar and Schneider (2014), p. 3.

[20]Ben-Shahar and Schneider (2011), pp. 649–749.

[21]Kim et al. (2013), p. 5.

be extended by measures which were to allow the customer to **understand the information** he was provided with.[22] Improvement of financial education and methods of providing information within the sale process became a focal point of new customer protection model.

The need for strengthen consumer protection became even more urgent once the studies revealed household decision making is increasingly financialized which implies that financial stability no longer automatically just extend to concerns about the solvency and liquidity of banking institutions, but also extend to the financial stability of individual households.[23] Therefore, ineffective customer protection may jeopardize stabilization of the financial markets. Successful improvement of the current customer protection regime not only should be considered in the individual customers' interest but also in public interest.

Notwithstanding the lessons learnt from financial crisis, in particular the one which concludes that the mere provision of information is not most effective consumer protection measure, the disclosure and transparency measures were continued to be strengthen. This time, however, the emphasis was to be shifted from provision of 'mere market information' to provision of 'personally tailored information'. In other words, providers of financial services should additionally provide customers with the information on benefits and risks related to the product and, most importantly, while providing the information, the customer's financial goals, knowledge and experience should be taken into account. A prime example of such approach is IDD Directive[24] which introduces a considerable amount of information duties of different nature. Interestingly enough, the IDD information requirements are based on the information duties introduced earlier by MiFID II with respect to the financial instruments and investors protection. The purpose of MiFID II provisions is the same: protection of the investors against misselling of financial products as well as improving their investment choices.

3.2 *Overview of the IDD's Information Duties Relevant for Non-Life Insurance*

The information duties introduced by IDD Directive are primarily of precontractual nature and can be divided into the following categories:

i. general information on the insurance distributor;
ii. information on the insurance product;

[22]Sovern (2010), p. 820f. The shift towards understanding of the information is also reflected in IDD Directive. See e.g. recital 42 of IDD Directive.

[23]Bieri (2014), p. 7; Ring (2018), pp. 34–36.

[24]Directive (EU) 2016/97 of the European Parliament and of the Council of 20 January 2016 on insurance distribution (recast)Text with EEA relevance, OJ L 26, 2.2.2016, pp. 19–59.

iii. information on the complaints handling procedures, the out-of-court complaint and redress procedures;
iv. identification of the customer's demands and needs and provision of advice or recommendation.[25]

The first category—**general information on the insurance distributor**—consists of insurance distributors' obligations to provide the customer with the information which helps to identify the distributor and makes the customer aware of who is he concluding the contract with. With this respect the following disclosures should be made: (i) identity and address of the insurance distributor, (ii) whether it is an insurance intermediary or insurer, (iii) whether it provides advice about the insurance products sold, (iv) the register in which an insurance intermediary has been included and the means for verifying that it has been registered, (v) whether the intermediary is representing the customer or is acting for and on behalf of the insurer (Article 18 of IDD Directive).

Besides the information ensuring identification of the insurance distributor, the customer should be also informed on any circumstances which could potentially cause a conflict of interests affecting the way in which insurance distributor provides information or advice. To this end, the insurance intermediary is obliged to disclose the following information: (i) whether it has a holding, direct or indirect, representing 10% or more of the voting rights or of the capital in a given insurer or whether that insurer or its parent undertaking has such holding in the insurance intermediary; (ii) the nature of the remuneration it receives in relation to the insurance contract and, in certain cases, also the amount of the fee or the method of its calculation; (iii) in relation to the contracts proposed or advised upon, whether or not it gives advice on the basis of a fair and personal analysis and whether or not it is under a contractual obligation to conduct insurance distribution business exclusively with one or more insurers. If not, it is obliged to provide the names of those insurers with which it may and does conduct business (Article 19 of IDD Directive).

The second category pertains to **information on the insurance product**. Here, the relevant obligations are more complex and do not limit to provision of a mere information. Namely, the main focus is given to the way the information is provided. First and foremost, it should be objective and 'customer tailored' each time. **'Customer tailored' information** means that it is provided in a comprehensible form to allow the customer to make an informed decision. The exact way of presenting the information depends on the information obtained from the customer, complexity of the insurance product being proposed and the type of customer, which is determined by the general assessment of the customer's knowledge and experience (Article 20 sec. 1 and 2 of IDD Directive).[26]

Secondly, besides the way of providing information should be each time adjusted to the personal type of customer, IDD Directive specifies the presentation methods as

---

[25]The literature recognizes obligation to identify customer's demands and needs as a special type of information duty. See Szczepańska (2015), pp. 207, 208.

[26]Pokrzywniak (2018), pp. 98, 99.

well. In relation to non-life insurance products,[27] the information should be provided by the way of **a standardised insurance product information document ('IPID').** It is precisely stipulated what kind of information should IPID contains (Article 20 sec. 8 of IDD Directive) and how should it look like (Article 20 sec. 7 of IDD Directive and Implementing Regulation No. 2017/1469[28]).

Additionally, certain information should be provided where an insurance product is offered together with an ancillary product or service which is not insurance (**cross-selling**). The customer should be informed whether or not it is possible to buy the different components separately (Article 24 of IDD Directive). Subsequently, depending on the situation, an adequate description of the different components, separate evidence of the costs and charges of each component, and in certain cases how interaction between the different components modifies the risk or the insurance coverage should be provided.

An important part of enhancing consumer protection plan is ensuring that consumers have access to adequate complaints handling and redress mechanisms that are accessible, affordable, independent, fair, accountable, timely and efficient. To this end, financial services providers and authorised agents were obliged to have in place mechanisms for complaint handling and redress.[29] In this vein, to make customers aware of how to execute their rights, IDD Directive introduces an obligation to inform customers on the **complaints handling procedures, the out-of-court complaint and redress procedures** (Article 18 of IDD Directive).

As seen above, first three categories of information duties contribute to the customer protection mostly by providing customer with more information. Thus, it is reasonable to claim that they reinforce the old customer protection regime based only on market transparency and information disclosures. The last category though—**identification of the customer's demands and needs and provision of advice or recommendation**—seems to address the need for understanding the information provided and taking reasonable (informed and economically justified)

[27]Although the obligation to provide IPID regards only non-life products, the information provided with respect to life products should be still compliant with the requirements set out by the Article 20 sec. 1 and 2 of IDD Directive. In turn, a detailed way of providing information on insurance-based investment products in the form of KID (Key Information Document) has been included in Regulation (EU) No 1286/2014 of the European Parliament and of the Council of 26 November 2014 on key information documents for packaged retail and insurance-based investment products (PRIIPs) (OJ L 352, 9.12.2014, pp. 1–23) and Commission Delegated Regulation (EU) 2017/653 of 8 March 2017 supplementing Regulation (EU) No 1286/2014 of the European Parliament and of the Council on key information documents for packaged retail and insurance-based investment products (PRIIPs) by laying down regulatory technical standards with regard to the presentation, content, review and revision of key information documents and the conditions for fulfilling the requirement to provide such documents (OJ L 100, 12.4.2017, pp. 1–52).

[28]Commission Implementing Regulation (EU) 2017/1469 of 11 August 2017 laying down a standardised presentation format for the insurance product information document (Text with EEA relevance), OJ L 209, 12.8.2017, pp. 19–23.

[29]G20 High Level Principles on Financial Consumer Protection, OECD, October 2011, available at: https://www.oecd.org/daf/fin/financial-markets/48892010.pdf [visited: 12.07.2019], p. 7.

decision by the customer. The relevant obligations do not limit to mere provision of information but, more importantly, they make insurance distributors to process certain information for the customer. Namely, the insurance distributor should specify, on the basis of information obtained from the customer, the demands and needs of the customer and subsequently propose an insurance contract consistent with that demands and needs. Moreover, if an advice in respect of insurance contract is provided, the insurance distributor shall provide the customer with a personalised recommendation explaining why a particular product would best meet the customer's demands and needs (Article 20 sec. 1 of IDD Directive). Wording of the discussed obligations seems to conclude that the liability and effort to ensure the desired 'understanding of information' has been attributed to the insurance distributors.

Finally, regardless content of the information, IDD Directive introduces a general rule due to which all the information provided should be fair, clear and not misleading, while marketing communications should always be clearly identifiable as such (Article 17 of IDD Directive).

4 Proportionality Test

The previous section has clarified that (i) effective **customer protection understood as making customer's decisions more reasonable and informed is a clear-cut objective**[30] of the EU's policy related to the financial markets and, (ii) in order to achieve this objective, the EU adopted certain **measures** among which **information duties** of different nature.

Once the objective and the measure have been identified, an attempt to verify whether or not the discussed measure is proportional can be made. The analysis presented below follows test of proportionality applied by the ECJ within the process of *ex post* control. In other words, first the author attempts to analyze whether the information duties introduced by IDD Directive (measure) are suitable and necessary to make customer's decisions more reasonable and informed (objective pursued by IDD Directive[31]). Subsequently, if the analysis results in confirming that the measure is both suitable and necessary, proportionality *sensu stricto* will be examined. For the sake of better presentation, the below analysis is summarized in the form of table. The table is inspired by the one used in the impact assessment reports which serve to analyze effectiveness and proportionality of the EU legislation.

[30]It applies specifically to the IDD Directive. See: the European Commission, Commission Staff Working Document. Impact Assessment. Accompanying the Document Proposal for a Directive of the European Parliament and of the Council on Insurance Mediation, Strasburg 3.7.2012, SWD (2012) 191 final, p. 27.

[31]See recitals 6, 7, 8, 10, 42, 44 of IDD Directive.

4.1 Are the Information Duties Introduced by the IDD Directive Suitable to Ensure the Customer's Protection?

To recap, the applied measure is deemed suitable only if it is possible to identify the **causal link between this measure and its objective** and if **the measure allows to achieve the intended objective**. A measure only fails to be suitable if it does not achieve any effect in relation to the intended objective or if it even hinders the achievement of that goal.[32] Thus, partial realization of the purpose is enough. As it has been mentioned at the beginning, it is plausible to assume that more information is better than less. Manifestly, it is impossible for the customer to take a conscious and reasonable decision with respect to the insurance product he knows nothing about. Since the information is anything which reduces uncertainty, it is therefore desirable to provide it to the customer. The causal link between information duties has been already identified and discussed e.g. by OECD and EIOPA.[33] Furthermore, the causal link between the information received by the customer (particularly its clarity, non-ambiguity and completeness) and the customer's reasonability has been demonstrated.[34]

In this case, suitability does not seem to be an issue. The above remarks supported with the institutional analysis should suffice to confirm that the broadly understood information duty constitutes a suitable measure to help customers take informed decisions and thereby to ensure customer protection.

4.2 Are the Information Duties Introduced by the IDD Directive Necessary to Ensure the Customer's Protection?

4.2.1 The Objective Will Not Come by Itself

To tackle the problem of necessity, it should be first clarified whether **the objective will not come about by itself**. Clearly, it cannot be reasonably expected that the customers will suddenly change the way they normally take the financial decisions if no steps will be taken in this respect. Furthermore, a lack of action at EU level not only would not achieve the objective but it could even result in an increase in the number of cases of misselling of insurance products and cases where consumers are

[32]Wendland (2018), p. 335.

[33]See e.g. G20 The Seoul Summit Document, p. 10, G20 High Level Principles on Financial Consumer Protection, OECD, October 2011, p. 6, EIOPA Consultation Paper on the proposal for Implementing Technical Standards on a standardised presentation format of the insurance product information document (EIOPA-CP-16/007), 2016.

[34]Fras (2018), p. 191.

led to take undue risks.[35] This is, among others, why the concept of 'legal information forcing' has been introduced.[36]

However, at this point, it should not be overlooked that as IDD Directive entered into force, numerous information duties have been already in place. The situation has been well illustrated by the European insurance and reinsurance federation—Insurance Europe which study demonstrates that besides IDD Directive's information duties, over 100 of disclosure requirements exist under other insurance related regulations.[37] Interestingly, not only does the study prove the abundance of the information duties but it also shows that they duplicate to certain extend. Bearing this in mind, a fair question to ask is whether the objective in question would have come by the means of former information duties implemented prior to the current ones.[38] If so, were IDD Directive's information duties necessary to achieve the objective? The author believes that the answer is negative, because the objective would have already been achieved. Following on from this argument, it could be assumed that IDD Directive's information duties serve here to improve the objective—not to achieve it. However, if that is the case, they would risk contributing to the information overload (see subparagraph 4.2.3. below). Nevertheless, since no study on the effectiveness of the information duties implemented prior to the IDD Directive has been made, this line of thinking is purely speculative.

4.2.2 The Objective Cannot Be Achieved by Other Measure Which Is as Useful as Measure Applied and Less Harmful for Other Interests

The decision on whether the measure is necessary needs to be preceded with confirmation that the objective cannot be achieved by other measure which is as useful as measure applied and less harmful for other interests. In terms of enhancing the process of customer's decision making within the financial market, a great potential has been attributed to **financial education.**[39] Certainly, it is recognized as a measure which is useful to help customers taking reasonable financial decisions.[40] It is believed that financial education improves financial literacy defined as a

[35]Lack of information can also result in misallocation and adverse selection. See: Loacker (2015), p. 57.

[36]Loacker (2015), p. 22 et seq.

[37]A. Hilliard, Issues arising from the implementation of the IDD, 7th AIDA Europe Conference, Warsaw, 13 April 2018, presentation available at: http://www.aida.org.uk/docs/Issues%20Arising%20from%20the%20Implementation%20of%20the%20IDD.pdf [visited: 12.07.2019].

[38]The author does not find any study which would evaluate the effectiveness of the information duties which have been in place so far.

[39]See e.g. G20 Leaders' Declaration, Sankt Petersburg 2013, pp. 19–20; 2014 Financial Inclusion Action Plan, 14 November 2014, p. 2. On financial education and its importance in the field of insurance see Xiao and Porto (2019), pp. 20–35.

[40]Kim et al. (2013), p. 5.

combination of financial awareness, knowledge, skills, attitude and behaviors necessary to make sound financial decisions and ultimately achieve individual financial wellbeing.[41] However, one could rightly note that, in contrast to information duties, it takes more time for financial education to achieve the objective. Possibly, this is the reason why financial education has been always considered supportive measure rather than the principal one.

If it is assumed that financial education is as useful as information duties, then the possible burdens that both measures bring should be compared. The comparison can be made with respect to costs each measure creates and their potential negative side effects. In terms of expenditures, it can be presumed that introduction and realization of financial education program would be more costly (though this should be subject to the economic analysis) and the burden of costs would be possibly shifted to the governments—not private entities. On the other hand, so far, no negative effect of financial education has been identified, while again, a major risk associated with information duties is information overload (see subparagraph 4.2.3. below).

4.2.3 Totality of Regulation

Whether or not the measure is necessary should be also verified from the perspective of totality of regulation which is believed to prevent from overlooking potential disproportion of the whole regulation while perfecting proportionality of particular provisions.[42]

According to the literature on proportionality, **the necessary regulation cannot cause unnecessary negative effects.**[43] Considering the negative effects of specific single information duty, it would be probably hard to indicate one. However, taking into account the totality of regulation and all the information duties introduced the conclusions may change dramatically. Indeed, what may be considered here as **unnecessary negative effect is the risk of information overload.**

The information overload within the context of insurance services has been already addressed.[44] It arises when the information provided is too numerous and complex to handle effectively. In terms of its consequences, it can be expected to be as harmful as lack of information. Why is it such a serious problem now and what

---

[41] Atkinson and Messy (2012), p. 13.

[42] Proportionality in Bank Regulation, A Report by the EBA Banking Stakeholder Group, p. 22. The aim of EBA Report is to offer alternative test of proportionality to improve application of proportionality in bank regulation. In this vein, 'totality of regulation' and 'excess complexity' have been proposed by the Banking Stakeholder Group of the European Banking Authority as an alternative criterion applied while assessing proportionality of bank regulation. Although the Report regards banking regulation, considerations presented therein may be equally applicable to the insurance regulation.

[43] Leanerts and van Nuffel (1999), p. 108.

[44] See e.g. Frank and Lamiraud (2009), pp. 550–562; Maśniak (2015), pp. 221–233; Kim et al. (2013), pp. 3–13.

might be the consequences of information overload? For one thing, the information age has off-loaded a great deal of the work previously done by professionals (e.g. insurance distributors, travel agents) onto all of the customers. A lot of service normally expected from companies has been transferred to the customer who, in order to render that service must receive, understand and process an unprecedented amount of information.[45] Beyond doing more work, i.e. dealing with continually increasing amount of information, the customers have to face more *changes* in information. This not only refers to e.g. insurance terms and conditions which may be subject to periodical amendments, but also to the form the information is provided in, e.g. IPID. Finally, living in a global economy exposes people not only to large amounts of information (the quantitative dimension) but also to information of very different types (the qualitative dimension),[46] which only adds to the difficulty of managing information received. The following situation may serve as an example of the above: a person seeking for non-life insurance coverage in Poland receives (i) **a full text of general terms and conditions** of insurance contract. These general terms and conditions are additionally accompanied with (ii) the **so-called "index"** in a form of table which is supposed to indicate the most important provisions of the GTC relevant for the customer to take an informed decision.[47] Currently, under IDD Directive the customer is also receiving (iii) **IPID**. Theoretically all these three documents contain the same information yet in a different form. Last but not least, in addition to this information regarding only non-life insurance product itself, the customer receives **information on the insurance distributor**. Information of different type and level of complexity, not to mention its amount.

The effects of information overload have been examined and the findings suggest that **too little information is no good, but so is too much**. In other words, the **customers** have finite limits for how much information they can absorb and process which leads to the fundamental conclusion that they **make faulty choices with more information.**[48] The literature confirms it by giving the example of the abovementioned index. Namely, it is claimed that instead of having better understanding of GTC, index makes customers confused and even more reluctant to read or understand GTC.[49] What additionally strengthens harmful effect of information

[45]Illich (1981).

[46]Overbye (2012), p. D3; Eppler and Mengis (2004), p. 5, 327.

[47]Obligation to include index in the general terms and conditions results from the Article 17 of the Polish act of 11 September 2015 on insurance and reinsurance activity (Journal of Laws of 2019, item 381 as amended).

[48]Not only decision quality and effectiveness are lowered due to information overload. Extensive analysis of the phenomenon shows a variety of negative effects, among which ignorance and high selectivity of information, loss of control over information, misinterpretation, loss of differentiation etc. See: Eppler and Mengis (2004), p. 5, 333; Jacoby (1977), pp. 569–573; Jacoby et al. (1974), pp. 33–42.

[49]Krajewski (2017).

overload is the fact that people are unable to ignore information that is irrelevant or incomprehensible.[50]

Having formulated the problem, the researchers started to search for the answer to the following question: how much information or complexity is optimal? Optimal complexity theory states that there is an inverted U function which can serve as a practical tool to assess the optimal amount of information needed to take a reasonable decision. The theory has been also proved empirically in a military exercise simulation.[51] These results have been further developed in another theory of George A. Miller known as "Magical Number 7"[52] which proves that human ability to process several information units at the same time is limited to 7 $\pm$ 2 units.

Another important study proves that the customer makes better decisions if he can choose which parameters to receive information about and how much.[53] It is justified by the fact that the customer can better choose information which is relevant to him but, most importantly, which he is best able to understand. *A contrario*, it results that the information which is irrelevant or incomprehensible causes information overload and interferes with making reasonable decision.

Finally, not only does information overload affect final result of decision-making, but primarily it tends to have negative impact on the already existing and processed information by eliminating it or by causing confusion.[54]

The totality of information duties may be burdensome also from the insurance distributors' perspective. Due to the recent surveys, the heavier regulation is perceived by the insurers as one of the greatest **entrepreneurial risk.**[55] Their main doubts arise over implementation costs and risk of compliance. The more numerous and complex is regulation, the higher is the risk.

4.2.4 Excess Complexity

Considering the problem through the totality of regulation (the quantitative dimension) encourages to assess necessity of the measure also through the prism of its complexity (the qualitative dimension). It should be determined **whether the measure is excessively and unnecessarily complex for the objectives** that are sought.[56] Is all the **content of information** provided to the customer under IDD Directive

[50]Kahneman et al. (1982).

[51]For details on the military exercise simulation see: Streufert et al. (1965), p. 736.

[52]G. A. Miller, The Magical Number Seven, Plus or Minus Two: Some Limits on our Capacity for Processing Information, Psychological Review, 63, pp. 81–97, available at: http://psychclassics.yorku.ca/Miller/.

[53]Ariely (2000), pp. 233–248.

[54]So called 'information cannibalism". See: Loacker (2015), p. 118.

[55]Insurance Banana Skins 2019, The CSFI survey of the risks facing insurers, https://www.pwc.com/gx/en/financial-services/assets/pdf/insurance-banana-skins-2019.pdf [visited: 20.07.2019].

[56]Proportionality in Bank Regulation, A Report by the EBA Banking Stakeholder Group, pp. 24, 25. See supra note 27.

indeed necessary for the customer to take fair decision? Would each customer be able to properly interpret and use the fact that an insurance intermediary has a holding representing 10% or more of the voting rights or of the capital in a given insurer? If disclosure of a particular information is intended to enhance the customer's ability to make decision, then his capacity to understand how the disclosed information is relevant to making decision becomes critical.[57]

Due to the survey by the financial services regulators in the U.K. and U.S., the main problem of the financial services customers is not a lack of information—quite opposite: what creates customers' confusion is too much information of a complex nature.[58] Clearly, what serves transparency (e.g. the above information on holding) does not always enhance understanding and legibility.

Finally, the ability of coping with the sheer amount of data and drawing the right conclusions is questioned not only with respect to the customers but also to other market players and supervisors. It is believed that overly complex regulations which generate a false sense of thoroughness may result in being a real source of **systemic risk**. It is argued that disclosure of too much information could actually reduce the effectiveness of previous disclosures[59] and ultimately reduce transparency.[60]

4.3 Is There an Appropriate Balance Between the Damage Suffered by the Customers (e.g. Consequences of the Information Overload) and Insurance Distributors (e.g. Costs) and the Benefit Obtained by Achieving Enhanced Customer Protection as a Consequence of Introducing the Information Duties?

Usually, when assessing proportionality of a measure, ECJ limits proportionality test to the test of suitability and necessity as they mostly give enough arguments to decide. Thus, the third test—proportionality *sensu stricto*—is used rarely. The same could happen also in this case. Previous paragraphs challenge information duties particularly as to their necessity in the sense of their amount and complexity. Following this, one could go a step further and claim that considering totality of regulation and the effects of information overload, information duties (as they are applied currently) cannot be recognized as necessary measure. Consequently, information duties do not result to be proportional and no need of proportionality *sensu stricto* test occurs.

[57]Ben-Shahar and Schneider (2011), p. 743.

[58]Diacon and Ennew (2001), p. 391.

[59]Jiang (2018), p. 503.

[60]Nebel (2004), p. 282.

Nevertheless, regardless the above possible assumption, it is worth to discuss at least one aspect of proportionality *sensu stricto*—the problem of **excessive burden** of the measure. With respect to the information duties, it seems that excessive burden could be considered in two situations: first—the negative effects of information overload (which have been already addressed) and second—costs. In terms of costs, a fair question to ask would be whether the expenditures made to adjust the insurance distributors' activity to the new requirements (information duties) are excessively burdensome for insurance distributors and especially for those who fall into small and medium-sized enterprises category.[61] Although EIOPA settled out its first impressions of the impact and costs of introducing a standardized presentation format for the IPID,[62] it is still hard to find a full costs assessment which would include all the newly introduced information duties.

5 Concluding Remarks

The above-presented test, modelled on the test of proportionality applied by the ECJ, examined proportionality of the information duties stemming from IDD Directive, relevant for non-life insurance only. The main result of the analysis is that **the measure (information duties) seems to be overused and thereby becomes disproportional**. Different empirical studies presented in this chapter support the thesis that the amount of information exceeds the insurance distributor's ability to describe it intelligibly and the customer's ability to understand it usefully. Consequently, information duties mostly fail to achieve the objective. The study also confirms previous academics' concerns about the necessity and expediency of the excessiveness of current insurance regulation in general.[63] On the side note, it is worth mentioning that the results of this study are likely to be even more evident if the study examines information duties relevant for life insurance, including investment based insurance products, as in this case IDD and other insurance regulation provide for additional number of even more complex information duties.

Summary of the above conducted test of proportionality has been also presented in the form of table which allows to grasp the whole picture (see Annex). The table identifies key elements of the test (i.e. objective, measures allowing to achieve the objective, benefits and detriments caused by each measure) in the first place. Having identified these elements, the table should be read as follows. First, a baseline

[61]The existing economic studies argue that the obligations relating to information entails substantial non-recurring and ongoing administrative expenditures not only for the distributors but also for the competent authorities of the member state and the customers themselves. See: Köhne and Brömmelmeyer (2018), p. 732.

[62]EIOPA, Consultation Paper on the proposal for Implementing Technical Standards on a standardised presentation format of the insurance product information document, EIOPA-CP-16/007, 1 August 2016, pp. 28, 29.

[63]Köhne and Brömmelmeyer (2018), p. 705.

scenario (measure No 0) is to prove that the objective will not come by itself and lack of action would only cause further detriments. Hence, an action is needed. Second, appropriateness of the measures No 1, 2 and 3 is assessed by comparing their benefits and detriments. As a result, it should be possible to tell whether the benefits of chosen measures outweigh its detriments. In order to do so, the benefits and detriments should be balanced, which may seem an impossible task. Namely, the biggest problem the balancing entails is to quantify both benefits and detriments. A certain value should be attributed to each benefit and detriment, taking account of the ultimate objective. Clearly, the subjectivity of this task only adds to its difficulty. For this reason, the table does not suggest any value and it is left to the reader to subjectively assess the overall balance.

Besides the balancing of benefits and detriments, each measure should be additionally assessed in terms of costs it generates. Cost effectiveness has been included in the table as a separate column, although, it could be rightly argued that costs constitute another detriment. Nevertheless, the costs have been separated for one major reason. Contrary to the abovementioned benefits and detriments, costs are quantifiable. Hence, it is possible to objectively compare costs generated by each measure. Here, the economic analysis may be of help. In fact, economic analysis should be an integral part of the test of proportionality as proportionality is believed to be more economical principle rather than legal one.[64] The table does take into account cost assessment factor, however, due to lack of the relevant information, the test cannot be recognized as completed in this part. Speaking of costs, it may be interesting to mention here the results of the study presented by the German government which recognized the 100 most costly information duties imposed by national law.[65] The study shows that the pre-contractual info duties are at 13th place, while the information to be provided during the duration of the insurance contract takes 8th place on the overall list. Noteworthy is also the fact that the study concerned only standardized information, which is considered cheaper than the individualized one.[66]

Despite the part regarding cost effectiveness, the author tried to compare the benefits and detriments on the basis of the weight of the evidence (empirical studies) and the importance of each factor. The majority of detriments are empirically proven while the benefits, which were indicted in the IDD Directive's impact assessment, often seem to be purely intuitive. Although a fair cost-analysis is needed to complete the results of this test, the author argues that the overall analysis questions proportionality of information duties. The test proves that the information duties are suitable to attain the objective, however, the same is not true for the test of necessity. Furthermore, even if one assumes that there is an appropriate balance between the benefits and detriments, it is still impossible to accept proportionality of the EU measure as it does not fulfil all three requirements jointly, i.e. lack of necessity. The

[64] See e.g. Portuese (2013).

[65] BT-Drucks 16/6826 of 24.10.2007.

[66] Loacker (2015), p. 44, 45.

author is aware that in order to successfully challenge the measure adopted by the EU, it needs to be *manifestly* inappropriate,[67] which information duty is surely not. Nevertheless, assuming that information duties do not comply with the principle of proportionality, the study would provide grounds to challenge the concept of disclosures and would serve as an incentive to revise totality of information duties included in the insurance regulation at both European and national level. For the potential process of revision, it is necessary to take into account the results of the insights from the neuroscience and behavioral economics which clearly show that it is next to impossible to fully control or influence the customer's decision making in a way that he or she would take only rational decisions. Bearing this in mind, the EU legislator would consider shifting from forcing further information requirements to searching for other measures which would improve the efficiency of information duties that are already in force—e.g. **financial education**. Benefiting from information duties naturally requires a certain willingness to read and understand the information provided. This, however, should not be taken for granted. Various studies have consistently found that consumers are often (apart from their difficulties in understanding the information provided) not willing to read the given material. In the insurance field this applies not only to general terms and conditions but also to rather short and clearly arranged documents like the key features documents.[68] One possible reason for which people are reluctant to read anything (even perfectly designed information) is that the insurance is unknown to majority of customers. **One is reluctant to a concept that he does not know nor understand.** Implementing financial education at the very beginning of basic education may serve as a tool to eliminate that reluctance and successfully improve the decision making of the next generation of customers.

Finally, the above analysis sheds some light on the quality of legislation. As it was depictured in the first paragraphs, the tendency to protect customer by 'feeding' him with more and more information of different forms and nature can be traced to the financial crisis of 2007–2010. This only proves the observance that 'catastrophes are probably the most important catalysts of new regulation'.[69] Having said this, it is also worth noting that a regulation which acts as a response to a market failure tends to be more severe in terms of quality and quantity. Bearing this in mind, it can be feared that growing adoption of transparency measures and information disclosures, including those introduced by the IDD Directive, result from political pressure, and a sense of duty to regulate rather than an in-depth search for the best measure preceded with a due impact assessment. If this is the case, it should not come as a surprise that the effectiveness or burden of information duties are rarely inquired. Even the available impact assessment report does not reflect much on the problem and proportionality of all the new information duties is rather taken for granted.

---

[67]Tor-Inge Harbo (2015), p. 24.

[68]Loacker (2015), p. 112.

[69]Bardach and Kagan (2017), p. 23.

Annex I

TEST OF PROPORTIONALITY			
PROBLEM: insurance coverage incompliant with customer's demands and needs → lack of the insurance coverage → negative influence on stabilization of financial market			
MEASURE	**OBJECTIVE** GENERAL OBJECTIVE: customer protection SPECIFIC OBJECTIVE: making customers' financial decisions more reasonable and informed by facilitating understanding the information and mechanisms		**COST EFFECTIVENESS**
	BENEFITS (EFFECTIVENESS)	**DETRIMENTS (NEGATIVE EFFECTS)**	
0 – Take no action (Baseline scenario)[70]	0	– identified problem will persist and could be aggravated by future market developments[71] – increase in the number of cases of mis-selling of insurance products and cases where customers are led to take undue risks[72]	N/A
1 – Information disclosures (i), (ii), (iii)	+ enhanced trust to insurance distributors[73] and higher transparency[74] (i), (iii) + clarity with regard to the principle-agent	• **INFORMATION OVERLOAD** and its consequences: – increased confusion – decision effectiveness (accuracy and	Potential system changes are needed to enable these disclosures. Yet it is estimated that the costs related to the

(continued)

[70]The aim of the baseline scenario is to answer the question of whether the objective will come by itself and to explain how the current situation would evolve without additional regulatory intervention.

[71]European Commission, Commission Staff Working Document Executive Summary of The Impact Assessment Accompanying the document Proposal for the Directive of European Parliament and of the Council on Insurance Mediation (SWD/2012/0192 final), Strasbourg, 3.7.2012, pp. 24, 25.

[72]Ibidem.

[73]Ibidem p. 18.

[74]Ibidem, p. 42.

TEST OF PROPORTIONALITY			
	relationship, including how this may impact on advice[75] (i) + facilitating comparison of insurance covers and prices[76] (i), (ii) + improved understanding and identification of the most important pieces of policy information (comprehensibility) by introducing standard presentation of IPID[77] (ii)	quality) lowered – increased difficulty in identification and selection of relevant information – loss of control over information – lack of critical evaluation and superficial analysis – loss of differentiation – higher time requirements for information handling • extension of sale process (iv) • administrative burden (compliance risk) • systemic risk • entrepreneurial risk	disclosures are not excessive.[78] The initial analysis results in non-excessive costs.[79]
2 – Identification of the customer's demands and needs and provision of advice or recommendation (iv)	+ enhanced customer's choice, confidence and quality of service received + improved comparability of offers[80] + improved understanding by customers of the services and products on offer[81]		Subject to further cost analysis
3 – Financial education programs	+ improved financial literacy	0	Subject to further cost analysis

Source: Produced by the author

[75]Ibidem, p. 42.

[76]Ibidem, p. 42.

[77]EIOPA, Final Report on Consultation Paper no. 16/007 on draft Implementing Technical Standards concerning a standardised presentation format for the Insurance Product Information Document of the Insurance Distribution Directive, EIOPA-BoS-17/055, 7 February 2017, p. 28. Interestingly, Poland has introduced similar measure prior to IPID (pl. skorowidz) which failed to achieve the objective.

[78]Ibidem, pp. 45, 49.

[79]Ibidem, pp. 30, 31.

[80]European Commission, Commission Staff Working Document Executive Summary of The Impact Assessment Accompanying the document Proposal for the Directive of European Parliament and of the Council on Insurance Mediation (SWD/2012/0192 final), Strasbourg, 3.7.2012, p. 71.

[81]Ibidem, p. 71.

References

Ariely D (2000) Controlling the information flow: effects on consumers' decision-making and preferences. J Consum Res 27(2):233–248

Atkinson A, Messy FA (2012) Measuring financial literacy: results of the OECD INFE pilot study. OECD Working Papers on Finance, Insurance and Private Pensions, 2012, No. 15. OECD Publishing

Bardach E, Kagan RA (2017) Going by the book: the problem of regulatory unreasonableness. Routledge, New York

Ben-Shahar O, Schneider CE (2011) The failure of mandated disclosure. Univ Pa Law Rev 159:647–749

Ben-Shahar O, Schneider CE (2014) The futility of cost benefit analysis in financial disclosure regulation. University of Chicago Law School, Coase-Sandor Institute for Law and Economics, Working Paper No. 680, 2D Series, Chicago

Bieri DS (2014) Financial Stability Rearticulated: Institutional Reform, Postcrisis Governance and the New Regulatory Landscape in the United States. GFURR Working Paper, August 2014

Craig P (2012) EU administrative law, 2nd edn. Oxford University Press, Oxford

Diacon S, Ennew C (2001) Consumer perceptions of financial risk. Geneva Pap Risk Insur 26 (3):389–409

Eppler MJ, Mengis J (2004) The concept of information overload: a review of literature from organization science, accounting, marketing, MIS, and related disciplines. Inf Soc 20:5

Frank RG, Lamiraud K (2009) Choice, price competition and complexity in markets for health insurance. J Econ Behav Organ 71(2);550–562

Fras M (2018) The principle and criterion of reasonableness in insurance. In: Malinowska K, Tarasiuk A (eds) Insurance challenges of Anno Domini 2018. Poltext sp. z o.o., Warsaw

Fung A, Graham M, Weil D (2008) Full disclosure, the perils and promise of transparency. Cambridge University Press, Cambridge, p 90

Harbo T (2015) The function of proportionality analysis in European Law. Brill Nijhoff, Boston; Nijhoff studies in EU law, volume 8, 2015

Hilliard A (2018) Issues arising from the implementation of the IDD. In: 7th AIDA Europe Conference, Warsaw, 13 April 2018, presentation available at: http://www.aida.org.uk/docs/Issues%20Arising%20from%20the%20Implementation%20of%20the%20IDD.pdf

Illich I (1981) Shadow work. Marion Boyars, London

Jacoby J (1977) Information load and decision quality. Some contested issues. J Mark Res 14 (4):569–573

Jacoby J, Speller DE, Berning CK (1974) Brand choice behavior as a function of information load: replication and extension. J Consum Res 1(1):33

Jiang L (2018) Disclosure's last stand? The need to clarify the 'informational interest' advanced by campaign finance disclosure. Columbia Law Rev 119:487, No.2

Kahneman D, Slovic P, Tversky A (1982) Judgment under uncertainty: heuristics and biases. Cambridge University Press, Cambridge

Kielholz WB, Nebel R (2005) Improving regulatory governance. Geneva Pap 30:34–42

Kim J, Braun B, Williams AD (2013) Understanding health insurance literacy: a literature review. Family Consum Sci Res J 42(1):3–13

Köhne T, Brömmelmeyer C (2018) The new insurance distribution regulation in the EU 0 A critical assessment from a legal and economic perspective. Geneva Pap Risk Insur Issues Pract 43 (4):704–739

Krajewski M (2017) Commentary to the Article 17 of the Polish act of 11 September 2015 on insurance and reinsurance activity. In: Szczepańska M, Wajda P (eds) Act on insurance and reinsurance activity. Commentary. Wolters Kluwer

Kunreuther H, Pauly MV (2018) Dynamic insurance decision-making for rare events: the role of emotions. Geneva Pap 43:335–355

Leanerts K, van Nuffel P (1999) Constitutional law of the European Union. Sweet and Maxwell, London

Loacker LD (2015) Informed insurance choice? The insurer's pre-contractual information duties in general consumer insurance. Edward Elgar Publishing

Maśniak M (2015) Doinformowanie czy przeciążenie informacyjne w stosunkach bancassurance, czyli o zakresie informowania ubezpieczonych (*Improving information or information overload in bancassurance. On the scope of information provided to insured persons*). In: Gnela B, Szaraniec M (eds) Informacja w prawie ubezpieczeń gospodarczych (*Information in insurance law*). Wolters Kluwer SA, Warsaw

Miller GA. The magical number seven, plus or minus two: some limits on our capacity for processing information. Psychol Rev 63. Available at: http://psychclassics.yorku.ca/Miller/

Nebel R (2004) Regulations as a source of systemic risk: the need for economic impact analysis. Geneva Pap Risk Insur 29(2):273–283

Overbye D (2012) Mystery of big data's parallel universe brings fear, and a thrill. The New York Times, June 5, p D3

Pokrzywniak J (2018) Obowiązek rozpoznania wymagań i potrzeb klienta (*Duty to identify demands and needs of client*). In: Pokrzywniak J (ed) Nowe zasady dystrybucji ubezpieczeń (*New rules for insurance distribution*). Wolters Kluwer Polska Sp. z o.o., Warsaw

Portuese A (2013) Principle of proportionality as principle of economic efficiency. Eur Law J 19 (5):612

Richter A, Ruß J, Schelling S (2019) Insurance customer behavior: Lessons from behavioral economics. Risk Manag Insur Rev 22:183–205. https://doi.org/10.1111/rmir.12121

Ring P (2018) The regulation and governance of financial advice in Europe – the implications for the retail financial advice sector and its consumers. In: Grima S, Marano P (eds) Governance and regulations. Contemporary issues. Contemporary Studies in Economics and Financial Analysis, Vol. 99. Emerald Publishing

Schwarcz SL (2011) Information asymmetry and information failure: disclosure problems in complex financial markets. In: Sun W, Steward J, Pollard D (eds) Corporate governance and the global financial crisis. International perspectives. Cambridge University Press

Sovern J (2010) Preventing Future Economic Crisis through Consumer Protection Law or How the Truth in Lending Act Failed the Subprime Borrowers, St John's School of Law, Legal Studies Research Paper Series, Paper 10-0189, December 2010

Streufert S, Suedfeld P, Driver MJ (1965) Conceptual structure, information search, and information utilization. J Personal Soc Psychol 2(5):736–740

Szczepańska M (2015) Analiza potrzeb klienta jako szczególny obowiązek informacyjny ubezpieczyciela (*Client's demands and needs analysis as an information duty of the insurer*). In: Gnela B, Szaraniec M (eds) Informacja w Prawie Ubezpieczeń Gospodarczych (*Information in the insurance law*). Wolters Kluwer SA, Warsaw

van Gerven W (1999) The effect of proportionality on the actions of Member States of the European community: national viewpoints from continental Europe. In: Ellis E (ed) The principle of proportionality in the laws of Europe. Hart, Oxford

Van Hulle K (2019) Solvency requirements for EU insurers. Solvency II is good for you. Intersentia

Wendland HM (2018) When good is not good enough: a comparative analysis of underinclusiveness and the principle of coherence under proportionality review. Maastricht J Eur Comp Law 25(3):332–356

Xiao JJ, Porto N (2019) Financial education and insurance advice seeking. Geneva Pap Risk Insur Issues Pract 44:20–35

Legislation

Directive (EU) 2016/97 of the European Parliament and of the Council of 20 January 2016 on insurance distribution (recast)Text with EEA relevance, OJ L 26, 2.2.2016, pp 19–59
Commission Implementing Regulation (EU) 2017/1469 of 11 August 2017 laying down a standardised presentation format for the insurance product information document (Text with EEA relevance), OJ L 209, 12.8.2017
Treaty on European Union (OJ C 326, 26.10.2012, p. 13–390)

Documents

EBA, Proportionality in Bank Regulation, A Report by the EBA Banking Stakeholder Group;2014 Financial Inclusion Action Plan, 14 November 2014
EIOPA, Consultation Paper on the proposal for Implementing Technical Standards on a standardised presentation format of the insurance product information document (EIOPA-CP-16/007), 2016
EIOPA (2019) Report on best practices on licensing requirements, peer-to-peer insurance and the principle of proportionality in an insurtech context. Publications Office of the European Union, Luxembourg
The European Commission, Commission Staff Working Document. Impact Assessment. Accompanying the Document Proposal for a Directive of the European Parliament and of the Council on Insurance Mediation, Strasburg 3.7.2012, SWD (2012) 191 final
Insurance Banana Skins 2019, The CSFI survey of the risks facing insurers, https://www.pwc.com/gx/en/financial-services/assets/pdf/insurance-banana-skins-2019.pdf
REP 632 A joint report from the Australian Securities and Investments Commission (ASIC) and the Dutch Authority for the Financial Markets (AFM): Disclosure: Why it shouldn't be default. 14 October 2019., available at: https://asic.gov.au/regulatory-resources/find-a-document/reports/rep-632-disclosure-why-it-shouldn-t-be-the-default/
Better regulation guidelines, Chapter III – Guidelines on impact assessment, available at: https://ec.europa.eu/info/law/law-making-process/planning-and-proposing-law/better-regulation-why-and-how/better-regulation-guidelines-and-toolbox_en
G20 The Seoul Summit Document
G20 High Level Principles on Financial Consumer Protection, OECD, October 2011., https://www.oecd.org/daf/fin/financial-markets/48892010.pdf
G20 Leaders' Declaration, Sankt Petersburg 2013

The Contribution of Product Oversight and Governance (POG) to the Single Market: A Set of Organisational Rules for Business Conduct

Pierpaolo Marano

1 Introduction

Product oversight and governance (POG) is one of the major innovations, if not the most significant, introduced by the Insurance Distribution Directive (IDD). It is somewhat unusual, however, that this novelty is not reflected both in the proposal for amending the Insurance Mediation Directive, which would later become the IDD and in the preliminary work carried out by the Commission for the drafting of that proposal. POG appeared in the IDD as a mere "copy and paste" from the Market in Financial Instruments Directive II (MiFID II). The initial draft of the MiFID II also did not contain any rules on POG. Thus, the entry of POG into European Union (EU) law was not accompanied by in-depth analyses of the EU bodies that decided to adopt that set of rules in the financial and insurance field.[1] Such a genesis of POG delivers a set of rules that should be investigated to understand the effects and usefulness.

POG is consistent, in principle, with the evolution in the EU approach to insurance regulation. Solvency II identified the protection of policyholders and beneficiaries as the main objective of supervision.[2] A prospective and risk-based approach is the basis of supervision that includes the verification on a continuous basis of the proper operation of the insurance or reinsurance business and of the

[1]However, see the *Opinion* issued by ESMA, *Structured retail products – Good practices for product governance arrangements*, March 2014, available at https://www.esma.europa.eu/sites/default/files/library/2015/11/2014-332_esma_opinion_u_structured_retail_products_-_good_practices_for_product_governance_arrangements.pdf.

[2]See Article 27 of Solvency II.

P. Marano (✉)
Catholic University of the Sacred Heart, Department of Legal Sciences, Milan, Italy
e-mail: pierpaolo.marano@unicatt.it

P. Marano, K. Noussia (eds.), *Insurance Distribution Directive*, AIDA Europe Research Series on Insurance Law and Regulation 3,
https://doi.org/10.1007/978-3-030-52738-9_3

compliance with supervisory provisions by insurance and reinsurance undertakings.[3] The IDD extended the set of rules on the proper operation of the insurance (and reinsurance) business and POG is a crucial component of this political choice. The set of rules on POG are addressed not only to insurance undertakings and distributors but also to the supervisory authorities. POG aims at anticipating customer protection at the design stage for product marketing, and it enables supervisory authorities to have a clearer picture of the businesses processes that are behind the products marketed to customers.

This chapter aims to investigate how POG fits into the overall EU insurance regulation. Thus, the first paragraph will analyse the origin of POG concept that can be attributed to the United Kingdom (UK). This "historical" research on the rules and underlying principles appears necessary given the absence of preliminary studies on POG at EU level before its introduction into the IDD. The second paragraph illustrates how IDD incorporated the POG devolving the adoption of the detailed rules to the Commission. The third and fourth paragraphs evaluate, respectively, the current and potential role that the new rules can play in building an authentic Single Market in the insurance sector.

2 The Origin of POG as a Regulatory Response Based on Principles of Businesses

The concept of POG was mainly developed in the UK,[4] as one of the regulatory responses to the failings in the UK regulatory framework on financial services, which emerged with the financial crisis.[5] The UK regulatory framework was based on the assumption that adequate consumer protection would be achieved provided sales processes were fair, and product feature disclosure was transparent. The UK authorities developed POG to complement such regulatory framework rather than replacing. They decided to require: (*i*) providers to demonstrate the value for

---

[3]See article 29(1) of Solvency II.

[4]Some inspiration can be found in the Resolution n. 9019104 of 2 March 2009 on illiquid investment products, which was issued by the Italian authority responsible for regulating the Italian financial market (CONSOB). The principle of "acting honestly, fairly and professionally in accordance with the best interest of customers" (see Article 19.1 MiFID) was interpreted in the sense of requiring issuers of illiquid investment products to design their commercial policy evaluating the compatibility of each product with the characteristics and needs of the customers to whom they are offered. Thus CONSOB requires the definition of business processes to allow, even in abstracts terms, the assessment of the financial needs of the selected target market compared to those satisfied by the products which should be offered to them, in the concrete selection phase of the products to be distributed and, more importantly, in the possible engineering phase. In addition, the activities above shall be approved by the administrative body and verified by the compliance function. See also Autorité des Marchés Financiers (AMF), *La commercialisation des instruments financiers complexes*, Position No 2010 - 05, of 15 October 2010.

[5]See Marano (2019), pp. 60 ff.

the customer of the products they are designing, and (*ii*) providers and distributors to take care of their customers. The new set of rules was based around the idea that a more structured design and marketing process, involving the board of directors and where company functions are always attentive to meeting customer needs and interests, should prevent the customer bias without the intervention of supervisory authorities. POG should allow supervised entities to be more aware of the embedded "value for customers" in their products, while supervisors can take rapid action to stop problems from growing and affecting large numbers of consumers, and to deter the creation of products likely to lead to consumer detriment.[6]

The UK authorities considered that POG was already embedded in principles on business conduct, but the regulatory intervention was deemed necessary to detail POG. This new supervisory approach has been completed turning some of the Financial Service Authority (FSA)[7] previously published material on treating customers fairly and the responsibilities of product providers and distributors into rules.[8] FSA Handbook related to "The Responsibilities of Providers and Distributors for the Fair Treatment of Customers" provided guidance for POG, which were inferred from some Principles of Businesses. Thus, principles operating prior to the financial crisis were deemed fit to found the new regulatory approach. These "evergreen" principles needed to be more detailed and, therefore, business conduct switched from a principle-based regulation to a detailed-based regulation.[9]

POG was built around four principles of businesses. The following can be considered like the principle that oversees all new regulatory architecture: A firm must conduct its business with due skill, care and diligence.[10] This principle permeates both the organisational structure of the firm and its approach to the customer, while the other three principles appear to be the application or specification of this general rule. One of them is more focused on organisational: A firm must take reasonable care to organise and control its affairs responsibly and effectively, with adequate risk management systems.[11] Another principle refers to the quality of the product/service offered to the customer: A firm must pay due regard to the interests of its customers and treat them fairly.[12] The other principle concerns the information flow with the customer: A firm must pay due regard to the information needs of its

[6]FSA, *Discussion Paper on Product Intervention*, January 2011, p. 16.

[7]The Financial Conduct Authority (FCA) replaced the Financial Services Authority (FSA) since 1 April 2013.

[8]See: FSA, *Treating Customers Fairly. Towards Fair Outcomes for Consumers*, July 2006; FSA, *Treating Customers Fairly. Structured Investment Products*, October 2009; FSA, *Finalised Guidance – Retail Product Development and Governance*, March 2012; FCA, *Structured Products: Thematic Review of Product Development and Governance*, March 2015; HM Treasury, *A New Approach to Financial Regulation: Judgement, Focus and Stability*, 2012. An analysis of the FSA Treating Customers Fairly Initiative is provided by Georgosouli (2011), pp. 405 ff.

[9]In a broader perspective, see Marcacci (2017), pp. 305 ff.

[10]See Principle of Business No. 2.

[11]See Principle of Business No. 3.

[12]See Principle of Business No. 6.

clients and communicate information to them in a way which is clear, fair and not misleading.[13]

The transition from a principle-based regulation to a detailed-based regulation leads as an obvious deduction that the rules have increased in number and detail. However, this finding is reductive compared to the real innovation that this transition entails: *these rules become an integral part of the organisation of insurance undertakings and their distributors. At the same time, supervision must ensure that the organisation of these entities also complies with these rules.*

Regarding providers,[14] the general principle together with the organisational principle and the principle of product/service quality, allow the UK authorities to affirm the following detailed rules that form the basis of POG. Providers shall identify the target market, namely which types of customer the product or service is likely to be suitable (or not suitable) for. Thus, the provider shall (*i*) stress-test the product or service to identify how it might perform in a range of market environments and how the customer could be affected, and (*ii*) have in place systems and controls to manage adequately the risks posed by-product or service design.

Moreover, the general principle under which a firm must conduct its business with due skill, care and diligence affects the information provided to distributors from providers. Such principle "implies" that providers shall (*i*) make clear if that information is not intended for customer use; and (*ii*) ensure the information is sufficient, appropriate and comprehensible in substance and form, including considering whether it will enable distributors to understand it enough to give suitable advice (where advice is given) and to extract any relevant information and communicate it to the end customer. As part of meeting this standard, the provider may wish to consider, about each distribution channel or type of distributor, what information distributors of that type already have, their likely level of knowledge and understanding, their information needs and what form or medium would best meet those needs (which could include discussions, written material or training as appropriate).

This principle is relevant when selecting a distribution channel, and it is complemented with those concerning the quality of the product/service offered to the customer, and the flow of information with the customer. In particular, a provider shall: (*i*) decide whether this is a product where customers would be wise to seek advice; (*ii*) review how what is occurring in practice corresponds to (or deviates from) what was initially planned or envisaged for the distribution of its products or services given the target market. This activity involves collecting and analysing appropriate management information such that the firm can detect patterns in

[13]See Principle of Business No. 7.

[14]FSA Handbook related to "The Responsibilities of Providers and Distributors for the Fair Treatment of Customers", which is availbale at https://www.handbook.fca.org.uk/handbook/document/rppd/RPPD_Full_20180103.pdf, specifies the term "provider" include persons who offer services such as portfolio management (through distributors or otherwise) as well as those who develop, manage or package products such as life insurance, general insurance or investment products or who develop or enter into home finance transactions (i.e. mortgages, home reversion plans and home purchase plans).

distribution as compared with the planned target market, and can assess the performance of the distribution channels through which its products or services are being distributed; (*iii*) act when it has concerns, for example by ceasing to use a particular distribution channel.

The above principles detailing the general one also incorporate the rules that are inferred for the information to customers. They request a provider to: (*i*) pay regard to its target market, including its likely level of financial capability; (*ii*) take account of what information the customer needs to understand the product or service, its purpose and the risks, and communicate information in a way that is clear, fair and not misleading; (*iii*) have in place systems and controls to manage effectively the risks posed by providing information to customers.

Those principles are also relevant, finally, for establishing detailed rules in the area of post-sale responsibility. Thus, a provider (*i*) in supplying information direct to the customer, must ensure that the information is communicated in a way which is clear, fair and not misleading; (*ii*) should periodically review products whose performance may vary materially to check whether the product is continuing to meet the general needs of the target market that it was designed for, or whether the product's performance will be significantly different from what the provider originally expected and communicated to the distributor or customer at the time of the sale. If this occurs, the provider should consider what action to take, such as whether and how to inform the customer of this (to the extent the customer could not reasonably have been aware) and of their option to seek advice, and whether to cease selling the product; (*iii*) should communicate to the customer contractual 'breakpoints' such as the end of a long tie-in period that may have a material impact on a customer that the customer cannot reasonably be expected to recall or know about already; (*iv*) should act fairly and promptly when handling claims or when paying out on a product that has been surrendered or reached maturity. In doing this, the provider should meet any reasonable customer expectations that it may have created about the outcomes or how the process would be handled; (*v*) must establish, implement and maintain effective and transparent customer complaint-handling systems.

The principles examined so far are also relevant for distributors. Regarding distributor responsibilities, the general principle as detailed by others, allows inferring several detailed rules in the area of financial promotions. Hence, distributors (*i*) shall have in place systems and controls to manage effectively the risks posed by financial promotions; and (*ii*) in passing on a promotion created by a provider, must act with due skill, care and diligence. A firm will not contravene the financial promotions rules where it communicates a promotion produced by another person provided the firm takes reasonable care to establish that another firm has confirmed compliance with the relevant detailed rules, amongst other matters.

Moreover, the general principle as detailed with those concerning the quality of the product/service offered to the customer, and the flow of information with the customer led to set up the following rules when providing information to a customer before or at the point of sale. Thus, providers: (*i*) shall consider, when passing provider materials to customers, whether it understands the information provided;

(*ii*) shall ask the provider to supply additional information or training where that seems necessary to understand the product or service adequately; (*iii*) shall not distribute the product or service if it does not understand it sufficiently, especially if it intends to provide advice; and (*iv*) when providing information to another distributor in a distribution chain, should consider how the further distributor will use the information, such as whether it will be given to customers. Firms should consider what information the further distributor requires and the reasonable level of knowledge and understanding of the further distributor and what medium may suit it best for the transmission of information.

The general principle as detailed with that related to the quality of the product/service offered to the customer is relevant when advising on the selection of a provider. Thus, distributors shall consider: (*i*) the nature of the products or services offered by the provider and how they fit with the customer's needs and risk appetite; and (*ii*) what impact the selection of a given provider could have on the customer in terms of charges or the financial strength of the provider, or possibly, where information is available to the distributor, how efficiently and reliably the provider will deal with the distributor or customer at the point of sale (or subsequently, such as when queries/complaints arise, claims are made, or a product reaches maturity).

The principles on organisational and the quality of the product/service offered to the customer allow to infer several rules in the area of post-sale responsibility. Hence, distributors: (*i*) shall comply with any contractual obligation it has to the customer, for example, to provide ongoing advice or periodic reviews. In connection with this, distributors should also consider their responsibility to maintain adequate systems and controls to deliver on such reviews; (*ii*) shall consider any implied or express representation they made (during meetings, correspondence or promotional material, for example) and, in particular, where a customer has reasonable expectations based on the prior statements of a distributor, the distributor should meet these expectations; (*iii*) where involved in handling claims or paying out on a product that has been surrendered or reached maturity, should meet any reasonable expectations that the distributor has created in the customer's mind about how the process would be handled; (*iv*) must establish, implement and maintain effective and transparent customer complaint-handling systems; and (*v*) shall pass any communications received from customers (intended for or suited to providers to act upon) to providers in a timely and accurate way.

In conclusion, the UK hands over the EU a set of organisational rules inferred from business conduct principles. POG embeds the customer's protection in the organisational rules applying to providers and distributors. Thus, firms are called to comply with internal procedures aiming at creating products that have a real value for the customers to whom they will be offered, and not just a value for the shareholders, directors and senior management of the undertaking. Moreover, POG aims at anticipating customer protection at the design stage for product marketing because it enables supervisory authorities to have a clearer picture of the businesses processes that are behind the products marketed to customers. The early knowledge of the design process should facilitate the supervisory authorities to exercise their intervention powers in order to prevent or reduce detriments arising from products that are not developed in the best interest of the customers.[15] To this purpose, authorities need to be properly equipped with skilled staff in order to quickly understand the design of the products,[16] if the intervention powers to be exercised promptly.[17]

3 The Transposition of POG in the EU Law: Organizational Rules for the Business Conduct

The EU fully embraced the set of rules on POG and their rationale as elaborated by the UK. POG was not included in the initial draft proposal of the IDD, which was issued by the European Commission in July 2012, and the introduction of POG for the insurance industry was not preceded by specific activity of the European Commission, even in terms of cost/benefit analysis. Notwithstanding this, the European Supervision Authorities (ESAs) adopted a Joint position on manufacturers' products oversight and governance processes in 2013, where the legal basis of EIOPA's involvement was founded (*i*) in the possibility that product governance provisions may be included in the Directive on insurance mediation (IMD) or any future legislative act replacing IMD and (ii) as part of the principle set forth by Recital 16 of the Directive Solvency II under which the main objective of insurance and reinsurance regulation and supervision is the "adequate protection of policyholders and beneficiaries".[18] This, because such a principle is supplemented by additional requirements in Articles 41(1) and 41(6) of Solvency II, which include having effective systems of internal control and governance to provide for sound and prudent management of the business.[19] IDD outlines the characteristic features of POG. They are supplemented by Commission Delegated Regulation (EU) 2017/2358 of 21 September 2017, which is based on the Technical advice provided by the EIOPA in February 2017.[20]

---

[15] Ferran (2012), pp. 264 ff. See also: Tomic (2018), pp. 229–255; Busch (2017), pp. 409–420; Colaert (2019), pp. 395–402.

[16] Brandt (2011), p. 8 noted "This is not to say that current supervisory staff are inadequate; however, it appears that what the FSA is proposing is a radical and challenging benchmark which requires a significant investment in resourcing levels, training and overall staff quality".

[17] About the genesis of product intervention, see Moloney (2012), pp. 186 ff.

[18] See also Van Hulle (2019), p. 10.

[19] See Joint Position of the European Supervisory Authorities on Manufacturers' Product Oversight & Governance Processes, at point 22. The Joint position is available at https://www.eba.europa.eu/documents/10180/15736/JC-2013-77+%28POG+-+Joint+Position%29.pdf.

[20] The Final report is available at https://eiopa.europa.eu/Publications/Reports/EIOPA%20Final_Report_on_IDD_Technical%20Advice.pdf. See also EIOPA, *Preparatory Guidelines on product oversight and governance arrangements by insurance undertakings and insurance distributors*, March 2016.

The interpretative questions arising from the formulation of the rules on POG are not analysed in this essay.[21] Here, the aim is to highlight the organisational nature of the new rules, that is, their characteristic of requiring manufacturers and distributors to adopt procedures and organisational structures through which carry out the process of design and distribution of products,[22] and the supervisory authorities to adopt a risk-based and forward-looking approach when monitoring the compliance with POG.

POG rules as detailed in the Commission Delegated Regulation (EU) 2017/2358 call manufacturers for a 'product approval process' covering the maintenance, operation and review of product oversight and governance arrangements for insurance products and for significant adaptations to existing insurance products before those products are brought to the market or distributed to customers, as well as rules for product distribution arrangements for those insurance products. The product approval process shall contain measures and procedures for designing, monitoring, reviewing and distributing insurance products, as well as for corrective action for insurance products that are detrimental to customers.[23] The product approval process shall be set out in a written policy ("product oversight and governance policy"), which shall be made available to the relevant staff. Manufacturers shall regularly review their product approval process to ensure that the process is still valid and up to date, and they shall amend the product approval process where necessary.[24] The relevant actions, which are taken by manufacturers about their product approval process, shall be duly documented, kept for audit purposes and made available to the competent authorities upon request.[25]

Product oversight and governance policy adds to policies already prescribed by Solvency II. Such a policy requires to be implemented in the organisation of the manufacture. Thus, the policy must be implemented by the operating units dealing with the design and distribution of products, and monitored by the internal control system. This policy will enable competent authorities to supervise and assess whether the regulated entities comply with the regulatory requirements on POG, thus promoting customer's protection in the end.[26] This is to say that such a policy is part of the system of governance of insurance undertakings that provides for sound and prudent management of their business. Thus, the written policy shall be the subject to prior approval by the administrative, management or supervisory body of

[21] A detailed analysis is provided by Marano (2019), p. 69 ff.

[22] In a broader perspective, this approach is qualified as "meta regulation" by Gunningham (2012), p. 135 ff. (Gunningham), p. 146 ff. (Coglianese et al), since legally force intermediaries to embrace specific management and control procedures, adopting a body of conduct of business rules approved under prudential supervision rationale.

[23] See Article 4 of Commission Delegated Regulation (EU) 2017/2358.

[24] See Article 4 of Commission Delegated Regulation (EU) 2017/2358.

[25] See Article 9 of Commission Delegated Regulation (EU) 2017/2358.

[26] See EIOPA, Final Report on Consultation Paper n. 16/006 on Technical Advice on possible delegated acts concerning the Insurance Distribution Directive, February 2017, p. 34.

the manufacturer or equivalent structure (in the case of two-tier systems)[27] as well as any material changes.[28] Moreover, the administrative, management or supervisory body of the manufacturer or equivalent structure: (*i*) is ultimately responsible for the establishment, subsequent reviews and continued compliance of the POG arrangements; and (*ii*) ensures that the POG arrangements are appropriately designed and implemented into the governing structures of the manufacturer.[29]

POG should include all decision-making processes (designing and developing) related to products that will be marketed or distributed to customers.[30] In the case of insurance undertaking playing a "passive" role or a non-exclusive role in the decision-making process, a distinction should be made whether the insurance undertaking has (*i*) contributed to the design of the product with another entity, or (*ii*) outsourced the design activities.

In the case sub (*i*), an insurance undertaking and an insurance intermediary are both manufacturers of the same product if the conditions listed in the Commission Delegated Regulation are met.[31] They are qualified as co-manufacturers, and they shall sign a written agreement that specifies their collaboration to comply with the requirements for manufacturers as referred to IDD,[32] the procedures through which they shall agree on the identification of the target market and their respective roles in the product approval process.

In the case sub (*ii*), manufacturers designate a third party to design products on their behalf and remain fully responsible for compliance with the product approval process.[33] The outsourcing to an entity other than an insurance intermediary falls outside the scope of the co-manufacturers rule. IDD prevents this entity from being regarded as a manufacturer.[34] Thus, insurance undertaking will be solely responsible for the outsourced activity,[35] and compliance with the product approval process. This clarification is relevant for insurance-based investment products because Regulation (EU) No 1286/2014 on Packaged Retail and Insurance-based Investment Product (PRIIP) provides a definition of PRIIPs manufacturer, which shall draw up for that product a key information document (KID) according to the requirements of that Regulation and shall publish the document on its website. Thus, if an insurance undertaking designates a third party (a PRIIP manufacturer) to design insurance products, the latter can be an entity falling outside the scope of POG, when such an entity is not an insurance intermediary. In this case, the insurance undertaking shall be the one entity to have to comply with POG rules because of the outsourcing of the

[27] See Article 41(3)(2) of Solvency II.

[28] See EIOPA, Final Report on Consultation Paper n. 16/006, cit., p. 35.

[29] See EIOPA, Final Report, cit., p. 35.

[30] Marano (2019), p. 69.

[31] See Article 2 of Commission Delegated Regulation (EU) 2017/2358.

[32] See Article 25(1) of IDD.

[33] See Article 4(5) of Commission Delegated Regulation (EU) 2017/2358.

[34] See Article 25(1) of IDD.

[35] See Article 49(1) of Solvency II.

manufacturer of an insurance-based investment product to an entity that cannot be considered as co-manufacturer.

In both cases, sub (*i*) and (*ii*), the activities required by the set of rules on POG are regarded as inherent in the organisation of the undertaking. They can be outsourced as other activities falling within the insurance production cycle or manufactured together by sharing their organisation between different entities.

Finally, the rules on POG also impact on the organisation of insurance intermediaries. If insurance intermediaries are co-manufacturers, the written agreement with the insurance undertaking/co-manufacturer has to specify the activities distributed between the two co-manufacturers within those listed in the set of rules on POG. Moreover, manufacturers have duties of properly selecting, informing and monitoring distribution channels. In contrast, distributors have to cooperate with manufacturers in monitoring the distribution of the insurance products to the identified target market, and they can set up or apply a specific distribution strategy. The co-operation between manufacturers and distributors has to be formalised in the product distribution arrangements.[36] These agreements will regulate the flow of information between the entities involved and coordinate the respective organisations. They should allow (*i*) distributors to transmit information that is eligible to support product monitoring and review carried out by manufacturers, (*ii*) manufacturers to accept what distributors report because they can verify the accuracy of the data communicated by distributors.[37]

4 POG and the Single Market in Insurance: The Current Effects

The previous paragraphs have highlighted that the set of rules on POG has been deduced from principles of conduct, and they become an essential part of the organisation of manufacturers and distributors. The transition from a principle-based regulation to a detailed-based regulation means that market's operators including supervisory authorities have to be organised to carry out their activities having in mind that products must include a real value for the customers ("target market"). POG seems capable of having multiple effects on the harmonisation process of insurance rules in the EU also contributing to their uniform interpretation, that is, to build up an effective Single Market. Some of these effects are obvious: POG is a tool for achieving better customer protection and coherent regulation for financial services across the UE. Other effects are less evident but no less criticial: POG extends the scope of harmonisation of organisational requirements and supports a convergent interpretation and application of the rules between supervisory authorities. This paragraph examines the effects that seem obvious, while the

[36]See Marano (2019), p. 84.

[37]See Marano (2019), p. 86.

following one explores some effects that seem to derive from the set of rules on POG.

Regarding better customer protection, the protection of policyholders and beneficiaries is the main objective of supervision in the EU as already noted. The set of rules on POG meets this goal by aligning the approach to products with that on capital requirements. In both cases, the aim is to *prevent* the harmful event *from occurring*.

In particular, POG introduced a risk-based and prospective approach similar to that of Solvency II. The latter Directive requires insurance undertakings to have in place an effective system of governance which provides for sound and prudent management of the business,[38] and an effective risk-management system to identify, measure, monitor, manage and report, on a continuous basis, the risks to which they are or could be exposed, and their interdependencies.[39] Thus, a sound and prudent management of the business cannot disregard effective risk management, where the risk-management system has to cover the risks to be included in the calculation of the Solvency Capital Requirement as well as the risks which are not or not fully included in the calculation thereof.[40] The risk assessment inherent in poorly designed products is part of the risk culture that insurance undertakings must introduce in their business processes and among the people who work for them. Undertakings have to supervise themselves, their processes, in order to prevent the design and distribution of products is detrimental to their customers. POG is a risk management tool that allows undertakings to prevent those risks by avoiding offering worthless products to customers.[41]

On the other hand, the supervision required by POG is similar to that arising from Solvency II. This latest Directive stated that supervision is based on a prospective and risk-based approach.[42] This approach includes the verification on a continuous basis of the proper operation of the insurance business and of the compliance with supervisory provisions by insurance undertakings in order to minimise disruption or loss on the part of policyholders.[43] POG is a tool that increases transparency to the supervisory authorities by improving their ability to understand and assess the process of manufacturing and distributing insurance products. POG discloses to the supervisory authority the persons/units involved in these processes, how the products are manufactured, and the purposes pursued with these products by the insurance undertakings. The advance knowledge of these processes is functional to

[38]See Article 41(1) of Solvency II.

[39]See Article 44(1) of Solvency II.

[40]See Article 44(2) of Solvency II.

[41]See EIOPA, *Preparatory Guidelines on product oversight governance*, cit., p. 4, which outlines that the organizational arrangements required under POG "have a substantial link to the system of governance under the Solvency II framework, requiring firms to have a sound and prudent management of the business under a risk based approach including an appropriate risk management system".

[42]See Van Hulle (2019), p. 372 f.

[43]Van Hulle (2019), p. 372.

early intervention by the authorities if they realise how the products or processes are likely to be detrimental to customers. POG is, therefore, likely to affect the approach of the authorities supervising market conducts. Authorities are now required to prevent bias from arising to the customers rather than repressing the conduct leading to such bias.

IDD achieves customer protection also aligning the rules on insurance with some of those on financial products and services introduced with the MiFID I, in 2004, and MiFID II. In particular, it was previously found that IDD introduced POG as a substantial "copy and paste" from MiFID II. The same can be said about the general principle under which distributors must always act honestly, fairly and professionally in accordance with the best interest of their customers, and most of the additional rules on customer protection for insurance-based investment products aiming at levelling the playing field with financial products as required by Solvency II. This approach of the EU legislator has been called as "Mifidization" of the EU regulatory framework on insurance, which refers to the impact of the regulation on financial products, mainly the rules laid down by MiFID Regulation also to the insurance sector.[44]

Although based on MiFID II, the application of the set of rules on POG needs to take into account the peculiarities of both non-life insurance and life insurance other than insurance-based investment products (IBIPs). While scenario analysis is required for IBIPs, it is reasonable that other insurance products will be tested mainly with qualitative methods rather than quantitative methods. The tests aim to assess whether the product will continue to respond, throughout its life, to the needs, characteristics and objectives of the target market identified. Qualitative methods in the form of a checklist must verify the adherence between predetermined lens (insurance needs and target) and product. They are also useful for verifying that all product-manufacturing steps have been respected. Quantitative methods, i.e. numerical analyses, should be mandatory for IBIPs and useful in support of quality tests and whenever they can confirm the correct manufacturing of the product that is being offered to the customer. POG does not list these methods. Thus, manufacturers have broad discretion in identifying and applying these methods taking into account the principle of proportionality. However, it is reasonable to expect that many manufacturers will follow particular methods with respect to specific products, while other methods will be taken as a reference for other products. This tendency towards uniform behaviour could be strengthened by the supervisory practices of the national authorities. EIOPA could then push towards convergent supervisory practices by selecting those methods that will be deemed more suitable for the objectives pursued by the POG rules, in compliance with the principle of proportionality. Hence, the manufacturing could be "standardised" across the EU not only for the process but also for products.

[44]Marano (2017b), p. 219 ff.; Marano (2017c), p. 415 ff. The current "Mifidization" concerns: (*i*) the sources of the regulation on insurance; (*ii*) the design and distribution of the insurance products; and (*iii*) customers' protection; while a potential field concerns the interpretation by the Courts.

The set of rules on POG aligned the Single Market on insurance to the Insurance Core Principles (ICPs) issued by the International Association of Insurance Supervisors (IAIS). The ICPs adopted on 1 October 2011 laid down provisions on product development that have been a point of reference for the EU legislator. These provisions were updated in the version released by IAIS in November 2017. The last version is affected by the adoption of the set of rules on POG in the IDD. In particular, ICP n. 19 refers to business conduct rules of either insurers or insurance intermediaries, and standard 19.5 states that the supervisor requires insurers to take into account the interests of different types of customers when developing and marketing insurance products. Concerning jurisdictions banning the power of approval from supervisors such as the EU, guidance 19.5.5 requests supervisors to issue guidance in terms of what is expected of insurers in this regard. The contents of the guidance are listed in guidance 19.5.5, and they mirror those set by EU law.[45] This identity is an outcome of the mutual influence between the EU regulation on insurance and the transnational regulation in the same field that is emerging after the global financial crisis.[46]

---

[45]This guidance may include the following: (*i*) development of products and distribution strategies should include the use of adequate information to assess the needs of different consumer groups; (*ii*) product development (including a product originating from a third party) should provide for a thorough assessment of the main characteristics of a new product and of the related disclosure documents by every appropriate department of the insurer; (*iii*) bringing a product or service to the market, the insurer should carry out a diligent review and testing of the product in relation to its business model, the applicable laws and regulations and its risk management approach. In particular, the policies, procedures and controls put into place should enable the insurer to:

- offer a product that delivers the reasonably expected benefits;
- target the consumers for whose needs the product is likely to be appropriate, while preventing, or limiting, access by consumers for whom the product is likely to be inappropriate;
- ensure that distribution methods are appropriate for the product, particularly in light of the legislation in force and whether or not advice should be provided;
- assess the risks resulting from the product by considering, among other things, changes associated with the environment or stemming from the insurer's policies that could harm customers; and
- monitor a product after its launch to ensure it still meets the needs of target customers, assess the performance of the various methods of distribution used with respect to sound commercial practices and, if necessary, take the necessary remedial action.

(*iv*) insurers should provide relevant information to intermediaries to ensure that they understand the target market (and thus reduce the risk of mis-selling), such as information related to the target market itself, as well as the characteristics of the product; (*v*) the intermediary should, in return, provide information to the insurer on the types of customers to whom the product is sold and whether the product meets the needs of that target market, in order to enable the insurer to assess whether its target market is appropriate and to revise its distribution strategy for the product, or the product itself, when needed.

[46]See Marano (2017a), p. 7.

4.1 The Potential Effects

The contribution of POG in building the Single Market in the insurance sector could be found in other less obvious forms.

The set of rules on POG extends the list of those affecting the organisation of the undertakings. IDD filled a gap of Solvency II in this respect. The latest Directive introduced improved governance and risk management requirements being aware that some risks may only be properly addressed through governance requirements rather than through the quantitative requirements reflected in the Solvency Capital Requirements.[47] Solvency II regulated general governance requirements, fit and proper requirements, risk management, internal control, outsourcing and prudent person principle.[48] Although customer protection was the cornerstone of the new regulation, a set of rules specifically addressed to the manufacture and distribution of products was missing in Solvency II. The organisational rules of POG finalise the principle of sound and prudent management to satisfy the interests and needs of the policyholders rather than to pursue the mere solvency of the insurance undertaking. The value of the insurer's solvency cannot be pursued without worrying—or worse at the expense—of creating value for insurer's customers, if the protection of policyholders and beneficiaries is the main objective of supervision in the EU as stated by Solvency II.

To qualify POG as a set of organizational rules, POG applies regardless of the Member State where the undertaking is based. POG is an integral part of the organization of the manufacturer incorporated in a specific Member State ("home country"). Thus, the home country authority must monitor compliance with POG even when the products are designed in that country and distributed in another Member State ("host country"). This supervision, however, refers to the activities of the manufacturer while those of the distributors are carried out by entities incorporated and operating under the law of the host country. As an organizational rule, POG should allow the home country authority to supervise *what* the manufacturer intends to distribute in the host country, but it is somewhat uncertain whether POG also allows supervision on *how* the products are distributed in the host country.

With this respect, POG can be described as a "circular process", where manufacturing cannot be separated from distribution, and vice versa, for the whole life cycle of the products. Monitoring of distribution, reviewing of the products and execution of remedial actions are all steps that postulate an information flow between distributors and manufacturers, which is subsequent to the marketing of the product. Products like the IBIPs have contents similar if not identical. Thus, these products may not vary considerably, when offered by a cross-border group between its subsidiaries/branches across Europe, at least in those national markets where potential customers have similar characteristics.

---

[47]See Recital 29 that adds: "An effective system of governance is therefore essential for the adequate management of the insurance undertaking and for the regulatory system".

[48]Siri (2017), p. 155 ff.

However, in the case of cross-border activities, each of the authorities involved—home and host—could have only a partial view of that circular process or get it late, because involving entities based in different countries. A proposal to fill this gap has already been formulated.[49] It consists in extending the supervision of colleges between authorities to the POG, when the affiliation to the group can influence the insurance distribution of subsidiaries and branches. In addition to the arguments supporting that proposal, the recent Regulation (EU) 2019/1238 of 20 June 2019 on a pan-European Personal Pension Product (PEPP) provides POG requirements almost identical to those of IDD.[50] Furthermore, it sets forth that the competent authorities and EIOPA shall exchange all information and documentation necessary to carry out their respective duties under such Regulation in accordance with Regulation (EU) No 1094/2010 establishing EIOPA, in particular to identify and remedy infringements of Regulation 2019/1238.[51] These infringements may also concern the rules on POG. Thus, the rules on the tasks and functioning of the college of supervisors and, more general, the exchange of information between authorities should be interpreted in favour of including the information related to POG, if not to push for the introduction of specific rules in this regard.

In addition to pushing for the adoption of rules governing when manufacturing and distribution take place in different Member States, the set of rules on POG can support a convergent interpretation of the EU regulation on insurance.

The UK experience revealed that POG was built around exiting principles, and the one permeating both organizational and conduct is the following: A firm must conduct its business with *due skill, care and diligence*. IDD sets forth the general principle under which insurance distributors always act *honestly, fairly and professionally* in accordance with the best interests of their customers. Although the wording of the two principles is different, the substantial similarities between the two seem obvious. The general principle introduced by IDD, which has been mostly implemented in the Member States by simply transcribing the wording into national laws, it is likely to have twofold relevance.

A first possible relevance concerns the individual contractual relationships between distributors and customers. That is, the ability to be taken as a reference by the judges in evaluating the distributor's conduct in the presentation, conclusion and execution of a specific insurance contract. However, this principle must be coordinated with those of good faith, fairness and diligence that have long been present in the private law of the Member States. Probably, two strands of interpretation will go against each other. A tendency will be to consider the general principle introduced by IDD as a mere repetition of the general principles of private law. As a result, the principle will be substantially irrelevant to the courts. Another trend is instead to believe that this general principle is different from those already provided by private laws. Such principle regulates the specific sub-legal system of the

[49] Marano and Siri (2018), p. 607 ff.

[50] See Article 25 of Regulation (EU) 2019/1238 of 20 June 2019.

[51] See Article 66(4) of Regulation (EU) 2019/1238 of 20 June 2019.

financial services since this rule is identical both in IDD and MiFID II. Should the latter tendency become established, the set of rules on POG would contribute to giving content to the principle in question. POG requires manufacturers to demonstrate that the product has been designed with customer interest in mind. The assessment of how the different steps of designing, monitoring and review activities have been carried out by manufacturer/distributor, could affect the decision of any dispute between manufacturer/distributor and the policyholder, at least in the event of national laws and judges allow to acquire such documentation even in judgement between the persons above.[52] This eventuality would have the advantage of facilitating the distinction between the case where the failure to achieve the best interests of that client may be attributed only to the distributor or depends on the characteristics of the product designed by the manufacturer.

Other potential relevance concerns the cooperation between supervisory authorities. This field seems more promising than the previous one in achieving a common Union supervisory culture and consistent supervisory practices.[53] Such cooperation is outside the private law and, therefore, it is less exposed to the conditioning of consolidated legal notions. The introduction of a general principle by European law allows these authorities to use common concepts that are detached from national principles and interpretations when they interact with each other and with EIOPA. Such a general principle also enables the authorities to fill it with detailed rules resulting from the relationship between EIOPA and national authorities. Moreover, the affirmation of a "common language" between authorities is likely to influence the individual contractual relationships, should the tendency to conceive the general principle as distinct from those already offered by private law prevail.

In general, a common understanding of the same legal rules by the authorities is a prerequisite for a common supervisory culture to be developed among them. The European System of Financial Supervision (ESFS) includes EIOPA and the competent or supervisory authorities on insurance in the Member States. The ESFS has been designed to overcome several deficiencies that emerged from the financial and economic crisis.[54] The main objective of the ESFS is to ensure that the rules applicable to the financial sector are adequately implemented to preserve financial stability and to ensure confidence in the financial system as a whole and sufficient protection for the customers of financial services. Thus EIOPA has been empowered of tasks and powers including to contribute to the consistent application of legally

[52]Marano (2019), p. 93.

[53]This is a goal that supervisory authorities must pursue: see Article 29 of Regulation (EU) No 1094/2010 of 24 November 2010 establishing EIOPA.

[54]See Recital No. 7 of Regulation (EU) No 1094/2010 of 24 November 2010, which lists: (*i*) no mechanism to ensure that national supervisors arrive at the best possible supervisory decisions for cross-border financial institutions; (*ii*) insufficient cooperation and information exchange between national supervisors; (*iii*) joint action by national authorities possible only as a result of complicated arrangements to take account of the patch work of regulatory and supervisory requirements; (*iv*) national solutions that are most often the only feasible option in responding to problems at the level of the Union; (*v*) different interpretations of the same legal text exist.

binding EU acts, in particular by contributing to a common supervisory culture, ensuring consistent, efficient and effective application of Solvency II and IDD.[55] In both cases, these rules are addressed to national authorities to strengthen a convergent application or interpretation of the EU law on insurance.

A convergent understanding of the set of rules on POG between authorities would reduce the legal uncertainty for supervised entities and facilitates the cross-border activities. Moreover, this convergence would support authorities in complying with challenges to the supervisory approach arising from POG. Also both Regulation (EU) No 1286/2014 on PRIIPs[56] and PEPP Regulation[57] attribute market monitoring duties and product intervention powers to the EIOPA and national supervisory authorities, and requests national authorities to cooperate and, without undue delay, provide each other with such information as is relevant for carrying out their duties under those Regulations and of making use of their powers. If the information in the KID does not reflect the characteristics of the product offered, the supervisory authority should exercise its power of intervention.[58] One of the conditions justifying the intervention of EIOPA is that national competent authority/authorities have not taken action to address the threat or the actions.[59] A common supervisory culture in which the rules on POG are uniformly understood and applied would make this replacement intervention merely hypothetical. This culture is positive for customer protection, which would be timelier, but this is also good for the same supervisors. Omission or delay in their intervention may well give rise to a liability to policyholders.[60]

Finally, POG aims at preventing customer detriment and, therefore, requires a risk-based and prospective approach to both manufacturers and supervisory authorities. This approach is also required in the case of cross-border business.[61] The organisational nature of the POG rules requires the authority of the home Member State to carry out the monitoring of the POG rules even if the products are distributed in another Member State. Manufacturers that intend to carry out the activity under the FOE regime have to provide the supervisory authority of the home Member State with information on the scheme of operations and the structure of the branch.[62] This

---

[55]EIOPA has the power to issue both guidelines under the "comply or explain" procedure, and non-binding opinions. See Marano (2017a), p. 13 f.

[56]See Articles 15, 16 and 17.

[57]See Article 63.

[58]See Article 24(1) of Regulation (EU) No 1286/2014 as referred to information required under Articles 8(3) and 10(1).

[59]See Article 16(2)(c) of Regulation (EU) No 1286/2014 and Article 65(3)(c) of Regulation (EU) 2019/1238.

[60]See Marano (2019), p. 93 f.

[61]Nevertheless, Van Hulle (2019), p. 22 f. outlines that supervision on cross-border business does not always work well in practice. Home Member States might not pay as much attention to business operations concluded by their (re)insurance undertakings in the host Member State as they do to business operations concluded by these undertakings on the domestic market.

[62]See Article 145(2)(b) of Solvency II.

information should also highlight how the set of rules on the POG is applied to products distributed in the host Member State. Otherwise, the authorization would incorporate potential damage for customers of the host Member State, for example, in the case manufacturer does not adopt any organisational supervision to ensure the products to be distributed taking into account the needs of the customers in the host country.

Although the scheme of operations does not need to be not provided in the case of activity carried out under the FOS regime, the related authorization procedure of the home country should be consistent with the aim of POG. The risk-based and forward-looking approach cannot make any distinction depending on the cross-border regimes. If the stakeholders have to wait until the authority of the host Member State establishes that a manufacturer pursuing business under the FOS regime in its territory is not complying with the legal provisions applicable to it in that Member State,[63] damage to customers has already occurred while the supervisory authorities may be held liable in addition to manufacturers. Above all, certainly, the Single Market would still be a goal rather than a reality.

References

Brandt P (2011) Product distribution round-up. Compliance Off Bull

Busch D (2017) Product Governance und produktintervention unter miFid ii/miFir. J Econ Bank Law 9:409–420

Coglianese C, Mendelson E (2012) Meta – regulation and self – regulation. In: Baldwin R, Cave M, Lodge M (eds) The Oxford handbook of regulation. Oxford University Press, Oxford

Colaert V (2019) Product intervention: a cross-sectoral analysis. In: Colaert V, Busch D, Incalza T (eds) European financial regulation. Levelling the cross-sectoral playing field. Hart

Ferran E (2012) Regulatory lessons from the payment protection insurance mis-selling scandal in the UK. Eur Bus Org Law Rev 13:247

Georgosouli A (2011) The FSA's 'Treating Customers Fairly' (TCF) initiative: what is so good about it and why it may not work. J Law Soc 38(3):405–427

Gunningham N (2012) Enforcement and compliance strategies. In: Baldwin R, Cave M, Lodge M (eds) The Oxford handbook of regulation. Oxford University Press, Oxford

Marano P (2017a) Sources and tools of the insurance regulation. In: Marano P, Siri M (eds) Insurance regulation in the European Union. Solvency II and beyond. Springer

Marano P (2017b) The "Mifidization": the sunset of life insurance in the EU regulation on insurance? In: Liber Amicorum in Honour of Joannis Rokas. NOMIKH ?I?ΛΙΟΘΗΚΗ, Athens

Marano P (2017c) La "Mifidización": El atardecer de los Seguros de vida en la normativa europea sobre seguros? Revista Española de Seguros

Marano P (2019) The product oversight and governance: standards and liabilities. In: Marano P, Rokas I (eds) Distribution of insurance-based investment products. Springer

Marano P, Siri M (2018) Cross-border insurance groups: towards a comprehensive supervision under solvency II. Geneva Pap Risk Insur Issues Pract 43(4)

Marcacci A (2017) European regulatory private law going global? The case of product governance. Eur Bus Org Law Rev 18:305–332

[63]See Article 155(1) of Solvency II.

Moloney N (2012) The legacy effects of the financial crisis on regulatory design in the EU. In: Ferran E, Moloney N, Hill JC, Coffee Jr JC (eds) The regulatory aftermath of the global financial crisis. Cambridge University Press, Cambridge

Siri M (2017) Corporate governance of insurance firms after solvency II. In: Marano P, Siri M (eds) Insurance regulation in the European Union. Solvency II and beyond. Springer

Tomic K (2018) Product intervention of supervisory authorities in financial services. In: Grima S, Marano P (eds) Governance and regulations. Contemporary issues. Emerald

Van Hulle K (2019) Solvency II requirements for EU insurers. Solvency II is good for you. Intersentia

Legislation

Commission Delegated Regulation (EU) 2017/2358 of 21 September 2017 supplementing Directive (EU) 2016/97 of the European Parliament and of the Council with regard to product oversight and governance requirements for insurance undertakings and insurance distributors. https://eur-lex.europa.eu/legal-content/EN/TXT/?uri=CELEX%3A32017R2358

Directive 2002/92/EC of the European Parliament and of the Council of 9 December 2002 on insurance mediation. https://eur-lex.europa.eu/legal-content/EN/TXT/?uri=CELEX%3A32002L0092

Directive (EU) 2016/97 of the European Parliament and of the Council of 20 January 2016 on insurance distribution (recast). http://data.europa.eu/eli/dir/2016/97/oj

Directive 2014/65/EU of the European Parliament and of the Council of 15 May 2014 on markets in financial instruments and amending Directive 2002/92/EC and Directive 2011/61/EU. http://data.europa.eu/eli/dir/2014/65/oj

Directive 2009/138/EC of the European Parliament and of the Council of 25 November 2009 on the taking-up and pursuit of the business of Insurance and Reinsurance (Solvency II). http://data.europa.eu/eli/dir/2009/138/oj

Regulation (EU) No 1094/2010 of the European Parliament and of the Council of 24 November 2010 establishing a European Supervisory Authority (European Insurance and Occupational Pensions Authority), amending Decision No 716/2009/EC and repealing Commission Decision 2009/79/EC. https://eur-lex.europa.eu/legal-content/EN/TXT/?uri=CELEX%3A32010R1094

Regulation (EU) No 1286/2014 of the European Parliament and of the Council of 26 November 2014 on key information documents for packaged retail and insurance-based investment products (PRIIPs). http://data.europa.eu/eli/reg/2014/1286/oj

Regulation (EU) 2019/1238 of the European Parliament and of the Council of 20 June 2019 on a pan-European Personal Pension Product (PEPP). https://eur-lex.europa.eu/legal-content/EN/TXT/?uri=uriserv:OJ.L_.2019.198.01.0001.01.ENG

Documents

Autorité des Marchés Financiers (AMF), *La commercialisation des instruments financiers complexes*, Position No 2010 - 05, of 15 October 2010. https://www.amf-france.org/en/node/59585

CONSOB, Resolution n. 9019104 of 2 March 2009 on illiquid investment products http://www.consob.it/documents/46180/46181/c9019104.pdf/64f86e70-2bb0-460a-8f60-3dd079b6341d

EIOPA, Final Report on Consultation Paper n. 16/006 on Technical Advice on possible delegated acts concerning the Insurance Distribution Directive, February 2017., https://eiopa.europa.eu/Publications/Reports/EIOPA%20Final_Report_on_IDD_Technical%20Advice.pdf

EIOPA, *Preparatory Guidelines on product oversight and governance arrangements by insurance undertakings and insurance distributors*, March 2016. https://www.eiopa.europa.eu/content/preparatory-guidelines-product-oversight-and-governance-arrangements-insurance-undertakings_en

ESAs, Joint Position of the European Supervisory Authorities on Manufacturers' Product Oversight & Governance Processes., https://www.eba.europa.eu/documents/10180/15736/JC-2013-77+%28POG+-+Joint+Position%29.pdf

ESMA, *Structured retail products – Good practices for product governance arrangements*, March 2014., https://www.esma.europa.eu/sites/default/files/library/2015/11/2014-332_esma_opinion_u_structured_retail_products_-_good_practices_for_product_governance_arrangements.pdf.

FCA, Structured Products: Thematic Review of Product Development and Governance, March 2015., https://www.fca.org.uk/publications/thematic-reviews/tr15-2-structured-products-thematic-review-product-development-and

FSA Handbook related to "The Responsibilities of Providers and Distributors for the Fair Treatment of Customers"., https://www.handbook.fca.org.uk/handbook/document/rppd/RPPD_Full_20180103.pdf

FSA, *Treating Customers Fairly. Towards Fair Outcomes for Consumers*, July 2006.; https://www.fca.org.uk/publication/archive/fsa-tcf-towards.pdf

FSA, *Treating Customers Fairly. Structured Investment Products*, October 2009., https://webarchive.nationalarchives.gov.uk/20130411080807/http://www.fsa.gov.uk/pubs/other/tcf_structured.pdf

FSA, *Discussion Paper on Product Intervention*, January 2011., https://www.fca.org.uk/publication/discussion/dp11_01.pdf

FSA, *Finalised Guidance – Retail Product Development and Governance*, March 2012. https://www.fca.org.uk/publication/finalised-guidance/fg12-09.pdf

HM Treasury, *A New Approach to Financial Regulation: Judgement, Focus and Stability*, 2012. https://www.gov.uk/government/consultations/a-new-approach-to-financial-regulation-judgement-focus-and-stability

IAIS, Insurance Core Principles., https://www.iaisweb.org/page/supervisory-material/icp-on-line-tool

The IDD and Its Impact on the Life Insurance Industry

Kyriaki Noussia

1 Introduction

Directive (EU) 2016/97 on Insurance Distribution of 20 January 2016,[1] ("IDD"), aimed to harmonise national provisions concerning the distribution of insurance and reinsurance products and insurance-based investment products ("IBIPs") by insurance intermediaries, insurance companies, their employees, and ancillary insurance intermediaries in the European Union.

The initial date of the implementation of the IDD and the application of the corresponding Delegated Regulations was ultimately postponed to 1 October 2018, for the insurance firms, so as to allow the market the necessary time needed for it to adapt. In turn, the European Parliament substantiated this request for postponement by the need to give insurance undertakings and insurance distributors more time to better prepare for a correct and effective implementation of the Directive and to implement the necessary technical and organisational changes to comply with the Delegated Regulations. The IDD aimed to improve the regulation of retail insurance sales and distribution practices across the single European market and to bring greater transparency and improved, more comprehensible, information to consumers, so as to help people ensure that they buy products that suit their needs. It

The original version of this chapter was revised. A correction to this chapter can be found at https://doi.org/10.1007/978-3-030-52738-9_17

[1]Directive (EU) 2016/97 of the European Parliament and of the Council of 20 January 2016 on insurance distribution (recast), available at http://data.europa.eu/eli/dir/2016/97/oj.

K. Noussia (✉)
University of Exeter, School of Law, Exeter, UK
e-mail: k.noussia@exeter.ac.uk

P. Marano, K. Noussia (eds.), *Insurance Distribution Directive*, AIDA Europe Research Series on Insurance Law and Regulation 3,
https://doi.org/10.1007/978-3-030-52738-9_4

serves as a minimum harmonisation Directive, meaning that Member States may "gold-plate" it, and, in doing so, impose higher standards and requirements, if they wish to do so.

Following the credit crunch of 2007/2008 lawmakers aimed at rebuilding the confidence of the investors into the financial markets.[2] Hence, any post-crisis regulation has as its overarching aim the prevention of any regulatory arbitrage which could lead to incentives to set up products solely to circumvent more stringent standards. The levelling of the playing field has attracted insurance products, especially those relating to life insurance or financial ones. This attraction has been mirrored at EU level[3] whereby Directive 2014/65/EU of 15 May 2014 on markets in financial instruments (MiFID II)[4] repealed the previous Directive 2004/39/EC (MiFID).[5] Recital 87 of MiFID II also outlined that in order to deliver consistent protection for retail clients and ensure a level playing field between similar products, it is important that IBIPs are subject to appropriate requirements and that any cross-sectorial inconsistencies which are detrimental to consumers are being addressed. To this effect, the IDD introduced some rules and principles contained in the final version of the MiFID II.

The IDD plays a significant role for the promotion of consumer protection within the distribution of insurance products across the EU, especially if one considers the fact that the MiFID II Directive does not cover the distribution of IBIPs. In particular, the IDD ensures a greater transparency of insurance distributors in relation to the price and costs of their products but also provides higher standards concerning product information and conduct of business ("COB") rules. In performing this function, the IDD provides many rules following the similar MiFID II rules. However, many differences still exist and pose a risk for segmentation or regulatory arbitrage.[6] Moreover, while the MiFID II Directive aspired to a maximum harmonisation, the IDD expressly aimed at a minimum harmonisation, allowing Member States to impose stricter rules for the protection of the customers.[7]

[2]G-20 Leaders (2008) and Śliwiński and Marano (2020).

[3]Marano (2017) and Śliwiński and Marano (2020).

[4]Directive 2014/65/EU of the European Parliament and of the Council of 15 May 2014 on markets in financial instruments and amending Directive 2002/92/EC and Directive 2011/61/EU, available at http://data.europa.eu/eli/dir/2014/65/oj.

[5]Directive 2004/39/EC of the European Parliament and of the Council of 21 April 2004 on markets in financial instruments amending Council Directives 85/611/EEC and 93/6/EEC and Directive 2000/12/EC of the European Parliament and of the Council and repealing Council Directive 93/22/EEC, available at http://data.europa.eu/eli/dir/2004/39/oj.

[6]Colaert (2015); Kern (2018), pp. 16–24.

[7]Recital 3 of the IDD.

The IDD aimed explicitly to harmonise national provisions concerning Insurance[8] and Reinsurance[9] Distribution across the Union,[10] and targeted not only, as previously, insurance brokers or intermediaries, but several types of persons or institutions which distribute IBIPs to third parties, such as agents, "bancassurance" operators, insurance undertakings, travel agents and car rental companies.[11] However, its overarching aim is that customers, regardless of the distribution channel, would benefit from the same level of protection and equal treatment.[12] In particular, in line with the MiFID II regime for financial instruments and structured deposits, within the IDD the regime of customer protection is ensured by specific provisions concerning the conduct of business rules and product governance requirements.[13]

As the Member States of the European Union begun to fully enact and enforce the provisions of the IDD, we started slowly witnessing changes in how insurance products are marketed and sold across Europe. History tells us that no matter how clever and careful the drafters of a body of law are, no one can precisely predict all the impacts that a body of regulations will cause in any particular market. In line with the above realisation, the fact that the IDD is a "minimum harmonization" directive, means that Member States can keep their own regulations applicable to intermediaries, in effect, so long as there is no conflict with the IDD.

In effect, The IDD arose out of a desire to give insurance customers equal protection regardless of the type of distributor from which they obtained insurance.[14] It seeks to level the playing field of protections for insurance customers by simplifying, consolidating, and expanding customer protections when needed. The IDD has the stated goal of focusing on "the area of the disclosure of information" to customers[15] and applies "to persons whose activity consists of providing insurance or reinsurance distribution services to third parties."[16]

The IDD aims at enhancing protections for customers and retail investors buying insurance products or insurance-based investment products. This purpose is in line

---

[8]'Insurance distribution' is defined as the "activities of advising on, proposing, or carrying out other work preparatory to the conclusion of contracts of insurance, of concluding such contracts, or of assisting in the administration and performance of such contracts". See Article 1(1) IDD.

[9]'Reinsurance distribution' is defined as the activities of advising on, proposing, or carrying out other work preparatory to the conclusion of contracts of reinsurance, of concluding such contracts, or of assisting in the administration and performance of such contracts, in particular in the event of a claim, including when carried out by a reinsurance undertaking without the intervention of a reinsurance intermediary. See Article 1(2) IDD.

[10]Recital 2 IDD.

[11]Recital 5 IDD; De Maesschalck (2017), pp. 63–65.

[12]Recital 6 IDD.

[13]Noussia and Siri (2019).

[14]Martinez and Marano (2020); Recital No 5 of the IDD highlights "agents, brokers and 'bancassurance' operators, insurance undertakings, travel agents and car rental companies" as examples of what a distributor is.

[15]See Recital No 6 of the IDD.

[16]See Recital No 11 of the IDD.

with the main objective of insurance and reinsurance regulation and supervision in the European Union, which is the adequate protection of policyholders and beneficiaries, as stated by Recital No.16 of the Directive 2009/138/EC of the European Parliament and the Council of November 25, 2009 on the taking-up and pursuit of the business of insurance and reinsurance (Solvency II). The IDD seeks to achieve the goal of enhancing customer protection by ensuring greater transparency of insurance distribution with regard to the price and costs of insurance products, requiring better and more comprehensible product information, and improving conduct of business rules, with particular attention to advice.

1.1 The Distributor's Remuneration

Unlike the MiFID II Directive, which considerably restricted the possibility for firms providing the service of investment advice on an independent basis and the service of portfolio management to accept and retain fees, commissions or any monetary and non-monetary benefits from third parties, and particularly from issuers or product providers, the IDD generally accepts such remuneration in connection with the distribution of an IBIP as long as the payment of fees, commissions or any non-monetary benefit does not have a detrimental impact on the quality of the relevant service and does not impair the distributor's duty to act honestly, fairly and professionally in accordance with the customer's best interests.

The IDD applies to customers and is accompanied by a broad range of mandatory disclosures of fees and conflicts by insurance intermediaries to customers. In particular, the intermediary has to disclose whether, in relation to the insurance contract, it works on the basis of a fee, a commission of any kind, any other type of remuneration and any combination of the above. Furthermore, to avoid distortion of competition by encouraging insurers to sell directly to customers rather than via intermediaries in order to avoid information requirements, insurers are required to provide information to customers about the nature of the remuneration their employees receive for the sale of insurance products.[17]

Additionally, insurance distributors shall not make any arrangement by way of remuneration, sales targets, or otherwise that could provide an incentive to itself or its employees to recommend a particular insurance product to a customer when the insurance distributor could offer a different insurance product which would better meet the customer's needs.[18]

Additional disclosure requirements apply in the case of insurance-based investment products. Distributors must provide additional information detailing any cost of distribution that is not already included in the costs specified in the key information documents (KID) for packaged retail and insurance-based investment products.

[17] Martinez and Marano (2020).

[18] See Article 17(3) of IDD.

This enables the customer to understand the cumulative effect that those aggregate costs have on the return on investment.[19]

The adoption of criteria based on the MiFID II Directive seemed like the best solution in many respects, i.e. firstly because it was considered as striking the appropriate balance between the interests of insurance distributors and those of their customers and because it was considered as enabling the necessary flexibility at National Competent Authority ("NCA") level.[20]

1.2 Distributors' Liabilities: Life Insurance

1.2.1 Scope of Distributors: Dual Responsibilities

The first impact of the IDD[21] directly follows from the new definition of the so-called "distributors". This term deliberately differs from the reference to the sole "intermediaries" mentioned in the previous Directive 2002/92/EC on insurance mediation ("IMD").[22] "Insurance distributor" is a term referring to any insurance intermediary, ancillary insurance intermediary and insurance undertaking, encompassing a large variety of persons or institutions, including the traditional agents, brokers and "bancassurance" operators, insurance companies, are subject to "equality of treatment" (i.e. same level of duties, obligations and liabilities) which are considered necessary so as to ensure customer protection. In short, anybody involved with insurance distribution, especially advising on, proposing, carrying out preparatory work to the conclusion of insurance or concluding insurance contracts, falls within the scope of IDD.

Because one of the objectives of the IDD was to guarantee an effective protection of customers across all financial sectors, and to guarantee that the same level of protection applies regardless of the channel through which customers buy an insurance product,[23] this explains why the IDD covers the distribution of not only non-life and life products, but also reinsurance products, and IBIPs. This also explains why the IDD applies to insurance distributors, when the previous Directive on insurance mediation, i.e. IMD, applied only to insurance intermediaries. Hence, based on the new definition of the insurance distributor, the IDD encompasses a larger number of firms than the IMD. This level playing field is considered a guarantee for customers to benefit from the same level of protection. In practice, however, it may lead to

[19]See Article 29 of IDD.

[20]EIOPA (2017).

[21]Directive (EU) 2016/97, op.cit.

[22]Directive 2002/92/EC of the European Parliament and of the Council of 9 December 2002 on insurance mediation, available at http://data.europa.eu/eli/dir/2002/92/oj.

[23]Commission 2012 staff working document executive summary of the impact assessment accompanying the document proposal for a Directive of the European Parliament and of the Council on insurance mediation.

situations of co-liability among the various types of distributors at stake where national legislations had operated a “clear-cut” in terms of liability before.

The IDD applies to insurance intermediaries, of course, but also to direct writers, i.e. to insurance undertakings which sell insurance products directly. The IDD, unlike the IMD, also expressly applies to certain activities conducted through price comparison websites. The IDD also applies to persons whose activity consists of the provision of information on one or more contracts of insurance in response to criteria selected by the customer, via a website or other media or of the provision of a ranking of insurance products or a discount on the price of an insurance contract, when the customer is able to directly or indirectly conclude an insurance contract at the end of the process.[24]

With regards to distribution agreements, beyond the respective obligations laid down in Regulation (EU) 2017/2358[25] with regard to the terms of the collaboration agreement between the insurance intermediary and the insurance company, such distribution agreements should be carefully reviewed on both sides, i.e. from the side of the intermediary and from the side of the insurance company, in order to precisely clarify their respective role, anticipate potential risk scenarios and achieve a good balance, especially as to their respective liability.

With regards to IBIPs, and on top of PRIIP’s Regulation EU/1286/2014,[26] as per the IDD, the distribution of IBIPs generates a full range of additional obligations for the distributors: (a) specific professional and organisational requirements must be abided by (art. 10, IDD). Buying an IBIP implies a risk and investors should be able to rely on the information and quality assessment provided. Insurance intermediaries and insurance undertakings that advise on, or sell, IBIPs to retail customers are to possess an appropriate level of knowledge and competence in relation to the products offered and their employees should be given adequate time and resources to be able to exhaustively inform the customers; (b) specific information standards (art. 29 & art. 30 of IDD and Regulation (EU) 2017/2358) aimed at addressing the investment embedded in IBIPs shall apply and include that the provision of appropriate information and the requirements for advice need to be suitable; (c) restrictions on remuneration (art. 28 & art. 29 of IDD and Regulation (EU) 2017/2359[27]) apply. The payment of remuneration (fee, commission, non-monetary benefits) in

[24]Article 1.2., Article 10.2. of the IDD; De Maesschalck (2017).

[25]Commission Delegated Regulation (EU) 2017/2358 of 21 September 2017 supplementing Directive (EU) 2016/97 of the European Parliament and of the Council with regard to product oversight and governance requirements for insurance undertakings and insurance distributors, available at http://data.europa.eu/eli/reg_del/2017/2358/oj.

[26]Regulation (EU) No 1286/2014 of the European Parliament and of the Council of 26 November 2014 on key information documents for packaged retail and insurance-based investment products (PRIIPs), available at http://data.europa.eu/eli/reg/2014/1286/oj.

[27]Commission Delegated Regulation (EU) 2017/2359 of 21 September 2017 supplementing Directive (EU) 2016/97 of the European Parliament and of the Council with regard to information requirements and conduct of business rules applicable to the distribution of insurance-based investment products, available at http://data.europa.eu/eli/reg_del/2017/2359/oj.

connection with the distribution of IBIPs should not have a detrimental impact on the quality of the relevant service. In order to fulfil this condition satisfactorily the distributor should develop, adopt and regularly review policies and procedures relating to conflict of interests and ensure that the customer is adequately informed about fees, commissions or benefits. When advice is provided to the customer the information on (1) all costs and related charges must be disclosed, as well as (2) information relating to the distribution of the product, (3) including the cost of advice.

1.2.2 Impact on International Activities (Free Passporting Service ("FPS"))

In spite of the willingness to establish a single internal market barriers to the taking up and pursuit of the activities of insurance and reinsurance intermediaries in the internal market remained up to the introduction of the IMD, and the inability for the latter to operate freely throughout the Community hindered the proper functioning of the single market in insurance. The IMD introduced a single passport for insurance intermediaries: it provided a registration system for all insurance intermediaries based on a whole range of binding professional requirements aimed at enhancing the protection of consumers in insurance matters and at facilitating cross-border activities. Registered insurance intermediaries will be allowed to take up and pursue the activity of insurance mediation within the EU by means of both freedom of establishment and of services[28] after going through a notification procedure.[29]

For the first time the IDD specifies in a very clear manner at several places that the stricter requirements of a Member State have also to be complied with, by insurance intermediaries operating under the freedom to provide services. Under the regime of the IMD there was no clarity about the national law governing the duty to inform or advise the client living abroad when the insurance intermediary was active form his home country through the free "passporting" service ("FPS").

The IDD has a wider scope than the IMD and applies to all insurance distributors, including insurance undertakings. However, they do not have to register[30] under the IDD and their passporting rights remain governed by the relevant domestic provisions implementing the Solvency II Directive. The IDD applies to ancillary intermediaries.[31] Registered ancillary insurance intermediaries under the IDD will be allowed to operate under freedom of service and/or establishment.

Under the IMD, once the intermediary had informed its home Member State of its intention to operate cross-border in one or more Member States under freedom of service and/or establishment for the first time, the home Member State authority was

[28] Article 3, IMD.

[29] Article 6, IMD.

[30] Article 3.1 (2) of the IDD.

[31] Ancillary intermediaries are defined under Article 2(4) of the IDD.

required, within 1 month of receiving the information, to notify the competent authorities of the relevant host Member States. It had also to advise the applicant intermediary that it had done this. The intermediary could only commence its activities 1 month after the date of notification. The IMD allowed an exemption for the host Member State to be notified. In practice, in cases where Member States chose to be notified —and they were a majority—this meant that an intermediary had to wait up to 2 months before being allowed to operate cross-borders. The approach of other Directives was more favourable: under MiFID for example an investment firm could go cross-border immediately upon notification by home to host Member States of the firm's intention to passport under freedom of service. The IDD, in two separate articles (Articles 4 and 6), details different notification requirements for freedom of service and/or establishment activities.

Like the IMD, the IDD requires the national registers to indicate the Member States in which "their" intermediaries conduct business under freedom of service or establishment activities. The IDD[32] also requires EIOPA to establish, publish on its website and keep up to date a single electronic register of intermediaries operating cross-border in their respective countries.[33] Under the IMD, the only power clearly given to host Member States over insurance intermediaries operating under freedom of service and/or establishment activities in their markets, was the one to adopt specific legal provisions to protect the general good.[34] The IMD did not, however, clearly divide competences between home and host member State competent authorities. The IDD clearly divides the oversight powers between the home and host Member States competent authorities over insurance intermediaries who are "passporting" in the EU and makes clear that in case of intermediaries' FOS activities, the home Member State competent authority will be responsible for ensuring compliance with all IDD requirements. The IDD goes even further and introduces new powers for host Member States to help them preventing the circumvention of their rules by insurance intermediaries.[35]

Intermediaries will also need to particularly focus on these national rules in the context of the information provided to policyholders, i.e. in respect of advice given and disclosure of remuneration schemes. Interestingly enough, in the context of "national law governing the situation", the IDD considers that stricter national provisions of the customer's habitual residence are the relevant ones. According to IDD (article 22 (2)), the provision of advice is mandatory if the customer's country of habitual residence so foresees. This may create inconsistent legal situations and requires anticipation measures by the stakeholders as Directive Solvency II,[36] in its

[32] Article 3(4), IDD.

[33] Audigier (2020).

[34] Article 6.3 and article 8.4, IMD.

[35] Article 9, IDD.

[36] Directive 2009/138/EC of the European Parliament and of the Council of 25 November 2009 on the taking-up and pursuit of the business of Insurance and Reinsurance (Solvency II) http://data.europa.eu/eli/dir/2009/138/oj.

article 178 on applicable law, expressly refers to the alternative provided for in Regulation Rome I,[37] namely the possibility for the policyholder to opt for the law of his nationality. Because the IDD aims at a so-called minimum harmonisation and because for the first time in the EU legislative framework, insurance intermediaries, are expressly reminded of their obligation to follow the stricter requirements of their policyholders' country of residence,[38] insurance intermediaries and employees of insurance undertakings will also need to comply with continuing professional training and development requirements—including knowledge of financial risks, of the insurance market, of applicable laws governing the distribution of insurance products such as consumer protection law and relevant tax law, of assessing customer needs, etc.. No doubt that such implementation may appear at first glance as too wide and burdensome, but it should be seen as a unique opportunity for all entities involved to (re-)negotiate distribution agreements, especially brokerage agreements, but also financial agreements such as asset management agreements, in order to achieve a good balance of liabilities between the professionals involved, to review risk management options and to look for sustainable business alternatives. In addition, the Regulations supplementing the IDD do not involve transposition measures. The automatic result is that distributors have had to directly abide by their scope of obligations as early as October 2018. This, at least, left the door open for maximum harmonisation of operational processes and adequate internal and external advice.

1.3 Inducements

According to the IDD, the insurance intermediary should inform the client whether, in relation to the insurance contract, any inducement,[39] i.e. any fee, commission or non-monetary benefit paid or provided by any party except the customer, is paid. The payment of inducements is only allowed if it '(a) does not have a detrimental impact on the quality of the relevant service to the customer, and (b) does not impair compliance with the insurance intermediary's or insurance undertaking's duty to act honestly, fairly and professionally in accordance with the best interests of its customers'.[40] This seems a less stringent discipline compared to that provided in MiFID II, which imposes specific bans and strict limitations to fees and commission

[37]Regulation (EC) No 593/2008 of the European Parliament and of the Council of 17 June 2008 on the law applicable to contractual obligations (Rome I) http://data.europa.eu/eli/reg/2008/593/oj.

[38]These stricter national rules will notably impact pre-contractual information duties, the type of advice to be given, the product documentation, authorised remuneration schemes and in particular the incentives gathered from underlying investment vehicles.

[39]Article 19(1)(e) IDD.

[40]Article 29(2) IDD.

paid in connection to financial advice.[41] All rebates are relevant, irrespective of their origin.

The insurance intermediary or insurance undertaking is required to consider the amount of inducement being paid in comparison to the value of the product or service being provided. Regardless of whether a personal recommendation is provided, a rebate should be assessed in accordance with Article 29(2), IDD.[42]

2 The Need for Regulation: Specific Professional and Organizational Requirements

Since the foundation of the European Community in 1957, many Directives, targeting a more integrated financial market and a harmonized approach, were issued.[43] In the past 25–30 years the financial market have undergone a deregulation process through the European Union's Third Generation Insurance Directive which was implemented in 1994. Creating a single European insurance market with a better diversification and a strong competition should have a positive effect on the choice of the policyholders with a variety of insurance products.[44]

The First Life Insurance Directive 1979/267[45] was codified by Directive 2002/83[46] and then repealed by Directive 2009/138[47] (Solvency II). Directive 2004/39 on markets in financial instruments ("MiFID") was followed by Directive 2014/65 ("MiFID II"). Directive 2002/92 on Insurance Mediation ("IMD") was the first Directive to impose specific obligations for the insurer and the distributor of investment products. The IMD was replaced by the IDD and was further exemplified the rules on the sale of investment products contained in MiFID II and in Regulation 1286/2014 on packaged retail and insurance-based investment products (PRIIPs Regulation).[48]

The IDD plays a significant role for the promotion of consumer protection within the distribution of insurance products across the EU, especially if considered that MiFID II does not covers the distribution of insurance-based products. In particular,

[41] Art 24(7) and (9) of MiFID II.

[42] EIOPA Q and A on Regulation (2018), No. 1635.

[43] Cummins et al. (2017), p. 67; Petsch (2019).

[44] Cummins et al. (2017), p. 66; Petsch (2019).

[45] First Council Directive 1979/267 1979 on the coordination of laws, regulations and administrative provisions relating to the taking up and pursuit of the business of direct life assurance Official Journal L 063, 13/03/1979 P. 0001–0018.

[46] Directive 2002/83 on life insurance, OJ L 345, 19.12.2002, p. 1–51.

[47] Directive 2009/138 (Solvency II), OJ L 335, 17.12.2009.

[48] Regulation (EU) No 1286/2014 of the European Parliament and of the Council of 26 November 2014 on key information documents for packaged retail and insurance-based investment products (PRIIPS) http://data.europa.eu/eli/reg/2014/1286/oj; Noussia and Siri (2019).

the IDD ensures a greater transparency of insurance distributors in relation to the price and costs of their products but also provides higher standards concerning product information and conduct of business (COB) rules.[49]

Some changes already began with the consideration of Solvency II[50] and a further significant transformation of the supervision of financial institutions occurred during the financial crisis in 2007 and 2008.[51] From then on, the European Commission is constantly working for a harmonization of the regulatory framework across the EU member countries. This implies implementing standards to react to a rapidly changing market.[52] Hence, the IDD was developed as a consequence of regulatory changes and in order to strengthen the consumer protection and establish a competitive and harmonized landscape of the insurance business in the EU. Even if the insurance business is traditionally seen as a stable financial sector, the liquidity liabilities within the banking industry increases the risk of contagious runs, and this also relates to partnerships and "bancassurance" and the subsequent cross-selling strategy, that is implied, which has initiated the development of complex risk management products and which also represents a challenge for the regulator to understand and evaluate them.[53]

Insurance companies offer products which are similar to saving products offered from banks. In doing so, they have, in the last years, transformed and positioned themselves as major actors within the financial market. New financial innovations modified the portfolios and increased the complexity of financial products. The liquidity risk and the systemic risk became higher. Life insurance products extended and became more similar to banking products. The new options within these products raised the liquidity of the liabilities. Because of these changes, there is now a clear difference to traditional insurance products, which has also revealed new levels of exposure.[54] In general, however, insurance companies have more liquid assets than banks, such as bonds, loans, real estate and equities, hence a lower liquidity risk.

The above realisations apart, the need to protect the interests of the policyholders and the overall stability of the financial system emphasizes the necessity of transparency through regulation, as the principle objective of supervision is the protection of the policyholder. Policyholders don't know how their paid premiums are used. Policyholders are as well not capable of evaluating the financial stability of the insurance company. Regulations should guarantee that the insurance company meets its obligations and protects the policyholder.[55] Any regulatory framework within the prudential authority needs to support the policyholders. Another reason for

[49]Noussia and Siri (2019).

[50]Cummins et al. (2017), p. 67; Petsch (2019).

[51]Doff (2008), pp. 196–198; Petsch (2019).

[52]Eling et al. (2007), p. 69; Petsch (2019).

[53]Das et al. (2003) and Petsch (2019).

[54]Lorent (2008) and Petsch (2019).

[55]OECD (1998), available at: http://www.oecd.org/regreform/sectors/1920099.pdf (04 April 2019).

prudential regulations is that claimholders will always demand the payment of their claims. A regulatory structure matters when the system suffers from agency problems and information asymmetries. Therefore, an external regulatory framework needs to be introduced. This structure creates synergies and is more efficient when it comes to functions and expertise. Additionally, it prevents regulatory gaps and duplicated control functions, while setting clear responsibilities and increasing the commitment of the supervisor.[56] Pertinent to the above need, the IMD information and conduct of business requirements were significantly amended by the requirements of Chapter V of the IDD. The stricter selling practices introduced, took the MiFID II Directive into account to ensure cross-sector consistency. This means that customers are now afforded equivalent levels of protection under the two regimes. Firms involved in the distribution of IBIPs have to comply with specific requirements set out in Chapter VI in addition to the Chapter V requirements in recognition of the fact that IBIPs are higher-risk products.

Hence, by the end of 2018 the IDD was fully implemented by all EU member states with the intention to harmonize the insurance business in the EU, provide the right incentives for sales agents and protect the policyholders via solving issues of transparency, information asymmetry and agency problems, and by creating incentives, a representation of the policyholder and the inversion of the production cycle.[57]

The IDD has three lists of subjects that it covers: general insurance, life insurance and insurance-based investment products. There is no further guidance, other than these three lists, published by the EU authorities and it is up to firms to interpret what the lists mean. For life insurance, the requirements are: minimum necessary knowledge of IBIPs, including terms and conditions and net premiums and, where applicable, guaranteed and non-guaranteed benefits; minimum necessary knowledge of advantages and disadvantages of different investment options for policyholders; minimum necessary knowledge of financial risks borne by policyholders; minimum necessary knowledge of policies covering life risks and other savings products; minimum necessary knowledge of organisation and benefits guaranteed by the pension system; minimum necessary knowledge of applicable laws governing the distribution of insurance products, such as consumer protection law and relevant tax law; minimum necessary knowledge of the insurance market and of the saving products market; minimum necessary knowledge of complaints handling; minimum necessary knowledge of assessing customer needs; conflicts of interest management; minimum necessary knowledge of business ethics standards; minimum necessary financial competency. For IBIPs, the requirements are: minimum necessary knowledge of policies including terms, conditions, the guaranteed benefits and, where applicable, ancillary risks; minimum necessary knowledge of organisation and benefits guaranteed by the pension system of the relevant Member State; knowledge of applicable insurance contract law, consumer protection law, data protection law,

[56]Gaganis and Pasiouras (2013).

[57]Petsch (2019).

data protection law, anti-money laundering law and, where applicable, relevant tax law and relevant social and labour law; minimum necessary knowledge of the insurance and other relevant financial services markets; minimum necessary knowledge of complaints handling; minimum necessary knowledge of assessing consumer needs; conflicts of interest management; minimum necessary knowledge of business ethics standards; and minimum necessary financial competency.[58]

3 Special Requirements Relating to Information, Advice, Remuneration

3.1 Information Requirement and the Duty to Act in the Customers' Best Interests

Ensuring the best interests of the customer is one of the motives of the IDD[59] and reflects the intention behind many of the obligations imposed on insurance distributors.

The concept of acting in the best interest of the customer adopted in the IDD Directive is not new and it reflects the obligations imposed under the MiFID Directive. The MiFID requirements for acting in the best interests of the customer focus primarily on customer information obligations in relation to the investment company providing the services, the financial instruments and the proposed investment strategies, which should include appropriate guidance and warnings about the risk associated with investment in such instruments or in relation to particular investment strategies, as well as information about the executors, costs and related fees. The aforementioned information should be structured in such a way that the customers or potential customers are able to understand the nature and risks of the investment service.[60]

The principle of the customer's best interest is also the core of the MiFID II Directive, where, as per Recital 71, investment companies should therefore understand the characteristics of the financial instruments they offer or recommend and develop effective strategies and arrangements to identify and review the categories of customers to whom products are to be delivered and services are to be provided. Member States should ensure that investment companies creating financial instruments guarantee that those products are developed in order to satisfy the specific needs of the target market, that they take reasonable steps to ensure that financial instruments are distributed within a specific target market, and that they periodically

---

[58]CII: Policy Briefing: Implementing the Insurance Distribution Directive: key provisions and analysis. March 2018, available at https://www.cii.co.uk/media/7775189/cii-policy-briefing-idd-implementation-22march2018.pdf.

[59]Malinowska (2018), p. 57.

[60]Paś (2020).

review the target market identification data and the performance of the products offered. Investment companies should also have adequate arrangements in place to obtain and understand relevant information regarding the product approval process, including the specific target market and the characteristics of the product they are offering or recommending.[61]

The IDD introduces a new obligation on insurance distributors to always act honestly, fairly and professionally, in accordance with the best interests of their customers (Article 17(1), IDD). One way in which insurance distributors are to comply with Article 17(1) is to ensure that they are not remunerated, and that they do not remunerate or assess the performance of their employees, in a way that conflicts with their duty to act in their customers' best interests (Article 17(3), IDD). In particular, the IDD explains that remuneration arrangements and sales targets should not provide an incentive to recommend a particular insurance product to a customer when a different product could be offered that would better meet the customer's needs (Article 17(3), IDD). The term "remuneration" is defined widely in Article 2 (1)(9) of the IDD to mean any commission, fee, charge or other payment, including an economic benefit of any kind, or any other financial or non-financial advantage or incentive offered or given in respect of insurance distribution activities.

All information related to the IDD, including marketing communications, addressed by an insurance distributor to customers or potential customers must be fair, clear and not misleading (Article 17(2), IDD). Article 17(2) states that its provisions are without prejudice to the Unfair Commercial Practices Directive (2005/29/EC) (UCPD).[62] Article 18 of the IDD provides for the obligation for general information. In good time before the conclusion of an insurance contract, an insurance intermediary or insurance undertaking must disclose to customers: (a) its identity and address, and the fact that it is an insurance intermediary or insurance undertaking, as appropriate; (b) whether it provides advice about the insurance products sold; (c) the procedures enabling customers and other interested parties to register complaints as referred to in Article 14; (d) the out-of-court complaint and redress procedures referred to in Article 15. In addition to the information listed above, an insurance intermediary must disclose to customers the register in which it has been included and the means for verifying that it has been registered and whether it is representing the customer or is acting for and on behalf of an insurance undertaking. In accordance with Article 19 of the IDD, there is a need for disclosing the nature of the remuneration received relating to the insurance contract, i.e. whether, in relation to the insurance contract, it works on the basis of a fee, i.e. the remuneration paid directly by the customer, or on the basis of a commission of any kind, i.e. the remuneration included in the insurance premium, or on the basis of other types of remuneration, including an economic benefit of any kind offered or given in connection with the insurance contract, or on the basis of a combination of any type of remuneration set out above. Where the fee is payable

---

[61] Paś (2020).

[62] Unfair Commercial Practices Directive (2005/29/EC) (UCPD).

directly by the customer, there is a need to disclose the amount of the fee or, where this is not possible, the method for calculating it. Also there is an obligation of disclosures for any payments made by the customer under the insurance contract after its conclusion, other than ongoing premiums and scheduled payments. Hence, an insurance undertaking need only communicate, in good time before the conclusion of an insurance contract, to its customers, the nature of the remuneration received by its employees relating to the insurance contract and any disclosures for any payments made by the customer under the insurance contract after its conclusion, other than ongoing premiums and scheduled payments.

As per the IDD, all information addressed by the insurance distributor to customers or potential customers should be "fair, clear and not misleading".[63] Articles 18 to 24, and 29 address the content, as well as the form and procedures that insurance distributors should perform in the disclosure of information to the client. First of all, before the conclusion of an insurance contract the insurance intermediary and undertaking should disclose: (i) its identity and address and that it is an insurance intermediary or undertaking; (ii) whether it provides advice about the insurance products sold; (iii) the procedures enabling customers and other interested parties to register complaints about insurance intermediaries and the out-of-court complaint and redress procedures.[64] Before the conclusion of the contract, the insurance distributor should specify the demands and needs of the customer, provide the customer with objective information about the insurance product in an understandable form, but also ensure that the contract proposed is consistent with the client's demands and needs.[65]

Recital 41 to the IDD explains that these disclosure obligations have been imposed on insurance undertakings to avoid the distortion of competition. Otherwise, insurance undertakings would have an advantage of avoiding disclosure obligations by selling direct to customers, rather than through intermediaries. The Commission's original IDD legislative proposal included more detailed and onerous remuneration disclosure provisions for intermediaries. However, these proved very contentious and were removed from the agreed text during the EU legislative process.

3.2 Advice Requirement

Where advice is provided before a specific insurance contract is concluded, an insurance distributor must provide the customer with a personalised recommendation (Article 20(1), IDD). Recital 45 to the IDD explains that this is in addition to specifying the customer's demands and needs. The personalised recommendation

[63] Article 17(2) IDD and Article 24(3) MiFID II.
[64] Article 18 IDD.
[65] Art 20 (1) IDD.

should explain why a particular product would best meet the customer's demands and needs. The details referred to in Article 20(1) IDD are to be adjusted according to both the complexity of the insurance product being proposed and the type of customer (Article 20(2), IDD). When an insurance intermediary informs a customer that it provides advice on the basis of a "fair and personal analysis", it must give advice on the basis of an analysis of a sufficiently large number of insurance contracts available on the market. This will enable the intermediary to make a personal recommendation on which insurance contract would be adequate to meet the customer's needs (Article 20(3), IDD). In the event the insurance intermediary gives its advice on the basis of a fair and personal analysis, it should advise on the basis of an analysis of a sufficiently large number of insurance contracts available on the market.[66] Moreover, the insurance intermediary should communicate the register in which it has been included and the means for verifying that it has been registered and whether it is representing the customer or it is acting for and on behalf of the insurance undertaking.[67]

The insurance intermediary should also provide information concerning potential conflict of interests, such as whether it has a holding, direct or indirect, representing 10% or more of the voting rights or of the capital in a given insurance undertaking, or whether a given insurance undertaking or parent undertaking of a given insurance undertaking has a holding, direct or indirect, representing 10% or more of the voting rights or of the capital in the insurance intermediary.[68] Similarly, in relation to the contracts proposed or advised upon, it should inform whether: (i) it gives advice on the basis of a fair and personal analysis; (ii) it is under a contractual obligation to conduct insurance distribution business exclusively with one or more insurance undertakings; or (iii) it is not under a contractual obligation to conduct insurance distribution business exclusively with one or more insurance undertakings and does not give advice on the basis of a fair and personal analysis.[69] Information concerning all costs and related charges should be promptly disclosed to the customers, to allow them to understand the overall cost as well as the cumulative effect on the return on the investment.[70]

In assessing whether the number of contracts and providers considered by an insurance intermediary is sufficiently large to constitute a fair and personal analysis, Recital 47 to the IDD explains that appropriate consideration should be given to the customer's needs, the number of providers in the market, the market share of those providers, the number of relevant insurance products available from each provider, the features of those products. The Recital goes on to state that the IDD should not prevent member states from requiring insurance intermediaries that wish to give

[66] Article 20(3) IDD.

[67] Article 18 (a) IDD.

[68] Article 19 (1) (a-b) IDD.

[69] Article 19(1)(c) IDD.

[70] Article 29(1) IDD.

advice on the basis of a fair and personal analysis to do so on an analysis of all the insurance contracts each intermediary distributes.

3.3 Exemptions from Information Requirements

Article 22(1) of the IDD explains that the information referred to in Articles 18, 19 and 20 does not need to be provided when an insurance distributor carries out distribution activities relating to the insurance of large risks. In addition, member states may decide that the information relating to insurance-based investment products referred to in Articles 29 and 30 does not need to be provided to professional clients (Article 22(1), IDD).

3.4 Stricter Information Provisions

The IDD[71] is a minimum harmonisation directive meaning that member states have the express option of maintaining or adopting stricter national provisions in a number of key areas, including in relation to the IDD[72] information provisions. Under Article 22(2) of the IDD, member states are allowed to gold plate the Chapter V information requirements provided the national provisions comply with EU law. In particular, member states may: (a) make the provision of advice referred to in Article 20(1) mandatory for the sales of any insurance products, or for certain types of insurance product (Article 22(2), IDD). In these cases, insurance distributors, including those exercising the free "passporting" service option, must comply with the stricter national provisions when concluding insurance contracts with customers who have their habitual residence or establishment in that member state, and limit or prohibit the acceptance or receipt of fees, commissions or other monetary or non-monetary benefits paid or provided to insurance distributors by any third party or a person acting on behalf of a third party relating to the distribution of insurance products (Article 22(3), IDD).

Any member state that proposes to apply and applies provisions in addition to those set out in the IDD must ensure that the administrative burden stemming from these provisions is proportionate with regard to consumer protection, and remains limited (Recital 52, IDD). Any member state that decides to exercise the discretion available under Article 22(2) must notify the Commission and EIOPA of its stricter national provisions (Article 22(2), IDD). To ensure a high level of transparency, EIOPA must ensure that the information it receives relating to national provisions is also communicated to customers, as well as insurance and reinsurance distributors

[71]Directive (EU) 2016/97, op. cit.

[72]Directive (EU) 2016/97, op. cit.

(Article 22(4), IDD). Member states must also ensure that their National Competent Authorities (NCAs) publish information about whether and how the member state has chosen to apply the stricter provisions (Article 22(2), IDD).

3.5 Information Conditions

Under Article 23(1) of the IDD, all pre-contract information to be provided in accordance with Articles 18, 19, 20 and 29 must be communicated to customers on paper; in a clear and accurate manner, comprehensible to the customer; in an official language of the member state in which the risk is situated or the member state of the commitment, or in any other language agreed by the parties; free of charge.

However, under Article 23(2) to (6), instead of providing this information to the customer on paper, it may be provided either: (a) using a durable medium other than paper, where the use of the durable medium is appropriate in the context of the business conducted between the insurance distributor and the customer; the customer has been given the choice between information on paper and on a durable medium, and has chosen the durable medium; and a paper copy of the information is provided to the customer on request and free of charge; or (b) by means of a website, if it is addressed personally to the customer, where the provision of the information by means of a website is appropriate in the context of the business conducted between the insurance distributor and the customer and it is considered appropriate if there is evidence that the customer has regular access to the internet, such as for example, if there is evidence that the customer has an email address; where the customer has consented to the information being provided by means of a website; where the customer has been notified electronically of the website's address, and the place on the website where the information can be accessed; where the information remains accessible on the website for such a period of time as the customer may reasonably need to consult it; and where a paper copy of the information is provided to the customer on request and free of charge. In the case of telephone sales, the pre-contract information given to the customer, including the Insurance Product Information Document ("IPID"), must be provided in accordance with EU distance marketing requirements. Moreover, even if the customer has chosen to obtain prior information on a durable medium other than paper, the information must be provided by the insurance distributor to the customer in accordance with Article 23(1) or (2) immediately after the conclusion of the insurance contract (Article 23(7), IDD).

3.6 New Information Requirements

For the sake of better consumer protection, insurance distributors will have to act honestly, fairly and professionally in accordance with the best interests of their customers. In particular, they cannot make any arrangements by way of remuneration or sales target that could provide an incentive to recommend a particular product to a customer when they could offer a different product that would meet the customer's needs better.

Regarding IBIPs, there is no ban on commission or fees introduced in the IDD. This situation should be welcomed as every intermediary has the right to be fairly remunerated for his or her services. The IDD however, requires from member states, in all cases of packaging, to ensure that an insurance distributor specifies the demands and needs of the customer in relation to the insurance products that form part of the overall package or the same agreement. The IDD explicitly recognises the differences between IBIPs and investment products and that IDD is the place to regulate them (Recital 10), but at the same time indicates that there is need for alignment with MiFID II and that, due to their specific character, there is need for a separate chapter on IBIPs (Recital 56).

Intermediaries and undertakings have to make (proportionate) arrangements to prevent conflicts of interest from adversely affecting the interests of their customers and must take steps to identify conflicts of interest.

Information regarding the distribution and all costs and related charges has to be provided in good time, before the conclusion of the contract. Where the MiFID II Directive requires benefits to enhance the quality of the service to the client,[73] and not against the criteria to act honestly, fairly, professionally and in the best interests of the client, the IDD allows them, if there is no detrimental impact on the quality of the service and it is not against the criteria to act honestly, fairly, professionally and in accordance with the best interests of its customers. In addition, the IDD explicitly foresees the possibility for member states to go beyond (e.g. prohibition of commissions, return to the client).

3.7 *Conflict of Interest*

The IDD and its delegated regulation[74] follow the MiFID II Directive provisions and those of its Delegated Regulation.[75] Article 23 of MiFID II, and article 28 of the IDD

[73]Commission 2012 staff working document executive summary of the impact assessment accompanying the document proposal for a Directive of the European Parliament and of the Council on insurance mediation; Directive 2014/65/EU of the European Parliament and of the Council of 15 May 2014 on markets in financial instruments and amending Directive 2002/92/EC and Directive 2011/61/EU http://data.europa.eu/eli/dir/2014/65/oj.

[74]Articles 3-7 of the Commission Delegated Regulation (EU) 2017/2359 of 21 September 2017 supplementing Directive (EU) 2016/97 of the European Parliament and of the Council with regard to information requirements and conduct of business rules applicable to the distribution of insurance-based investment products, http://data.europa.eu/eli/reg_del/2017/2359/oj.

[75]Commission Delegated Regulation (EU) 2017/565. See also the Explanatory Memorandum, Commission Delegated Regulation (EU) 2017/2359, p. 3.

does not define or prohibit conflicts of interest. However, in the relevant Delegated Regulation[76] we find provisions specifying certain situations which should be taken into account in the assessment of conflict of interest,[77] and the requirement for insurance intermediaries and insurance undertakings to establish, implement and maintain specific conflicts of interest policy to be followed for the identification, prevention and management of such conflicts of interest.[78] In particular, insurance intermediaries and insurance undertakings shall assess whether they, a relevant person or any person directly or indirectly linked to them by control, have an interest in the outcome of the insurance distribution activities, in the event such an interest: (a) is distinct from the customer's or potential customer's interest in the outcome of the insurance distribution activities; and (b) has the potential to influence the outcome of the distribution activities to the detriment of the customer.[79]

As for the conflict of interest policy, this should include the circumstances, related to the specific insurance distribution activity, which constitute or may give a rise to a conflict of interest which could damage the customers' interest, as well as the procedures to be followed and the measure to be adopted for the management of such conflicts.[80] The policy should be assessed and periodically reviewed, on an at least annual basis, and amended in case of any deficiency.[81] As regard to the insurance intermediaries, who are under a contractual obligation to conduct insurance distribution business exclusively with one or more insurance undertakings,

[76]Commission Delegated Regulation (EU) 2017/2359 of 21 September 2017 supplementing Directive (EU) 2016/97 of the European Parliament and of the Council with regard to information requirements and conduct of business rules applicable to the distribution of insurance-based investment products, http://data.europa.eu/eli/reg_del/2017/2359/oj.

[77]Article 3 of the Commission Delegated Regulation (EU) 2017/2359 of 21 September 2017 supplementing Directive (EU) 2016/97 of the European Parliament and of the Council with regard to information requirements and conduct of business rules applicable to the distribution of insurance-based investment products, http://data.europa.eu/eli/reg_del/2017/2359/oj.

[78]Article 4 of the Commission Delegated Regulation (EU) 2017/2359 of 21 September 2017 supplementing Directive (EU) 2016/97 of the European Parliament and of the Council with regard to information requirements and conduct of business rules applicable to the distribution of insurance-based investment products, http://data.europa.eu/eli/reg_del/2017/2359/oj.

[79]Article 3(2) of the Commission Delegated Regulation (EU) 2017/2359 of 21 September 2017 supplementing Directive (EU) 2016/97 of the European Parliament and of the Council with regard to information requirements and conduct of business rules applicable to the distribution of insurance-based investment products, http://data.europa.eu/eli/reg_del/2017/2359/oj.

[80]Article 4(2) of the Commission Delegated Regulation (EU) 2017/2359 of 21 September 2017 supplementing Directive (EU) 2016/97 of the European Parliament and of the Council with regard to information requirements and conduct of business rules applicable to the distribution of insurance-based investment products, http://data.europa.eu/eli/reg_del/2017/2359/oj.

[81]Article 7(1) and Recital 5 of the Commission Delegated Regulation (EU) 2017/2359 of 21 September 2017 supplementing Directive (EU) 2016/97 of the European Parliament and of the Council with regard to information requirements and conduct of business rules applicable to the distribution of insurance-based investment products, http://data.europa.eu/eli/reg_del/2017/2359/oj.

EIOPA has clarified that the conflict of interest policy remains a requirement under the responsibility of that intermediary.[82]

As in MiFID II, the disclosure of a conflict of interest should be avoided, except for the situations in which the organizational and administrative arrangements are insufficient for the prevention of risks of damage to the interests of the customer.[83] In such a case, the disclosure should be made on a durable medium and include sufficient detail,[84] which means that it should provide a specific description of the conflict of interest in question, explain its general nature, sources, and associated risks for consumers, and state that the organizational and administrative arrangements established within the conflict of interest policy are not sufficient to ensure, with reasonable confidence, the prevention of such risks.[85] Finally, the senior management of the insurance distributors should receive, at least annually, written reports on the situations in which a conflict of interest arose, and of these the insurance intermediary of undertaking should keep a record.[86]

4 Product Oversight and Governance

Article 25 of IDD sets Product Oversight and Governance ("POG") rules forth and the European Commission is empowered to adopt delegated acts to further specify the principles set out in this article, taking into account in a proportionate way the activities performed, the nature of the insurance products which were sold and the nature of the distributor. Thus, POG rules of the IDD are supplemented by Commission Delegated Regulation (EU) 2017/2358 of 21 September 2017,[87] which is based on the Technical advice provided by the EIOPA in February 2017.

[82] EIOPA (2018).

[83] Article 6(1) and Recital 5 of the Commission Delegated Regulation (EU) 2017/2359 of 21 September 2017 supplementing Directive (EU) 2016/97 of the European Parliament and of the Council with regard to information requirements and conduct of business rules applicable to the distribution of insurance-based investment products, http://data.europa.eu/eli/reg_del/2017/2359/oj.

[84] Article 28(3) of the Directive (EU) 2016/97, op. cit.

[85] Article 6(2) and Recital 5 of the Commission Delegated Regulation (EU) 2017/2359 of 21 September 2017 supplementing Directive (EU) 2016/97 of the European Parliament and of the Council with regard to information requirements and conduct of business rules applicable to the distribution of insurance-based investment products, http://data.europa.eu/eli/reg_del/2017/2359/oj.

[86] Article 7(2) and Recital 5 of the Commission Delegated Regulation (EU) 2017/2359 of 21 September 2017 supplementing Directive (EU) 2016/97 of the European Parliament and of the Council with regard to information requirements and conduct of business rules applicable to the distribution of insurance-based investment products, http://data.europa.eu/eli/reg_del/2017/2359/oj.

[87] Commission Delegated Regulation (EU) 2017/2358 of 21 September 2017 supplementing Directive (EU) 2016/97 of the European Parliament and of the Council with regard to product oversight

The Commission Delegated Regulation[88] specifies the criteria and practical details for the application of POG rules, affirming that these rules are mainly addressed at manufacturers of insurance products and oblige them to maintain, operate and review a POG policy in order to ensure on a continuous basis that all insurance products marketed are appropriate for their specific target market. Insurance distributors have to support this by operating product distribution arrangements to ensure that they have all the information needed to sell the product in line with the POG policy set by the manufacturer. The POG rules are built around both the manufacturer and the distributor because the POG imposes separate duties to both of them, as well as general provisions. In addition, the same entity can play the role of manufacturer and distributor.[89]

The product oversight and governance (POG) rules in the IDD are a mere duplication of the rules in MiFID II, albeit with some slight differences.[90] The set of rules on POG do not address a specific life insurance product. POG sets the duty for disclosure to the supervisory authority of the way in which the products are manufactured and the purposes actually pursued with these products by the insurance undertakings.[91] Hence POG allows for the implementation of transparent and auditable product approval frameworks for new products the design of which is not compromised by profit or time pressures. With regards to "bancassurance", manufacturers have to provide assistance where sales were conducted through banks, without relying on the assumption that banking staff in sales functions had the necessary product knowledge.

For the life insurance sector, the rules on POG guarantee the design and distribution of products that satisfy the interests and needs of customers belonging to the target market and to whom those specific products are distributed, and safeguards the customer's protections to the point of sale as it forges the protection of customers with respect to poorly designed products. Manufacturers are the main recipients of POG rules. Both insurance undertakings and insurance intermediaries can qualify as manufacturers depending on the role they play in designing insurance products.[92] In the case of insurance undertaking playing a "passive" role or a non-exclusive role in the decision-making process, a distinction should be made whether the insurance undertaking has (i) outsourced the design activities or (ii) contributed to the design of the product with another entity.

---

and governance requirements for insurance undertakings and insurance distributors http://data.europa.eu/eli/reg_del/2017/2358/oj.

[88]Commission Delegated Regulation (EU) 2017/2358 of 21 September 2017 supplementing Directive (EU) 2016/97 of the European Parliament and of the Council with regard to product oversight and governance requirements for insurance undertakings and insurance distributors http://data.europa.eu/eli/reg_del/2017/2358/oj.

[89]Marano (2019).

[90]Marano (2019, 2020).

[91]Marano (2020) and Śliwiński and Marano (2020).

[92]See Article 25(1) of the Directive (EU) 2016/97 of the European Parliament and of the Council of 20 January 2016 on insurance distribution (recast) http://data.europa.eu/eli/dir/2016/97/oj.

The IDD does not rule out that the co-manufacturing is done by two insurance undertakings without involving an insurance intermediary. This is the case of a life insurance product combining two different classes, e.g. unit-linked and assurance on survival to a stipulated age or on earlier death, each of them managed by one of the two insurance undertakings, whilst the product is distributed through the distribution channel selected by one of the undertakings.

Articles 9 and 10 of Commission Delegated Directive (EU) 2017/593 of 7 April 2016[93] supplementing MiFID II could be a useful reference for the Member States as regulation on financial products deals with this issue. The IDD shall not affect a Member State's law in respect of insurance and reinsurance distribution activities pursued by insurance and reinsurance undertakings or intermediaries established in a third country and operating on its territory, provided that equal treatment is guaranteed to all persons carrying out insurance and reinsurance distribution activities on that market.[94] The principle of equal treatment therefore requires national legislation to apply POG rules to products marketed in the country without taking into account the nationality of the manufacturer. Thus, the same principle can apply in the case of activities carried out by insurance entities based in third countries.[95]

5 Impact of the IDD

An essential focus of regulatory supervision is market conduct in insurance distribution, which is challenged by the IDD through the imposing of minimum advice quality and transparency standards for insurance distribution within EU member states. The IDD also implies that the member states may implement even stricter rules where necessary.

At first glance, it seems that the Europeanisation of the regulatory and supervisory system will lead to greater transparency for policyholders, new minimum standards for certain rules of cross-border business, more and better tools to supervise insurance intermediaries and general rules to sanction intermediaries that breach the provisions of the IDD, and ensure that insurance products with investment elements are protected in a similar way to other financial investment products in the EU. The new minimum harmonisation also equalises costs across various sales channels, largely through increased transparency to consumers, hopefully reducing barriers to the pursuit of fair insurance purchases.[96] Overall, a solid regulatory framework can

---

[93]Commission Delegated Directive (EU) 2017/593 of 7 April 2016 supplementing Directive 2014/65/EU of the European Parliament and of the Council with regard to safeguarding of financial instruments and funds belonging to clients, product governance obligations and the rules applicable to the provision or reception of fees, commissions or any monetary or non-monetary benefits, http://data.europa.eu/eli/dir_del/2017/593/oj.

[94]See Article 1(6) of the Directive (EU) 2016/97, op.cit.

[95]Marano (2019).

[96]Klumpes and Schuermann (2011).

enhance the efficiency of insurance markets and lead to lower costs of insurance coverage. The U.S., where insurance is still regulated at the state level, might benefit from a unified regulatory framework. The new EU framework may thus serve as an example for the U.S.

Nevertheless, ensuring compliance with legal requirements implies bureaucratic costs, which are ultimately borne by the policyholders, and the implementation of the new IDD involves some major challenges for many EU countries. An important question to be addressed is whether this new EU-wide harmonisation regulation is an expedient and cost-efficient solution. The benefits of harmonised rules might not always outweigh the substantial costs of implementation, which will be different in each EU Member State. While such increased bureaucracy is unavoidably associated with a certain amount of costs involved in the process of meeting regulatory goals, "inefficient" regulation may lead to unnecessary costs. Inappropriate regulatory provisions might even result in useful insurance products disappearing from the market since potential policyholders are no longer willing to pay the resulting higher premiums.[97] However, there are diverse and conflicting provisions in different areas in the U.S. as well, which might also result in additional costs (for instance, compliance costs) that are passed on to consumers and may lead to rising prices and possibly even to the disappearance of certain products from the market.

In the case of the new IDD, potentially high administrative costs for the involved parties in some Member States might arise, for instance through the introduction of the new online EU insurance distribution register. The design of such an online register, as well as its continued maintenance, may amount to additional costs for the insurance supervisor. A second example, for non-life insurance products is the Insurance Product Information Document ("IPID"), which will incur costs of developing the setting-up of the document technology infrastructure to manage the population of documents, as well as ongoing costs related to the circulation and renewal of IPIDs and other costs of record keeping.[98]

Another challenge is the alignment of new IDD requirements with other legal provisions, which might overlap, or be redundant or even contradict IDD requirements, and might ultimately lead to further unnecessary bureaucracy costs. Insufficiently harmonised parallel reform measures or lack of coordination between regulations circulated on different regulatory levels might result in a shortcoming of legal certainty and could bring about new risks and costs for the insurance industry. An example is the alignment of IDD requirements with MiFID II standards. In particular in the life insurance market, requirements have to be imposed to conform to MiFID II rules.[99] Some other requirements such as the assessment to

[97]GDV (2015), p. 19.

[98]Final Report on Consultation Paper no. 16/007 on draft Implementing Technical Standards concerning a standardised presentation format for the Insurance Product Information Document of the Insurance Distribution Directive (EIOPA-BoS-17/055), available at https://register.eiopa.europa.eu/Publications/Reports/IDD%20Final%20Report%20on%20draft%20ITS%20on%20IPID.pdf; Köhne and Brömmelmeyer (2018).

[99]Clifford Chance (2013) and Köhne and Brömmelmeyer (2018).

ascertain the suitability and appropriateness of a product (Art. 30 IDD) might impose an additional administrative burden.

Moreover, the expected increase in reporting and disclosure requirements might involve excessive bureaucracy and it remains questionable whether the aspired goal of strengthened consumer protection can be reached. Not least, the additional administrative expenditure might imply a rise in premiums to the full detriment of consumers. The new regulatory changes do not take fully into account that some consumers are competent enough to research and purchase investment options and insurance products themselves. These consumers will prefer to buy insurance directly from insurance companies or via the Internet. With some insurance products disappearing from the marketplace for the above reasons, these consumers are clearly made worse off by some requirements of the new IDD. Additionally, future continuing professional training requirements might prove costly for insurance intermediaries.[100] These costs will likely be passed on to consumers through fees or taxes. The additional costs to consumers may be worthwhile if increased education and transparency reduce the likelihood of bad advice by intermediaries. However, a potentially unintended consequence of the regulation is that stricter standards may lead insurance distributors to engage in defensive selling practices (i.e. recommending more insurance than is needed) in order to avoid professional liability claims. This motivation may be strengthened if the practice also leads to more commission income.

5.1 Impact with Regards to the Life Insurance Sector

The EU financial services regulation is increasingly cross-sectoral. The IDD introduces additional requirements for insurance-based investment products with the collective asset and the long term orientation being important differentiators of life insurance contracts and retail investment products. In relation to collective asset, ownership, retail investors individually purchase units or shares, whereas policyholders typically do not acquire the underlying assets of their life insurance contract but a contractual right towards the insurance undertaking. This contractual right materialises upon occurrence of the insured event such as death, disability, and longevity. The ownership of the underlying assets is held by the insurance undertaking which protects policyholders from the ‘timing risk’, i.e. when to buy and to sell. By concluding an insurance contract, the policyholder joins the community of insured, sharing all risks and costs based on the principles of solidarity and risk pooling. The policyholder’s capital market and biometric risk, which are independent from each other, are pooled and coordinated by the insurance undertaking. As a result, policyholders receive twin benefits from investment and insurance protection under a single integrated contract. In relation to long term orientation, the holding

[100]Hogan Lovells (2017) and Köhne and Brömmelmeyer (2018).

period of retail investment products is defined *ex post* and comprises often only a few years, including the option to exit at any time. By contrast, the holding period of life insurance contracts is defined *ex ante* and usually comprises several decades with restricted exit options. The long term orientation of life insurance is further underlined by the fact that customer intervention during the contract period is usually fairly limited, and contractual option(s) such as lump-sum payment or annuities can be exercised typically only at maturity.

Notwithstanding the differences outlined above, the IDD reflects an individual and short term approach. In relation to the correlation between product distribution and dealing on own account any potential conflicts of interest shall be assessed by taking into account whether the insurance distributor 'is likely to make a financial gain, or avoid a financial loss, to the potential detriment of the customer.

In contrast to the distribution of retail investment products, there is typically no correlation between the profit/loss made by the policyholder and the profit/loss made by the insurer. Therefore, it deserves further scrutiny whether, and how, this conflict of interest situation should be upheld in an insurance context. In relation to periodic assessments, insurance distributors shall inform their customers whether a periodic assessment of the suitability of the insurance-based investment products will be carried out.[101] However, life insurance contracts are characterised by a long term orientation that precludes short-term customer intervention. Quite the contrary, *ex post* changes to insurance contracts, such as surrender or withdrawal, mostly imply disadvantages with regards to costs and fiscal treatment.

In the customer's best interest, the stable, long term character of life insurance should not be undermined by artificial volatility caused by short-term customer intervention. In relation to periodic reports, at least annually, the customer has to be informed about any 'transactions' that have been undertaken on his behalf. In an insurance context, the wording 'on behalf' seems unsuitable as any investment activity by insurers is typically carried out on behalf of the entire community of insured. In the insurance sector, this issue could be resolved by specifying that this provision only applies to 'transactions made upon explicit request of the individual customer.'[102]

5.2 Assessment of Suitability

The IDD provides specific conduct of business rule, not derived from MiFID IIregime, known as the demands and needs test. The scope of this test is not prescribed in the IDD or the Delegated Regulation[103] and is subject to national implementation. However, EIOPA provided some guidance regarding minimum

[101] IDD, Art. 29(1)(a).

[102] Pscheidl (2018).

[103] Commission Delegated Directive (EU) 2017/593, op. cit.

expectations for this test and how it may relate to the assessment of suitability.[104] Recital 7 of Delegated Regulation 2017/2359[105] clarifies that the assessments of suitability and appropriateness are without prejudice to the obligation, for insurance intermediaries and insurance undertakings, to consider and specify, prior to the conclusion of any insurance contract, on the basis of information obtained from the customer, and the demands and needs of that customer.

The demands and needs test provides a protection for customers to avoid cases of mis-selling (Recital 44, IDD) and it applies to all insurance contracts, not just IBIPs. Article 30, IDD applies "without prejudice" to the demands and needs test as covered by Article 20(1), IDD. The demands and needs test has to be performed in any event prior to the conclusion of the contract and is distinct from the suitability assessment in advised cases, and the suitability assessment can also be provided at any time during the customer relationship. The assessment of demands and needs is required whether or not advice is being provided and the specifying of the demands and needs would not amount to a suitability assessment. Depending on the national implementation, where advice is being provided, the demands and needs test and assessment of suitability could be seen as a continuum, rather than as a break.

The main information concerning the customer's needs, typically includes, for example, personal information (age, profession, place of residence etc.) or the information particularly linked to the type of product requested. This information should enable the insurance intermediary or insurance undertaking to assess whether certain products can be offered or not according to their capacity of meeting the demands and needs of the customer. This could lead to a selection of a range of comparable products for consideration during the suitability assessment where advice is being given or during the appropriateness assessment where no advice is given.

Where the customer is provided with advice the information, which will be obtained by the insurance intermediary or the insurance undertaking, will need to include other more specific and detailed elements, like the customer's financial situation, including their ability to bear losses, their investment objectives, including their risk tolerance, and other correlated information. Under the IDD and the Delegated Regulation,[106] the provisions concerning the assessment of suitability and appropriateness are almost identical to the corresponding provisions under MiFID II and its specific Delegated Regulation.[107] In particular, the suitability assessment requires that the insurance intermediary or undertaking, in the case of sales with advice, gathers information about their client's knowledge, experience,

[104]EIOPA (2018).

[105]Commission Delegated Regulation (EU) 2017/593 op.cit.

[106]Articles 9-19 of the Commission Delegated Regulation (EU) 2017/2359 op.cit.

[107]Commission Delegated Regulation (EU) 2017/565 of 25 April 2016 supplementing Directive 2014/65/EU of the European Parliament and of the Council as regards organisational requirements and operating conditions for investment firms and defined terms for the purposes of that Directive, available at http://data.europa.eu/eli/reg_del/2017/565/oj.

investment objective and risk tolerance—in order to recommend to the client the IBIPs that are best aligned with the client's profile,[108] which means that it meets the client's investment objectives, risk tolerance, financial situation and that its nature and characteristics are adequate in respect to the client's knowledge and experience.[109]

The insurance intermediary or undertaking should adopt measures to ensure that the information collected about the clients is reliable, and communicate them that the suitability assessment is performed in their best interest.[110] It should then provide the customer with the so-called 'suitability statement', which includes an outline of the advice given, as well as information about how the recommendation meets the customer's investment objectives, risk tolerance, financial situation, knowledge and experience.[111]

The appropriateness requirement provides that, in the event of sales requiring no advice, the insurance intermediary or insurance undertaking gathers information on the client to assess if the product or services offered or demanded were appropriate for the customer.[112] In the event the product is deemed not appropriate for the customer, the insurance intermediary or insurance undertaking should warn the customer or potential customer.[113] Article 19(3) of Delegated Regulation 2017/2359 contains requirements for records to be kept in relation to the appropriateness assessment, in particular regarding the result of the assessment, warnings given to the customer and storage in an accessible manner for future reference. As under MiFID II, this assessment is not required concerning non-complex products as defined by MiFID II.[114] However, due to the specific structures of insurance products, the Commission Delegated Regulation under IDD provides, among the criteria for non-complex IBIPs, an additional condition concerning products including a specific guarantee.[115]

Moreover, the insurance intermediary or insurance undertaking should establish a record of documents agreed with the customer containing rights and obligations of the parties, as well as other terms related to the provision of services to the customer. The customer should also be provided with periodic reports on the service, which include a number of communications proportionate to the type and complexity of the IBIP involved.[116]

[108] Article 30(1) of the IDD.

[109] Article 9(2) of the Commission Delegated Regulation (EU) 2017/2359 op.cit.

[110] Article10 and 11 of the Commission Delegated Regulation (EU) 2017/2359 op.cit.

[111] Article 14(1) of the Commission Delegated Regulation (EU) 2017/2359 op. cit.

[112] Article 30(2) of IDD and Article 14 of the Commission Delegated Regulation (EU) 2017/2359 op. cit.

[113] Noussia and Siri (2019).

[114] Article 30(3) IDD and 25(4)(a) MiFID II.

[115] Article 16(a) of the Commission Delegated Regulation (EU) 2017/2359.

[116] Articles 30(4) and (5) IDD.; Noussia and Siri (2019).

6 A Comparison of the EU and U.S. Insurance Distribution Regulatory Regime

Whilst the IDD attempts to reduce cross-sectoral and cross-border inconsistencies by establishing a more uniform regulatory framework in the European insurance market, via the introduction to insurance distribution systems of minimum quality standards and disclosure requirements to insurance distribution systems, "the U.S. insurance regulation mostly continues to be the purview of state government, leading to cumbersome and conflicting provisions as well as higher compliance costs".[117]

The new IDD attempts to reduce cross-sectoral and cross-border inconsistencies by establishing a more uniform regulatory framework in the European insurance market. For this purpose, minimum quality standards and disclosure requirements are introduced to insurance distribution systems. In contrast, "U.S. insurance regulation mostly continues to be the purview of state government, leading to cumbersome and conflicting provisions as well as higher compliance costs".[118]

"In the US, insurance regulation is almost entirely the responsibility of the individual states, the individual state insurance commissioners and the National Association of Insurance Commissioners (NAIC). The NAIC drafts the model insurance laws, however the NAIC Model Acts are mainly advisory tools. The primary body of law applied to insurance intermediaries is the Producer Licensing Model Act (PLMA)".[119]

"The most striking difference between the PLMA and the IDD is that the PMLA is written from the perspective of the individual U.S. state legislators constitutes a suggestion of an advisory body whereas the IDD is a mandatory Directive".[120]

The IDD also enhances standards related to information requirements and conduct of business rules (Chapter V, IDD). The IDD marks another step in further harmonising the European market for insurance regulation and creating a level playing field. It imposes new requirements which broaden the scope of regulatory oversight of insurance distribution channels as well as imposing new constraints on business conduct, including continuing professional training for sales people and compensation disclosure to enhance market conduct regulation. "Chapter V of the IDD delineates the information requirements for intermediaries, and the rules applicable to their business conduct. Section 12 of the PLMA lists prohibited actions which can lead to an insurance intermediary's license revocation and a civil penalty. Despite that the IDD language is written in a prescriptive manner and the PLMA is written in a proscriptive manner, there are some similarities."[121] Article 17 of the

[117]Defever (2021), p. 198; Hofmann et al. (2018).

[118]Defever (2021), p. 198; Hofmann et al. (2018).

[119]Defever (2021), p. 198.

[120]Defever (2021), p. 200.

[121]Defever (2021), p. 201.

IDD requires that insurance distributors always act honestly, fairly and professionally in accordance with the best interests of their customers. Section 12 A. (8) of the PLMA forbids an insurance producer from using fraudulent, coercive, or dishonest practices, or demonstrating incompetence, untrustworthiness or financial irresponsibility in the conduct of business. "What is strikingly missing from the PLMA is the requirement that U.S. insurance intermediaries act with the best interests of their customers, as is required of European intermediaries. Another requirement present in the IDD that is glaringly absent from the PLMA is that marketing be "fair, clear, and not misleading."[122] The PLMA places only two restrictions on the remuneration of insurance producers—one, that a producer must be licensed in order to receive commissions, and two, that the producer must disclose a compensation agreement with an insurer if the producer is also receiving compensation from the customer.[123] In contrast, the IDD mandates that Member States shall ensure that distributors and their employees are not remunerated in a way that conflicts with their duties to act in accordance with the best interest of their customers;[124] that they reveal business holdings that create conflicts;[125] that they reveal whether advice is based on fair and personal analysis or not, or whether there is exclusivity with an insurance company;[126] and that they reveal the nature of remuneration received, i.e. fee, commission, or other, and the amount, and whether it ties to employee remuneration."[127]

In terms of regulatory scope, the IDD allows insurance intermediaries to sell products across multiple EU Member States where previously parity did not always exist. The U.S. has attempted to provide some kind of uniformity in cross-state producer licencing with the GLB Act (passed in 1999)[128] and NARAB II Regulation (passed in 2015).[129] Additionally, the IDD introduces minimum requirements for all distributors of insurance and reinsurance policies, including direct sales, agents, brokers and others, to comply with new disclosure and training requirements to enhance consumer protection independent of the distribution channel. Nevertheless, the IDD is a minimum harmonisation Directive leaving the Member States with the opportunity to implement even stricter rules. U.S. intermediary regulation is not uniform between retail, wholesale and reinsurance sales. Individual state and national laws govern these transactions separately, which may impact consumer protection measures differently, depending on the distribution channel.

The IDD requires insurance distributors to be registered with a competent authority in their home member state (Art. 3(1) IDD), and member states have to implement an online EU insurance distribution register and ensure that a single

[122]IDD Art. 17, 2.

[123]Defever (2021), pp. 201–202.

[124]IDD Art. 17, 3.

[125]IDD Art. 19, 1. (a) and (b).

[126]IDD Art. 19, 1. (c).

[127]IDD Art. 19, 1. (d), (e), 2., and 4.; Defever (2021), pp. 201–202.

[128]Gramm–Leach–Bliley Act (GLBA), also known as the Financial Services Modernization Act of 1999, (Pub.L. 106–102, 113 Stat. 1338, enacted November 12, 1999).

[129]NARAB II Regulation, Public Law No: 114-1 (01/12/2015).

information point exists.[130] Similarly, in the U.S. all intermediaries have to obtain a licence (depending on the type of insurance, e.g., a Property and Casualty licence, or a Life, Accident and Health licence) in order to sell insurance.

According to the IDD, a basic level of advice quality has to be guaranteed, and continuing education of insurance intermediaries is required, but Member States may impose additional standards on producers. The NARAB Board in the U.S. imposes minimum continuing professional training standards for licenced producers, but individual states may vary their re-licencing standards for the intermediaries licenced there. Many states require a portion of continuing education to focus on ethics, but otherwise licencees may choose their own training so that the actual training may lead to considerable differences regarding the knowledge and competency of intermediaries.

With regards to information requirements and conduct of business the IDD provides strengthened consumer protection and requires from the intermediary to inform the consumer of any potential conflicts of interest before the insurance contract is finalised (e.g., Art. 18 IDD). These disclosure requirements exceed any standard disclosures provided by U.S. insurance intermediaries. As part of this disclosure, the IDD imposes additional standards on insurance producers related to compensation, i.e. they need disclose to the consumer the amount of compensation they receive for the sale of the insurance product (Art. 19 IDD); previously, this compensation disclosure requirement varied by EU member state. In the U.S. there is no standard requirement to disclose producer compensation, but again this varies by state, leaving consumers with a certain lack of clarity regarding their rights.[131]

Moreover, in the EU, compensation of insurance distributors may be a commission paid by the insurer, a fee paid by the insured, or any other remuneration within the contract, but always provided that this does not conflict with the distributor's duties to act in the best interest of its customers (Art. 17(3) IDD). In addition, in the U.S. there is not just one standard compensation scheme for insurance intermediaries: compensation varies with regard to the type of insurance sold and the nature of the relationship between the producer and insurer. Beside the standard commissions, intermediaries can also receive a contingent commission.

Other new IDD disclosure requirements to improve consumer protection are requirements that are placed on insurance distributors in relation to advice and how this advice is provided. Depending on the complexity of the insurance product and consumer type, there is a requirement to specify the demands and needs of the customer and provide objective information in a comprehensible format. For certain non-life insurance products this has to be summarised in the IPID, which mandates policy-level disclosures (e.g., coverages, exclusions and restrictions) to the insured. In the U.S. there is no comparable standard document, and requirements vary by state. Whether intermediaries have a duty to advise their client also depends on the state.

---

[130] Köhne and Brömmelmeyer (2018) and Hogan Lovells (2017).

[131] Scism (2012) and Köhne and Brömmelmeyer (2018).

Furthermore, the IDD requires insurance undertakings to comply with new POG requirements to ensure certain suitability for the defined target market and a focus on consumer protection measures. In addition, consistency between Member States is ensured.

Similar to non-life insurance products, the IDD also enhances the information and disclosure requirements for IBIPs. Additionally, insurance intermediaries must assess the suitability and appropriateness of the product for the customer (Art. 30 IDD), which again highlights the increased focus on consumer protection in the EU and aims to improve the alignment and consistency between the regulation of financial and insurance markets. In the U.S., life insurance contracts may be subject to regulation by (1) the Securities and Exchange Commission if the contracts qualify as *securities* that are not exempt under the U.S. federal securities laws, and (2) by the U.S. Department of Labor if they are offered in connection with employee benefit plans.

While insurance regulation in the U.S. continues to be the purview of state government, some federal regulation and standardised practices affect insurance distribution systems nationally. Most notably, the NARAB II regulation (passed in 2015)[132] provides reciprocity between states for licenced insurance providers. However, insurance regulation in the EU appears to consistently move towards more harmonisation across Member States. The IDD marks another change in the divide between EU regulatory uniformity and U.S. regulatory dispersion and can maybe set an example for the U.S.

An essential focus of regulatory supervision is market conduct in insurance distribution, which is challenged by the IDD through the imposing of minimum advice quality and transparency standards for insurance distribution within EU member states. The IDD also implies that the member states may implement even stricter rules where necessary.

At first glance, it seems that the Europeanisation of the regulatory and supervisory system will lead to greater transparency for policyholders, new minimum standards for certain rules of cross-border business, more and better tools to supervise insurance intermediaries and general rules to sanction intermediaries that breach the provisions of the IDD, and ensure that insurance products with investment elements are protected in a similar way to other financial investment products in the EU. The new minimum harmonisation also equalises costs across various sales channels, largely through increased transparency to consumers, hopefully reducing barriers to the pursuit of fair insurance purchases.[133] Overall, a solid regulatory framework can enhance the efficiency of insurance markets and lead to lower costs of insurance coverage. The U.S., where insurance is still regulated at the state level, might benefit from a unified regulatory framework. The new EU framework may thus serve as an example for the U.S.

[132]NARAB II Regulation, Public Law No: 114-1 (01/12/2015).

[133]Klumpes and Schuermann (2011).

"The primary difference between the IDD and the PLMA is that the IDD is mandatory and the PLMA is voluntary. Due to its advisory nature, the PMLA has been inconsistently adopted and inconsistently enforced. The bodies of regulations applying to insurance producers remain in a piecemeal state, and the PMLA has done very little to close the gaps".[134]

"The takeaway for EU Member States should be that uniformity will not be achieved until and unless they adopt and apply the mandatory penalties provided in the IDD and achieve a sufficient level of transparency to aid consumers in avoiding bad actors, and to act as a deterrence to producers. The IDD's more prescriptive, rules-based insurance regulations will be the first of their kind to be applied across such a wide and diverse territory like the EU Member States."[135]

The benefits of the new IDD can only be evaluated after introduction of the Directive when a direct comparison with the status quo becomes possible. It seems that some of the envisaged provisions include redundancies for several Member States and will lead to duplicate requirements, which may make implementation even more complicated. However, some important questions remain: Do consumers feel better informed? Do consumers make better decisions? Can important losses be prevented? An important challenge is that the insurance industry in Europe might fail to recognise the integration of borderless markets. As argued by Schiro[136] many insurance markets continue to transcend borders such that national regulation may increasingly spill over from one local jurisdiction to another, thereby leading to the risk of conflicting regulations.

Nevertheless, the IDD will, despite the challenges of implementation, likely help to establish a harmonisation of European insurance markets through more uniform standards and regulation. This will reduce legal uncertainties and facilitate fair competition between insurance companies and intermediaries in different EU Member States. Notably, consumer protection across all financial sectors can be improved by aligning the regulatory system for insurance and financial markets. All in all, the new IDD will enhance the efficiency of European insurance markets. Through more uniform and consistent regulation, in conjunction with extended transparency requirements, it can ensure that consumers throughout the EU are equally well protected. Therefore, these more uniform regulations could set an example for dispersion in U.S. insurance regulation.

[134]Defever (2018); Defever (2021), p. 215.

[135]Defever (2018).

[136]Schiro (2006) and Köhne and Brömmelmeyer (2018).

7 Conclusions

At the age of transparency, the IDD has a direct application in the life insurance sector in relation to the improvement of quality of products delivered to the customers.[137] The IDD acts as a minimum harmonisation directive, allowing stricter rules at national level to be imposed. It promotes transparency and the insured's customer's protection and in doing so accomplishes a large harmonization impact and effect in the insurance industry overall, in line with the view for a single harmonised market.

The requirements set by the IDD for life insurance products require a minimum necessary knowledge of IBIPs, of the various financial risks, of the life policies and of the organisation and benefits guaranteed by the various investments products. Insurance distributors need always act honestly, fairly and professionally in accordance with the best interests of their customers and disclose their general personal information and redress and opt out procedures so as to enhance transparency. A duty to advise and provide a personalised recommendation as needed also exists. The IDD allows insurers to accept and retain fees, commissions or any monetary and non-monetary benefits from third parties, and particularly from issuers or product providers regarding the distribution of an IBIP as long as the payment of such remuneration does not impact negatively the provision of insurance and does not impair the distributor's professional capacity and obligations. The IDD also introduces additional requirements for IBIPs with the collective asset and the long term orientation being important differentiators of life insurance contracts and retail investment products.

Overall, following the wave of other regulatory changes, such as MiFID II and PRIIPS Regulation,[138] the IDD intends to strengthen consumer protection, improve the competitive landscape of the European insurance industry, and reduce cross-sectoral inconsistencies. The IDD also introduces product oversight and governance requirements similar to MiFID II. In relation to assessing the suitability and appropriateness of this is conducted by insurance companies that provide advice to customers on IBIPs so as to enable them to recommend to the customer or potential customer the IBIPs that are suitable for that person. IBIPs are an essential feature of insurance industry. However, it has not always been easy to make them widely known to the wider public due to the slow opening of the market for financial services within the EU. IDD will hopefully provide a more harmonized and more efficient legal framework, fostering the convergence of investor protection within the financial sectors as a whole.[139]

---

[137] Śliwiński and Marano (2020).

[138] Regulation (EU) No 1286/2014 of the European Parliament and of the Council of 26 November 2014 on key information documents for packaged retail and insurance-based investment products (PRIIPs), http://data.europa.eu/eli/reg/2014/1286/oj.

[139] Noussia and Siri (2019).

To be able to make a critical assessment of the IDD, the individual rules and regulations must be evaluated in terms of their sense and appropriateness. As far as the IBIPs are concerned, it is problematic that the scope of their regulation remains doubtful and that apart from the unresolved problem of classifying existing life insurance products in relation to IBIPs, the IDD also remains vague in terms of the further distinction between complex and non-complex IBIPs, which renders the application of IDD and IDD-related provisions even more complicated.[140]

The legislator provides for an IDD evaluation to be carried out after 3 years. However, this is questionable and difficult to achieve due to a lack of market-wide costs. Hence, future research will be required with regards to the individual rules and regulations so as to achieve a verification of the level of target achievement at before and at an early stage from the introduction of the rules, and thereafter at certain intervals.[141]

References

Audigier I (2020) Insurance Distribution Directive and cross-border activities by insurance intermediaries in the EU. In: Marano P, Noussia K (eds) Insurance Distribution Directive: promises and reality. Springer, Cham

Colaert V (2015) European banking, securities and insurance law: cutting through sectoral lines? Common Market Law Rev 52:1579–1616

Cummins J et al (2017) Competition, efficiency and soundness in European life insurance markets. J Financ Stab 28:66–78

Das MUS, Podpiera R, Davies N (2003) Insurance and issues in financial soundness, IMF Working Papers: Working Paper No. 03/138. International Monetary Fund, Washington, D.C.

De Maesschalck N (2017) The Insurance Distribution Directive: what does it change for intermediaries and for others? In: Marano P, Siri M (eds) Insurance regulation in the European Union. Palgrave Macmillan, Cham

Defever KM (2018) Comparative analysis of European Union and United States insurance law systems – with emphasis on consumer protection law, (2018). Eur J Commer Contract Law 10:9–27

Defever KM (2021) Enaction of Chapter VII of the Insurance Distribution Directive: what can Member States learn from the enforcement failures of the United States? In: Marano P, Noussia K (eds) Insurance Distribution Directive. AIDA Europe Research Series on Insurance Law and Regulation, vol 3. Springer, Cham. https://doi.org/10.1007/978-3-030-52738-9_9

Doff R (2008) A critical analysis of the solvency II proposals. Geneva Papers Risk and Insur Iss Practice 33(2):193–206

Eling M, Schmeiser H, Schmit JT (2007) The solvency II process: overview and critical analysis. Risk Manag Insur Rev 10(1):69–85

Gaganis C, Pasiouras F (2013) Financial supervision regimes and bank efficiency: international evidence. J Bank Financ 37(12):5463–5475

GDV (2015) Regulation in the insurance industry: opportunities and challenges from an economic perspective. Economic issues and analyses (7). German Insurance Association (GDV), Berlin

[140]Köhne and Brömmelmeyer (2018).

[141]Köhne and Brömmelmeyer (2018).

Hofmann A, Neumann JK, Pooser D (2018) Plea for uniform regulation and challenges of implementing the new Insurance Distribution Directive. Geneva Paper Risk Insur Iss Pract 43:740–769. https://doi.org/10.1057/s41288-018-0091-6

Kern (2018) Marketing, sale and distribution. Mis-selling of financial product. A study requested by the ECON Committee, Directorate-General for Internal Policies PE 618.996

Klumpes PJM, Schuermann S (2011) Corporate, product and distribution strategies in the European life insurance industry. Geneva Papers Risk Insur Iss Pract 36(1):50–75

Köhne P, Brömmelmeyer C (2018) The new insurance distribution regulation in the EU—a critical assessment from a legal and economic perspective. The Geneva papers on risk and insurance - issues and practice. Palgrave Macmillan, The Geneva Association, vol 43(4), pp 704–739

Lorent B (2008) Risks and regulation of insurance companies: is solvency II the right answer?, Working Papers CEB 08–007. RS, Université Libre de Bruxelles

Malinowska K (2018) Customer's best interest as a rule in insurance contracts, considerations against new regulations on insurance distribution. In: Malinowska K, Tarasiuk A (eds) Insurance challenges of Anno Domini 2018. Publikacja jubileuszowa AIDA, Warszawa, p 57

Marano P (2017) Sources and tools of the insurance regulation. In: Marano P, Siri M (eds) Insurance regulation in the European Union: solvency II and beyond. Palgrave Macmillan, London, pp 5–30

Marano P (2019) The product oversight and governance: standards and liabilities. In: Marano P, Rokas I (eds) Distribution of insurance-based investment products. The EU regulation and the liabilities. Springer, Berlin, pp 59–96

Marano P (2020) The contribution of Product Oversight and Governance (POG) to the single market: a set of organizational rules for business conduct. In: Marano P, Noussia K (eds) Insurance Distribution Directive: a legal analysis. Springer, Berlin

Martinez L, Marano P (2020) The new EU rules on insurance customer/policyholder protection viewed against the NAIC model acts. Global Jurist 20190039:1934–2640. https://doi.org/10.1515/gj-2019-0039. ISSN (Online)

Noussia K, Siri M (2019) The legal regime and the relevant standards. In: Marano P, Rokas I (eds) Distribution of insurance-based investment products. The EU regulation and the liabilities. Springer, Berlin, pp 28–56

Paś I (2020) Ensuring the customer's best interest in the Polish insurance market. In: Marano P, Noussia K (eds) Insurance Distribution Directive: promises and reality. Springer, Berlin

Petsch V (2019) The necessity for regulating the insurance market considering the implementation of the IDD (September 12, 2019). 2019 ENTRENOVA conference proceedings. SSRN: https://ssrn.com/abstract=3490486

Pscheidl D (2018) Implementing IDD across the EU—first findings and the way forward. ERA Forum 19:205–217. https://doi.org/10.1007/s12027-018-0524-5

Schiro J (2006) External forces impacting the insurance industry: threats from regulation. Geneva Papers Risk Insur Iss Pract 31(1):25–30

Scism L (2012) Insurance fees, revealed. Wall Street J, 30 Mar 2012

Śliwiński A, Marano P (2020) Innovation in life insurance: the economic landscape and the Insurance Distribution Directive. In: Borda M, Grima S, Kwiecien I (eds) Life insurance in Europe. Risk analysis and market challenges. Springer, Berlin

Legislation

Commission Delegated Regulation (EU) 2017/2358 of 21 September 2017 supplementing Directive (EU) 2016/97 of the European Parliament and of the Council with regard to product oversight and governance requirements for insurance undertakings and insurance distributors. http://data.europa.eu/eli/reg_del/2017/2358/oj

Directive (EU) 2016/97 of the European Parliament and of the Council of 20 January 2016 on insurance distribution (recast). http://data.europa.eu/eli/dir/2016/97/oj

Directive 2009/138/EC of the European Parliament and of the Council of 25 November 2009 on the taking-up and pursuit of the business of Insurance and Reinsurance (Solvency II). http://data.europa.eu/eli/dir/2009/138/oj

Directive 2014/65/EU of the European Parliament and of the Council of 15 May 2014 on markets in financial instruments and amending Directive 2002/92/EC and Directive 2011/61/EU. http://data.europa.eu/eli/dir/2014/65/oj

European Commission (2016) Commission Delegated Regulation of 30 June 2016 supplementing Regulation (EU) No 1286/2014 of the European Parliament and of the Council on key information documents for packaged retail and insurance based investment products (PRIIPs) by laying down regulatory technical standards with regard to the presentation, content, review and revision of key information documents and the conditions for fulfilling the requirement to provide such documents (C(2016)3999 final)

Regulation (EC) No 593/2008 of the European Parliament and of the Council of 17 June 2008 on the law applicable to contractual obligations (Rome I). http://data.europa.eu/eli/reg/2008/593/oj

Regulation (EU) No 1286/2014 of the European Parliament and of the Council of 26 November 2014 on key information documents for packaged retail and insurance-based investment products (PRIIPs). http://data.europa.eu/eli/reg/2014/1286/oj

Documents

CII: Policy Briefing: Implementing the Insurance Distribution Directive: key provisions and analysis. March 2018, https://www.cii.co.uk/media/7775189/cii-policy-briefing-idd-implementation-22march2018.pdf

Clifford Chance (2013) How to distribute insurance products in the current regulatory environment. February 2013, London, https://www.cliffordchance.com/briefings/2013/02/how_to_distributeinsuranceproductsinth.html

EIOPA (2017) Technical Advice on possible delegated acts concerning the Insurance Distribution Directive, 1/2/2017, EIOPA-17/048. https://eiopa.europa.eu/Publications/Consultations/EIOPA%20Technical%20Advice%20on%20the%20IDD.pdf

EIOPA (2018) Q and A on Regulation - Answers - Commission Implementing Regulations laying down Implementing Technical Standards, (EU) 2017-2359 Info requirements and conduct of business rules applicable, published on: July 16 2018. https://eiopa.europa.eu/Pages/Guidelines/Q-and-A-on-Regulation-Answers-Commission-Imple0menting-Regulations.aspx

G-20 Leaders (2008) Washington, D.C. Summit—Leaders' Statement. http://www.nytimes.com/2008/11/16/washington/summit-text.html?pagewanted=all

Hogan Lovells (2017) Insurance Distribution Directive...one year to go, http://viewer.zmags.com/publication/f42cbb3c#/f42cbb3c/1

OECD (1998) Competition and related regulation issues in the insurance industry. http://www.oecd.org/regreform/sectors/1920099.pdf. 04 Apr 2019

Practice Note (2020) Insurance Distribution Directive (IDD), Practical Law UK Practice Note 4-544-5805, Thomson Reuters. https://uk.practicallaw.thomsonreuters.com/4-544-5805?transitionType=Default&contextData=(sc.Default)&firstPage=true#co_anchor_a675177

Insurance-Based Investment Products: Regulatory Responses and Policy Issues

Michele Siri

1 Introduction

Investor protection can be defined as the set of rules and principles expected to preserve the interests and the rights of a person in its role as the investor or the defensive protection of the vulnerable investor against unscrupulous market participants.[1] The aim of investor protection regulation is to allow investors to make informed financial decisions which are better aligned with their interests and profile. Following the financial turmoil in 2007, and considered the increasing complexity of financial markets, the EU has strengthened its regulatory efforts in setting a proper level of protection and transparency in the area of investment services.[2] In particular, by introducing the Directive on Markets in Financial Instruments (MiFID),[3] the related Markets in Financial Instruments Regulation (MiFIR),[4] the Insurance Distribution Directive (IDD)[5] and the Regulation on key information documents for packaged retail and insurance-based investment products (PRIIPs),[6] the EU has

[1]Clarck (1976), p. 26.

[2]Colaert (2017a), pp. 229–244; Moloney (2015), pp. 736–765; Moloney (2010).

[3]Directive 2004/39/EC (MiFID I), recently revised by Directive 2014/65/E (MiFID II). See Liverse (2016), p. 45. See also Moloney (2014), chapter IX.

[4]Regulation 648/2012/EU.

[5]Directive 2016/97/EU. See Hofmann et al. (2018), p. 740 ss.; Köhne and Brömmelmeyer (2018), p. 704 ss.; Ramharter (2016), p. 221 ss.

[6]EU Regulation 1286/2014/EU of 26 November 2014 on key information documents for packaged retail and insurance-based investment products (PRIIPs).

M. Siri (✉)
University of Genoa, Law Department, Genoa, Italy
e-mail: michele.siri@unige.it

P. Marano, K. Noussia (eds.), *Insurance Distribution Directive*, AIDA Europe Research Series on Insurance Law and Regulation 3,
https://doi.org/10.1007/978-3-030-52738-9_5

recently provided the main—sometimes overlapping—criteria to be followed by financial intermediaries in conducting their activities.

The IDD plays a significant role in the promotion of consumer protection within the distribution of insurance products across the EU, especially considering that MiFID II does not cover the distribution of insurance-based products. In particular, the IDD ensures greater transparency by insurance distributors in relation to the price and costs of their products but also provides higher standards as regards product information and conduct of business (COB) rules. In performing this function, the IDD provides many rules echoing the corresponding MiFID II rules. However, many differences persist and present a risk of segmentation and regulatory arbitrage.[7] Moreover, while MiFID II aspires to a maximum harmonisation, the IDD expressly aims at a minimum harmonization (as stated in Recital 3), which means that any Member State can impose stricter rules to protect customers. The IDD has been supplemented by two delegated regulations—based on the European Insurance and Occupational Pensions Authority (EIOPA) Technical Advice to the Commission[8]—concerning product oversight and governance requirements for insurance undertakings and insurance distributors, information requirements and conduct of business rules.

The IDD aims explicitly to harmonise national provisions concerning insurance and reinsurance distribution across the European Union, and targets not only—as in the past—insurance brokers or intermediaries, but several types of persons or institutions which distribute insurance-based investment products (IBIPs) to third parties, such as agents, 'bancassurance' operators, insurance undertakings, travel agents and car rental companies. However, customers—regardless of the distribution channel—should benefit from the same level of protection and equal treatment. In particular, in line with the MiFID II regime for financial instruments and structured deposits, within the IDD regime customer protection is ensured by specific provisions concerning the conduct of business rules and product governance requirements.[9] In this regard, since the IDD empowers the Commission to adopt specific Delegated Acts concerning such requirements, on February 2016, the European Commission requested the EIOPA for its technical advice for the development of IDD Delegated Acts. Two Commission Delegated Regulations were published in autumn 2017 and specifically targeted conduct on business rules for IBIPs and product and oversight governance applicable to all insurance contracts, including IBIPs.[10]

[7]Kern (2018), p. 31; Colaert (2017b), pp. 589 ss.

[8]EIOPA 17/048, Technical Advice on Insurance Distribution Directive (1 February 2017). See Noussia (2019), pp. 119–136.

[9]Rokas and Siafarika (2019), p. 3 ss.

[10]Respectively, Commission Delegated Regulation (EU) 2017/2359 of 21 September 2017 supplementing Directive (EU) 2016/97 of the European Parliament and of the Council with regard to information requirements and conduct of business rules applicable to the distribution of insurance-based investment products; and Commission Delegated Regulation (EU) 2017/2358 of 21 September 2017 supplementing Directive (EU) 2016/97 of the European Parliament and of the

2 Disclosure of Information

Traditionally, product information has been sectoral or even product-specific, with a change of approach only recently represented by the PRIIPs Regulation.[11] In the PRIIPS Regulation, the Key Information Document (or KID) is a basic information leaflet on the essential features of a wide range of packaged retail and insurance-based investment products such as structured products, insurance-based investment products or investment funds that retail investors can buy directly from manufacturers of those products or indirectly through financial intermediaries, by means of the internet, or otherwise.[12]

The PRIIPs KID must be made available to retail investors prior to any sale, either in a paper format or through a durable medium or a website. The KID is required to contain pre-contractual information to help the retail investor understand the features of the product and compare it with other products. This includes comprehensive information on the product's objectives and how it will achieve them, on its risk-reward profile (including maximum possible loss) and the assumptions on which this is based, on all costs to be directly or indirectly borne by the retail investor, and on the product's recommended holding period.[13] By capturing a wide variety of retail investments, PRIIPs seeks to ensure comparability across and within sectors as well as across borders, without imposing specific requirements in relation to business models, product designs or legal forms.

Solvency II contains a series of pre-contractual disclosure requirements which have to be complied with by insurance undertakings. These include general information about the applicable law and the insurance company and, in the case of life insurance, a series of basic elements of information on the contract, such as coverage, terms of the contract, conditions for termination, payment of premiums, an indication of surrender and paid-up values, tax arrangements, and rules on complaint handling. The insurance undertaking must also inform policyholders about their right to cancel the contract within a cooling-off period.[14]

The IDD provides a set of basic disclosure rules which apply to the distribution of all insurance products. These require the provision of information to the customer about the insurance intermediary or insurance undertaking selling the product, about the provision of advice and about the remuneration received in relation to the insurance contract. The insurance distributor must also gather information from

Council with regard to product oversight and governance requirements for insurance undertakings and insurance distributors.

[11]Colaert (2019), p. 303 ss.

[12]Kyriaki and Siri (2019), p. 39 ss.; Colaert (2016).

[13]Articles 5–12 PRIIPs Regulation. See also for further details about the KIID's content, Commission Delegated Regulation (EU) 2017/65313. As far IBIPs are concerned, see EIOPA, Costs and past performance, 2020 Report, April 2020.

[14]Articles 183ff Solvency II.

the customer in order to establish his/her insurance demands and needs.[15] If the insurance product sold is an IBIPs, the insurance intermediary or insurance undertaking has to comply with the additional requirements set out in the IDD.[16] These requirements are largely aligned to those of MiFID II and include disclosure of all costs and charges in an aggregated form under the same conditions as provided in MiFID II.[17] However, contrary to MiFID II,[18] the requirements set out in the IDD are not further detailed in Level 2 legislation.

3 Conflicts of Interest

The IDD and its delegated regulation[19] follow MiFID II provisions and those of its delegated regulation.[20] Neither Article 23 of MiFID II or Article 28 of the IDD defines or prohibits conflicts of interest. However, in the relevant delegated regulations, we find provisions specifying certain situations which should be taken into account in the assessment of conflicts of interest,[21] and the requirement for insurance intermediaries and insurance undertakings to establish, implement and maintain specific conflicts of interest policy to be followed for the identification, prevention and management of such conflicts of interest.[22] In particular, insurance intermediaries and insurance undertakings shall assess whether they, a relevant person or any person directly or indirectly linked to them by control, have an interest in the outcome of the insurance distribution activities, in the event such an interest: (a) is distinct from the customer's or potential customer's interest in the outcome of the insurance distribution activities; and (b) has the potential to influence the outcome of the distribution activities to the detriment of the customer.[23]

As for the conflicts of interest policy, this should include the circumstances—related to the specific insurance distribution activity—which constitute or may give rise to a conflict of interest which could damage customers' interest, as well as the procedures to be followed and the measure to be adopted for the management of such

---

[15] Articles 18ff IDD.

[16] Articles 26ff IDD. Please see Noussia and Siri (2019), p. 39 ss.

[17] Article 24 MiFID II. About MiFID II disclosure rules, among others: Della Negra (2019), p. 34ff.

[18] Articles 44ff Commission Delegated Regulation (EU) 2017/565.

[19] Articles 3–7 Commission Delegated Regulation (EU) 2017/2359.

[20] The above-mentioned Commission Delegated Regulation (EU) 2017/565. See also the Explanatory Memorandum, Commission Delegated Regulation (EU) 2017/2359, p. 3.

[21] Article 3 Commission Delegated Regulation (EU) 2017/2359 and Article 33 Commission Delegated Regulation (EU) 2017/565.

[22] Article 4 Commission Delegated Regulation (EU) 2017/2359. For investment firms, *cf.* Article 34 Commission Delegated Regulation (EU) 2017/565.

[23] Article 3(2) Commission Delegated Regulation (EU) 2017/2359.

conflicts.[24] The policy should be assessed and periodically reviewed, on an at least annual basis, and amended in case of any deficiency.[25]

As regards insurance intermediaries, who are under a contractual obligation to conduct the insurance distribution business exclusively with one or more insurance undertakings, EIOPA has clarified that the conflicts of interest policy remain a requirement under the responsibility of that intermediary.[26] EIOPA considers it essential that intermediaries who distribute exclusively on behalf of one or more insurance undertakings are required to establish, implement and maintain an efficient conflicts of interest policy, set out in writing and suited to their size and organisation and the nature, scale and complexity of their business in accordance with Article 4 (1) of Delegated Regulation 2017/2359. This requirement "does not prohibit intermediaries who distribute exclusively on behalf of one or more insurance undertakings, from receiving assistance and guidance from an insurance undertaking to which they are tied, in developing a conflicts of interest policy". However, EIOPA holds that the regulatory responsibility of establishing, implementing and operating the policy remains with the insurance intermediary.

As in MiFID II,[27] the disclosure of a conflict of interest should be limited to situations in which the organisational and administrative arrangements are insufficient to prevent the risks of damage to the interests of the customer.[28] In such a case, the disclosure should be made on a durable medium and include sufficient detail,[29] which means that it should provide a specific description of the conflicts of interest, explain its general nature, sources, and associated risks for consumers, and state that the organizational and administrative arrangements established within the conflicts of interest policy are not sufficient to ensure, with reasonable confidence, the prevention of such risks.[30] Finally, the senior management of the insurance distributors should receive, at least annually, written reports on the situations in which a conflict of interest arose, and of these the insurance intermediary of undertaking should keep a record.[31]

In EIOPA's view,[32] an insurance intermediary or insurance undertaking is not exempted from further managing conflicts of interests if it discloses the conflicts of interest to the consumer. The legal basis for such conclusion is the Recital 5 of

[24] Article 4(2) Commission Delegated Regulation (EU) 2017/2359.

[25] Article 7(1) and Recital 5 Commission Delegated Regulation (EU) 2017/2359. *Cf.* Article 34 (5) Commission Delegated Regulation (EU) 2017/565.

[26] EIOPA, Q&A on Regulation (2018), No. 1622.

[27] Article 34(4) of the Commission Delegated Regulation (EU) 2017/565.

[28] Article 6(1) and Recital 5 Commission Delegated Regulation (EU) 2017/2359.

[29] Article 28(3) IDD.

[30] Article 6(2) and Recital 5 Commission Delegated Regulation (EU) 2017/2359.

[31] Article 7(2) and Recital 5 Commission Delegated Regulation (EU) 2017/2359. Cf. Article 35 Commission Delegated Regulation (EU) 2017/565.

[32] EIOPA, Q&A on Regulation (2018), No. 1625. See also No. 1627 as regards to the application of proportionality in relation to the measures set out in the IDD for managing conflicts of interest.

Delegated Regulation 2017/2359 which clarifies that the disclosure of conflicts of interest by an insurance intermediary or an insurance undertaking cannot exempt it from the obligation to maintain and operate the organisational and administrative arrangements that are the most effective means of preventing damage to customers. EIOPA considers, being "disclosure [. . .] a measure of last resort", that the insurance intermediary or insurance undertaking has to take "all reasonable steps to prevent the conflicts of interest from adversely affecting the interests of its customers and only when the conflicts of interests cannot be prevented, disclosure of the conflicts of interest to the customer is expected". As part of the disclosure, EIOPA considers it important that "the customer is advised that organisational and administrative measures established to prevent or manage conflicts of interest are not sufficient to ensure, with reasonable confidence, that risks of damage" to the interests of the customer will be prevented. Such a report is not addressed to the insurance undertaking, given the reference in Art. 7 only to report on conflicts of interest to their senior management of the intermediary.

4 Inducements

According to the IDD, the insurance intermediary should inform the client whether, in relation to the insurance contract, any inducement,[33] i.e. any fee, commission or non-monetary benefit paid or provided by any party except the customer, is paid. The payment of inducements is allowed (and insurance intermediaries and insurance undertakings are regarded as fulfilling their obligations) if it '(a) does not have a detrimental impact on the quality of the relevant service to the customer, and (b) does not impair compliance with the insurance intermediary's or insurance undertaking's duty to act honestly, fairly and professionally in accordance with the best interests of its customers'.[34] This seems a less stringent discipline compared to that provided in MiFID II, which imposes specific bans and strict limitations to fees and commission paid, especially in connection with independent financial advice and portfolio management.[35]

However, inducements rules in the insurance sector appear stricter when looking at EIOPA's interpretation of IDD provisions: in fact, any sort of rebates can be considered an inducement, irrespective of their origin. Thus, even receiving rebates with different rates from fund managers is covered and such rebates must be assessed under Article 29(2) IDD to ensure that they do not have a detrimental impact on the quality of the relevant service to the customer and that do not impair compliance with the insurance intermediary's or insurance undertaking's duty to act honestly,

[33] Article 19(1)(e) IDD. About this part, please see Noussia and Siri (2019), p. 47 ff.

[34] Article 29(2) IDD.

[35] Art 24(7), (8) and (9) MiFID II. For a comparison between MiFID II and IDD as regards inducements, see Colaert and Incalza (2019), p. 377.

fairly and professionally in accordance with the best interests of its customers.[36] Furthermore, a rebate should be assessed in accordance with Article 29(2), IDD regardless of whether a personal recommendation is provided.[37]

Moreover, EIOPA states that the insurance undertaking which receives the rebate is obliged to consider "all relevant factors which may increase or decrease the risk of a detrimental impact on the quality of the relevant service to the customer, and which have potential to impair compliance with the insurance undertakings duty to act honestly, fairly and professionally in accordance with the best interests of its customers, including the fact that different rates are received from fund managers". Insurance undertakings must also take into account EIOPA's Opinion on monetary incentives and remuneration between providers of asset management services and insurance undertakings[38] in which the risk of customer detriment related to the practice of receiving rebates from asset managers is addressed, including the application of the Product Oversight and Governance requirements.[39]

As requested by the IDD,[40] the Commission further specified in a delegated act the criteria for assessing whether inducements paid or received increase the risk of a detrimental impact on the quality of the relevant service.[41] In particular, an inducement has to be considered to have a detrimental impact on the quality of the relevant service to the customer when "it is of such a nature and scale that it provides an incentive to carry out insurance distribution activities in a way that is not in compliance with the obligation to act honestly, fairly and professionally in accordance with the best interests of the customer".[42] Furthermore, insurance distributors should conduct an overall analysis taking into account "all relevant factors which may increase or decrease the risk of a detrimental impact on the quality of the relevant service to the customer', as well as 'any organizational measures taken by the insurance intermediary or insurance undertaking carrying out distribution activities to prevent the risk of detrimental impact".[43]

The insurance intermediary or insurance undertaking is required to consider the amount of inducement being paid in comparison to the value of the product or service being provided. EIOPA holds that insurance intermediaries and insurance undertakings need to consider whether "the customer is receiving value for the

---

[36]EIOPA, Q&A on Regulation (2018), No. 1630.

[37]EIOPA Q&A on Regulation (2018), No. 1633.

[38]EIOPA, Opinion on Monetary Incentives and Remuneration Between Providers of Asset Management Services and Insurance Undertakings, 17/295 (2017).

[39]EIOPA Q&A on Regulation (2018), No. 1632 and 1633. About product governance, see *in this volume* Marano P, The Contribution of Product Oversight and Governance (POG) to the Single Market: A Set of Organizational Rules for Business Conduct. In the MiFID II/MiFIR legislation, see Busch (2016), p. 123 ss. As regards to the EU insurance supervisory law, see also Dreher (2019), p. 79 ss.

[40]Article 29(4) IDD.

[41]Article 8 Commission Delegated Regulation (EU) 2017/2359.

[42]Article 8(1) Commission Delegated Regulation (EU) 2017/2359.

[43]Article 8(2) Commission Delegated Regulation (EU) 2017/2359.

payment in relation to the services they have received".[44] In any case, the amount of the inducement being paid should not be disproportionate and not excessive to the services being provided.[45]

EIOPA considers important that insurance intermediaries and insurance undertakings demonstrate compliance with Article 8 of Delegated Regulation 2017/2359, which requires the same to perform an overall analysis of the inducement schemes, taking into account any relevant factors that may increase or decrease the risk of detriment to customers.[46] Regarding the frequency of such assessments, EIOPA recommends that "insurance intermediaries and insurance undertakings consider all relevant factors which may increase or decrease the risk of a detrimental impact on the quality of the relevant service to the customer or risk of impairing compliance with the intermediary's or insurance undertaking's obligation to act fairly, honestly and professionally in accordance with the best interests of the customer, and assess for themselves at what frequency the assessment is required in order to maintain continual compliance with the criteria set out in Article 29(2), IDD". For example, if there are no changes or modifications to the inducement scheme, the frequency can be appropriately extended, where no other indicators (such as customer complaints or others) give reason to do so. Anyway, the details of the assessment should be recorded in order to demonstrate and enable competent authorities to monitor that the inducement complies with the criteria set out in Article 29(2) IDD.[47]

Anyway, despite the ambition to set up a level playing field between IBIPs and other financial investments, IDD requirements for inducements are opposite to those applied by MiFID II. While inducements are banned unless explicitly permitted, the IDD presumes they are permitted and are prohibited if they determine a 'detrimental impact' on the distributor's quality of the service.[48] A further dis-alignment with MiFID II refers to the absence of an enhanced regime in case of the distributor of an IBIP provides advice on an independent basis. Under the IDD, in fact, Member States have the discretion to introduce a specific regime in this respect to better protect investors. Again, differences between national implementation rules remain and as far as the distribution of the IBIP is concerned the gold plating measures have the effect of fragmenting the internal market in the financial services at large.

[44]EIOPA Q&A on Regulation (2018), No. 1631.

[45]In this respect, EIOPA reiterates that in case of a rebate from a fund manager, insurance undertakings should consider again the already mentioned EIOPA's Opinion on monetary incentives and remuneration between providers of asset management services and insurance undertakings in which the risk of customer detriment related to the practice of receiving rebates from asset managers are addressed (Q&A No. 1631),

[46]EIOPA Q&A on Regulation (2018), No. 1623.

[47]Ibidem.

[48]Colaert and Incalza (2019), p. 386.

5 Demands and Needs Test

IDD provides specific conduct of business rules, not derived this time from MiFID II regime, known as the demands and needs test. The scope of this test is not prescribed in the Directive or the Delegated Regulation and it is subject to national implementation. However, EIOPA has provided some guidance regarding minimum expectations for this test and how it may relate to the assessment of suitability.[49] Recital 7 of Delegated Regulation 2017/2359 clarifies that the assessments of suitability and appropriateness are without prejudice to the obligation, for insurance intermediaries and insurance undertakings, to consider and specify, before the conclusion of any insurance contract, on the basis of information obtained from the customer, the demands and needs of that customer. The main information concerning the customer's needs, typically includes, for example, personal information (age, profession, place of residence, etc.) or the information particularly linked to the type of product requested. This information should enable the insurance intermediary or insurance undertaking to assess whether certain products can be offered or not, according to their capacity of meeting the demands and needs of the customer. This could lead to a selection of a range of comparable products for consideration during the suitability assessment where advice is being given or during the appropriateness assessment where no advice is given.

The 'demands and needs' test provides protection for customers to avoid cases of mis-selling (Recital 44, IDD), and it applies to all insurance contracts, not just IBIPs. Article 30, IDD applies "without prejudice" to the demands and needs test as covered by Article 20(1), IDD. The 'demands and needs' test has to be performed in any event prior to the conclusion of the contract and is distinct from the suitability assessment in advised cases, and the suitability assessment can also be provided at any time during the customer relationship. The evaluation of demands and needs is required whether or not advice is being provided and the specifying of the demands and needs would not amount to a suitability assessment. Depending on the national implementation, where advice is being provided, the demands and needs test and assessment of suitability could be seen as a continuum, rather than as a break. However, it is not clear whether a qualitative and timely suitability assessment would cover the demands and needs test.[50] Since the 'demands and needs' test is subject to national implementation, a more extensive guidance from EIOPA would be in the interest to avoid the internal market fragmentation.

[49]EIOPA, Q&A on Regulation (2018), No. 1638.

[50]Busch et al. (2019), p. 366.

6 Suitability and Appropriateness Assessment

As already mentioned above, the insurance intermediary or insurance undertaking has, in addition, to gather, as part of the advice process, information about the customer's knowledge and experience in the relevant investment field, the customer's financial situation and his or her investment objectives, in order to be able to recommend to the customer insurance-based investment products that are suitable for the investor. In case of advice provided to the client, the distributor has to consider other more specific and detailed elements, like the customer's financial situation, including their ability to bear losses, their investment objectives, including their risk tolerance, and other correlated information. In the EIOPA view, the final outcome should be a personalised recommendation where it is specifically explained why that particular product best meets the customer demands and needs.

Under the IDD and its Delegated Regulation,[51] the provisions concerning the assessment of suitability and appropriateness are almost identical to the corresponding provisions under MiFID II and its specific Delegated Regulation.[52] In particular, the suitability assessment requires that the insurance intermediary or undertaking, in the case of sales with advice, gathers information about their client's knowledge, experience, investment objective and risk tolerance—in order to recommend to the client the IBIP that is best aligned with the client's profile.[53] To be recommended, the IBIP has to meet the client's investment objectives, risk tolerance, financial situation and that its nature and characteristics are adequate with respect to the client's knowledge and experience.[54]

If the insurance product is not suitable for the individual customer or the suitability cannot be determined, but the customer still wishes to conclude the contract it is up to the Member State's implementation law to establish if the contract can still be concluded. In the EIOPA's view, Paragraphs 5 and 6 of Article 9 of the Delegated Regulation 2017/2359 cover the cases where a recommendation cannot be made due to the insurance intermediary or the insurance undertaking not obtaining the necessary information or there being no products that are suitable for the customer or potential customer.[55] In these circumstances, the customer may agree to proceed with concluding the contract as a sale without advice (in conformity with the applicable rules of national law), and subject to an assessment of appropriateness unless it is possible to sell the contract on an execution only basis (see recital 12 of Delegated Regulation 2017/2359). Where the distributor cannot obtain the necessary information to assess the appropriateness of the contract, the distributor shall warn the customer that the contract might not be appropriate. Only when the customer asks to proceed with concluding the contract despite this warning, the distributor

[51] Article 30 IDD and Articles 9–19 Commission Delegated Regulation (EU) 2017/2359.

[52] Articles 9ff MiFID II and articles 54ff Commission Delegated Regulation (EU) 2017/565.

[53] Article 30(1) IDD and Article 9 Commission Delegated Regulation (EU) 2017/2359.

[54] Article 9(2) Commission Delegated Regulation (EU) 2017/2359.

[55] EIOPA Q&A on Regulation (2018), No. 1639.

may perform the sale. In all cases, Article 20(1) IDD provides that any contract proposed must always be consistent with the demands and needs of the customer. The insurance intermediary or undertaking should adopt measures to ensure that the information collected about the clients is reliable, and communicate to the same that the suitability assessment is performed in their best interest.[56] It should then provide the customer with the so-called 'suitability statement', which includes an outline of the advice given, as well as information about how the recommendation meets the customer's investment objectives, risk tolerance, financial situation, knowledge and experience.[57]

The appropriateness requirement provides that, in the event of sales requiring no advice, the insurance intermediary or insurance undertaking gathers information on the client to assess if the product or services offered or demanded were appropriate for the customer.[58] In the event the product is deemed not appropriate for the customer, the insurance intermediary or insurance undertaking should warn the customer or potential customer. EIOPA believes that the level of detail will be case-specific and depend upon the individual circumstances of the sale including the nature of the product or service offered or demanded, the risks involved and the knowledge and experience of the customer.[59] It is worth noting that Article 17(1) of Delegated Regulation 2017/2359 requires that the information obtained shall include information to the extent appropriate to the nature and type of product or service offered or demanded. Therefore, it should relate to the product overall, including where relevant, such as in the case of a unit-linked insurance contract, the underlying investment assets. Article 19(3) of Delegated Regulation 2017/2359 contains requirements for records to be kept in relation to the appropriateness assessment, in particular regarding the result of the assessment, warnings given to the customer and storage in an accessible manner for future reference. As under MiFID II, this assessment is not required concerning non-complex products as defined by MiFID II.[60] However, due to the specific structures of insurance products, the Commission Delegated Regulation under IDD provides, among the criteria for non-complex IBIPs, an additional condition concerning products including a specific guarantee.[61]

Moreover, the insurance intermediary or insurance undertaking should establish a record of documents agreed with the customer containing rights and obligations of the parties, as well as other terms related to the provision of services to the customer. The customer should also be provided with periodic reports on the service, which include a number of communications proportionate to the type and complexity of the IBIP involved.[62] In the context of periodic reporting to customers, the insurance

[56] Article 10 and 11 Commission Delegated Regulation (EU) 2017/2359.

[57] Article 14(1) Commission Delegated Regulation (EU) 2017/2359.

[58] Article 30(2) IDD and Article 14 Commission Delegated Regulation (EU) 2017/2359.

[59] EIOPA Q&A on Regulation (2018), No. 1636.

[60] Article 30(3) IDD and 25(4)(a) MiFID II.

[61] Article 16(a) Commission Delegated Regulation (EU) 2017/2359.

[62] Articles 30(4) and (5) IDD.

intermediary is also expected to develop and provide 'adequate reports on the service provided'. There could be some overlapping between the insurance intermediary primarily responsible for reporting to customers on costs and charges and providing periodic reports to customers, and the insurance undertaking which is always responsible for delivering information on the product, as required under the Solvency II Directive. According to EIOPA, with regard to the obligations to provide appropriate reporting under Articles 29(1) and 30(5), IDD and Article 18 of Delegated Regulation 2017/2359, it will depend upon who is providing the service.[63] This may generally be expected to be an insurance intermediary, except where the insurance undertaking is providing services when distributing directly. Thus, the insurance undertaking remains always responsible for delivering information required by Article 185 of Directive 2009/138/EC (Solvency II).[64]

7 Non-complex Insurance-Based Investment Products

Drawing from the relevant provisions in the IDD (Articles 30(3) (a), 30(6)) and MiFID II (Article 57) although an assessment of the suitability or appropriateness of an IBIP for the customer by the insurance distributor is generally required as part of an advised or non-advised sale (IDD Article 30 (1),(2)), Member States are allowed (IDD Article 30(3)) to derogate from these obligations and not to require either a suitability or appropriateness test to be conducted, where various conditions are satisfied. Such sales ("execution-only") although carried out only at the initiative of the customer still require the insurance distributor to specify the demands and needs of the customer prior to the conclusion of the contract (IDD Article 20(1)). One of the conditions specified in Article 30(3) to determine whether an IBIP can be distributed as an execution-only sale relates to the complexity of the IBIP. IBIPs can be considered non-complex when they only provide investment exposure to the financial instruments deemed non-complex under MiFID II and do not incorporate a structure which makes it difficult for the customer to understand the risks involved (IDD article 30(3)(a)(i)).

In accordance with Article 25(8) of MiFID II, the Commission is empowered to adopt delegated acts on the criteria to identify "other non-complex financial instruments" referred to in Article 25(4)(a)(vi) of the same Directive. Also, Article 30(3)(a)(ii) of IDD acknowledges the possibility that IBIP may not fall within the scope of Article 30(3)(a)(i), but may still be deemed a non-complex product. EIOPA has considered that where an IBIP incorporates a structure which makes it difficult for the customer to understand the risks involved, it is in all cases not fit for distribution via an execution-only sale.[65] EIOPA's evidence-gathering has shown that there are

[63]EIOPA, Q&A on Regulation (2018), No. 1645.

[64]Articles 30(4) and (5) IDD.

[65]EIOPA 17/048, Technical Advice on Insurance Distribution Directive (1 February 2017), at 72ff.

only a limited number of IBIP types currently sold on an execution-only basis. Whilst numerous Member States allow for the sale of certain products on a non-advised basis, only a limited number allow for products to be sold by means of execution-only transactions. In relation to the criteria for the assessment of other non-complex financial instruments, EIOPA has included in its technical advice the relevant provisions of the Commission Delegated Regulation under MiFID II, where these criteria address product features, which are considered to be equally applicable to IBIPs. However, in these cases, it has been still necessary to modify some of the MiFID II requirements to reflect the insurance sector appropriately. In particular, regarding the provision in point (d) of the technical advice, given that exit penalties have been a feature of long-term IBIPs that are considered to have led to consumer detriment, this is intended to exclude products with unreasonable exit charges, including fiscal penalties. Regarding the nature of any guarantee provided by the insurance undertaking, where the latter provides a guarantee regarding the surrender and maturity value of an IBIP, the customer is not fully exposed to the performance of the financial instruments in which the insurance undertaking has invested or to which the customer's benefits are linked. In view of this, depending on the nature of the guarantee, IBIPs could be regarded as non-complex, even though the contract may provide investment exposure that is not limited to financial instruments deemed non-complex under MiFID II. In this case, EIOPA has considered that, as a minimum, the customer should be guaranteed to receive, at both surrender and maturity, at least the amount of the premiums that they have paid, minus legitimate costs levied.[66]

In accordance, EIOPA has issued the following technical advice: "An IBIP shall be considered as non-complex for the purposes of Article 30(3)(a)(ii) of Directive (EU) 2016/97 if it satisfies all of the following criteria: (a) the contractually guaranteed minimum surrender and maturity value is at least the amount of premiums paid by the customer minus legitimate costs levied; (b) it does not incorporate a clause, condition or trigger that allows the insurance undertaking to materially alter the nature, risk or pay-out profile of the IBIP; (c) there are options to surrender or otherwise realise the IBIP at a value that is available to the customer; (d) it does not include any explicit or implicit charges which have the effect that, even though there are technical options to surrender the IBIP, doing so may cause unreasonable detriment to the customer, because the charges are disproportionate to the cost to the insurance undertaking of the surrender; (e) it does not in any other way incorporate a structure which makes it difficult for the customer to understand the risks involved".[67]

Contracts for IBIPs can be difficult to understand for consumers. Distributors, either insurance undertakings or insurance intermediaries, play therefore an important role in processing information for the consumer and guiding consumers in

[66]EIOPA 17/048, Technical Advice on Insurance Distribution Directive (1 February 2017), at 75–76.

[67]EIOPA 17/048, Technical Advice on Insurance Distribution Directive (1 February 2017), at 77.

choosing suitable insurance policies. Prior to the advent of the IDD, consumer protection standards for the sales of insurance-based investment products were not considered sufficient at EU level to reduce the risk of mis-selling of those products, as the IMD did not contain specific rules for the sale of life insurance products with an investment element. This was in spite of the fact that these products are generally more complicated and present higher risks for retail consumers than other insurance products. Hence, IDD has stipulated additional conduct of business rules for the sale of IBIPs, and it provided for the case that differentiation should exist between complex and non-complex IBIPs.

Where an IBIP is considered non-complex, Member States may allow insurance distributors to not undertake some of the assessments (suitability and appropriateness) during the sales process that is normally necessary for the distribution of IBIPs. The EIOPA technical advice on the criteria to be used to assess "other non-complex IBIPs" aimed to facilitate the identification of "other non-complex IBIPs", such that only those products for which the risks are readily understood by customers, can be sold by execution-only. It also aimed to promote the consistent application of the IDD with respect to the identification of "other non-complex insurance-based investments" to be consistent with the line taken in the delegated acts expected to be adopted under Article 25(8) of MiFID II. Those aims are aligned with those under the IDD, i.e. the aim of improving insurance regulation in a manner that will facilitate market integration, the aim of establishing the conditions necessary for fair competition between distributors of insurance products and the aim of strengthening consumer protection, in particular with regards to IBIPs. It follows that an overly strict approach would not only be disadvantageous for insurance undertakings and insurance intermediaries, but also for customers and potentially for NCAs.

Hence, the adoption of criteria based on MiFID II seemed like the best solution in many respects, i.e. firstly because it was considered as striking the appropriate balance between the interests of insurance distributors and those of their customers and because it was considered as enabling the necessary flexibility at NCA level via the provision of criteria for other "non-complex insurance-based investments" at EU level. Not least, at the customer level, it seemed reasonable to prevent insurance undertakings and insurance intermediaries from making insurance products available for sale via execution-only which do not meet the criteria, while enabling customers to execute an order for products if the criteria are met.[68]

[68]EIOPA, Technical Advice on possible delegated acts concerning the Insurance Distribution Directive, 1/2/2017, EIOPA-17/048. About this part, please see Noussia and Siri (2019), p. 47 ff.

8 Sustainable Finance and IBIPs

The EU initiatives for the promotion of sustainable finance[69]—started in the end of 2016 with the appointment of the High-Level Expert Group (HLEG) on sustainable finance and formally launched in March 2018 with the adoption of the action plan on 'Financing Sustainable Growth',[70] is going to reshape the regulatory framework related to the distribution of IBIPs, with particular regard, on the one hand, to disclosure rules, and on the other, to Solvency II and IDD framework in relation to the integration of sustainability preferences and considerations in rules concerning investment advice, prudent person principle, conflicts of interest and target market assessment.

As to the first aspect—disclosure rules—the new Regulation (EU) 2019/2088 ('ESG Disclosure Regulation')[71] provides for financial market participants—including insurance undertakings which make available an IBIP[72]—and financial advisers—comprising insurance intermediaries and insurance undertaking providing advice with regard to IBIPs[73]—new sustainability-related disclosure duties towards end investors. In particular, the new rules, by applying a cross-sectorial approach, introduce a set of pre-contractual and on-going disclosure duties for a vast range of financial entities, concerning the consideration of sustainability factors, impacts and risks in the investment decision-making and advisory processes. The main aim of the regulation, aside from the reduction of market fragmentation and inefficiencies,[74] is the diminution of information asymmetries that could ultimately prevent end investors from making fully informed investment decisions.[75] As a consequence, transparency duties are imposed to financial market participants and financial advisers in relation to: (i) the integration of sustainability risks[76] in investment decision-making processes or investment/insurance advice[77] and in their remuneration policies;[78] (ii) the consideration of adverse sustainability impacts of their decision-making/

---

[69]Siri and Zhu (2019), pp. 1–23.

[70]EU Commission Communication, Action Plan: Financing Sustainable Growth, COM (2018) 97 final (March 2018).

[71]Regulation (EU) 2019/2088 of 27 November 2019 on sustainability-related disclosures in the financial services sector disclosure regulation.

[72]Article 2(1)(a) ESG Disclosure Regulation.

[73]Article 2(11)(a)(b) ESG Disclosure Regulation. It should be noted that Art. 17 exempts financial advisers which employ fewer than three persons from the application of the regulation.

[74]Recital 9 ESG Disclosure Regulation.

[75]Recitals 9, 10 and 20 ESG Disclosure Regulation.

[76]'Sustainability risk' is defined as "an environmental, social or governance event or condition that, if it occurs, could cause an actual or a potential material negative impact on the value of the investment". Article 2(22) ESG Disclosure Regulation.

[77]Articles 3 and 6 ESG Disclosure Regulation.

[78]Article 5(1) ESG Disclosure Regulation.

advisory processes and at the financial product level;[79] the (iii) the subsistence of sustainable investment[80] as the main objective of a financial product;[81] and (iv) the promotion of environmental or social characteristics in investment decision-making and in advisory processes.[82]

Such rules—which will apply as from 10 March 2021—will undoubtedly enhance transparency and prevent the diffusion of green-washing practices. However, the effectiveness of the new regulation is strictly connected to the prior finalization of the regulation on the establishment of a framework to facilitate sustainable investment (the 'Taxonomy Regulation'), which will establish uniform criteria to determine whether an economic activity is to be considered sustainable.

As to the second aspect, on 30 April 2019 EIOPA published the technical advice to the EU Commission[83] on the integration of sustainability risks and factors in the delegated acts under Solvency II and the IDD with specific reference to organizational requirements, operating conditions, risk management (under Solvency II), and target market assessment (under IDD).[84] It should be noted that, for the preparation of the technical advice, EIOPA has closely liaised with ESMA to ensure consistency across sectors to the extent possible.[85] A first key proposal is made in relation to the integration of sustainability in the prudent person principle of Article 132 of the Solvency II Directive, within which insurance and reinsurance undertakings shall take into account sustainability risks when assessing the security, quality, liquidity, and profitability of the portfolio as a whole. In particular, EIOPA calls for the introduction of new requirements concerning the integration of sustainability risks by insurance and reinsurance undertakings in their investment decisions and underwriting practices, as well as the consideration of the potential long-term impact of their investment strategy and decisions on sustainability factors.[86]

---

[79] Article 4 and 7 ESG Disclosure Regulation.

[80] A 'sustainable investment' is defined as "an investment in an economic activity that contributes to an environmental or [. . .] to a social objective [. . .], provided that such investments do not significantly harm any of those objectives and that the investee companies follow good governance practices [. . .]. Recital 17 ESG Disclosure Regulation.

[81] Articles 9, 10 and 11 ESG Disclosure Regulation.

[82] Articles 10 and 11 ESG Disclosure Regulation.

[83] On 24 July 2018, the European Supervisory Authorities received a formal request from the Commission to provide technical advice supplementing the initial package of proposals and to assist the Commission on potential amendments to, or introduction of, delegated acts under Directive 2009/65/EC (UCITS), Directive 2009/138/EC (Solvency II), Directive 2011/61/EU (AIFM), Directive 2014/65/EU (MiFID II) and Directive 2016/97/EU (Insurance Distribution Directive—IDD) with regard to the integration of sustainability risks and sustainability factors. See Letter from DG FISMA on sustainability risks and factors, FISMA C4 SG/acg (2018)4365900.

[84] EIOPA (2019) Technical Advice on the integration of sustainability risks and factors in the delegated acts under Solvency II and IDD, 30/04/2019, EIOPA-BoS-19/172.

[85] EIOPA (2019) Technical Advice on the integration of sustainability risks and factors in the delegated acts under Solvency II and IDD, 30/04/2019, EIOPA-BoS-19/172, at 4.

[86] EIOPA (2019) Technical Advice on the integration of sustainability risks and factors in the delegated acts under Solvency II and IDD, 30/04/2019, EIOPA-BoS-19/172, at 25.

Further amendment proposals concern conflict of interests rules under the IDD, as EIOPA calls for the integration of ESG considerations in the identification of conflicts of interest whose existence may damage the interests of the customer, and suggests that when insurance distribution is carried out in relation to IBIPs, insurance undertakings and insurance intermediaries should take all appropriate steps to identify and manage any conflicts of interest that may arise in relation to ESG considerations and in the course of any insurance distribution activities.[87] In respect to product oversight and governance, EIOPA calls for the amendment of the IDD Delegated Regulation 2017/2358, suggesting the introduction of a clear reference to ESG considerations and preferences. In particular, according to EIOPA's policy proposals, ESG factors should be taken into account by manufacturers throughout the entire target market assessment of each insurance product, but also in the context of product testing, monitoring and review processes and with regard to distribution arrangements.[88]

Finally, on 4 January 2019, the European Commission published draft rules to ensure—by amending the IDD—that investment firms and insurance distributors take sustainability considerations and preferences into account when providing advice to their clients on IBIPs.[89] In particular, the Commission proposed to amend the IDD by requiring insurance intermediaries and insurance undertakings to assess their customers and potential customers' ESG preferences as a part of their suitability assessment, but also to explain in the suitability statement provided to customers how their recommendation took into account such preferences. The new delegated regulation has not been published yet, but it will enter into force 20 days after its publication on the Official Journal of the European Union and will apply 18 months after it enters into force.

However, some commentators raised many concerns with such proposal, especially in relation to the concept of 'ESG preferences', defined by the delegated regulation as "a customer's or potential customer's choice as to whether and which environmentally sustainable investments, social investments or good governance investments should be integrated into his/her investment strategy".[90] In particular, many stakeholders required further clarification or even substitution of such wording, since its vagueness could lead to divergent approaches by retailers and

---

[87]EIOPA (2019) Technical Advice on the integration of sustainability risks and factors in the delegated acts under Solvency II and IDD, 30/04/2019, EIOPA-BoS-19/172, at 33. See Marano (2019), pp. 59 ff.

[88]EIOPA (2019) Technical Advice on the integration of sustainability risks and factors in the delegated acts under Solvency II and IDD, 30/04/2019, EIOPA-BoS-19/172, at 37.

[89]Draft Commission Delegated Regulation (EU) …/… amending Delegated Regulation (EU) 2017/2359 with regard to environmental, social and governance preferences in the distribution of insurance-based investment products.

[90]Draft Commission Delegated Regulation (EU) …/… amending Delegated Regulation (EU) 2017/2359 with regard to environmental, social and governance preferences in the distribution of insurance-based investment products, Article 1(1).

ultimately to increased confusion among clients.[91] Moreover, such definition seems inconsistent with the one provided in the draft delegated regulation amending MiFID II, as it seems to assume that all customers have ESG preferences, while it should be clarified—as done in the draft delegated regulation amending MiFID II—that customers may or may not have ESG preference.[92]

As one may infer from this brief overview of EU legislative proposals and measures on sustainable finance, the integration of ESG considerations, risks and preferences in the distribution of IBIPs requires, again, the challenging implementation of a cross-sectorial approach, where the need for legal certainty has to coordinate with the flexibility required in the light of the peculiarities of each financial sector and of the novelty of the still-evolving sustainable financial market.

9 Policy Issues and Next Steps

As outlined in the introduction, current IBIPs investor protection rules in EU legislation rely on sectoral rules largely derived from the MiFID II paradigm. The "silo" approach is, at least partially, a consequence of the market structure at the level of distributors of insurance-based financial products. The long-term horizon of life insurance products as well as the variety of distribution channels in life insurance markets, including agents and brokers, need flexibility and proportionality in respect of intermediaries providing advice in the financial sector.[93] However, significant differences between the legal frameworks affect the decision-making of retail investors. In particular, the rules related to disclosure, suitability assessment and inducements, may not work as intended and probably affect the decision-making of retail investors when they shop around for savings product.[94]

At the same time, the PRIIPs "horizontal" framework has proven somehow not adequate to address the legal differences across the variety of retail investment products. As others have already observed, the existing protection regime may result in efficiency losses and information asymmetries. As regards these shortcomings, a cross-sectoral mapping exercise could identify possible redundancies, inconsistencies, overlaps and gaps and evaluate the extent to which those issues could hinder retail investors from taking sound investment decisions. This comparison may add

---

[91] See feedbacks on Commission Delegated Regulation (EU) . . ./. . . amending Delegated Regulation (EU) 2017/2359 with regard to environmental, social and governance preferences in the distribution of insurance-based investment products, available at https://ec.europa.eu/info/law/better-regulation/have-your-say/initiatives/1185-Institutional-investors-and-asset-managers-duties-regarding-sustainability/feedback?p_id=237222.

[92] Draft Commission Delegated Regulation (EU) . . ./. . . of XXX amending Delegated Regulation (EU) 2017/565 as regards the integration of Environmental, Social and Governance (ESG) considerations and preferences into the investment advice and portfolio management.

[93] Pscheidl (2018), p. 211 ss.

[94] Busch et al. (2019), p. 343 ss.

value to a review of the existing disclosure regime only if the type of the legislative instrument applied in each piece of the current rules is also included in the scope. For instance, as described above, rules on pre-contractual and on-going disclosure requirements are set out in the MiFID II, IDD, PRIIPs, Solvency II, as well as in national legislation. Without a common core at EU level, hopefully, encapsulated in an EU Regulation, a further step in the harmonisation process would be proven costly and ultimately unsatisfactory. As a benchmark, the new pre-contractual and on-going disclosure requirements set out in the PEPP Regulation should be tested to uniform the comparability of information items, both across products and across the Member States. The new PEEP information document may represent a tool to assess the clarity and comprehensiveness of the information documents of the IBIPs as well the other PRIIPs products.

Notwithstanding the merits of a deep cross-sectoral harmonisation of all the information documents in scope of the PRIIPs Regulation, a further step to enhance the investor protection at least in the insurance sector for all the IBIPs products rely on the different approaches at national level related to the rules for the demands and needs test and the suitability assessment for retail investors. The IDD does not provide strict rules for the timing of the suitability assessments, presumably assuming that before each transaction with a client both a 'demands and needs' test and a suitability assessment have to be performed by the distributor. As the corresponding MiFID II rules show, the information gathered from a client may be part of a portfolio of data covering different transactions. Thus, a further step should be to provide clear rule enabling and encouraging the distributor to undertake one suitability assessment for more than one transaction.

Moreover, it would be highly recommended to rethink the process of collecting information through the demands and needs test or the suitability assessment from 'a client perspective'. If the questionnaires to be answered by retail investors are compiled with the assistance, and somehow under the influence of the distributor, uniform guidelines should be provided, as for financial instruments under the MiFID II/MIFIR package, to enhance the effectiveness of the information collection. Under MiFID II, a firm is entitled to rely on the information provided by retail clients and must take reasonable steps to ensure that the information collected is reliable.[95] The actual high-level Delegated Regulation should be complemented by EIOPA Guidelines with the aim of increasing the effectiveness of the 'demands and needs' test or the suitability assessment from a client perspective and foster the supervisory convergence between a variety of market practices at the national level.

Among others, the IBIPs Guidelines we propose should include the means used to gather information about the retail investor with proper guidance depending on the way adopted to collect the information. According to behavioural studies, the guidelines should be specifically designed to be applied to a written questionnaire, or online profiling with or without human interaction, or by means of an interview.

[95]ESMA (2018) Guidelines on certain aspects of the MiFID II suitability requirements, 6/11/2018, ESMA 35-43-1163.

Furthermore, the information needed with regards to the retail investor's knowledge and experience, financial situation and investment objectives should be identified and the style of the advisory dialogue should also be set, in terms of the clarity and comprehensibility of the questions posed relating the preferences, economic situation, and risk-profile.

A further step to enhance the quality of the process of the collection of information from a client perspective requires special attention to the comprehensibility of the suitability reports and the suitability statements.[96] The IDD Level 2 Delegated Regulation should be complemented by guidelines recognising good market practices about the comprehension and usefulness of the suitability reports and suitability statements provided to retail investors. Furthermore, from a client perspective, not only the content and the information needed should be identified but we also need to ensure the clarity and comprehensibility for the retail investor of such information, also as regards the decision to choose the more costly or complex financial instrument over an equivalent one.

10 Conclusion

The chapter has aimed to analyse the recent reform of the EU regulatory framework in regard to IBIPs. The actual regime provided for IBIPs offers stronger protection to all customers, regardless of the distribution channel. In line with the EU plan to provide consistent cross-sectorial investor protection across all Member States, many provisions under the IDD are based on the corresponding rules under MiFID II, even though some differences remain and should be further elaborated in connection to the inconsistencies, overlaps and gaps in the investor protection as far as the distribution of the IBIPs is concerned. Furthermore, several Member States have exercised the discretions given by the IDD for the IBIPs mainly to gold plate investor protection measures. However, such an uncoordinated approach undermines the internal market. Therefore, the chapter advises EIOPA to use its powers to coordinate the diverging Member States' measures and ensure transparency about the measures NCAs have taken in this respect.

The European Commission is already required to review, by 2021, the IDD, assessing the specific characteristics of insurance-based investment products. Focusing on the long-term purpose and the variety of insurance-based investment products, we need to design and implement a tailored regime combining life insurance products regulation and conduct of business rules under a cross-sectorial regulatory framework of investor protection.

[96] Article 14 (1), (2) and (3) Commission Delegated Regulation (EU) 2017/2359.

References

Busch D (2016) Product governance and product intervention under MiFID II/MiFIR. In: Busch D, Ferrarini G (eds) Regulation of the EU financial markets: MiFID II and MiFIR. Oxford University Press, pp 123–146

Busch D, Colaert V, Hellinger G (2019) As 'assist-your-customer obligation' for the financial sector? In: Colaert V, Busch D, Incalza T (eds) European financial regulation. Levelling the cross-sectoral playing field. Hart Publishing, pp 343–375

Clarck R (1976) The soundness of financial intermediaries. Yale Law J 86(1):4–103

Colaert V (2016) The regulation of PRIIPs: great ambition, insurmountable challenges. J Financ Regul 2(2):203–224

Colaert V (2017a) Building blocks of investor protection: all-embracing regulation tightens its grip. J Eur Consum Mark Law 6:229–244

Colaert V (2017b) MiFID II in relation to other investor protection regulation: picking up the crumbs of a piecemeal approach. In: Busch D, Ferrarini G (eds) Regulation of the EU financial markets: MiFID II and MiFIR. Oxford University Press, pp 589–611

Colaert V (2019) Product information for banking, investment and insurance product. In: Colaert V, Busch D, Incalza T (eds) European financial regulation. Levelling the cross-sectoral playing field. Hart Publishing, pp 303–315

Colaert V, Incalza T (2019) Conflicts of interest and inducement in the financial sector. In: Colaert V, Busch D, Incalza T (eds) European financial regulation. Levelling the cross-sectoral playing field. Hart Publishing, pp 377–393

Della Negra F (2019) MiFID II and private law. Hart

Dreher M (2019) Produktfreigabeverfahren und Versicherungsaufsichtstrecht. In Dreher M, Wandt M (eds) Das interne Produckfreigabeverfahren Solvency II in der Rechtsanwendung, 2018. VVW GmbH, Karlsruhe, pp 79–122

Hofmann A, Neumann JK, Pooser D (2018) Plea for uniform regulation and challenges of implementing the new Insurance Distribution Directive. Geneva Pap Risk Insur Issues Pract 43:740–769

Kern A (2018) Marketing, sale and distribution. Mis-selling of financial products. A study requested by the ECON Committee, Directorate-General for Internal Policies PE 618.996

Köhne T, Brömmelmeyer C (2018) The new insurance distribution regulation in the EU—a critical assessment from a legal and economic perspective. Geneva Pap Risk Insur Issues Pract 43:704–739

Kyriaki N, Siri M (2019) The legal regime and the relevant standards. In: Marano P, Rokas I (eds) Distribution of insurance-based investment products. Springer, Cham, p 39 ss

Liverse K (2016) The scope of MiFID II. In: Busch D, Ferrarini G (eds) Regulation of the EU financial markets: MiFID II and MiFIR. Oxford University Press, pp 27–48

Marano P (2019) The product oversight and governance: standards and liabilities. In: Marano P, Rokas I (eds) Distribution of insurance-based investment products. Springer, Cham, pp 59–96

Moloney N (2010) How to protect investors. Lessons from the EC and the UK. Cambridge University Press

Moloney N (2014) EU securities and financial markets regulation. Oxford University Press

Moloney N (2015) Regulating the retail markets. In: Moloney N, Ferran E, Payne J (eds) The Oxford handbook of financial regulation. Oxford University Press, pp 736–765

Noussia K (2019) The legal framework regarding the distribution of insurance-based investment products: the EU and UK approach. J Int Bank Law Regul 33(4):119–136

Noussia K, Siri M (2019) The legal regime and the relevant standards. In: Marano P, Rokas I (eds) Distribution of insurance-based investment products. Springer, Cham, pp 27–58

Pscheidl D (2018) Implementing IDD across the EU—first findings and the way forward. ERA Forum 19:205–217

Ramharter M (2016) Aktuelle und zukünftige Fragen der Lebensversicherung zwischen Zivil- und Aufsichtsrecht – Information und Beratung nach der Richtlinie (EU) 2016/97 über Versicherungsvertrieb. ZVersWiss 105:221–254

Rokas I, Siafarika A (2019) The notion of insurance-based investment products. A cross-sectoral legal approach in Europe. In: Marano P, Rokas I (eds) Distribution of insurance-based investment products. Springer, Cham, pp 3–25
Siri M, Zhu S (2019) Will the EU Commission successfully integrate sustainability risks and factors in the investor protection regime? A research agenda. Sustainability 11:1–23

Legislation and Other Legal Instruments

EIOPA (2017) Technical Advice on possible delegated acts concerning the Insurance Distribution Directive, 1/2/2017, EIOPA-17/048
EIOPA (2017) Opinion on Monetary Incentives and Remuneration Between Providers of Asset Management Services and Insurance Undertakings, 17/295
EIOPA (2018) Q&A on Regulation (EU) No 2017-2359
EIOPA (2019) Technical Advice on the integration of sustainability risks and factors in the delegated acts under Solvency II and IDD, 30/04/2019, EIOPA-BoS-19/172
ESMA (2018) Guidelines on certain aspects of the MiFID II suitability requirements, 6/11/2018, ESMA 35-43-1163
EIOPA, Costs and past performance, 2020 Report, April 2020
EU Commission Communication, Action Plan: Financing Sustainable Growth, COM (2018) 97 final (March 2018)
EU Commission Delegated Regulation (EU) 2017/565 of 25 April 2016 supplementing Directive 2014/65/EU of the European Parliament and of the Council as regards organisational requirements and operating conditions for investment firms and defined terms for the purposes of that Directive
EU Commission Delegated Regulation (EU) 2017/2359 of 21 September 2017 supplementing Directive (EU) 2016/97 of the European Parliament and of the Council with regard to information requirements and conduct of business rules applicable to the distribution of insurance-based investment products
EU Commission Delegated Regulation (EU) 2017/2358 of 21 September 2017 supplementing Directive (EU) 2016/97 of the European Parliament and of the Council with regard to product oversight and governance requirements for insurance undertakings and insurance distributors
EU Draft Commission Delegated Regulation (EU) . . ./. . . amending Delegated Regulation (EU) 2017/2359 with regard to environmental, social and governance preferences in the distribution of insurance-based investment products
EU Draft Commission Delegated Regulation (EU) . . ./. . . of XXX amending Delegated Regulation (EU) 2017/565 as regards the integration of Environmental, Social and Governance (ESG) considerations and preferences into the investment advice and portfolio management
EU Directive 2004/39/EC of 21 April 2004 on markets in financial instruments amending Council Directives 85/611/EEC and 93/6/EEC and Directive 2000/12/EC of the European Parliament and of the Council and repealing Council Directive 93/22/EEC (MiFID I)
EU Directive 2009/138/EC of 25 November 2009 on the taking-up and pursuit of the business of Insurance and Reinsurance (Solvency II)
EU Directive 2014/65/EU of 15 May 2014 on markets in financial instruments and amending Directive 2002/92/EC and Directive 2011/61/EU (MiFID II)
EU Directive 2016/97/EU of 20 January 2016 on insurance distribution (IDD)
EU Regulation 1286/2014/EU of 26 November 2014 on key information documents for packaged retail and insurance-based investment products (PRIIPs)
EU Regulation 2019/2088/EU of 27 November 2019 on sustainability-related disclosures in the financial services sector disclosure regulation

Part II
The Insurance Distribution Directive as a "Benchmark" for National Legislators

The Notion of "Employee" in the IDD: A Harmonized Interpretation Based on the EU Law

Anna Tarasiuk and Bartosz Wojno

1 Introduction

The general aim of the European Union's ("**EU**") regulations, regardless of their level, is to harmonize certain aspects of public and private relationships. Since EU directives are supposed to be implemented to the national laws of the EU Member States, the notions used in directives, if not explained in the directive itself, can cause interpretation problems. This may apply, in particular, when certain notions have well recognized meanings under national legislation, or in the case of gold-plating regulations, introduced by a Member State.

This chapter is devoted to the interpretation of the concept of an "employee of insurance undertaking", which was used in the Directive on insurance distribution,[1] adopted in 2016 ("**IDD**"). It deals with the problem of the concept of an employee of an insurance undertaking in terms of the type of legal relationship and the scope of activities that are allowed to be performed only by such employees.

The intention of the authors of this chapter is to demonstrate that, in accordance with the previous case law of the European Court of Justice/Court of Justice of the European Union, the concepts contained in EU directives should be interpreted in accordance with EU law, taking into account its autonomy and its aim

[1]Directive (EU) 2016/97 of the European Parliament and of the Council of 20 January 2016 on insurance distribution (recast) text with EEA relevance (O.J. L 26, 2.2.2016, pp. 19–59).

A. Tarasiuk (✉)
Kozminski University, Warsaw, Poland

Lyszkiewicz Tarasiuk Kancelaria Radcow Prawnych Sp.p., Warsaw, Poland
e-mail: anna.tarasiuk@ltlegal.pl

B. Wojno
Lyszkiewicz Tarasiuk Kancelaria Radcow Prawnych Sp.p., Warsaw, Poland
e-mail: bartosz.wojno@ltlegal.pl

P. Marano, K. Noussia (eds.), *Insurance Distribution Directive*, AIDA Europe Research Series on Insurance Law and Regulation 3,
https://doi.org/10.1007/978-3-030-52738-9_6

(harmonization of legal systems of Member States). However, a simple translation of a particular term used in an EU directive into the language of a Member State may give rise to an incentive for that term to be interpreted in the context of a local legal system. As such approach may seem to be natural at first sight, it may lead to results rather unexpected by a European lawmaker.

When analysing the definition of an "employee", the risks related to the interpretation of this concept have been pointed out, using the example of the IDD implementation into Polish law in this respect. As regards the scope of activities that may be performed only by such employee, it has been attempted, in particular, to distinguish those activities that may constitute distribution activities, within the meaning of the IDD, by way of using rational criteria, including the risk of causing loss to a customer, if an activity is performed in an unprofessional or unfair manner. Since a clear indication of those activities, which are subject to the IDD's requirements, is fundamental from the point of view of legal certainty as a condition for the development of insurance market, the authors expect that relevant authorities of the European Union Member States will adopt a similar interpretation which will, in turn, be translated into appropriate jurisprudence.

2 Brief Historical Background

The development of the European insurance regulations in the period of its 50 years of history has followed certain defined paths. As regards insurance undertakings, the European lawmaker has concentrated on the issues related to management of insurance activities, prudential regulation, and the enhancement of a single market within the Community.[2] The latter aim, understood as facilitating effective exercise of freedom of establishment and freedom to provide services, almost at the same time, had served as the basis for the introduction of the first European regulation regarding the activities of insurance intermediaries as very important market players responsible for the delivery of insurance products to customers.[3]

The protection of customers' interests has always been the most important objective of those regulations. The facilitation of financial and organisational position of insurance undertakings enhances public trust to insurance providers as

[2]Please see three generations of insurance directives, starting with the First Council Directive 73/239/EEC of 24 July 1973 on the coordination of laws, regulations and administrative provisions relating to the taking-up and pursuit of the business of direct insurance other than life assurance (O.J. L 228, 16.8.1973, pp. 3–19) and the First Council Directive 79/267/EEC of 5 March 1979 on the coordination of laws, regulations and administrative provisions relating to the taking up and pursuit of the business of direct life assurance (O.J. L 63, 13.3.1979, pp. 1–18).

[3]Council Directive 77/92/EEC of 13 December 1976 on measures to facilitate the effective exercise of freedom of establishment and freedom to provide services in respect of the activities of insurance agents and brokers (ex ISIC Group 630) and, in particular, transitional measures in respect of those activities (O.J. L 26, 31.1.1977, pp. 14–19).

reputable debtors under insurance contracts. The possession of adequate capital and organisational resources by insurance undertakings is, therefore, the basic condition for effectively safeguarding the policyholders' interest. On the other hand, easy access to the whole European market also serves the interest of customers as it allows for a wider selection of insurance products and providers of insurance coverage, enabling the customers to meet their insurance-related expectations for competitive prices. The activities of insurance intermediaries are crucial from that point of view as they make it possible to connect insurance undertakings and entities interested in insurance services, without the need to establish separate sale structures by insurance undertakings.

However, the legal instruments aimed at the implementation of the protection of customers' interests have been limited, as the insurance private law, in particular insurance contracts, remain (with certain exceptions[4]) the sole competency of the Member States of the European Union and, consequently, local regulations. By the same token, the process of offering insurance product and concluding an insurance contract had for many years fallen beyond the scope of legal regulations at the European level. The European lawmaker introduced certain (but still very basic) information obligation of insurance undertakings in relation to life insurance.[5] The sales of insurance products (as a part of financial market) using the means of distance communication had followed a separate path and also remained limited to particular issues only (information obligations and a right to withdrawal from the contract), comprising only the protection of consumers (non-professionals) as a particular group of customers.[6]

The Directive on insurance mediation[7] ("**IMD**"), adopted in 2002, had been the first step as regards the introduction of a complex regulation in relation to the process of offering and concluding insurance contracts. It comprised provisions related to professional requirements of insurance intermediaries and an enforcement mechanism of those requirements,[8] the intermediaries' liability towards their customers (including the protection of cash flows between a customer and an intermediary), as

---

[4]E.g. Council Directive 87/344/EEC of 22 June 1987 on the coordination of laws, regulations and administrative provisions relating to legal expenses insurance (O.J. L 185, 4.7.1987, pp. 77–80) currently repealed by Directive 2009/138/EC of the European Parliament and of the Council of 25 November 2009 on the taking-up and pursuit of the business of Insurance and Reinsurance (Solvency II) (O.J. L 335, 17.12.2009, pp. 1–155).

[5]See regulation introduces by Article. 31 of Council Directive 92/96/EEC of 10 November 1992 on the coordination of laws, regulations and administrative provisions relating to direct life assurance and amending Directives 79/267/EEC and 90/619/EEC (OJ L 360, 9.12.1992, pp. 1–27).

[6]Directive 2002/65/EC of the European Parliament and of the Council of 23 September 2002 concerning the distance marketing of consumer financial services and amending Council Directive 90/619/EEC and Directives 97/7/EC and 98/27/EC (OJ L 271, 9.10.2002, pp. 16–24).

[7]Directive 2002/92/EC of the European Parliament and of the Council of 9 December 2002 on insurance mediation (O.J. L 9, 15.1.2003, pp. 3–10).

[8]Article 3 par. 3 of the IMD: "*Member States shall ensure that registration of insurance intermediaries - including tied ones - and reinsurance intermediaries is made subject to the fulfilment of the professional requirements laid down in Article 4.*"

well as information obligation of insurance intermediaries. The declared aim of the IMD was the "*completion of the single market for financial services and (...) the enhancement of customer protection*".[9]

After the implementation of the IMD it became clear that there was a need of further development of the European legislation covering the interactions between customers and providers of insurance products from the legal side. In 2010 the Committee of European Insurance and Occupational Pension Supervisors[10] ("**CEIOPS**") published the CEIOPS Advice to the European Commission on the revision of the Insurance Mediation Directive (2002/92/EC) ("**CEIOPS Advice**"), comprising a broad analysis of the regulatory framework of insurance mediation, and recommended possible legislative steps. In particular, it deliberated the future scope of a new regulation (at that time called the "IMD2"), by stating that: "*The majority of Members support the inclusion of direct sales by insurance undertakings in the scope of IMD2. The main rationale for their inclusion is to ensure consumer protection. Members are in favour of a "level playing-field" in this respect. Members regard the protection afforded to consumers should be the same regardless of the sales channel through which they choose to purchase their insurance. Members were unanimous in their view that employees of insurance undertakings should not be registered under IMD2.*"[11]

Consequently, the final effect of review of the IMD resulted in including "direct sales" of insurance products by insurance undertakings into the scope of the new regulation—the IDD. According to recital 6 of the IDD, "*Consumers should benefit from the same level of protection despite the differences between distribution channels. In order to guarantee that the same level of protection applies and that the consumer can benefit from comparable standards, in particular in the area of the disclosure of information, a level playing field between distributors is essential.*" The equal treatment of sales channels has also been confirmed in recital 7 (second sentence) of the IDD: "*Insurance undertakings which sell insurance products directly should be brought within the scope of this Directive on a similar basis to insurance agents and brokers.*" Moreover, the European lawmaker has emphasized that "*There is a benefit to consumers if insurance products are distributed through different channels and through intermediaries with different forms of cooperation with insurance undertakings, provided that they are required to apply similar rules on consumer protection. Such concerns should be taken into account by the Member* States *in the implementation of this Directive.*"[12]

---

[9]Recital 8 of the IMD.

[10]Ref: CEIOPS CCP-59/10, https://register.eiopa.europa.eu/CEIOPS-Archive/Documents/Advices/20101111-CEIOPS-Advice-on-IMD-Revision.pdf (last access: 29.05.2020).

[11]CEIOPS Advice, p. 23.

[12]Recital 16, second and third sentence of the IDD.

3 Application of the IDD to Employees of Insurance Undertakings

It is clear that the intention of the IDD was to improve the requirements towards insurance intermediaries and to extend those requirements also towards insurance undertakings that perform direct sales of the insurance products. There is no doubt that there are substantial differences as regards the distribution of insurance products performed by intermediaries and by insurance undertakings themselves. Those differences result from the specific nature of each insurance undertaking and its business, as well as its status of a regulated entity under legal provisions concerning the conduct of insurance business. The complexity of the core activity of an insurance undertaking (including not only the sales, but also the whole process of "manufacturing" of insurance products and their governance at the level of a risk borne by an insurance undertaking and at the level of individual insurance contracts), as well as the regulatory requirements related to that activity, result in interactions between different legal regimes applicable to a given insurance undertaking. The number of legal regimes and their interactions sometimes may lead to legal uncertainty in the context of the provisions of the IDD. One of the examples is the exact identification of the activities subject to the legal rules on insurance distribution and the manner of application of those rules.

The notion "*insurance distributor*" under the IDD is understood as "*any insurance intermediary, ancillary insurance intermediary or insurance undertaking*".[13] An "insurance undertaking" has been defined as "*an undertaking as defined in Article 13 point 1 of Directive 2009/138/EC of the European Parliament and of the Council*".[14]

Although the insurance undertaking itself is an insurance distributor, as a corporate entity it operates in the insurance market through natural persons duly authorized to perform activities with legal effect for the insurance undertaking. The regulatory requirements regarding insurance undertakings may apply in three different dimensions: the legal obligations may be imposed towards the insurance undertaking itself, its governing bodies (such as members of the management board, or its shareholders), or the staff of an insurance undertaking at the operational level. The IDD applied a mix of all the three dimensions. Therefore, the provisions of the IDD refer to an insurance undertaking as an entity (e.g. the obligations related to product oversight and governance), but also include certain rules directly addressed to its management board (directors), and its employees.

According to Article 10 § 1 of the IDD "*Home Member States shall ensure that insurance and reinsurance distributors and employees of insurance and reinsurance undertakings carrying out insurance or reinsurance distribution activities possess appropriate knowledge and ability in order to complete their tasks and perform their*

[13]Article 2 § 1 point 8 of the IDD.

[14]Article 2 § 1 point 6 of the IDD.

duties adequately." The same rule applies to continuing professional training and development requirements in order to maintain an adequate level of performance.[15] Moreover, according to the IDD "*Member States need not apply the requirements referred to in paragraph 1 and in the first subparagraph of this paragraph to all the natural persons working in an insurance or reinsurance undertaking, or insurance or reinsurance intermediary, who pursue the activity of insurance or reinsurance distribution, but Member States shall ensure that the relevant persons within the management structure of such undertakings who are responsible for distribution in respect of insurance and reinsurance products and all other persons directly involved in insurance or reinsurance distribution demonstrate the knowledge and ability necessary for the performance of their duties.*"[16] Similar rules have been laid down in the IDD as regards the requirement of good repute.[17]

The regulatory requirements applicable to the key persons (mainly management) of an insurance undertaking constitute a solution that has already been broadly used in the provisions of Directive 2009/138/EC on the taking-up and pursuit of the business of Insurance and Reinsurance[18] ("**Solvency II Directive**"). It should be noted here that imposing obligations on other personnel members of the insurance undertaking constituted a new approach. This may be explained by a different object of regulations: as Solvency II Directive is concentrated on prudential governance of insurance undertakings in order to facilitate their financial solvency, the IDD focuses on the environment of direct interactions between insurance distributors and customers. In the case of insurance distributors, the focus on the aforementioned interactions requires the lawmaker to impose a regulatory burden directly on the persons involved in relations with customers, due to the fact that the actions undertaken by such persons constitute a key risk factor to the detriment of the interest of the customers.

It should be clearly pointed out that—although not directly specified in the provisions of the IDD—the insurance undertaking takes full responsibility for any actions undertaken by its employees, involved in insurance distribution activity. The insurance undertaking is the insurance distributor and any action undertaken by its employee related to the distribution of insurance products is to be treated as an action undertaken by the insurance undertaking itself. It applies to both the liability for losses suffered by customers under private law regime, and the administrative liability connected with possible supervisory sanctions under public law.

The application of the regulatory requirements to employees of insurance undertakings requires identification of a definition of an "employee of the insurance

[15]Article 10 § 2 first subparagraph of the IDD.

[16]Article 10 § 2 fifth subparagraph of the IDD.

[17]Article 10 § 3 of the IDD.

[18]Directive 2009/138/EC of the European Parliament and of the Council of 25 November 2009 on the taking-up and pursuit of the business of Insurance and Reinsurance (Solvency II) (O.J. L 335, 17.12.2009, pp. 1–155).

undertaking" and the identification of activities of the employee carrying out insurance distribution activity that fall within the scope of the IDD.

4 Defining an "Employee of the Insurance Undertaking": Contractual Relations

The IDD does not provide for a definition of an "employee of the insurance undertaking". What is more, there is no provision which would contain a reference to national legislation as regards the understanding of that notion.

The notion of an "employee" with reference to insurance undertakings[19] appears in a number of provisions of the IDD: simply as "*their (insurance undertakings) employees*",[20] "*employees of insurance and reinsurance undertakings carrying out insurance or reinsurance distribution activities*",[21] "*employees of insurance or reinsurance undertakings who are engaged in insurance or reinsurance distribution*".[22]

Moreover, the IDD mentions also "*natural persons working in an insurance undertaking*",[23] "*staff directly involved in insurance distribution*"[24] and "*natural persons not directly involved in insurance distribution*"[25] (the latter to apply to all kinds of insurance distributors). Those notions demonstrate that the IDD is not fully consistent as regards its wording.

Since the IDD does not differentiate between the above meanings or provide any legal reasons to differentiate between the above notions, one should assume that an "*employee*" means the same as (or at least is included in the scope of the meaning of) a "*natural person working in*" or the "*staff*" or "*natural persons*" and that the "*employee of insurance undertaking*" should be understood as a natural person who works for an insurance undertaking.

The IDD remains silent as regards the type of a legal relation between the insurance undertaking and the "employee". The identification of the type of an "employment" relationship seems to be relevant since it may be an invitation to an excessively narrow, or expanded, interpretation, especially in view of the national

---

[19]The IDD mentions also "employees of insurance and reinsurance intermediaries" (art. 10 § 2 of the IDD) and "employees of insurance distributors" (art. 10 § 3 second subparagraph, art. 17 § 3 of the IDD), therefore some issues deliberated in this article may have relevance also to employees of all kinds of insurance distributors, however issues related to employees of insurance companies are the most complicated from legal point of view.

[20]Article 2 § 1 point 3, art. 3 § 1 second subparagraph, art. 10 § 2 first and second subparagraph, art. 19 § 4 of the IDD.

[21]Article 10 § 1 of the IDD.

[22]Article 10 § 2 subpar. of the IDD.

[23]Art. 10 par. 2 subpar. fifth, art. 10 par. 3 subpar. third of the IDD.

[24]Art. 10 par. 3 subpar. third of the IDD.

[25]Art. 10 par. 3 subpar. third of the IDD.

legislations of the EU Member States. It is also of utmost importance from the point of view of the management of human resources of insurance undertakings as they are subject to rules of a free market economy and should be allowed to make use of work of natural persons under different types of legal relations (allowed by national legislations).

The IDD neither provides for an exact definition of an "employee", nor allows to define it by national legislation, or to interpret in accordance with national legislation of the EU Member States. Consequently, a widely accepted approach in the European case law that prohibits the pursuit of the meaning of a given notion in the provisions of a national legislation should be applied. Such an approach has a very long history and is well based in the legal system of the European Union. It has been stated in the grounds of a judgement of the European Court of Justice (the "**Court**") of 18.01.1984 Ekro[26]: "*The need for a uniform application of Community law and the principle of equality require that the terms of a provision of Community law which makes no express reference to the law of the Member States for the purpose of determining its meaning and scope must normally be given an independent and uniform interpretation throughout the Community; that interpretation must take into account the context of the provision and the purpose of the relevant regulations.*" In many judgments that have been adopted after the cited case, the same conclusion has been repeated as the basic principle of interpretation of European law.[27]

The autonomy of understanding of notions used in the provisions of European law is fundamental for its uniform application in all Member States. If a national authority, or a national court refers to the national legislation in order to determine the understanding of a given notion, there would be a risk of different interpretations of the provision of European law among individual Member States. This would result in a different application of those provisions, putting into question the idea of adopting such regulations, in particular as regards the facilitation of freedom of establishment and freedom to provide services, which are usually based on mutual recognition of national regimes related to particular types of economic activity. Therefore, as the consequence of the autonomy of European law, the concept of autonomic meanings of notions, independent from national legal systems, used in the provisions of the European law, has been established by the Court.

Therefore, the notion of an "employee" under the IDD cannot be explained by a simple reference to national legislations, in particular national labour (employment) law.[28] To be more specific, it would be against the principle recognized by the Court

---

[26]Case 327/82.

[27]As examples see Cases: C-287/98, C-467/08.

[28]Please see the Explanatory Statement to the Polish Act on Insurance Distribution that simply translates the word "employee" into Polish and referred to the employee in the meaning of the Polish Labour Code. The Polish Act on Insurance Distribution itself does not provide for any definition of an employee, but the justification to the draft act includes an improper assumption that the "employee of an insurance undertaking" shall be regarded an "employee" in the meaning of the Polish Labour Code.

to limit the notion of an "employee" only to persons employed on the basis of a contract of employment as understood in the national law, and to exclude persons providing work under other types of contract (usually civil law contracts). A common, European, meaning of an "employee" should be sought instead, taking into account the context of the provisions and the purpose of the IDD.

The EU lawmaker's intention, as expressed in the IDD, was the sole enhancement of the protection of customers in the process of distribution of insurance products. In other words, the concept of the IDD was to introduce the rules providing conditions aimed at preventing the situations that can be detrimental for the interests of customers. In order to achieve it, the lawmaker imposed certain obligations, that need to be fulfilled during the process of insurance distribution by insurance undertakings and, consequently, by natural persons acting on behalf of such insurance undertakings. Those obligation include, among other things, the provision of information about the distributor and the product offered, the performance of an analysis of demands and needs of the customer. The fulfilment of those obligations must be performed with the application of professional knowledge, and the distributors in question are obliged to act honestly and fairly, bearing in mind the best interest of customers as the ultimate condition.[29] Such expectations of the EU lawmaker may be achieved if the persons acting on behalf of an insurance undertaking are of good repute and have sufficient professional qualifications, as well as if there are adequate control mechanisms in place within the insurance undertaking that allow to identify, mitigate or counteract any risks related to the actions undertaken by such persons. It is also clear that full responsibility for any consequences of the distribution acts rests within the insurance undertaking, in particular as regards any losses suffered by a customer.

Taking the above into account, it seems clear that the type of a contract between the insurance undertaking (acting as an insurance distributor) and the natural persons conducting insurance distribution activities on behalf of an insurance undertaking need to be regarded as irrelevant from the point of view of the purposes of the IDD. The "employee" may meet the requirements of professional knowledge and good repute, irrespective of the nature of a contractual relation with the insurance undertaking. If such nature of the contract or the applicable contractual provisions do not exclude the effective control of an insurance undertaking over the distribution activity of the "employee" (in order to manage risks related to insurance distribution), it is difficult to find, on the basis of the IDD provisions, legal arguments that would require a differentiation between various types of contracts allowed by the national legislation of the EU Member States or, in particular, recognize a contract other than a contract of employment (in particular, various civil law contracts) as not allowed under the IDD.

The above conclusion seems to be supported by those provisions of the IDD which do not refer to an "employee" but—having undoubtedly the same intention—to "natural persons working", or the "staff". Such an approach makes it possible to

---

[29]Article 17 § 1 of the IDD.

maintain that there has been no intention of a narrow approach towards a type of a legal relation between an employee and an insurance undertaking.

It should, therefore, be underlined that when the IDD refers to the "*employees of insurance undertakings*", it does not impose an obligation to limit the possible contractual relation between the employee and insurance undertaking, exclusively to a contract of employment. Other types of contracts are also allowed, as far as they do not preclude an effective fulfilment of requirements provided for in the IDD.

The above conclusion seems to be coherent with the understanding of an "*employee*" under other legal regulations of European law. The extensive interpretation of the notion "*worker*" (as an equivalent of an "*employee*") has been adopted under art. 39 of the Treaty establishing the European Community. As stated in the grounds of the judgment of the Court dated 17.07.2008 Raccanelli:[30] "*(...) it must be noted that the Court has consistently held that the concept of 'worker' within the meaning of Article 39 EC has a specific Community meaning and must not be interpreted narrowly. Any person who pursues activities which are real and genuine, to the exclusion of activities on such a small scale as to be regarded as purely marginal and ancillary, must be regarded as a 'worker'. The essential feature of an employment relationship is, according to that case-law, that for a certain period of time a person performs services for and under the direction of another person in return for which he receives remuneration (see, in particular, Case 66/85 Lawrie-Blum [1986] ECR 2121, paragraphs 16 and 17; Case C-138/02 Collins [2004] ECR I-2703, paragraph 26; and Case C-456/02 Trojani [2004] ECR I-7573, paragraph 15).*" It is worth noticing that the factor of a "*direction of another person*" may be connected with the contractual possibility of control, allowing the insurance undertaking to verify, if the activities of the employee are compliant with the requirements of the IDD. Therefore, the concept of "*employment*" elaborated by the Court in the Raccanelli case seems to fit into the purposes of the IDD, as leaves the "*employer*" (being the insurance undertaking) the possibility to influence the actions of the "*employee*" in order to manage the risks related to insurance distribution.

In light of the conclusion drawn, it should be underlined that defining "employee" under the IDD still may raise doubts in various national approaches transposing the IDD. For example, the Polish Act on Insurance Distribution[31] (the "**AID**") does refer to an "*employee conducting distribution activity in the insurance undertaking*" but does not provide a definition of such "employee", neither by defining this notion in the glossary of the AID nor by a reference to any legal act, such as the Polish Labour Code[32] (the "**PLC**"). The mere lack of the definition should not constitute a problem since the pro-EU interpretation should be applied. However, the explanatory statement to the draft AID that constitutes a legal requirement before any legal act is adopted by the Polish Parliament, included a reference to the PLC exactly and only in terms of the "*employee conducting distribution activity in the insurance*

[30]Case C-94/07.

[31]Act dated 15 December 2017 on insurance distribution (uniform text: J.L. 2019 item 1881).

[32]Act dated 27 June 1974 Labour Code (uniform text: J.L. 2019 item 1040, as amended).

undertaking". Evidently, the explanatory statement to the draft act (i.e. the bill) does not constitute legal provisions or any official or binding interpretation but may be, and often is, an indicator of the approach of the Polish lawmaker. Since the explanatory statement cannot be changed after the law has been passed and the statement itself should provide a lead to the interpretation of the provisions of the act, some representatives of the Polish legal doctrine tend to follow the assumption that the notion of an "employee" in the meaning of AID is the same as in the PLC. Such an approach, in the opinion of the authors of this chapter, for the reasons already presented, should be regarded as incorrect and may cause unnecessary interpretation problems.[33]

An entirely different approach is exemplified by the UK Financial Conduct Authority, which seems to apply an extensive understanding of the definition of an "employee". According to Chapter 28 the FCA's Handbook "*Insurance distribution: specific knowledge, ability and good repute requirements*", in relation to minimum knowledge, ability and good repute requirements for carrying out insurance distribution activities, the 'employee' in the said chapter: (1) is not restricted to an individual working under a contract of employment; and (2) includes (without limitation) any natural or legal person whose services are placed at the disposal of the firm, under an arrangement between the firm and a third party; and (3) also includes appointed representatives and their employees.[34] The same, extensive, approach is used in Chapter 4.2[35] of the FCA Handbook.

The conclusion is that the IDD does not force insurance undertakings to use employees only on the basis of contracts of employment. In order to perform distribution activities, insurance undertakings may make use of the employees under different types of contracts (also a variety of civil law contracts). There may appear a question on a grey area between an employee representing the insurance undertaking and natural persons being an insurance intermediary (or ancillary insurance intermediary) acting on behalf of the insurance undertaking. The answer lies within the legal definition of an insurance intermediary[36] (and an ancillary insurance intermediary[37]) under the IDD. That definition refers to a "*natural or legal person, who, for remuneration, takes up or pursues the activity of insurance distribution*". The specific nature of services of an insurance intermediary (an ancillary insurance intermediary) is that an intermediary "*takes up or pursues the activity of insurance distribution*" which means that it has a status of a legally independent entrepreneur.

[33]Unfortunately, the Polish Financial Supervisory Authority has not presented its official standpoint so far.

[34]SYSC 28.1.

[35]In TC 4.2 'employee': (1) is not restricted to an individual working under a contract of employment; and (2) includes (without limitation) any natural or legal person whose services are placed at the disposal of the firm, under an arrangement between the firm and a third party; and (3) also includes appointed representatives and their employees. https://www.handbook.fca.org.uk/handbook/TC/4/2.html# (last access 29.05.2020).

[36]Article 2 § 1 point 3 of the IDD.

[37]Article 2 § 1 point 4 of the IDD.

The activity of insurance intermediary is therefore conducted somehow independently (from the insurance company) and at the economic risk of the intermediary, while an employee acts under the direction and control of the employer, the latter bearing the economic risk of the activity conducted with use of employees.

5 Scope of Distribution Activities Performed by Employees of Insurance Undertakings

Another part of the discussed definition of the "employee of insurance undertaking" is the determination, as precisely as possible, of the scope of distribution activities that—when performed—make the employee in question subject to the regime of the IDD.

Several provisions of the IDD contain clear and unambiguous regulations that only an employee (directly) involved into distribution activity is the addressee of the obligations imposed in the IDD (and consequently in the national legislation implementing the IDD).

A definition of "*insurance distribution*" provided in Article 2 sec. 1 (1) of the IDD indicates that: "*insurance distribution means the activities on, proposing, or carrying out other work preparatory to the conclusion of contracts of insurance, of concluding such contracts, or of assisting in the administration and performance of such contracts, in particular in the event of a claim (...)*".

The wide definition of "*insurance distribution*" is then limited by Article 2 sec. 2 of the IDD, which excludes the following activities from its scope:

a) the provision of information on an incidental basis in the context of another professional activity where:
   (i) the provider does not take any additional steps to assist in concluding or performing an insurance contract;
   (ii) the purpose of that activity is not to assist the customer in concluding or performing a reinsurance contract;
b) the management of claims of an insurance undertaking or of a reinsurance undertaking on a professional basis, and loss adjusting and expert appraisal of claims;
c) the mere provision of data and information on potential policyholders to insurance intermediaries, reinsurance intermediaries, insurance undertakings or reinsurance undertakings where the provider does not take any additional steps to assist in the conclusion of an insurance or reinsurance contract;
d) the mere provision of information about insurance or reinsurance products, an insurance intermediary, a reinsurance intermediary, and insurance undertaking or a reinsurance undertaking to potential policyholders where the provider does not take any additional steps to assist in the conclusion of an insurance or reinsurance contract.

The starting point for the interpretative considerations on what activities carried out by an employee of an insurance undertaking can be classified as distribution activities should be the purpose of the IDD. We need to, therefore, return to recital 7[38] (second sentence) and recital 6[39] (first sentence) of the IDD. Additionally, a concept of distribution activities should be interpreted on the basis of the criteria quite similar to those previously applied to insurance mediation in the IMD, as the concept of the IDD is to introduce equal treatment of mediation and direct sales. In the IMD,[40] mediation activities have been defined as *"activities of introducing, proposing or carrying out other work preparatory to the conclusion of contracts of insurance, or of concluding such contracts, or of assisting in the administration and performance of such contracts, in particular in the event of a claim"*. On the grounds of this definition, IDD exemplified that the distribution activities are the acts initiating the first contact with the customer but preceding the proposal to use the insurance service. Thus, in the classification of an employee's activity in an insurance undertaking, it is possible to rely on an assessment of those activities through the prism of the activities of a competent insurance intermediary. As such, distribution activities of an insurance undertaking correspond to the activities of the insurance intermediary as to its subject-matter, and they differ mainly as regards the entity which carries out those activities.

On the basis of recital 32 of the IDD,[41] one should assume that distribution activities should, in principle, relate to substantive transactions relating to the preparation, conclusion of an insurance contract or the performance thereof, that is to say, those areas of activity which are most relevant and necessary for the insurance contract to be concluded, or performed.

The analysis of recital 28 of the IDD should lead to the same conclusion: *"It is important to guarantee a high level of professionalism and competence among (...) the employees of insurance and reinsurance undertakings who are involved in activities preparatory to, during and after the sales of insurance and reinsurance policies. Therefore, the professional knowledge of intermediaries and ancillary insurance intermediaries and of the employees of insurance and reinsurance undertakings needs to match the level of complexity of those activities (...)."*

It should be noted that a similar classification was made before the introduction of the IDD (indeed, with regard to the facts before the introduction of the IMD) for the purposes of tax regulation in the case-law of the Court. The Court, in the grounds for

[38] *"Insurance undertakings which sell insurance products directly should be brought within the scope of this Directive on a similar basis to insurance agents and brokers"*.

[39] *"Consumers should benefit from the same level of protection despite the differences between distribution channels"*.

[40] Article 2 (3) (first sentence) of the IMD.

[41] *"Member States should not need to consider as relevant persons those managers or employees not directly involved in the distribution of insurance or reinsurance products. Concerning insurance and reinsurance intermediaries and undertakings, all employees directly involved in the distribution activity should be expected to possess an appropriate level of knowledge and competence, with certain exceptions, such as for those who are devoted solely to administrative tasks (...)."*

the judgment of 3 March 2005—Arthur Andersen[42] stated, with regard to the activities relating to "*handling insurance applications, assessing the risks to be insured, determining whether a medical examination is required, deciding whether to accept the risk where such an examination is deemed unnecessary, issuing, managing and rescinding insurance policies and making amendments to contracts and modifying premiums, receiving premiums, managing claims, setting and paying commission for insurance agents and maintaining contact with them, handling aspects relating to reinsurance and supplying information to insured parties and insurance agents and to other interested parties, such as the tax authorities*" and that "*although they contribute to the essence of the activities of an insurance company, (...) they do not constitute services that typify an insurance agent either*". Consequently, the Court has held that "'*back office' activities, consisting in rendering services, for payment, to an insurance undertaking do not constitute the performance of services relating to insurance transactions carried out by an insurance broker or an insurance agent within the meaning of that provision.*" That judgment concerns tax law, which enjoys a specific terminological autonomy, but in the context of the legal considerations, the Court also took into account the relevant European rules on insurance mediation[43] on measures to facilitate the effective attainment of freedom of establishment and freedom to provide services in relation to the activities of insurance agents and brokers, which defined intermediation in a manner very similar to the one specified in the IMD (and, possibly, similar to the definition of insurance distribution under the IDD). Consequently, the view that a number of activities connected with ensuring the operations of an insurance undertaking, including a possibility of concluding and performing insurance contracts, but not directly linked to the offering of insurance cover to customers and the conclusion and performance of insurance contracts, should not be classified as distribution activities.

Since the objectives of introducing the IDD was to protect the interests of customers, it should be underlined that the key manifestations of the activity of the insurance distributor are related to interactions with the customer. An example of such interaction is the client's demands and needs analysis, or a proposal to conclude an insurance contract on such basis (Article 20 (1) of the IDD). Such activity is, naturally, manifested in a number of detailed activities (e.g. asking questions about the customer's needs, serving the necessary documents, clarifying their content, receiving information about the insured risk). On a contrary, it is difficult to imagine acts which would form part of a legally defined insurance distribution and which would not involve a (direct or indirect) contact with the customer. Even if certain activities are carried out internally at the distributor concerned (e.g. an estimate of the value of the subject-matter of the insurance), such activity should be regarded as having no practical significance as a manifestation of the distribution of insurance until the result is presented to the customer. Consequently, it must be assumed that

[42]Case C-472/03.

[43]Council Directive 77/92/EEC of 13 December 1976.

only those activities which may affect the interests of customers by shaping the area of their rights or obligations, or affecting their conduct, must be regarded as the distribution of insurance.

The abovementioned interaction with the customer should not cover all possible acts performed by way of a direct contact with the customer. Firstly, simple technical or representation activities may be carried out by way of a direct contact with the customer which may not be classified as a part of a set of insurance distribution designations. Secondly, it may be that a person who does not actually carry out the activity (including insurance distribution) is directly in contact with the customer, but merely provides the customer with certain information without affecting its content.

The previously mentioned recital 7 of the IDD provides that "(. . .) *the protection of consumers requires an extension of the scope of that Directive to all sales of insurance products. Insurance undertakings which sell insurance products directly should be brought within the scope of this Directive on a similar basis to insurance agents and brokers*."

Consequently, the extension to insurance undertakings as insurance distributors of requirements which, before the entry into force of the IDD, had been applicable only to insurance intermediaries, is explained precisely by the need to protect the interests of customers.

The essential requirements referred to the above regulations concern the organisation and functioning of insurance distributors, in particular the integrity and professional knowledge of the persons carrying out distribution activities.[44]

Consequently, distribution of insurance should be regarded only as such activity in which the criteria of fairness and professional knowledge must be met, as conditions for effective consumer protection. This means that the distribution of insurance is the activity in which the failure to comply with the aforementioned criteria may jeopardise the effective protection of consumers. In other words, insurance distribution includes those activities, whose flawed (unprofessional, unfair) performance is likely to harm the interests of customers.

On the other hand, the manifestations of the activity of the persons employed in an insurance undertaking, which are not required to comply with the requirements relating to integrity and professional knowledge should not be regarded as distribution activities. This will include, for example, the activities of a technical nature, e.g. the mere service of a document or the provision of information which is not substantively relevant to the interests of the customer. The activities which fall within the scope of the exemption covered by Article 87 sec. 2 point (c) of the IDD should not be regarded as distribution activities, either. In such a case, there is only a preliminary association between the parties to a potential insurance contract in the future, in particular, an initial interest on the part of the customer as regards a mere possibility of obtaining insurance cover. Since the specification may, or may not, take place in the later stages of the distribution process, the mere invocation of

[44]Article 10 of the IDD.

interest has not apparently been regarded by the European legislation as an act to be carried out by a person with verified professional knowledge of insurance products.

Consequently, technical activities should not be classified as distribution activities, if they consist of entering contracts in the register, commissioning or printing of letters, addressing or dispatching them, registering declarations, the physical service of letters, etc.

In this context, the concept of the '*assistance in the administration of contracts'*, which forms part of the definition of insurance distribution, should not be read as the performance of technical activities, but as the activities of a substantive nature affecting the performance of insurance contracts, including those affecting the decision-making process of the customer.

The separation of the "administration of contracts" from the technical activities of an employee conducting distribution activities in an insurance undertaking should always be clearly specified. By way of an example, the delivery of the general conditions of insurance can be regarded as a purely technical act (if physically delivered by a courier) but in itself (delivery, or lack of delivery) directly affects the insurance undertaking's liability and thus affects the conclusion or performance of an insurance contract. Failure to deliver the general conditions of insurance will most likely be the liability of an employee of the insurance undertaking involved in the preparation of the procedures for service of documents or a substantive review of the proper performance of that obligation or an insurance undertaking employee performing a distribution activity directly, which included the delivery of the general conditions of insurance to the customer.

Another problematic issue as regards the identification of an employee conducting distribution activity in an insurance undertaking is the fact that the distribution of insurance products is a complex activity and the customer-related documentation can be developed in several stages and by different persons in a given insurance undertaking. In particular, it may be the case that one person develops a draft content of the information provided to the customer or the statement made to such customer, while another person approves the prepared content, reviewing it once more as a person authorized to represent the insurance distributor, and consequently bears organisational and substantive responsibility for the information or the declaration made.

The IDD rules do not address such a situation; they merely provide that the Member States do not have to apply the requirements regarding the integrity and professional knowledge to "*all the natural persons working in an insurance or reinsurance undertaking, or insurance or reinsurance intermediary, who pursue the activity of insurance or reinsurance distribution, but Member States shall ensure that the relevant persons within the management structure of such undertakings who are responsible for distribution in respect of insurance and reinsurance products and all other persons directly involved in insurance or reinsurance distribution demonstrate the knowledge and ability necessary for the performance of their duties.*[45]"

There may be some doubts about the classification of the activities of persons employed in an insurance undertaking which relate to the sphere of governance of an insurance product. The regulation of product governance is a novelty in the context of the IDD (there were no similar regulations in the IMD). It should be assumed that, although product governance is a regulated area in the IDD, it does not apply to the distribution of insurance and should not be treated as such by the local legislation.

Firstly, one can assume that the addressee of product governance obligations would be an entity which creates a given insurance product, and not the insurance distributor. An insurance product, according to Article 25 of the IDD, is manufactured by an insurance undertaking and sometimes also by an insurance intermediary. However, it may be the case that the product manufacturer remains completely separate from the distributor, for example in a situation where the product has been developed by an insurance undertaking and the distributors are simply insurance intermediaries.

Secondly, it is clear from the IDD rules that the product governance issues have been separated from the product distribution issues, since their launch times differs. According to Article 25 sec. 1 paragraph 1 of the IDD, that can be treated as a good example: "*Insurance undertakings, as well as intermediaries which manufacture any insurance product for sale to customers, shall maintain, operate and review a process for the approval of each insurance product, or significant adaptations of an existing insurance product,* ***before it is marketed or distributed to customers***."

Consequently, product governance is a process carried out by the manufacturer of an insurance product, which is separate from the distribution of that product. There are only functional compounds between product management and distribution processes, i.e. proper product governance allows its distribution in a legally compliant manner, and the experience of distribution processes can improve the solutions adopted in the framework of product governance.

The same approach should be applied to underwriting activities of insurance undertakings. Such activities are specific to insurance business (risk assessment and accepting), and are not part of insurance distribution, although are performed in relation to a particular potential customer, in order to determine, whether the insurance cover should be granted or not. Still, it is a part of internal process within the insurance undertaking, and not a part of process of offering an insurance product. Such approach seems to have certain recognition by the European Insurance and Occupational Pension Authority ("**EIOPA**"). In one of its "Questions & Answers"[46] it referred to "EIOPA Final Report on Public Consultation No. 14/017 on Guidelines on the System of Governance" stating (in explanatory text for Guideline 61): "where an insurance intermediary is mandated to write insurance business or to settle claims on behalf of the undertaking, this is an outsourced service and, as such, the

[45] Article 10 sec. 2 paragraph 5 of the IDD.

[46] https://www.eiopa.europa.eu/content/1994_en?source=search (access 31.05.2020).

arrangement is caught by the Solvency II outsourcing requirements. The typical intermediation activities of an insurance intermediary, i.e. introducing, proposing or carrying out other preparatory work for the conclusion of insurance contracts, or concluding such contracts, or assisting in the administration and performance of such contracts, in particular in the event of a claim, as set out in the IDD, are not subject to the outsourcing requirements. In the case of outsourcing of underwriting activities, the application of the outsourcing requirements needs to be analysed taking into consideration the specific requirements applicable under the IDD". It seems that EIOPA separates underwriting activities and mediation (or, extensively, sales) activities as having different nature and, as such, subject to different legal regimes.

Another issue that can cause difficulties in defining the scope of activities falling within a definition of an "employee conducting distribution activity" is the "*professional management of claims*". The IDD does not specify what the "*professional management of claims*" means, but recital 14 of the IDD literal reading applies not to the general management of claims but to a "professional" one and made "on behalf of an insurance or reinsurance undertaking". It looks like this recital relates to the entities that perform certain functions, not as insurance distributors, but as performers of other professional activity.

On the basis of the principle of rationality of the European legislation, one should consider that the word 'professional' that appears in the text has not found its way there by accident. At the same time, the element of professional performance of the activity is also specified in Article 2 sec. 2 of the IDD. In light of the foregoing, one could conclude that, professional claims handling—in the understanding of the EU legislator—is only the handling of claims of an insurance undertaking by a third party and not by a group of employees of an insurance undertaking.

6 Conclusions

The IDD does not provide for a definition of an "*employee of an insurance undertaking*", nor does it include an indication of how this term should be interpreted; it also does not point out to any reference to a national legislation. The IDD also does not indicate one type of legal relationship between the insurance undertaking and the "employee". The above should lead to a conclusion that the notion of the "employee" in the IDD should be interpreted in the context of EU legislation and case law, and not in the context of national legislation of the EU Member States.

Summing up, as regards the definition of an "*employee of an insurance undertaking conducting distribution activity*", the IDD does not provide for an obligation that the distribution activity in an insurance undertaking can only be performed by the "employees" employed on the basis of a contract of employment. This notion should be understood in a much wider manner, as any legal relationship that has been concluded between an insurance undertaking and the person that is to perform distribution of insurance products. Provided the local regulations of the EU Member States do not provide for some limitations within gold-plating practices, the insurance undertakings may benefit from the contractual freedom; they may employ persons performing distribution acts under different types of contracts of provision of work for a contractor of such work. The IDD itself has not introduced any limitations in this respect.

Another issue which may result in a legal uncertainty for insurance undertakings is the scope of their activities (and the activities of their employees) falling within the regime of the IDD as the acts of insurance distribution. The definition of insurance distribution remains very extensive and depending on the interpretation of the notion, some activities may be regarded, or not, as examples of distribution activities. Ultimately, taking the purposes of the IDD into account, the scope of application of the regulation of the IDD should be limited to those actions, which are conducted by way of a (direct or indirect) contact with a customer, where such contact is intended to establish insurance coverage, or to execute the existing insurance contract, and, eventually, the actions undertaken by an employee of an insurance undertaking may exert influence on the interest of the customer (it may be detrimental if such actions are unfair or unprofessional in nature).

Legal Acts

Act dated 15 December 2017 on insurance distribution (uniform text: J.L. 2019 item 1881).

Act dated 27 June 1974 Labour Code (uniform text: J.L. 2019 item 1040, as amended).

Directive (EU) 2016/97 of the European Parliament and of the Council of 20 January 2016 on insurance distribution (recast) text with EEA relevance (O.J. L 26, 2.2.2016, pp. 19–59).

First Council Directive 73/239/EEC of 24 July 1973 on the coordination of laws, regulations and administrative provisions relating to the taking-up and pursuit of the business of direct insurance other than life assurance (O.J. L 228, 16.8.1973, pp. 3–19).

First Council Directive 79/267/EEC of 5 March 1979 on the coordination of laws, regulations and administrative provisions relating to the taking up and pursuit of the business of direct life assurance (O.J. L 63, 13.3.1979, pp. 1–18).

Council Directive 77/92/EEC of 13 December 1976 on measures to facilitate the effective exercise of freedom of establishment and freedom to provide services in respect of the activities of insurance agents and brokers (ex ISIC Group 630) and, in particular, transitional measures in respect of those activities (O.J. L 26, 31.1.1977, pp. 14–19).

Council Directive 87/344/EEC of 22 June 1987 on the coordination of laws, regulations and administrative provisions relating to legal expenses insurance (O.J. L 185, 4.7.1987, pp. 77–80).

Council Directive 92/96/EEC of 10 November 1992 on the coordination of laws, regulations and administrative provisions relating to direct life assurance and amending Directives 79/267/EEC and 90/619/EEC (OJ L 360, 9.12.1992, pp. 1–27).

Directive 2002/65/EC of the European Parliament and of the Council of 23 September 2002 concerning the distance marketing of consumer financial services and amending Council Directive 90/619/EEC and Directives 97/7/EC and 98/27/EC (OJ L 271, 9.10.2002, pp. 16–24).

Directive 2002/92/EC of the European Parliament and of the Council of 9 December 2002 on insurance mediation (O.J. L 9, 15.1.2003, pp. 3–10).

Directive 2009/138/EC of the European Parliament and of the Council of 25 November 2009 on the taking-up and pursuit of the business of Insurance and Reinsurance (Solvency II) (O.J. L 335, 17.12.2009, pp. 1–155).

Treaty on the Functioning of the European Union.

Case Law: European Court of Justice

Judgment of the Court (Fifth Chamber) of 18 January 1984, Ekro BV Vee- en Vleeshandel v Produktschap voor Vee en Vlees, Case 327/82.

Judgment of the Court of 19 September 2000, Grand Duchy of Luxemburg v Berthe Linster, Aloyse Linster and Yvonne Linster, C-287/98.

Judgement of the Court (Third Chamber) of 21 October 2010, Padawan SL v Sociedad General de Autores y Editores de España (SGAE), C-467/08.

Judgment of the Court (Fifth Chamber) of 17 July 2008, Andrea Raccanelli v Max-Planck-Gesellschaft zur Förderung der Wissenschaften eV, C-94/07.

Judgment of the Court (First Chamber) of 3 March 2005, Staatssecretaris van Financiën v Arthur Andersen & Co. Accountants c.s., Case C-472/03 Arthur Andersen.

Other Sources

CEIOPS CCP-59/10, https://register.eiopa.europa.eu/CEIOPS-Archive/Documents/Advices/20101111-CEIOPS-Advice-on-IMD-Revision.pdf (last access: 29.05.2020).

EIOPA Q&A: https://www.eiopa.europa.eu/content/1994_en?source=search (access 31.05.2020).

The UK Financial Conduct Authority Handbook, https://www.handbook.fca.org.uk (last access 31.05.2020).

Ensuring the Customer's Best Interest in the Polish Insurance Market

Wojciech Paś

1 Introduction

Among the changes introduced by the Insurance Distribution Directive[1] (hereinafter referred to as the Insurance Distribution Directive or the IDD Directive), it is certainly worth noting that Member States of the European Union are obliged to ensure that, when providing the distribution of insurance, insurance distributors always act honestly, fairly and professionally, in accordance with the best interest of their customers. This obligation results from Article 17 (1) of the aforementioned Directive and has been implemented into the Polish legal system in the form of Article 7 (1) of the Act on Insurance Distribution,[2] which constitutes a reflection of the provision of the Directive in this respect. The main objective of this provision adopted by the European legislator is to try to limit the risk of misselling by insurance distributors, i.e. offering insurance products that are not adequate to the needs and requirements of the specific customer. The sources of misselling distinguished by the European legislator include mainly the remuneration policy of persons responsible for the distribution of insurance products, as indicated in Recital 46 of the Insurance Distribution Directive. According to the European legislator, such a policy should not affect the ability of such persons to act in the best interests of their customers. However, performance-based remuneration itself should not constitute an incentive to offer a particular product to the customer.

The views expressed in this publication are those of the author and do not express the official position of the institution in which he is employed.

[1]Directive (EU) 2016/97 of the European Parliament and of the Council of 20 January 2016 on insurance distribution (Official Journal of the European Union, L 26, 2 February 2016).

[2]Polish Act of 15 December 2017 on Insurance Distribution (i.e. Journal of Laws 2018.2210).

W. Paś (✉)
PZU SA, Warsaw, Poland

P. Marano, K. Noussia (eds.), *Insurance Distribution Directive*, AIDA Europe Research Series on Insurance Law and Regulation 3,
https://doi.org/10.1007/978-3-030-52738-9_7

The distribution of insurance products under the regime of the Insurance Distribution Directive should be carried out through a test of the customer's requirements and needs based on information received from him or her.[3] Any insurance product offered to the customer should always meet his or her requirements and needs. The distribution of adequate insurance products to customers is one of the solutions adopted in the Insurance Distribution Directive, which aims to achieve the fundamental objectives of the Directive, such as increasing the protection of customers in the financial market and restoring their confidence in that market. The Insurance Distribution Directive itself is part of a series of legislative initiatives taken at the European level, designed to increase consumer protection in the insurance market.[4]

In Sect. 2, I interpret the principle of the customer's best interest in light of European and Polish insurance law and Polish supervisory practice, in particular, how this principle is understood in the IDD and MiFID, and what the relationship is between these two legal systems. Next, I analyse the best interest in light of the PFSA's recommendations and the supervisory sanctions which may be applied by the PFSA in the event of a breach of this principle.

The last section is devoted to ensuring the customer's best interest in the Polish insurance market. Within this section, I indicate what actions should be taken to ensuring this principle as well as the impact of the distributor remuneration system on ensuring the application of this principle.

2 The Principle of the Customer's Best Interest in Light of European and Polish Financial Markets Law and Polish Supervisory Practice

2.1 European and Polish Insurance Law

First of all, it should be stated that the principle of acting in the best interest of the customer is a new obligation resulting from insurance law. The previous Insurance Mediation Directive did not impose this obligation on insurance intermediaries.[5]

Ensuring the best interests of the customer is one of the motives of the IDD and appears repeatedly in the provisions thereof.[6] It is the intention behind many of the obligations imposed on insurance distributors, starting with management and prevention of conflicts of interest by insurance distributors in a manner which ensures that they do not adversely affect the interests of customers, through a system of remuneration of distributors which should not adversely affect their ability to act in

[3]In accordance with Recital 44 of the Insurance Distribution Directive.

[4]Mrozowska-Bartkiewicz (2016), pp. 112–113.

[5]Directive 2002/92/EC of the European Parliament and of the Council of 9 December 2002 on insurance mediation, Official Journal of the European Union, L 9, 15 January 2003, p. 245.

[6]Malinowska (2018), p. 57.

accordance with the best interests of the customer. It also refers to cross-selling practices which must not lead to a situation where the interests of customers are not properly taken into account.

Article 7 (1) of the Act on Insurance Distribution is the main source of the obligation imposed on insurance distributors to act in the best interest of the customer present in the Polish law. Pursuant to this provision, when distributing insurance policies, an insurance distributor shall act honestly, reliably and professionally, in accordance with the best interests of customers. An insurance distributor within the meaning of the Act on Insurance Distribution is an insurance company, an insurance agent, an agent offering supplementary insurance or an insurance broker.

The development of principle of the customer's best interest is reflected in the requirements relating to the remuneration policy of insurance distributors.[7] Pursuant to Article 7 (2) of the Act on Insurance Distribution, the method of remunerating insurance distributors and persons with whom the insurance agency activities or insurance brokerage activities are performed, as well as persons with whom the insurance company's distribution activities are performed, may not be contrary to the obligation to act in accordance with the best interests of customers, in particular, an insurance distributor may not make arrangements concerning remuneration, sales targets or other arrangements that could constitute an incentive to propose a specific insurance agreement or insurance guarantee agreement to the customer in a situation where the insurance distributor could propose another agreement that would be better suited to the customer's needs.

Another expression of the principle of the best interest of the customer consists in the requirements relating to the prevention of conflicts of interest by an insurance agent, insurance broker and insurance company in the course of distribution of insurance based-investment products, which are regulated in Article 15 of the Act on Insurance Distribution. In light of this provision, the aforementioned distributors are obliged to make use of organisational solutions aimed at preventing conflicts of interest in such a way that they do not have a negative impact on the interests of customers. Such solutions should be proportional to the business activity conducted and proposed insurance agreements as well as the type of distributor. Within the adopted solutions, distributors referred to in Article 15 of the Act on Insurance Distribution should undertake actions to identify conflicts of interest between them, including their management board members, proxies, employees or other persons related to them, and their customers, or between their customers, arising in the course of conducting business in the distribution of insurance-based investment products. In the event that organisational solutions are not sufficient to avoid the risk of customer detriment, the aforementioned distributors shall, before the conclusion of the insurance contract, disclose the general nature or sources of conflict of interest to the customer, including in particular whether the commission received under the insurance contract depends on the volume of insurance contracts concluded. The information is to be provided on a durable medium and must include appropriate data and

[7]Ziemniak (2019), p. 35 and subsequent.

information taking into account the type of customer and enabling the customer to make an informed decision about the activity of the insurance distributor in relation to which the conflict of interest has arisen.

The principle of the customer's best interest is also subject to the requirements of both Commission Delegated Regulation (EU) 2017/2358 of 21 September 2017 regarding product supervision and management requirements for insurance companies and insurance distributors[8] and Commission Delegated Regulation (EU) 2017/2359 of 21 September 2017 regarding information requirements and rules of business operations applicable to the distribution of insurance-based investment products.[9]

The requirement for the manufacturer of insurance products to provide all relevant information concerning those products, including information on the product approval process, the specific target market and the suggested distribution strategy, constitutes the implementation of the principle of the customer's best interest under the Regulation with regard to product supervision oversight and governance requirements for insurance companies and insurance distributors. At the same time, manufacturers and distributors of insurance products should take appropriate action when they determine that a product does not correspond or no longer corresponds to the interests, objectives and characteristics of a particular target market. The best interest of customers is also one of the criteria that should be taken into account in the approval process of an insurance product, i.e. at the stage of its development. The main source of obligations related to the principle of the best interest of the customer under the Regulation with respect to information requirements and business rules applicable to the distribution of insurance-based investment products is prevention and management of conflicts of interest and evaluation of incentives as well as incentive schemes under Article 8 of the Regulation.

The principle of acting in the customer's best interest itself can often interact with the existing rules of insurance law in the EU Member States, such as the principle of good faith.[10] Such a situation may mean that the principle of acting in the customer's best interest may *de facto* constitute a repetition of the existing rules of insurance law[11] or an emanation of those rules.[12] Irrespective of how it interacts with the existing rules of insurance law, it will also undoubtedly create new obligations for insurance distributors, which may contribute to the harmonisation of legislation in

[8]Commission Delegated Regulation (EU) 2017/2358 of 21 September 2017 supplementing Directive (EU) 2016/97 of the European Parliament and of the Council with regard to product oversight and governance requirements for insurance undertakings and insurance distributors, *OJ L 26, 2.2.2016, p. 19.*

[9]Commission Delegated Regulation (EU) 2017/2359 of 21 September 2017 supplementing Directive (EU) 2016/97 of the European Parliament and of the Council with regard to information requirements and conduct of business rules applicable to the distribution of insurance-based investment products, *OJ L 145, 30.4.2004, p. 1.*

[10]Malinowska (2018), p. 64 et seq.

[11]Marano (2017b), p. 11 and subsequent.

[12]Malinowska (2018), p. 71.

the EU and may also affect the relationship between the supervisory authority and the insurance distributor.[13] In this context, the principle of acting in the customer's best interest will be a sort of a model of conduct for an insurance distributor in the course of its business and will be subject to assessment by a supervisory institution in accordance with the adopted model.[14] From this perspective, it is desirable and justified for the stability and safety of insurance distributors that supervisory authorities publish their views on their understanding of the principle of acting in the customer's best interest, together with examples of actions which are either consonant with or contrary to this principle.

2.2 *MiFID*

It seems that the provisions of Directive 2004/39/EC on markets in financial instruments (MiFID Directive)[15] and Directive 2014/65/EU on markets in financial instruments[16] could have been the reference point for the adoption of obligations related to acting in the best interest of the customer for insurance distributors, as could be indicated by Recital 10 of the IDD Directive, which states the need to ensure effective consumer protection in all financial sectors and the need to ensure the harmonisation of regulations. The concept of acting in the best interest of the customer adopted in the IDD Directive reflects the obligations imposed under the MiFID Directive. Pursuant to Article 19 of the MiFID Directive, Member States require that, when providing investment services and/or, where appropriate, additional services to customers, an investment company shall act honestly, fairly and professionally in accordance with the best interests of customers. The aforementioned provision is the source of the obligations associated with investment companies acting in the best interests of their customers.

The MiFID requirements for acting in the best interests of the customer focus primarily on customer information obligations in relation to the investment company providing the services, the financial instruments and the proposed investment strategies, which should include appropriate guidance and warnings about the risk associated with investment in such instruments or in relation to particular investment strategies, as well as information about the executors, costs and related fees. The aforementioned information should be structured in such a way that the customers or potential customers are able to understand the nature and risks of the investment

[13]Malinowska (2018), p. 11 et seq.

[14]Malinowska (2018), p. 11 et seq.

[15]Directive 2004/39/EC of the European Parliament and of the Council of 21 April 2004 on markets in financial instruments (amending Council Directives 85/611/EEC and 93/6/EEC and Directive 2000/12/EC of the European Parliament and of the Council and repealing Council Directive 93/22/EEC)—(MiFID).

[16]Directive 2014/65/EU of the European Parliament and of the Council of 15 May 2014 on markets in financial instruments and amending Directive 2002/92/EC and Directive 2011/61/EU.

service and the specific type of financial instrument offered and thus to make informed investment decisions. Another area related to acting in the best interest of the customer is the obligation to examine the knowledge and experience of the customer in the field of investment relevant to the specific type of product or service, his/her financial situation and investment objectives in order to allow the investment company to determine whether the proposed investment service and financial instrument are appropriate for the customer. At the same time, when an investment company concludes that a product or service is not appropriate for the customer or potential customer, it must advise the customer of that fact. A similar obligation is imposed on the investment company in the event that the customer refuses to provide information about his/her knowledge and experience or if this information is insufficient for assessing suitability; in such a case the investment company is required to warn the customer that it is unable to assess the suitability of a particular product or service.

The principle of the customer's best interest is also the core of the MiFID II[17] system of regulations, including in particular Directive 2014/65/EU on markets in financial instruments, which expands the scope of obligations related to this principle.[18] In particular, in accordance with Recital 71 of Directive 2014/65/EU, investment companies should therefore understand the characteristics of the financial instruments they offer or recommend and develop effective strategies and arrangements to identify and review the categories of customers to whom products are to be delivered and services are to be provided. Member States should ensure that investment companies creating financial instruments guarantee that those products are developed in order to satisfy the specific needs of the target market, i.e. end-customers, within a specific customer category, that they take reasonable steps to ensure that financial instruments are distributed within a specific target market, and that they periodically review the target market identification data and the performance of the products offered. Investment companies offering or recommending financial instruments which are not products developed by them should also have adequate arrangements in place to obtain and understand relevant information regarding the product approval process, including the specific target market and the characteristics of the product they are offering or recommending. Such an obligation should apply without prejudice to any adequacy or suitability assessment to be carried out subsequently by the investment company in the course of providing investment services to each customer based on his or her personal needs, characteristics and objectives.

The overriding objective of the obligation to act in the customer's best interest is to protect investors from misconduct, which is not safeguarded by other more specific MiFID II requirements.[19] Thus, a breach of the general requirement related to the obligation to act in the best interests of the customer does not necessarily

[17]Malinowska (2018), p. 59.

[18]Malinowska (2018), p. 59.

[19]Della Negra (2019), p. 34 and subsequent.

involve a breach of more specific requirements. The purpose of the duty to act in the customer's best interest is to safeguard the interests of the client in a comprehensive manner, which is not may be guaranteed by more specific requirements.[20]

Preventing asymmetry of information between a professional such as an investment firm or intermediary firms and a client is also identified as one of the objectives of the rules regarding the conduct of business in MiFID II.[21]

Under MiFID II, the customer's best interest is perceived through the implementation of the requirements set out in Articles 24–25 of MiFID II, consisting primarily in the assessment of the suitability and adequacy of instruments and reporting to clients.[22] Moreover, the principle of acting in the best interests of its clients under MiFID II is also implemented by the product governance requirements.[23]

2.3 *MiFID vs. IDD*

Undoubtedly, the MiFID regulations have influenced the shape of European insurance law, as can be seen in Recital 10 of the IDD, which states that there is a need to ensure effective consumer protection in all financial sectors and to ensure the harmonisation of rules. This phenomenon has been described in publications as "Mifidization" of European insurance law and is manifested by its impact on: (a) the sources of insurance law, (b) the insurance product management system, (c) customer protection, (d) interpretations of the rules on life insurance by the EU national courts.[24]

The adoption of similar legal solutions for MiFID-regulated investment products and IDD-regulated insurance-based investment products is intended to prevent regulatory arbitrage and thus to avoid encouraging the creation of financial products that are not subject to a more stringent legal regime.[25]

The best example of the impact of the MiFID on European insurance law is the Commission Delegated Regulation (EU) 2017/2358 of 21 September 2017 with regard to product oversight and governance requirements for insurance undertakings and insurance distributors, which reflects the legal framework adopted under the MiFID.[26]

This includes in particular requirements relating to the management of insurance products for manufacturers and distributors of insurance products, such as the obligation to construct a relevant target market and a relevant "antigroup", i.e. the

[20]Della Negra (2019), p. 34 and subsequent.

[21]Della Negra (2019), p. 27 et seq.

[22]Gortsos (2018), p. 68 and subsequent.

[23]Gortsos (2018), p. 71 et seq.

[24]Marano (2017a), p. 219 et seq.

[25]Marano (2017a), p. 221 et seq.

[26]Marano (2017a), p. 222 et seq.

customer group for which the insurance product will generally not be suitable given their needs, characteristics and objectives.

Although similar legal solutions have been adopted in both the MiFID and the IDD, there are also some differences between these legal systems (e.g. a regulation concerning incentives) which may contribute to the creation of a regulatory arbitrage within this framework.[27] It is also significant that the MiFID II system is based on the maximum harmonisation of EU law within the legal orders of the Member States, as opposed to the IDD system, which is based on minimum harmonisation of the law, which means that EU Member States may introduce more restrictive regulations.[28] Examples of such legal solutions adopted in selected EU Member States which increase the requirements for insurance distributors compared to the IDD regulation were presented in the EIOPA report—*Report analysing national General Good rules in the context of the proper functioning of the Insurance Distribution Directive (IDD) and the internal market.*[29]

The objectives of both legal systems, i.e. the IDD and the MiFID, are generally complementary. Their core is to provide greater protection for recipients of financial products. Nevertheless, it should be agreed that the creation of regulations for financial institutions should take into account the specific nature of the products they create.[30] The nature of insurance products is different from that of other products related strictly to investment. Therefore, similar legal solutions in the financial market should be adopted while taking into account the specificity of a particular business sector.

2.4 Polish Supervisory Practices on the Insurance Market

Although the obligation to act in the best interest of the customer did not exist until the Act on Insurance Distribution came into force in Polish insurance law, the obligation to act as an insurance intermediary taking the best interest of the customer into account was already included in the recommendations of the Polish Financial Supervision Authority (PFSA) for insurance companies concerning their product management systems, in force since 1 July 2016. At this point, it should be noted that the PFSA's recommendations are not universally binding provisions of law, and constitute solely an expression of supervisory expectations addressed to insurance or reinsurance companies with respect to their operations. In this sense, a supervisory recommendation is an indication of what approaches by an insurance or reinsurance company are approved by the supervision authority and therefore not questioned by

[27] Kern (2018), p. 31; Noussia and Siri (2019), p. 42 and subsequent.

[28] Kern (2018), p. 31 et seq.

[29] https://eiopa.europa.eu/Pages/News/EIOPA-examines-national-general-good-rules.aspx.

[30] Cousy (2017), p. 48 et seq.

the PFSA.[31] As a consequence, recommendations constitute an expression of how the PFSA perceives certain areas of an insurance company's activity, and actions by the supervised entity to the contrary may, in situations specified in legal regulations, result in the initiation of supervisory proceedings.[32] However, it should be emphasised that the simple non-compliance of an insurance company with a recommendation cannot constitute the basis for imposing supervisory sanctions by the PFSA. Violation of the applicable provisions of law is a circumstance that constitutes the basis for the application of supervisory instruments by the PFSA. However, it is possible that a specific recommendation will adopt the content of a legal standard.[33]

2.5 *Responsibility Linked to the Principle of the Customer's Best Interest in the Polish Legal System*

The above may have a special significance in the context of the insurance companies' implementation of the requirements resulting from the Act on Insurance Distribution, including the obligation to act in accordance with the customer's best interest. This is because the authority responsible for supervision of the performance of actions taken in the area of insurance and reinsurance distribution is the Polish Financial Supervision Authority, which is entitled to apply supervisory sanctions in the event of the distributors' failure to fulfil certain obligations. One of the bases for the PFSA to apply supervisory sanctions referred to in Article 84 (1) of the Act on Insurance Distribution is the distributors' violation of the obligation to act in the best interest of the customer, i.e. violation of the rule specified in Article 7 (1) of the Act on Insurance Distribution.[34]

---

[31] Wojno (2017a).

[32] Wojno (2017a).

[33] Wojno (2017a).

[34] In this situation, the PFSA may choose from among the following administrative decisions:

1. issue a public statement indicating the person responsible for the violation and the nature of the violation;
2. order the insurance or reinsurance distributor to cease the violation and refrain from repeating it;
3. suspend a member of the management board of an insurance or reinsurance distributor who is a legal person and is responsible for the violation for a period not exceeding 6 months;
4. impose a fine on an insurance or reinsurance distributor who is a legal person, not exceeding the amount of PLN 21,827,500 or 5% of annual net revenues on the sale of goods and services and financial operations or—in the event of an insurance or reinsurance company—5% of the gross premium written, disclosed in the last financial statements for the financial year, approved by the approval authority of the insurance or reinsurance distributor, or twice the amount of benefits obtained or losses avoided as a result of the violation, if these can be determined;
5. impose a fine on an insurance or reinsurance distributor who is a natural person, not exceeding the amount of PLN 3,055,850 or twice the amount of benefits obtained or losses avoided as a result of the violation, if these can be determined;

Applying the sanction referred to above may be preceded by the issuance of a recommendation by the PFSA against a distributor committing a violation under Article 84 (3) of the Act on Insurance Distribution. The application of supervisory measures by the PFSA is this authority's prerogative, but not its obligation.[35] Nevertheless, the supervisory authority's obligation under Article 85 of the Act on Insurance Distribution is to take into account significant circumstances related to the breach when selecting the type and amount of the supervisory measure.[36]

Notwithstanding the above, it is also worth mentioning the consequences under civil law of the non-adaptation of an insurance product by the distributor to the demands and needs of a customer, which may take different forms depending on the situation.[37]

2.6 Best Interest in Light of the PFSA's Recommendations

Referring to the obligation to act as an insurance intermediary, and taking into account the best interest of the customer referred to in the PFSA recommendations concerning the product management system, it should be pointed out that, in accordance with Recommendation No. 19.2, *In the case of an intermediary for whom the amount of commission depends exclusively on the level of sales, the Company should ensure and demonstrate that the manner of determining the commission does not interfere with the intermediary's obligation to act in the best interest of the customer.* These recommendations also refer to other obligations of the insurance company, which may be perceived as the elements of acting in the best interest of the customer. This applies especially to the obligation to distribute the specific insurance products to a specific target market and to identify an "antigroup", i.e. a group of customers for whom the product will not be adequate. In the preamble

6. withdraw the authorisation to conduct brokerage activity from an entity performing such activity, who violates the law, or remove an insurance agent or an agent offering supplementary insurance, who violates the law, from the register of insurance agents.

[35]Wojno (2017b).

[36]These circumstances include:

1. the gravity and duration of the violation;
2. the degree of responsibility of the insurance distributor or reinsurance distributor;
3. the financial situation of the insurance distributor or reinsurance distributor;
4. the amount of benefits obtained or the amount of losses avoided—when these can be determined;
5. the amount of losses incurred by customers and other persons in connection with the infringement—in the case when these can be determined;
6. the insurance or reinsurance distributor's willingness to cooperate with the supervisory authority;
7. the measures taken by the insurance or reinsurance distributor to prevent a repeated violation of the law;
8. the previous violations committed by the particular insurance or reinsurance distributor.

[37]See more in Kucharski (2019).

to the aforementioned recommendation, which constitutes a kind of statement of reasons for its issuance, the supervisory authority first of all pointed to the need to ensure an effective product management system covering the full product life cycle, i.e. from the moment of its design to the moment of its withdrawal from the market and fulfilment of contractual obligations by the insurance company, which have an impact not only on the financial results and solvency of the insurance company, but also on the quality of the insurance company's relations with its customers. It seems that the last element may have been crucial for the PFSA's need to issue the recommendations in question, taking into account the scale of missellings in the distribution of insurance products[38] in recent years as well as in the context of the related risk for insurers. As the PFSA points out in the preamble to the recommendation, the quality of the product management system affects many important areas in the activity of insurance companies and may involve many different types of risks. The PFSA's recommendations are meant to indicate supervisory expectations concerning prudent and stable product management, including the risks associated with this process. In the context of the above, it is also worth mentioning the PFSA's parallel recommendations for insurance companies concerning product adequacy, which refer to the company's obligation to offer insurance customers investment products that meet both the needs and capabilities of those customers (in accordance with Recommendation No. 8). This should be preceded by an examination of the customer's knowledge, experience in the field of life insurance and his or her financial situation. According to the PFSA, these recommendations aim to increase the level of customer protection in the area of insurance-based investment products by ensuring an appropriate information policy towards them and to match them to their needs and capacities.

The need for insurance companies and insurance intermediaries creating an insurance product to identify the target market and the "antigroup" is also clearly highlighted in the EIOPA's preliminary guidelines on product oversight and governance arrangements by insurance undertakings and insurance distributors, published on 13 April 2016.[39] In light of the preamble to the EIOPA guidelines, product supervision and management arrangements play a key role in customer protection and are intended to limit the risk of misselling by, *inter alia*, distributing insurance products to the target market. At the same time, the European supervisory body points out that they constitute a key element of the regulatory requirements of the Insurance Distribution Directive. It is important to underline that the EIOPA guidelines are preliminary in nature. Nevertheless, it should be noted that Poland has declared its willingness to comply with the guidelines through the PFSA

[38]Orlicki (2016), p. 4.

[39]Preparatory Guidelines on product oversight and governance arrangements by insurance undertakings and insurance distributors. https://eiopa.europa.eu/Pages/Guidelines/Preparatory-Guidelines-on-product-oversight-and-governance-arrangements-by-insurance-undertakings-and-insurance-distributor.aspx.

recommendations concerning the product management system and recommendations concerning product adequacy testing.[40]

3 Ensuring the Customer's Best Interest in the Polish Insurance Market

The obligation on the insurance distributor to act in the best interest of the customer, as laid down in the IDD and subsequently reflected in the Act on Insurance Distribution, is not an entirely new obligation for insurance companies. This obligation, although it had not been present previously in insurance law, had been reflected in the recommendations of the Polish Financial Supervision Authority for insurance companies relating to the product management system and product adequacy testing, which have been in force since 1 July 2016. The PFSA's recommendations were certainly inspired by the MiFID regulations, as well as the proposed EIOPA preliminary guidelines on product oversight and governance arrangements by insurance undertakings and insurance distributors and IDD regulations. The introduction of new requirements for insurance companies was caused by irregularities in the Polish insurance market in the area of distribution of insurance-based investment products. The main source of these irregularities was misselling.[41]

This may be significant in the context of meeting the insurance distributors' obligation to act in the best interest of the customer. One of the intentions behind the adoption of the aforementioned recommendation by the PFSA was to improve the relations of customers with insurance companies, and in particular to prevent the risk of misselling and ensure the usefulness of insurance for policyholders and the insured.[42] These values also seem to have guided the European legislator, as can be seen in particular Recitals of the IDD. In this context, the realisation of the customer's best interest in the course of insurance distribution should be seen as ensuring the adequacy of the product to the customer's needs and requirements. In this sense, an insurance product offered to a customer should meet his or her needs and requirements for the desired insurance coverage. It seems that the intensity of efforts to ensure the customer's best interest should depend on the type of distributor offering a particular insurance product to the customer.[43] This is because the role of an insurance agent is different from that of an insurance broker.

[40] Preparatory Guidelines on product oversight and governance arrangements by insurance undertakings and insurance distributors. https://eiopa.europa.eu/Pages/Guidelines/Preparatory-Guidelines-on-product-oversight-and-governance-arrangements-by-insurance-undertakings-and-insurance-distributor.aspx.

[41] Communication from the Polish Financial Supervision Authority regarding the issued recommendations: https://www.knf.gov.pl/o_nas/komunikaty?articleId=54879&p_id=18.

[42] Orlicki (2016), p. 9.

[43] Also in: Malinowska (2017), pp. 120–121; Orlicki (2017), p. 24.

Acting in accordance with the best interest of the customer is interpreted by Polish legal doctrine as such a course of action that is "fair, honest, with regard to the highest level of reliable and exhaustive information and with regard to the customer's needs, on the basis of a professional analysis carried out in accordance with Article 8 (1) of the Act on Insurance Distribution".[44] This procedure should be characterised by the fulfilment of all the obligations resulting from the Act on Insurance Distribution, and its effect should be to propose an optimal insurance contract (i.e. one which is adequate to the needs and requirements of the customer), taking into account the type of distributor.[45] The duty to act in the customer best interest of the client is a guarantee to safeguard her/his rights in situations when this is not guaranteed by more specific duties.

3.1 Actions Aimed at Ensuring the Customer's Best Interests

The first step towards ensuring the customer's best interest, appropriate for each type of distributor, is first of all be to determine the needs and requirements of the customer in order to identify an adequate insurance product. Establishing the needs and requirements of the customer would seem to be an indispensable element for acting in his or her best interest.[46] The lack of knowledge of the customer's expectations regarding the desired insurance coverage makes it impossible for the distributor to offer an insurance product meeting his or her needs. Moreover, the obligation of the insurance distributor to determine the customer's requirements and needs prior to conclusion of the insurance contract on the basis of the information obtained from the customer is laid down in Article 8 (1) of the Act on Insurance Distribution. In accordance with that provision, *before an insurance contract or an insurance guarantee contract is concluded, the insurance distributor must, on the basis of the information received from the customer, identify his requirements and needs and provide objective information on the insurance product in an intelligible form in order to enable the customer to make an informed decision.* The aim of the analysis of the customer's needs and expectations should be to identify the subject of the coverage and the risks the customer wants to insure against.[47]

Another element common to each type of distributor, the objective of which is ensuring the best interest of the customer, is to ensure compliance of the proposed insurance agreement with the needs and expectations of the customer in terms of insurance coverage, which has been specified in Article 8 (3) of the Act on Insurance Distribution. Nevertheless, it seems that the implementation of this obligation should take into account the specificity of each distributor. Compliance with this obligation

---

[44]See Nowak (2018), p. 72 et seq.

[45]Ziemniak (2019), p. 38.

[46]See more: Pokrzywniak (2018), p. 71 et seq.

[47]See Tarasiuk and Wojno (2018), p. 7.

by an insurance agent acting in the name and on behalf of an insurance company and an insurance broker acting in the name and on behalf of a customer should be assessed differently. The specificities of the different distribution channels are also recognised by the European legislator who, in Recital 17 of the IDD, states that *this Directive should take into account the differences in the types of distribution channel. It should, for example, take into account the characteristics of insurance intermediaries who are under a contractual obligation to conduct insurance distribution business exclusively with one or more insurance undertakings (tied insurance intermediaries) which exist in certain Member States' markets, and should establish appropriate and proportionate conditions applicable to the different types of distribution.("...")*.

In this context, it should be stated that assessment of the fulfilment of the obligation to act in the best interests of the customer should be seen from the perspective of the distributor type. The role of an insurance broker should be to ensure that the maximum conditions of insurance coverage for its customer are provided. Other distributors, including insurance agents, who act in the name and on behalf of the insurance company should pursue the best interests of the customer by ensuring that the product is adequate to the customer's needs and capacities, in particular by ensuring the usefulness of the insurance product for the customer.[48] At this point it should be emphasised that the obligation to act in the best interest of the customer applies to all actions performed by an insurance distributor in the course of insurance distribution.

3.2 Distributor's Remuneration and the Customer's Best Interests

In my opinion, one main factor that may affect the activity of an insurance distributor in accordance with the best interest of the customer is how the distributor is remunerated. This has also been recognised by the European legislator as indicated in Recital 46 of the IDD. According to the European legislator, such a policy should not affect their ability to act in the best interests of their customers. However, performance-based remuneration itself should not constitute an incentive to offer a particular product to the customer. This principle has been reflected in the provisions of the IDD Directive and the Act on Insurance Distribution. Pursuant to Article 7 (2) of the Act on Insurance Distribution, *the method of remunerating insurance distributors and persons with whom the insurance agency activities or insurance brokerage activities are performed, as well as persons with whom the insurance company's distribution activities are performed, may not be contrary to the obligation to act in accordance with the best interests of customers, in particular, an insurance distributor may not make arrangements concerning remuneration,*

[48]Orlicki (2016), p. 9; Paś (2018), p. 57.

sales targets or other arrangements that could constitute an incentive to propose a specific insurance agreement or insurance guarantee agreement to the customer in a situation where the insurance distributor could propose another agreement that would be better suited to the customer's needs. This requirement is already present in the PFSA's product management system recommendations. On the basis of Recommendation No. 19.2, the insurance company should ensure and demonstrate that the manner of determining the commission does not interfere with the intermediary's obligation to act, with consideration of the customer's best interest.

In light of the above, the rules relating to the remuneration of insurance distributors should be designed in such a way that they do not encourage misselling and thus are not contrary to the duty to act in the best interests of the customer.[49] The above should be perceived in terms of ensuring that the insurance product is adequate to the customer's needs and capacities. Thus, it seems unacceptable to construct remuneration rules that will motivate insurance distributors to distribute insurance products which do not meet the needs of their customers. However, it should be noted that insurance-based investment products are additionally subject to specific requirements set out especially by Commission Delegated Regulation (EU) 2017/2359 of 21 September 2017 regarding information requirements and rules of business operations applicable to the distribution of insurance-based investment products.

3.3 Ensuring the Best Interest of the Customer as a Way to Limit Misselling

The distributors' implementation of the principle of the best interest of the customer should be seen as an imperative to deal with customers in a way that does not result in the distribution of insurance products which are not adequate to the needs and expectations of customers. In this context, the fulfilment of the obligation to act in the best interest of the customer could be treated as compliance with the prohibition of practices infringing on the collective interests of customers in the form of misselling in financial services, laid down in the Polish legal system in Article 24 (1) in conjunction with Article 24 (2)(4) of the Act on Competition and Consumer Protection.[50] In light of those provisions, it is prohibited *to propose to customers that they purchase financial services which do not meet their needs as determined with regard to the information available to the trader concerning the characteristics of those customers or to propose to them that they purchase those services in a manner which does not correspond to their nature.* The explanatory memorandum to the inclusion of financial service misselling in the catalogue of

[49]Ziemniak (2019), p. 35 et seq.

[50]Ustawa z dnia 16 lutego 2007 r. o ochronie konkurencji i konsumentów (Act of 16 February 2007 on competition and consumer protection) (uniform text: Journal of Laws of 2017, item 229).

practices affecting collective customer interests explains the prohibition of inadequate financial services as follows: "The planned regulation, introducing a ban on offering financial services that do not meet the needs the consumers they are offered to, determined with regard to the information available to the trader about the characteristics of these consumers or proposing they purchase these services in a manner that does not correspond to their nature, is aimed at forcing traders to behave ethically when offering financial products to consumers. They must assess their products in terms of their suitability for certain groups of consumers and direct them to the groups for which the product is actually intended, in a manner which is not misleading and in conformity with the accepted principles of morality".[51] Consequently, it can be concluded that proper implementation of the best interests of the customer will certainly reduce the risk of breaching the ban on the misselling of financial services, including in the area of insurance distribution.[52]

4 Conclusion

The obligation to act in accordance with the best interests of the customer is not a new obligation for the participants in the Polish insurance market. It has already been reflected in the PFSA's recommendations concerning product management systems. This obligation should be qualified as an imperative to deal with customers in a manner that does not result in the distribution of insurance products which are not adequate to the needs and expectations of customers. Proper implementation of the best interest of the customer will certainly reduce the risk of violating the ban on misselling of financial services. It seems that the intensity of efforts to ensure the customer's best interest should depend on the type of distributor offering a particular insurance product to the customer. The fulfilment of this obligation by insurance distributors should be assessed from the perspective of ensuring that the product is adequate to the needs and expectations of the customer, in particular guaranteeing that the insurance is useful for the customer, which means that it is adequate to his/her needs and capacities to cover his/her expected insurance cover. The duty to act in the customer's best interest is a guarantee to safeguard her or his rights in situations when this is not guaranteed by more specific duties.

[51] Wędrychowska-Karpińska and Wiercińska-Krużewska (2016).

[52] Orlicka (2015), p. 48.

References

Cousy H (2017) Changing insurance contract law: an age-old, slow and unfinished story. In: Marano P, Siri M (eds) Insurance regulation in the European Union. Solvency II and beyond. Palgrave Macmillan

Della Negra F (2019) MiFID II and private law: enforcing EU conduct of business rules. Bloomsbury Publishing

Gortsos C (2018) Stricto Sensu Investor Protection under MiFID II: a systematic overview of Articles 24-30. Cambridge Scholars Publishing

Kern A (2018) Marketing, sale and distribution. Mis-selling of financial product. A study request by the ECON Committee

Kucharski B (2019) Cywilnoprawne konsekwencje niedostosowania przez dystrybutora produktu ubezpieczeniowego do wymagań i potrzeb klienta (Civil law consequences of the non-adjustment of an insurance product by the distributor to the demands and needs of a customer), "Prawo asekuracyjne" v. 3/2019, Warszawa

Malinowska K (2017) Najlepszy interes klienta – rozważania na tle ustawy o dystrybucji ubezpieczeń (Customer's best interest – considerations against new regulations on insurance distribution). In: Gnela B, Szaraniec M (eds) Dystrybucja usług ubezpieczeniowych. Wybrane zagadnienia prawne (Distribution of insurance services. Selected legal issues). Warsaw

Malinowska K (2018) Customer's best interest as a rule in insurance contracts, considerations against new regulations on insurance distribution. In: Malinowska K, Tarasiuk A (eds) Insurance challenges of Anno Domini 2018. Publikacja jubileuszowa AIDA 2018, Warszawa

Marano P (2017a) The 'Mifidization': the sunset of life insurance in the EU regulation on insurance? Liber Amicorum for Professor Ioannis Rokas, NOMIKH BIBΛIOΘHKH, Athens

Marano P (2017b) Sources and tools of the insurance regulation in the European Union. In: Marano P, Siri M (eds) Insurance regulation in the European Union. Solvency II and beyond. Palgrave Macmillan

Mrozowska-Bartkiewicz B (2016) Jakie zmiany dla polskiego rynku ubezpieczeń przyniesie Dyrektywa w sprawie dystrybucji ubezpieczeń? (What changes will the Directive on insurance distribution bring to the Polish insurance market?). Wiadomości Ubezpieczeniowe v. 2/2016, Warsaw

Noussia K, Siri M (2019) The legal regime and the relevant standards. In: Marano P, Rokas I (eds) Distribution of insurance-based investment products. The EU regulation and the liabilities. Springer

Nowak J (2018) In: Czublun P (ed) Ustawa o dystrybucji ubezpieczeń. Komentarz. Insurance Distribution Act. Comment. CH Beck, Warszawa

Orlicka J (2015) Zakaz stosowania klauzul abuzywnych i missellingu w znowelizowanej ustawie o ochronie konkurencji i konsumentów (Prohibition on the application of abusive clauses and misselling in the revised consumer and competition protection act). Prawo Asekuracyjne v. 4/2015

Orlicki M (2016) Projektowanie typu ubezpieczenia ("produktu ubezpieczeniowego") według rekomendacji KNF dla zakładów ubezpieczeń dotyczących systemu zarządzania produktem (Insurance type (insurance product) design pursuant to the PFSA's recommendations for insurance companies about product management system), Prawo Asekuracyjne v. 3/2016

Orlicki M (2017) Aksjologia dystrybucji ubezpieczeń – kryteria uznawania działań dystrybutora za zgodne z prawem i etyczne (Axiology of insurance distribution - criteria for considering the distributor's activities legal and ethical). In: Gnela B, Szaraniec M (eds) Dystrybucja usług ubezpieczeniowych. Wybrane zagadnienia prawne (Distribution of insurance services. Selected legal issues). Warszawa

Paś W (2018) Obowiązek działania przez agenta ubezpieczeniowego zgodnie z najlepiej pojętym interesem klienta a jego lojalność wobec zakładu ubezpieczeń (The insurance agent's obligation to act in accordance with the customer's best interests in the context of his loyalty to the insurance company). In: Malinowska K, Tarasiuk A (eds) Insurance challenges of Anno Domini 2018. Publikacja jubileuszowa AIDA 2018, Warszawa

Pokrzywniak J (2018) Obowiązek rozpoznania wymagań i potrzeb klienta (Obligation to identify customer requirements and needs). In: Pokrzywniak J (ed) Nowe zasady dystrybucji ubezpieczeń (New rules for insurance distribution). Warsaw

Tarasiuk A, Wojno B (2018) Analiza wymagań i potrzeb klienta w procesie dystrybucji ubezpieczeń (Demands and needs analysis in the process of insurance distribution). Prawo asekuracyjne 3/2018, Warszawa

Wędrychowska-Karpińska A, Wiercińska-Krużewska A (2016) Komentarz do art. 24 ustawy o ochronie konkurencji i konsumentów (Commentary on article 24 of the act on competition and consumer protection). In: Stawicki A, Stawicki E (eds) Ustawa o ochronie konkurencji i konsumentów (Competition and Consumer Protection Act). Comment, wyd. II

Wojno B (2017a) Komentarz do art. 365 ustawy o działalności ubezpieczeniowej i reasekuracyjnej (Commentary to Article 365 of the Polish act on insurance and reinsurance activity). In: Szczepańska M, Wajda P (eds) Ustawa o działalności ubezpieczeniowej i reasekuracyjnej (Polish act on insurance and reinsurance activity. Commentary). Warsaw

Wojno B (2017b) Komentarz do art. 362 ustawy o działalności ubezpieczeniowej i reasekuracyjnej (Commentary to Article 362 of the Polish act on insurance and reinsurance activity). In: Szczepańska M, Wajda P (eds) Ustawa o działalności ubezpieczeniowej i reasekuracyjnej (Polish act on insurance and reinsurance activity. Commentary). Warsaw

Ziemniak MP (2019) Wynagrodzenie pośrednika ubezpieczeniowego w kontekście ustawy o dystrybucji ubezpieczeń. Zagadnienia wybrane (Remuneration of insurance intermediary in the context of insurance distribution act. Selected issues). "Wiadomości Ubezpieczeniowe" v. 2/2019, Warszawa

Insurance Distribution Carried Out by Insurers in Spain

Javier Vercher-Moll

1 Introduction

When legal operators embark on the study of insurance law, they must delineate which part of this regulatory block will be the object of their study. The law of private insurance can be defined as "*the set of legal norms that specifically discipline the status of the private insurer, that of its collaborators and that of the insurance contract*".[1] This is an area in which rules of public and private law converge, and this convergence is most acute in the hierarchy of applicable sources.[2]

The status of the private insurance entrepreneur is currently regulated by *Law 20/2015, of July 14, on the organization, supervision and solvency of insurance and reinsurance entities*, which transposes *Directive 2009/138/EC of the European Parliament and of the Council of 25 November 2009 on the taking-up and pursuit of the business of Insurance and Reinsurance (Solvency II)*. The collaborators of the insurer, whose activity is focused on the distribution or production of insurance, either directly by the insurer or through a third party, is regulated mainly by *Law 26/2006, of July 17, of insurance and private reinsurance mediation*, which transposes *Directive 2002/92/EC of the European Parliament and of the Council of 9 December 2002 on insurance mediation* into the Spanish legislation. Finally, the insurance contract constitutes the third regulatory block of the private insurance system, and it is regulated by *Law 50/1980, of October 8, on the Insurance Contract*.

This study has been carried out as part of the Research Project I+D "Hacia una protección del cliente más global". AICO2019/075. Generalitat Valenciana.

[1] Sánchez Calero (1961), p. 14.
[2] Del Caño Escudero (1971), p. 11.

J. Vercher-Moll (✉)
University of Valencia, Valencia, Spain
e-mail: javier.vercher@uv.es

P. Marano, K. Noussia (eds.), *Insurance Distribution Directive*, AIDA Europe Research Series on Insurance Law and Regulation 3,
https://doi.org/10.1007/978-3-030-52738-9_8

The legal regime applicable to the insurer can be divided into four fundamental sections: access to the insurance activity, that is, the insurance company's capacity to insure the assets of the insured party before an accident; the exercise of the activity, that is the guidelines that exist to safeguard the solvency of the insurance company so that it can provide the compensation to which it is contractually obliged; the system of infractions and penalties designed to prevent situations created by the insurance company that could endanger the solvency of the entity, or harm the insurance market in general; and finally, the intervention regime of the insurance entity that can the revoke its administrative authorization, and order its dissolution and liquidation.

A novel feature of this regulatory regime, and one that has not been the subject of attention to date, is the sale of insurance by the insurance company itself, a matter regulated by the new *Directive (EU) 2016/97 of the European Parliament and of the Council of 20 January 2016 on insurance distribution*. A priori, such regulation could be seen as superfluous because it is obvious that the insurer, as a commercial company, can offer and sell its services just like any other. In this sense, it would seem that nothing new is added by art. 10 of the Directive, given that it simply recognizes the factual circumstance that insurance companies demonstrate their corporate objective by contracting their products with customers.

However, despite this apparent superficiality, the justification for the article is that it imposes the same contractual obligations on all operators that offer insurance, so that differences between them are overcome for the benefit of uniformity.[3]

The preparatory work that led to the Directive[4] evidences the concern of the European Commission for mediation in private insurance. The objectives of the Directive are : to attempt to resolve the differences in consumer protection that depend on where the product is purchased, to eliminate conflicts of interest between the consumer and the seller of insurance products occasioned by the remuneration of the latter; to overcome deficiencies in the information provided on the insurance product, whether due to bias caused by the insurance seller's system of compensation, or by insufficient technical training of the insurance sales personnel; to regulate the penalties that may be imposed in relation to the sale of insurance; and to promote access to cross-border markets, both through the free provision of services and the right of freedom of establishment.

The Directive attempts to answer the criticisms made by legal scholars[5] regarding *Directive 2002/92/EC of the European Parliament and of the Council of 9 December 2002 on insurance mediation*, which excluded the sale of insurance through the insurance company itself from the mediation activity. Thus, insurance companies are now considered to be insurance distributors, which places them on equal terms with respect to other distributors.

[3]Hofmann et al. (2018), p. 743.

[4]COM (2012) 360 final, SWD (2012) 191 final.

[5]Bataller Grau (2007), pp. 112–113.

The new Directive establishes the same conditions of competition for all insurance distributors, which benefits insurance consumers, as it makes it easier for them to enjoy the same level of protection despite the obvious differences between the distribution channels. It is an example of the phenomenon known as "Mifidization", after the Mifid regulations for the sale of insurance.[6]

The term "Mifidization" refers to the increase of consumer protection standards in insurance, even though the Mifid regulations do not apply to a specific insurance product. This impact on insurance affects the legal regulatory sources of insurance, the design of insurance products and their distribution, the protection of consumers, and the interpretation of the regulations governing life insurance.[7]

From the 2002 Directive up until the present day the legal panorama of the insurance business has changed radically. The reforms introduced in the areas relating to contractual information and the supervision and solvency of insurance entities, together with the constant evolution of the case-law interprets the insurance contract, obliges us to explain the transcendence of this precept within the existing regulatory framework.

From a contractual point of view, insurance companies that contract directly with their clients must act on equal terms with respect to other insurance distributors, so that there is no distinction with regard to their the duty to provide information on insurance products.[8]

In order to ensure equality among insurance distributors, the Directive also introduces an important novelty, as it requires compliance with certain subjective criterion of the employees of any company that distributes insurance, as well as of their insurance sales directors and managers. It is therefore pertinent to consider whether the regulation represents, not only a reformulation of the system of governance of insurance companies, but also whether, in attention to the principles of corporate governance and supervision it contains, the Directive will require the reformulation of the internal infrastructure of insurance companies, the concepts of the honourability and aptitude that must be shown by their employees, and the powers granted to the supervisory authorities of the Member States.

The problems posed by the Directive are not simple, because they might entail an urgent reform of current regulations.

From the perspective of corporate governance, it is worth asking whether the four fundamental areas that make up the governance system of insurance companies have become obsolete. The direct sale of insurance by insurers requires the creation of a new, autonomous area to complement the companies' systems of governance, and this begs the question of whether the reform of corporate governance is therefore necessary.

---

[6]Marano (2017b), p. 10.

[7]Marano (2017a), p. 416.

[8]Quintans Eiras (2018), pp. 373–420; Miranda Serrano (2017), pp. 287–320; Peñas Moyano (2017), pp. 321–340.

The Directive requires certain subjective requirements of sales staff. They must have sufficient knowledge, skills and honorability to perform such work. These criteria deserve further examination as they contain important details regarding the training that the employees of the insurance company must have, who must possess the quality of honorability and what it means to be honorable in this context.

In any case, the Directive is a minimum standard. It lays down the minimum bases for Member States to transpose the Directive into their national law. This can generate both benefits and drawbacks. As a benefit, States may increase the level of consumer protection but, as a disadvantage, this may result in the level of protection of insurance consumers not being the same in each country.

2 Governance System of Insurance Companies

Articles 258 to 272 of the Commission Delegated Regulation (EU) 2015/35 establish the regulation for the system of governance of insurance companies. All insurers and reinsurers are required to have an effective system of governance that guarantees the sound and prudent management of the activity and that is proportionate to its nature, volume and the complexity of its operations.

The company's system of governance must encompass the following functions: risk management, compliance verification, and internal and actuarial audits. In addition, it must contain written corporate governance policies that will include, among others, a transparent and appropriate organizational structure, with a clear distribution and adequate separation of functions, effective mechanisms to guarantee the transmission of information, and remuneration policies and practices adapted to suit the characteristics of the companies.[9]

Remuneration is one of the areas focused upon in the new Directive. Article 17.3 determines that "*insurance distributors are not remunerated or do not remunerate or assess the performance of their employees in a way that conflicts with their duty to act in accordance with the best interests of their customers. In particular, an insurance distributor shall not make any arrangement by way of remuneration, sales targets or otherwise that could provide an incentive to itself or its employees to recommend a particular insurance product to a customer when the insurance distributor could offer a different insurance product which would better meet the customer's needs*". This provokes a situation which, as legal scholars have pointed out, leads to the coexistence of two types of remuneration: fixed remuneration for salaries or fees and variable remuneration based on the commissions earnt on the volume of insurance policies sold.[10]

The question which needs to be examined here is how article 10 fits into the system of corporate governance outlined in the Directive, as, from a first reading of

[9]Tapia Hermida (2016), pp. 331–350.

[10]Hofmann et al. (2018), p. 749.

the text, direct sales do not seem to have a place within the framework of internal functions it creates for insurance companies.

It goes without saying that the Directive imposes a series of minimum requirements for the corporate governance of insurance companies, and that, having delimited these functions as those that are essential for the healthy and prudent management of insurance entities, the law requires that insurance companies incorporate them into their organizational structures. The exact area in which direct sales can best be included needs to be established, and this task entails an analysis of each of the areas covered by the Directive.

Risk management includes all the strategies, procedures and information processing necessary to identify, measure, monitor, manage and continuously report on the risks to which, both individually and in aggregate, the company faces. The risk management system must be effective and fully integrated into the organizational and decision making structures of the company, and has to cover directors or those that exercise managerial authority over the company. Insurance and reinsurance companies have to establish a risk management function to facilitate the application of the system.

The compliance verification function must advise management about compliance with any legal, regulatory and administrative provisions affecting the company, as well as compliance with its internal regulations. This has to include evaluations of the impact of any modifications of the legal environment on the company's operations and the determination and evaluation of compliance risk.

The internal audit includes checking the adequacy and effectiveness of the internal control system and other elements of the company's governance system. The internal audit function should be objective and independent of the operational functions. The conclusions and recommendations derived from the internal audit must be notified to the management body, which will determine what actions should be taken with respect to each of them and ensure that such actions are carried out.

Finally, with respect to the actuarial function, this must be carried out by people who have sufficient knowledge of actuarial and financial mathematics, in accordance with the nature, volume and complexity of the risks inherent to the activity of insurance or reinsurance companies, and who can accredit relevant experience in relation to professional and other applicable standards.

Having briefly examined these four fundamental functions of the entities, it is pertinent to question whether there is a place for direct sales in any of them according to their nature. In the opinion of the author, the direct sales of an insurance company are the maximum expression of the deployment and development of the company's corporate purpose. Direct sales generate risks that must be controlled and monitored by the risk management unit, so a priori, the sale of insurance could be channeled through this area. However, maintaining such a position would result in diminishing the importance of the risk function, which monitors not only those risks derived directly from the corporate purpose, but also those of any another nature that are not related to the sales activity.

It is therefore worth pondering whether director sales should constitute a specific area that must necessarily be provided, in the image and likeness of other functions, with specific policies and procedures.

3 A New Area?

If I analyze the organizational structure of the insurance companies that operate in the Spanish market, I may observe the enormous development enjoyed by the commercial units in recent decades. Not surprisingly, it is a function of great importance because, as previously indicated, it implies the deployment of the company's corporate purpose.

Direct sales by insurance companies will involve the creation of a specific area, equipped with specific policies, with appropriate and updated procedural manuals, as well as, with an orderly and modern infrastructure. All of this is necessary in order to: respect the rights of customers, quickly and efficiently manage the coverage or claims, and minimize the risks and, therefore, the damages that can be generated to the company itself, as well as improving the efficiency of management so as to maximize the company's profit.

This area should be controlled by the other areas that make up the insurance company's governance system. I can consider that the commercial area is the place where the activity of the insurance company is fully developed. It is the area that is in contact with the company's client: the one that contracts, the one that knows the daily needs of the clients, etc. For all these reasons, the rest of the areas of the government system must control this area from different prisms.

The compliance area must review insurance contracts, abusive clauses, customer information, contract updates, etc. The risk area must review the company's risk limit according to the volume of insurance policies, must also review the accident rate, must review if there are claims against the insurance company, must create a contingency plan exclusively for the commercial area, etc.

The actuarial area must review the matching of flows with the accident rates, so that the insurer can pay the indemnities to the insured. The internal audit area must review the policies of the commercial area, the updating of its procedure manuals, the benefits it generates for the insurer, proposals for improvement in the management of the commercial area, etc.

An efficient management of the commercial area will be important for the future development of the insurance company. On the one hand, this area will provide important information to the marketing area in order to know how to design advertising, to emphasize the characteristics of the company's insurance policies, to orient advertising towards certain groups of people. On the other hand, the information from the commercial area will also be important for the development of new businesses, that is, to know the new needs of the insurance company's clients and, therefore, to create insurance policies that adjust to the new needs of the insured.

Finally, the commercial area will offer information on the reputational value that the insurer has in the insurance market. If the commercial area has direct contact with the client, thanks to the surveys, it will be able to know the clients' opinion about the company. This information is important for the insurance company's management team. Managers will be able to evaluate not only the insurance company's turnover, but also people's opinions about the company.

Thus, according to article 17 of the Directive, advertising communications made by insurance companies to customers or potential customers must be accurate, clear and not misleading, as well as clearly identifiable as such. Consequently, the decisions of the clients will be informed, that is, the client will have full conviction of the insurance product that he/she is going to contract. In this point, the insurance sales area has an important responsibility, given that it knows the type of clients and their needs, to not target consumers with biased advertising communications designed to affect the free decision making capacity of customers or prospective customers. In this sense, it must promptly inform the Marketing Area of the limits of the advertisements it creates.

The fundamental idea contained in article 20 of the Directive is that before the conclusion of an insurance contract, the insurance distributor must specify, based on information obtained from the client, the requirements and needs of said client and provide the client with objective information about the insurance product in a comprehensible manner, so that the client can make an informed decision.

At this point, I should focus on the analysis of the subjective requirements of the employees of the insurance company, because the new Directive emphasizes the technical capacity of the people who distribute insurance through the company, in order to strengthen the company's governance system and guarantee the rights of its customers.

4 The Requirements of Good Repute

Article 10 of the Directive is dedicated to regulating the details of the distribution activity by insurance companies. In its first paragraph, it states that insurance companies must ensure that the employees who participate directly in insurance distribution activities, the people responsible for the distribution activity, or, where appropriate, those who are part of the management body responsible for the distribution activity, meet the requirement of commercial and professional honorability.

Without prejudice to the analysis of the requirement of commercial and professional honorability, the article refers directly to a group of people that form the core of the distribution activity within the company.

The subjective requirements demand that the staff affected by them have sufficient authority to manage the destiny of part of the company.[11] That is, unlike the regulations applicable to entities operating within the financial markets, the Directive amplifies the reach of certain subjective requirements to the collective, given that the person who has effective contact with the client shall also be subject to assessment.

To assess a person's commercial honor, it is necessary to study the commercial history, the sanctions imposed, the investigations on the person, etc. The problem is that there is no mathematical rule that solves whether a person has a good reputation. The Spanish regulations have made an important effort to detail the Directive, in order to determine whether the persons responsible for the commercial area, and the employees, have a good commercial reputation. In any case, it will be the supervisor of each country who will have the capacity to determine whether a director or an employee of the commercial area of the insurer is honorable.

The aforementioned persons must meet the requirements of commercial and professional honorability provided in art. 2.19 of the Spanish Law 3/2020.[12] The definition of these concepts offered in this article indicates that they consist of the "*quality applicable to those that have observed a personal trajectory of respect for commercial or other laws that regulate economic activity and business life, as well as to good commercial, financial and insurance practices. Said condition shall apply to those persons who do not have a criminal record for having committed criminal offences related to the exercise of financial activities, and who have not been sanctioned in the administrative field in insurance, banking, the securities market, Public Finance, Social Security, Competition Law, the movement of capital, economic transactions abroad, money laundering and the financing of terrorism and the protection of consumers and users, for the commission of offences classified as very serious or serious. The disqualification from the exercise of public or administrative positions and from the management of financial entities, as well as that declared in accordance with Law 22/2003, of July 9, on Insolvency, until the period of fixed disqualification, or the state of bankrupt or not rehabilitated bankrupt in the case of insolvency proceedings prior to the entry into force of the aforementioned law, shall also be considered as circumstances that do not allow for compliance with the honorability requirement*".

From a first reading of this paragraph, it would seem that the requirement of honorability is based on a broad concept, whose margin of appreciation by the *Dirección General de Seguros y Fondos de Pensiones* is extensive. However, it can be reduced to a series of specific and relatively simple questions. In effect, any person who does not have a criminal record, or who has not received sanctions or disqualification from the exercise of public office or from the administration and

---

[11]Vercher Moll (2016), p. 350.

[12]Real Decreto-ley 3/2020, de 4 de febrero, de medidas urgentes por el que se incorporan al ordenamiento jurídico español diversas directivas de la Unión Europea en el ámbito de la contratación pública en determinados sectores; de seguros privados; de planes y fondos de pensiones; del ámbito tributario y de litigios fiscales.

management of financial companies as a result of the commission of infractions or crimes of an economic nature is considered to be honorable.

The definition offered here is less broad than those contained in the regulations of the entities that operate in the financial market,[13] because it appears to establish a clear distinction between the governing bodies, which have effective management as general directors and/or director's delegates, of the persons appointed to sell insurance within the company. However, in order to make an integrative interpretation of the Spanish Draft with the regulatory and supervisory regulations of the companies that operate in the financial market, the *Dirección General de Seguros y Fondos de Pensiones* seems to make a broad interpretation of the subjective requirements. However, this is not the "*mens legis*" of the Directive, because the subject of the requirement is an employee of the insurance entity, and the degree of requirement cannot be compared to that contained in (for example) Law 20/2015.

5 The Appropriate Knowledge

Apart from the requirement of honorability, art. 10.2 of the Directive imposes the obligation "*that insurance and reinsurance intermediaries and employees of insurance and reinsurance undertakings and employees of insurance and reinsurance intermediaries comply with continuing professional training and development requirements in order to maintain an adequate level of performance corresponding to the role they perform and the relevant market*".

In addition, the Directive states that the "*member States need not apply the requirements referred to all the natural persons working in an insurance or reinsurance undertaking, or insurance or reinsurance intermediary, who pursue the activity of insurance or reinsurance distribution, but Member States shall ensure that the relevant persons within the management structure of such undertakings who are responsible for distribution in respect of insurance and reinsurance products and all other persons directly involved in insurance or reinsurance distribution demonstrate the knowledge and ability necessary for the performance of their duties*".

The Spanish Law 3/2020 indicates in article 139 that insurance companies must ensure that employees directly involved in distribution activities, the person responsible for the distribution activity or, where appropriate, at least half of the people who are part of the management body responsible for the activity of distribution, possess appropriate knowledge and skills by passing training courses.

The recipients of this mandate are the insurance companies, and it applies to the same people as the honorability requirement, that is, the employees involved in the distribution of insurance products, the person responsible for said distribution or, at least half of the people who are part of the management body responsible. However,

[13] Vercher Moll (2017), p. 120.

the literal tenor of the precept is surprising, not because of the training requirement, whose purpose is satisfying the demands of the knowledge requirement, but because it does not place all the people to whom the aforementioned knowledge requirement is demanded on equal terms.

It is logical that employees, who have direct contact with the client are required to have certain knowledge, because it supposes a definite guarantee for the client or potential client. In this sense it is similar to article 25 of the (now repealed) *Law 26/2006, of July 17, on insurance and private reinsurance mediation*, according to which the banking-insurance operator was obliged to establish a training program for employees that participated directly in insurance mediation. However, article 139 of the Spanish Law 3/2020 suffers from the same logical defect as article 25 did, because it does not seem reasonable that only half of the management body responsible for the distribution activity has to possess the appropriate knowledge and skills in this matter.

This requirement means breaking one of the most basic principles of corporate governance. Indeed, valuable work has been carried out by legal scholars[14] in order to increase controls and ensure the sound and prudent management of commercial companies. In this regard, one could mention of the Proposal of the Businessmen's Circle of October 1996, the Code of Good Governance in Spain (Olivencia Code of 1998), the Aldama Report of 2003, the Unified Code of Good Governance of 2006 (Code Conthe) and its update in June 2013 and the Code of listed companies of February 2015 (Rodríguez Code).

It is the management body responsible for the distribution activity that must provide the greatest guarantees in terms of knowledge and fitness for the position, since otherwise the operational risk[15] of the company is increased, which may lead to a violation of clients' rights, as well as incurring sanctions imposed by the *Dirección General de Seguros y Fondos de Pensiones*, so the proper conclusion to draw is that all the people who compose the management body responsible for the distribution activity should possess appropriate knowledge and skills.

6 Professional Training

In order to maintain the adequate knowledge and skills for staff in the insurance distribution function, article 10.2 of the Directive includes the following obligation "*home Member States shall ensure that insurance and reinsurance intermediaries and employees of insurance and reinsurance undertakings and employees of insurance and reinsurance intermediaries comply with continuing professional training and development requirements in order to maintain an adequate level of performance corresponding to the role they perform and the relevant market.*

[14]Díaz Ruiz (2010), pp. 263–290; Esteban Velasco (2010), pp. 267–290.

[15]Vercher Moll (2018), pp. 143–162.

To that end, home Member States shall have in place and publish mechanisms to control effectively and assess the knowledge and competence of insurance and reinsurance intermediaries and employees of insurance and reinsurance undertakings and employees of insurance and reinsurance intermediaries, based on at least 15 hours of professional training or development per year, taking into account the nature of the products sold, the type of distributor, the role they perform, and the activity carried out within the insurance or reinsurance distributor.

Home Member States may require that the successful completion of the training and development requirements is proven by obtaining a certificate".

This obligation is included in art. 139.2 of the Spanish Law 3/2020, which states that insurance companies must establish continuous training plans. However, the legal classificatory structure of the article could be improved because in the third paragraph it indicates that these training plans will be adapted to bases determined by the *Dirección General de Seguros y Fondos de Pensiones*. However, this point is a minor issue, the important one is the obligation imposed on the insurance company.

The continuous training programs must be adapted: to the products distributed, to the function staff perform and to the activities they carry out, and the training programs established must indicate, at least, the requirements to be fulfilled by the people for whom they are created and the means to be employed for their execution. The documentation corresponding to the training programs will be available at the *Dirección General de Seguros y Fondos de Pensiones.*

Therefore, in the opinion of the author, and in line with the distinctions between the staff who occupy the function of distributing the products, it is possible to differentiate various stages of training for employees depending on a host of factors: the type of product, the regulations that affect it, the client's rights and obligations, the procedure to be followed; the people responsible for the distribution activity and/or the people who are part of the management body responsible for the distribution activity. In addition to the aforementioned matters, the training must take account of the existing contingency plans, the company's governance system, the distribution of functions, the firm's procedures and policies, the alert systems in place for warning of outdated products, etc.

Finally, as already indicated, the *Dirección General de Seguros y Fondos de Pensiones* will establish, by resolution, the general lines and basic principles that, in terms of their content, organization and execution, will have to be met by the initial and continuous training programs for the employees of insurance companies, for the people responsible for the distribution activity as well as, where appropriate, for the people who are part of the management body responsible for the distribution activity.

7 The Policies and Procedures

Article 10.8 of the Directive establishes that "*insurance and reinsurance undertakings shall approve, implement and regularly review their internal policies and appropriate internal procedures. Insurance and reinsurance undertakings shall identify a function to ensure the proper implementation of the endorsed policies and procedures*".

This generic obligation is specified in art. 25 of the Directive. In its first paragraph, it states that the "*insurance undertakings, as well as intermediaries which manufacture any insurance product for sale to customers, shall maintain, operate and review a process for the approval of each insurance product, or significant adaptations of an existing insurance product, before it is marketed or distributed to customers. The product approval process shall be proportionate and appropriate to the nature of the insurance product. The product approval process shall specify an identified target market for each product, ensure that all relevant risks to such identified target market are assessed and that the intended distribution strategy is consistent with the identified target market, and take reasonable steps to ensure that the insurance product is distributed to the identified target market*".

Article 139.4 of the Spanish Law 3/2020, states that insurance companies will periodically approve, apply and review their internal policies and appropriate internal procedures. Likewise, insurers must determine a function that guarantees the correct execution of the approved policies and procedures, and the name of the person responsible for that function should be made available to the *Dirección General de Seguros y Fondos de Pensiones*.

This article, in fact, does not introduce any novelty, since the mandate that insurance companies should have appropriate policies and procedures is an obligation that is regulated in Law 20/2015, which transposes the Solvency II Directive. Perhaps, the only novelty at this point is given by the need for such documentation to be developed within the distribution function of the company's products.

In any case, as article 65.2 of Law 20/2015 states, the "*governance system will include written corporate governance policies that will include, among others, a transparent and appropriate organizational structure, with a clear distribution and adequate separation of functions, effective mechanisms to ensure the transmission of information, and remuneration policies and practices appropriate to the characteristics of the companies*"; so that it is a global obligation within the company that affects all of its functions.

Therefore, the policy of the commercial area should reflect the general principles of the company's commercial area and, in addition, the principles for approving specific insurance products. These principles should be set out in procedural manuals for the approval of insurance policies that the company wishes to market.

As a general rule, the policies of the commercial areas of insurance companies usually establish operating principles. With the clients: the company will be transparent, explain the insurance premium, explain the conditions of the contract, methods of payment of the premium, not oblige the client to contract, explain the contracting procedure to the client, clarify doubts to the client about the insurance policy. About the company's image: transmitting confidence to the client, training the commercial network about the insurance product and about the regulations, hiring highly competitive managers. On other insurance companies: watch over the products of other insurance companies, do not discredit other companies, etc.

Article 139 indicates that the *Dirección General de Seguros y Fondos de Pensiones* will be informed of the name of the person responsible for the review of the policies and procedures. In the opinion of the author, this function can be assumed by the internal auditor, given that the evaluation is carried out within the company according to its functions.

Article 66.4 of Law 20/2015 indicates that "*insurance and reinsurance companies will have an effective internal audit function, which will include checking the adequacy and effectiveness of the internal control system and other elements of the company's governance system and will be carried out in accordance with the provisions of the regulation of management, supervision and solvency of insurance and reinsurance companies and of the account audit activity*", however, it emphatically states that "*the internal audit function must be objective and independent of the operational functions*", which leads us to distinguish between the internal audit function and the person responsible for executing the policies and procedures regarding the distribution of products.

Finally, it should not be overlooked that the norm does not require any subjective requirements for the person responsible for that function. At this point, given that the activity consists in the control of policies and procedures, which is nothing more than the deployment of the company's corporate purpose in the market, it would appear that the previously studied requirements should be equally applicable and enforceable on the person in charge of the control function of policies and procedures.

8 The Supervision of the DGSFP

To conclude, the article 139 of the Spanish Law 3/2020 gives the *Dirección General de Seguros y Fondos de Pensiones* (DGSFP) broad powers of control over insurance companies with regard to the distribution of their products. Thus, on the one hand, this Public Administrative body will have control over the registry that insurance companies must establish to enroll employees who participate directly in insurance distribution activities, as well as the person responsible for the distribution activity or, where appropriate, the people who are part of the management body responsible for the distribution activity. On the other hand, the insurance companies will register in the Register of the *Dirección General de Seguros y Fondos de Pensiones* the person responsible for the distribution activity and, where appropriate, the people who are part of the management body responsible for the activities of distribution.

However, the most important question is what happens if the DGSFP considers that an employee of the company does not have a good reputation or adequate knowledge to distribute the insurer's insurance. This can be a major problem because the insurer may have to dismiss the employee if he or she is not reputable. Perhaps, there is no problem if the employee does not have sufficient knowledge, because the insurance company can provide training in this regard.

Spanish labour law does not regulate what happens when a company employee does not have a good reputation. The question is whether or not the dismissal is lawful. In this situation, the insurance company will have to supervise its employees in order to know if they have a good reputation or not. In this regard, if the DGSFP considers that an insurance company employee does not have a good reputation, the insurance company may have to dismiss the employee. It would be advisable to synchronise insurance distribution regulations with labour regulations.

9 Conclusions

The new European Directive creates a major transformation in the distribution of insurance. From a structural point of view, the new requirements for insurance companies are of incalculable impact at the moment. The main beneficiary of the reform is the client of the insurer, the reasons are of diverse nature but, fundamentally, because the client will be advised and informed in a prudent way before contracting an insurance policy. The client will be able to understand what he/she is contracting with the insurance company. In addition, the company's insurance salesmen must be knowledgeable, skilled and honest, which guarantees the best advice to the client.

In addition, the Directive controls all persons or companies distributing insurance. The Directive regulates both the conditions of access to the distribution market and the conditions of operation. This facilitates public control and supervision, which is carried out on the entire financial system, of any form of distribution of insurance products, whether directly by the insurer or by any other intermediary.

Perhaps there is a discrepancy between the Directive and the rules governing the insurance contract. The information obligations for the client are duplicated, those of the new Directive and those of the insurance contract. In addition, the Solvency II Directive also contains an obligation for the insurer to inform the client about the insurance contract. This leads to overprotection which is not necessary. The most important thing is that there should be an orderly information statute for the client.

Therefore, the question is: How many more information obligations will the client be more protected? In any case, these obligations aim to increase transparency in the insurance market as a guarantee of confidence, stability and good marketing of products. The important thing is that the distributor knows the customer and his needs, mainly because there are many clients with limited financial education and sometimes they do not really know their risks to be insured.

The new Insurance Distribution Directive stimulates the need to reform all Solvency II regulations. The governance system established by the Solvency II Directive was a major step forward in creating insurance companies with transparent structures. The requirements to have policies and procedures in each area of the governance system allowed for improved company management and for supervisors in each country to better perform their monitoring task. However, the new Directive advises that the Solvency II regulations should be reformed.

The direct distribution made by the insurer and the new obligations for its employees make it advisable to create a specific area in the insurance company's governance system. The day to day shows how the insurers have a commercial area in their system of governance, but if I analyze the new Directive, it would be advisable to create a specific area more technical. The characteristics of this area could be at the same level as the other areas of the system of governance, such as the area of regulatory compliance, the actuarial area, the risk area, etc. This would increase the transparency of the insurer's structure.

Definitely, all these new demands are causing a profound reform in the corporate governance of insurance companies. The minimum requirements for the governance of insurance companies should be extended in order to recognise a new area of governance. The new area would be for the sale of the company's insurance products and the company would have its own standardised policies and procedures.

New requirements for insurance company employees who sell insurance are welcome. If the insurance company's management is required to be knowledgeable, skilled and honest, it is no exaggeration to say that lower-ranking employees are also required to be knowledgeable, skilled and honest, especially since the employees who distribute the insurance have daily contact with the customer. If the Solvency II regulation establishes the "fit and proper" principle for the insurance company's management, the same principle now applies to the employees who distribute the insurance. Obviously, the regulations cannot require the same knowledge of the insurance company's management as of the employees, but this is an important step towards the professionalization of the employees.

In order to ensure that employees comply with the requirements, the regulations establish continuous training for them. This idea is important, above all because insurance regulations, both life and non-life, are constantly developing and changing. Recycling knowledge will benefit customers, mainly because they will get better advice and because their rights will not be violated. In addition, employees will be able to understand which clauses in the insurance contract are illegal, so they will not use these clauses. Therefore, the insurance company's employees will also carry out quality control of the products that the insurer offers to the public.

On the other hand, new demands on the knowledge, skills and reputation of employees increase the internal risks of the insurance company. Auditors should analyse whether employees who distribute insurance are actually trained to do so. In order to avoid problems, the insurance company should hire employees with the appropriate knowledge or conduct training courses and examinations.

The supervisory bodies of each country will be able to know the employees who distribute insurance. This control will enable employees to complete a questionnaire to determine whether they can distribute insurance or need further studies to do so. In addition, the supervisors in each country will be able to sanction the insurance companies if the employees do not meet the requirements of knowledge, aptitude and honesty. Therefore, the principle of "fit and proper" is established for the employees of the insurance company that distributes insurance products.

In short, transparency, both in customer information and in the insurer's governance system, is the key to consumer satisfaction and confidence. Furthermore, it influences consumer loyalty, which is in the insurer's interest. Obviously, maintaining high levels of transparency entails costs, but this is a benefit for the insurer in the long term because it offers a good reputation image. In today's competitive insurance market, reputational risk is a major risk that insurers must control and mitigate.

References

Bataller Grau J (2007) La ley de ¿mediación? de seguros y reaseguros privados: su ámbito de aplicación. In: Comentarios a la Ley de mediación de seguros y reaseguros privados. Thomson-Civitas, Cizur Menor, pp 112–113
Del Caño Escudero F (1971) Derecho Español de Seguros. Imp. Góngora, Madrid
Díaz Ruiz E (2010) Códigos de conducta y mercados financieros: cuestiones generales. In: Códigos de conducta y actividad económica: una perspectiva jurídica. Marcial Pons, Madrid, pp 263–290
Esteban Velasco G (2010) Una aproximación a los códigos de buen gobierno en el marco y heterogéneo fenómeno de los códigos de conducta. In: Códigos de conducta y actividad económica: una perspectiva jurídica. Marcial Pons, Madrid, pp 267–290
Hofmann A, Neumannm JK, Pooser D (2018) Plea for uniform regulation and challenges of implementing the new Insurance Distribution Directive. In: The Geneva Papers, 43, Geneva, p 740
Marano P (2017a) La "Mifidización": el atardecer de los seguros de vida en la normativa europea sobre seguros? Revista Española de Seguros 171–172:416
Marano P (2017b) Sources and tools of the insurance regulation in the European Union. In: Insurance regulation in the European Union, solvency II and beyond. Palgrave Macmillan, Cham, p 10
Miranda Serrano L (2017) Transparencia en la contratación de seguros: condiciones generales y particulares. Revista Española de Seguros 171–172:287–320
Peñas Moyano MJ (2017) El deber general de información de los aseguradores a los tomadores, asegurados y beneficiarios. Revista Española de Seguros 171–172:321–340
Quintans Eiras MR (2018) Información como motor de la protección del asegurado en la comercialización de seguros. Revista Española de Seguros 175:373–420
Sánchez Calero F (1961) Curso de Derecho del Seguro Privado. Ediciones Nauta, Bilbao
Tapia Hermida AJ (2016) Los puntos críticos del proceso de implantación del sistema de gobierno de las entidades aseguradoras. Revista Española de Seguros 167:331–350
Vercher Moll J (2016) Las condiciones de acceso al mercado de las entidades aseguradoras. Marcial Pons, Madrid
Vercher Moll J (2017) Los requisitos subjetivos de los que ostentan la dirección efectiva en las sociedades del mercado financiero. Revista de Derecho Bancario y Bursátil 146:120
Vercher Moll J (2018) La transcendencia jurídica de la gestión de riesgos en las entidades de crédito. Revista de Derecho Bancario y Bursátil 150:143–162

Enaction of Chapter VII of the Insurance Distribution Directive: What Can Member States Learn from the Enforcement Failures of the United States?

Kathleen M. Defever

1 Introduction

We are entering a new era of insurance regulation, in which our economic systems continue to grow larger and more profitable, and the authorities tasked with regulation of insurance markets are facing more intense, complex challenges. Most people would agree that an overall increased prosperity is positive and beneficial for society—but in a capitalistic, free market-based system, when more wealth is created and concentrated, this creates more acute market powers. Market power per se is not problematic, but market leaders need the guidance of governmental authorities in order to ensure that their choices and methods geared toward profit maximization are not also causing damage to their own societies. With governmental regulation, economic activity can be guided with the aim of helping all of society to be richer and happier, as a whole.

In the European Union, insurance regulation was recently increased when the Commission issued the Insurance Distribution Directive (IDD), to regulate the methods in which insurance intermediaries are allowed to sell insurance products to consumers.[1] The IDD marks a significant progression toward increased uniformity of regulation across the entire European Union, and is more far-reaching in terms of regulatory detail. The IDD requires very specific actions of every insurance intermediary engaged in commerce in the EU member states, and prescribes specific

[1]Directive (EU) 2016/97 of the European Parliament and of the Council of 20 January 2016 on insurance distribution (recast), Text with EEA relevance.

K. M. Defever (✉)
DePaul University College of Law, Chicago, IL, USA

University of Connecticut School of Law, Hartford, CT, USA
e-mail: kathleen@defeverlaw.com

P. Marano, K. Noussia (eds.), *Insurance Distribution Directive*, AIDA Europe Research Series on Insurance Law and Regulation 3,
https://doi.org/10.1007/978-3-030-52738-9_9

punishments for infringements. In the United States, the current regulations applicable to intermediaries have been in place for several decades or more, so enough time has passed to gain insight into whether these regulations have been successful, and to what degree. We will particularly assess the enforcement regimes in the United States, and discuss their overall lack of effectiveness.

2 Broad Landscape of the Unites States' Regulation of Insurance Intermediaries

In the United States, insurance regulation is almost entirely the responsibility of the individual states. Typically, the U.S. Congress regulates all commerce which crosses state lines, and this would definitely include insurance sales.[2] However, because individual states regulated insurance commerce for nearly a century before Congress contemplated federal regulation, it was decided that the states would be allowed to continue their regulatory regimes and Congress would only intervene when it was necessary.[3] Since then, Congress has only intervened on a few topics of insurance, such as terrorism insurance, flood insurance, employee retirement plans, and group health and disability coverages.

Most insurance regulation originates with the individual state insurance commissioners, who collectively comprise the National Association of Insurance Commissioners (NAIC). The NAIC drafts the model insurance laws which are then typically adopted, in part or in full, by the individual states. However, there is no requirement that the states adopt these model laws, and no requirement that the adopted laws are enforced. NAIC model acts are merely advisory tools, and despite their careful drafting, they have had little success in achieving uniformity of American insurance laws.

The primary body of law applied to insurance intermediaries in the United States is the Producer Licensing Model Act (PLMA), authored by the NAIC and adopted in some form by 40 states.[4] The Act is meant to govern "the qualification and procedures for the licensing of insurance producers," and "simplif[y] and organize some statutory language to improve efficiency... and reduce costs associated with issuing and renewing insurance licenses."[5] The PLMA defines an insurance producer as "a person required to be licensed under the laws of this state to sell, solicit or negotiate insurance."

In part, the PLMA details recommended licensing procedures, supplies reasons for revocation or denial of licenses, addresses which types of paid commissions are

---

[2]Gibbons v. Ogden (1824); United States v. South-Eastern Underwriters Association (1944).

[3]"[N]o act of Congress shall be construed to invalidate, impair, or supersede any law enacted by any State for the purpose of regulating the business of insurance... unless such Act specifically relates to the business of insurance."; 15 U.S.C. §1012(b).

[4]Producer Licensing Model Act (2005), National Association of Insurance Commissioners, found at: https://www.naic.org/store/free/MDL-218.pdf.

[5]Relevant material quoted from Section 1. Purpose and Scope, PLMA (2005).

allowed, and outlines recommended compensation disclosures. While the PLMA does briefly address how violations of the Act may be handled by state insurance commissioners, it mostly leaves the details to the individual states. This will be addressed further in Sects. 4 and 5.

In the United States, legislatively-drafted insurance regulations like the PLMA are bolstered by the common law system, otherwise known as case law, or court-issued decisions.[6] Ostensibly, where the legislators have failed, the courts can act as a "check and balance"[7] and issue proclamations which bolster—or which put into question—the regulations. However, these two branches of government (legislative and judiciary) are only able to bolster and improve one another when each branch is working efficiently. As we will discuss, the current system of United States "checks and balances" is not operating efficiently and is unable to build and support the level of regulatory clarity and enforcement which is needed to sustain an optimally healthy economic environment for insurance intermediaries and their customers.

3 Insurance Distribution Directive Overview

The Insurance Distribution Directive is the successor of the Insurance Mediation Directive (IMD),[8] and as such is wider in scope and more specific in commandment. The primary relevant objectives listed in the recitals are as follows—minimum harmonization among the Member States; increased consumer protection and better information provision for customers—including the creation of a standardized insurance product information document, comparable standards which bring consumers more predictability, analysis of the consumers "demands and needs" before sale, and provision of personalized advice for customer; ensuring the orderly pursuit of insurance business and fair treatment by regulatory authorities; creation of a single information point for registers of insurance intermediaries; coordination of Member State licensing provisions; establishment of out-of-court redress procedures; protection of consumers from intermediary conflicts of interest; transparency of intermediary remuneration; a new product development governance procedure[9]; and the provision of different methods of enforcement, including monetary sanctions and criminal sanctions.

---

[6]*See* Viscusi, Kip, *Regulation through Litigation* (2002) for more detailed discussion on this concept.

[7]Definition of U.S. concept of "checks and balances" can be found at: https://legaldictionary.net/checks-and-balances/, last visited September 25, 2019.

[8]Directive (EU) 2002/92/EC of the European Parliament and of the Council of 9 December 2002 on insurance mediation.

[9]Notably, in the United States product oversight and governance is managed by the individual state insurance commissioners through entirely separate insurance codes which generally apply to insurance companies and their products—product oversight and governance is not addressed in the PLMA.

The IDD is applicable to insurance and reinsurance distribution, which specifically is defined as the "activities of advising on, proposing, or carrying out other work preparatory to the conclusion of contracts of insurance, of concluding such contracts, or of assisting in the administration and performance of such contracts, in particular in the event of a claim,[10] including the provision of information concerning one or more insurance contracts in accordance with criteria selected by customers through a website or other media... when the customer is able to directly or indirectly conclude an insurance contract."[11] An insurance intermediary is defined as a natural or legal person who, for remuneration, pursues the activity of insurance distribution.[12]

4 Comparing the Producer Licensing Model Act with the Insurance Distribution Directive

The most striking difference between the PLMA and the IDD is that the PMLA is written from the perspective of the individual U.S. state legislators and/or their insurance commissioner, so that the PLMA can be directly adopted by the individual states. Everything in the PLMA is merely a suggestion being made by an advisory body. The IDD, on the other hand, is a mandatory directive authored by the EU Commission, a legislative body with the authority to require the Member States to adopt legislation. Therefore, the language varies considerably.

4.1 Organizational Requirements

Chapter IV of the IDD lays out Organizational Requirements for the Member States. In Article 14, Member States are required to set up procedures for customers to register complaints about insurance distributors, and "in all cases, complainants shall receive replies." Further, Member States are required to ensure that an effective, impartial, and independent out-of-court redress procedure is available for the settlement of customer-intermediary disputes.[13] There are no such requirements in the PLMA. However, most U.S. States have created an Office of the Insurance

[10]The addition of the language "in particular in the event of a claim" has been rightly criticized for creating confusion, as the insurance distribution directive is otherwise focused on the production and sales of insurance products, i.e. their distribution. The processing of insurance claims is an entirely separate undertaking from the sales and distribution of products and policies. *See* Pscheidl (2018), p. 208.

[11]IDD Article 2, 1. (1).

[12]IDD Article 2, 1. (3).

[13]IDD Article 15.

Commissioner (or similar), and that office does handle consumer complaints. The process is entirely voluntary for the individual state officials, and there is no procedural guarantee that the complaint will receive a reply. Additionally, the U.S. states do not make out-of-court complaint and redress procedures available for settlement purposes, beyond the limited service they typically provide to register a complaint, notify the insurer or intermediary of the complaint, and then advise the customer on a course of action. This process is widely criticized as non-effective toward resolution, and correspondingly is seldom even initiated by consumers.

4.2 Duties of Insurance Intermediaries/Producers

Chapter V of the IDD delineates the information requirements for intermediaries, and the rules applicable to their business conduct. Section 12 of the PLMA lists prohibited actions which can lead to an insurance intermediary's license revocation and a civil penalty. Despite that the IDD language is written in a prescriptive manner and the PLMA is written in a proscriptive manner, there are some similarities.

Article 17 of the IDD requires that insurance distributors "always act honestly, fairly and professionally in accordance with the best interests of their customers." Section 12 A. (8) of the PLMA forbids an insurance producer from "using fraudulent, coercive, or dishonest practices, or demonstrating incompetence, untrustworthiness or financial irresponsibility in the conduct of business..." Notably while the IDD requires "professionalism," the PLMA forbids "incompetence, untrustworthiness or financial irresponsibility," which although differently described, seem to be similar standards. What is strikingly missing from the PLMA is the requirement that U.S. insurance intermediaries act "with the best interests of their customers," as is required of European intermediaries.

Another requirement present in the IDD that is glaringly absent from the PLMA is that marketing be "fair, clear, and not misleading."[14] This is a much stricter standard than the usual prohibition of fraud found in all U.S. common law. The EU appears to be requiring a shift toward "good behavior," or marketing that is more protective of the customer, while the U.S. is merely prohibiting "bad behavior". All of the 50 U.S. states have the unfettered ability to write stricter laws, since the PLMA is advisory and the federal government does not monitor insurance intermediaries. But, in reality, the average state struggles to enforce the basic PLMA provisions, much less create stricter regulations.[15]

The PLMA places only two restrictions on the remuneration of insurance producers—one, that a producer must be licensed in order to receive commissions, and two, that the producer must disclose a compensation agreement with an insurer if the

[14]IDD Art. 17, 2.

[15]This is based on the general knowledge and understanding of the author. Regulatory activities in a specific state may vary.

producer is *also* receiving compensation from the customer.[16] In contrast, the IDD mandates that Member States shall ensure that distributors and their employees are not remunerated in a way that conflicts with their duties to act in accordance with the best interest of their customers[17]; that they reveal business holdings that create conflicts[18]; that they reveal whether advice is based on fair and personal analysis or not, or whether there is exclusivity with an insurance company[19]; and that they reveal the nature of remuneration received, i.e. fee, commission, or other, and the amount, and whether it ties to employee remuneration.[20]

Beyond these requirements, the IDD includes numerous other new regulations of the activities of insurance intermediaries that are not addressed in the PLMA. Briefly, the IDD now requires a product information document that supplies information to the customer in a comprehensible form which allows the customer to make an informed decision; when advice will be given by the insurance distributor, they must specify the demands and needs of the customer based on the information that the customer provides, and the contract proposed shall be consistent with these demands and needs, and the result of an analysis of a sufficiently large number of insurance contracts available on the market.[21] In comparison to the sparse prohibitions of the PLMA, these IDD regulations are very detailed and specific. Additionally, the IDD now requires a product review process within each insurance distributor's company operations, and provides that sanctions shall apply to any infringements.[22]

4.3 Sanctions, Penalties, and Other Measures

Because the nature of the PMLA is advisory, specific sanctions are not prescribed as they are in the IDD. However, the PMLA does provide suggested penalties for violations of the duties of insurance producers within Section 12—"[t]he insurance commissioner may place on probation, suspend, revoke or refuse to issue or renew an insurance producer's license or may levy a civil penalty in accordance with [state law]." The PMLA clarifies that nothing in the Act prohibits the commissioner from releasing final, adjudicated actions to be open to public inspection.[23] Section 19 further clarifies that individual states retain full authority for enforcement, reassuringly indicating "The insurance commissioner may, in accordance with [state law],

[16]PLMA Sect. 13 and Sect. 18.

[17]IDD Art. 17, 3.

[18]IDD Art. 19, 1. (a) and (b).

[19]IDD Art. 19, 1. (c).

[20]IDD Art. 19, 1. (d), (e), 2., and 4.

[21]IDD Art. 20.

[22]IDD Art. 25.; *See also* footnote 10.

[23]PLMA Sect. 15, F. (5).

promulgate reasonable regulations as are necessary or proper to carry out the purposes of this Act."

Section VII of the IDD, titled "Sanctions and Other Measures," is far more exhaustive and detailed than the PMLA. At the outset, the Commission made it clear that Member States can keep their own criminal sanctions, as long as they provide notice to the Commission.[24] This is similar to Section 19 of the PLMA, only American states do not need to report their regulations to the NAIC or any federal government body. Additionally, European Union Member States are *required* to publish sanctions when they are imposed[25]—as opposed to the PLMA "allowance" that commissioners *may* make the sanctions public.

Where the IDD significantly departs from the PLMA is Article 33, 2. The Commission requires Member States to ensure that their competent authorities have the power to impose *at least* the following additional administrative sanctions and other measures: an order requiring the responsible person to cease the conduct and desist from a repetition; withdrawal of the insurance intermediary's registration; ban on certain management functions; and the imposition of particular sanctions. For a legal person, i.e. an insurance corporation, the maximum pecuniary sanctions are at least €5mil or up to 5% of total annual turnover, or up to two times the amount of profits gained (or losses avoided) due to the breach. For a natural person, i.e. an individual intermediary, the maximum pecuniary sanctions are at least €700,000 or up to two times the amount of profits gained (or losses avoided) due to the breach. Then, in numeral 4 of Article 33, Member States are specifically allowed to have additional sanctions or other measures, and are allowed higher levels of administrative pecuniary sanctions than those provided in that same article. This leads one to question the use of the word "maximum" where Article 33 had already listed specific monetary penalties.

Article 34, titled "Effective Application of Sanctions and Other Measures," provides mandatory guidance to Member States applying sanctions, requiring that competent authorities shall take into account "all relevant circumstances, including where appropriate..."... the gravity and duration of the breach, the degree of responsibility of the responsible person, the financial strength of the responsible person, the importance of profits gained or losses avoided, the losses for customers, level of cooperation of the responsible person with authority, any measures taken to prevent repetition of breach, and any previous breaches. The IDD has taken a large step toward a significantly more strict, rules-based body of regulations that prescribes specific penalties, but the PMLA lacks any provisions that reach beyond the suggestion of a general "allowance" for state insurance commissioners to create their own penalty schemes.

---

[24]IDD Art. 31.

[25]And report them to EIOPA, Art. 32.

5 How the United States Enforces Insurance Intermediary Regulations

As mentioned, the enforcement of insurance regulations in the United States falls almost entirely to the individual states. The lack of a powerful federal insurance authority leaves the U.S. insurance market in a fractured, and arguably chaotic, status of affairs.[26] Despite the NAIC's attempt to create uniformity, none of their model laws are mandatory, and therefore are not fully adopted or enforced within the states. An insurance intermediary/producer is primarily subject to the regulations of the state their business is domiciled in.

The state Office of the Insurance Commissioner[27] enforces intermediary regulations. These regulations are embedded into state statutes, or codes. According to the NAIC, 40 states have adopted the PLMA in a form which mirrors the NAIC-drafted version. However, upon closer examination, this representation is in error—a fact we will address further in the Alabama section. The ten non-adopting states have their own "related activity," which may or may not be similar to the PLMA, but upon closer examination, may also mean the state has *more stringent* regulations than the PLMA, i.e. California. Clearly, while the NAIC does provide a helpful list of states and their supposed adoption status, the list is only a starting point. To find the precise rules for any state, careful research is necessary. The inaccuracy of the list raises some serious doubts about how much progress the NAIC has actually made toward their goal of uniformity.

Another, equally important source of insurance intermediary law is the American common law, i.e. lawsuits handled by the courts. Generally, the state courts are tasked with interpreting the state's existing statutes. However, many states allow *only* the insurance commissioner to enforce the PLMA, circumventing the ability of consumers to file a lawsuit based on a violation of the PLMA, and preventing courts from enforcing the provisions. While this further weakens the effectiveness of the PLMA, it does not entirely prevent a harmed plaintiff from bringing a lawsuit against an insurance intermediary. U.S. courts also apply and interpret general principles of law such as fraud, misrepresentation, breach of contract, tortious conduct, etc.

As a result, analyzing enforcement requires a two-pronged approach, because enforcement actions can be initiated by both the state's insurance commissioner and the state courts. To understand the effectiveness of the enforcement of the insurance intermediary laws in the United States, we will look at the enforcement structures and records of three states—California, Michigan, and Alabama. These states were chosen due to their insurance sales market share—California being one of the largest

[26]After the economic recession of 2007–2009, an oversight body called the Federal Insurance Office was created, but it was granted only advisory powers.

[27]Or, Department of Insurance.

markets, Michigan in the middle range, and Alabama with one of the smaller markets.[28]

5.1 California Enforcement

California (CA) is one of the ten states that has not adopted the PMLA in a manner similar to the NAIC's recommended format. However, this is because California has detailed insurance regulations applicable to producers that date from decades before the PMLA was drafted.[29] Chapter 5 of the CA Insurance Code, titled "Production Agencies" is applicable to insurance intermediaries/producers. The Code begins with more extensive and detailed definitions of relevant terms than suggested by the PLMA—most importantly of "agent" and "broker"—the two most common types of insurance intermediaries in the United States.

Section 1621 defines "insurance agent" as a "person who transacts insurance... on behalf of an admitted insurance company." An "insurance broker" is defined as "a person who, for compensation and on behalf of another person, transacts insurance... with, but not on behalf of, an admitted insurer."[30] Whether a producer is classified as an agent or a broker will determine which regulations, and thus which penalties, are applicable to them. While these California definitions seem very clear and simple, in practice the classifications cause much confusion and lend a great deal of uncertainty to the regulations, translating into a lack of customer trust.

5.1.1 Duties of California Insurance Intermediaries/Producers

Article 6 of the CA Insurance Code covers "License Qualifications," and lists disqualifying factors which echo both the PMLA and the IDD, such as "lacking in integrity," knowing or willful misstatements, previous fraudulent activity or dishonesty, "incompetency or untrustworthiness," "knowing misrepresentation of an insurance policy terms or effect," failure to perform required duties, and criminal convictions.[31] The CA Code goes a step further and grants the commissioner the broad power to deny an intermediary's application if "the granting of the license will be against public interest."[32] Further, licenses can be revoked if a producer has induced a client to grant them a monetary benefit such as a loan, or the inclusion of

---

[28] Property and Casualty Insurance Industry 2018 Direct Premiums Earned—California, $78.45 billion; Michigan, $19.65 billion; Alabama, $8.8 billion; National Association of Insurance Commissioners 2019.

[29] Cal. Ins. Code §§1621 to 1758.994 (1959/2016).

[30] Cal. Ins. Code § 1623.

[31] Cal. Ins. Code § 1668.

[32] Cal. Ins. Code § 1668 (b).

the producer as a beneficiary in the customer's will or trust.[33] There are no broad prohibitions or disclosure requirements applicable to the commissions and fees of agents or brokers in California.

5.1.2 California Sanctions, Penalties, and Other Measures

The California Department of Insurance's Investigation Division handles administrative enforcement, and refers crimes to local California prosecutors. Any infringement of the insurance code can lead to ordered restitution, imposed fines, and penalties.[34] Administrative fines delineated by the CA Insurance Code range from $200 to $500. Administrative remedies also include suspension or revocation of producer licenses and cease and desist orders. Enforcement through civil courts can entail the seizure of a business, and criminal prosecution might bring incarceration, probation, and community service. Civil penalties cannot exceed $1000 per day or per violation, up to a maximum of $50,000.[35] While these amounts might be sufficient deterrence for individual producers, they will not deter large companies. Fortunately, the Insurance Commissioner is authorized to incrementally increase these amounts with an advance notice, and larger penalties are imposed under the authorization of other California statutes and common law, which are well-developed in the State of California.[36]

The penalties which are enforced by the CA Department of Insurance are available on the Department's website, but to see them you need to search for a specific party name. This is an impediment to full transparency, as consumers are not able to compare enforcement records between the various producers and their employers, and cannot see the full breadth of investigative and enforcement work which is performed by the CA Insurance Commissioner's Investigative Division. Without a more full and effective transparency, consumers are unable to keep their representatives accountable.

5.1.3 California Case Law

Enforcement through civil or criminal courts can yield an almost unlimited range of potential penalties, from large monetary judgments in civil court to many years of imprisonment after a criminal trial. While the availability of strong enforcement

---

[33]Cal. Ins. Code § 1668.1.

[34]Cal. Ins. Code § 1746(g).

[35]Cal. Ins. Code § 1748.5.

[36]*See, for example* the March 9, 2006 Marsh USA (Marsh & McLennan Companies, Inc.) Decision and Order, which cites the California Insurance Code, criminal law, and common law principles (here, of agency) in the imposition of certain fines but an overall settlement of $100,000,000; http://www.insurance.ca.gov/0250-insurers/0500-legal-info/0600-decision-ruling/0100-precedential/upload/marsh-usa-inc.pdf, last visited September 30, 2019.

through the judicial system is typically viewed as a significant benefit for American consumers, under the current economic and legal circumstances it primarily results in additional uncertainty, confusion, and frustration.

First, consumers are not well-equipped to know the status of common law as it applies to insurance intermediaries. In fact, a review of precedential case law applicable to intermediaries in California yields conflicting decisions and unclear interpretations, particularly with regard to the definitions of "agent" and "broker," and defining their specific duties. The state of CA has also created a third, unusual category called "dual agency."[37] When the judiciary struggles to make bright line rules regarding the duties of intermediaries, it becomes next to impossible for a consumer to be certain of which duties are owed to them from their chosen agent or broker, and whether they have a legitimate claim of wrongdoing.

Second, California is one of the states in which the consumer does not have standing to file suit when their producer has violated the CA Insurance Code—they can only sue based on common law violations. While this may not have a significant impact when the violation is minor, because the consumer can report this to the Department of Insurance and hope they negotiate a resolution, it becomes highly problematic in the case of complex violations or ongoing patterns of dishonesty or abuse.[38] Insurance commissioners do not have a proactive record of enforcing claims which require long-term, heavy investigation and evidentiary analysis.[39]

Finally—and the most problematic factor for U.S. common law enforcement—the judicial system is not currently a viable option for the pursuit of justice for the vast majority of Americans. Lawsuits have become too expensive to be maintained by all but the very wealthiest of American citizens, and the alternatives of mediation or arbitration are also prohibitively expensive.[40]

5.1.4 California Enforcement Summary

Although California should be commended for its very detailed and well-thought insurance code, the resulting enforcement lacks in (1) transparency, (2) deterrence, and (3) breadth, because (a) it does not address or aid prosecution of common law violations, which are a fundamental, critical judicial balance and support to U.S. legislation, (b) the commissioner is not proactively enforcing all legislative acts, and particularly not those which cover repeated and widespread patterns of abuse, and (c) the insurance code cannot be enforced through private lawsuits.

[37] *U.S. Fidelity & Guar. Co.* (2008) at 1122-23.

[38] Particularly those which are covered by the Unfair Trade Practices Act (which applies to producers) or the Unfair Claims Settlement Practices Act (which can implicate producers)—both drafted by the NAIC and adopted by the state of California.

[39] Defever (2018), p. 17.

[40] Defever (2018), p. 17.

5.2 Michigan Enforcement

Michigan (MI) is one of the 40 states that is listed as having adopted the PMLA in a manner similar to the NAIC's recommended format. Chapter 12 of the MI Insurance Code, titled "Agents, Solicitors, Adjusters, and Counselors" is applicable to insurance intermediaries/producers.[41] The state of Michigan uses different definitions than both California and the PLMA. While the PLMA does not attempt to define the different types of producers, and CA goes an extra step and delineates definitions for both agents and brokers—the state of Michigan takes a different approach altogether and defines an "agent" as "an insurance producer." Agents are then further broken down into the subsections "agent of the insured" and "agent of the insurer".

The word broker appears never to be used in the context of insurance sales in Michigan—all insurance sales and negotiations are performed by agents. However, there is an additional status of "solicitor". A solicitor works for a licensed agent/producer, and "may solicit applications for insurance and collect premiums on behalf of a licensed insurance producer resident... if he or she is so authorized to act by a written contract with the insurance producer, the contract specifies the extent of his or her authority to act, he or she is licensed to act as a solicitor... and the insurance producer has notified the director[42] of the contract."[43] There are also specific rules regarding how an agent for the insured and an agent for the insurer are allowed to contract. An agent of the insured may only obtain coverage for a customer through an agent of the insurer if "the agent of the insured has a relationship with the agent of the insurer under a written contract... [which] must specify the extent of the agent of the insured's authority to act and require the maintenance of an amount of professional liability insurance...".[44]

The State of Michigan also licenses "insurance counselors," which are defined as those who "provide advice, counsel, or opinion with respect to benefits promised, coverage afforded, terms, value, effect, advantages, or disadvantages of a policy of insurance...".[45] It is unclear exactly how counselors differ from agents, but the code section does mention that the definition of counselor is not meant to prohibit the customary advice offered by a licensed insurance agent.

If one compares these Michigan-defined relationships with the defined relationships of agent and broker in California, as well as the usage of the terms "intermediary" and "distributor" in the IDD (which does also utilize the words broker and agent), it is easy to understand why uniformity is a high priority on both continents. If the regulators and experts struggle to keep track of basic terms, how can we ever expect customers to feel confident?

---

[41]M.C.L.A. §§ 500.1201 to 500.1247.

[42]Director refers to Michigan's director of licensing.

[43]M.C.L.A. § 500.1211 (1) "Contract requirements for solicitor and agent of insured".

[44]M.C.L.A. § 500.1211 (2).

[45]M.C.L.A. § 500.1232.

5.2.1 Duties of Michigan Insurance Intermediaries/Producers

The license qualifications for Michigan insurance solicitors and consultants are more specific than the role of an agent, and appear quite thorough. While all three roles require education and training, the solicitors and consultants also are investigated by the insurance commissioner to ensure they have a reasonable understanding of the insurance products and state insurance laws, intend to act in good faith, are honest and trustworthy, and possess a good business reputation and good moral character.[46] These standards appear to generally echo the California license qualifications, only the terminology is much broader and leaves a great deal more discretion to the insurance commissioner.

Solicitors are also required to act as a fiduciary for all monies received or held in their capacity as a solicitor, and are not allowed to pay referral fees or any type of commission to someone who procures business for them.[47] Consultants are not fiduciaries, but they must disclose their fee to the customer, and if they are receiving a commission from an insurer when they act as an agent to procure coverage, they must disclose that commission. Again, these are interesting qualifications in that they seem to partly mirror the IDD and partly the CA requirements.

Licensed insurance producers are subject to penalties if they "violate any insurance laws or regulation..."; attempt to obtain a license through misrepresentation or fraud; improperly withhold or convert any money received in the course of business; intentionally misrepresent insurance terms have committed any insurance unfair trade practice or fraud; use fraudulent, coercive, or dishonest practices; or demonstrate incompetence, untrustworthiness, or financial irresponsibility in the conduct of business.[48] These requirements are a close replica of Section 12 of the PLMA. The regular use of commissions and service fees in Michigan are not directly addressed, but implicitly authorized.[49]

5.2.2 Michigan Sanctions, Penalties, and Other Measures

The penalties for violations of the insurance code in Michigan range from merely license revocation and cease and desist orders to civil fines or restitution for the injured. Unlike California, no criminal prosecution is mentioned. Civil fines cannot be more than $1000 for each violation, unless the violator knew or reasonably should have known of their violation—then the commissioner can impose up to $5000 per violation. No combination of fines can exceed $50,000. Civil fines are also imposed if a person knowingly violates a cease and desist order—no more than $20,000 for

[46]M.C.L.A. § 500.1214(3) and M.C.L.A. § 500.1234(3).

[47]M.C.L.A. § 500.1216.

[48]M.C.L.A. § 500.1239 (1).

[49]*See* M.C.L.A. §500.1240 which explains that commissions and fees are forbidden when the producer is unlicensed.

each violation, and no more than a total of $100,000.[50] These monetary penalties are similar to the civil fines available under the CA Insurance Code.

Restitution for the insured is available to cover incurred losses, damages, or other harm, and no monetary limit is provided. The commissioner can also require a refund of any overcharges. The unlimited availability of restitution is relatively comparable to the IDD's allowance for the penalty of up to twice the amount of the profits gained, or losses avoided, because of the violator's breach.[51] However, the specifically delineated civil penalties of both Michigan and California are incredibly small compared to the IDD's limits in the hundred of thousands, or several million, euros.

Despite the low penalties, the State of Michigan is doing an excellent job with transparency of insurance code enforcement. Every quarter they publish a detailed, web searchable enforcement report in PDF format which lists all enforcement actions taken. A clear table with descriptive headers is used, indicating the name of the violator, their case number, the type of license or registration, the date of the commission's action, the specific action taken, the reason for the action, the type of file closure used, the date of file closure, and the fines and penalties imposed. Some examples of the "reason[s] for action" are "Misconduct of Business, M.C.L § 500.1239(1)(d)" and "Unlawful Behavior of an Agent, M.C.L. 500.1239(1)(b)(e)". The specific citation of the legal clause used for enforcement is unambiguous. Fines and penalties range from "Revoke License" to "$8,000 Civil Penalty."[52] To be fair, California's database of violators did provide links to the actual legal documents which support the penalty imposed, but again, that is only if you already know the name of the violator. The Michigan approach is much clearer and easy to navigate—much more consumer-friendly.

5.2.3 Michigan Case Law

Like California case law, Michigan case law struggles with a lack of clarity. Also like California, the definitions of agent and broker are raised in Michigan courts, which is interesting given that the word "broker" never appears in the Michigan insurance statutes.[53] For an insurance consumer, this will be utterly confusing.

Overall, the status of insurance case law in the United States is in a conflicted and confusing state. A reading of the chapters "Negligence Claims by Insureds" and "Broker Liability" in the treatise *Law of Commercial Insurance Agents and Brokers* reveals that some state courts assert that customers cannot be expected to know the requirements of proper care applicable to agents or brokers,[54] but that other state

[50] M.C.L.A. § 500.1244.

[51] IDD Art. 33, 1. (f) (ii).

[52] *See* https://www.michigan.gov/difs/0,5269,7-303-20594_46950%2D%2D-,00.html, last visited September 29, 2019.

[53] *Cleveland Indians Baseball Co. v. New Hampshire Ins. Co.*, (2013) at 640.

[54] *Todd v. Malafronte*, (1984) at 466.

courts believe that insurance "is not a field that is so highly technical that the public cannot understand at least the general nature of an agent's responsibilities."[55] While some courts only require expert testimony regarding the duties of agents and brokers when the insurance claims are complex, California requires expert testimony regarding these duties because "the standard of care is beyond the common knowledge of the layperson".[56]

U.S. states clearly do not agree on the basic elements of insurance law. The common law system supplies very little support for the insurance codes—sometimes even undermining or confusing them by introducing additional concepts like dual agency in California, or the undefined role of broker in Michigan.

5.2.4 Michigan Enforcement Summary

Michigan is doing an admirable job with enforcements and transparency. A review of their quarterly enforcement summaries reveals a great deal of activity investigating and penalizing offenders. However, the penalties could certainly be higher, particularly in the case of legal persons, i.e. companies. Penalties which have a maximum of $100,000 will not be effective deterrence to large companies. Also, if the commissioner is merely ordering the intermediary to return the improper gain, but not adding a large amount of restitution, the intermediary may not hesitate to attempt to cheat the laws again. Fortunately, although the penalties have very low caps, there are clauses like the one allowing restitution which allow additional amounts to be added.

5.3 Alabama Enforcement

The NAIC also lists Alabama as a state which has adopted the PLMA in a substantially similar manner, but upon further research, this is potentially misleading. The NAIC lists Chapter 7 of the Alabama Insurance Code as the PLMA "Model adoption." However, from 1991 to 2013, Alabama has repealed 19 of the 61 sections in Chapter 7. While it would be difficult to tell if the repealed sections were accurate and/or essential matches of the PLMA, there is a demonstrated lack of substance in Alabama's Insurance Code.

Alabama adds yet another mix of insurance terms to our pool – using primarily the words "producer" and "service representative". There is no mention of brokers,

[55] *Atwater Creamery Co. v. Western Nat. Mut. Ins. Co.*, (1985) at 279.

[56] *Law of Commercial Agents & Brokers, Chapter 2 - Negligence Claims by Insureds* (2017 Supplement) at 57.

consultants, solicitors, or distributors.[57] Agents are mentioned, but not defined or singled out as subject to the code. The term producer is defined as "a person required to be licensed under the laws of this state to sell, solicit, or negotiate insurance." A service representative is defined as "a natural person, other than an officer, manager, or managing general agent of the insurer, employed on salary... by the insurer [or] managing general agent... to work for... producers in selling, soliciting, or negotiating insurance in the insurer..., but only in the property lines of authority."[58]

When compared with the definitions of the IDD, California, and Michigan, the closest matches we have for the Alabama definition of producer are "insurer's agent" or perhaps "solicitor" in Michigan, or simply "agent" in California. Service Representatives appear to be merely employees of Alabama producers, but more highly regulated than they would be in other states. Also, the use of the word agent to describe the employer of the service representative adds another layer of confusion.

PLMA adoption has failed to provide consistency amongst basic insurance terms. This failure results in each state regulating completely different actors who perform entirely different scopes of activity, and with different regulatory methods.

5.3.1 Duties of Alabama Insurance Intermediaries/Producers

The duties of Alabama "licensees," as they are called, are very similar to those of licensed Michigan producers, which in turn echo the suggested terms of Section 12 of the PLMA.[59] The only significant standout is a clause authorizing a penalty when a licensee induces, persuades, or advises "any policyholder to surrender or cause to be cancelled any policy of insurance issued to the policyholder by any authorized insurer in exchange for a policy offered by the licensee where the surrender or cancellation shall result to the financial detriment of the policyholder."[60] While most of Section 12 of the PLMA is quite broad, this is an example of Alabama adopting those recommended general clauses, but then adding the state's own, more specific and narrow regulation. Unfortunately, this is the only notable example of the Alabama legislature doing so. However, the Michigan and Alabama adoption of Article 12 indicate that the PLMA has assisted in some uniformity, even if with that one article, only.

Like Michigan and California, Alabama requires education and training for their equivalents of intermediaries/producers. They also require fingerprinting and a criminal history check.[61] If a license applicant has been convicted of a felony, a review committee considers multiple factors before making a recommendation to the

---

[57]Brokers and Solicitors appear to have been mentioned in the Repealed sections, but these have not been replaced.

[58]Ala. Code 1975 § 27-7-1 (5) and (20).

[59]*See* the last paragraph of section 4.2.1.

[60]Ala Code 1975 § 27-7-19(6).

[61]Ala. Code 1975 § 27-7-4.4 and § 27-7-5.

Commissioner regarding approval or disapproval of the application. The factors are reminiscent of the factors prescribed in IDD Article 34[62] to be considered before applying sanctions to intermediaries who violate the law, only here, they are used to screen for the degree of criminality of a potential licensee. For example, the Alabama Review Committee considers (among others) the following factors: the nature and severity of the offense(s); the particular circumstances of the offense(s); the nature and extent of injury or loss to other persons or property; whether the offense(s) are related to insurance; the sentence imposed; the time that has elapsed since the conviction or sentence; any aggravating or mitigating factors; and any relevant evidence tending to demonstrate contrition or rehabilitation.[63] Where the state of Alabama will allow those with criminal pasts a chance to work as an insurance intermediary, the EU Commission is revoking the licenses of—and placing very large sanctions upon—those very same individuals.

Monetary commissions are allowed in Alabama, with some restrictions. Licensees are not allowed to share their commissions unless they are a producer sharing with other licensed producers for the same kinds of insurance or insurance classifications.[64] Producers seem to have a fiduciary duty of some degree, as they are required to keep premiums and funds being held for others in a trust fund, "in a fiduciary capacity".[65]

5.3.2 Alabama Sanctions, Penalties, and Other Measures

Alabama fines an unlicensed "person who sells, solicits, or negotiates insurance" with a fine up to three times the premium received.[66] A similar penalty applies to an insurer or producer who pays "any commission or other valuable consideration to a person for services as a producer or service representative" who is unlicensed (three times the commission paid).[67] If a producer or service representative submits a false or fraudulent application for license renewal, the license can be suspended or the licensee "may be subject to a civil fine in an amount not to exceed $10,000.

The penalties for "licensees" violating the provisions of § 27-7-19 (echoing Article 12 of the PLMA) are license suspension, probation, revocation, and/or a civil fine in an amount not to exceed $10,000 per violation. There is no overall cap on fines, so if there are multiple violations the fines can add up significantly.[68]

Alabama does post an "Annual Fraud Bureau Report" from the previous year, on the Department of Insurance website. However, the report is a short, five-page PDF

---

[62] *See* last para., section 3.3 herein.

[63] Ala. Admin. Code § 482-1-146-.07.

[64] Ala. Code 1975 § 27-7-35.

[65] Ala. Code 1975 § 27-7-36.

[66] Ala. Code 1975 § 27-7-4 and § 27-7-35.1.

[67] Ala. Code 1975 § 27-7-4.1 and § 27-7-35.1.

[68] Ala. Code 1975 § 27-7-19 (b) and (c).

document containing some generalizations regarding the results of the different investigations, such as "unfounded," "lack of resources," and "presented for prosecution". There is no additional information about the investigations—not the nature of the violation, not the name of the offender, not the code provision at issue, no list of penalties... nothing additional. Alabama's enforcement is completely lacking in transparency, to the great detriment of consumers.

5.3.3 Alabama Case Law

Alabama courts offer little to no interpretive support for the Alabama insurance code chapter applicable to producers. As discussed in the California and Michigan sections, this is unfortunate because (1) the state codes are not exhaustive and would benefit from clarification and supplementation, most particularly the sparse Alabama code, and (2) the overall lack of litigation by harmed consumers is a direct result of the exorbitant costs of American lawsuits.

5.3.4 Alabama Enforcement Summary

Alabama's use of penalties that are multiples of the amount illegally received is similar to the IDD penalties of Article 33 prescribing sanctions up to two times the profits gained. These style penalties are effective because they ensure not only the illegal profit is taken away, but a proportional punishment is imposed. While Alabama seems to have some basic penalties in place, the lack of publication of enforcement activities renders it is impossible to know if the insurance code is being enforced sufficiently.

6 Structures for Enforcement in the United States and the European Union

As we can see, the enforcement structures of the U.S. and the EU are very different. In the United States, federal law has very little cohesive effect, due to the federal government declining to use its powers to legislate insurance law. Regulation falls to the individual states, where a combination of state statutes and court-created common law comprise the body of insurance regulations. The state insurance commissioners collectively meet as the National Association of Insurance Commissioners and draft advisory acts like the PMLA which the states can elect to adopt and use as they choose. However, the nature of these advisory acts renders them principles-based in a similar fashion to the IDD's predecessor the IMD, and we can see through these examples that principles-based regulations are not able to support effective enforcement.[69]

In the EU, the equivalents of the U.S. federal law are the Directives promulgated by the Commission of the European Union. The Commission has authored several mandatory acts regulating the business of insurance, most recently the IDD. Member States are required to adopt the IDD and integrate it into their individual state insurance law regimes. As the Commission issues new Directives and updates the previous ones, the regulations are shifting away from their principles-based origins and becoming more rules-based. This shift will have a major impact on the enforcement mechanisms of the Member States because while principles-based regulations rely on self-enforcement by the actors, rules-based regulations require the Member States to enforce specific rules.

7 What Can Member States Learn from the Enforcement Failures of the United States?

The primary difference between the IDD and the PLMA is that the IDD is mandatory and the PLMA is voluntary. Due to its advisory nature, the PMLA has been inconsistently adopted and inconsistently enforced. As we discovered through our analysis of three very different states, California, Michigan, and Alabama, even in the instances where the basic principles of an article in the PMLA are adopted, they are significantly altered to suit the individual state's perceived needs. The bodies of regulations applying to insurance producers remain in a piecemeal state, and the PMLA has done very little to close the gaps. Even in the event that the PMLA was uniformly adopted in all 50 states, the incredible differences in the state enforcement regimes would still lend uncertainty, uneven application, and inconsistent results.

The takeaway for EU Member States should be that uniformity will not be achieved until and unless they adopt and apply the mandatory penalties provided in the IDD, and achieve a sufficient level of transparency to aid consumers in avoiding bad actors, and act as a deterrence to producers. The IDD's more prescriptive, rules-based insurance regulations will be the first of their kind to be applied across such a wide and diverse territory as the EU Member States. Insurance scholars are voicing concern that the IDD has taken the new regulations a step too far, and the immense costs of complying with the minimum harmonizations will be crippling to the Member States and cause damage the insurance economy.[70] However, as can be seen in the U.S. example, stricter rules are needed for the protection of consumers and the health of the insurance market.

---

[69] *See* Ferran, Ellis, *Regulatory Lessons from the Payment Protection Insurance Mis-selling Scandal in the UK* (2012) for analysis of this phenomena as it occurred in the UK.

[70] *See* De Maesschalck (2017); *See* Hofmann et al. (2018).

Despite the cultural homogeneity of the U.S. states, insurance regulations remain principle-based and uniformity of enforcement under the current regime has widely failed. As the EU moves forward with the IDD, it is now the United States that should be asking what can be learned from the EU's inevitable failures and successes in the application of the IDD.[71]

References

Alabama Administrative Code § 482-1-146-.07

Alabama Insurance Code 1975 § 27-7-1 to § 27-7-44

Atwater Creamery Company v. Western National Mutual Insurance Company, 366 N.W.2d 271, 279 (Minn. 1985)

California Insurance Code §§1621 to 1758.994 (1959/2016)

Cleveland Indians Baseball Company., L.P. v. New Hampshire Ins. Co., 727 F.3d 633, 640 (6th Cir. 2013) (Michigan law)

De Maesschalck N (2017) The Insurance Distribution Directive: what does it change for intermediaries and for others? In: Marano P, Siri M (eds) Insurance regulation in the European Union. Palgrave Macmillan, pp 59–77

Defever KM (2018) Comparative analysis of European Union and United States insurance law systems – with emphasis on consumer protection law. Eur J Commer Contract Law (Paris Legal Publishers) 2018-2/3:9–27

Directive (EU) 2002/92/EC of the European Parliament and of the Council of 9 December 2002 on insurance mediation

Directive (EU) 2016/97 of the European Parliament and of the Council of 20 January 2016 on insurance distribution

Ferran E (2012) Regulatory lessons from the payment protection insurance Mis-selling scandal in the UK. Eur Bus Org Law Rev (Cambridge University Press) 13(2):247–270

Gibbons v. Ogden, 22 U.S. 1 (1824)

Hofmann A, Neumann JK, Pooser D (2018) Plea for uniform regulation and challenges of implementing the new Insurance Distribution Directive. The Geneva Papers, Palgrave Macmillan, pp 740–769

In the Matter of the Licenses and Licensing Rights of Marsh USA, Inc., d.b.a. Marsh Risk and Insurance Services, et al., Decision and Order of the Insurance Commissioner of the State of California, March 9, 2006

Michigan Compiled Laws, §§ 500.1201 to 500.1247 (1980/2018)

Producer Licensing Model Act (2005) National Association of Insurance Commissioners

Pscheidl D (2018) Implementing IDD across the EU – first findings and the way forward. ERA Forum 19:205–217

Todd v. Malafronte, 3 Conn. App. 16, 484 A.2d 463, 466 (1984)

U.S. Fidelity & Guarantee Company v. Lee Investments LLC, 551 F. Supp. 2d 1114, 1122-23 (E.D. Cal. 2008)

Unfair Claims Settlement Practices Act (1997) National Association of Insurance Commissioners

Unfair Trade Practices Act (2004) National Association of Insurance Commissioners

United States v. South-Eastern Underwriters Association, 322 U.S. 533 (1944)

---

[71] *See* Hofmann et al. (2018) for the same conclusion after a detailed comparison and analysis of EU and U.S. insurance distribution regulations.

Viscusi WK (2002) Regulation through Litigation, AEI-Brookings Joint Center for Regulatory Studies
Weimer, BD Hagglund CE, Whitman AF (2017) Law of commercial insurance agents and brokers. Thomson West
15 U.S.C. §1012(b)

What Can the Insurance Distribution Directive "Offer" the South African Microinsurance Model?

Samantha Huneberg

1 Introduction

The European Union (EU) has recently introduced the Insurance Distribution Directive (IDD)[1] which replaces the previous Insurance Mediation Directive.[2] This new directive will regulate how insurers and firms design as well as market various insurance products in the EU.[3] This new directive is aimed at enhancing consumer protection when purchasing insurance products within the EU market.[4] The IDD is expected to be beneficial to consumers in the insurance market, as consumer protection is the main theme throughout the directive.

Similarly, South Africa has provisions in the Policyholder Protection Rules[5] (PPRs) specifically aimed at regulating the product design of insurance products.[6] The newly amended PPRs[7] contain rules on the product design of both life and non-life insurance[8] products as well as new provisions on microinsurance.[9]

[1]Directive (EU) 2016/97 of the European Parliament and of the Council of 20 January 2016.

[2](2002/92/EC).

[3]See the purpose of the directive.

[4]There is a very strong emphasis on treating consumers fairly despite the distribution channels chosen to purchase the product.

[5]As promulgated in terms of section 55 of the Short-term Insurance Act 53 of 1998.

[6]See rule 2 of the 2018 PPRs.

[7]Of 2018. As amended in terms of GN 996 in *GG* 41928 of 28 September 2018.

[8]In chapter 3, rule 2. This chapter will only consider the microinsurance and product design rules in terms of non-life insurance.

[9]Chapter 3, rule 2A of the 2018 PPRs.

S. Huneberg (✉)
University of Johannesburg, Johannesburg, South Africa
e-mail: shuneberg@uj.ac.za

P. Marano, K. Noussia (eds.), *Insurance Distribution Directive*, AIDA Europe Research Series on Insurance Law and Regulation 3,
https://doi.org/10.1007/978-3-030-52738-9_10

It appears as if the trend of consumer protection in insurance is growing internationally. The IDD is to have far-reaching consequences in terms of how insurance products are designed and sold within the various EU markets. As far as the current regulations in South Africa are concerned, the newly amended PPRs are also strongly geared towards consumer protection and this is especially evident with the introduction of the new rules on microinsurance.[10] Microinsurance is finally recognised as a formal type of insurance product within the South African market and this is to have widespread consequences for a large portion of the South African market.

Microinsurance is known as insurance with lower premiums and therefore also lower coverage.[11] Microinsurance refers to insurance products that provide coverage to low-income earners and households (this would be considered the mass market in South Africa).[12] A microinsurance policy therefore provides protection to individuals who generally have little savings.[13] These types of insurance policies are now managed in accordance with generally accepted insurance practices in South Africa.[14]

The fact that microinsurance has now been identified as a formal insurance product in South Africa is laudable due to the fact that the country's population consists of a large number of low-income earners. Insurance policies are renowned for being cumbersome, generally one-sided in favour of the insurer, and can be difficult to understand for the layman. This means that many vulnerable and financially illiterate consumers are being take advantage of by unscrupulous insurers. The newly amended PPRs are aiming to regulate microinsurance as well as provide concrete rules on the product design of insurance products in order to promote these products to a larger portion of the population. These provisions are therefore seeking to protect policyholders from insurers.[15]

However, the question arises whether the current rules on microinsurance in South Africa are indeed realistic and within reach, in light of the consequences facing these consumers? Can more be done in order to provide better coverage of microinsurance products to these specific consumers? This chapter seeks to answer these questions by analysing certain provisions of the IDD and ultimately asking whether the South African microinsurance model can learn or take away something of value from the provisions of the IDD? It was mentioned above that the IDD is specifically aimed at regulating how insurers design and sell products to the EU market and therefore, the provisions may be of value to the South African model of

[10]See rule 2A of the 2018 PPRs.

[11]Hunt (2019) What is Microinsurance? The Balance https://www.thebalance.com/what-is-microinsurance-4165961. Accessed 13 July 2019.

[12]Millard (2012), p. 665.

[13]See the National Treasury's Policy Document on the South African microinsurance regulatory framework July 2011.

[14]See rule 2A of the 2018 PPRs.

[15]See chapter 2, rule 1 of the 2018 PPRs which deals with the fair treatment of policyholders.

microinsurance, which should ultimately aim at inclusivity and consumer protection for these particular consumers.

2 The Insurance Distribution Directive

2.1 Introduction

As was mentioned in paragraph 1 above, the IDD was introduced in the EU market in January 2016.[16] This directive replaces the previous Insurance Mediation Directive.[17] The IDD focuses strongly on the concept of 'insurance distribution'. This concept refers to the selling, the proposed selling, advice on or preparing in any way, the conclusion of an insurance contract.[18] The IDD is strongly geared towards the fair treatment of all policyholders and the Recital specifically states in paragraph 6 that,

> Consumers should benefit from the same level of protection despite the differences between distribution channels. In order to guarantee that the same level of protection applies and that the consumer can benefit from comparable standards, in particular in the area of the disclosure of information, a level playing field between distributors is essential.[19]

From the above, it is evident that the IDD is focuses strongly on the various distribution channels through which insurance is sold to policyholders, therefore ensuring that policyholders are treated equally whether purchasing insurance through an intermediary, broker or other operators.[20] The Directive mentions that a level playing field should be achieved through the implementation of the provisions of the IDD.[21]

The purpose of the IDD is for consumers to ultimately benefit from its provisions through improved sales standards[22] and the extension of those standards to new areas of protection.[23] Before specific provisions of the Directive will be considered, it is necessary to consider the scope of application of the Directive. For purposes of

---

[16]Directive (EU) 2016/97.

[17](2002/92/EC).

[18]EU Rules of Insurance Distribution https://ec.europa.eu/info/business-economy-euro/banking-and-finance/insurance-and-pensions/insurance-distribution_en. Accessed 13 July 2019. See also Chapter 1, Article 2 of the IDD for the full definition.

[19]See paragraph 6 of the 2016/97 Directive (EU).

[20]Interestingly, the directive covers travel agents, car rental companies, and 'bancassurance' operators. See paragraph 5 of the Recital to the directive. The IDD therefore regulates the activities of insurance intermediaries, insurance companies, their employees, ancillary insurance intermediaries as well as online distribution. Evidently, the directive will have a greater impact in terms of the distribution channels than its previous counterpart. See also paragraph 7 and 8 of the Directive.

[21]Paragraphs 6 and 16.

[22]Paragraph 6.

[23]For example, to insurance-based investment products.

this chapter, only specific sections of the IDD will be considered which are relevant to the comparison with microinsurance provisions in South Africa.

2.2 Scope of Application

Chapter 1, article 1 of the Directive sets out the scope of application. The previous Insurance Mediation Directive applied to the regulation of insurance intermediaries, whereas the IDD now has a much broader application.[24] This wider application applies to all sellers of insurance products, including insurance undertakings that sell directly to customers; firms who are not insurers and whose activities include advising on, proposing, concluding, carrying out other work prior to the conclusion of a contract of insurance or assisting in the administration and performance of contracts of insurance—intermediaries and lastly, ancillary insurance intermediaries.[25]

It is also necessary to consider those transactions to which the IDD does not apply. Paragraph 13 states that the Directive will not apply "to mere introducing activities consisting of the provision of data and information on potential policyholders to insurance or reinsurance intermediaries or undertakings or of information about insurance or reinsurance products or an insurance or reinsurance intermediary or undertaking to potential policyholders."[26] It also does not apply "to persons with another professional activity, such as tax experts, accountants or lawyers, who provide advice on insurance cover on an incidental basis in the course of that other professional activity, nor should it apply to the mere provision of information of a general nature on insurance products, provided that the purpose of that activity is not to help the customer conclude or fulfil an insurance or reinsurance contract. This Directive should not apply to the professional management of claims on behalf of an insurance or reinsurance undertaking, nor to the loss adjusting and expert appraisal of claims."[27]

[24]See article 1 (2).

[25]Paragraphs 5 and 8.

[26]Paragraph 13. This exemption has been transposed by HM Treasury into Article 33B of The Financial Services and Markets Act 2000 (Regulated Activities) Order 2001 (RAO). New guidance has been added into the FCA Handbook that Article 33B only will cover "those situations where a person provides existing information they hold on potential policyholders (for example their name and contact details) but does not extend to information they obtain from other means such as pre-purchase questioning". This wording suggests that activities falling under this exemption will be limited in nature and provide only a slight extension to existing exclusions such as the provision of information on an incidental basis (Article 72C RAO) and arrangements enabling parties to communicate (Article 27 RAO).

[27]Paragraph 14.

Worth noting is article 1, paragraph 3 which importantly states that the "Directive shall not apply to ancillary insurance intermediaries carrying out insurance distribution activities where all the following conditions are met:

(a) the insurance is complementary to the good or service supplied by a provider, where such insurance covers:
    (i) the risk of breakdown, loss of, or damage to, the good or the non-use of the service supplied by that provider; or
    (ii) damage to, or loss of, baggage and other risks linked to travel booked with that provider;
(b) the amount of the premium paid for the insurance product does not exceed EUR 600 calculated on a pro rata annual basis;
(c) by way of derogation from point (b), where the insurance is complementary to a service referred to in point (a) and the duration of that service is equal to, or less than, three months, the amount of the premium paid per person does not exceed EUR 200."[28]

The Directive also does not apply to insurance and reinsurance distribution activities located outside the Union.[29]

Whilst the IDD makes no specific mention of the concept of microinsurance, it is not clear whether the directive would in fact apply to microinsurance products as these types of insurance products are not a common feature in the EU.[30] However, if we apply paragraph 3 of article 1 to microinsurance, then it would appear that the IDD would not be applicable to microinsurance where the insurance is complementary to the goods or services provided by a service provider, as long as the other conditions of paragraph 3 are met. This is based on the fact that there is a cap on the amount of the premium paid in this specific instance. This is a key feature in microinsurance, the premiums paid are set in accordance with the maximum amount of coverage provided in terms of the microinsurance policy.

Therefore, microinsurance products may very well fall within the other areas of scope within the IDD but because these types of insurance products are not a common feature in the market, it is unclear at this stage whether the rules in the IDD would in fact apply to microinsurance products. However, this is not a primary concern of this chapter. Rather, the focus of this chapter is to analyse certain provisions of the IDD relating to the product design of insurance products in general and seek to answer the question of whether any of these provisions can be helpful in the design and selling of microinsurance products in South Africa.

The first relevant provisions of the IDD to consider are the provisions relating to disclosure requirements.

---

[28]Read together with article 1(4).

[29]Article 1(6).

[30]Take note that Belgium has implemented specific legislation on microinsurance.

2.3 Disclosure Requirements of the IDD

It is interesting to note that article 17 in chapter 5 of the Directive starts off by stating that "insurance distributors must always act honestly, fairly and professionally in accordance with the best interests of the customer." This already indicates the theme of consumer protection which the Directive seeks to achieve.

The disclosure requirements in terms of the IDD impose a wider range of obligations on insurance firms.[31] Article 18 sets out general information to be provided by an intermediary or undertaking. The disclosure requirements state that anyone acting as a distributor must confirm whether they are acting as an insurer or an intermediary;[32] intermediaries must state whether they are acting on behalf of the customer or the insurer;[33] where intermediaries are contractually obliged to conduct business with one (or, even more) insurers, they are now under a pro-active duty to provide the customer with the name of the insurer; intermediaries must disclose the "nature and basis", or type and origin, of the remuneration that they receive in relation to the contract of insurance in question;[34] and insurers are required to disclose the "basis" of the remuneration paid to their employees.[35]

From the above it is clear that the new disclosure requirements in terms of the IDD require insurance firms and intermediaries to reconsider their current sales scripts and client documentation and to ultimately make considerable amendments where necessary, so that the firms are in line with the current requirements of the IDD. This thus requires all insurance firms selling insurance products to conform to the necessary disclosure requirements and ensure that the way in which they sell insurance products are currently in line with the provisions of the directive.[36]

Now that the disclosure requirements of the IDD have been considered, it is necessary to evaluate the relevant provisions on consumer needs. The reason for this is due to the fact that in microinsurance, the consumers' needs are of the utmost importance when designing these types of insurance products.

2.4 Consumer Needs

Under the IDD, all insurance distributors are now required to specify consumers' demands and needs based upon information obtained from them.[37] They must also ensure that the insurance policy proposed or recommended to the customer is

[31] See Paragraph 21.
[32] Paragraph 40.
[33] Article 18(a)(v).
[34] Paragraph 41.
[35] Paragraph 46.
[36] See article 18 and 19.
[37] Paragraph 44. See article 20.

consistent with those demands and needs.[38] These new obligations will require insurance distributors to be more active when assessing demands and needs with customers prior to the insurance being sold.[39]

In the case where no personal recommendation or advice is being made to the customer (or rather non-advised sales are undertaken), the Directive states that the customer should be given the relevant information about the product to allow the customer to make an informed decision.[40] This means that a product information document should provide standardised information about non-life insurance products.[41] Article 20(6) states that the insurance product information document referred to in paragraph 5 shall be drawn up by the manufacturer of the non-life insurance product.[42] The intermediary should explain the key features of the insurance product as well as the fact that its staff should be given appropriate time and resources to do so.[43] For example, in the case of a motor insurance policy, the consumer should be informed about the types and levels of cover or excess.[44] Under article 20(7), all the necessary information required for the insurance product information document is set out. Under this paragraph, it requires these documents to be short, laid out in a clear manner, be written in official languages of Member States, be accurate and not misleading, and include a statement to the effect that complete pre-contractual and contractual information on the product is provided in other documents.[45] These requirements are all aimed at ensuring that the customer is receiving all the necessary information regarding the insurance product and that they understand exactly what they are entering into.

In the instance where insurance firms provide personal recommendations to customers, this also requires them to provide a personalised explanation of why a particular insurance policy would best meet the customer's demands and needs.[46] Under article 20(3), it is mentioned that it is essential that customers know whether they are dealing with an intermediary who gives advice on the basis of a fair and personal analysis.[47] The intermediary must take into account the needs of the customer, the number of providers in the market, the market share of those providers and the number of relevant insurance products available from each provider.[48] This provision therefore ensures that products are appropriate for specific customers, that

[38]Paragraph 45. See article 20(1).

[39]Paragraph 44.

[40]Paragraph 48. See article 20(4).

[41]Paragraph 48. See article 20(5).

[42]See article 20(6).

[43]Paragraph 48. See article 20(7).

[44]See article 20(8).

[45]See article 20(7).

[46]Paragraph 47. See article 20(1)-(3).

[47]See article 20(3).

[48]Paragraph 47. See article 20(3).

their needs have been taken into account in terms of the entire market and that the best insurance product for their needs is being offered to them.

Article 20, as a whole, aims to ensure that customers' needs are taken into account when selling various insurance products, that customers understand the type of product they are purchasing and that all the necessary information about the product is conveyed to the customer in the form of a product information document.[49] The fact that this document must be short,[50] easy to read and written in official languages of the Member States is commendable.[51] This ensures that customers of all backgrounds, that being whether financially literate or not, should be capable of understanding the contract and its content. This guarantees consumer protection for all, various types of consumers.

Interestingly, on 21 August 2017 a further regulation was implemented which sets out a standardised presentation format for the insurance product information document. The regulation works in conjunction with the IDD and sets out specific standards which must be adhered to by the insurance product manufacturers. The regulation states that the format of the document must contain the manufacturers name and logo.[52] As far as the length of the document is concerned, it shall be set out on two sides of A4-sized paper when printed.[53] The format of the document must also be according to a specific order of content as suggested in article 4. The document must also have specific headings as set out in the regulation.[54] The regulation therefore ensures that all insurance manufacturers are bound by the same set of rules therefore ensuring that the product information document is consistent and standardised throughout. Consumers will therefore be treated equally and receive the same document despite the manufacturer of the product.

Article 23 also states that information provided to the customer must be communicated on paper, in a clear and accurate manner, in an official language and free of charge. This means that customers can obtain all the necessary information on the insurance product in a clear manner.[55]

---

[49]See Commission implementing regulation 2017/1469 on 21 August 2017.

[50]Set out on both sides of an A4 document. See article 3 of the Commission implementing regulation 2017/1469 on 21 August 2017.

[51]See the Commission implementing regulation 2017/1469 on 21 August 2017. Article 5 says that it must be presented in plain language, no jargon may be used.

[52]Article 1.

[53]Article 3.

[54]Article 6.

[55]Take note that the IDD contains specific rules on cross-selling in article 24. However, cross-selling is not of importance when it comes to microinsurance in the South African market and therefore will not be discussed in detail. The provisions on cross-selling state that The IDD states that where the insurance product is the 'primary' product offered in the package, then the distributors must inform customers whether it is possible to purchase each component separately. If this is in fact the case, the customer must be provided with appropriate information on these different components; a description of how the interaction between the different components changes the risk or the insurance coverage, and evidence of separate costs and charges for each component. Where the insurance is the 'ancillary' product, distributors will need to ensure that the

2.5 Product Oversight and Governance Requirements

Article 25 of the directive contains provisions relating to a product approval process. The article states that undertakings as well as intermediaries which manufacture insurance products for sale to customers must maintain, operate and review a process for the approval of each product, or even relating to significant adaptations of an existing product, before it is marketed or distributed to customers.[56]

This approval process must specify the target market for each product, identify the risks associated with the product for the target market, and ensure that the intended distribution strategy is consistent for the target market.[57] Therefore, it is the responsibility of the insurance undertaking or intermediary to take reasonable steps to ensure that the insurance product is distributed according to the target market.

Further, on 21 September 2017, the EU issued the delegated Regulation 2017/2358 that deals specifically with product oversight and governance requirements for insurance undertakings and insurance distributors. The regulation sets out rules on product governance issues for both manufacturers and distributors.[58] Therefore, the regulations contains concise rules on the manufacturing of insurance products,[59] the product approval process,[60] the target market,[61] product testing and monitoring and review processes,[62] and distribution channels utilised.[63]

This regulation therefore compels both manufacturers as well as distributors to adhere to the specific rules as contained in the regulation. Customers will benefit from this in that they will receive fair treatment and standardised services from both.

The provisions on product oversight are of relevance to microinsurance products as the rules on the target market and the actual product review process will be of major importance when microinsurance products are being sold and marketed to the correct market.

---

non-insurance elements are available to be purchased by customers on the same terms, but without the insurance.

[56]See article 25(1).

[57]See article 5(1) of the Delegated Regulation 2017/2358 of 21 September 2017.

[58]See chapters II and III respectively.

[59]Article 3 of Delegated Regulation 2017/2358 of 21 September 2017.

[60]Article 4.

[61]Article 5.

[62]Article 6 and 7 respectively.

[63]Article 8.

2.6 Pre-Contractual Information

Under article 20, the manufacturer of a non-life insurance product, such as a motor insurance or home contents policy, is required to draw up a document called the Insurance Product Information Document (IPID), which insurance distributors must provide to the customer prior to the conclusion of the insurance contract.

According to article 20(8), the insurance product information document shall contain information about the type of insurance, a summary of the insurance cover, main risks, sum insured, the means of payment of premiums, main exclusions, obligations at the start of contract, obligations during the term of contract, obligations when a claim is made, the term of the contract and means if terminating the contract.

Worth noting is that this information is given to the customer before the contract is concluded, therefore assisting the customer in making an informed decision. The actual contract is delivered to the customer once they have entered into the contract. Therefore, the pre-contractual document does not replace the actual contract. This is a very beneficial practice for the customer as it provides the customer with a brief and easy to read summary of the product and allows the customer to make an informed decision.

2.7 Preliminary Remarks

The above paragraphs considered certain provisions from the IDD which would be of value to the microinsurance market in South Africa. From the above, it is evident that the IDD regulates the way various insurance products are designed and sold either by insurance intermediaries, or directly by insurance undertakings and even through other "ancillary insurance intermediaries".[64] Clearly, consumer protection is the theme throughout the directive. It sets out the information that should be given to consumers before they sign an insurance contract;[65] provides customers with a summary of the product before the contract is concluded and therefore allows them to make informed decisions. These features of the IDD can be of use in the South African microinsurance industry as it would allow low-income earners the opportunity to understand the product before purchasing the insurance cover.

[64]Paragraph 2.1. highlighted the importance of the various distribution channels in insurance and the whole point of the IDD is to enhance consumer protection despite through whom insurance is bought. See article 18. "Ancillary insurance intermediaries" are businesses offering insurance as an add-on to products and services proposed by them. Typical examples include travel agencies or airlines offering travel insurance or sellers of electrical appliance proposing insurance against theft and damage.

[65]Article 18.

As far as preliminary remarks regarding the Directive are concerned, it is evident that the IDD is aimed at ensuring the all insurance products, despite the chosen distribution channel, must be appropriately designed for each customer by taking into account their needs and that approval processes are carried out at all levels by all distributors in order to ensure that consumer protection is achieved. This will be of major significance to the microinsurance market in South Africa.

With this in mind, it is now necessary to consider the rules in South Africa on microinsurance and then evaluate these rules according to the high standard of the IDD provisions. However, before looking at the rules in South Africa, the concept of microinsurance on an international level will be considered.

3 The Concept of Microinsurance

3.1 Introduction

Microinsurance may be viewed as a recent or 'new' concept.[66] Some of the first countries to implement specific regulations on microinsurance are: India, which was the first in 2005, followed by the Philippines in 2006,[67] Peru in 2007, Mexico in 2008, Taiwan in 2009, and Brazil in 2012.[68] The concept of microinsurance is aimed at financial inclusivity.[69] It is trite that insurance is generally taken out by people who can afford it. More affluent consumers are generally in a position to afford insurance. It can be quite costly and this does not allow low income earners the opportunity to afford insurance. This is where microinsurance comes in. Microinsurance is insurance aimed at providing coverage for low-income earners.[70] These types of earners are especially prevalent in emerging markets where insurance may not be as established as other more developed markets.[71] Therefore, in order for microinsurance to succeed in emerging markets, it is essential that these policies are specifically designed with the correct target market in mind. Microinsurance products and policies must be designed for a different group from the current, average consumer.

[66]In South Africa, microinsurance provisions were only enacted as recently as 2018. However, the IAIS in its 2007 policy document states that it is fact not a new concept as things like funeral insurance and mutual insurance have existed for a long time.

[67]Philippine Insurance Commission (2010) Regulations for the provisions of microinsurance products and services. Manila, Philippines.

[68]Biener et al. (2013), p. 2.

[69]Biener et al. (2013), p. 2.

[70]The IAIS states in its policy document on microinsurance that low-income earners differ from country to country and is generally based a country's state of development.

[71]For example, in South Africa.

Microinsurance can be defined as “a financial arrangement designed to protect low-income people against specific perils in exchange for regular premium payments proportionate to the likelihood and cost of risk involved”.[72]

Microinsurance needs to take the specific interests of its consumer into account when developing the regulation and supervision of these products.[73] The principles behind microinsurance are to develop specific insurance policies with the aim of enhancing access to financial services for more vulnerable consumers, to create awareness around these financial products for these consumers, promoting education as well as to enact well-defined laws aimed at the financial inclusivity of these low-income earners.[74] In order for microinsurance to work, these factors need to be taken into account.

3.2 *Microinsurance on an International Level*

International insurance bodies, such as the International Association of Insurance Supervisors (IAIS), have considered the importance of microinsurance. In June 2007, the IAIS published a policy document, Issues in Regulation and Supervision of Microinsurance, aimed at providing a thorough and realistic view on the implementation of microinsurance.[75] This policy document considers the fundamental issues aimed at enhancing a legal framework for microinsurance on an international level. The document explains the current state of microinsurance which is being developed for the low-income population on the basis of practical and prudent insurance business principles, as well as the importance of its role in developing inclusive financial systems particularly within emerging markets, and lastly, why this type of insurance product needs to be regulated and supervised along professional lines.[76]

[72]Churchill and Matul (2007), pp. 1–3.

[73]Churchill and Matul (2007), pp. 1–3.

[74]Churchill and Matul (2007), pp. 1–3.

[75]International Association of Insurance Supervisors and CGAP Working Group on Microinsurance (2007) *Issues in Regulation and Supervision of Microinsurance*. Available at https://www.google.co.za/url?sa=t&rct=j&q=&esrc=s&source=web&cd=2&ved=2ahUKEwihqKiQx_boAhULQhUIHXeACP0QFjABegQIAhAB&url=https%3A%2F%2Fwww.iaisweb.org%2Ffile%2F34275%2Fissues-paper-in-regulation-and-supervsion-of-microinsurance-june-2007&usg=AOvVaw340q6Oe8yb_D9kNa5i0oEp. Accessed 30 August 2019.

[76]International Association of Insurance Supervisors and CGAP Working Group on Microinsurance (2007) *Issues in Regulation and Supervision of Microinsurance*. Available at https://www.google.co.za/url?sa=t&rct=j&q=&esrc=s&source=web&cd=2&ved=2ahUKEwihqKiQx_boAhULQhUIHXeACP0QFjABegQIAhAB&url=https%3A%2F%2Fwww.iaisweb.org%2Ffile%2F34275%2Fissues-paper-in-regulation-and-supervsion-of-microinsurance-june-2007&usg=AOvVaw340q6Oe8yb_D9kNa5i0oEp. Accessed 30 August 2019.

Importantly, the IAIS states that microinsurance is not limited to any type of insurance product or line or service provider.[77] Therefore, microinsurance can take the form of life or non-life insurance and can be distributed through any of the appropriate channels.

The Institute of Insurance Economics in Switzerland has also emphasised the importance of growing microinsurance and the need for such products in emerging markets. There is still a very large portion of the world that does not have access to insurance products. It is estimated that worldwide, four billion people do not have access to insurance products.[78] Therefore, the Institute published reports on microinsurance and made recommendations as to how these products can be specifically designed and marketed for the appropriate consumers.

The Regulation in Microinsurance Markets: Principles, Practice, and Directions for Future Development outlines specific features that microinsurance products should encompass.[79] The paper importantly highlights that insurance policies being sold are increasing yearly. The ILO indicated that the number of policies sold between 2009 and 2012 increased from 135 million to 500 million.[80] This is a significant increase and indicates the prevalence of the uptake of policies. However, even in light of these numbers, there is still a vast portion of the market worldwide that do not have access to insurance products due to that fact that for most, insurance is a luxury. Microinsurance appears to be the most viable initiative in penetrating this unserved market.[81] Some of the key features that the paper outlines which are necessary for the development of microinsurance policies are financial literacy, risk management procedures, consumer protection measures and highly effective regulatory frameworks which supports the growth of the microinsurance market.[82]

Consumer protection appears to be at the forefront of the development of this market.[83] This concept is highlighted by Llanto, in which he states that “any regulatory system around microinsurance products should encourage consumer

---

[77]*Ibid* at page 5.

[78]International Association of Insurance Supervisors and CGAP Working Group on Microinsurance (2007) *Issues in Regulation and Supervision of Microinsurance*. Available at https://www.google.co.za/url?sa=t&rct=j&q=&esrc=s&source=web&cd=2&ved=2ahUKEwihqKiQx_boAhULQhUIHXeACP0QFjABegQIAhAB&url=https%3A%2F%2Fwww.iaisweb.org%2Ffile%2F34275%2Fissues-paper-in-regulation-and-supervsion-of-microinsurance-june-2007&usg=AOvVaw340q6Oe8yb_D9kNa5i0oEp. Accessed 30 August 2019.

[79]Biener et al. (2013), pp. 2–3.

[80]ILO (2012).

[81]Biener et al. (2013), p. 2.

[82]Biener et al. (2013), pp. 2–5.

[83]The IAIS mention in their policy document that consumer protection is vital to the proper implementation of such policies. See page 6 of the International Association of Insurance Supervisors and CGAP Working Group on Microinsurance (2007) *Issues in Regulation and Supervision of Microinsurance*. Available at https://www.google.co.za/url?sa=t&rct=j&q=&esrc=s&source=web&cd=2&ved=2ahUKEwihqKiQx_boAhULQhUIHXeACP0QFjABegQIAhAB&url=https%3A%2F%2Fwww.iaisweb.org%2Ffile%2F34275%2Fissues-paper-in-regulation-and-

protection as a whole".[84] It is therefore evident that consumer protection is one of the fundamental principles of effective microinsurance policy implementation.[85]

It is therefore clear that microinsurance is to have profound benefits for low-income earners, essentially offering these consumers access to a product which they never had access to before. The success of microinsurance is based on various factors, especially with regard to a proper and fair regulatory framework. The regulatory framework for any microinsurance products should be aimed at consumer protection.

3.3 Principles for an Effective Microinsurance Model

The IAIS highlighted specific principles for the successful implementation of microinsurance in their 2007 policy document. The policy document mentions the following principles as essential for the proper implementation of microinsurance: developing a microinsurance policy and promoting its implementation; facilitating the availability of key information/statistical data on microinsurance business; promoting learning processes and dialogue among relevant sectoral stakeholders; enacting clear laws and regulations in accordance with internationally accepted standard that encourage insurance coverage for low-income households and its compliance while limiting regulatory arbitrage, contributing to the policy dialogue with government so that social insurance schemes are working in conjunction with microinsurance; developing clear policies to enhance access to financial services which can be used as a basis for discussion with legislators, and also between government departments and supervisors; limiting moral hazard and fraud by promoting awareness, and putting in place controls and incentive systems; and promoting consumer education and raising awareness to instill an insurance culture among low-income households.[86]

These principles as highlighted by the IAIS in 2007 are crucial for microinsurance models to succeed. It is now necessary to consider the microinsurance model in South Africa and deliberate exactly what it entails for consumers and the insurance industry as a whole.

---

supervsion-of-microinsurance-june-2007&usg=AOvVaw340q6Oe8yb_D9kNa5i0oEp. Accessed 30 August 2019.

[84]Llanto (2007), pp. 61–86.

[85]Llanto (2007), pp. 61–86.

[86]See page 6 of the International Association of Insurance Supervisors and CGAP Working Group on Microinsurance (2007) *Issues in Regulation and Supervision of Microinsurance*. Available at https://www.google.co.za/url?sa=t&rct=j&q=&esrc=s&source=web&cd=2&ved=2ahUKEwihqKiQx_boAhULQhUIHXeACP0QFjABegQIAhAB&url=https%3A%2F%2Fwww.iaisweb.org%2Ffile%2F34275%2Fissues-paper-in-regulation-and-supervsion-of-microinsurance-june-2007&usg=AOvVaw340q6Oe8yb_D9kNa5i0oEp. Accessed 30 August 2019.

4 Microinsurance in South Africa

4.1 History of Microinsurance

Microinsurance is a fairly recent concept in the South African insurance industry.[87] South Africa has always differentiated between indemnity insurance and non-indemnity insurance, long-term insurance and short-term insurance,[88] and most recently through the enactment of the Insurance Act,[89] life and non-life insurance.[90]

However, it is evident from the above classifications that microinsurance was never recognised as a formal insurance product. So when did microinsurance first come into the picture? In 2008, the South African National Treasury put forward the idea of microinsurance when it first released a discussion paper on the future of this type of insurance in South Africa for public comment.[91] This discussion paper was then supported by written-comments and proposals given by participants, which were evaluated and taken into consideration by the Treasury.[92] In July 2011, after significant consultation, the National Treasury published a policy document on microinsurance[93] in which a comprehensive policy framework was set out.[94] The framework emphasised that there were three features of the insurance industry that needed urgent reform; namely, the need to promote better access for South Africans to affordable insurance products that meet the risks they specifically face, the need for consumers to better match the products that they buy with their insurance needs and the strengthening of consumer protection in general.[95] Financial inclusion for the mass market was the objective of the framework.[96]

This is where the concept of microinsurance was born and thereafter became a formally recognised insurance product with the Insurance Act (IA)[97] and PPRs

---

[87]Microinsurance was only enacted in 2018 but first received attention back in 2008 when the National Treasury set out a discussion paper on the matter.

[88]Reinecke et al. (2013), p. 10.

[89]18 of 2017.

[90]The Insurance Act defines "life insurance business" as any activity conducted with the purpose of entering into or meeting insurance obligations under a life insurance policy and "non-life insurance business" as any activity conducted with the purpose of entering into or meeting insurance obligations under a non-life insurance policy.

[91]National Treasury (2008) The future of microinsurance regulation in South Africa discussion paper. www.treasury.gov.za, Accessed 13 July 2019. See also Millard (2012), p. 665.

[92]Millard (2012), p. 665.

[93]National Treasury (2011) The South African Microinsurance Regulatory Framework accessed at www.treasury.gov.za. Accessed 13 July 2019.

[94]Millard (2012), p. 665.

[95]National Treasury *The South African Microinsurance Regulatory Framework* 1. See also Millard (2012), p. 665.

[96]Millard (2012), p. 665.

[97]18 of 2017.

regulating this new type of insurance. The IA defines microinsurance in section 1 as follows:

> 'microinsurance business' means insurance business:
>
> (a) conducted in respect of any of the following classes and sub-classes of insurance business set out in Schedule 2:
>
> (i) life insurance business, classes 1, 3, 4 or 9; and
> (ii) non-life insurance business, in the sub-class personal lines in:
> (aa) classes 1, 2, 3, 9, 11, 14 or 17; and
> (bb) class 10, but only to the extent that the insurance obligations directly relate to the classes referred to in item (aa); and
>
> (b) in the case of life insurance business and class 14 referred to in paragraph (a) (ii) (aa), in respect of which the aggregate value of the insurance obligations relating to each life insured under an insurance policy does not exceed the maximum amounts prescribed; and
> (c) in the case of non-life insurance business other than class 14 referred to in paragraph (a) (ii) (aa), in respect of which the aggregate value of the insurance obligations under an insurance policy does not exceed the maximum amounts prescribed; and
> (d) in respect of which the aggregate value of the insurance obligations under all insurance policies issued by the same insurer to the same policyholder does not exceed the maximum amounts prescribed under paragraphs (b) and (c).

The Act also defines who a "microinsurer" is and states that it is, "an insurer licensed to conduct only microinsurance business".[98]

In the non-life insurance sphere, microinsurance is available in the form of motor, property, agriculture, legal expense, certain liability policies, consumer credit, certain accident and health policies and reinsurance products.[99] It appears from the above-mentioned forms of microinsurance policies that a lot more consumers will now have access to insurance products that meet their specific needs. This ultimately means that a larger portion of the South African population will now have access to these products.[100] The 2018 PPRs contain concise rules on this type of insurance product and importantly, sets out the rules on the application of the provisions,[101] the structure of the policy,[102] the variation and renewal of such a policy,[103] waiting

[98]See section 1 of the Insurance Act 18 of 2017.

[99]See Table 2: Classes and sub-classes of Insurance Business: Non-life Insurance" in terms of the Insurance Act 18 of 2017. See also Millard (2012), p. 665, 667.

[100]Financial inclusion is paramount to this newly recognised insurance product.

[101]Rule 2A.2.

[102]Rules 2A.4.

[103]Rule 2A.5.

periods,[104] exclusions,[105] excesses,[106] claims,[107] the reinstatement rules,[108] and rules on the reporting of a new product.[109]

The insurance market in South Africa is one of the largest on the continent.[110] The South African insurance market accounted for USD 42 billion of the total premiums written of the global market in 2016.[111] PWC compiled a report in which they stated that South Africa has the highest insurance penetration levels in Africa and is a relatively more mature market, which might point to fewer opportunities for growth in the future.[112] However, the increasing growth in premiums tell a different story. Long-term gross written premiums rose from US$15.8 bn in June 2016 to US$19.3 bn in June 2017, while short-term insurers experienced growth from US$4.0 bn to US$4.9 bn over the same period.[113] This proves that there is major growth on the cards for South Africa and Africa as a whole, especially if the microinsurance market can be tapped. In South Africa, there are also very few big insurers that dominate the market, making entrance for smaller businesses very difficult.[114]

In terms of the microinsurance market in South Africa, the population in the country consists of a vast majority of low-income earners as well as people who are exposed to luxuries such as insurance on a daily basis.[115] A large part of the population is not considered "financially literate" and this means that many South Africans do not understand financial products and the consequences of these types of products.[116] This is where microinsurance is to have a significant impact.

---

[104]Rule 2A.6.

[105]Rule 2A.7.

[106]Rule 2A.8.

[107]Rule 2A.9.

[108]Rule 2A.10.

[109]Rule 2A.12.

[110]PWC Report "Ready and Willing: African insurance industry poised for growth" September 2018. Available at https://www.pwc.co.za/en/assets/pdf/south-african-insurance-2018.pdf. Accessed 6 January 2020. This also illustrates why a chapter on South Africa is included in an international European book.

[111]PWC Report "Ready and Willing: African insurance industry poised for growth" September 2018. Available at https://www.pwc.co.za/en/assets/pdf/south-african-insurance-2018.pdf. Accessed 6 January 2020.

[112]PWC Report "Ready and Willing: African insurance industry poised for growth" September 2018. Available at https://www.pwc.co.za/en/assets/pdf/south-african-insurance-2018.pdf. Accessed 6 January 2020. The top four life insurers are very dominant and account for 52% of the market, while the top non-life players control 56% of the market.

[113]PWC Report "Ready and Willing: African insurance industry poised for growth" September 2018. Available at https://www.pwc.co.za/en/assets/pdf/south-african-insurance-2018.pdf. Accessed 6 January 2020.

[114]*Ibid* at page 18.

[115]Mpedi and Millard (2010), p. 508.

[116]Nanziri and Olckers (2019), p. 2.

The financial literacy of South Africans was put to survey by the National Income Dynamics Study and it was found that only 40.57% of South Africans are financially literate.[117] It was further found that peoples financial literacy increases when they go on to study a diploma or degree and that household incomes also had an effect on financial literacy.[118] The survey found that 63.3% of households with an income of R30,000 or more per month are financially literate compared to only 34.1% in households of R5000 per month or less.[119] This proves that low-income earners, the possible microinsurance consumer, is not always financially literate and therefore, there is a need that these products are designed correctly for these specific consumers.

A further study conducted by the Financial Services Board in 2015 showed that about 69% of adult South Africans do not have emergency funds to cover their expenses for 3 months in case of sickness, job loss, economic downturn or other emergency.[120] When surveying people about insurance products the study revealed that only 38% percent of South Africans indicated that they do not hold at least one insurance product in 2015 compared to 62% of adults who hold at least one insurance product.[121] Only 51% of South African adults are aware of insurance products.[122] The most popular type of insurance product held was funeral insurance with 28% of adults holding an account with a burial society.[123]

From the above it is therefore apparent that there is a need for microinsurance products for low-income earners in South Africa. These consumers also require protection from risks but it is essential that microinsurance products are designed and sold differently to these consumers in order to cater for their needs.

4.2 *Policyholder Protection Rules on Microinsurance*

4.2.1 Introduction

Microinsurance is now recognised as a formal type of insurance product in South Africa.[124] Since the promulgation of the Insurance Act,[125] microinsurance is regulated by statute and the specific rules on how these products are to be structured

---

[117]Nanziri and Olckers (2019), p. 2.

[118]Nanziri and Olckers (2019), p. 2.

[119]Nanziri and Olckers (2019), p. 2.

[120]Roberts et al. (2016), p. 9.

[121]Roberts et al. (2016), p. 9.

[122]Roberts et al. (2016), p. 9.

[123]Roberts et al. (2016), p. 9.

[124]See the Insurance Act 18 of 2017 as well as the 2018 PPRs.

[125]18 of 2017.

and carried out are outlined in the PPRs.[126] Chapter 3 of the 2018 PPRs regulates microinsurance. Rule 2A has been included and the rule regulates various aspects of microinsurance.[127] These rules are to have a profound impact on low-income earners and households.

The PPRs have set stringent rules as to how these types of policies may be designed, marketed[128] and sold to low-income earners in South Africa. In addition, all non-life insurance products are regulated by the 2018 PPRs which also include rules on product design as well as disclosure requirements.[129]

4.2.2 Specific Rules on Microinsurance

4.2.2.1 Outline

Rule 2A of the 2018 PPRs contains comprehensive guidelines on all aspects of microinsurance.[130] These rules will be dealt with in further detail below. Rule 2A.2 starts off with setting out the application of the rule and states that,

> This rule applies to any microinsurance policy and applies concurrently with, and in addition to, all other rules set out in these Policyholder Protection Rules. If there is an inconsistency between any provision of this rule and any other rule in these Policyholder Protection Rules, the provision of this rule prevails.

In terms of the use of the term 'microinsurance' rule 2A.3 states that, "An insurer, other than a microinsurer, or any person acting on behalf of that insurer may not use the term 'microinsurance' or any derivative thereof in respect of a policy or in any advertisement in respect of a policy."

4.2.2.2 Structure of the Policy

The structure of a microinsurance policy is significant as it is important to note exactly how these types of products are designed with the specific consumer in mind. Rule 2A.4 states that a microinsurance policy may not have a contract term of more than 12 months and also that the value of the policy benefits under a microinsurance policy may not exceed the maximum amounts as prescribed by the Prudential Authority. The rule also makes mention of the fact that such a policy must, upon expiry of its contract term, either be automatically renewed; or terminated in

[126] See rule 2A in terms of the Short-term Insurance Act Policyholder Protection Rules.

[127] Including claims, excesses, reporting of new products and the structure of these policies.

[128] Rule 10 sets out the rules for the advertising of insurance products.

[129] Rule 2 and rule 11 respectively.

[130] Every aspect from the structure of the policy, to waiting periods, to exclusions is dealt with in rule 2A.

accordance with the requirements set out in these Rules.[131] A microinsurance policy may not provide that any of the policy benefits thereunder is subject to the principle of average.[132]

Therefore, microinsurance policies may not have a contract term more than 12 months and the monetary cap introduced under the section gives effect to the very basic principle of microinsurance: that is that the value of the policy should not exceed a specific amount.[133] The fact that a microinsurance policy is valid for a 12-month period does not appear to be any different from other short-term insurance contracts, as most short-term policies are valid for a period of 12 months and are then renewable after that period has expired.[134]

4.2.2.3 Waiting Periods

A waiting period is for the most part a regular feature in insurance contracts. These periods usually provide for a time period which has to elapse before a benefit will be paid to the policyholder.[135]

As far as waiting periods for microinsurance policies are concerned, rule 2A.6 states that, "a microinsurance policy, underwritten under the accident and health class of non-life insurance business as set out in Table 2 of Schedule 2 to the Insurance Act, may not impose a waiting period exceeding the shorter of one quarter of the term of the policy or 6 months, in respect of which policy benefits are payable on the happening of a death, disability or health event resulting from natural causes".[136] Additionally, a microinsurance policy may also not impose a waiting period in respect of policy benefits payable on the happening of a death, disability or health event resulting from an accident.[137] Furthermore, a microinsurance policy may also not impose a waiting period when it is renewed.

---

[131] Rule 2A.4.3.

[132] See rule 2A.4.1.–2A.4.4.

[133] Caps under microinsurance policies are limited to R100,000 for life insurance and R300,000 for non-life insurance. See also Millard (2012), p. 665, 667.

[134] Millard (2012), p. 665, 667. As far as the variation and renewal of a microinsurance policy goes, rule 2A.5.1 states that the terms, conditions or provisions of a microinsurance policy may not be changed or varied during the first 12 months after inception of the policy, unless the microinsurer can demonstrate that there are reasonable actuarial grounds to change or vary the terms, conditions or provisions of the microinsurance policy or that the variation will be to the benefit of the policyholder or member of a group scheme concerned; and the variation is done in accordance with rules 11.6.3 and 11.6.4.

[135] Millard (2012), p. 665, 668.

[136] Rule 2A.6.1.

[137] Rule 2A.6.2.

4.2.2.4 Exclusions

Exclusion clauses are another common feature in insurance policies. Exclusion clauses generally provide that the liability of the insurer will be excluded in specific instances.[138] The policyholder should be aware of any exclusion clauses as contained in the policy as these clauses directly affect the liability of both parties to the contract.[139] Policyholders should be aware of instances where the insurer will not cover them. This is generally in line with consumer protection provisions. As far as microinsurance policies are concerned, rule 2A.7.1. states that a microinsurance policy in respect of which the aggregate value of the policy benefits is R120,000 or less may not impose any exclusions or conditions limiting the liability of the microinsurer, other than exclusions or conditions relating to:

(a) unlawful conduct, provided that such exclusions may only be applied or relied on if there is a direct link between the cause of the loss and the unlawful conduct;
(b) special risks referred to in the Conversion of the SASRIA Act, 1998 (Act 134 of 1998);
(c) the condition of any asset insured at inception of the policy, other than exclusions relating to the wear and tear of the asset;
(d) the maintenance and usage of the insured asset under a policy that insures against unforeseen mechanical or electrical component failure;
(e) consequential loss; or
(f) any combination of (a) to (e).

From the above it is evident that the exclusion rules relating to microinsurance policies ensure that exclusions in these policies are limited to specific instances of unlawful conduct and general unlawfulness.

Rule 2A.7.2 then provides that a microinsurance policy in respect of which the aggregate value of the policy benefits exceeds R120,000 may impose exclusions or conditions, in addition to those set out in rule 2A.7.1(a) to (f), limiting the liability of the microinsurer if the microinsurer is able to demonstrate that such exclusions or conditions will:

(a) not unreasonably erode the value of the benefits under the policy, taking into account the nature of the policy benefits;
(b) continue to render the policy being suitable for targeted policyholders; and
(c) not compromise the consistent delivery of fair outcomes to the policyholders or members.

Once again, reaching an equitable balance between the insurer and policyholder appears to be the aim of the provision.

---

[138]Reinecke et al. (2013), pp. 241 and 112 state that parties to an insurance contract should be in agreement on the identities of the parties to the contract the performances to be rendered by each of them. In addition, the authors state that "[c]onsensus about performance requires unanimity about the existence and meaning of the proposed terms of the contract, such as warranties, suspensive and resolutive conditions, exclusions, time clauses and any other terms affecting the parties' respective obligations."

[139]Reinecke et al. (2013), pp. 241–242. See also Millard (2012), pp. 668–669.

4.2.2.5 Excesses

An excess clause provides that a policyholder must bear the first portion of the loss himself.[140] In principle, this means that a policyholder will only be able to claim if the loss suffered is more than the excess required to be paid in terms of the policy.[141] In terms of microinsurance, such policies should contain an excess that is proportionate to the loss suffered. In terms of rule 2A.8.1, it is mentioned that microinsurance policies may only provide one standard excess per risk event covered under a particular class of non-life insurance business.[142]

Additionally, rule 2A.8.2 specifies that if an excess is payable under a microinsurance policy, such excess must be disclosed to a policyholder or member of a group scheme, or a potential policyholder or potential member of a group scheme in accordance with rules 11.4.1, 11.5.1[143] and 17.10. Therefore, excess payments must be disclosed to the prospective policyholder before the contract is entered into. The PPRs further regulate the disclosure of excess payments.[144] The fact that excesses must be disclosed to microinsurance policyholders is indispensable to these policyholders as they do not always have the finances readily available at any given time.

Excess amounts should be proportional to the loss suffered[145] and rule 2A.8.3 states that where any excess is payable under a microinsurance policy in respect of which the aggregate value of the policy benefits is R120,000 or less, the excess may not exceed the lower of 10% of the value of the policy benefits, payable for the risk event as set out in the policy[146] or R1000.[147] Where the aggregate value of the policy benefits exceeds R120,000, the excess payment may not exceed 10% of the value of the policy benefits, payable for the risk event as set out in the policy. An additional

---

[140] Reinecke et al. (2013), pp. 327–328 and 242.

[141] *Ibid.*

[142] Rule 2A.8.1. As referred to in Table 2 of Schedule 2 of the Insurance Act.

[143] These rules regulate pre-contractual disclosure of all contractual terms, including excess payments.

[144] Rule 17.10 provides that "Where any excess is payable by the policyholder, the excess:

(a) must be clearly disclosed to the policyholder as required by rules 11.4.2*(d)*(iii) and 11.5.1*(c)*(iii);
(b) must be disclosed to the claimant as required by rule 17.8.3;
(c) must be fair and reasonable; and
(d) may not constitute an unreasonable barrier to a claimant, taking into account the reasonably assumed circumstances and expectations of the average targeted policyholder and claimant in respect of the policy concerned."

[145] Reinecke et al. (2013), pp. 327–328.

[146] Rule 2A.8.3(*a*).

[147] Rule 2A.8.3(*b*).

requirement in the new rules provides for an annual inflation-linked escalation of these values.[148]

In light of the above provisions it appears as if the rules on excess amounts for microinsurance policies are very much in line with the purpose of microinsurance, in that the aimed target market are given value for money, especially where the amount of money these consumers have, is the key consideration.

4.2.2.6 Claims Process

Claims stage is a critical period in the insurance relationship.[149] Usually policyholders only become aware of certain contractual provisions which may impact them negatively at this stage.[150]

In terms of microinsurance policies, rule 2A.9.1 states that subject to rule 2A.9.2, a microinsurer must, within 2 business days after all required documents in respect of a claim under a microinsurance policy have been received, assess and make a decision whether or not the claim submitted is valid,[151] and authorise payment of the claim,[152] repudiate the claim,[153] or dispute the claim and notify the insured of any dispute.[154]

In the case where an insurer disputes a claim submitted by the policyholder, the insurer must, within 14 business days after expiry of the period referred to in rule 2A.9.1 investigate the claim further,[155] come to a decision whether the claim submitted is in fact valid,[156] and then make a decision as to whether to pay or repudiate the claim.[157] It must be kept in mind that these types of policyholders do not have the additional resources lying around to simply cover a loss and therefore they are strongly relying on the insurance coverage taken out. Insurers should therefore comply with the short time-frames in order to compensate the policyholder efficiently and effectively.

A noteworthy provision in the rules comes out in rule 2A.9.3. This rule stipulates that a microinsurer may not reject a claim under a microinsurance policy on the basis

---

[148]Rule 2A.8.5. The amounts referred to in this rule escalates annually, from the effective date of this rule, by the Consumer Price Index (CPI) annual inflation rate published by Statistics South Africa, as defined in section 1 of the Statistics Act, 1999 (Act 6 of 1999).

[149]Reinecke et al. (2013), p. 320.

[150]Reinecke et al. (2013), p. 322. For example, forfeiture clauses generally only come to the knowledge of the policyholder when they submit a claim at claims stage.

[151]Rule 2A.9.1(a).

[152]Rule 2A.9.1(b)(i).

[153]Rule 2A.9.1(b)(ii).

[154]Rule 2A.9.1(b)(iii).

[155]Rule 2A.9.2(a).

[156]Rule 2A.9.2(b).

[157]Rule 2A.9.2(c).

that the policyholder did not disclose if the microinsurer did not specifically request the policyholder to disclose that information before the inception of the policy. This is to have far-reaching consequences for microinsurance policyholders. Evidently, insurers now have to play a more active role in the pre-contractual disclosure phase and must ask the necessary questions.[158] Therefore, disclosure requirements for non-life microinsurance products are very much pro-consumer and seek to protect the consumers in a real manner. Obviously, rule 2A.9 will be a game changer for the consumer in protecting their rights at claim stage.

4.2.2.7 Reinstatement

The concept of reinstatement of insurance policies occurs when a policy has lapsed due to the non-payment of the premium within the days of grace.[159] The payment of premiums is always a cause for concern in insurance policies. Where an insurer reinstates a policy, reinstatement is in effect a renewal of the contract on the same terms as before and insurers may specify formalities before considering the reinstatement of a lapsed policy.[160]

In terms of microinsurance policies, rules 2A.10.1(a) and (b) stipulate that if a microinsurance policy has lapsed due to the non-payment of premium and the microinsurer reinstates such policy, the microinsurer must do so on at least the same terms as the policy that had lapsed and may not impose a waiting period under the reinstated policy. Additionally, rule 2A.10.2 stipulates that if a microinsurer enters into a new microinsurance policy with the same policyholder or member of a group scheme within 2 months after a microinsurance policy has lapsed due to the non-payment of premium, the microinsurer may not impose a waiting period under such new policy.[161]

Therefore, the rules on reinstatement of policies are very much pro-consumer and afford the policyholder a fair amount of protection.

Now that the concept of microinsurance on an international level as well as in terms of South African law has been considered, it is necessary to now focus on the provisions of product design in South Africa. The IDD highlights the importance of product design in insurance products as well as the sales side of these products. The evaluation of the provisions of the IDD above illustrated the importance of taking customers' needs into consideration and product approval processes.[162] Interestingly

[158]This appears to be in line with the recent decision in *Mahadeo v Dial Direct Insurance Ltd* 2008 4 SA 80 (W).

[159]Reinecke et al. (2013), p. 105.

[160]Reinecke et al. (2013), p. 105.

[161]Rule 2A.10.3 stipulates that rule 2A.10.2 does not apply where the policyholder or member of a group scheme had not completed a waiting period imposed under the lapsed policy, in which case the microinsurer may impose a waiting period not exceeding the unexpired part of the waiting period under the lapsed policy.

[162]See paragraph 2 above.

enough, South Africa has included concise rules on product design in the PPRs. These rules also demonstrate the importance of both approval processes and consumer needs. Therefore, these rules will be evaluated below and once these rules have been clarified, the question of whether South Africa can learn or take away anything of value from the IDD provisions, will be deliberated.

4.3 Policyholder Protection Rules on Product Design

Rule 2 in the 2018 PPRs deals with the product design of various insurance products.[163] In terms of non-life insurance products, rule 2 places specific rules and restrictions on insurers when developing these products. The rule starts off by stating that insurers when developing products must make use of adequate information on the needs of identified types, kinds or categories of policyholders or members;[164] insurers must undertake a thorough assessment, by competent persons with the necessary skills, of the main characteristics of a new product, the distribution methods intended to be used in relation to the product and the disclosure documents related thereto in order to ensure that the product, distribution methods and disclosure documents[165]:

(i) are consistent with the insurer's strategic objectives, business model and risk management approach and applicable rules and regulations;
(ii) target the types, kinds or categories of policyholders or members for whose needs the product is likely to be appropriate, while mitigating the risk of the product being used by types, kinds or categories of policyholders or members for whom it is likely to be inappropriate; and
(iii) take into account the fair treatment of customers; and insurers that are subject to white labelling arrangements, must undertake due diligence in the assessment in respect of the governance, resources and operational capability of the persons with whom the insurer has such arrangements and ensure compliance with paragraph (b) above.[166]

Rule 2.2 goes further and states that "before an insurer starts to market, offer or enter into specific policies in respect of a new product, a senior manager of the insurer must in writing approve the product and confirm that the product, distribution methods and disclosure documents meet the principles set out in rule 2.1(b)."[167]

---

[163]These rules thus apply to all non-life insurance products including microinsurance products.

[164]Rule 2.1. (a).

[165]Rule 2.1. (b).

[166]Rule 2.1. (c).

[167]See rule 2.2. Also, take note that rule 2.3. states that 2.3 this rule only applies to the development of any new product as of 1 January 2018 and any material change in design of an existing product."

In summary, it is evident that the rules on product design as set out in the 2018 PPRs are strongly geared towards making sure that various non-life insurance products are designed with the correct consumer in mind. Insurers can no longer design insurance products for a broad market. Rather, they now need to make sure that they can identify the needs of various types of consumers and design insurance products with these specific consumer needs in mind. They also need to do appropriate research on their consumers, identify various distribution channels to be used when marketing the specific products to the consumers as well as always ensuring the customers are treated fairly throughout the entire process.[168]

It is thus clear that rule 2 also identifies the various distribution channels through which products may be marketed to consumers and also takes into account the disclosure requirements for consumers.[169] This is similar to what the IDD sets out in its provisions and rules. The IDD focuses strongly on making sure that consumers are treated equally in the designing and marketing of insurance products, despite the different distribution channels used by insurers.[170]

Therefore, rule 2 in the 2018 PPRs encompasses many of the same principles as in the IDD, in that insurance products should be designed with a specific market in mind as well as the fact that the product should be marketed to the correct market and that customers are treated fairly throughout the entire process. This means that in the realm of microinsurance, these now formalised insurance products must be designed for low-income consumers and should be specifically geared towards them.

4.4 Disclosure Requirements in Terms of the PPRs

Rule 11 of the 2018 PPRs provides for certain disclosure requirements, similar to what we see in the IDD. In terms of rule 11.3.1, it is required that insurers provide communication to policyholders in plain language, which must not be misleading, in an appropriate medium, clear and readable print sizing and monetary amounts must be provided in monetary terms.

Further, rule 11.3.2. states that an insurer must take reasonable steps to ensure that a policyholder is given appropriate information about a policy in good time so that the policyholder can make an informed decision about the policy prior to inception and throughout the duration of the policy.[171]

[168]See rule 2.3.

[169]Take note that rule 11.3.2. specifically states that policyholders must be given appropriate information about a policy in good time so that the policyholder can make an informed decision about the policy prior to inception and throughout the policy.

[170]See paragraph 2.2. above.

[171]This applies to intermediaries too in terms of rule 11.3.6 and 11.3.7. What is considered good time will depend on the importance of the information in the policyholder's decision making process and the point at which it is considered most useful. See further rule 11.3.4.

Also of significance is rule 11.4.1(a) which states that where the insurer provides a policyholder, or intermediary, before a policy is entered into, with a policy quotation or similar communication that purports to provide detailed information to the policyholder, and it may be reasonably expected that the policyholder will rely on such information to make a decision whether to enter into the policy or not, the quotation or communication must include information as set out in rule 11.4.2.[172]

Interestingly, this rule puts the burden on both the insurer as well as an intermediary. Therefore, insurers must give the intermediaries the information and then it can be expected that the intermediaries must relay this information to the consumer. It must be noted that intermediaries are governed by the Financial Advisory and Intermediary Services Act[173] and FAIS requires intermediaries to also disclose relevant information to the consumer before the contract is concluded in terms of the General Code of Conduct.[174]

This is similar to the disclosure requirements as set out in the IDD, however, one noticeable difference is that the IDD makes specific mention of the length of this document which can be vital to microinsurance consumers who may benefit from a short-concise document outlining the important aspects of the policy.

Evaluation of the product design and disclosure requirements for microinsurance products.

If we apply the provisions of product design in the PPRs specifically to microinsurance products, then it is safe to say that non-life microinsurance products must be designed by insurers in a way that takes into account exactly what these consumers require from such products, that insurers identify exactly who their market is and what they need from insurance products and then design the products accordingly.[175]

Insurers must also consider the exact distribution channels of microinsurance products in order to ensure that the correct market is identified and that the best distribution channels for these consumers are utilised. It is also essential that insurers design microinsurance products in a manner that promotes the fair treatment of these customers at all times.[176] In addition, it is crucial that a senior manager approves the microinsurance product before it is specifically marketed or offered to the

[172]This rule states that the insurer must provide the policyholder with the name of the insurer, type of policy, nature and extent of policy benefits, any charges or fees levied against the policy, premium payable, frequency of premium, cooling-off rights, exclusions or limitations and any circumstance which could give rise to a conflict of interest.

[173]37 of 2002.

[174]See section 3(1) of the GCC which requires that providers must, when rendering a financial service such as giving advice, must ensure that such advice is factually correct, provided in a plain language, given timeously so as to allow the consumer to make an informed decision, must be adequate and appropriate for the consumer taking into account their level of knowledge, must be provided in writing if so requested by the consumer etc.

[175]Rule 2.1.

[176]Rule 2.

consumers.[177] The role of the senior manager in this instance is to confirm that the product, its distribution channels and disclosure of all necessary documents meet the principles of rule 2.1(b). Therefore, there is an approval process in place, similar to what we see in article 25 of the IDD.

The provisions on microinsurance specifically appear to be pro-consumer and aim to protect the consumers in almost every aspect. Although some of the provisions in rule 2A are quite similar to other short-term (non-life) policies, such as the time period of 12 months or the waiting period provisions, it is still evident that the rules are strongly based on the protection of the consumer. From the product design stage of microinsurance policies, to the advertising and selling of these products, all the way to claims management procedures, the PPRs apply and therefore, consumer protection is the idea throughout. Therefore, microinsurance consumers will also receive the benefits of disclosure as set out in rule 11, ensuring that they receive adequate information before the inception of the policy in order to make an informed decision.

However, is this sufficient in protecting the needs of microinsurance consumers? Is there not more that can be done to personalise these products for the consumer? This is where the IDD comes in. The following paragraph will ask the ultimate question of, what can South Africa learn or take away from the IDD?

5 What Can South Africa Take Away from the IDD to Enhance the Current Microinsurance Provisions?

The IDD is a comprehensive piece of legislation. The directive is specifically aimed at providing uniform rules on product design and the sales of insurance products across various distributors. The emphasis and inclusion of various distributors is significant as this is broadening the application of the directive to more products and providers. Therefore, creating a fairer insurance market for all customers. The analysis of the directive above highlighted the most significant aspects of the directive. It is evident that the customer comes first and that insurance products are designed specifically taking into account the interests and needs of a target market. The distributors of the insurance products must then ascertain if a single customer falls within the target market of the specific product. If they do fall within the target market, then distributors can adapt the product based on the customer's needs. This therefore ensures that the customer is in fact receiving a product which takes their personal needs into account. This is a commendable feature of the directive. No longer can insurers sell one single product for every customer. Rather, products must be designed according to the target market, which is selected by insurers in accordance to the customer's needs. This is to have far-reaching benefits for the customer. The fact that the directive also encompasses more distributors who must comply

[177] Rule 2.2.

with the directive ensures that customers are receiving the same and fair treatment across all suppliers and distributors. Therefore, customers do not need to worry that because they are dealing with an intermediary, and not directly with an insurer, that they might not be receiving the same advice or treatment. This ensures fairness on all levels of distribution.

One of the most significant features of the directive is the product information document that customers must receive before the contract is concluded. The fact that customers must receive a document that is short, concise, not misleading, accurate, in an official language and which explains to the customer what the product entails, is in fact the most far-reaching provision of the directive. This document allows consumers, at the pre-contractual stage, to make an informed decision. It appears as if this specific provision can be of most value to the South African microinsurance model. Although the PPRs have rule 11.3 and 11.4 which deal with disclosures at the pre-contractual stage, the IDD is far more specific in the fact that it must be a two (2) page document and that it must be in an official language. These two factors can have a significant impact on potential microinsurance consumers.

It was stated above that the vast majority of the population in South Africa are not financially literate and are low-income earners. Thus, making microinsurance a viable option for many people. However, we also face the barrier of most of these consumers not speaking or understanding the English language. South Africa has 11 official languages and therefore, the majority of the population do not speak or understand English. It is trite that insurance policies in South Africa are generally stipulated in English. This will prove to be a major obstacle to the microinsurance consumer. Therefore, South Africa would benefit from following this provision of the directive aimed at providing product information documents that are concise and in an official language.

If South Africa were to follow this approach as adopted in the IDD then that would mean that microinsurance consumers should receive a specific document which is short, concise, not misleading, in plain language, in one of the official languages of the country, and which clearly sets out what the policy entails and what insurance product the consumer is covered for. This would have extensive benefits for the consumer. By receiving a document that is easy to understand, that is in a language they speak and that is short and concise, this can reduce the uncertainties and issues that come about through long-winded policies which are difficult for the layman to understand.

This is a crucial feature which can enhance consumer protection in the microinsurance sphere. It is evident that the current PPRs are very much on track with the IDD in terms of product design, disclosure requirements and the fact that products must be designed with consumers needs in mind. South Africa also follows a similar process of product approval for insurance products. The PPRs currently state that insurance products must go through an approval process by a senior manager who will ensure that the products have been correctly designed for a specific consumer and that their needs were taken into account. However, we do not see a similar provision in the PPRs to that of the product information document as contained in the IDD with regards to the length of the document and the language requirement.

Therefore, if we come back to the question of this chapter which asked, what can the IDD offer the South African microinsurance market? It then becomes clear that following the provisions as set out in article 20 will provide microinsurance consumers in South Africa with significant protection. Article 20(4) also specifically makes mention of the "type of customer", this is something that the PPRs should also make mention of. It needs to be remembered that all customers are different, therefore we cannot apply the same selling and advice standards to all customers. Products should be sold differently according to the type of customer.

Article 20(6) state that for non-life insurance products, the information referred to in paragraph 4 shall be provided by way of a standardised insurance product information document. Paragraph 7 then sets out what the document should entail. Paragraph 8 goes even further by stating exactly what kind of information the document should encompass. It states that it should contain information about the type of insurance, the cover provided, the main risks (included and excluded), premiums and duration of payments, obligations on terms of the contract, what happens when a claim is made, the duration of the contract and terminating the contract.

Although South Africa has similar provisions in rule 11.3.2. and rule 11.4.2 of the PPRs, it would have more of an impact on consumers to have a very short document, being restricted to 2 pages, and in an official language of the consumer. The two rules are also currently applicable to intermediaries too and therefore, the obligation will extend to intermediaries to provide consumers with a standardised insurance product document, as in line with the current rules 11.3.6 and 11.4.1. of the PPRs, as well as in terms of the FAIS General Code of Conduct.

The benefit of providing a standardised insurance product information document to the microinsurance consumer should outweigh the cost of having to prepare such a document. As far as the cost implication goes for the insurer in developing the standardised insurance product information document for the consumer, it is submitted that there will not be any major financial burden on the insurer in developing this document. Currently, rule 11.4.1. of the PPRs allows for insurers to supply policyholders with a quotation or similar communication before the policy is entered into which enables the policyholder to make an informed decision, and this does not come with any additional cost to the policyholder. Rule 11.4.2. sets out the information which must be contained in this quotation or communication and the list is extensive. Once again, no mention of fees to the policyholder is made mention of. Insurers provide this information free of charge to consumers. Therefore, it is submitted that producing a standardised insurance product information document for microinsurance consumers will not cause a financial burden and will only assist the consumers in making an informed decision as to whether to enter into the policy or not. Providing the document in an official language should not affect the consumer as in terms of the National Credit Act[178] section 63 states that every consumer has the right to receive documents in an official language to the extent that it is reasonable having regard to usage, practicality, expense, regional circumstances and the balance of the needs of the population. Section 65(3) of the Act then goes on to state that a credit provider must not charge a fee for the original copy of any document required to be delivered to a consumer in terms of this Act. Therefore, the NCA makes it clear that documents may be requested in an official language and that the provider may not charge a fee for such documents. If we apply this to another financial sector, the insurance industry, then it is not irrational to assume that insurers are to provide consumers with an information document at the pre-contractual stage in an official language at no cost to the consumer. Rather, insurers should focus on this vast untapped market that is capable of bringing in significant revenue for the insurer.

6 Conclusion

The product design of insurance products is no longer an easy or effortless task for insurers. Insurers used to be in control of the process of product design and they were previously the ones who could set the tone of how various types of insurance products were designed and marketed to the public. This is no longer the case. The IDD, in the EU market, and the PPRs in terms of South African legislation, are both setting clear and concise rules on exactly how various insurance products are to be designed and marketed to the public. Consumer protection is at the forefront of both of these pieces of legislation. Insurers and intermediaries must now follow strict rules when designing and marketing insurance products. The fact that the EU as well as South Africa have recognised the importance of protecting consumers, at various phases of any insurance product lifecycle, is commendable.

With specific regard to microinsurance products, this means that these more vulnerable consumers are now afforded additional protection in the design of these specific insurance products. Microinsurance policyholders can now be guaranteed that the policies are designed with their specific needs accounted for. However, there is more that can be done in the sales of these products to protect consumers. By following the IDD in terms of its momentous provision of the insurance product information document, South Africa can ensure better and more personalised protection for microinsurance consumers. South Africa should provide a similar document for its microinsurance consumers and the PPRs should make mention of taking into account the type of customer purchasing the product.

It is pertinent to remember that not all customers are the same and therefore it is necessary to take different types of customers' needs into account. The South African microinsurance model can only benefit from taking the provisions

[178] 34 of 2005.

of article 20 of the IDD into account when selling microinsurance products. This will ensure a higher level of consumer protection as a whole for consumers which have for the most art been excluded from the insurance industry for all this time.

References

Articles, Documents and Textbooks

Biener C, Eling M, Schmit J (2013) Regulation in microinsurance markets: principles, practice, and directions for future development. Working Papers on Risk Management and Insurance No 127

Churchill C, Matul M (eds) (2007) Protecting the poor: a microinsurance compendium, vol II. International Labour Organization, Geneva

Hunt J (2019) What is Microinsurance? The Balance https://www.thebalance.com/what-is-microinsurance-4165961

ILO (2012) Microinsurance coverage expanding at breathtaking pace according to ILO and the Munich Re Foundation. ILO Press Release, ILO, Geneva, Switzerland

International Association of Insurance Supervisors and CGAP Working Group on Microinsurance (2007) Issues in Regulation and Supervision of Microinsurance. Available at https://www.google.co.za/url?sa=t&rct=j&q=&esrc=s&source=web&cd=2&ved=2ahUKEwihqKiQx_boAhULQhUIHXeACP0QFjABegQIAhAB&url=https%3A%2F%2Fwww.iaisweb.org%2Ffile%2F34275%2Fissues-paper-in-regulation-and-supervsion-of-microinsurance-june-2007&usg=AOvVaw340q6Oe8yb_D9kNa5i0oEp. Accessed 30 Aug 2019

Llanto G (2007) Policy and regulatory issues and challenges in microinsurance: a Philippine case. Philipp J Dev 34(1):61

Millard D (2012) Harnessing the informal economy: some reflections on National Treasury's Policy Document on the South African Microinsurance Regulatory Framework. THRHR 665

Mpedi L, Millard D (2010) Bridging the Gap: the role of microinsurance in a comprehensive social protection system in South Africa. Obiter 508

Nanziri LW, Olckers M (2019) Financial literacy in South Africa (2019) 2. (SALDRU Working Paper Number 242 Version 1/NIDS Discussion Paper 2019/9)

PWC Report "Ready and Willing: African insurance industry poised for growth" September 2018. Available at https://www.pwc.co.za/en/assets/pdf/south-african-insurance-2018.pdf

Reinecke MFB, van Niekerk JP, Nienaber PM (2013) South African insurance law. LexisNexis, South Africa, p 10

Roberts B, Struwig J, Gordan S (2016) Financial literacy in South Africa: results from the 2015. S Afr Soc Attitudes Surv, 9

Legislation

Financial Advisory and Intermediary Services Act 37 of 2002

Insurance Act 18 of 2017

Insurance Distribution Directive (EU) 2016/97

National Credit Act 34 of 2005

Policyholder Protection Rules 2018

Part III
The Interplay Between the Insurance Distribution Directive and Other Regulations/Sciences

The Interplay Between the GDPR and the IDD

Viktoria Chatzara

1 Introduction

The operation of the European Union insurance industry during the last years has been deeply disrupted by the adoption in 2016 and the entry into force in 2018 of the General Data Protection Regulation (the "GDPR")[1] and the Insurance Distribution Directive (the "IDD"),[2] which have caused significant changes to the EU and national markets. In some cases these changes have even affected non-EU market players, as in the case of the GDPR provisions, the scope of which also covers companies established outside the EU, but offering products or services to EU-located individuals or monitoring the behavior of individuals within the EU.[3] In other cases the implementation of the new rules has resulted in radical transformations of the insurance market.[4]

[1]Regulation (EU) No. 2016/679 of the European Parliament and of the Council of 27 April 2016 on the protection of natural persons with regard to the processing of personal data and on the free movement of such data, and repealing Directive 95/46/EC (General Data Protection Regulation).

[2]Directive (EU) No. 2016/97 of the European Parliament and of the Council of 20 January 2016 on insurance distribution (recast).

[3]See in this relevance Article 3(2) of the GDPR, as well as Guidelines 3/2018 on the territorial scope of the GPDR (Article 3)—Version adopted after public consultation by the European Data Protection Board (EDPB) on 12 November 2019, and available at: https://edpb.europa.eu/sites/edpb/files/files/file1/edpb_guidelines_3_2018_territorial_scope_after_public_consultation_en_1.pdf.

[4]As, for example, in the case of the Greek Law 4583/2018 transposing the IDD, Article 5 par. 7 of which prohibited the cooperation between insurance agents and insurance brokers, thus obliging

V. Chatzara (✉)
Rokas Law Firm, Athens, Greece
e-mail: v.chatzara@rokas.com

P. Marano, K. Noussia (eds.), *Insurance Distribution Directive*, AIDA Europe Research Series on Insurance Law and Regulation 3,
https://doi.org/10.1007/978-3-030-52738-9_11

1.1 Similar Origins and Parallel Lives

Both the GDPR and the IDD have parallel "life stories", as they both come to respectively replace previously applicable EU laws on data protection (namely the Directive 95/46/EC) and on insurance mediation (namely the Directive 2002/92/EC), aiming to address any issues that rose from the implementation of the previous laws, and also to modernize the applicable legal framework in the data protection and insurance distribution field.

As a coincidence that added to the regulatory compliance burden of the insurance industry participants that were affected by these new sets of rules, both the GDPR and the IDD were enacted in 2016 (May and January respectively), and became effective in 2018 (May and October[5]). With respect to the GDPR, although it granted the national legislators the possibility to adopt more detailed and/or stricter provisions in relation to certain issues,[6] for which it is often mentioned as "hybrid" Regulation, its provisions became directly applicable and enforceable, as provisions of an EU Regulation. On the contrary, in order for IDD to become applicable, the national law measures transposing it into the legal orders of each Member State needed to be enacted.

Root Causes and Aims Both the GDPR and the IDD were adopted by the European Union in the aftermath of the severe financial crisis of 2008, and during the groundbreaking intrusion of technological solutions in the insurance and, generally, the financial services sector. Particularly with respect to the financial sector, legislators and regulators aimed to minimize the possibility for any future systemic risks, increase corporate transparency requirements and strengthen consumer protection.[7] In relation to the data protection field, the different implementation of Directive 95/46/EC across the Member States led to inconsistencies that created complexity, legal uncertainty and increased administrative costs,[8] and thus the need for reform.

As far as the GDPR is concerned, its enactment and entry into force is considered to be the most significant change in personal data protection law during the last

---

market players to reform the structure of existing distribution networks that widely consisted up to now of both agents and brokers.

[5]According to the provisions of Directive (EU) 2018/411 that transferred the deadline for the national laws transposing the IDD to be enacted to 1 July 2018, and the date since which said national measures had to apply, to 1 October 2018 at the latest.

[6]Such as the processing of employees' personal data, the processing of special categories of personal data, any restrictions to the rights granted to data subjects, etc. Such implementing, more detailed provisions, have been adopted, for example in Greece, by virtue of Law 4624/2019, which caused the need for further compliance measures to be taken, in order for the data processing operations to be aligned with the national law provisions as well.

[7]Emond and Tereza (2019).

[8]European Commission – Fact Sheet, *Questions and Answers – Data protection reform*, 21 December 2015, available at: http://europa.eu/rapid/press-release_MEMO-15-6385_el.htm.

20 years,[9] updating and modernizing the principles of the 1995 Directive. Taking into account the needs that triggered its enactment the main aims of the GDPR, as declared in its text, are on the one hand the provision of adequate protection to individuals, who are expected to gain more control over their personal data,[10] and, on the other hand, the facilitation of businesses with the reduction of the administrative costs.[11] At the same time, the GDPR provisions also seem to have taken into consideration the rapid technological developments that have increased the scale of data collection and sharing,[12] and that are expected to further take place and add to the challenges of personal data protection. In this regard, personal data protection obligations are being described in the GDPR provisions in such a generic and broad manner (e.g. with the use of general legal terms, such as "appropriate technical and organizational measures", reference to the "state of the art", etc.) that allows their constant adaptation to any further technological advances.

The IDD provisions, on the other hand, were included in the financial services legislative texts that aim at minimizing any future systemic crises from taking place. As such, its main objectives include the minimum harmonization of insurance distribution regulation across the EU, and the enactment of consistent prudential standards and of elevated conduct standards.[13] At the same time, the IDD operates as a tool aiming to the enhancement of the EU Single Market in the insurance sector, thus, intending to create a level playing field for all different insurance distribution channels,[14] reduce any cross-sectoral differences and improve the competitiveness level of the EU insurance market.[15] Further to the above, the IDD provisions also

[9]Patel (2017).

[10]See Recitals No. 10 et. seq. of the GDPR.

[11]See Recital No. 9 of the GDPR, as well as reference to the benefits of the new provisions in the Communication from the Commission to the European Parliament and the Council, *Stronger protection, new opportunities – Commission guidance on the direct application of the General Data Protection Regulation as of 25 May 2018*, COM(2018) 43 final, 24 January 2018, available at: https://eur-lex.europa.eu/legal-content/EN/TXT/?qid=1563892565511&uri=CELEX:52018DC0043.

[12]Truli (2016).

[13]PwC, *Hot Topic – Insurance Distribution Directive – Are you ready? – Update February 2018*, PwC, February 2018, available at: https://www.google.com/url?sa=t&rct=j&q=&esrc=s&source=web&cd=15&cad=rja&uact=8&ved=2ahUKEwjznMqu2MjjAhVQqaQKHWNXCKMQFjAOegQICRAC&url=https%3A%2F%2Fwww.pwc.co.uk%2Ffinancial-services%2Fassets%2Fpdf%2Finsurance-distribution-directive-are-you-ready-january2018.pdf&usg=AOvVaw0GzYf6-KfmQ38U2v5sovEG.

[14]In this context, the scope of the IDD not only covers insurance intermediaries, but also insurance undertakings, when engaging in direct sales to customers – see Article 1(2) in conjunction with Article 2(1)(1) of the IDD.

[15]Deloitte, *Insurance Distribution Directive (IDD): the MiFID of insurance*, 2017, available at: https://www.google.com/url?sa=t&rct=j&q=&esrc=s&source=web&cd=9&ved=2ahUKEwjznMqu2MjjAhVQqaQKHWNXCKMQFjAIegQIARAC&url=https%3A%2F%2Fwww2.deloitte.com%2Fcontent%2Fdam%2FDeloitte%2Fgr%2FDocuments%2Ffinancial-services%2Fgr_insurance%2520distribution%2520directive_noexp.pdf&usg=AOvVaw2KmAlxEQC4lOigxnILyLXk.

intend to improve consumer protection,[16] providing for enhanced precontractual information and conflicts of interest obligations.

Law and Regulatory Supplements Apart from the main legal texts of the GDPR and the IDD (and their national harmonizing laws), a series of secondary, implementing hard and soft law texts has been adopted to supplement the data protection and insurance distribution regulatory framework. From a data protection law perspective, several Guidelines on specific issues arising from the GDPR provisions[17] had already been adopted by the Working Party of Article 29 (of the Directive 95/46/EC), and have now been endorsed by the newly established European Data Protection Board (EDPB), that continues issuing additional Guidelines, Opinions and other tools concerning the implementation of the GDPR.[18] The GDPR provisions are further supplemented by national law provisions regulating more specific issues, as mentioned above, as well as by virtue of regulatory decisions and guidance issued by the competent national Data Protection Authorities, in a way that the affected insurance market participants still need to take into account any national legal and regulatory particularities that may apply to their operations and which are evolving on an ongoing basis.

Similarly with respect to the IDD, the European Commission has issued (on the basis of relevant authorizations provided in the IDD provisions) delegated[19] and implementing acts[20] which regulate specific issues, e.g. more detailed rules on the Product Oversight and Governance (POG) obligations, a standardized template for the Insurance Product Information Document (IPID), etc. Given that the IDD is a minimum harmonization directive (in the sense that Member States may provide for more stringent obligations on insurance distributors), and that its provisions do not (as a rule) apply directly, but need to be harmonized by virtue of national measures, which are the ones applicable, insurers and intermediaries falling into the scope of the new rules will need to examine what national IDD laws they need to comply with, particularly in case they engage in cross-border activities, given that conduct supervision falls into the ambit of the host regulator's supervision.[21] In parallel,

[16]EIOPA, *Annual Report 2016*, published on 15 June 2017, available at: https://eiopa.europa.eu/publications/annual-reports.

[17]Such as the interpretation and implementation of the transparency notion under the GDPR, the Data Protection Impact Assessment, the Data Protection Officer, the data portability right, etc.

[18]See a list of the applicable Guidelines endorsed and/or adopted by the EDPB at: https://edpb.europa.eu/our-work-tools/general-guidance/gdpr-guidelines-recommendations-best-practices_en.

[19]Available at: https://eur-lex.europa.eu/search.html?DB_DELEGATED=32016L0097&qid=1563887687983&DTS_DOM=ALL&type=advanced&lang=en&SUBDOM_INIT=ALL_ALL&DTS_SUBDOM=ALL_ALL.

[20]Available at: https://eur-lex.europa.eu/search.html?qid=1563887688536&DTS_DOM=ALL&type =advanced&DB_IMPLEMENTING=32016L0097&lang=en&SUBDOM_INIT=ALL_ALL&DTS_SUBDOM=ALL_ALL.

[21]In this sense, an insurance distributor established in Germany, but selling insurance in France, will have to comply (for its France-related operations) with the applicable French IDD provisions, and

EIOPA is also empowered and proceeds with issuing soft law guidelines concerning the implementation of IDD provisions, which should be also taken into account.[22] As a result, also with respect to the IDD, market participants need to consider any applicable national law and regulatory derogations, in order to ensure their compliance with the new regime.

1.2 Impact on Insurance Activities

As noted above, both the GDPR and the IDD radically reform the previously applicable data protection and insurance mediation laws, significantly affecting the operations of both insurance undertakings and intermediaries. The transformation projects undertaken by the affected companies in light of the new rules touch upon and affect all functions, departments and activities, from the ones concerning the relations with customers, business partners and other third-parties, to the ones pertaining exclusively to internal organizational and operational issues.

Internal Effects From an internal aspect, insurers have been required to amend any existing or to adopt new policies and procedures regulating their data collection and processing activities, to identify and implement the appropriate legal bases for each processing activity, to incorporate the privacy by design and by default notions in the procedures and guidelines they follow when designing new activities, to appoint a Data Protection Officer, to conduct data protection impact assessments (when required under the applicable provisions), and to amend their privacy notices and related documentation to customers according to the new information obligations.[23] At the same time, the IDD and its national transposing measures have obliged the affected parties to draft and adopt additional policies and procedures (e.g. POG policies, insurance distribution policies, etc.), to appoint responsible key persons for the insurance distribution activities, and even to proceed with the certification of such key persons and other involved employees.[24]

---

with the German IDD provisions with respect to any products it sells in Germany—see in this regard also PwC, *Hot Topic – Insurance Distribution Directive – Are you ready? – Update February 2018*, as above.

[22]See in this relevance: https://eiopa.europa.eu/consumer-protection/insurance-distribution-directive.

[23]See Patel (2017).

[24]For example in Greece, under the previously applicable law, the employees of insurance undertakings did not need to be certified as to their professional knowledge. According to the Greek law transposing the IDD, the insurance undertaking's employees that are directly involved in the insurance distribution activities, as well as the persons assigned with the responsibility for such activities, have now been required to take exams organized by the Bank of Greece (the Greek Regulatory Authority) and have their professional knowledge and experience certified.

Impact on External Relations With respect to any external relations, insurers have been required to re-evaluate the consent declarations they had been using, and even to request that their customers would grant them anew any necessary consents (or to identify a different, more appropriate legal basis for the processing of personal data). The relations between insurers and intermediaries have also been scrutinized from a data protection law perspective, causing some times debates between the parties, as it was necessary to determine whether they constitute controller-to-processor or controller-to-controller relations, in order to further assess what, if any, GDPR compliance measures needed to be taken.[25] The IDD provisions similarly impact on almost all external relations in the context of the insurance business: depending on the exact national law requirements, any cooperation agreements between insurers and intermediaries need to be reexamined and duly amended, to reflect any obligations arising for each party from the new rules. With respect to the distributor-customer relation, the IDD elevates the customer's best interest as an overarching principle, in the sense that the interests of the customers are required to be taken into account precontractually, as customers need to be proposed insurance products which are suitable and appropriate for them at the time of purchase, but also throughout the life cycle of a product.[26] In this relevance, insurance distributors are required to prepare appropriate procedures and documentation, to be able to proceed with the specification of the customer's demands and needs, to provide advice concerning an insurance product,[27] and to explain the link between the proposed product and the customer's demands and needs.[28]

Compliance Projects It derives from the above that the entry into force of the GDPR and the IDD regulatory frameworks has caused insurers and intermediaries to engage in long, time-consuming and burdensome compliance projects, which have even gone as far as to completely restructure their operations. Although relating to different policy and law sectors, the GDPR and IDD sets of rules affect each other, and compliance with both these frameworks is intrinsically interconnected: to advise a customer on an insurance product according to the IDD, data collection and

[25]KPMG, *The GDPR and key challenges faced by the Insurance industry*, February 2018, available at: https://www.google.com/url?sa=t&rct=j&q=&esrc=s&source=web&cd=1&cad=rja&uact=8&ved=2ahUKEwjMg4fw_cjjAhUQKlAKHYK3AHsQFjAAegQIBBAC&url=https%3A%2F%2Fassets.kpmg%2Fcontent%2Fdam%2Fkpmg%2Fie%2Fpdf%2F2018%2F03%2Fie-gdpr-for-insurance-industry.pdf&usg=AOvVaw0bmREPmoGtekQSR5_7t2gz.

[26]Bernardino (2016).

[27]Particularly in cases where national laws on IDD render obligatory the provision of advice, in the sense of a personalized recommendation.

[28]Caroline Veris and Patricia Goddet – Deloitte, *Insurance Distribution Directive – 2018: a challenging year for the European insurance sector*, Performance magazine issue 25, available at: https://www.google.com/url?sa=t&rct=j&q=&esrc=s&source=web&cd=1&cad=rja&uact=8&ved=2ahUKEwjBq6mxvcvjAhVbURUIHfeZBXcQFjAAegQIAhAC&url=https%3A%2F%2Fwww2.deloitte.com%2Fcontent%2Fdam%2FDeloitte%2Flu%2FDocuments%2Ffinancial-services%2FInsurance%2Flu-insurance-distribution-directive-2018-challenging-year-european-insurance-sector-012018.pdf&usg=AOvVaw3gvYcV6eDFpDwSB2_x-B7j.

processing needs to take place, thus the relevant procedure needs to take into account the GDPR requirements. The same applies in other aspects as well. Considering that data collection and processing is crucial for the insurance business, in the context of numerous operations ranging from risk assessment and premium calculation to claims payment,[29] it is self-evident that any IDD-related compliance actions need to be designed bearing in mind the GDPR requirements and the relevant compliance actions already undertaken.

Such interplay becomes even more evident and the parallel compliance with both frameworks imperative with the expansion of insurance technology (InsurTech) solutions: the use of InsurTech and, particularly, of Internet of Things (IoT) applications in the insurance industry expands and covers all areas from risk assessment to policy and premium re-evaluation and to claims evaluation, and results in an exponential increase of the volume of personal data collected and processed by insurers. In this regard, InsurTech applications need to be designed in a way that safeguards compliance with the applicable data protection principles and requirements in general, but also ensures that any IDD-related requirements (such as the obligation to act in the customer's best interest) are also respected.

This chapter does not aim to exhaustively track down all the possible aspects and cases where GDPR and IDD rules interact, or to propose adequate solutions in the questions which such interaction may pose. Its aim is to highlight some characteristic examples of functions and procedures where such interplay is evident, and lay down some initial thoughts concerning the particular aspects of such interaction that arise and must be taken into account.

2 GDPR and IDD Interaction Affecting Internal Functions

The new data protection and insurance distribution regulatory frameworks establish new, enhanced obligations on the insurers and intermediaries falling into their scope. These cause them to undertake remedial measures affecting first of all their internal organization and operations. The new sets of rules have caused the radical amendment of their internal policies and procedures or the adoption of new ones, the creation of new internal positions and, in general, have added up to the already heavy internal governance obligations that were imposed on the affected parties, particularly on insurers by virtue of the Solvency II regime.

In this relevance, and considering that data collection and processing has always been at the core of the insurance business, any remedial measures aiming to ensure compliance with the IDD provisions shall be also examined as to whether they

[29] Insurance Europe, *GDPR is around the corner: time for final checks by insurers – An overview of insurers' obligations under the General Data Protection Regulation*, May 2018, available at: https://www.insuranceeurope.eu/sites/default/files/attachments/GDPR%20is%20around%20the%20corner.pdf.

encompass personal data processing, in which case, they should be designed and implemented bearing also in mind the applicable GDPR provisions and obligations. All the more so, to the extent that the use of InsurTech solutions that lead to increased volumes of data input to insurers and more direct and frequent insurer-customer interaction and data transmission is integrated in the newly developed functions. At the same time, any GDPR-related compliance measures need to be drafted taking account of the particularities stemming from the nature of the relevant insurance business.

2.1 Product Oversight and Governance Requirements for Manufacturers

One of the characteristic—if not the most characteristic—examples of internal organization obligations described in the IDD[30] and its implementing provisions,[31] with significant interaction with the GDPR-related obligations, are the newly established Product Oversight and Governance (POG) obligations for insurance undertakings and insurance distributors.[32] POG requirements constitute one of the most important novelties in the EU insurance distribution regulation enacted by virtue of the IDD, aligning in this respect insurance regulation with the respective provisions already applicable in other financial services sectors.[33] POG arrangements are considered to be part of the company's system of governance (though not being considered as constituting a new key function for insurers[34]), comprising of internal processes, functions and strategies aiming to ensure a correct design of insurance products, thus intrinsically linked with the Solvency II corporate governance framework and filling a gap thereof from a customer protection point of view.[35]

---

[30]Article 25 of the IDD.

[31]Namely the provisions of the Commission Delegated Regulation (EU) 2017/2358 of 21 September 2017 supplementing Directive (EU) 2016/97 of the European Parliament and of the Council with regard to product oversight and governance requirements for insurance undertakings and insurance distributors (the "POG Regulation").

[32]The discussion around the GDPR and the POG-related obligations and their interplay concerns cases where POG-related activities and procedures entail the collection and processing of personal data, and not exclusively of statistical and/or fully anonymized data.

[33]Thus constituting a good example of the so-called "Mifidization" of the insurance regulation, as POG requirements were first included in the MiFID II text. See in this respect Prof. Pierpaolo Marano, *The "Mifidization": The Sunset of Life Insurance in the EU Regulation on Insurance?*, Liber Amicorum for Professor Ioannis Rokas, 2017.

[34]EIOPA, *Preparatory Guidelines on product oversight and governance arrangements by insurance undertakings and insurance distributors*, EIOPA-BoS-16-071, 18 March 2016, available at: https://eiopa.europa.eu/Pages/Guidelines/Preparatory-Guidelines-on-product-oversight-and-governance-arrangements-by-insurance-undertakings-and-insurance-distributor.aspx.

[35]EIOPA's Preparatory Guidelines on POG, as above.

As described in the applicable provisions, the POG requirements aim to ensure effective customer protection, a level playing field for all market operators, equal conditions of competition and an appropriate standard of consumer protection,[36] in line with the general EU insurance regulation objectives of protection of policyholders and beneficiaries.[37] In this regard, the intended outcome of effective POG requirements is the correct identification of the target market for each insurance product, as well as the design of more targeted insurance products, better suited for the insurance demands and needs of the respective target market. The design and adaptation, however, of insurance products to their target market, as well as the effective monitoring of insurance products throughout their life span, requires the collection and processing of significant volumes of data, including personal data. Said activities, in their turn, fall directly into the scope of the GDPR, which evidences the interdependence between these two sets of rules.

2.1.1 Product Approval Process

The core POG-related obligations on insurers and intermediaries qualifying as manufacturers of insurance products[38] consist in that said manufacturers shall adopt, implement and review an appropriate "Product Approval Process" regulating the development and distribution of new products and significant adaptations to existing insurance products. Such Product Approval Process shall be designed having in mind the principle of proportionality, in the sense that it shall be relatively simple for straightforward and non-complex products, and more complex in case of more sophisticated products that may entail higher risk for the customers.[39]

The main elements that should be included in a Product Approval Process can be summarized in the definition of: (a) the "insurance product" or the "material change" to an insurance product, (b) the methods used to identify the target market for the insurance product and the risks relevant to said target market, (c) the methods used to determine the appropriate distribution strategy and the information to be provided to the distributors, (d) the methods used to ensure that the insurance product is distributed to the identified target market, and (e) how the insurance product will be monitored and reviewed.[40]

---

[36] Recital (1) of the POG Regulation.

[37] Recital (16) of the Solvency II Directive (Directive 2009/138/EC).

[38] According to Article 3(1) of the POG Regulation, insurance intermediaries are considered to be manufacturers *"where an overall analysis of their activity shows that they have a decision-making role in designing and developing an insurance product for the market"*, while under par. 2 of the same Article, such decision-making role is deemed to exist if the intermediary autonomously determines the essential features and main elements of an insurance product (e.g. coverage, price, costs, risk, target market, etc.), which are not substantially modified by the insurer providing coverage for the insurance product.

[39] Recital (2) of the POG Regulation.

[40] BaFin, *Product approval process: Requirements for product manufacturers and distributors*, 02.03.2018, available at: https://www.bafin.de/dok/10523912.

Target Market Identification The identification of the appropriate target market and of the demands and needs thereof in the context of the Product Approval Process requires the collection and processing of significant data volumes by manufacturers (Big Data), including personal data. Target markets shall be identified at a sufficiently granular level depending on the characteristics and risk profile of their members, as well as on the complexity and nature of the respective insurance product.[41]

A strong trend in the insurance sector towards increasingly data-driven business models, in the context of which traditional data sources (e.g. demographic data, exposure data) are being combined with new sources like IoT-deriving data, online media data, etc., is being documented,[42] and is expected to impact on the insurance product design procedures and result in better segmentation of the different target markets. Insurers are seen to be taking advantage of the technological advances in order to address any asymmetric information phenomena they have been facing until recently, due to which they were not able to offer insurance products reflecting accurately the risk profile of their customers.[43,44]

In this relevance, Product Approval Processes are expected to further incorporate in the product design functions the use of new and innovative data sources and Big Data Analytics (BDA) tools, aiming to better understand the customers' needs and characteristics, define further segmented target markets, develop more tailored products and services, and proceed with more accurate risk assessments. The impact of advanced BDA tools has already been evident in this regard, with the appearance and continuous development of usage-based insurance products, particularly in motor and health insurance.[45]

Product Testing At the same time, in the course of the Product Approval Process, and before proceeding with distributing a new insurance product, manufacturers shall test their insurance products appropriately, including scenario analysis, in order

[41]Filip Oller, KPMG Luxembourg, *Product Oversight and governance requirements under IDD*, 24 October 2017, available at: https://blog.kpmg.lu/product-oversight-and-governance-requirements-under-idd/.

[42]EIOPA, *Big Data Analytics in Motor and Health Insurance: A Thematic Review*, 2019, available at: https://eiopa.europa.eu/Pages/News/EIOPA-reviews-the-use-of-Big-Data-Analytics-in-motor-and-health-insurance.aspx.

[43]Porrini (2017).

[44]For example EIOPA stated that, in case of motor liability insurance products, which are mandatory for consumers and which may limit product differentiation, require less granularity and detail in terms of the identified target market, while in the case of insurance-based investment products (IBIPs), which are more complex, the identification and description of the appropriate target market should be more detailed.

[45]In this context, and with the integration of IoT tools into the insurance value chain, the process is leading to the identification of insurance demands and needs on a completely individual basis in relation to each customer, and to the design of completely personalized insurance products.

to assess whether the product meets the identified needs, objectives and characteristics of the target market throughout its lifetime. Such product testing operations may need to go, depending on the nature and the characteristics of the product tested, up to the point of testing the product on a pilot group, to examine whether it meets the expectations of the target customers or not,[46] in which case personal data will once again be collected and processed.

2.1.2 Product Monitoring Phase

Apart from the obligations related exclusively to the design phase of an insurance product, the Product Approval Process shall also provide for and regulate the continuous and regular monitoring of a product launched in the market, with the aim to ensure that it continues meeting the intended customers' demands and needs, and that it does not cause any adverse effects to the customers. In this regard manufacturers shall proceed with regular reviews of the products and identify any factors that may significantly alter the demands and needs or the characteristics of the identified target market, or the main features, the coverage and the guarantees of the insurance product.[47] In the same context, manufacturers shall document and take account of any circumstances that may adversely affect the customers of an insurance product, and proceed with taking appropriate measures to mitigate such adverse effects, informing at the same time the customers and the distributors of such remedial measures.[48]

All the above mentioned monitoring and review actions that take place in the after-sales service phase, and with a view to being efficient and to truly add to customer protection, as is the aim of the POG obligations, require further collection and processing of personal data determining the exact circumstances that may materially affect the characteristics of the insurance product or the target market, or that may cause adverse effects to the customers. In order to further assist in the collection and evaluation of such data, insurers have also introduced technological tools in the post-sales service and assistance sectors, such as automated answers in their call centers, robotized customer service evaluation, to generate insights about complaint management, fraud detection and customer authentication issues.[49]

[46]EIOPA, *First set of Questions & Answers on the Application of the Insurance Distribution Directive*, 11.07.2018, available at: https://eiopa.europa.eu/Pages/News/EIOPA-publishes-first-set-of-Questions%2D%2DAnswers-on-the-Application-of-the-Insurance-Distribution-Directive.aspx.

[47]Article 7(1) of the POG Regulation.

[48]Article 7(3) of the POG Regulation.

[49]EIOPA, *Big Data Analytics in Motor and Health Insurance: A Thematic Review*, as above.

2.2 *Product Distribution Arrangements*

POG provisions impose further obligations on both manufacturers and distributors concerning the distribution of insurance products. The measures to be taken to ensure compliance with said obligations similarly entail data processing issues, in a way that the design and implementation of POG compliance measures needs to take into account any applicable GDPR-related aspects so as to ensure compliance with the respective data protection obligations as well.

2.2.1 Choice and Audit of Appropriate Distribution Channels

The identification of the target market by manufacturers under the Product Approval Process impacts upon the choice of the distribution channels to be used, as they must be appropriate for said target market.[50] The choice of appropriate distribution channels may also entail data collection and processing activities on behalf of the manufacturer, particularly in the event that the affected distributors are individuals, and to the extent that the choice of appropriate distributors is deemed to require the processing of information on the key persons being responsible for the insurance distribution activities.

In the same context, manufacturers provide the distributors with information on their Product Approval Process and the objectives thereof, and ensure that their products are being distributed in accordance with said Process, namely, in accordance with the identification of the target market for each product, i.e. whether the insurance products are being distributed on said target market.[51] Nevertheless, this obligation does not automatically result in a strict prohibition to distributors to sell an insurance product outside the target market, neither does it oblige manufacturers to take any measures against distributors proceeding with such sales, in any case. On the contrary, according to EIOPA's guidance, in cases of distribution outside the target market, manufacturers need to assess whether there are any adverse consequences for the customers outside the target market, who were provided with the product and take corrective measures, in case of such adverse effects, in order to mitigate them.[52] Such assessment, however, evidently entails personal data collection and processing activities, aiming to assess the possibility for any adverse effects on the specific customers.

[50] Article 8(1) of the POG Regulation.

[51] Article 8(3) of the POG Regulation.

[52] EIOPA, *First set of Questions & Answers on the Application of the Insurance Distribution Directive*, as above.

2.2.2 Product Distribution Arrangements

In terms of distributors, the POG Regulation provides that they shall also have in place specific product distribution arrangements with the aim to ensure that they obtain from the product manufacturer all information required on the specific features of the insurance product and the identified target market, aiming to prevent and mitigate customer detriment, support a proper management of conflicts of interest and ensure that the objectives, interests and characteristics of customers are duly taken into account.[53] Furthermore, insurance distributors are required to ensure that the distribution strategies they follow are in line with the distribution strategies and target markets identified by the product manufacturer.

For these objectives to be achieved, insurance distributors will need to collect and process customers' personal data so that they assess whether any conflicts of interest may arise, and to evaluate the customers' characteristics, demands and needs, so that they assess whether each customer falls into the relevant target market, and propose appropriate insurance products. The volume of personal data collected in this context increases exponentially with the use of new technologies (IoT, connected devices), that are being more and more included in the design of new distribution strategies and methods. As such, product distribution arrangements need to be drafted and designed in a way that takes into account the necessary data processing activities for their efficient implementation, as well as any related GDPR (and other data protection) obligations.

Reporting to the Manufacturer The obligations which IDD and its implementing POG Regulation pose on distributors extend throughout the life span of the insurance product. Distributors shall monitor and notify the manufacturer of any indication that the insurance product is not in line with the target market's demands and needs, or in any event that they become aware of any circumstances that may adversely affect the customers.[54] For distributors to fully comply with these obligations, they shall monitor the performance of the insurance products they distribute during their whole term, by maintaining contact with the relevant customers, and by collecting and processing adequate and appropriate data, that will allow them to duly evaluate the product's performance and conformity with the insurance demands and needs of the identified target market. Should such alignment not occur or cease, distributors will also have to transfer the relevant data to product manufacturers, in order for appropriate measures to be taken. Similar data transfers will have to take place in case of adverse effects caused by or due to product characteristics to the customers.

All the above, indicatively stated, personal data collection and processing activities will have to be duly designed in the product distribution arrangements adopted by insurance distributors, in a way that takes into consideration the GDPR-deriving

[53] Article 10(1) and (2) of the POG Regulation.

[54] Article 11 of the POG Regulation.

data protection obligations. More to that, the issue of the legal capacity under the GDPR, in which insurance distributors act when processing such personal data and transferring them to the product manufacturers, should be also examined, as further data protection implications may arise, that may even affect the form of the cooperation between the distributors and the manufacturers.

2.3 *Related Data Protection Issues*

As derives from the above brief analysis, compliance with the POG and product distribution obligations requires the design, adoption and implementation of a series of internal policies, procedures and activities that encompass personal data collection and processing and, as such, fall into the scope of the GDPR provisions. In this respect, the design of any appropriate IDD compliance measures should not take place without also taking into account any relevant GDPR implications, and without ensuring compliance with the new data protection framework as well.

2.3.1 Privacy by Design and by Default

A key element of the GDPR's risk-based approach and its focus on the accountability principle[55] is the adopted legal obligation for data controllers[56] to put in place appropriate technical and organizational measures designed to implement data protection principles, both at the time of the determination of the means for processing and at the time of the processing itself (privacy by design), and for ensuring that, by default, only personal data which are necessary for each specific processing purpose are being processed (privacy by default).[57] The notion of privacy by design, as the idea of integrating data protection principles at the design of any system, service, product or process, and throughout their lifecycle, is not a new one, as the need to be proactive in considering any privacy requirements has been acknowledged long before the GDPR.[58] Nevertheless, it was by virtue of the

[55]In the sense that data controllers must ensure and be able to demonstrate compliance with the GDPR provisions.

[56]I.e. of the persons that, alone or jointly with others, determine the purposes and means of the processing of personal data—see Article 4(7) of the GDPR.

[57]Article 25 of the GDPR.

[58]The term "privacy by design" was originally used by Ann Cavoukian, the Information and Privacy Commissioner in Ontario, Canada, and was broken down in the so-called "seven foundational principles": 1. Proactive not Reactive, Preventative not Remedial; 2. Privacy as the Default Setting; 3. Privacy Embedded into Design; 4. Full functionality—positive sum, not zero sum; 5. End-to-end security—full lifecycle protection; 6. Visibility and transparency—keep it open; 7. Respect for user privacy—keep it user-centric. See in this respect: https://www.ipc.on.ca/wp-content/uploads/2018/01/pbd.pdf.

GDPR provisions that the privacy by design notion transformed from a "best practice" (as it was considered under the previous regime) to a legal obligation.

General Principles and Guidelines As a legal obligation, the privacy by design and by default notions shall be embedded in the design of all activities that may entail personal data processing operations, including in the design of the Product Approval Processes and the product distribution arrangements of manufacturers and distributors respectively (POG-related obligations, policies and procedures in general), taking into account the nature, scope, context, purposes and complexity of the relevant activities, the state of the art and costs of implementation of any measures, and the risks that the processing operations may cause to individuals. Data controllers shall implement appropriate technical and organizational measures and necessary safeguards, designed to implement the applicable data protection principles in an effective manner and to protect the rights and freedoms of data subjects.[59]

In practice, compliance with the privacy by design and by default principles could be achieved by ensuring that data protection outcomes are achieved, when drafting the POG-related policies and procedures, such as[60]:

- Considering data protection issues as part of the product approval process and product distribution arrangements;
- Rendering data protection an essential component of the above mentioned policies and procedures;
- Ensuring that only the personal data that are needed for the POG-related purposes are being processed[61];
- Ensuring that any IT systems, services, etc. being employed in POG arrangements safeguard personal data protection;
- Disclosing both within and outside the organization the identity and contact details of the persons responsible for data protection (such as the Data Protection Officer);
- Adopting a simple language policy for any public documents, such as the notices explaining to the customers the processing of their personal data for purposes relating to product design and monitoring;

[59]See Guidelines 4/2019 on Article 25, "Data Protection by Design and by Default" of the European Data Protection Board, adopted on 13 November 2019—Version for public consultation, available at: https://edpb.europa.eu/sites/edpb/files/consultation/edpb_guidelines_201904_dataprotection_by_design_and_by_default.pdf. To be noted that the final relevant guidance of the EDPB on the privacy by design and by default notions, along with practical guidelines for their effective implementation, after the public consultation, was not made publicly available by March 2020.

[60]Information Commissioner's Office, *Guide to the General Data Protection Regulation (GDPR) – Accountability and Governance – Data Protection by design and by default*, 22.05.2019, available at: https://ico.org.uk/for-organisations/guide-to-data-protection/guide-to-the-general-data-protection-regulation-gdpr/accountability-and-governance/data-protection-by-design-and-default/.

[61]For instance, distributors, when designing the procedures for reporting any adverse circumstances to product manufacturers, shall ensure that only the personal data relating to and adequately describing such adverse circumstances will be transferred to the product manufacturers.

- Providing customers/data subjects with appropriate tools, so that they can determine whether their personal data are being properly processed.

As a result, apart from ensuring that the minimum requirements set by the IDD and the POG Regulation are met, insurers and intermediaries shall also ensure that any data processing operations are also taking place in the context of a design process integrating data protection principles in both the design and operational phase thereof. Furthermore, measures to mitigate any risks to the affected individuals, taking into account the state of the art and the cost of implementation, shall be also selected and implemented throughout the POG arrangements; such measures shall be appropriate and effective, in the sense that they must assist the data controller in ensuring and being able to demonstrate compliance with the GDPR. Equally important, the appropriate data protection safeguards shall be implemented into the processing activities described in the applicable POG arrangements.[62]

Manufacturer—Distributor Relations Taking into account that the privacy by design and by default obligations refer to data controllers, the issue of whether an insurance distributor qualifies as an individual (or joint) data controller or as a data processor acting on behalf of the manufacturer-data controller, and to what extent, becomes of importance even at the stage of designing appropriate and adequate product distribution arrangements. Should the insurance distributor be characterized as a data controller, the case is quite simple as it will bear complete responsibility in embedding privacy by design and by default into its product distribution arrangements. The issue, however, becomes a bit more complicated, in case the distributor is considered to be joint controller with the manufacturer, in the sense that they jointly determine the means and purposes for the processing activities in the context of the product distribution. In this case their cooperation agreement should also contain a specific description of the roles and responsibilities undertaken by each of them in terms of the data protection obligations and, namely, the ones stemming from the rights granted to data subjects by the GDPR, and the ones concerning the provision of appropriate information to them.[63] More to that, the possibility for the distributor to be considered to act as data processor[64] on behalf of the manufacturer (who is acting as the data controller), should also not be precluded, particularly in cases where the distributor does not have any discretionary powers and exclusively follows the guidelines and mandates of the manufacturer when it comes to product distribution activities. In such case, would the distributor as a data processor not have to comply with the privacy by design and by default obligations when designing its product distribution arrangements? Or would the manufacturers, as data controllers,

[62]European Data Protection Supervisor (EDPS), *Opinion 5/2018 – Preliminary Opinion on privacy by design*, 31 May 2018, available at: https://edps.europa.eu/data-protection/our-work/publications/opinions/privacy-design_en.

[63]Article 26 of the GDPR.

[64]I.e. as the person which processes personal data on behalf of the data controller—see Article 4 (8) of the GDPR.

have to ensure that the distributors-data processors they choose to cooperate with design and operate their processes in a way that safeguards personal data protection, thus indirectly obliging distributors to endorse privacy by design and by default principles in any case whatsoever? What additional provisions and safeguards would have to be included in the cooperation agreement between the manufacturer and the distributor, in order to duly reflect such controller-processor relation[65]?

In the same context, issues concerning the privacy requirements implemented by each one of the parties involved and, particularly, any inconsistencies between the different privacy arrangements, should be also identified and addressed, in a way that the different privacy settings are duly respected by all parties, particularly in cases involving BDA. The solution of "automated policy definition and enforcement", in a way that one party cannot refuse to follow the policy of another party in the same chain, could be examined in this direction.[66]

Third Party Providers Rapid technological advancements and the increasing penetration of InsurTech solutions throughout the insurance value chain impacts the product design phase as well. Product approval and monitoring processes quickly incorporate InsurTech tools, aiming to collect through them the adequate and appropriate data needed to achieve their goals. Although many insurers directly invest in technological research and innovation, others cooperate with InsurTech providers in order to purchase or obtain rights to use appropriate tools. Even in this case, and though InsurTech providers would not directly be seen as falling into the scope of the obligation to abide with privacy by design and by default principles, they would have to (and insurers and intermediaries cooperating with them should examine whether they do) design their products in a way that enables data controllers to implement all necessary measures to ensure data protection.[67]

Privacy-Enhancing Technologies In the same relevance, and as a means to assist them in ensuring the integration of data protection principles into their product approval and distribution arrangements, manufacturers and distributors should consider using privacy-enhancing technologies (PETs), i.e. technologies that embody fundamental data protection principles, by minimizing personal data use,

---

[65]Particularly in light of Article 28 of the GDPR regulating the controller-processor relationship, and par. (3) thereof, providing for the minimum contractual provisions that shall be included in the agreement or other legally binding document to be executed between them.

[66]ENISA, *Privacy by design in big data – An overview of privacy enhancing technologies in the era of big data analytics*, December 2015, available at: https://www.enisa.europa.eu/publications/big-data-protection.

[67]EDPS, *Opinion 5/2018 – Preliminary Opinion on privacy by design*, as above. See also in this relevance Recital 78 of the GDPR, stating that: "*When developing, designing, selecting and using applications, services and products that are based on the processing of personal data or process personal data to fulfil their task, producers of the products, services and applications should be encouraged to take into account the right to data protection when developing and designing such products, services and applications and, with due regard to the state of the art, to make sure that controllers and processors are able to fulfil their data protection obligations . . .*".

maximizing data security, and empowering individuals.[68] Despite the fact that they have not yet become a standard and widely-used component in system design, PETs such as encryption, protocols for anonymous communications, attribute-based credentials, etc.,[69] could be incorporated into the product approval and distribution policies designed and implemented in light of the new IDD obligations, ensuring at the same time compliance with the applicable GDPR provisions.

Privacy by Design in Big Data Analytics Product design and monitoring processes in large scale are expected to require the collection and use of big data by product manufacturers, thus giving rise to increased privacy concerns. As a result, increased privacy by design arrangements will need to be integrated in the design and implementation of the relevant product approval and distribution procedures. In this relevance, the notion of "selectiveness" could assist in ensuring GDPR compliance: its accurate implementation would ensure that only the information that is actually needed for a specific analysis is securely being accessed and processed (instead of collecting all possible data to feed the analysis).[70]

Privacy by Default In the same time, the privacy by default notion, as elaborated in the relevant GDPR provisions, is intrinsically linked with the data minimization and the purpose limitation principles,[71] according to which data controllers shall ensure that they process only the personal data required for the specific processing purpose, and that they do not proceed with any further processing of the personal data for purposes other than the specific, legitimate ones they collected the personal data for (which shall be further notified to the data subjects concerned). In this sense, and in order to comply with both the privacy by default obligations, and the obligations to abide by the general processing principles of the GDPR, POG-related arrangements encompassing personal data processing shall be designed in a way that personal data processing is limited to the personal data that are necessary for the correct and sufficiently granular identification of the target market, for the adequate monitoring of the insurance product's performance, and for no further processing purposes (such as, for example evaluation of a customer's behavior).

---

[68]See ICO's GDPR guidance on privacy by design and by default, as above. ENISA refers to PETS as *"software and hardware solutions, i.e. systems encompassing technical processes, methods or knowledge to achieve specific privacy or data protection functionality or to protect against risks of privacy of an individual or a group of natural persons"*—see also in this respect: https://www.enisa.europa.eu/publications/big-data-protection.

[69]ENISA, *Privacy and Data Protection by Design – from policy to engineering*, December 2014, available at: https://www.enisa.europa.eu/publications/privacy-and-data-protection-by-design.

[70]ENISA, *Privacy by design in big data – An overview of privacy enhancing technologies in the era of big data analytics*, as above.

[71]As provided in Article 5(1) of the GDPR.

2.3.2 Transparency and Information Issues

Another set of major issues arising from the GDPR provisions and concerning the collection and use of personal data in the course of the implementation of POG-related arrangements, refers to the obligations of data controllers to duly inform the affected individuals of the processing their personal data undergo, in line with the general principle of transparency of the data processing activities.[72] Transparency constitutes an overarching principle in the GDPR constellation,[73] applying irrespectively of the legal basis applicable and throughout the processing activities, to three central areas:

- The provision of information to data subjects related to fair processing of their personal data, i.e. before or at the start of the data processing activity (when the personal data is being collected either from the data subject or otherwise obtained);
- Any communications between the data controllers and the data subjects in relation to their rights under the GDPR, i.e. throughout the processing period; and
- Facilitating the data subjects to exercise their rights, or at other specific points during the processing period, such as when data breaches occur, or in case of other material changes to the processing.[74]

Transparency Concerns in POG Arrangements Personal data processing in the context of product design and product monitoring and evaluation activities, particularly in the cases involving massive data collection through connected devices, or big data analytics, could raise transparency concerns. Traditional notice mechanisms, such as simple privacy notices, written forms, etc., are considered to be inadequate to provide proper transparency and control over the personal data processing activities.[75] Particularly in the case of BDA tools being employed, the transparency concerns are more elevated, as many firms encounter difficulties in

[72]As provided in Article 5(1)(a) of the GDPR.

[73]Although not defined in the GDPR provisions, the notion of transparency is described in Recital 39 of the GDPR, according to which: *"It should be transparent to natural persons that personal data concerning them are collected, used, consulted or otherwise processed and to what extent the personal data are or will be processed. The principle of transparency requires that any information and communication relating to the processing of those personal data be easily accessible and easy to understand, and that clear and plain language be used. That principle concerns, in particular, information to the data subjects on the identity of the controller and the purposes of the processing and further information to ensure fair and transparent processing in respect of the natural persons concerned and their right to obtain information and communication of personal data concerning them which are being processed ...".*

[74]Working Party 29, *Guidelines on transparency under Regulation 2016/679*, 17/EN, WP260 rev.01, adopted on 29 November 2017 and last revised and adopted on 11 April 2018, as endorsed by the EDPB, available at: https://edpb.europa.eu/our-work-tools/general-guidance/gdpr-guidelines-recommendations-best-practices_en.

[75]ENISA, *Privacy by design in big data – An overview of privacy enhancing technologies in the era of big data analytics*, as above.

adequately and properly explaining some complex data processing tools and procedures.[76]

POG arrangements shall be designed so as to ensure that affected data subjects are provided with the appropriate information on the processing of their personal data,[77] in a way that complies with the transparency requirements.[78] Namely, any information solutions to be adopted, shall ensure that the information or communication to the data subjects must be concise, transparent, intelligible and easily accessible, using clear and plain language, must be in writing or by other means, including (where appropriate) by electronic means or even orally where requested by the data subject, and generally free of charge. It is crucial, when designing the way of providing the required information, that it is clearly differentiated from any non-privacy related information (such as other precontractual information to be provided under the IDD provisions), and that the necessary information is provided in a way that prevents information fatigue of the individuals. Data subjects must be able to duly determine in advance the scope and the possible repercussions of their personal data processing activities, in a way that they are not surprised at a subsequent stage. However, given that the GDPR increased information obligations add to the existing obligations to provide precontractual information to the customers that derive from the applicable insurance regulation (e.g. the load of information prescribed by the IDD and the Solvency II Directive), the problem of providing overwhelming information to the customers arises, which, in its turn, may lead to opposite results than the intended customer-data subject protection.[79]

Information Obligations In this relevance, insurers and intermediaries are ultimately obliged to think out of the box and manufacture alternative methods and means of providing the required information to the customers. The use of InsurTech solutions throughout the insurance value chain, which grants insurance market players the possibility to develop a direct and continuous relation and communication with their customers could be also employed in order to address any transparency concerns that may arise from encompassing data processing operations into the product design and monitoring procedures to be implemented.

GDPR provisions already grant data controllers the discretion to provide the required information via electronic tools, where appropriate (which could be the case, for example, where customers agree to connect with their insurer by means of connected devices). In such cases, the transparency goals could be achieved by employing not (or not only) plain textual communications, which do not seem to

[76]EIOPA, *Big Data Analytics in Motor and Health Insurance: A Thematic Review*, as above.

[77]As set out in Articles 13 and 14 of the GDPR (depending on whether the personal data are being collected directly from the data subjects or from other sources).

[78]A description of the transparency requirements, in the form of the general rules applying to any information and/or communications to the data subjects, is provided in Article 12 of the GDPR.

[79]Tarasiuk (2019).

adequately and efficiently address the evolution of services,[80] but also by incorporating into the design of the product offering and monitoring phases layered approaches (which can provide information to the users at different stages of the processing and at different levels of detail), maybe even in combination with standardized icons, pictograms and other visualization tools, which are provided for in the GDPR, where appropriate.[81] In this regard, the integration of technological advances into the adopted POG-related arrangements, should not only aim at increasing the amount and frequency of data input from the customers, but should also be employed in a way that assists in achieving compliance with the GDPR transparency obligations.

2.3.3 Other Privacy-Related Implications

The extensive collection and use of personal data for the purposes of efficient POG arrangements in line with the relevant IDD provisions enhances already existing or triggers new GDPR-related obligations.

Data Protection Impact Assessment According to the GDPR, a Data Protection Impact Assessment (DPIA) is a process designed to describe the processing activity, assess the necessity and proportionality of said processing activity, identify the risks to the rights and freedoms of the affected individuals, and assist in defining the appropriate measures to mitigate said risks. In this relevance, DPIAs are considered to be tools assisting the data controllers with their accountability obligations, as they not only help them comply with their GDPR obligations, but also to demonstrate and prove compliance at any point.[82] As described in the GDPR provisions, a DPIA is mandatory only in cases the contemplated processing activity is likely to result in a high risk to the rights and freedoms of natural persons,[83] particularly when new data processing technologies are employed, and, in any case, in the processing operations the national Data Protection Authorities have included in their lists of processing activities requiring the conduct of DPIAs.

In the case of data processing operations taking place in the course of product design and monitoring activities, they would most likely be considered as triggering the obligation for a DPIA, particularly in case of systematic and extensive evaluation

---

[80]Indicatively, it was shown that, in order for an average user to read the privacy policies for all visited web services, he/she would need to spend approximately 30 working days per year. See ENISA, *Privacy by design in big data – An overview of privacy enhancing technologies in the era of big data analytics*, as above.

[81]Working Party 29, *Guidelines on transparency under Regulation 2016/679*, as above.

[82]Working Party 29, *Guidelines on Data Protection Impact Assessment (DPIA) and determine whether processing is "likely to result in a high risk" for the purposes of Regulation 2016/679*, adopted on 4 April 2017, 17/EN, WP 248, and endorsed by the EDPB, available at: https://edpb.europa.eu/our-work-tools/general-guidance/gdpr-guidelines-recommendations-best-practices_en.

[83]Article 35(1) of the GDPR.

of personal data including automated decision-making processes, large scale processing of special categories of data or even of simple personal data, matching or combination of different datasets, innovative use of technological solutions, or in case the data processing may prevent the data subjects from exercising their rights or using a service/contract.[84] As a result, the design of the product approval process and the product distribution arrangements, shall be accompanied by a Data Protection Impact Assessment, in accordance with the relevant GDPR provisions and guidance, including at least the following information concerning the relevant data processing activities:

- a systematic description of the processing operations (e.g. nature, scope, context and purposes of the processing, personal data categories, recipients and retention period, functional description of the processing activity, etc.);
- an assessment of the necessity and proportionality of the processing activity (e.g. identification of the measures taken contributing to the necessity and proportionality, and to the rights of the data subjects, including definition of specified, legitimate and explicit purposes, data minimization measures, etc.);
- identification of the risks to the rights and freedoms of the data subjects concerned (e.g. reference to the origin, nature, particularity and severity of the risks, to the potential impacts to the data subjects, etc.);
- identification of the appropriate measures envisaged to mitigate the above mentioned risks; and
- reference to any third party involvement and input to the DPIA (e.g. advice of the DPO, views of the data subjects or their representatives, etc.).

Depending on the data activities envisaged in the course of the product approval, distribution and monitoring arrangements, and on the severity of the risks to the data subjects that may arise thereof, the risk mitigating measures may not be considered to sufficiently reduce the potential risks from the envisaged processing activities. In such case, manufacturers or distributors (as the case may be) will have to consult with the competent Data Protection Authority before launching the contemplated data processing activities, which may even conclude that said processing activities shall not take place at all.[85]

Further to the above, if the product design, distribution and monitoring activities deem to require a DPIA, such Assessment shall take place primarily at the design stage of such processes. However, the DPIA, as well as the compliance with all GDPR obligations, is not prescribed as an one-off exercise, but rather as a

[84]These data processing activities are included in the indicative examples of operations that trigger the obligation for a DPIA according to Article 35(3) of the GDPR, the WP 29 Guidelines on DPIA, while most of these categories have been included in the lists of activities triggering the DPIA obligations, issued by the national Data Protection Authorities—see, indicatively, the relevant list issued by the Hellenic Data Protection Authority (HDPA) in its Decision 65/2018, published in Government Gazette B' 1622/10.05.2018, available at: https://www.dpa.gr/portal/page?_pageid=33,239286&_dad=portal &_schema=PORTAL.

[85]The provisions of Article 36 of the GDPR are of relevance.

continuous exercise that has to be repeated regularly, in order to ensure continuous compliance of the relevant data processing activities with the GDPR provisions.[86] In the context of such regular review and re-evaluation as to the adequacy of the DPIA findings, the measures taken to mitigate any risks to the data subjects may also have to be duly updated, in line with the state of the art developments.[87]

Data Protection Officer The GDPR provisions establish a new position in the organizational structure of data controllers and processors, the Data Protection Officer (DPO), the appointment of whom is obligatory in case the core activities of the data controller/processor consist of processing operations, which require large scale, regular and systematic monitoring of data subjects, or large scale processing of special categories of personal data.[88] Insurance undertakings, given the significance of data collection and processing activities for their insurance business, are among the categories of data controllers falling into the scope of the obligation to appoint a DPO. Such obligation is further enhanced in the event that additional data processing activities are designed to be included in the functions of the insurance company, in the course of its product design, distribution and monitoring activities. The DPO, as described in the relevant GDPR provisions,[89] monitors the compliance of the company with its GDPR obligations, and shall be involved, from the earliest stage possible in all issues relating to data protection, including where a DPIA is being carried out.[90] As such, the manufacturer's and/or the distributor's DPO (as the case may be), shall be included in the design of the product approval, distribution and monitoring arrangements, so that he/she may identify the privacy-related issues that may arise therein, and assist the company in ensuring compliance with the related GDPR obligations.

Records of Processing Activities Under the GDPR provisions, data controllers are obliged to maintain records of the data processing activities they undertake in writing (including in electronic form), which shall be made available upon request to the competent Data Protection Authority.[91] In this respect, the data processing operations taking place in the course of the product design, distribution and monitoring functions, shall be also duly recorded in such records, which shall contain references to the processing purposes, the categories of the personal data and data subjects involved, the categories of recipients to whom personal data are being disclosed,

---

[86]Working Party 29, *Guidelines on Data Protection Impact Assessment (DPIA) and determine whether processing is "likely to result in a high risk" for the purposes of Regulation 2016/679*, as above.

[87]Bieker et al. (2017).

[88]See in this relevance the provisions of Article 37 of the GDPR.

[89]Articles 38–39 of the GDPR.

[90]Working Party 29, *Guidelines on Data Protection Officers (DPOs)*, adopted on 13 December 2016, last revised and adopted on 5 April 2017, 16/EN, WP 243 rev. 01, as endorsed by the EDPB and available at: https://edpb.europa.eu/our-work-tools/general-guidance/gdpr-guidelines-recommendations-best-practices_en.

[91]See Article 30 of the GDPR in this relevance.

where applicable information on any cross-border data transfers to countries outside the EEA, the envisaged retention periods for the different data categories, and a general description of the adopted technical and organizational security measures being implemented.

The new IDD framework on insurance distribution provides for new internal governance obligations on both insurers and insurance intermediaries falling into its scope. Such new obligations include the need for insurance manufacturers to adopt and implement appropriate Product Approval Processes, which may also provide for procedures to effectively monitor the performance of the insurance products being released in the markets, while insurance distributors shall similarly adopt and implement appropriate product distribution arrangements. Taking into account the goals which these new procedures aim to accomplish, in terms of defining appropriate and sufficiently granular target markets for the insurance products depending on the characteristics, the demands and needs of the respective customers, and ensuring that the products are duly distributed in the relevant target market, and continue being aligned with the insurance demands and needs without causing any adverse effects to the customers, as well as the fact that data collection and processing has always been of utmost importance for the development of insurance business, it becomes self-evident that product design, distribution and monitoring requires corresponding and extensive data collection and processing operations. As a result, compliance with the relevant IDD obligations must be designed and achieved in a way that compliance with the applicable GDPR obligations is at the same time ensured.

In this relevance, the privacy by design and by default notions and their practical implications should be taken particularly into account during the design of the relevant POG-related policies and procedures, in the sense that the GDPR data processing principles (especially the principles of data minimization, purpose limitation and data safety) shall be embedded into the new policies, as an integral part thereof. Particularly in case of the use of InsurTech and BDA tools, any transparency concerns shall be properly and adequately addressed, in order to ensure that the data subjects are aware of the nature, scope and consequences of the data processing activities that concern them, and are not taken by surprise at a subsequent stage. Technological advances should be employed aiming to further enhance the transparency factor, where and as appropriate. The design and implementation of the new POG-related operations shall be duly monitored as to its compliance with the GDPR by the company's appointed DPO, while a DPIA seems to be obligatory before and during the course of the new or enhanced data processing activities. The details of such processing activities should be also duly documented, in records of data processing activities having the minimum content prescribed in the relevant GDPR provisions.

3 GDPR and IDD Implications in the External Relations

The IDD provides for elevated conduct obligations on insurance distributors, aiming to an enhanced level of customer protection. In this context, and in order to duly comply with the obligation to always act in the best interest of the customers, insurance distributors are legally obliged to collect and process personal data of their customers (and potential customers), so that they may identify such best interest and act accordingly. As already discussed, such conduct obligations extend—from a time perspective—not only at a pre-contractual stage, but also throughout the term of the relationship with the customer. In this relevance, compliance with said IDD-deriving obligations needs to be designed and implemented bearing in mind the GDPR-related obligations that may ensue.

At the same time, the cooperation between insurers and intermediaries requires, under the relevant IDD provisions, the exchange of information containing personal data, thus creating further data protection challenges. The definition of the exact nature of the relationship between insurers and intermediaries in light of the applicable GDPR provisions also poses crucial questions that may affect their cooperation as a whole. Similarly, IDD and GDPR provisions have the potential to affect the relations between competitors, creating new questions.

3.1 Relations with Customers

The IDD provisions, aiming to achieve the main goal of strengthening consumer protection attribute a key role to the principle of transparency governing insurance distribution by tightening the rules on information provided by insurance distributors, providing for obligations concerning information duties, conflicts of interest, disclosure of remuneration systems, etc.[92] The effective and full compliance with these obligations requires either the disclosure of personal data to the customers, or the collection and processing of personal data from the customers, in the various stages of the distributor—customer relation.

3.1.1 Choice of Insurance Product: Risk Assessment

The general principle applicable on the relationship between insurance intermediaries and their customers under the IDD constellation is that intermediaries shall always act having in the mind the best interest of their customers.[93] In this context, distributors are required to determine the insurance demands and needs of their customers, on the basis of the information received from them, and always propose

[92]Malinowska (2016).

[93]Article 17(1) of the IDD.

an insurance contract that is consistent with such identified demands and needs,[94] while in case advice[95] is provided to the customer in relation to an insurance product,[96] the distributor shall also explain the reasons why the proposed insurance product is better suited for the customer. The obligations to duly explain to the customer the reasons why the proposed insurance product fits their demands and needs intend to further enhance the transparency in the insurance distribution process, to the benefit always of the customer. Particularly in the case of cross-selling, the above mentioned identification of demands and needs must result in proposing a bundle of products that better suits the customer as a whole.[97]

In this context, the IDD compliance measures to be taken, shall be designed in a way that ensures the adequate identification of the customer's insurance demands and needs and of the appropriate insurance product to be offered. Any product distribution arrangements outlining the steps to be taken up to the proposal of a specific insurance product to the customer, shall determine the information that needs to be provided by the customer, the means to be used in this context, and the way in which the collected information will be translated into specific insurance demands and needs. However, also with a view to the customer relations of the company, given that such identification of each customer's particular characteristics requires the collection and processing of personal data, the design and implementation of such procedures will need to take into account the applicable GDPR obligations. Namely, also these relevant procedures will have to be drafted in accordance with the privacy by design and by default principle, ensuring particularly that only the personal data required to achieve the specific processing purpose of determining the customer's insurance demands and needs are collected, and that such data are not subject to any further processing. Furthermore, the relevant distribution arrangements will also need to be designed in a transparent way, in the sense that the customers will have to be provided with all the required information on the relevant processing of their personal data. Distributors will also need to define the appropriate legal basis for the processing of such personal data, depending mainly on whether any special categories of personal data are being collected.[98]

[94]Article 20(1) of the IDD.

[95]In the sense of a personalized recommendation to the customer.

[96]To be noted that national legislators have taken advantage of the discretion provided by the relevant IDD provisions and have rendered the provision of advice obligatory in certain cases. The Greek Law 4583/2018 transposing IDD, for instance, provides that all insurance distributors are obliged to provide advice to their customer, with respect to all insurance products (except from large risk insurance).

[97]As determined in Article 24(6) of the IDD.

[98]In which case, according to Article 9 of the GDPR, more stringent conditions will apply, in order for the distributors to be able to duly establish the legitimate collection and processing of such special categories of personal data.

The Case of Insurance-Based Investment Products IDD[99] and its implementing provisions[100] contain more stringent obligations on distributors that sell insurance-based investment products (IBIPs). Namely, the distribution of IBIPs shall be based on a suitability and appropriateness assessment of the proposed IBIP for the specific customer. The relevant IDD provisions state that the distributor shall seek additional information on the customer's particular characteristics, such as information on the customer's knowledge and experience on the investment sector, on his/her financial status, including his/her ability to suffer losses,[101] on his/her investment goals and risk tolerance level,[102] etc., in order to have a reasonable basis for determining that their personal recommendation to the customer meets his/her investment objectives (including his/her risk tolerance), as well as his/her financial situation (including the ability to suffer losses), and is such that the customer has the necessary knowledge and experience in the investment field relevant to the specific type of product or service. It is beyond any doubt that the suitability and appropriateness assessment required in the case of IBIPs distribution entails a significant amount of personal data processing activities, which shall be designed and performed in a way that respects the GDPR provisions as well, as described above. To be noted, however, that fragments of the fundamental GDPR data processing principles have already been included in the provisions of the IBIPs Regulation, according to which it must be ensured that the level of information collected shall be appropriate to the specific type of product or service being considered for the specific customer, in line with the data minimization principle of the GDPR. In this regard the privacy by design and by default notions shall be complied with during the design of the appropriate compliance measures with the IBIPs-related IDD provisions, not only because of the GDPR obligations, but even because of the IDD obligations themselves.

Risk Assessment and Premium Calculation When examining which is the most suitable insurance product to be proposed to each customer, distributors shall also undertake the respective risk assessment exercise, in the sense that they shall evaluate the relevant parameters of each case and evaluate the risk to be undertaken, so that the appropriate premium is also charged.[103] National insurance laws already

---

[99]Chapter VI, Articles 26–30 of the IDD.

[100]Namely the provisions of the Commission Delegated Regulation (EU) 2017/2359 of 21 September 2017 supplementing Directive (EU) 2016/97 of the European Parliament and of the Council with regard to information requirements and conduct of business rules applicable to the distribution of insurance-based investment products (the "IBIPs Regulation").

[101]Such as information on the source and extent of the customer's regular income, assets (including liquid assets), investments and real estate property, and regular financial commitments—see Article 9(3) of the IBIPs Regulation.

[102]Such as information on the length of time for which the customer wishes to hold the investment, his/her preferences regarding risk taking, the risk profile, and the purposes of the investment—see Article 9(4) of the IBIPs Regulation.

[103]See Persatuan Insurans Am Malaysia, *How will I be assessed and what is risk profiling?*, 2019, available at: http://www.piam.org.my/phased-liberalisation-section/how-will-i-be-assessed-risk-profiling/.

acknowledge the need for the risk to be insured to be properly and adequately known beforehand to the insurer by providing for precontractual information obligations on the prospective policyholders as well.[104] With respect to the new IDD obligations on distributors, the risk assessment and premium calculation exercise is a crucial part in the procedure towards providing sound advice to their customers in relation to the ultimately proposed insurance product and, as such, the procedures and means for this evaluation shall be designed in line with the overarching IDD principle of bearing the customer's best interest in mind.

In this regard, risk assessment and even risk profiling is a procedure requiring the collection and processing of personal data, both on the insurance history of the customer, and on the current conditions. Distributors are able to take advantage of the new technological advances, such as the IoT, and use the possibilities being offered by connected devices to have access to a significantly large volume of data, so that they may better understand the individual risk profile of each customer, and align their proposals accordingly. The integration, however, of such advances into the risk assessment operations, must take place in a way aligned with the GDPR principles; distributors must carefully determine the personal data they need, to proceed with an accurate risk analysis, and collect from the customers the data that is appropriate, adequate and necessary for such purposes, in line with the data minimization principle. The use of connected devices is going to result in a significantly increased inflow of personal data, which the insurers must be duly prepared, not only to appropriately collect, but also to duly process, for the purposes for which it was collected.[105] In this regard, appropriate safeguards will also need to be implemented, in order to ensure that no further processing takes place, unless the customers—data subjects have been duly informed for any additional processing purposes and such further processing takes place lawfully and according to the GDPR provisions.

3.1.2 Precontractual Information Obligations

Another area where the IDD and the GDPR provisions interact and affect the relation between distributors and their customers is the issue of the precontractual information to be provided to the customers, so that they may make a duly informed decision on the insurance contract to be executed.

Information Overload The IDD provisions aim as already mentioned above, to enhance customer protection. To that end, they require for extensive precontractual

[104]For example, the Greek Insurance Contract Act (ICA – Law 2496/1997) in its Article 3 provides that the policyholder shall disclose to the insurer, before the conclusion of the contract, any and all information and circumstances he/she is aware of that are objectively material for the assessment of the risk, while adverse results are provided for the case that the policyholder does not comply.

[105]Cindy Maike, *Insurance risk assessment in a connected world*, 09.01.2019, Horton Works, available at: https://hortonworks.com/blog/insurance-risk-assessment-in-a-connected-world/.

information to be provided to the customers, in due time before the conclusion of the contract, concerning the identity and other capacities of the distributor, the specific characteristics of the insurance product being offered, etc. In this respect the IDD has introduced the Insurance Product Information Document (IPID), in relation to non-life insurance products. The IPID is a short, standardized document which conveys the minimum critical information on the insurance type, the insurance cover, the premiums to be paid, the exceptions from the cover, etc.[106] In this regard, the IDD provisions have significantly added to the already existing precontractual information obligations under other insurance regulatory texts, such as the Solvency II and the PRIIPs Regulation[107] in terms of the products falling within its scope, while in case of consumer insurance products, additional information obligations arise from the applicable EU consumer protection Directives[108] and their national implementing measures. The GDPR provisions further add to the above mentioned information obligations, as they oblige distributors to disclose to their customers a significant number of information concerning the personal data being processed, the processing purposes, the data recipients, the legal bases of the processing the customers' rights under the GDPR, etc. From this point, the interplay between the IDD and the GDPR provisions, which both aim, at the bottomline, at the effective protection of the individuals (in their capacity as insurance customers and data subjects at the same time), puts such protective goal at risk. Customers are being overwhelmed with information, which simply becomes confusing, with the effect that their ability to be properly informed and make appropriate decisions when purchasing insurance products may be obstructing.[109]

[106]The IPID's specific standardized form and content has been elaborated in the Commission Implementing Regulation (EU) 2017/1469 of 11 August 2017 laying down a standardized presentation format for the insurance product information document (the "IPID Regulation"). With respect to the IPID, its very limited size, in combination with the information it needs to contain under the IDD and the IPID Regulation provisions, have caused significant problems to insurers at the implementation phase, as they could not design the IPID in a way compliant with all its requirements. For example, in case of insurance products with multiple covers, insurers were required to determine and choose which covers would be considered to be the "main" ones and be included in the IPID, and which ones not, in a way that could be deemed to be arbitrary.

[107]Regulation (EU) No 1286/2014 of the European Parliament and of the Council of 26 November 2014 on key information documents for packaged retail and insurance-based investment products (PRIIPs).

[108]Such as the Directive 2000/31/EC of the European Parliament and of the Council of 8 June 2000 on certain legal aspects of information society services, in particular electronic commerce, in the Internal Market ("Directive on electronic commerce"), or the Directive 2002/65/EC of the European Parliament and of the Council of 23 September 2002 concerning the distance marketing of consumer financial services and amending Council Directive 90/619/EEC and Directives 97/7/EC and 98/27/EC.

[109]See a relevant analysis in Insurance Europe, *Submission to the online REFIT Platform tool on information overload, duplication and paper requirements*, October 2017, available at: https://www.insuranceeurope.eu/submission-online-refit-platform-tool-information-overload-duplication-and-paper-requirements.

Conflicts of Interest The information to be provided to the customer at a precontractual stage include, among others, information on possible conflicts of interest between the distributor on the one hand and the customer on the other. From a general point of view, the IDD provides that intermediaries shall inform the customer of any close links they may have with an insurer, or of any exclusive cooperation.[110] Particularly with respect to the distribution of IBIPs, distributors shall establish and implement an effective conflicts of interest policy, aiming to identify the circumstances that constitute or may result in such a conflict, and to determine the procedures to be followed and measures to be adopted in order to manage such conflicts of interest and prevent them from harming the customers,[111] including notifying the customer of any particular conflict of interest that may arise.[112] In the context of ensuring that customers are duly informed of any potential conflicts of interest causes, the IDD provisions oblige distributors to inform their customers on the remuneration they receive in relation to the insurance product they propose. Particularly insurers proceeding with insurance distribution activities are obliged to inform the customers of the nature or, in some cases, of the actual relevant remuneration their employees shall receive. This aspect of the IDD compliance requirements may not entail (or not exclusively refer to any) any further processing of customers' personal data, but does entail personal data processing in terms of disclosing personal data of the distributor and its employees (as the case may be) to the customers. As such, any IDD compliance measures shall be also designed and implemented in a way that respects and ensures compliance with the applicable GDPR provisions: for instance, any personal data disclosure shall not extend beyond the data necessary for the purpose of complying with the relevant IDD obligations, while the data subjects concerned (e.g. employees, directors, etc.) shall be duly informed of the relevant data processing activities.

3.2 Relations with Other Insurance Market Players

The IDD and the GDPR provisions are changing the relationship between the insurance distributors and their customers, both aiming to enhance the level of trust towards the insurance market. At the same time, issues are similarly arising from the interplay of the IDD with the GDPR provisions, with regard to the relations between the different participants in the insurance value chain.

---

[110] Article 19 of the IDD.

[111] See Articles 3–8 of the IBIPs Regulation for more details on the particular obligations of the distributors in relation to the prevention and management of the conflicts of interest.

[112] Which may concern the customer and any "relevant person" of the insurance distributor, such as a director, partner, manager, employee or other natural person; for a detailed definition of the "relevant person" notion for the purposes of conflicts of interest management in the IDD constellation, see Article 2(1) of the IBIPs Regulation.

3.2.1 Insurer: Intermediary Relation

In the course of the insurance distribution process, the effective cooperation between insurers and intermediaries requires significant data processing activities, namely, exchange of personal data from one to another, throughout the life cycle of the insurance contract. At a precontractual stage, intermediaries are required to collect adequate and appropriate data from the prospective customer and transfer them to the insurer, so that the latter may proceed with the necessary risk assessment exercise, decide whether to accept the risk or not, and properly calculate the proposed premium. During the term of the insurance contract, insurers and intermediaries are required, under the POG-related provisions, to monitor the performance of the product in order to determine whether it continues being in line with the target market's characteristics, while intermediaries shall notify the insurer (i.e. product manufacturer) of any circumstances falling to their attention, that may adversely affect the customer, and the insurer in its turn shall inform the intermediary of any measures taken to duly address such circumstances. Similarly, in case of any risk occurrence event, intermediaries are required to act in the best interest of their customers, collecting and forwarding to the insurer any personal data required for the due satisfaction of the insurance claim.

In the course of the above described activities, intermediaries are seen as collecting and transferring to insurers the necessary personal data for the drafting, conclusion, monitoring and execution of the insurance contract, as such activities are also described in the IDD provisions. In most of the occasions, such collection and transfer of data takes place on the basis of standardized forms and means established by the insurer and made available to the intermediaries the insurer cooperates with for the distribution of its products. Such scheme of collection and transfer of personal data, apart from the need to be designed and implemented to comply with the IDD provisions, also needs to take into account the relevant GDPR obligations.

The major question that arises in this regard is the capacity under which each party operates and, particularly, whether the intermediary will be considered as acting as data processor on behalf of the insurer—data controller, or if the intermediary acts as an independent data controller on its own accord, or if both cases could be applicable—up to a point each one. The delimitation between these concepts is of paramount importance, as it is the data controller that is mostly responsible to ensure compliance with the GDPR provisions, while the data processor only needs to comply with limited provisions of the GDPR applicable directly to it. Furthermore, under the GDPR constellation, should a controller-processor relationship seem to exist, the insurer-intermediary cooperation in terms of personal data activities will have to be regulated under a legally binding agreement, containing specific content, while the insurer as a data controller will be able to give documented instructions to the intermediary,[113] but will also bear responsibility for any data processing activities undertaken by the intermediary on its behalf. The issue of the delimitation between the notion of controller, as the person actually determining the purposes and means of the data processing activities, and of processor, given its complexity and the vast number of grey areas that apply,[114] has caused many controversies between intermediaries and insurers in the course of the GDPR compliance projects undertaken, and still remains to be resolved and its practical implications to be seen.

3.2.2 Relations Between Competitors

Some of the new obligations and tools under the IDD and the GDPR provisions may also potentially affect the relationship between insurance distributors, regardless of their capacity as insurers or intermediaries. The most characteristic example of the way in which the new frameworks may cause issues is the combination of the IDD obligation to propose an insurance product that suits the particular characteristics of the customer, with the data portability right under the GDPR.

According to the newly established data portability right,[115] customers have the right (under the conditions prescribed in the applicable provisions) to request that a distributor provides them with their personal data they have provided to the distributor, in a structured, commonly used and machine-readable format, or that the distributor transfers such personal data directly to another distributor. In this regard, a distributor, in the course of collecting the necessary information on a potential customer, in order to determine his/her insurance demands and needs, could ask from said customer to make use of the right to data portability, and provide the distributor will all personal data from another distributor. Such request could possibly mean that the first distributor is required to provide to the new distributor information that could contain personal data concerning the customer but created by the first distributor (such as a complex insurance profile created by compiling raw data). In this respect, such a request would cause the first distributor to embark in a complex exercise in order to determine which personal data they are obliged to provide to the customer (or directly to the new distributor), and which ones they may withhold.[116] The outcome of such exercise, however, cannot preclude beyond any

---

[113] Which could go up to the point of requesting that the intermediary deletes all personal data and any copies thereof concerning a specific customer or categories of customers, thus, interfering directly with the intermediary's clientele.

[114] Some guidance and criteria on the delimitation of these two notions are found in the Working Party 29, *Opinion 1/2010 on the concepts of "controller" and "processor"*, 00264/10/EN WP169, available at: https://ec.europa.eu/justice/article-29/documentation/opinion-recommendation/index_en.htm.

[115] Under Article 20 of the GDPR.

[116] Guidance concerning the personal data that would fall into the ambit of such obligation and the ones that could be exempted can be found in the Working Party 29, *Guidelines on the right to data*

doubt the disclosure of commercial secrets from one distributor to another, such that may grant the new distributor an unjustified competitive advantage against the other.

The new IDD and GDPR provisions and the interaction between these two sets of rules impacts the activities throughout the cycle of the insurance distribution: from a precontractual stage up to the satisfaction of any insurance claims. Alongside the new policies and procedures that need to be adopted and implemented, the new insurance distribution and data protection frameworks impact upon the relations between the insurance distributors and their customers, but also between distributors themselves. Compliance with the IDD obligations to propose products that are in line with the customer's individual characteristics, as well as to continuously monitor the product's performance and alignment with their insurance demands and needs, has increased the amount of personal data that need to be collected and processed. As such, the relevant IDD compliance measures need to be designed under the privacy by design and by default principles, taking also account of the other applicable GDPR provisions.

Similarly, the new rules give rise to novel or newly arising issues concerning the relations between insurers and intermediaries. The matter as to whether an intermediary may be characterized as data controller or processor may seem to be a typical, bureaucratic one, but its practical implications are of utmost importance for both parties, as they touch upon the issue of who does the insurance clientele *belong* to. At the same time, compliance with some IDD obligations, such as determining the insurance profile of a customer, may be achieved more easily by taking advantage of some possibilities provided under the GDPR provisions. However, new issues may still arise as to the extent up to which it will be ethical and in line with the honest transactional practices to make use of such new tools, and from what point onwards they could result in distorting the competition between insurance distributors.

4 Summary and Conclusions

The GDPR and the IDD, along with their EU and national implementing provisions, Guidelines, etc., have radically transformed the previously applicable laws on data protection and insurance mediation/distribution, aiming to address shortcomings and deficiencies of the respective previously applicable laws, and to enhance the protection provided to individuals and insurance customers respectively. Such changes impacted on the functioning of the private insurance market in the EU altogether, in some cases causing structural modifications in the market and the cooperation between market players. Furthermore, the need to ensure compliance with the new rules has significantly disrupted the operations of both insurers and intermediaries.

---

portability, 16/EN WP 242 rev. 01, adopted on 13 December 2016 and last revised and adopted on 5 April 2017, endorsed by the EDPB, and available at: https://edpb.europa.eu/our-work-tools/general-guidance/gdpr-guidelines-recommendations-best-practices_en.

Their almost simultaneous adoption and entry into force triggered some lengthy, time and resources consuming, and burdensome compliance projects that interact with each other in numerous occasions, as the compliance measures concerning the implementation of the IDD provisions need to take into account the requirements set out in the GPDR provisions as well.

GDPR and IDD remedial measures affect first of all the internal operations and functions of insurers and intermediaries, adding to the already extensive corporate governance requirements, as they have caused the amendment and/or adoption of policies and processes (either explicitly provided in the new rules, or implicitly required for compliance with them), the establishment of new key functions and roles in the organizational structures, etc. The Product Oversight and Governance (POG) requirements constitute one of the most characteristic examples where the required IDD compliance measures entail the adoption of extensive data collection and processing operations. The identification of the appropriate target market on the basis of the particular insurance characteristics of its members, the design of insurance products targeting specific insurance demands and needs, and the continuous monitoring of their performance and alignment with the targeted demands and needs require the analysis of increasing data volumes. At the same time, determining the appropriate distribution strategy for each target market, and notifying the product manufacturer of any potential adverse effects the product may cause to consumers, similarly consist of data processing activities. In this regard, any IDD compliance measures have to be designed also in the light of the GDPR obligations, particularly taking account of the privacy by design and by default notions.

In the same way, the new IDD and GDPR provisions affect the relationship between insurance distributors and their customers, between insurers and intermediaries, and even between distributors themselves (i.e. operating in the same level of the insurance value chain). In terms of the relations with their customers, insurers are required under the IDD provisions to always act in the best interest of their customers, determine their insurance demands and needs and ensure that any product they propose suits them, while there are national transposing laws rendering obligatory the provision of advice, in the sense of a personal recommendation. In this regard, IDD compliance throughout the life cycle of the distributor-customer relation requires extensive personal data collection and processing and, thus, needs to be designed and implemented bearing in mind the need to also ensure compliance with the applicable GDPR obligations. As far as the relations between distributors are concerned, IDD provisions require in several cases the exchange of information, including personal data, between them, in a way that triggers the question of the capacity in which each party acts: is the distributor a data processor acting on behalf of the manufacturer or not? And, if yes, to what extend? What would be the practical implications of each response in terms of managing the clientele and the related personal data? At the same time, the use of new GDPR tools may assist in ensuring compliance with IDD obligations, but could raise new issues between insurance distributors when acting as competitors in the market, as it could lead to the disclosure of sensitive commercial secrets of one competitor to another, granting as such competitive advantage to the latter.

The GDPR and the IDD impact on the operation of insurers and intermediaries should not be seen exclusively as two separate procedures and issues to be tackled. The interaction between these two new sets of rules is evident in all relevant aspects, as any measures aiming to the compliance with one of them shall take into consideration and duly integrate the requirements of the other one, in a way that compliance with them is safeguarded as well. The need to combine the requirements of both the GDPR and the IDD into the remedial actions undertaken often constitutes a complex exercise, requiring the cooperation of different functions of the organization. To that end, the rapid integration of technological developments, namely new InsurTech solutions, into the insurance value chain and the daily operations of insurance distributors should be the focal point of this intricate combination of the data protection and insurance distribution requirements, as they may provide assistance to market participants in ensuring their full compliance in the most efficient way.

References

Bernardino G (2016) Exploring new horizons for the benefit of the citizens in the European Union. In: Keynote and Welcome Speech, EIOPA 6th Annual Conference, Frankfurt. Available at: https://eiopa.europa.eu/Publications/Speeches% 20and%20presentations/2016-10-18%20EIOPA%20Annual%20Conference.pdf

Bieker F, Friedewald M, Hansen M, Obersteller H, Rost M (2017) A process for data protection impact assessment under the European general data protection regulation. In: Conference Paper, 4th Annual Privacy Forum, Frankfurt/Main, Germany. Available at: https://www.researchgate.net/publication/319276698_A_Process_for_Data_Protection_Impact_Assessment_under_the_European_General_Data_Protection_Regulation.

Deloitte (2017) Insurance Distribution Directive (IDD): the MiFID of insurance. Available at: https://www.google.com/url?sa=t&rct=j&q=&esrc=s&source=web&cd =9&ved=2ahUKEwjznMqu2MjjAhVQqaQKHWNXCKMQFjAIegQIARAC&url=https%3A%2F%2Fwww2.deloitte.com%2Fcontent%2Fdam%2FDeloitte%2Fgr%2FDocuments%2Ffinancial-services%2Fgr_insurance%2520distribution%2520directive_ noexp.pdf&usg=AOvVaw2KmAlxEQC4lOigxnILyLXk.

Emond I, Tereza K (2019) European Union regulation of insurance industry in the aftermath of the financial crisis. Lawyer Q Int J Legal Res 1(2) Available at: https://tlq.ilaw.cas.cz/index.php/tlq/article/view/330/336

European Commission (2015) Fact Sheet, Questions & Answers – Data protection reform, 21.12.2015. Available at: http://europa.eu/rapid/press-release_MEMO-15-6385_el.htm

European Commission (2018) Communication to the European Parliament and the Council. In: Stronger protection, new opportunities – Commission guidance on the direct application of the General Data Protection Regulation as of 25 May 2018, 24.01.2018. Available at: https://eur-lex.europa.eu/legal-content/EN/TXT/?qid=1563892565511&uri=CELEX:52018DC0043

Insurance Europe (2017) Submission to the online REFIT Platform tool on information overload, duplication and paper requirements, October 2017. Available at: https://www.insuranceeurope.eu/submission-online-refit-platform-tool-information-overload-duplication-and-paper-requirements

Insurance Europe (2018) GDPR is around the corner: time for final checks by insurers – An overview of insurers' obligations under the General Data Protection Regulation, 05.2018. Available at: https://www.insuranceeurope.eu/sites/default/files/attachments/GDPR%20is%20around%20the%20corner.pdf.

KPMG (2018) The GDPR and key challenges faced by the Insurance industry, 02.2018. Available at: https://www.google.com/url?sa=t&rct=j&q=&esrc=s&source= web&cd=1&cad=rja&uact=8&ved=2ahUKEwjMg4fw_cjjAhUQKlAKHYK3AHsQFjAAegQIBBAC&url=https%3A%2F%2Fassets.kpmg%2Fcontent%2Fdam%2Fkpmg%2Fie%2Fpdf%2F2018%2F03%2Fie-gdpr-for-insurance-industry.pdf&usg=AOv Vaw0bmREPmoGtekQSR5_7t2gz

Maike C (2019) Insurance risk assessment in a connected world, 09.01.2019, Horton Works. Available at: https://hortonworks.com/blog/insurance-risk-assessment-in-a-connected-world/

Malinowska K (2016) Insurance transparency and protection regime under the Insurance Distribution Directive. Insurance Review 4/2016. Available at: https://www.google.com/url?sa=t&rct=j&q=&esrc=s&source=web&cd=1&cad=rja&uact=8&ved=2ahUKEwjztv6fu9LjAhUDwqYKHexAB1AQFjAAegQIABAC&url=https%3A%2F%2Fpiu.org.pl%2Fwp-content%2Fuploads%2F2017%2F05%2FWU-2016-04-06-Malinowska-en.pdf&usg=AOvVaw1x7RazC-YDA5le4xFKCQpH

Marano P (2017) The "Mifidization": The Sunset of Life Insurance in the EU Regulation on Insurance? Liber Amicorum for Professor Ioannis Rokas, NOMIKH ΒΙΒΛΙΟΘΗΚΗ, Athens, pp. 219–234

Oller F, KPMG Luxembourg (2017) Product Oversight and governance requirements under IDD, 24.10.2017. Available at: https://blog.kpmg.lu/product-oversight-and-governance-requirements-under-idd/

Patel C (2017) GDPR: main points of the law and its impact on insurance. LexisNexis. Available at: https://blogs.lexisnexis.com/insurance-insights/2017/08/gdpr-main-points-of-the-law-and-its-impact-on-insurance/

Persatuan Insurans Am Malaysia (2019) How will I be assessed and what is risk profiling? Available at: http://www.piam.org.my/phased-liberalisation-section/how-will-i-be-assessed-risk-profiling/

Porrini D (2017) Regulating Big Data effects in the European insurance market. Insur Mark Comp 8 (1) Available at: https://www.researchgate.net/publication/324084745_Regulating_Big_Data_effects_in_the_European_insurance_market

PwC (2018) Hot Topic – Insurance Distribution Directive – Are you ready? – Update February 2018. Available at: https://www.google.com/url?sa=t&rct=j&q =&esrc=s&source=web&cd=15&cad=rja&uact=8&ved=2ahUKEwjznMqu2MjjAhVQqaQKHWNXCKMQFjAOegQICRAC&url=https%3A%2F%2Fwww.pwc.co.uk%2Ffinancial-services%2Fassets%2Fpdf%2Finsurance-distribution-directive-are-you-ready-january2018.pdf&usg=AOvVaw0GzYf6-KfmQ38U2v5sovEG

Tarasiuk A (2019) Consumer insurance – recent regulatory tendencies. In: 20th AIDA Serbia Conference Proceedings, "Insurance Law and Practice – Current Trends, Future Challenges"

Truli E (2016) The General Data Protection Regulation and civil liability, MPI Oct. 21-22, 2016

Veris C, Goddet P—Deloitte (2018) Insurance Distribution Directive – 2018: a challenging year for the European insurance sector. Performance magazine issue 25. Available at: https://www.google.com/url?sa=t&rct=j&q=&esrc=s&source =web&cd=1&cad=rja&uact=8&ved=2ahUKEwjBq6mxvcvjAhVbURUIHfeZBXcQFjAAegQIAhAC&url=https%3A%2F%2Fwww2.deloitte.com%2Fcontent%2Fdam%2FDeloitte%2Flu%2FDocuments%2Ffinancial-services%2FInsurance%2Flu-insurance-distribution-directive-2018-challenging-year-european-insurance-sector-012018.pdf&usg=AOvVaw3gvYcV6eDFpDwSB2_x-B7j

Regulatory Guidance and Decisions

BaFin (2018) *Product approval process: Requirements for product manufacturers and distributors*, 02.03.2018, available at: https://www.bafin.de/dok/10523912

EIOPA (2019) *Big Data Analytics in Motor and Health Insurance: A Thematic Review*, available at: https://eiopa.europa.eu/Pages/News/EIOPA-reviews-the-use-of-Big-Data-Analytics-in-motor-and-health-insurance.aspx

EIOPA (2018) *First set of Questions & Answers on the Application of the Insurance Distribution Directive,* 11.07.2018, available at: https://eiopa.europa.eu/Pages/News/EIOPA-publishes-first-set-of-Questions%2D%2DAnswers-on-the-Application-of-the-Insurance-Distribution-Directive.aspx

EIOPA (2017) *Annual Report 2016*, 15.06.2017, available at: https://eiopa.europa.eu/publications/annual-reports.

EIOPA (2016) *Preparatory Guidelines on product oversight and governance arrangements by insurance undertakings and insurance distributors*, EIOPA-BoS-16-071, 18.03.2016, available at: https://eiopa.europa.eu/Pages/Guidelines/Preparatory-Guidelines-on-product-oversight-and-governance-arrangements-by-insurance-undertakings-and-insurance-distributor.aspx

ENISA (2015) *Privacy by design in big data – An overview of privacy enhancing technologies in the era of big data analytics*, 12.2015, available at: https://www.enisa.europa.eu/publications/big-data-protection

ENISA (2014) *Privacy and Data Protection by Design – from policy to engineering*, 12.2014, available at: https://www.enisa.europa.eu/publications/privacy-and-data-protection-by-design

European Data Protection Board (2019) *Guidelines 4/2019 on Article 25 Data Protection by Design and by Default – Version adopted for public consultation*, 13.11.2019, available at: https://edpb.europa.eu/sites/edpb/files/consultation/edpb_guidelines_201904_dataprotection_by_design_and_by_default.pdf

European Data Protection Board (2018) *Guidelines 3/2018 on the territorial scope of the GDPR (Article 3) – Version adopted after public consultation*, 12.11.2019, available at: https://edpb.europa.eu/sites/edpb/files/files/file1/edpb_guidelines_3_2018_territorial_scope_after_public_consultation_en_1.pdf

European Data Protection Supervisor (2018) *Opinion 5/2018 – Preliminary Opinion on privacy by design*, 31.05.2018, available at: https://edps.europa.eu/data-protection/our-work/publications/opinions/privacy-design_en

Hellenic Data Protection Authority (2018) *Decision 65/2018 – List of activities requiring DPIA*, Government Gazette B' 1622/10.05.2018, available at: https://www.dpa.gr/portal/page?_pageid=33,239286&_dad=portal&_schema=PORTAL

Information Commissioner's Office (2019) *Guide to the General Data Protection Regulation (GDPR) – Accountability and Governance – Data Protection by design and by default*, 22.05.2019, available at: https://ico.org.uk/for-organisations/guide-to-data-protection/guide-to-the-general-data-protection-regulation-gdpr/accountability-and-governance/data-protection-by-design-and-default/

Information and Privacy Commissioner of Ontario (2018) *Privacy by design – seven foundational principles*, 01.2018, available at: https://www.ipc.on.ca/wp-content/uploads/2018/01/pbd.pdf

Working Party 29 (2017a) *Guidelines on transparency under Regulation 2016/679*, 17/EN, WP260 rev. 01, 29.11.2017 (revised 11.04.2018), available at: https://edpb.europa.eu/our-work-tools/general-guidance/gdpr-guidelines-recommendations-best-practices_en

Working Party 29 (2017b) *Guidelines on Data Protection Impact Assessment (DPIA) and determine whether processing is "likely to result in a high risk" for the purposes of Regulation 2016/679*, 17/EN, WP 248, 04.04.2017, available at: https://edpb.europa.eu/our-work-tools/general-guidance/gdpr-guidelines-recommendations-best-practices_en

Working Party 29 (2016a) *Guidelines on Data Protection Officers (DPOs)*, 13.12.2016 (revised on 05.04.2017), 16/EN, WP 243 rev. 01, available at: https://edpb.europa.eu/our-work-tools/general-guidance/gdpr-guidelines-recommendations-best-practices_en

Working Party 29 (2016b) *Guidelines on the right to data portability*, adopted on 13.12.2016 (revised on 05.04.2017), 16/EN, WP 242 rev. 01, available at: https://edpb.europa.eu/our-work-tools/general-guidance/gdpr-guidelines-recommendations-best-practices_en

Working Party 29 (2010) *Opinion 1/2010 on the concepts of "controller" and "processor"*, 00264/10/EN, WP 169, available at: https://ec.europa.eu/justice/article-29/documentation/opinion-recommendation/index_en.htm

Regulating Telematics Insurance

Role for the IDD to Complement the GDPR on Improving Consumer Data Protection in the Context of Telematics Insurance

Freyja van den Boom

1 Introduction

As insurance providers are increasingly developing and adopting data driven innovations there is a need for a better understanding how to regulate against potential harm caused.[1] A good example is the development of usage-based insurance products or 'Telematics' where through a device, data obtained from the vehicle (such as speed, time and location) is used by insurers for various purposes including more adequate risk assessments and personalized pricing.[2] Despite the benefits for

[1]Acknowledged for example by the European Parliament stating that [..] *Notwithstanding all the benefits, FinTech confronts us with essential questions of a regulatory societal nature.* European Parliament (2017) *Draft Report on FinTech: the influence of technology on the future of the financial sector* (2016/2243 (INI) [online] http://www.europarl.europa.eu/; Also OECD (2017), 'Technology and innovation in the insurance sector', OECD [online] https://www.oecd.org/pensions/Technology-and-innovation-in-the-insurance-sector. pp. 27–39; On the role of policy and regulation in InsurTech . See IAIS (2018), 'Issues Paper on Increasing Digitalization in Insurance and its Potential Impact on Consumer Outcomes [online] https://www.iaisweb.org/page/supervisory-material/issues-papers##. More specific on the challenges posed by Telematics See Troncoso et al. (2011) Providing many examples of the problems caused by data innovations including telematics see O'Neil (2016). And Pasquale (2015).

[2]Barone and Bella (2004); Bordoff and Noel (2008) See for an introduction to connected cars and data: Kerber (2018). Derikx et al. (2016), pp. 73–81 | 26: 73. For an introduction how insurance use of risk pooling works see Smith and Kane (1994), pp. 1–27.

F. van den Boom (✉)
Bournemouth University, Centre for Intellectual Property Policy and Management, Poole, UK
e-mail: fvandenboom@bournemouth.ac.uk

P. Marano, K. Noussia (eds.), *Insurance Distribution Directive*, AIDA Europe Research Series on Insurance Law and Regulation 3,
https://doi.org/10.1007/978-3-030-52738-9_12

consumers to potentially obtain lower premiums and improve their driving, there are serious privacy concerns about the increased use of vehicle data by insurers.[3]

Vehicle data will generally constitute personal data, and especially in combination with advanced data analytics, processing thereof by insurers may have serious consequences for (potential) consumers.[4] Without adequate regulation in place, the uptake and benefits for consumers regarding telematics insurance may be limited. Based on the assumption that well-informed consumers make better decisions about insurance products and services, this raises questions about what information should be provided and specifically whether current regulations enable the sharing of relevant information by insurers to consumers.[5]

To inform the current debate on telematics regulation with insight on the scope of relevant requirements for information disclosure, this contribution analyses two recent regulatory developments at EU level.

- The EU General Data Protection Regulation (GDPR) which applies to the processing of personal data in general;[6]
- The EU Insurance Distribution Directive (IDD) which specifically regulates consumer insurance distribution.[7]

Following a brief introduction to Telematics insurance, the key requirements of the GDPR and IDD are discussed and the scope of information disclosure

[3]Acquisti et al. (2015); Koops et. al (2016); Leenes et al (2018) Other concerns include the need to better inform consumers about consequences especially of innovative products that people have no experience with. This includes for example making it clearer to consumers of telematics that their premium could increase as well as be cancelled as a result of bad driving scores. See General Accident Telematics Car Insurance Terms and Conditions '*If a score of below 50 is recorded [...] we reserve the right to cancel your policy [..]* [online] https://help.generalaccident.com/media/1090/telematicsterms.pdf.

[4]On the discussion behind the general understanding that vehicle data is personal data see The Fédération Internationale de l'Automobile (FIA) (2017) Legal Memorandum on Connected Vehicles and Data [online] https://www.fiaregion1.com/wp-content/uploads/2017/06/20170516-Legal-Memorandum-on-Personal-Data-in-Connected-Vehicles-www.pdf. On the challenges for understanding privacy risks by consumers see Solove (2006) p 505. Specific regarding privacy concerns and telematics: see Pogarcic Mataija and Van Schoubroeck (2016) *Telematics insurance: legal concerns and challenges in the EU insurance market.* More generally see Tene and Polonetsky (2013), p. 239.

[5]At the time of writing the EU directive on modernizing consumer law part of the 'new deal for consumers' was not yet adopted and therefore not taken into consideration. It is however highly relevant given its aim 'to adapt EU consumer protection legislation to the realities of the digital era'. See for more background information and most important developments the Council of the EU (2019) EU consumers' protection to be reinforced, Press release [online] https://europa.eu/!uc86NQ.

[6]Regulation (EU) 2016/679 on the protection of natural persons with regard to the processing of personal data and on the free movement of such data.

[7]Directive (EU) 2016/97 of the European Parliament and of the Council of 20 January 2016 on insurance distribution (recast) *OJ L 26, 2.2.2016, pp. 19–59.* Köhne and Brömmelmeyer (2018).

concluding with the proposed role for the IDD to complement the GDPR in the context of telematics insurance.[8]

What is argued for here is that both the GDPR and the IDD require a broad interpretation of the information necessary to improve consumer and personal data protection; and that insurers should consider taking an integrated approach towards the information requirements for effective and efficient compliance.[9]

2 Telematics Insurance and the General Data Protection Regulation

2.1 Telematics Insurance

Modern vehicles are increasingly equipped with advanced sensor and communication technologies generating vast amounts of data on the way it functions as well as driving style and habits of its users.

Having access to this data in combination with increasingly advanced data analytics has made it possible for insurers to innovate and develop new products and services including insurance based on actual driving behavior of consumers or 'telematics' insurance.[10]

The data vehicles generate can be obtained by insurers in several ways for example by installing a telematics device such as a dongle in the policyholder's vehicle.[11] Relevant types of data insurers may collect include when, where, how and how long the car was used as research shows that for example late night and long-distance driving, speeding and heavy braking all correlate with an increase in accident risk.[12]

[8]A note on the use of 'consumer' and 'customer' in the IDD. It seems that the IDD uses them interchangeably; (compare for example Recital 5 and 6 IDD) their meaning is not the same. The GDPR instead only refers to customers, however, for readability this text will use the term consumer to refer to the driver buying telematics car insurance for their own use unless otherwise noted.

[9]The Financial Conduct Authority '*We see firms being clear and transparent in their dealings with all consumers as key to well-functioning markets*'. Financial Conduct Authority (2015); Schaeken Willemaers, Gaetane (2014)

[10]It is expected that by 2020 most European insurers will have adopted telematics. Ptolomeus (2016) Global Usage-based Insurance Study Abstract [online] https://www.ptolemus.com/wp-content/uploads/2019/07/UBIStudy2016.pdf.

[11]Other ways include the use of smartphone apps or obtain the data (with permission from the manufacturers) directly from in vehicle systems. Handel et al. (2014); Ohlsson et al. (2015) For a brief introduction how telematics works see https://www.octotelematics.com/insurance-telematics-resources/what-is-insurance-telematics/.; and regarding insurance use of telematics, see Fan and Wang (2017), pp. 1–5

[12]See As already identified by Dorweiler in 1929 certain information would be more predictive but unattainable at the time. Dorweiler (1929), p. 337 See further Weiss and Smollik (2012), p. 5 and Conners, J & Feldblum, S. (1998). *Personal Automobile: Cost Drivers, Pricing, and Public Policy*.

Telematics enables insurers to improve their risk assessment and optimize their pricing accordingly.[13] As the assessment is based on actual driving data from the individual this may lead to more precise risk pooling or even to fully personalized insurance pricing.[14] Another potential advantage is that insurers can monitor the data and provide drivers with feedback on their driving, this way insurers may be able to reduce the risk of moral hazard as well as improve road safety when drivers are sufficiently incentivized, for example through a bonus or premium deduction to improve their driving.[15]

Despite the benefits of telematics for both insurers and consumers the uptake has been slow which in part can be explained by the concerns people have raised about privacy and security.[16]

As insurers differ in what data they consider relevant for their risk and policy assessment there is discussion over what data they should be allowed to have access to. Controversial concerning telematics is the collection of GPS location data for example.[17] Especially given that such data when monitored over longer periods may reveal sensitive information and possibly protected characteristics as well as increase the risk for such data to be used for a non-risk related analysis and premium setting.[18]

In response to these concerns, the remains of this section provides an analysis to what extent privacy and data protection regulation helps consumers to become better informed and address some of their concerns about the way insurers obtain and process data in the context of providing telematics insurance.

On the difference between factors and proxies concluding that traditional data provides proxies and do not provide a full understanding of the underlying factors that influence automobile insurance loss costs. Karapiperis et al. (2015).

[13]Handel et al. (2014); Ohlsson et al. (2015).

[14]Paefgen, J., Kehr, F., Zhai, Y., Michahelles, F. (2012). *Driving behavior analysis with smartphones: Insights from a controlled field study.* And Lajunen et al. (1997), pp. 3–16.

[15]Driving less careful after having obtained insurance is an example of moral hazard. See Shavell (1979); On how in-vehicle smart driving system can lead to significant improvements in driving behaviors see Birrell et al. (2014), pp. 1801–1810; On the opportunity to provide driver feedback: Dijksterhuis et al. (2016), pp. 1158–1170. For a good overview of all the issues see Tselentis et al. (2016), pp. 362–371; Husnjak et al. (2015), pp. 816–825.

[16]Weiss and Smollik (2012), p. 35; LexisNexis® Risk Solutions, *Telematics insurance helps cut young driver casualty rates by 35%,* 14/11/2018 [online] https://risk.lexisnexis.co.uk/about-us/press-room/press-release/20181114-young-driver#_edn2; Despite their concerns people are willing to share data when there are strong incentives to do so. Derikx et al. (2015).

[17]European Data Protection Board (2020), *Guidelines 1/2020 on processing personal data in the context of connected vehicles and mobility related applications. Version 01, note 43 p 10.*

[18]Collinson P. (2017) Motoring myths: what 'black boxes' reveal about our driving habits, The Guardian,[online] Available at: https://www.theguardian.com/money/2017/dec/16/motoring-myths-black-boxes-telematics-insurance. See also Solove (2006)

On what data from vehicles may be of use for insurers in the context of risk assessments see Thomas (2012); Geneva Association (2018) "*Big Data and Insurance: Implications for Innovation, Competition and Privacy*", March 2018, Available at: https://www.genevaassociation.org/research-topics/cyber-and-innovation-digitalization/big-data-and-insurance-implications-innovation.

2.2 *The General Data Protection Regulation (GDPR)*

When an insurer wants to use vehicle data, which is generally considered personal data in the context of insurance, they will likely fall under the scope of the General Data Protection Regulation (GDPR).[19] The GDPR lays down rules relating to the protection of natural persons, about the processing of personal data and rules relating to the free movement of personal data.[20] In particular, the first principle of the GDPR on data processing to be lawful, fair and transparent is relevant to understand the scope of the information requirements for insurers.[21] The principle of transparency is considered relevant in understanding information to be made available to enable consumers to become aware of; verify and challenge the lawfulness of the processing of personal data and automated decision-making processes.[22]

Under the GDPR insurers as data controllers are required to make certain information available either directly or upon a specific request for access to data from consumers.[23] The GDPR states that information must be given *[..] in a concise, transparent, intelligible and easily accessible form*, using *clear and plain language,* avoiding for example legalese or vague terms.[24]

The principle of transparency further requires that insurers provide enough information to enable consumers to make use of their rights under the GDPR which includes the right to access. Because the GDPR does not provide much further guidance what constitutes sufficient there are different interpretations of the level of detail and access to be provided which will be discussed further below.

In light of its aims including for consumers to make better informed decisions about personal data processing, the GDPR requires that information must be made

---

[19]*This Regulation applies to the processing of personal data [..].* Article 2(1)GDPR. Whereas *'personal data' means any information relating to an identified or identifiable natural person ('data subject');* Article 4(1) Location data, which is generally collected from the vehicle, is mentioned as an example of personal data. (FIA) (2017).

[20]Art 1(1) GDPR.

[21]Art 5(1)a GDPR. *'Personal data shall be: processed lawfully, fairly and in a transparent manner in relation to the data subject."* Transparency was already taken as a key element for processing to be considered fair as processing should not be done in a way that would be considered misleading data subjects for example. See Carey p. 42; The Art. 29 Data Protection Working Party (2017), *Guidelines on the Right to Data Portability*, 16/EN WP 242 rev.01 (hereinafter WP29).

[22]Article 5; 12 and Recital 39 GDPR. WP29 (2016) *Guidelines on Transparency* P.6; Cruz Villalon (2015) *"the requirement to inform the data subjects about the processing of their personal data, which guarantees transparency of all processing, is all the more important since it affects the exercise by the data subjects of their right of access to the data being processed, [..]*Opinion AG Cruz Villalon, 9 July 2015 (1) Case C-201/14 *Smaranda Bara and Others;* Court of Justice of the European Union: Judgment in Case C-201/14 / *Smaranda Bara and Others*; paragraph 74.

[23]Consumers have specific rights to information including the right to access; to rectification, the right to data portability and rights regarding automated decision making. Articles 12–23 GDPR.

[24]Article 12 GDPR and Recital 39 GDPR; WP29 (2016) *Guidelines* on *Transparency* P. 9 [..] *The information provided to a data subject should not contain overly legalistic, technical or specialist language or terminology'.*

available to consumers about the collection, use and consequences of processing personal data by insurers.[25] The GDPR requires insurers to provide the following information;[26]

- the identity and the contact details of the controller and, where applicable,
  - of the controller's representative;
  - of the data protection officer;
- the purposes and the legal basis for the processing; [27]
- the recipients or categories of recipients of the personal data
- the storage period, or if that is not possible, the criteria used to determine that period;
- the existence of applicable rights including the following:
  - to request from the controller access to; rectification; erasure of personal data and/or data portability
  - to request from the controller restriction of processing and/or to object to processing
  - to withdraw consent at any time
  - to lodge a complaint with a supervisory authority;
- If there is an obligation to provide personal data to the insurer because of statutory or contractual requirement and what the possible consequences are when they fail to do so.
- When insurers make use of automated decision-making, including profiling, referred to in Article 22(1) and (4) they must inform consumers thereof and give meaningful information about the logic involved, as well as the significance and the envisaged consequences of such processing.

---

[25]Recital 58 of the GDPR emphasizes the need for transparency to be particularly relevant in situations [..] where the proliferation of actors and the technological complexity of practice make it difficult for the data subject to know and understand whether, by whom and for what purpose personal data relating to him or her are being collected, Article 5; 12 and Recital 39 GDPR. WP29 (2016) Guidelines on Transparency P.6; Cruz Villalon (2015) "the requirement to inform the data subjects about the processing of their personal data, which guarantees transparency of all processing, is all the more important since it affects the exercise by the data subjects of their right of access to the data being processed, [..]Opinion AG Cruz Villalon, 9 July 2015 (1) Case C-201/14 Smaranda Bara and Others; Court of Justice of the European Union: Judgment in Case C-201/14 / Smaranda Bara and Others; paragraph 74.

[26]When personal data is collected directly from the consumer (art 13 GDPR).

[27]Where applicable the legitimate interests pursued by the controller or by a third party. Article 12,18 GDPR; Recital 60 GDPR Further processing of personal data is allowed when the repurpose is compatible with the initial one depends on identifiable link between the two purposes; reasonably expectations for the data subject; the consequences and safeguards to mitigate potential harm or detriment to the data subject. See further, Soussan G, Woolfson P, Terruso D (2016) p. 24 mentioning the example of 'insurance link' investigation where data collected for fraud could not be used for policy quotation purposes.

Also, when personal data is not obtained directly from the consumer but indirectly for example using data brokers, insurers must also inform consumers about[28]

- The categories of personal data [obtained];
- The source of the personal data and if applicable, whether it came from publicly accessible sources.

It remains difficult without clear practical guidance provided by the GDPR or case law, for insurers to know what the level of granularity of the data and information detail is required to be compliant. This is problematic given that insurers face fines for non-compliance and consumers may not receive sufficient information for them to take well-informed decisions.[29] This contribution focusses on the latter, proposing to interpret the scope of information necessary as broad as possible to effectively empower consumers with control over the processing of personal data concerning them.[30]

To comply with the GDPR insurers must enable consumers to better understand the product on offer and depending on the legitimate ground for processing to give informed consent for the processing of their personal data and/or to challenge the collection and processing effectively making use of their rights when personal data is processed for insurance processes.[31] Therefore when considering what information to provide; the level of detail must be sufficient for consumers to know what personal data is collected and how their personal circumstances, behaviour and characteristics have influenced decision making for them. To enable consumers to validate and agree to the use of their personal data for processing they must be able to check whether the (proposed) processing is lawful and fair. Which means that they need to be able to challenge whether the information used is correct and whether the decision-making process is accurate. Furthermore, they should be made aware and better informed about the risks and potentially negative consequences for them personally which for example include being informed about the risks for bias, discrimination and system failure.[32]

When it comes to personal data the level of detailed information about that data should be at the level of the individual so they can become aware what data about

---

[28] Art 14 GDPR.

[29] Art 77–84 GDPR on remedies, liabilities and penalties. Insurers may refuse to provide certain information because they consider this to fall under the exception when this information would otherwise have helped consumers to decide whether or not to buy certain type of insurance given the potential harm.

[30] A recent survey shows that consumers do want to know about how their personal data is being processed McCauley (2018); See further Kamleitner and Mitchell (2018), who discuss information overload and report that visualizing data streams could be helpful in increasing consumer understanding about what happens to data after consent is initially given. Kamleitner and Mitchell (2018), pp. 91–118. Insurance Council of Australia (2015, 2017)

[31] Article 12,18 GDPR; Recital 60 GDPR.

[32] See Goodman and Flaxman (2017); Edwards and Veale (2017).

them is used and whether this data is correct and relevant for the purpose. Providing consumers with only categories does not allow them to do so.[33]

When data is obtained from other sources consumers should be made aware that this is the case and provided with what personal data is received, how it is being processed by the insurer and what the risks and consequences are for them of the insurer processing this data. Furthermore, they must be informed who the source is and how to contact them to challenge the data accuracy and the lawfulness and fairness of its processing by this specific source.

Insurers themselves may not have (access to) information from third parties. For example, in the case of the use of credit or fraud scores obtained from third parties, insurers are unlikely to have access to what personal data and process are used to derive these scores. Although one could argue that insurers must have access or obtained this information themselves given their responsibility to understand and ensure their decision-making processes are compliant and for example not based on biased data. Consumers should be able to verify the validity of the personal data processing including when a decision is based on data from third parties such as credit or fraud scores. Which is why they need to be able to obtain relevant information including the personal data and processing used that has established such score either directly from the insurer or when the insurer cannot provide this, the contact details of the source and/or third party who can.[34]

When it comes to information about the legal ground for processing the level of detail should allow for a comprehensible explanation why the chosen legal ground is the most appropriate for the proposed processing considering the purpose. Considering that consumers, based on the information given, must be able to understand which of the six legal grounds the insurer has chosen and why for them to challenge the lawfulness of the processing and personal data collected for the said purpose.[35]

---

[33]For example, many insurers state they collect 'date of birth' and 'address' but without knowing what information is on file consumers cannot correct if there is a mistake.

[34]It is often the case that this information includes proprietary information that the insurer may not have access to themselves so the insurer does not know how these scores were calculated nor can they then assess whether this data is accurate. This raises challenges for insurers considering they can be held accountable towards consumers when they base their decision-making on inaccurate information which may lead to discriminatory outcomes and adverse effects. If insurers could hide behind not having access to how these scores are calculated, they would shift it on the consumer to challenge the source of the data which would be too heavy a burden for them to bare.

[35]It can be argued that a privacy policy informing consumers that "personal data will be used to improve the service", without specifying what personal data is used is not specific enough to comply with the GDPR. Article 6 GDPR Recitals (47), (48) and (49), GDPR. Insurers report that they mostly rely on the legal basis of the performance of the contract, compliance with a legal obligation and legitimate interest for processing personal data of consumers. Consent is used only for processing health data as well as for direct marketing purposes. Insurance Europe response [...] p. 5, Soussan G, Woolfson P, Terruso D (2016), pp. 18–23 also legal duty may be applicable p 21 Note that Member States remain free to specify how this provision applies in their national law. See also Court of Justice of the EU, Joined Cases C-468/10 and C-469/10, ASNEF and FECEMD, 24 November 2011 regarding a Spanish law rule which restricted processing under the basis of legitimate interest only to information that was already in the public domain.

When it comes to information for consumers about risks and consequences of processing must enable them to decide whether to buy the insurance and what coverage. It should also include how certain personal data influences insurance decisions including their risk assessment. Providing information about how data contributes to the decision-making processes outcomes but also how accurate these processes are is heavily discussed in the context of the scope of the GDPR requirement on the right to meaningful information about the logic involved with automated decision-making.

A broad interpretation requires the following: If a potential consumer is refused insurance for example because they have a negative fraud score, they should be able to obtain information on why this is including how reliable the decision is. As insurers increasingly adopt more advanced automated processes for decision making there is concern that these processes become too opaque and can no longer be explained in terms of how the data being put in correlates to the outcome. As it should be possible to explain to the consumer how their insurance needs which are based on their current situation and behavior are met by the insurance product this could become problematic when an explanation about the process to offer the insurance product and at what price cannot be given. This would not only make it impossible for consumers to challenge whether personal data processing is fair and lawful but also reduce the opportunity for them to change their situation and reduce their risk exposure.[36]

Providing consumers with meaningful information would not only help improve the overall risk in society but also gives consumers the choice whether to buy certain insurance and from which insurer stimulating competition based not only on price but also coverage and possibly the level of privacy protection as well as improve consumer trust in insurance more generally when they are no longer confronted with consequences they were not sufficiently aware of.

Concerning the products potential for negative personal consequences, as discussed in the previous section Telematics may not be beneficial for higher risk drivers who instead of being rewarded could be faced with higher premiums compared to when they would purchase more traditional forms of car insurance. Improving their understanding on insurance products and whether it addresses their needs taking into consideration these and other consequences would in this case probably have led to the consumer not opting for Telematics. Proposed is to help consumers make better choices by making available

- the risk assessment of their needs and demands and how the (proposed) insurance product meets their needs but also where it doesn't; and

[36]Grouped under three data processing stages Van Ooien et al. have identified a list of threats to individual control over personal data processing which consumers should be made aware of. See van Ooijen and Vrabec (2016), p. 95 specifically on the severe consequences to be explained when consumers would withdraw consent for example it may not be possible to obtain new coverage with a new provider on similar terms, *e.g.* the loss of "no claims bonus" for motor insurance. See, Soussan G, Woolfson P, Terruso D (2016) p. 20.

- what changes they could make to influence risk factors that are under their control.[37]

Concerns about a broad scope of the information disclosure requirements is that it could not only harm consumers by causing information overload but lead to administrative burden for insurers as well as their need for keeping certain information confidential.[38] Because the GDPR takes into consideration the different rights and freedoms involved including the insurers' freedom to conduct business the scope of information requirements must remain balanced and proportionate.[39]

2.3 GDPR Discussions on the Scope of Information Requirements

Ongoing discussions on the scope of the right for consumers to access personal data; on the scope of the data portability right and the limits of processing personal data for profiling are briefly presented here to illustrate the lack of consensus about the scope of the GDPR requirements.[40]

Based on the *right to request for data portability* a consumer may request their insurer to send a copy of (a subset of) personal data provided by the consumer to another insurer.[41] According to the interpretation of the article 29 working party, this would include the vehicle data as this is data (in)directly provided to the insurer by the consumer but for example not the insurers 'risk score based upon the analysis of

[37]For example, how their driving behaviour or habits including whether they drive much late at night or park their car outside will influence the outcome of the insurers decision making process.

[38]Concerns about the risk for information overload raised by Insurance Europe (2016) Insight Briefing *Better, not more information for consumers.* Further research discusses whether people indeed understand how algorithms work. Bucher (2017); On the problem of 'informed' consent Custers et al. (2013), pp. 435–457. On the problem of information complexity and how the GDPR contributes to solving problems regarding information asymmetry regarding processing see Van Ooijen and Vrabec (2019), pp. 91–107.

[39]The right to privacy is not an absolute right and requires an appropriate balance between the different rights and freedoms. Recital 4 GDPR. On the concerns to protect trade secrets in light of the GDPR see Malgieri (2016), pp. 102–116.

[40]Contribution from the multistakeholder expert group on one year of GDPR application (Multistakeholder expert report 2019), Multistakeholder Expert Group to support the application of Regulation (EU) 2016/679, Report 13 June 2019 pp. 5–9.

[41]Article 20(1)a GDPR conditions include only data provided by and based on specific legal grounds have to be provided to the data subject. Excluded from the scope is data which are derived or inferred from the personal data provided by the data subject. The WP29 gives a broad interpretation of what data is considered to be 'provided by'. See Article 29 Data Protection Working Party (2017), *Guidelines on the Right to Data Portability,* 16/EN WP 242 rev.01. For critical analysis and concerns raised about the scope and effectiveness of the right in practice see Zanfir (2012), p. 149 Graef et al. (2013), pp. 53–63; Swire and Lagos (2013), p. 335.

the telematics data as this is considered inferred data.[42] A sufficiently broad scope of what personal data falls under the scope for data portability would allow consumers to more easily switch and stimulate competition between insurers. However, it could also harm competition as insurers have warned for the consequences of having to share too much information considering the risk to disclose valuable information. For example, on factors used for target market selection and risk assessments insurers are concerned about the potential risks for fraud and unfair competition. As a result, insurers may become reluctant to contribute to the development of data standards and interoperability required for further innovations or to continue to offer certain insurance products which would be detrimental to consumers.[43]

Considering their rights regarding *automated decision-making*, insurers are required to inform consumers whether they make use of profiling for example and give meaningful information about the logic involved but no provision explains what this means or how this should be done in practice.[44] There is much debate if it is and will continue to be possible to explain processes which make use of advanced analytics. Especially when data and computer science experts are no longer able to understand let alone explain how an algorithm reaches a certain outcome.[45] Which has led to some proposing that these systems, therefore, should not be used by insurers for critical decision-making when this would have significant effects on people's lives. As insurance decisions about whether to accept or reject an application or insurance claim may have a significant effect, insurers must take caution when innovating their decision-making processes.[46] Although insurers may not yet

[42]The Article 29 Working Party (Art. 29 WP) was an advisory body on the GDPR. On 25 May 2018, it has been replaced by the European Data Protection Board (EDPB).

[43]Multi stakeholder expert report, (2019) n 41; On the perspective of insurers see Insurance Europe (2017) *contribution to the Article 29 Working Party guidelines on the right to data portability*, Position paper, 26 January 2017; for general concerns about the broad scope see Meyer (2017) *European Commission, experts uneasy over WP29 data portability interpretation* [Available online] https://iapp.org/news/a/european-commission-experts-uneasy-over-wp29-data-portability-interpretation-1/.

[44]Articles 13,14,22 GDPR. The GDPR acknowledges that automated decision-making, including profiling can have serious consequences for individuals, however in order to fall under the scope of the general prohibitions the effects must be legal or similarly significant which the GDPR does not further define. Article 29 Data protection Working Party (2017) *Guidelines on Automated individual decision-making and Profiling for the purposes of Regulation 2016/679*, WP 251, p. 7 The GDPR defines profiling as: *any form of automated processing of personal data consisting of the use of personal data to evaluate certain personal aspects relating to a natural person, in particular to analyse or predict aspects concerning that natural person's performance at work, economic situation, health, personal preferences, interests, reliability, behaviour, location or movements*; Article 4(4) GDPR.

[45]The need for, and lack of, explainable AI has been gaining much attention lately as an emerging field in machine learning seef or example DARPA's program on XAI [online at https://www.darpa.mil/program/explainable-artificial-intelligence] but the concerns are not new see for a good introduction: Wachter et al. (2017), 10.1126.

[46]Article 22 GDPR. The GDPR does provide a number of exceptions, including the "necessity to perform or enter into a contract". See further Article 29 Data protection Working Party (2017)

have implemented automated decision-making this is likely to change in the future so there is an urgent need to understand the scope of the requirements and potential exceptions for insurers to be able to adopt and benefit from innovations without harming consumers rights to privacy and data protection.[47]

Whether insurance innovations such as telematics using personal data and advanced processing are stifled or enabled and if these are going to be beneficial for consumers may further depend on the outcome of the discussions on the scope of GDPR requirements.[48]

3 Telematics Insurance and the Insurance Distribution Directive

Instead of a one size fits all industries solution to the questions about the scope of the GDPR information requirements;[49] a sector-specific approach is called for taking into consideration sector-specific demands and needs which is more likely to improve industry-wide compliance and protection without stifling innovation.[50]

Guidelines on Automated individual decision-making and Profiling for the purposes of Regulation 2016/679, WP 251. See for proposed guidance on the scope in the context of insurance BIPAR (2016), p. 36. In response however Insurance Europe raises concerns about the impact of the guidelines for adoption of innovative processes. Insurance Europe (2019) Insight Briefing EU General Data Protection Regulation: one year on, Insurance Europe aisbl, June 2019. The insurance industry has also raised concerns about a too narrow interpretation as proposed by the EDPB guidelines which would discourage insurers from further developing and using innovative beneficial automated processes.

[47]There is a trend towards increasingly data-driven business models throughout the insurance value chain in motor insurance. See EIOPA (2018) *BDA thematic review* p6 In this context it is important insurers (together with their DPO) consider a risk and impact assessment. See Bipar (2016), p. 43 based on their recordkeeping requirements. '*Before a controller processes data, it should decide, with its DPO, how risky the processing is likely to be to the rights and legitimate expectations of data subjects. If the risk is high, the controller should carry out an impact assessment to evaluate the origin, nature, particularity and severity of the risk.* Examples include: *processing using new technology; innovative techniques, such as profiling; and large-scale processing of special categories of data or data relating to criminal convictions and offences.'*

[48]Insurance Europe raised concerns on the impact that certain GDPR provisions can have on the use of innovative technologies in the sector considering that legal uncertainty stifles innovation in insurance. See Insurance Europe (2019) *Position Paper Response to EC stocktaking exercise on application of GDPR,* COB-DAT-19-032; p. 9 On the negative effect of the GDPR on the development and use of AI in Europe: Wallace and Castro (2018), March 27, 2018.

[49]Confirming a no one size fits all approach the Geneva Association (2018) "*Big Data and Insurance: Implications for Innovation, Competition and Privacy",* March 2018, https://www.genevaassociation.org/research-topics/cyber-and-innovation-digitalization/big-data-and-insurance-implications-innovation. p. 16.

[50]Recognizing the need for such a sector specific approach taking account of '*the specific features of the various processing sectors and the specific needs of micro, small and medium-sized enterprises.'* Article 40 GDPR; and the need for a national scope Member States may maintain or

What the previous section showed is that without consensus it will remain difficult for insurers to know what information they must give to (potential) consumers regarding their processing of personal data for insurance purposes. To help understand the insurance sector and find the adequate scope for information requirements that provide a balance between the need for information from consumers and the need to protect information by insurers this section takes such an approach through an analysis of the EU Insurance Distribution Directive (IDD).[51]

The focus is on key IDD information requirements specific for insurers and how these may complement the GDPR with a better understanding of the challenges within the insurance industry. To better understand these requirements for insurers to disclose information to consumers; we will first briefly discuss relevant product oversight and governance requirements as these are necessary to understand what information has become available after which specific requirements of the IDD on what information must be made available for consumers in the context of telematics.

3.1 The Insurance Distribution Directive (IDD)

The EU Directive on Insurance Distribution (IDD) aims to improve the way insurance products are sold so that they will bring real benefits to consumers in the EU.[52] The IDD requires greater transparency on pricing and costs of insurance products; better and more comprehensive information to improve consumer decision making and transparency and business conduct rules to prevent the mis-selling of insurance products to consumers.[53]

introduce more specific provisions to adapt the application of certain GDPR rules for specific processing situations, including determining more precisely the conditions under which the processing of personal data is lawful. Article 6(2) GDPR; Recital 10 GDPR and Recital 98 GDPR referring to codes of conducts to facilitate the effective application of the GDPR by considering the characteristics of sector specific processing and the specific needs of micro, small and medium enterprises. *''Codes could calibrate the obligations of controllers and processors, taking into account the risk likely to result from the processing for the rights and freedoms of natural persons.*

[51]Directive 2016/97/EU of the European Parliament and of the Council of 20 January 2016 on insurance distribution (recast), [2016) OJ L 26/19 (the IDD).

[52]*[..] In order to guarantee that the same level of protection applies and that the consumer can benefit from comparable standards, in particular in the area of the disclosure of information, a level playing field between distributors is essential.* Recital 6 IDD; Recital 2 IDD. For a critical analysis of the background and IDD requirements in relation to its aims see De Maesschalck (2017), pp. 59–79; Hofmann et al. (2018), pp. 740–769; Köhne and Brömmelmeyer (2018). Marano (2019a),; Schaeken Willemaers, Gaetane (2014).

[53]EU Publications (2016) *Insurance distribution — new rules from 2018,* Document 32016L0097 [online] https://eur-lex.europa.eu/legal-content/en/LSU/?uri=CELEX:32016L0097.

The IDD requires insurers to comply with the general principle to act:

- honestly, fairly and professionally;[54] and
- in accordance with the best interests of their customers.[55]

This applies not only to information disclosure but the entire process of developing, testing, and distributing insurance products in the EU.

Important to note here is that the IDD only provides minimum harmonization of national provisions allowing the EU Member States to provide for a higher level of consumer protection proportionate to additional administrative burdens.[56] Member States could for example require insurers to disclose specific information such as ratings and risk factors for consumers to become better informed about insurance products such as Telematics.

3.2 IDD: Product Oversight and Governance (POG) Requirements

The POG requirements contribute to improving insight and transparency about insurance products in several ways. Although the IDD POG requirements are addressed at insurers and distributors they are important for the question about what data is available and how much must be shared with consumers.

To improve consumer protection and to offer products that are in their best interest, insurers are held under the IDD to have a proportionate and appropriate product approval process in place for each insurance product.[57]

---

[54]Insurers must prioritize the interest of consumers when designing, developing and distributing insurance products to prevent the miss-selling of insurance products to consumers Article 17 (1) IDD As an example of how this has been implemented nationally see for the UK the FCO Handbook article ICOBS 2.5.-1. Financial Conduct Authority (2015)

[55]Article 19; 20 IDD insurers must avoid selling insurance products which do not meet the consumers' insurance demands and needs. Although Insurance-based investment products are not dealt with here the EIOPA specifically refers to a suitability/appropriateness assessment for insurers to ensure that not more information is requested from the consumer than needed (or duplicated) to provide good quality advice to the consumer. The EIOPA considers this will further enhance the quality of service provided to the consumer, strengthening the framework for proper selling practices. See consideration 8 of the EIOPA, Final Report on Consultation Paper no. 16/006 *on Technical Advice on possible delegated acts concerning the Insurance Distribution Directive.*

[56]Article 11(2) IDD and Recital 3 IDD.

[57]Article 25 IDD: *"[...]to the nature of the insurance product.* Recital 55 IDD: For specific guidelines how to comply in practice see the EIOPA (2016) *Preparatory Guidelines on product oversight and governance arrangements by insurance undertakings and insurance distributors*. For detailed analysis of the POG requirements see further Marano (2019b). The EU Regulation and the Liabilities, in Marano, P., Rokas, I. (ed.), Distribution of Insurance-Based Investment Products. The EU Regulation and the Liabilities, Springer, Cham 2019: pp 59–96.

To comply manufacturers of insurance products must for each insurance product do the following:[58]

- Identify the target market based on the needs and demands of consumers.;[59]
- Assess the risks and costs involved;
- Design a distribution strategy consistent with the identified target market reaching only those consumers with needs and demands best served by the product.[60]
- Regularly review to ensure that marketed products remain to serve the needs of the market and the distribution strategy remains appropriate.[61] Distributors are therefore held to provide insurers with any relevant information to do so.[62]

To enable distributors to fully understand the products they intend to sell; insurers are held to share information about their product approval processes including on the target market; the proposed distribution strategy and any circumstances which might cause a conflict of interest to the detriment of the consumer.[63] The information provided to distributors must be clear, complete and up to date.[64]

The IDD also requires both insurers and insurance distributors to document their actions and to make this available upon request to authorities.[65] Although this is not

[58]Insurers are considered manufacturers when they have a decision-making role in designing and developing products for the market. Article 3(1) IDD regulation. Which is assumed when they can autonomously determine *the essential features and main elements of an insurance product, including its coverage, price, costs, risk, target market and compensation and guarantee rights, [..]* Art 3(2) IDD Regulation.

[59]'Article 5(1) IDD Regulation *'[..] be identified at a sufficiently granular level, taking into account the characteristics, risk profile, complexity and nature of the insurance product [..]* Recital 5 and 6 IDD Regulation further explain that (5) The identification of the target market means *describing a group of customers sharing common characteristics at an abstract and generalized level in order to enable the manufacturer to adapt the features of the product to the needs, characteristics and objectives of that group of customers. (6) The level of granularity of the target market and the criteria used to define the target market [..] should be relevant for the product and should make it possible to assess which customers fall within the target market.*

[60]Article 5(1) Recital 5 and 6 IDD Regulation.

[61]Article 25(1) IDD.

[62]Art 25(1) IDD; The IDD Regulation states that '*Insurance distributors becoming aware that an insurance product is not in line with the interests, objectives and characteristics of its identified target market or becoming aware of other product-related circumstances that may adversely affect the customer shall promptly inform the manufacturer [..]*' and that '*[..]insurance distributors shall upon request provide manufacturers with relevant sales information, including, where appropriate, information on the regular reviews of the product distribution arrangements.*' Art 10,11 IDD Regulation.

[63]Art 8 IDD; Recital 10 IDD information must be given to distributors [..] *to fully understand the products they intend to distribute, so that they can carry out their distribution activities in accordance with the best interest of their costumers, in particular by providing professional advice*'. Recital 55 IDD: *"[..]be able to understand the characteristics and identified target market of those products. [..].*

[64]Art 8(2) IDD Regulation.

[65]Art 9;12 IDD Regulation.

directly information to be shared with consumers it does require insurers and distributors to keep records and generally be well informed themselves of adverse effects for their consumers as a result of their products and services.[66]

Compliance with the IDD requires insurers to become better informed themselves and may increase the necessity to gather and analyze personal data to understand and continue to assess their products concerning the target market and to document their steps for accountability purposes.[67] These efforts, however, may contradict with some of the data protection principles they must adhere to under the GDPR such as the principle of data minimization, storage limitation and privacy by design. This issue has been identified and will be discussed further below.

3.3 IDD: Information Disclosure Requirements

Under the IDD insurers must provide consumers with relevant information about the insurance product in a comprehensible form;[68] If a consumer is offered a contract this must be consistent with their insurance demands and needs.[69] The IDD further states that the information given must be fair, clear and not misleading.[70]

To decide what information consumers need, insurers must take into consideration the complexity of the insurance product and the type of consumers it is for.[71] For example when it comes to new and innovative insurance products like telematics, consumers require more information to understand how telematics works and what the consequences are when they do not maintain a safe driving score based on criteria set by their insurer. The rise in complaints about the perceived

---

[66]As insurers may not collect information about protected characteristics such as gender or race they would not be able to monitor the impact of decisions including whether to reject applications or claims has on these groups of vulnerable consumers in society including whether insurance for these groups remains accessible and affordable.

[67]Article 7(3) of Delegated Regulation 2017/2358, for example states that manufacturers are held to monitor their products during its lifetime for any circumstances related to the insurance product that may have a material adverse affect on the consumer. See further EIOPA Q&A on appropriate product testing requirements [accessed online] https://eiopa.europa.eu/Pages/Guidelines/Q-and-A-on-Regulation-Answers-Delegated-Regulation.aspx.

[68]Article 20 IDD [..] *objective information about the insurance product in a comprehensible form to allow that customer to make an informed decision.*

[69]In this regard the IDD introduces specific disclosure requirements to inform consumers about any relationship between the insurer and distributor or other circumstance that could be an incentive not to receive recommendations which are not in their best interest to avoid conflicts of interest Article 17 (3) IDD.

[70]Art 17(2); 20(7) and 23 IDD. Somewhat similar to the art 5(1)a GDPR principle of lawfulness, fairness and transparency where the latter requires information and communication relating to the processing of personal data to be easy to understand using clear and plain language. Article 12 GDPR and Recital 39 GDPR.

[71]Art 20(1) and Art 20 (2) IDD.

unfairness of telematics insurance illustrates such a lack of understanding especially amongst young people of their policy requirements which could be improved through better and more comprehensible information.[72]

The IDD contains several information requirements based on which information must be provided to consumers the following is relevant with respect to non-life insurance products such as motor vehicle insurance:

The insurance intermediary must give consumers relevant information including about the following:[73]

- The intermediaries' identity and address;
- whether the communication constitutes advice about the insurance products sold and if so a personalised recommendation explaining why this is the best product for the customer considering their demands and needs.
- whether the proposed contract or advice is based on a fair and personal analysis;[74]
- the rights of the consumer to complain and information about procedures for redress.
- possible conflicts of interest and remunerations.[75]

The IDD introduced a new information requirement for insurers to help consumers get better informed about non-life insurance products. The Insurance Product Information Document (IPID) is meant to give consumers key information about the product in a way that allows them to easily obtain relevant information and compare between different insurers. The IPID contains the following information:

- key information about the type of insurance;
- a summary of the insurance cover, including
  - the main risks insured,
  - the sum and,
  - the geographical scope, if applicable;

[72]Frost, J., 2018. *Rise in telematics complaints down to 'sub-standard' market entrants – Mike Brockman*. Insurance Times, [online] Available at: https://www.insurancetimes.co.uk/rise-in-telematics-complaints-down-to-sub-standard-market-entrants-mike-brockman/1427294.article; Recital 71 GDPR on fairness.

[73]Art 18–20 IDD.

[74]Art 20(3). [..]on the basis of an analysis of a sufficiently large number of insurance contracts available on the market to enable it to make a personal recommendation, in accordance with professional criteria, regarding which insurance contract would be adequate to meet the consumer's needs.

[75]This includes information to be provided about the register in which it has been included and how to verify; whether the intermediary is representing the consumer or is acting for and on behalf of the insurance undertaking; The names of insurance undertakings with whom the distributor has a contractual obligation for exclusivity. The names of insurance undertakings with whom the distributor has a contractual obligation for exclusivity; and Information about remuneration received including whether consumers must pay a fee and/or any other payments See art 18–19 IDD.

- the means and duration of the payment of the premiums;
- the obligations at the start and during the term of the contract;
- the obligations if a claim is made and main exclusions where claims cannot be made;
- the term of the contract including the start and end dates of the contract;
- the means of terminating the contract.

With respect to insurance based investment products there are additional requirements.[76]

3.4 *Product Oversight and Governance*

The Product Oversight and Governance requirements are relevant as they require insurers to conduct testing and monitoring of their insurance products to make sure these are and remain appropriate for their specific target market. To facilitate the implementation of the IDD, the European Commission adopted two Delegated Regulations which contain implementing measures.

The delegated regulation on Product oversight and governance requirements for insurance undertakings and insurance distributors specifies the criteria and practical details for the application of the POG rules, based on the European Insurance and Occupational Pensions Authority (EIOPA) technical advice.[77]

In addition, the EIOPA as well as many other (national) authorities and organizations such as the Financial Conduct Authority (FCA) have developed guidance on issues of interpretation or application of the IDD and its implementing measures. Their interpretation of the scope of the POG are useful insofar that they require insurers to obtain certain information which under a broad interpretation of the scope of the information requirements towards consumers should be made available.

To ensure consistent and effective application the EIOPA published their responses to questions about the POG product testing requirements.[78] To ensure that insurance product meets the identified needs, objectives and characteristics of the target market insurers must undertake appropriate product testing.[79] The product

[76]Which fall outside the scope of this research. For an analysis of the IDD requirements for these products see: Marano (2019b).

[77]The two Delegated Regulations cover Product oversight and governance requirements for insurance undertakings and insurance distributors; and Information requirements and conduct of business rules applicable to the distribution of insurance-based investment products (IBIPs).

[78]EIOPA, Answers to (EU) 2017–2358 product oversight and governance requirements for insurance: 11 July 2018 (accessed online) These answers by the EIOPA are however not legally binding and do not prevent national competent authorities from maintaining or introducing stricter standards on a national level.

[79]Delegated Regulation 2017/2358.

should be tested on all relevant dimensions. This should according to EIOPA, in particular, include assessments of:

- how the product works;
- its performance;
- its risk/reward profile,
- price and coverage; and
- information to consumers.

Considering the relevant information it contains the EIOPA recommends insurers to include their product scenario analysis. Another good practice, according to EIOPA, for insurers who use driving behavior for premium setting, to know what information consumers must be given is to take into account the level of information available to the consumers belonging to that target market and the consumer's financial literacy.[80] Further good practices proposed are consumer testing to help assess the comprehensibility by consumers of insurance products and to analyse consumer complaints about similar products.[81]

In the UK, the Financial Conduct Authority (FCA) gives practical examples of what they consider to be IDD compliant advice for UK insurers.[82] According to the FCA, advice given by an insurer to a potential consumer, which includes proposing all available insurance products with only a generic statement for each product on what type of needs it will meet, is most likely non- compliant. Unless the insurer can show that they have identified, and all the products offered are consistent with, the consumers demands and needs.[83] Undertaking a demand and needs test for each consumer before providing advice on what insurance products are suitable may however lead to some insurers collecting more not fewer personal data about potential consumers which may be problematic in the context of the GDPR principles.

[80]Article 5 (3) Delegated Regulation 2017/2358: However, the requirement to assess the product performance should not be understood as an interference with the manufacturer's freedom to set premiums or as price control in any form.

[81]See EIOPA (2018) Answers to (EU) 2017–2358 product oversight and governance requirements for insurance, [online] https://eiopa.europa.eu/Pages/Guidelines/Q-and-A-on-Regulation-Answers-Delegated-Regulation.aspx.

[82]FCA (2017) *Insurance Distribution Directive Implementation* – Consultation Paper I (CP17/7).

[83]FCA (2018) *IDD: delivering clear, fair outcomes for consumers from the insurance sector* [online] https://www.fca.org.uk/firms/insurance-distribution-directive/idd-delivering-clear-fair-outcomes-consumers-insurance-sector.

3.5 Information Disclosure: The Insurance Product Information Document

As mentioned, the IDD requires insurers to provide consumers with a simple, standardized Insurance Product Information Document (IPID) for non-life insurance products. The IPID, which is a new requirement introduced by the IDD for insurers, presents for each type of insurance product what the key characteristics of the product are.[84] These include what is and what is not insured; what is covered and any restrictions on coverage; key obligations for the policyholder including payment and finally information about the start, end and policy cancellation. As the IPID only contains key product information it does not replace the need for consumers to receive more detailed information including when they receive an offer for a product how the product complies with their specific needs and demands. The IPID format includes a statement that all the necessary pre-contractual and contractual information is available elsewhere.[85]

The key information provided for on the IPID aims to enable consumers to quickly understand what the insurer offers and to compare between different insurers.[86] However, and despite that most stakeholders welcomed the IPID and its purpose, there are serious concerns about whether in its current form the IPID is effective and proportionate. If it is not effective it poses disproportioned administrative burdens for insurers to maintain. Main concerns include whether consumers are better informed and enabled to make comparisons as well as the potential risk for an overreliance by consumers on the basic information contained in the IPID which could result in consumers becoming less instead of better informed about the specificities of their insurance if they do not or no longer read the main insurance policy documents.[87]

Research shows that the IPID may not present potential consumers with key information necessary for them to make an informed decision. A brief comparison illustrates serious differences in interpretations of what insurers consider to be key information to be shared with consumers. For example with respect to telematics car insurance a comparison between the IPD from a Dutch and a UK car insurance provider the UK IPID mentions that the policy may be cancelled as a result of

---

[84]Article 20(8) IDD specifies which information the insurance product information document should contain; which includes the type of insurance it relates to, the main risks insured and excluded from its cover, geographical scope and whether consumers have any contractual obligations for example regarding the claim's procedure.

[85]Article 2 IPID Regulation.

[86]Recital 3:[..] *to provide customers with product information which is easy to read, understand and compare,* Commission Implementing Regulation (EU) 2017/1469 laying down a standardized presentation format for the IPID, C/2017/5544, OJ L 209, 12.8.2017, pp. 19–23 (hereinafter IPID Regulation).

[87]As researchers have for example shown that easier-to-read insurance contract terms inflate estimates of the compensation that will be awarded in the case of an accident. Van Boom et al. (2016), pp. 187–197; Davis (1977), pp. 841–920; Pander Maat et al. (2009).

breaching policy terms or severe traffic violations the Dutch IPID only mentions that driving behavior may lead to a premium reduction but not that a traffic violation could lead to the policy being cancelled immediately.[88]

Considering the impact, it has for a consumer when their insurance coverage is being cancelled this should be considered key information.

Currently the IPID does not allow consumers to make comparisons given the different interpretations of what information should be given.[89] Important is, therefore, also to continue to monitor signs of overreliance on the limited information contained in the IPID as it could result in consumers becoming less informed about insurance products which is against its aim and purpose.

4 The GDPR and IDD Proposed Information Requirements

This final section presents the analysis based on the previous sections about the scope of requirements under the GDPR and IDD; the interplay between the GDPR and the IDD presenting an overview of key challenges and opportunities regarding the provision of information to improve consumer and data protection in the context of innovations in consumer insurance. Looking at the role of the IDD considering the aims of the GDPR, to what extent do the GDPR and the IDD complement and/or contradict each other concerning information requirements to enable better-informed decision-making regarding innovations in insurance products and services.

4.1 Interaction Between the GDPR and IDD

The IDD as it aims to take into consideration the specificities of the insurance industry providing a balanced approach to stakeholder interests will improve the understanding of the scope of the GDPR information disclosure requirements for insurance products and innovations thereof. However, due to a lack of consensus amongst experts and practitioners, uncertainty about key requirements and the interpretation thereof remains which may limit the developments and adoption of otherwise beneficial innovations in the insurance industry.

---

[88] VIVAT Schadeverzekeringen N.V., *Fairzekering - Autoverzekering WA + Beperkt Casco* [online] https://verzekeringskaarten.nl/fairzekering/Autoverzekering-WA and Aioi Nissay Dowa Insurance Company of Europe (insurethebox) *Insurance Product Information Document* [online] https://www.insurethebox.com/wp-content/uploads/2018/09/itb_IPID_v1.pdf.

[89] Research shows that even when a standardized format is used insurers differ in the level and type of information they provide, which makes it impossible for consumers to compare between different insurers. See in this volume: Brofeldt, A. and Kolding-Krøger, B, *"The promised increase in customer protection under the IDD. Customers' demands and needs and comparable pre-contractual information in form of a standardised IPID"*.

To consider the IDD requirements to better understand the scope of the GDPR requirements for insurers may help to reduce the risk of excessive and disproportionate interpretations of the scope for information to be provided to consumers in the context of insurance.[90] This combined approach will provide a (more) balanced understanding of the different interests involved, and characteristics of, the insurance industry required for better compliance with the GDPR requirements.

4.1.1 Better Informed Decision Making

Based on the understanding that greater transparency and better and more comprehensible information about insurance products and the processing of personal data will enable consumers to make better-informed decisions and contribute to consumer and privacy protection.[91]

The IDD, when implemented in a way that enables adequate information to be made available to consumers regarding the processing of personal data, has the potential to contribute to improved and informed decision-making about innovative insurance products such as telematics that require personal data processing.[92] By providing consumers with key information not only about how their insurance products and services cover their demands and needs but also how their behavior affects their risk score and what they could do to obtain a more favorable result in terms of lower premium or lower chance of ever needing to call upon insurance benefits not only consumers but insurers as this would improve the level of understanding how insurance works and trust people have in the industry.

[90]The GDPR acknowledges the need for sector specific interpretations of the requirements encouraging certification and codes of conduct. Article 40 GDPR '[..] *encourages the drawing up of codes of conduct intended to contribute to the proper application of this Regulation, taking account of the specific features of the various processing sectors and the specific needs of micro, small and medium-sized enterprises.* And Recital 98(1) GDPR [..] *to facilitate the effective application of this Regulation, taking account of the specific characteristics of the processing carried out in certain sectors.'*

[91]Confirming conclusions reached by Hofmann et al. (2018) who concluded that: *All in all, the new IDD will enhance the efficiency of European insurance markets.*: 'and that: *Through more uniform and consistent regulation, in conjunction with extended transparency requirements, it can ensure that consumers throughout the EU are equally well protected*' p. 766.

[92]See in this regard the objectives of the IPID to ensure that the consumer has the relevant information about a non-life insurance product to allow him to easily compare between different product offers and to make an informed decision about whether or not to purchase the product, which not only contributes to the general aim of better informed consumers but also to help avoid consumer lock in with one service provider as is the aim of the right to data portability under the GDPR. EIOPA (2017) *Draft Implementing Technical Standards* p. 3.

4.1.2 Improve Accountability and Responsible Business Practices

The IDD contributes with specific requirements not only to improve better-informed decision-making by consumers but also to improve the understanding of the requirements for insurers and distributors on what information should be made available under the scope of both the GDPR and the IDD.

4.1.3 Balancing Information Requirements

In practice insurers are challenged to find the right balance between the need for data collection for analysis and monitoring purposes while complying with the data protection principles of data minimization, privacy by default and by design.

The IDD requires insurers to understand the needs and demands of consumers not only to provide for adequate products but also to know what information consumers need to make informed decisions regarding what insurance to purchase. Although this could be taken as an incentive to collect vast amounts of personal data, collecting more than the minimum amount of personal data required to comply with the IDD, would be in breach of the GDPR where the principle of data minimization protects consumers against the risks involved of too excessive data collection.[93] In practice insures must be able to explain why certain data collection is appropriate and not excessive for understanding their target market and consumers' demands and needs.[94] Taking into consideration that insurers are required to regularly review whether their products remain adequate and distribution remains appropriate for the identified target market(s). Insurers and their distributor must, therefore, monitor for any adverse effects on (potential) consumers and the market including on the availability and affordability of insurance for vulnerable groups. This requires again the collection of personal data to gain relevant insights. For example, monitoring the impact of their acceptance criteria on its potential for bias or discrimination of protected groups. As the IDD requires insurers to document their actions including steps taken to avoid adverse effects insurers may risk non-compliance with the IDD as well as face fines based on the GDPR.

The above examples illustrate why it is important for insurers not to have separate compliance procedures for the IDD and the GDPR but to integrate them in their product development and decision-making processes from the beginning. This will help reduce any overlap and administrative duplications and the risk for

[93]"Personal data shall be: adequate, relevant and limited to what is necessary in relation to the purposes for which they are processed (data minimisation)" Article 5(1)(c) GDPR Considering that the principles of data minimisation and purpose specification are difficult to reconcile with the prospect of big data analyses. The Geneva Association (2018), p. 16.

[94]As this could be used as an argument to collect ever more personal data collecting data to better understand consumers' demands and needs for example must be balanced against the GDPR notion of data protection by design and privacy principles of data minimization and purpose limitation. Art 5 GDPR.

non-compliance being able to explain and justify the collection and processing of personal data.[95]

4.1.4 Information Disclosure: Proposed Scope

The GDPR and the IDD, when interpreted with a sufficiently broad scope regarding the information disclosure requirements for insurers towards consumers, would include all information required for consumers to make better decisions which insurance product would best meet their needs. It would also enable them to hold insurers accountable for providing adequate safeguards to mitigate any adverse effects or to provide redress when things do negatively impact people's lives. Adequate information disclosure will contribute to reducing the risks for bias, and discrimination when disclosure includes having access to challenge decisions made by insurers using automated processes. If there is no means to provide explanations that help consumers understand how decisions are made that affect them including what they should do to reduce their risk, arguably these systems should not be used for critical processes.[96]

4.2 Information Disclosure: GDPR and IDD Integration for Better Compliance

Compliance with the IDD should contribute to the aim of the GDPR to enable consumers to become well informed and better protected against harm from personal data processing by insurers by bringing a sector-specific interpretation and balance for the scope of the GDPR.[97]

---

[95]The need for a coherent application of the applicable regulatory framework is acknowledged by the EP in the context of avoiding competitive disadvantages for insurers. European Parliament (2017), p. 10; See in this volume Chatzara, V., *"The interplay between the GDPR and the IDD"*.

[96]There is a lively discussion on explainability of AI and accountability for the adoption of increasingly sophisticated and opaque automated decision-making. Whether such systems should be adopted by insurers is subject to debate as there is much disagreement about the legal requirements; about the level of explain-ability of different methods and their potential adverse effects or what safeguards should be in place. Furthermore promising solutions are starting to be proposed. For a good understanding of what explainable AI entails Price Waterhouse Copper (2018) explainable AI; the DARPA XAI Program https://www.darpa.mil/attachments/XAIProgramUpdate.pdf ; Project ExplA which is a collaboration between the UK Information Commissioner's Office and The Alan Turing Institute to create practical guidance to assist organisations with explaining artificial intelligence (AI) decisions to the individuals affected who have recently published a report and guidelines of what they consider relevant for explainability. [Accessed online] https://ico.org.uk/about-the-ico/research-and-reports/project-explain-interim-report/.

[97]See in this regard the objectives of the IPID to ensure that the consumer has the relevant information about a non-life insurance product to allow him to easily compare between different

As such the IDD requirements which are specific for the insurance sector and the more general requirements under the GDPR on transparency and information disclosure should be considered by insurers not in isolation but complementing each other. Considering the consequences, if an insurer decides not to make or have the required information available, they not only risk non-compliance with the IDD but could also face fines based on the GDPR.[98] As such it important for insurers to consider both the IDD and the GDPR requirements together and not have separate processes for compliance.[99] This combined approach will provide a (more) balanced understanding of the different interests involved, and characteristics of, the insurance industry which would contribute also to a better understanding of and compliance by insurers with the GDPR requirements.

Returning to the main concern on whether consumers can obtain the information that allows them to make informed decisions regarding telematics insurance the following can be said:

4.2.1 The IDD Contributes to Transparency in and About Insurance

Transparency of, and information on, personal data processing by insurers will enable consumers to become better informed when it comes to telematics and other innovations within insurance where the processing of personal data is necessary.[100] Although it is argued here that generally more information is required to be made available by insurers than is currently being done in practice, this has to be proportionate taking into consideration the consequences for insurers including additional administrative burdens and risks for unfair competition.[101]

---

product offers and to make an informed decision about whether or not to purchase the product, which not only contributes to the general aim of better informed consumers but also to help avoid consumer lock in with one service provider as is the aim of the right to data portability under the GDPR. EIOPA (2017) Draft Implementing Technical Standards p. 3.

[98]The ICO and The Alan Turing Institute provide insights on the risks for not making information available. For more information see https://ico.org.uk/about-the-ico/news-and-events/blog-ico-and-the-alan-turing-institute-open-consultation-on-first-piece-of-ai-guidance/.

[99]As proposed also by Chatzara, V. (2019) note 94. The need for a coherent application is also acknowledged by the European Parliament in the context of avoiding competitive disadvantages for insurers legislation in place. European Parliament (2017), p. 10.

[100]Researchers warn for overly restrictive provisions as they may *[. . .] decrease insurance companies' ability to develop product innovations, thereby reducing the range of products available in the marketplace.* Hofmann et al. (2018), p. 765.

[101]Relevant discussions and concerns about the unclear scope of the GDPR access rights include for example the issue of trade secrets Malgieri (2016), pp. 102–116. Arguing for the need for more information to be shared and proposing a new data protection right, the 'right to reasonable inferences' needed to enable adequate control for consumers over personal data; and Wachter and Mittelstadt (2018); On the other hand see Hofmann et al who warn that the expected increase in reporting and disclosure requirements might add to what is already excessive bureaucracy for insurers. Hofmann et al. (2018) referring to GDV (2015).

4.2.2 Recommendations: Self-Regulation Regarding Information Disclosure

Despite concerns raised about the uncertainty as a result of the lack of clearer guidance on how to comply with the GDPR requirements, it does not seem likely that this will happen nor that it would be desirable given the different national and sector specific needs and demands regarding what information is required. The Insurance Industry should continue to take a proactive approach to address any legal uncertainties about the scope for information to be provided compliant with the GDPR and IDD. The absence of legal clarity and specific requirements also provides opportunities for the insurance sector to develop standards and industry specific codes of conduct regarding the GDPR information requirements.[102]

The EDPS considers codes to: '*[. . .] represent an opportunity to establish a set of rules which contribute to the proper application of the GDPR in a practical, transparent and potentially cost effective manner that takes on board the nuances for a particular sector and/or their processing activities.*'[103] The development of sector specific initiatives including codes and certifications to '*enhance transparency and compliance* and to contribute to *'the proper application of the Regulation'* is encouraged under the GDPR.[104]

An industry-wide approach, developing practical guidelines based on a shared interpretation of the scope, is recommended which could be done in the form of standard developments and/or the insurance code of conduct focusing specifically on information disclosure compliance with both the GDPR and the IDD.[105] The IPID could also play a more prominent role here by including information regarding

---

[102]Referring to codes of conduct the EDP considers this an opportunity for '[. . .] *specific sectors to reflect upon common data processing activities and to agree to bespoke and practical data protection rules, which will meet the needs of the sector as well as the requirements of the GDPR.'* And that such codes could be, [..] *a practical, potentially cost effective and meaningful method to achieve greater levels of consistency of protection for data protection rights* 'EDPG Guidelines 1/2019 on Codes of Conduct and Monitoring Bodies under Regulation 2016/679 p. 4.

[103]EDPG Guidelines 1/2019 *what are the benefits of codes'* p. 7 and more specifically *36. Codes will need to specify the practical application of the GDPR and accurately reflect the nature of the processing activity or sector. They should be able to provide clear industry specific improvements in terms of compliance with data protection law. They will need to set out realistic and attainable standards for all their members, and they will need to be of a necessary quality and internal consistency to provide sufficient added value[..]* and *37. [..] aim to codify how the GDPR shall apply in a specific, practical and precise manner. The agreed standards and rules will need to be unambiguous, concrete, attainable and enforceable (testable).*

[104]See Article 40(1) of the GDPR that specifically encourages the setting up of codes of conduct [..] 'intended to contribute to the proper application of this Regulation, taking account of the specific features of the various processing sectors and the specific needs of micro, small and medium-sized enterprises.' Articles 40 and 41 and Recitals 98, 100 of the GDPR. See for more detail and guidance and more recent for drafting, amending or extending sector specific codes the EDPG Guidelines 1/2019.

[105]See also Van Ooijen and Vrabec (2019) who argue for codes of conduct to help mitigate deficiencies that remain entrenched in the GDPR.

personal data processing to allow consumers to compare insurers also on the level of privacy protection they provide.

4.2.3 Recommendations: Include Privacy Information/Icons on the IPID

To stimulate more competition amongst insurers the level of privacy protection they offer could be monitored, compared and communicated to consumers. Research shows that icons can be used to 'effectively communicate complex and lengthy privacy policies to consumer.'[106] This could be done through the IPID to help potential consumers make more informed decisions which insurers to choose based on their level of use and protection of personal data.[107] Research on privacy icons shows that it is promising in helping consumers become better informed.[108]

To conclude: as both the GDPR and the IDD are recent developments, it remains to be seen how national implementation and proposed interpretations in the sector will play out in practice.[109] Monitoring the developments following the implementation of the GDPR and the IDD, therefore, remains essential for the insurance industry to see whether a broader scope of information disclosure will improve consumer (data) protection without negatively affecting, for example, insurers' incentives for and investments in developing innovative insurance products and interoperability.[110]

---

[106]See Edwards, L. Abel, W. (2014) The Use of Privacy Icons and Standard Contract Terms for Generating Consumer Trust and Confidence in Digital Services Create Working Paper 2014/15 (October 2014); Proposing a Risk-Based approach for the selection, design and implementation of privacy icons having identified that consumers mostly lack understanding of the risks related to processing; Efroni et al. (2019), pp. 352–366.

[107]See for an example of a Dutch Telematics insurers' privacy statement on the collection of personal data: [online] https://verzekeringskaarten.nl/fairzekering/autoverzekering-beperkt-casco.

[108]Hoepman presents an analysis of initiatives and proposes what characteristics to take into consideration when deciding what elements of a privacy policy, and essential aspects on the what, where and how of the processing of personal data, must be represented by an icon See Jaap-Henk Hoepman *Using icons to summarise privacy policies: an analysis and a proposal.* September 21, 2016 [accessed online] https://blog.xot.nl/2016/09/21/using-icons-to-summarise-privacy-polices-an-analysis-and-a-proposal/.

[109]The Multistakeholder Expert Group reports that [the impact the Regulation should have on business practices still has to fully materialise and that they see a need to move from the implementation to the enforcement stage. Multistakeholder Expert Group to support the application of Regulation (EU) 2016/679. Report. 13 June 2019. Page 5.

[110]The need to monitor insurance practices especially pricing strategies is widely recognized see FCA (2018) *FCA launches general insurance market study [online]* https://www.fca.org.uk/news/press-releases/fca-launches-general-insurance-market-study See for an interesting initiative to obtain insights: The Dutch Association (of Insurers) has developed the solidarity monitor against the background of the debate over the possible undesired effects of the use of big data by insurers, to be able to analyse how the spread in premiums are developing and to what extent consumers remain insurable. Their reports can be found online https://www.verzekeraars.nl/media/4115/solidarity-

Acknowledging that the insurance industry has specific challenges when it comes to compliance with the information requirements under the GDPR this chapter aimed to provide an analysis of the requirements under the GDPR and the IDD specific for insurers. What the analysis shows there is concern about the scope of information to be made available by insurers to consumers considering the aims of both the GDPR and the IDD. A too-broad interpretation of what information and level of detail must be provided may impede the insurers' ability to innovate and remain competitive while still providing affordable insurance to as many people as possible. A too narrow interpretation would not allow consumers to become well informed and/or challenge decisions made by insurers when these may have an adverse effect. Finding this balance for information required to be made available by insurers is further challenged when regulation overlaps, contradicts or leaves room for interpretation.[111] As legal uncertainties may stifle what would otherwise be beneficial innovations based on personal data and automated decision-making there is a clear need for more research that looks at the specific challenges for the insurance industry.

Annex I

Based on the analysis Table 1 presents examples of what information needs to be made available to consumers to comply with the broad scope of information requirements under the GDPR and the IDD.

Table 1 Information requirements and examples under the IDD and the GDPR

GDPR
• Detailed and personalized information about personal data processing.[a] • What personal data being processed. *Example:* instead of stating (general) types of data, consumers should be given access to what specific personal data is being processed by the insurer in the context of their insurance.[b] Otherwise it would not be possible for consumers to become aware or correct any mistakes or object to certain data being used for purposes they do not agree with. • What purpose and the legal ground for each data is used. *Example:* consumers may want to know whether their insurer uses certain data for purposes unrelated to the risk they seek to insure including the use of personal data for unfair price

(continued)

monitor-2017.pdf; On the challenges for interoperability see for example Kerber and Schweitzer (2017).

[111] A concern raised by Insurance Europe about contradicting regulations where not much attention has been paid when developing new regulations to existing requirements resulting in a mismatch of requirements and disproportionate burdens for insurers to comply. Insurance Europe (2019) *Making EU insurance regulation that works and benefits consumers.*

Table 1 (continued)

GDPR
discrimination.[c] • Who provided the data. *Example*: when decisions are made based on data obtained from third parties such as credit or fraud scores consumers have to right to obtain (upon request) detailed information about who these third parties are and what data they have provided in order to assess whether this data is correct.[d] *Exception:* when it is not possible to identify the origin because various sources have been used, general information should be provided.[e] • What processing takes place. *Example:* whether profiling takes place information of such profiling and the consequences of such profiling[f] *Example:* when algorithms are used consumers should be provided with information how these algorithms work and their reliability in order for them to understand, challenge but also change the outcome of decision-making processes.[g] If a consumer doesn't have access to what personal information led to what decision they cannot change their behavior to reduce their risk or challenge the outcome of decision-making processes. • What the risks are and impact of providing personal data Detailed information explaining the risks and consequences of processing personal data and consequences when personal data is not or no longer provided;[h] *Example:* for consumers to make an informed decision whether to buy insurance they must also know what the risks are including what happens for example if they do not maintain what the insurer considers a good driving score. Having their insurance cancelled may lead to consumers no longer being able to obtain affordable insurance in the future.
IDD
• Detailed information about key aspects of the insurance product. The IPID only requires informing consumers about the main characteristics for them to quickly understand and compare insurance products of different insurers.[i] • Relevant information about the Insurance process Relevant information on insurers 'internal processes, functions and strategies for designing and bringing products to the market, monitoring and reviewing them over their life cycle.[j] This may include information about target market and negative target market sectors and reasoning behind choices made why these are (not) appropriate product reviews to check if the product performance may lead to consumer detriment and, in case this occurs, what actions will be taken to change its characteristics and mitigate the detriment; characteristics of the target market, and of the product distribution channels arrangements.[k] • The risk assessment process Having access to detailed information regarding the analysis of their personal data and how this influences their risk score is relevant for a consumer to be able to understand what needs and demands the insurer has taken into consideration but also to challenge the decisions made by the insurer which may have a serious effect for consumers when they are for example refused insurance because of data they do not know and have no way of challenging whether the data and processes are lawful, accurate and fair. Relevant risks and circumstances which are related to the product and give rise to the risk of consumer detriment[l] • The process and outcome of the demands and needs tests For advice-based insurance: as a minimum the analysis of the demands and needs of the consumer should be made available for consumers to understand and challenge the appropriateness of the recommendations. In general (and proposed as a best practice) insurers should always make the demands and needs test based on which the insurer identified the products (negative) target markets available for consumers for them to challenge any decisions regarding the appropriateness of products.[m]

(continued)

Table 1 (continued)

GDPR
• Information on possible conflict of interest/remuneration Consumers must be informed about any relationship between the insurer and distributor or other circumstance that could be an incentive not to be recommended those products which are not in their best interest.[n]

[a]*[. . .] the right to know [..] the purposes for which the personal data are processed, where possible the period for which the personal data are processed, the recipients of the personal data, the logic involved in any automatic personal data processing and, at least when based on profiling, the consequences of such processing* Recital 63 GDPR

[b]Article 8 and article 9(1)b: [..] *all available information on their origin, on the preservation period as well as any other information that the controller is required to provide in order to ensure the transparency of processing.;* 9(1)c *'[..] knowledge of the reasoning underlying data processing where the results of such processing are applied to him or her;"* Modernised Convention 108

[c]'The principles of fair and transparent processing require that the data subject be informed of the existence of the processing operation and its purposes.' And [..] *any further information necessary to ensure fair and transparent processing'.* Recital 60 GDPR. Countries for example are banning certain pricing practices as it raises concern about discrimination and fairness. See in this regard the FCA presenting their investigation on unfair price discrimination in general insurance. *Occasional paper 22* available online https://www.fca.org.uk/publications/research/price-discrimination-financial-services

[d]Recital 60 GDPR

[e]Recital 61 GDPR

[f]Recital 60 GDPR *'Where the personal data are collected from the data subject, the data subject should also be informed whether he or she is obliged to provide the personal data and of the consequences, where he or she does not provide such data.'*

[g]Referring to CoE law is that certain essential information has to be compulsorily provided including any additional information that is necessary to ensure fair data processing or that is useful for such purpose, such as [..] *the knowledge of the reasoning underlying the data processing.* Explanatory Report of Modernised Convention 108, para. 68 in Handbook (2019), p. 121

[h]Recital 61 GDPR. Art29 WP takes the position that insurers 'should *[..] spell out in unambiguous language what the most important consequences of the processing will be: in other words what kind of effect will the specific processing [..] actually have on a data subject? Such a description of the consequences of the processing should not simply rely on innocuous and predictable "best case" examples of data processing, but should provide an overview of the types of processing that could have the highest impact on the fundamental rights and freedoms of data subjects in relation to protection of their personal data.* 'WP29 (2016) *Guidelines on Transparency* P.8 nr 9

[i]And must reference that *complete pre-contractual and contractual information about the non-life insurance product is provided to the customer in other documents.* Article 2 IPID Regulation

[j]Art 1.12 EIOPA Guidelines EIOPA (2016) *Preparatory Guidelines on product oversight and governance arrangements by insurance undertakings and insurance distributors*

[k]Prepatory Guideline 14 Objectives of the product distribution arrangements: *The product distribution arrangements should aim to prevent and mitigate customer detriment, support a proper management of conflicts of interests and should ensure that the objectives, interests and characteristics of customers are duly taken into account.* EIOPA (2016) *Preparatory Guidelines on product oversight and governance arrangements by insurance undertakings and insurance distributors,* p. 11

[l]Prepatory Guideline 19. 1.36 EIOPA (2016) *Preparatory Guidelines on product oversight and governance arrangements by insurance undertakings and insurance distributors* p. 10

[m]EIOPA (2016) Preparatory Guidelines on product oversight and governance arrangements by Insurance undertakings and insurance distributors (POG Guidelines)

[n]'By way of remuneration, sales targets or otherwise'. Article 17 (3) IDD

References

Acquisti A, Brandimarte L, Loewenstein G (2015) Privacy and human behavior in the age of information. Science 347(6221):509–514

Article 29 Data Protection Working Party (2017) Guidelines on the Right to Data Portability, 16/EN WP 242 rev.01

Barone G, Bella M (2004) Price-elasticity based customer segmentation in the Italian auto insurance market. J Target Meas Anal Mark 13:21–31

Birrell S, Fowkes M, Jennings P (2014) Effect of using an in-vehicle smart driving aid on real-world driver performance intelligent transportation systems. IEEE Trans 15(4):1801–1810

Bordoff J, Noel PJ (2008) Pay-as-you-drive auto insurance: a simple way to reduce driving related harms and increase equity. The Brookings Institution, Washington, DC

Bucher T (2017) The algorithmic imaginary: exploring the ordinary affects of Facebook algorithms. Inf Commun Soc 20(1)

Conners J, Feldblum S (1998) Personal automobile: cost drivers, pricing, and public policy

Custers B, van Der Hof S, Schermer B, Appleby-Arnold S, Brockdorff N (2013) Informed consent in social media use-the gap between user expectations and EU personal data protection law. SCRIPTed 10:435–457

Davis J (1977) Protecting consumers from overdisclosure and gobbledygook: an empirical look at the simplification of consumer credit contracts. Virginia Law Rev 63(6):841–920

Derikx S, de Reuver M, Kroesen M, Bouwman H (2015) Buying-off privacy concerns for mobility services in the Internet-of-things era. In: Proceedings of the 28th Bled eConference, Bled, Slovenia, 7–10 June

Derikx S, de Reuver M, Kroesen M (2016) Can privacy concerns for insurance of connected cars be compensated? Electr Mark 26(1):73–81 | 26: 73

Dijksterhuis C, Lewis-Evans B, Jelijs B, Tucha O, de Waard D, Brookhuis K (2016) In-car usage-based insurance feedback strategies. A comparative driving simulator study. Ergonomics 59 (9):1158–1170

Dorweiler P (1929) Notes on Exposure and Premium Bases. CAS Proceedings1929 XVI(33):337

Edwards L, Veale M (2017) Slave to the algorithm? Why a 'right to an explanation' is probably not the remedy you are looking for. Duke Law Technol Rev 16(1):1–65

Efroni Z, Metzger J, Mischau L, Schirmbeck M (2019) Privacy icons. Eur Data Protect Law Rev 5 (3):352–366

EIOPA (2016) Preparatory Guidelines on product oversight and governance arrangements by insurance undertakings and insurance distributors

EIOPA (2018) Q and A on Regulation - Answers - Commission Implementing Regulations laying down Implementing Technical Standards, (EU) 2017–2359

European Parliament (2017) Draft Report on FinTech: the influence of technology on the future of the financial sector (2016/2243 (INI)

Fan C, Wang W (2017) A comparison of underwriting decision making between telematics enabled UBI and traditional auto insurance. Adv Manage Appl Econ 7:1–5

Financial Conduct Authority (2015) Developing our approach to implementing MiFID II conduct of business and organizational requirements, Discussion Paper DP15/3

GDV (2015) Regulation in the insurance industry: Opportunities and challenges from an economic perspective. Economic Issues and Analyses, No. 7. German Insurance Association (GDV), Berlin

Goodman B, Flaxman S (2017) European Union regulations on algorithmic decision-making and a "right to explanation". AI Magazine 38(3):50–57

Graef I, Verschakelen J, Valcke P (2013) Putting the right to data portability into a competition law perspective law: the journal of the higher school of economics. Ann Rev 2013:53–63

Handel P, Ohlsson J, Ohlsson M, Skog I, Nygren E (2014) Smartphone-based measurement systems for road vehicle traffic monitoring and usage-based insurance. IEEE Syst J 8 (4):1238–1248

Hofmann A, Neumann JK, Pooser D (2018) Plea for uniform regulation and challenges of implementing the new Insurance Distribution Directive. Geneva Pap Risk Insur Issues Pract 43(4):740–769. 30p

Husnjak S, Perakovic D, Forenbacher I, Mumdziev M (2015) Telematics system in usage based motor insurance. Proc Eng 100:816–825

Insurance Council of Australia (2015) Too Long; Didn't Read. Enhancing General Insurance Disclosure. Research findings report

Insurance Council of Australia (2017) Consumer Research on General Insurance Product Disclosures, Research findings report

Kamleitner B, Mitchell VW (2018) Can consumers experience ownership for their personal data? From issues of scope and invisibility to agents handling our digital blueprints. In: Peck J, Shu S (eds) Psychological ownership and consumer behavior. Springer, Cham, pp 91–118

Karapiperis D, Birnbaum B, Brandenburg A, Harbage R, Obersteadt A (2015) Usage-based insurance and vehicle telematics: insurance market & regulatory implications. The National Association of Insurance Commissioners and the Center for Insurance Policy and Research

Kerber W (2018) Data governance in connected cars: the problem of access to in-vehicle data. J Intellect Prop Inf Technol Electr Commer Law

Kerber W, Schweitzer H (2017) Interoperability in the Digital Economy. Journal of Intellectual Property, Information Technology and Electronic Commerce Law (Jipitec); MAGKS, Joint Discussion Paper Series in Economics, No. 12-2017

Köhne T, Brömmelmeyer C (2018) The new insurance distribution regulation in the EU—a critical assessment from a legal and economic perspective. Geneva Pap Risk Insur Issues Pract 43 (4):704–739. 36p. https://doi.org/10.1057/s41288-018-0089-0

Koops BJ, Newell BC, Timan T, Skorvanek I, Chokrevski T, Galic M (2016) A typology of privacy. Univ Pa J Int Law Rev 38:483

Lajunen T, Karola J, Summala H (1997) Speed and acceleration as measures of driving style in young male drivers. Percept Motor Skills 85:3–16

Leenes R, van Brakel R Gutwirth S, De Hert P. (2018) Data protection and privacy: the internet of bodies (computers, privacy and data protection. Hart, Oxford, pp 249–276

Maesschalck ND (2017) The Insurance Distribution Directive: what does it change for intermediaries and for others? In: Marano P, Siri M (eds) Insurance regulation in the European Union. Palgrave Macmillan, pp 63–65

Malgieri G (2016) Trade secrets v personal data: a possible solution for balancing rights. Int Data Priv Law 6(2):102–116

Marano P (2019a) Navigating InsurTech: the digital intermediaries of insurance products and customer protection in the EU. Maastricht J Eur Comp Law 26(2):294–315

Marano P (2019b) The product oversight and governance: standards and liabilities. In: Marano P, Rokas I (eds) Distribution of insurance-based investment products. Springer, Cham

McCauley D (2018) What the Internet of Things means for consumer privacy. Briefing paper, The Economist Intelligence Unit Limited 2018

Meyer D (2017) European Commission, experts uneasy over WP29 data portability interpretation. The Privacy Advisor. Retrieved from https://iapp.org/news/a/european-commission-experts-uneasy-over-wp29-data-portability-interpretation-1/

O'Neil C (2016) Weapons of math destruction: how big data increases inequality and threatens democracy. Crown, New York

Ohlsson J, Händel P, Han S, Welch R (2015) Process innovation with disruptive technology in auto insurance: lessons learned from a smartphone-based insurance telematics initiative BPM-Driving Innovation in a Digital World. Springer, pp 85–101

Paefgen J, Kehr F, Zhai Y, Michahelles F (2012) Driving behavior analysis with smartphones: Insights from a controlled field study

Pander Maat H, De Boer N, Timmermans C (2009) De gebruiksvriendelijkheid van hypotheekinformatie: Een lezersonderzoek. Universiteit Utrecht, Utrecht

Pasquale F (2015) The black box society. Harvard University Press, Cambridge

Schaeken Willemaers, Gaetane (2014) Client Protection on European Financial Markets – From Inform Your Client to Know Your Product and Beyond: An Assessment of the PRIIPs Regulation, MiFID II/MiFIR and IMD 2 Revue Trimestrielle de Droit Financier
Shavell S (1979) On moral hazard and insurance. In: Dionne G, Harrington SE (eds) Foundations of insurance economics. Huebner international series on risk, insurance and economic security, Vol 14. Springer, Dordrecht
Smith ML, Kane SA (1994) The law of large numbers and the strength of insurance. In: Insurance, risk management, and public policy. pp 1–27. https://doi.org/10.1007/978-94-011-1378-6
Solove D (2006) A taxonomy of privacy. Univ Pa Law Rev 154:477–560
Soussan G, Woolfson P, Terruso D (2016) The GDPR from an insurance and financial intermediation perspective. BIPAR and Steptoe & Johnson LLP
Swire P, Lagos Y (2013) Why the right to data portability likely reduces consumer welfare: antitrust and privacy critique. Maryl Law Rev 72(2):335, pp 347–349
Tene O, Polonetsky J (2013) Big data for all: privacy and user control in the age of analytics. Northwest J Technol Intellect Prop 11:239
Thomas GR (2012) Non-risk price discrimination in insurance: market outcomes and public policy. Geneva Pap Risk Insur Issues Pract 37(1):27–46
Troncoso C, Danezis G, Kosta E, Balasch J, Preneel B (2011) Pripayd: privacy-friendly pay-as-you-drive insurance. IEEE Trans Depend Secure Comput 8(5):742–755
Tselentis DI, Yannis G, Vlahogianni EI (2016) Innovative insurance schemes: pay as/how you drive. Transp Res Proc 14:362–371
Van Boom WH, Desmet P, Van Dam M (2016) "If It's Easy to Read, It's Easy to Claim"—the effect of the readability of insurance contracts on consumer expectations and conflict behaviour. J Consum Policy 39(2):187–197
van Ooijen I, Vrabec H (2016) Does the GDPR enhance consumers' control over personal data? An analysis from a behavioural perspective. J Consum Policy 42(1):95
Van Ooijen I, Vrabec HUJ (2019) Does the GDPR enhance consumers' control over personal data? An analysis from a behavioural perspective. J Consum Policy 42(1):91–107
Wachter S, Mittelstadt B (2018) A right to reasonable inferences: re-thinking data protection law in the age of big data and AI. Columbia Bus Law Rev
Wachter S, Mittelstadt B, Floridi L (2017) Transparent, explainable, and accountable AI for robotics. Sci Robot 2:10.1126
Wallace N, Castro D (2018) The impact of the EU's new data protection regulation on AI. Center for Data Innovation
Weiss J, Smollik J (2012) Beginner's roadmap to working with driving behavior data. Casualty Actuarial Soc E-Forum 2(1):35
Zanfir G (2012) The right to data portability in the context of the EU data protection reform. Int Data Priv Law 2(3):149

Considering the IDD Within the EU Legal Framework on ADR Systems

Flaminia Montemaggiori

1 Introduction

The favour towards alternative dispute resolution (ADR) methods arose in the United States in the mid-seventies to underline, in the face of the crisis of access to justice, the need to use tools other than judicial measures to ensure consumer protection and to decongest the judicial system.[1] Since then, these mechanisms have also spread throughout the EU, including a heterogeneous range of methods and procedures, such as mediation, various forms of arbitration, Ombudsman, etc.

Directive 2016/97/EU of 20 January 2016 on insurance distribution (IDD) also provides for the establishment of adequate out-of-court complaint and redress procedures for the settlement of disputes between customers and insurance distributors. The directive is therefore added to the other sectoral directives of the financial system aimed at ensuring the establishment of adequate ADR procedures for disputes concerning banking and financial services.

In this sense, the IDD represents the last step, in a chronological sense, of the growing attention of EU institutions towards out-of-court procedures, deemed as appropriate and effective tools to ensure better access to justice especially for consumer disputes.

Alongside the sectoral directives laying down the obligation for Member States to implement such systems, there are other European legislative measures of a cross-cutting nature, as they aim to define the basic principles of ADR procedures:

Opinions expressed are views of the author.

[1] Sander (1976), p. 111 ss. More details in paragraph 2.

F. Montemaggiori (✉)
IVASS (Italian Supervisory Authority for Insurance Sector), Insurance Ombudsman's Technical Secretariat, Rome, Italy
e-mail: flaminia.montemaggiori@ivass.it

P. Marano, K. Noussia (eds.), *Insurance Distribution Directive*, AIDA Europe Research Series on Insurance Law and Regulation 3,
https://doi.org/10.1007/978-3-030-52738-9_13

reference is made to Commission Recommendations 98/257/EC and 2001/310/EC, the 2002 Green Paper, the harmonisation of Consumer ADR systems pursued by Directive 2013/11/EU and the regulation of mediation laid down by Directive 2008/52/EC.

In addition to regulatory actions, a number of networks aimed at facilitating the resolution of transnational disputes and promoting cooperation between ADR entities have been launched at European level, such as the ECC-Net for consumers[2] and the Fin-Net concerning financial services disputes.[3]

By means of legislative measures and networks of organisations, consumers will therefore have, at least abstractly, the tools to be able to obtain effective and low-cost protection of their rights, especially in the case of small claims for which the use of a judicial solution might appear disproportionate in terms of time and costs.[4]

This protection is now guaranteed for the insurance sector by the IDD, which, as already mentioned, achieves full coverage by ADR procedures in all financial sectors where consumer rights are involved. Of course much will depend on the Member States' implementation of the directive, especially concerning the most characterising issues such as the subjective scope of application (which subjects will have to adhere to the system), the nature of the disputes that may be taken into account, dispute settlement procedures, sources of financing, etc.

Many choices will necessarily be influenced by the different national legal traditions and the specific purpose of public supervision of the financial sector, to which the insurance sector belongs. However, a positive effect for the insurance sector could still be expected: considering the high level of conflict between customers and insurance distributors and the burden of those disputes on legal litigations, the creation of an effective ADR system could lead to deflationary effects for judicial litigations and related costs, with potential downside effects on premiums charged to policyholders.[5] It would also strengthen the relationship of trust between insurance operators and customers and consumer confidence in the financial system with a view to its soundness and stability. Finally, the "educational role" of the new body's decisions should not be underestimated: on the one hand, they could have a

---

[2]The European Consumer Centres Network (ECC–Net) provides free help and assistance in dispute resolution when the consumer and trader involved are based in two different European countries (Member States, plus Iceland and Norway), https://ec.europa.eu/info/live-work-travel-eu/consumers/resolve-your-consumercomplaint/european-consumer-centres-network_en.

[3]Fin-Net is a network of national organisations responsible for out of court settling consumer complaints in the area of financial services, https://ec.europa.eu/info/business-economy-euro/banking-and-finance/consumer-finance-and-payments/retail-financial-services/financial-dispute-resolution-network-fin-net_en.

[4]The use of ADR methods is a question of justice policy that has important consequences for both the quality and efficiency of judicial outcomes. For more details: BEIS (2018), "Resolving consumer disputes: ADR and the court system"; ELI-ENCJ (European Network of Councils for the Judiciary) (2018), "The relationship between formal and informal justice: The courts and ADR"; EU Commission (2018a), "Capacity-building grants for ADR entities".

[5]In this sense the legislative decree report on the IDD implementation in Italy.

preventive and dissuasive effect on similar violations, on the other hand they could be a tool for undertakings to monitor product adequacy over time.

2 ADR Systems from the USA to the EU: Distinctive Features and Common Purpose

ADR systems refer to a heterogeneous category of "alternative" techniques and procedures to the ordinary dispute resolution system, aimed at ensuring easy access to justice and quick and effective dispute resolution.

It is an informal justice that spread quickly in the common law countries, mainly the American system and later the English one, due to the characteristics of these legal systems, including the absence of a rigid codification of principles in which to channel any disputes. In particular, the movement that was born in the United States in the 1960s and that would then spread throughout Europe is based on the idea that the solution to the justice crisis, which was too congested, was to be found in the use of other dispute resolution measures.[6]

This ideology was conventionally codified at a conference held in 1976 in Minneapolis entitled "*National conference on the causes of popular dissatisfaction with the administration of justice*". Many speeches formulated, in the face of the discouraging situation of the judicial system, a series of proposals aimed at removing some disputes from the Courts to be redirected to other decision-making bodies outside the jurisdictional system.[7] In the minds of the movement, an effective resolution of the dispute would have been achieved in terms of cost, timing and accuracy of the investigation. Access to protection would also have been guaranteed, especially for less well-off citizens who could have brought to the attention of a third party those disputes which, because of the cost of the proceedings, they would not have brought before the courts.

The transition from the cultural movement to legislative initiatives was short, with the adoption in 1980 of the Dispute Resolution Act and, in 1998, of the Alternative Dispute Resolution Act, with which ADR systems were favoured and financed by federal legislation.[8] The result has been the proliferation of "customised" dispute resolution procedures in the USA, i.e. made-to-measure with respect to the dispute to be resolved. The ideology then spread to Europe, where, however, such systems have been slow to develop due to cultural resistance linked to

[6]The movement was linked to the ideology of a group of intellectuals, including Warren Burger (Chief Justice) and Frank Sander (Professor of Harvard Law School). See in particular Sander (1976) cit. On the topic see also: Twining (1993), p. 380 e ss; Cappelletti (1993), pp. 282–296; Della Noce (2002), p. 545.

[7]In particular, Sander's intervention on the "multi-door court house", in which the consumer request would no longer be filed in the court, but in a dispute resolution center which would redirect it to the most appropriate resolution mechanism. See Kessler and Finkelstein (1988), p. 577.

[8]Crownie (2001), p. 1768.

the traditional role of the judge or due to the different experiences of other European countries on the timing of justice. Despite the diversity of forms and procedures, ADR systems appear to converge towards a fast and effective dispute resolution.

The speed is determined by the fact that these schemes use simplified procedures that can overcome the structural rigidity of the process; they are concluded in a short time and are based on affordable costs. Such systems therefore appear to be useful tools for resolving small claims against which traditional judicial instruments may not appear appropriate. The effectiveness is given by the specific competences of the decision-making bodies of ADR systems that, therefore, could be the most appropriate instrument for disputes with a high degree of technicality. Such procedures also aim to maintain or, where appropriate, restore professional and personal relations between the parties once the dispute has been resolved.

Therefore, if the objective is common, the forms in which these techniques are structured are extremely different. It is possible, however, to trace them back to two fundamental models, depending on whether they aim to define the dispute by an agreement between the parties (as mediation) or by a decision of a third party (as arbitration).

Arbitration thus constitutes the archetype of "heteronomic" ADR models, based on the knowledge and decision of the cause by a third party, having received a mandate from the parties that commit to accept that solution. The model is based on the private will that, through an agreement or an arbitration clause, establishes to refer the decision of a dispute, that has already arisen or may arise in the future, not to the judge but to qualified third impartial parties.

Mediation is a procedure in which a neutral third party, without decision-making power, assists the parties with conflicting interests in finding a mutually acceptable solution. The mediator therefore does not seek to impose his point of view but merely helps the parties to reach an agreement that aims to please all the contenders.

The alternatives relating to the conciliation method are more widespread, tending to compose the dispute through a solution agreed by the parties and not imposed by a third party foreign to the interests at stake. The culture of compromise has been more successful than the culture of decision, because it sets up a channel of communication between the parties who will maintain their relationship.

3 The Main EU Regulatory Actions Regarding ADR Systems

The interest of European institutions in ADR systems has been and is still considerable. The actions carried out over a period of 20 years are part of the European Union policies aimed at guaranteeing an area of freedom, security and justice, functional to the smooth running of the internal market and the strengthening of judicial cooperation.[9] A European judicial area where the protection of rights can take place not only in judicial procedures but also in alternative ways of resolving disputes. In the intention of the European legislator, alternative dispute resolution should create that virtuous circle that would lead undertakings to behave according to the standards required by the Union and consumers to purchase goods and services, confident of finding prompt protection of their rights.[10]

This is why ADR systems are placed in the context of policies aimed at improving access to justice:[11] it happens, in fact, that this right which is normally guaranteed to citizens by the constitutional charters, ends up constituting a mere formal right, devoid of effectiveness. It would also be more appropriate to talk about instruments that are not alternative but complementary to justice, as they may sometimes be the most appropriate means for certain types of disputes and thus extend the area of protection afforded to citizens for their rights. All in order to guarantee access to justice, enshrined as a fundamental right in Article 6 of the European Convention for the Protection of Human Rights and Fundamental Freedoms—ECHR[12] and enshrined as a general principle of the European law in Article 47 of the Charter of Fundamental Rights of the European Union—CFR.[13]

The inefficiency of the justice service could also produce serious economic consequences, as the efficiency of the processes is one of the indicators of the ease of investing in some countries of the world.[14]

ADR systems are therefore a political priority for European institutions, which must ensure their development and quality. The EU legislative bodies have therefore

[9]Article 81, par. 2, lett. g) Treaty on the Functioning of the European Union (TFEU) according to which the European Parliament and the Council adopt measures to ensure "the development of alternative methods for dispute resolution". About the EU initiatives on ADR system: Gill et al. (2017), Sirena (2018), Creutzfeldt (2013).

[10]The need to ensure adequate protection to consumers requires that rules conferring rights empowering consumers, when they engage in economic activities in the EU's Single Market, should be followed up by procedural rules and legislative and non-legislative tools that aim to make the enforcement of consumer rights in the Member States more effective (Report from the Commission on the application of Directive 2013/11/EU, Brussels, COM (2019) 425 final, p. 1).

[11]Access to justice acts as a corollary of the fundamental rights conferred by the European law: the European legislative framework cannot create rights without providing their holders with mechanisms which ensure their effective exercise.

[12]The ECHR is an international convention to protect human rights and political freedoms in Europe, entered into force on 3 September 1953 with the establishment of the European Court of Human Rights. Article 6 provides the right to have your case dealt with a fair and public hearing and within a reasonable time by an independent and impartial judge established by law". See more in "European Court of Human Rights, Guide on Article 6".

[13]The CFR enshrines political, social, and economic rights for EU citizens. It applies to the EU Institutions and its member states when implementing EU law. The right to an effective remedy and a fair trial was raised by the Court of Justice to the rank of a general principle of the European law (judgment of 15 May 1986 in Case 222/84 Johnston) and was enshrined in Article 47 of the CFR.

[14]World Bank ranking "World Bank doing business 2019". Other indicators are the ease of starting a business, getting a loan, the tax system, etc.

progressively identified the minimum quality standards with which the different systems must comply.

A first comparative study is the Commission's 1993 Green Paper, which sets out the legal and out-of-court procedures for consumer disputes for each Member State.[15] The Commission Recommendation 98/257/EC of 30 March 1998A[16] represents a milestone in the ADR theorisation process, and identifies seven principles to which the various ADR procedures must adhere: independence[17] (of the decision-making body), transparency (of the procedure), debate between the parties, legality,[18] effectiveness,[19] freedom and representation. However, its scope is limited to ADR systems that envisage settlement of the dispute through the intervention of third parties who propose or impose a solution.[20]

European institutions' interest in ADR systems has been growing in parallel with the development of cross-border trade, in particular e-commerce, strongly linked to the degree of confidence among consumers about the effectiveness of the exercise and protection of the rights acquired. The out-of-court settlement of disputes is intended as a means of making the exercise of the right to the free movement of goods and services within the European Union effective. As citizens' exchanges and mobility intensify, cross-border disputes, often characterised by conflicts of laws and jurisdictions, are increasing.

The following Recommendation 2001/310/EC of 4 April 2001[21] focuses on the principles to be followed by out-of-court procedures characterised by the intervention of a third party which facilitate the resolution of a consumer dispute by bringing the parties together and assisting them, i.e. by making informal suggestions on settlement options, in reaching a solution by common consent (recital 9). The principles are: impartiality, transparency, effectiveness and fairness.[22] Therefore,

---

[15]Green Paper "Consumer access to justice and the settlement of consumer disputes within the single market, COM/93/576FINAL.

[16]Commission Recommendation 98/257/EC of 30 March 1998 on the principles applicable to the bodies responsible for out-of-court settlement of consumer disputes [1998] OJ L 115/31.

[17]It provides that where the decision is taken by an individual, the independence shall be guaranteed if the person appointed possesses the abilities required to carry out his function and if a period of office of sufficient duration is granted; when a collegiate body, the independence must be ensured by giving equal representation to consumers and professionals.

[18]The legality requires the decision taken by the body may not result in the consumer being deprived of the protection afforded by the mandatory provisions of the law of the State in whose territory the body is established.

[19]Effectiveness of the procedure is ensured through measures guaranteeing that the consumer has direct access to the procedure, free of charges or of moderate costs, only short periods elapse between the referral of a matter and the decision.

[20]Recital: "...this recommendation ..... does not concern procedures that merely involve an attempt to bring the parties together to convince them to find a solution by common consent".

[21]Commission Recommendation 2001/310/EC of 4 April 2001 on the principles for out-of court bodies involved in the consensual resolution of consumer disputes [2001] OJ L 109/56.

[22]The fairness should be safeguarded by allowing the parties to provide any necessary and relevant information, treated as confidential unless they expressly agree otherwise. (recital 15).

the ADR solution may be less favourable than the result that could be achieved by the application of legal rules, without prejudice to the consumer's freedom, duly informed, to accept the proposal or not.

Several European acts were subsequently adopted to clarify specific aspects of ADR procedures with regard to the different methods that can be used.[23]

In 2002, the Commission renewed its interest in ADR procedures with the adoption of the Green Paper, in which the promotion of such methods is set out as a political priority for EU institutions.[24] The document focused on ADR schemes in civil and commercial matters "other than arbitration" where a neutral third party handles the dispute.[25]

The mediation model therefore begins to assume autonomy, to then be codified in the Directive 2008/52/EC on mediation in civil and commercial disputes concerning available rights.[26] This gives mediation a central role in the system of out-of court resolution instruments in order to ensure better access to justice and contribute to the smooth running of the internal market. The Directive was therefore an important milestone in the introduction and use of mediation procedures in the EU, although its implementation differed considerably between Member States, depending on the prior existence of national mediation systems and the extent of the culture of mediation. The Directive encourages the use of mediation but also ensures a balanced relationship between mediation and judicial proceedings (Art. 1). The court may invite the parties to use mediation to settle the dispute, without prejudice to national law making the use of mediation compulsory both before and after the start of judicial proceedings. Especially in cases where recourse to mediation is mandatory, the right to an effective remedy and a fair trial, as provided for in Article 47 of the Charter of Fundamental Rights, should not be precluded. Parties to a written agreement resulting from mediation, or one of them with the explicit consent of the others, could request that the content of their agreement is made enforceable; except if the content of the agreement is contrary to the law of the Member State in

[23]The "Communication from the Commission of 4 April 2001 on widening consumer access to ADR", COM (2001) 161, states that the ADR procedures can be entrusted to both public and private authorities, as ombudsman, complaints committee, etc. The "European Parliament Report on action taken on the Community policy on out-of-court settlement of consumer disputes", (A5-0134-2001), stresses that at first attempts should be made to solve the dispute directly between the consumer and the traders before resorting to extra-judicial solutions.

[24]Green Paper on alternative dispute resolution in civil and commercial law, Brussels, 19.04.2002 COM (2002) 196 final.

[25]The Commission pointed out that the development of these new forms of dispute resolution had to be considered as a consensual form of social pacification more than the recourse to a judge or an arbitrator.

[26]Directive 2008/52/EC of the European Parliament and of the Council of 21st May 2008 on certain aspects of mediation in civil and commercial matters. See Commission report on the implementation of the directive, that shows that almost all Member States have extended the scope of their measures transposing the Directive beyond cross-border to domestic cases. See De Palo et al. (2014), Menkel-Meadow (2015).

which the request is made or if that law does not provide for enforceability (recital 19).

The guarantee that consumers can refer to "quality" ADR entities for all types of contractual disputes with traders was reached by Directive 2013/11/EU on Alternative Dispute Resolution (ADR Directive).[27] This is also part of European initiatives to complete the internal market; aimed at removing direct and indirect obstacles to its functioning and strengthening citizens' confidence in the means of protecting their rights.

This directive stems from the finding that, despite the Commission's recommendations of 1998 and 2001, ADR had not yet sufficiently and consistently developed in the EU. Disparities in coverage (existence of different ADR systems), in quality and knowledge of ADRs among Member States therefore represented a barrier to the internal market and were identified as one of the reasons why many consumers avoided cross-border purchases due to fearing that any disputes with undertakings could not be resolved easily, quickly and affordably.[28] The absence of high-quality ADR procedures in a Member State also placed undertakings at a competitive disadvantage compared with those in other Member States, which could resolve disputes with consumers in a quicker and cheaper way. It was therefore considered necessary to achieve an harmonisation, even if minimal, of Consumer ADR systems by imposing requirements and quality standards of the procedures and bodies in charge of their management regardless of the residence of consumers within the EU.

The Directive provides for a minimum harmonisation approach, leaving wide discretion to Member States in providing for additional measures to ensure a higher level of consumer protection.

The Directive is also linked to Regulation (EU) No. 524/2013 on online disputes, entered into force on 9 January 2016 with the aim of establishing a Europe-wide online platform offering consumers and traders a single out-of-court entry point for the settlement of online disputes, through ADR entities linked to that platform.[29] They are therefore two interlinked and complementary legislative instruments in the sense that only entities meeting the requirements of the Directive can be considered as ADR entities and, as such, can be registered and thus operate on the ODR platform.[30]

---

[27]Directive 2013/11/EU of the European Parliament and of the Council of 21 May 2013 on alternative dispute resolution for consumer disputes. See Biard (2019), pp. 109–147; Biard (2018), pp. 171–196; Cortes (2018), pp. 82–88; Loos (2016).

[28]See "Study on the use of ADR in the EU of 16 October 2009", (pp. 56–63; 112.115; 120–121). As announced in the Commission's Communication 'A New Deal for Consumers' of 11 April 2018 (COM[2018] 183 final), strengthening this consumer ADR/ODR framework is a priority in the Commission's endeavour to complement the EU enforcement toolbox, make the existing enforcement tools fully effective and make EU consumer law deliver its full potential.

[29]Regulation (EU) n. 524/2013 of the European Parliament of the Council of 21 May 2013 on online dispute resolution for consumer disputes (Regulation on consumer ODR).

[30]The 'ODR platform' was launched on 15 February 2016 (http://ec.europa.eu/odr). The first report was published by the Commission on 13 December 2017 (COM 2017,744 final). About 24,000

The Directive applies to national and cross-border ADR procedures. The outcome of the dispute shall be entrusted to an ADR entity, permanently established, which will propose or impose a solution or bring the parties together in order to facilitate an amicable solution.[31]

Given the cross-cutting scope of the ADR Directive, the question of the relationship with Directive on mediation arises.

Directive 2013/11 provides that the ADR Directive applies horizontally to all types of ADR procedures, including those covered by mediation Directive and that its provisions prevail in the event of a conflict over any other existing Union legal acts already containing provisions concerning out-of-court dispute resolution, however without prejudice to the mediation Directive (recital 19 and article 3, paragraph 2).

In addition to the above described regulatory actions, the Commission has also planned the creation of two European networks to facilitate consumer access to ADR procedures for cross-border disputes. Although they have the same purpose, their functioning differs greatly: the ECC-Net is a consumer information and assistance structure with contact points ("clearing houses") in each Member State,[32] while the network for out-of-court settlement of cross-border financial services disputes (Fin-Net Financial Services Complaints Network) links national competent bodies which are required to comply with the requirements of the Recommendation 98/257/EC.[33]

---

complaints were lodged, mainly in the clothing sector, air tickets and technological products. On the topic: EU Commission (2018b). "Grants for ADR entities, online traders and online marketplaces to upgrade the applicants' software to work with the ODR platform"; Cortes and Lodder (2014).

[31]The Directive only concerns disputes between consumers and traders, while the ODR Regulation also applies to disputes triggered by traders towards consumers, if the Member State allows the resolution of such disputes through an ADR entity. The Directive applies to disputes concerning contractual obligations arising from sales or service contracts both online and offline, whereas the regulation refers only to online contracts.

[32]The aim of ECC-Net is to provide consumers entering into cross-border disputes with information about their rights and obligations. A consumer will submit the claim to its national contact point; it will liaise with the contact point partner in the other MS to reach an amicable solution.

[33]On this subject: Commission "Fin-Net activity report 2016". Since 2001, the European Commission has promoted the creation of the Fin-Net among ADR entities active in the banking, financial and insurance sectors. 60 ADR entities are currently members of Fin.Net (EU, Iceland, Liechtenstein and Norway). The arrangements for the participants collaboration are covered by a Memorandum of Understanding, in force since 16 May 2016, that provides for network members, temporary members (for which recognition is pending), affiliated (ADR entities operating in countries where the Directive in not applicable, e.g. in Switzerland).

4 The Role of the IDD Directive Within the EU Legal Framework on ADR Procedures

The IDD is the last step, in a chronological sense, of the European ADR legislative process described above[34]: it therefore provides for the establishment of adequate out-of-court complaint and redress procedures for the settlement of disputes between customers and insurance distributors. It is one of those sector-specific provisions, with particular reference to the banking and financial sector, which require Member States to set up ADR systems and require intermediaries to provide information on their existence and on the activation of the procedure in order to protect the weakest part of the negotiating relationship.[35]

With the IDD and its delegated regulations, the European legislator finalised the second most important act aimed at modernising insurance supervision since the introduction, only a few years ago, of the new prudential supervision known as "Solvency II regime".[36]

The strengthening of undertakings' capital adequacy is now followed by a redesign of the means for distributing insurance products. Both interventions have a unique and shareable intent: the construction of a market of more solid and robust undertakings, a more efficient distribution chain, better informed and protected consumers.

The IDD aims to strengthen and consolidate the existing rules of the Insurance Mediation Directive (IMD, Directive 2002/92). Where the IMD applied to the

---

[34]Directive 2016/97 of the European Parliament and of the Council of 20 January 2016 on insurance distribution. The IDD aims to strengthen and consolidate the existing rules of the Insurance Mediation Directive (IMD) introduced in early 2005 and designed to encourage competition between insurance firms, as well as ensure appropriate levels of protection for customers, across the EU. See Castle (2019), pp. 97–125; Hofmann et al. (2018), pp. 740–769; Pscheidl (2018), pp. 205–217; Maesschalck (2017), pp. 59–77; Christofilou (2016), pp. 267–298; Malinowska (2016), pp. 89–100; Bernardino (2015), p. 7.

[35]The obligation for MS to set up ADR systems in the field of banking and financial services derives from several provisions with an increasing degree of prescriptiveness: e.g. Directives 2002/65/EC (concerning the distance marketing of consumer financial services) and 2007/64/EC (on payment services, repealed by directive 2015/2366/EU), stated that Ms "shall promote the setting up or development of adequate and effective out-of-court complaints and redress procedures", while directive 2008/48/EC (on consumer credit agreements) provided for a formal obligation ("member States shall ensure that adequate and effective out-of-court complaint and redress procedures [. . .] are put in place"). Similar obligation can be found in Directive 2014/65/EU (on markets in financial instruments, article 75).

[36]The solvency II framework includes the Directive 2009/138/EC, the Delegated Regulation 2015/35/EU directly applicable in the MS, the (EIOPA) European Insurance Supervisory Authority's Guidelines, not binding third-level measures. Solvency II sets out a EU-wide set of capital and risk management requirements that match with the objective of consumer protection. The solvency assessment of an undertaking is based on the combination of three-pillar requirements, similar to Basel II for the banking sector: quantitative (capital requirements), qualitative (focused on the system of governance) and transparency. On the topic, see; Marano and Siri (2018), pp. 594–614; Marano and Siri (2017), cit; Swain and Swallow (2015), p. 145.

regulation of insurance intermediaries, the IDD applies to the wider regulation of insurance 'distributors'. This means that it applies to all sellers of insurance products, including insurance undertakings that sell directly to customers; any person whose activities consist of assisting in the administration and performance of insurance contracts, including those acting on behalf of insurers—e.g., claims management activities; ancillary insurance intermediaries; websites or other media used to provide information about insurance contracts with comparison services, where the customer is able to directly or indirectly conclude an insurance contract. The directive is finalised to regulate the way insurance products are designed and sold both by insurance intermediaries and directly by insurance undertakings and ensure that consumers have the same level of protection regardless of the distribution channel.

For this purpose, IDD lays down the information that should be given to consumers before they sign an insurance contract; it imposes conduct of business and transparency rules on distributors, through provisions referring to the product design process on the basis of the target market (Product Oversight Governance) and the customer profiling (demand and need test).

With regard to ADR systems, Article 15 of IDD strengthens in the provisions of Article 11 of the IMD, by requiring Member States to establish (and not only to promote) adequate and effective out-of-court complaint and redress procedures for the resolution of disputes between insurance distributors and customers relating to the rights and obligations arising from the Directive. The provision is aimed to make the rules on transparency, conduct of business and consumer protection more effective and to avoid them becoming mere declarations of principle.[37]

5 Issues About Implementing the ADR System in the Insurance Sector

Many issues could arise from the implementation of Article 15 of the Directive in Member States. The generic formulation of the provision allows possible different configurations of the new system of out-of-court dispute settlement in the insurance sector, also having regard to the minimum harmonisation of the Directive 2013/11/EU.

[37]In the sense of a strengthening of the consumer protection, referring to the impact of the EU regulation on financial products, mainly the rules laid down by MiFID II, to the insurance sector and more specifically with regard to life insurance, see Marano (2017).

5.1 The System's Setting

First, the ADR system's setting up. In the extreme variety of the category and in the fundamental distinction between procedures based on an agreement of the parties and those centred on the decision of a third party, the reality of Ombudsmen could be particularly important.[38] These bodies act in financial sectors (especially in the banking field), with a different degree of institutionalisation and coordination with the institutional objectives of the sectoral supervisory authorities. In the financial sector, the complementarity of ADR systems with supervisory authorities' objectives is marked, especially with regard to the links between disputes over the intermediary's misconduct and the supervision of conduct of business. The design of the ADR entity stemming from the IDD will be affected by its possible specific competence in the insurance sector or by the use of another out-of-court system already active in the banking and financial sector.[39] It will be important for this entity if its staff is established within the sectoral supervisory authority: there could be problems in the coordination between the activity of the ADR body and the Authority; on the other hand, however, the Authority could be able to use the information deriving from the ADR activity for the purpose of supervising intermediaries.[40]

If there will be an out-of-court system centred on the decision of a third party, the choice could be made between a single or collegial body, with the need to guarantee the requirement of independence in both cases. This topic should be addressed on the basis of the ADR Directive, which provides that, when the decision is taken

---

[38]See Creutzfeldt (2016), Hodges (2014), pp. 593–608; Lener (2018). See also Schwarcz (2009), p. 735, that suggests that the British FOS (Financial Ombudsman Service) may offer a model for improving consumer dispute resolution in realms beyond insurance.

[39]At the beginning of 2017, a survey on the main characteristics of the members of Fin-Net was carried out upon the Italian Banking Supervisory Authority (Bank of Italy)'s initiative (see Italian Banking Ombudsman, Annual Report 2017, p. 44). The survey, which involved 48 ADR schemes from 27 member states, shows that Fin-Net members vary in the scope of their jurisdiction and in their procedures. For about half of the ADR schemes, their jurisdiction extends exclusively to disputes concerning only one financial sector (banking, investment or insurance services). Just over a third have jurisdiction over more than one sector. Only a few schemes also accept non-financial disputes. See also Cymand (2017), which shows that the currently existing ADR schemes in the area of financial services either cover financial services in particular sectors (i.e., Banking Ombudsman in Italy, Insurance Ombudsman in Germany, Ombudsman of the Authority of Financial Markets in France), all financial services sectors (Financial Ombudsman Service in United Kingdom, the Consumer Complaints Manager of the Malta Financial Services Authority, Financial Services Complaints Institute in Dutch) or handle consumer complaints in general (National Board for Consumer Complaints in Sweden, State Consumer Protection Authority in Lithuania).

[40]The survey previously described shows that in many cases the supervisory authorities for the purpose of supervising intermediaries use information obtained through the ADR scheme's activity. In some cases, the ADR entity report to the competent authority any conduct of intermediaries in breach of sectoral legislation. Sometimes, the ADR scheme is established within the supervisory authority. In other countries the data transmitted by ADRs are only statistical, as they don't include information concerning individual cases.

individually, such subject must have the necessary competences and be appointed for a period of office of sufficient duration to ensure the independence of his actions, while if collegial, equal representation of consumers and market traders is to be respected. The latter consideration could involve important appraisals considering that in the insurance field there is a complex distribution system that sees both undertakings and intermediaries involved in the relationship with the customer. The involvement of both parties in distribution disputes is frequent. It could be relevant for the composition of the collegial body and for the number of members to be designated as representatives of undertakings and intermediaries.

5.2 *The Adherent Subjects*

From the point of view of market operators joining the system, they could be subject by law to the jurisdiction of the new IDD ADR or could join it on a voluntary basis and subject to certain conditions.[41] In particular, the question of the adhesion of EU companies operating in another Member State could arise. The item is linked to the transnational nature of insurance disputes because of the large number of EU companies operating in different countries both under the freedom of establishment and under the freedom to provide services. For this reason, cross-border disputes in the insurance sector, in the sense of a dispute between a policyholder of a Member State and an insurance undertaking with head office in another Member State, might be very common. In this regard, article 15 of the IDD recommends that Member States shall ensure that European ADR bodies cooperate in the resolution of cross-border disputes. In the same direction, Directive 2013/11/EU provides that the handling of cross-border disputes shall be carried out through forms of cooperation between ADR entities and the strengthening of relevant European networks, including Fin-Net in which the new IDD ADR should also take part. The purpose of this network is therefore to provide consumers with easy access to ADR in cases regarding cross-border financial services: in other words, it enables consumers wishing to act against an intermediary in another Member State to ask to the ADR operating in their own State, that, through the network, will put the consumer in contact with the equivalent ADR system of the country in which the intermediary operates. A different line of thought could instead be based considering the supervision carried out by the host member state on transparency and fairness of behaviour and on compliance with the rules of general interest. That kind of supervision could request EU companies to adhere to the host ADR system. In the same direction, if the insurance contracts of these companies operating in another country provide that the law and jurisdiction of the State in which they operate shall apply,

[41] In the aforementioned survey of the Fin-Net ADR systems, almost two thirds of cases the intermediaries' participation in the system is mandatory; in certain cases adhesion may be mandatory or voluntary depending on the issue involved.

the contract could be considered binding also for the adhesion to the ADR system of the host country.

5.3 The Customers

The meaning of "customer" should also be considered, since no definition can be found both in the IDD and in the ADR Directive. Although referring to the customer, the ADR Directive only defines the consumer as a natural person who acts for purposes different from entrepreneurial, commercial, or professional activity. It will therefore be necessary to consider whether the definition of customer will cover only the insured persons and the policyholder, as the persons who have or have had a contractual relationship[42] with an undertaking or an intermediary with regard to insurance services, or will have to include other subjects, such as persons who are entitled to receive insurance benefits or to claim compensation for the damage suffered (injured persons). The meaning of customer will depend on which disputes are handled with the IDD ADR system.

5.4 The Nature of Disputes

With regard to the nature of disputes, article 15 of the IDD refers to disputes between customers and insurance distributors concerning the rights and obligations arising under this Directive. The dispute could concern an action or omission relating to the activities of the insurance sector subject to regulation and supervision. The scope will depend on the national implementation of the provision: it could be limited to disputes arising from the violation of the rules of conduct inherent to insurance distribution (i.e. infringement of disclosure rules, a choice perhaps consistent with the wording of the Directive), or it could be extended to the determination of the rights and obligations deriving from an insurance contract (i.e. coverages, exclusions), to be evaluated whether to include the right to compensation for damage suffered.[43] If the request were to concern the payment of a sum of money, it might be useful to provide for a limitation on the amounts. With regard to claiming damages, if they were included, it should be interesting to understand how the IDD ADR body could handle the evidence requirements: whether it could ask for external technical advice to ascertain the event or to quantify the damage suffered or could conduct

[42]It will be useful to understand whether the complainant is a customer or a potential customer and if the system covers both the contractual and the pre-contractual phases, with the protection of legitimate expectations.

[43]It will be interesting to evaluate if only financial loss or also pain and suffering, damage to reputation, distress or inconvenience.

independent audits. It is a fact that the parties of the dispute should have to prove the circumstances that they use as the grounds for their request or explanations. If additional evidence or explanations are required, the ADR might request the parties to provide them. The decisions should be based upon the documents provided by the parties (complainant and intermediary) during the investigation.[44]

A time limit could also be envisaged, limiting the competence of the new ADR system to disputes arising within a limited time frame. This is in order to ensure the functionality of the new system, which would be undermined if decisions were to be taken on situations that are too far in the past. This would also help to speed up and streamline the ADR procedure, since it is more likely that questions would be resolved quickly if they refer to recent issues, for which documentation can be easily retrieved.

5.5 *The Procedure*

Concerning the procedure, the dispute should be free of charge to the claimant,[45] while the financing of the system should be charged to the intermediaries subject to the IDD ADR jurisdiction. They should be required to contribute to it, with a fixed or variable fee related, for example, to the size of the intermediary or the number of claims filed against them.

Normally before submitting a dispute to the IDD ADR body, the customer should lodge a dispute with the insurance undertaking or intermediary, to solve the dispute directly, preserving the relationship of trust with the insurance operator. The ADR procedure should not be started too long after the complaint has been lodged.[46]

Finally, the ADR procedure could end in different ways, depending on the nature of the system adopted: if no agreement between the parties could be reached, the parties could be referred to the ordinary legal process, while in the event of a system

---

[44]In line with the speed of the procedure and the summary knowledge of out-of-court system. In this regard, recital 25 (directive 2013/11) provides that "In order to ensure that ADR entities can operate effectively, those entities should have the possibility of maintaining or introducing . . . procedural rules that allow them to refuse to deal with disputes in specific circumstances, for example where a dispute is too complex and would therefore be better resolved in court."

[45]Under ADR directive, services must be provided at low or no costs to consumers. However, a nominal fee for consumers might encourage responsible use and adequate engagement with the dispute resolution process.

[46]In line with Directive 2013/11/UE, recital 50: In order to avoid an unnecessary burden being placed on ADR entities, Member States should encourage consumers to contact the trader in an effort to solve the problem bilaterally before submitting a complaint to an ADR entity. See also article 5, par. 4 lett. e): Member States may, at their discretion, permit ADR entities to maintain and introduce procedural rules that allow them to refuse to deal with a given dispute on the grounds that the consumer has not submitted the complaint to the ADR entity within a pre-specified time limit, which shall not be set at less than one year from the date upon which the consumer submitted the complaint to the trader.

with a third party with decision-making powers, the question of the effectiveness of ADR decisions would arise.[47] The decisions regarding the substance of the dispute could be a recommendation, not binding, not being appealed. In the case of a decision that totally or partly satisfies the consumer's request, it could establish the term within the insurance undertaking or intermediary is advised to take all actions pointed out. However, if the intermediary does not comply with a decision, its non-compliance would be made public.[48] Such negative publicity could deter new customers from contacting the negligent undertaking or intermediary, indirectly inducing the latter to respect the ADR recommendations.[49]

6 Closing Remarks

The impetus provided by the European Union regarding ADR was decisive for the definition of the general principles in ADR systems. The different procedures that have been and will be implemented by Member States often reflect national legal traditions and the specific purpose of public supervision of the financial sector. However, ADR systems are growing strongly, both as a response to mistrust in the justice system and because they seem to be the most appropriate way to settle consumer disputes.[50]

---

[47]The ADR Directive acknowledges the competence of Member States to determine whether ADR entities established on their territories are to have the power to impose a solution (recital 4). See also Creutzfeldt and Bradford (2016): "in term of decision acceptance (..) people care, on average, more about the way a decision was reached than about its substantive content, and, moreover, that they are more likely to accept even unfavourable decisions if they feel they were reached in a procedurally fair way". The decision acceptance is strongly linked with the perception of fairness and impartiality of the procedure.

[48]See Green Paper on ADR in civil and commercial law, cit, 31: In the field of consumer protection law, the third party can be called upon to adopt a formal position on the solution to the dispute in the form of a decision which can be binding on a party. This is the case for clients' ombudsmen who were appointed by certain professional sectors such as banks and insurance companies and whose decisions are binding on the companies who are affiliated to the scheme. In this case, the effectiveness of the decision taken can essentially be measured in terms of marketing. If these professionals do not in fact comply with these decisions, they run the risk that this decision will be published, or if they are affiliated to a commercial system which, for example, awards quality labels, they may be excluded from this system.

[49]In the above-mentioned survey of Fin-Net ADR, it appears that in most of the schemes, the procedure ends with a recommendation or a non-binding decision, and the parties are free to bring the dispute before the courts. In some cases a financial intermediary's non-compliance with a decision is made public. However, one-third of the schemes have the authority to issue binding decisions which, in the event of non-compliance, may be enforced by the judicial authorities (e.g. if the decision is accepted by the client and if the value of the dispute does not exceed fixed thresholds).

[50]On 11 and 12 June 2018, the European Commission hosted the ADR Assembly 2018 which brought together representatives of notified European ADR entities (according to the Directive 2013/11/EU), ADR competent authorities, ODR contact points, European Consumer Centres,

Through sectoral and cross-cutting legislative measures and networks, consumers will thus have appropriate tools to obtain effective and low-cost protection of their rights, particularly in the case of small claims, where the use of a judicial solution would be disproportionate. Considering the burden of insurance disputes on legal litigations, the establishment of an effective ADR system, faster and cheaper than ordinary judicial routes, should have important deflationary effects of judicial litigation and related costs, with potential positive and downside effects on the premiums charged to policyholders.

The financial education that could be carried out by IDD ADR towards the customer-consumer will be important, in order to spread the culture of awareness and the supervision and monitoring of the proper behaviour of undertakings and insurance intermediaries. This objective, together with the functioning of the new out-of-court resolution system, should strengthen the relationship of trust between insurance operators and customers and the reputation of the insurance sector, as well as reinforce consumer confidence in the financial system with a view to its soundness and stability.

The new IDD ADR system's decisions could have a dissuasive effect on similar breaches, and could lead insurance operators to modify certain practices found to be incorrect as sanctioned by the ADR system. In this sense, the educational function of such decisions could be fulfilled.[51] The appeals submitted to the new system could also be used by insurance companies to monitor the adequacy of products to the target market's needs over time: the recurrence of similar requests could in fact reveal an inadequate profiling of the product for the target customers.

Time and the practical application of the new rules will show whether and how effective the new measures aimed to implement an ADR system in the insurance sector will be. Much will depend on the scope of the nature of the disputes that may be analysed by the IDD ADR system. The extent of the knowledge of the new ADR system among consumers will be equally important for the effectiveness of the new tool.[52] However, the relative flexibility of the EU Member States in adopting more

consumer organisations, business associations and other stakeholders. Diversity in the ADR sector was seen by delegates to be positive both at individual level (diverse models may allow service users choose from a range of dispute resolution options) and at systemic level (competition in the sector can contribute to higher standards overall).

[51]In accordance with the accountability measures laid down in directive 2013/11/EU, article 7, par. 2, lett. b 2.: member States shall ensure that ADR entities make publicly available on their websites their annual activity reports, which shall include any systematic or significant problems that occur frequently and lead to disputes between consumers and traders; such information may be accompanied by recommendations as to how such problems can be avoided or resolved in future, in order to raise traders' standards and to facilitate the exchange of information and best practices.

[52]In line with the results of the 2018 ADR assembly previously mentioned, the need for a deep awareness and understanding appears as a fundamental also for the IDD ADR system, by publishing decisions, using social and traditional media and communication as a vital part of quality case-handling, educating and empowering consumers and ensuring transparency in the dispute resolution process. In fact, overlapping, geographical and sectoral competencies of ADR bodies may be confusing for service users and allow "forum shopping" by consumers. Differences in approach

stringent rules—in respect of IDD previsions—may lead to a lack of uniformity and consistency.[53] The jungle of competing systems with skills interlinked with other neighbouring sectors (financial, banking and insurance) may not help. For the time being, we can only hope that such an opportunity will not be lost and that the new out-of-court insurance dispute resolution instrument will effectively strengthen customer protection and the efficiency of the financial system.

References

ADR Assembly. https://www.europeanresolution.com/adr-assembly-2018-brussels-11-12-june/

BEIS (2018) Resolving consumer disputes: ADR and the court system. https://assets.publishing.service.gov.uk/government/uploads/system/uploads/attachment_data/file/698442/Final_report_Resolving_consumer_disputes.pdf

Bernardino G (2015) Insurance distribution in a challenging environment. Speech at the European Federation of Insurance Intermediaries (BIPAR), Brussels, p 7. https://eiopa.europa.eu/

Biard A (2018) Monitoring consumer ADR in the EU: a critical perspective. Eur J Priv Law 2:171–196. academia.edu.documents/56294395

Biard A (2019) Impact of Directive 2013/11/EU on Consumer ADR quality: evidence from France and the UK. J Consum Policy 42:109–147. https://link.springer.com/article/10.1007/s10603-018-9394-z

Cappelletti M (1993) ADR processes within the framework of the world-wide access-to justice movement. Mod Law Rev 56:282–296. https://onlinelibrary.wiley.com/doi/pdf/10.1111/j.1468-2230.1993.tb02673.x

Castle H (2019) ADR and insurance-based investment products. In: Marano R (ed) Distribution of IBIPS. Springer, Cham, pp 97–125

Christofilou A (2016) ODR and insurance. In: Marano P, Rokas I, Kochenburger P (eds) The "Dematerialized" insurance. Springer, Cham, pp 267–298

Cortes P (2018) Consumer ADR in Spain and the UK. EuCML 2:82–88. http://academia.edu.documents/59203344

Cortes P, Lodder A (2014) Consumer dispute resolution goes online: reflection on the evolution of European law for out-of-court redress. Maastricht J Eur Comp law 15(1), SSRN-id2414098

Creutzfeldt N (2013) The origins and evolution of consumer dispute resolution systems in Europe. In: Hodges C, Stadler A (eds) Resolving mass disputes. https://ssrn.com/abstract=2441069

Creutzfeldt N (2016) What do we expect from an Ombudsman? Narratives of everyday engagement with the informal justice system in Germany and the United Kingdom. Int J Law Context 12 (4):437–452. https://doi.org/10.1017/S1744552316000203

Creutzfeldt N, Bradford B (2016) Dispute Resolution Outside of Courts: Procedural Justice and Decision Acceptance Among Users of Ombuds Services in the UK. https://onlinelibrary.wiley.com/doi/pdf/10.1111/lasr.12234

Crownie CH (2001) The ADR Act of 1998: implementing a new paradigm of justice. N Y Law Rev 76:1768. https://www.nyulawreview.org/wp-content/uploads/2018 /08/NYULawReview-76-6-Crowne.pdf

between dispute resolution bodies might be a factor that contributes to poor public understanding of ADR.

[53]For further discussion in this direction, on the basis of a comparison with the Model Acts promulgated by the National Association of Insurance Commissioners (NAIC) in the United States, see Martinez and Marano (2020).

Cymand D (2017) ADR Mechanism in the area of financial services in EU. Financ Law Rev 2. https://czasopisma.bg.ug.edu.pl/index.php/flr/article/view/2109
De Palo G, D'Urso L, Trevor M, Branon B, Canessa R, Cawyer B, Reagan L (2014) 'Rebooting' the Mediation Directive: Assessing the limited impact of its implementation and proposing measures to increase the number of mediations in the EU. http://www.europarl.europa.eu/ReData/etudes/etudes/join/2014/493042/IPOL-JURI_ET%2820 14%29493042_EN.pdf
Della Noce DJ (2002) Mediation theory and policy: the legacy of the pound conference. Ohio State J Disp Resolut 17. https://kb.osu.edu/bitstream/handle/1811/87146/OSJDR_V17N3_545.pdf
ELI-ENCJ (European Network of Councils for the Judiciary) (2018) The relationship between formal and informal justice: The courts and ADR. www.europeanlawinstitute.eu/fileadmin/user_upload/p_eli/Publications/ADR_Statement.pdf
EU Commission (2018a) Capacity-building grants for ADR entities. http://ec.europa.eu/research/participants/portal/desktop/en/opportunities/cp/topics/cons-adr-2018.html
EU Commission (2018b) Grants for ADR entities, online traders and online marketplaces to upgrade the applicants' software to work with the ODR platform. https://ec.europa.eu/inea/en/connecting-europe-facility/cef-telecom/apply-funding/2018-cef-te lecom-call-odr
European Court of Human Rights, Guide on Article 6. https://www.echr.coe.int/Documents/Guide_Art_6_criminal_ENG.pdf
Gill C, Creutzfeldt N, Williams J, O'Neill S, Nial V (2017) Confusion, gaps and overlaps: a consumer perspective on ADR between consumer and businesses. www.citizensadvice.org.uk/Global/CitizensAdvice/Consumer%20publications/Gaps%20overlaps%20consumer%20confusion%20201704.pdf
Hodges C (2014) Consumer ombudsmen: better regulation and dispute resolution. ERA Forum, 15
Hofmann A, Neumann JK, Pooser D (2018) Plea for uniform regulation and challenges of implementing the new IDD. Geneva Pap Risk Insur 43:740–769
Italian Banking Ombudsman, Annual Report 2017. https://www.arbitrobancariofinanziario.it/abf/relazioneannuale/index.html?com.dotmarketing.htmlpage.language=3
Kessler G, Finkelstein LJ (1988) The evolution of a multi-door courthouse. Cath U Law Rev 37:577. http://scholarship.law.edu/lawreview/vol37/iss3/2
Lener R (2018) The Securities and Financial Ombudsman. A brief comparison with the Banking and Financial Ombudsman. https://fchub.it/wp-content/uploads/2018/05/Lener-1.pdf
Loos M (2016) Consumer ADR after Implementation of the ADR Directive: Enforcing European Consumer Rights at the Detriment of European Consumer Law. https://papers.ssrn.com/sol3/paperscfm?abstract_id=2685651
Maesschalck N (2017) The IDD: what does it change for Intermediaries and others. In: Marano P, Siri M (eds) Insurance regulation in the EU: solvency II and beyond. Palgrave Macmillan, pp 59–77. https://academia.edu.documents/58268329
Malinowska K (2016) Insurance transparency and protection regime under the IDD. Insur Rev 4:89–100. https://piu.org.pl/wp-content/uploads/2017/05/WU-2016-04-06-Malinowska-en.pdf
Marano P (2017) The 'Mifidization': the sunset of life insurance in the EU regulation on insurance? Liber Amicorum for Professor Ioannis Rokas, NOMIKH BIBΛIOΘHKH, Athens, pp. 219–234
Marano P, Siri M (2017) Insurance regulation in the European Union: Solvency II and Beyond. Palgrave Macmillan. https://academia.edu.documents/58268329
Marano P, Siri M (2018) Cross-border insurance groups: towards a comprehensive supervision under Solvency II. Geneva Pap Risk Insur: Issues Pract 44:178
Martinez L, Marano P (2020) The new EU rules on insurance customer/policyholder protection viewed against the NAIC model acts. Global Jurist. https://doi.org/10.1515/gj-2019-0039
Menkel-Meadow CJ (2015) Mediation, Arbitration, and ADR. UC Irvine School of Law Research Paper No. 2015-59. https://ssrn.com/abstract=2608140
Pscheidl D (2018) Implementing IDD across the EU—first findings and the way forward. ERA Forum 19:205–217
Report from the Commission on the application of Directive 2013/11/EU, Brussels, COM(2019) 425 final, p. 1

Report from the Commission on the implementation of the directive 2008/52/EC. http://www.europarl.europa.eu/doceo/document/A-8-2017-0238_IT.html
Sander F (1976) Address before the national conference on the causes of popular dissatisfaction with the Administration of justice: varieties of dispute processing. Fed Rules Decis 70
Schwarcz D (2009) Redesigning consumer dispute resolution: a case study of the British and American approaches to insurance claims conflict. Tul Law Rev 83:735. http://scholarship.law.umn.edu/faculty_articles/571
Sirena P (2018) ADR Systems in the Banking and Financial Markets. Osservatorio del diritto civile e commerciale, n. 2. https://www.rivisteweb.it/doi/10.4478/91897
Study on the use of ADR in the EU of 16 October 2009, pp 56–63; 112.115; 120–121. http://ec.europa.eu/consumers/redrescons/adrstudy.pdf
Swain R, Swallow D (2015) The prudential regulation of insurers under Solvency II, Bank of England. Q Bull Q2:145. http://www.bankofengland.co.uk/
Twining W (1993) Alternative to what? Theories of litigation, procedure and dispute settlement. In: Anglo-American Jurisprudence: some neglected classics. Mod Law Rev 56:380 e ss. https://onlinelibrary.wiley.com/doi/pdf/10.1111/j.1468-2230.1993.tb02679.x
World Bank doing business 2019. https://www.doingbusiness.org/

Legislation

Green Paper Consumer access to justice and the settlement of consumer disputes within the single market, COM/93/576FINAL
Commission Recommendation 98/257/EC of 30 March 1998 on the principles applicable to the bodies responsible for out-of-court settlement of consumer disputes [1998] OJ L 115/31
Commission Recommendation 2001/310/EC of 4 April 2001 on the principles for out-of court bodies involved in the consensual resolution of consumer disputes [2001] OJ L 109/56
Communication from the Commission of 4 April 2001 on widening consumer access to ADR, COM (2001) 161
Green Paper on alternative dispute resolution in civil and commercial law, Brussels, 19.04.2002 COM (2002) 196 final
Directive 2008/52/EC of the European Parliament and of the Council of 21st May 2008 on certain aspects of mediation in civil and commercial matters
Directive 2009/138/EC of the European Parliament and of the Council of 25 November 2009 on the taking-up and pursuit of the business of Insurance and Reinsurance (Solvency II) (Official Journal of the European Union L 335/1)
Directive 2013/11/EU of the European Parliament and of the Council of 21 May 2013 on alternative dispute resolution for consumer disputes
Regulation (EU) n. 524/2013 of the European Parliament of the Council of 21 May 2013 on online dispute resolution for consumer disputes (Regulation on consumer ODR)
Directive 2016/97 of the European Parliament and of the Council of 20 January 2016 on insurance distribution (Official Journal of the European Union L 26/19)
Legislative decree report on the IDD implementation in Italy, 2018., http://documenti.camera.it/apps/nuovosito/attigoverno/Schedalavori/getTesto.ashx?file=0516_F001.pdf&leg=XVII#pagemode=none

IDD and Distribution Risk Management

Jorge Miguel Bravo

1 Introduction

Insurance companies use a wide range of distribution methods to target their customers (captive career agents, salaried employees, independent agents, brokers, corporate agents, insurance specific debit/credit cards, call centres, affinity group distribution—microfinance, retail outlets, post office, work site marketing, bancassurance, labour unions-, cell phone/PDA, kiosks, internet, e-commerce, work site and direct marketing), the relative importance of which depends upon the size and segmentation of the market, the available technological resources and innovation, competition and industry development and customer preferences.

Insurance distribution is currently at a turning point, as seen by the drastic changes in both the variety of emerging channels and transformation within channels. These distribution changes are driven by several key market forces including: (i) changing customer preferences and customer empowerment, with significant customer dissatisfaction and mistrust towards incumbents in the aftermath of the financial crisis and the deteriorating reputation of the financial services industry, increasing the willingness among customers (particularly the youngest) to try out new products and providers; (ii) connectivity and data, with customers increasingly connected and using mobile devices, demanding digital offerings, (iii) digital transformation and advancing technology (FinTech & InsurTech), with increasing infrastructure replacement, monetization of data and disintermediation of the value chain; (iv) an aging population, (v) new and more strict market regulations and increased

J. M. Bravo (✉)
NOVA IMS - Universidade Nova de Lisboa, Lisbon, Portugal

Université Paris-Dauphine PSL, Paris, France

MagIC, CEFAGE-UE & BBVA Pensions Institute, Lisbon, Portugal
e-mail: jbravo@novaims.unl.pt

P. Marano, K. Noussia (eds.), *Insurance Distribution Directive*, AIDA Europe Research Series on Insurance Law and Regulation 3,
https://doi.org/10.1007/978-3-030-52738-9_14

regulatory scrutiny; and (vi) challenging market environment, poor market performance and economic uncertainty (e.g., low interest rate environment), that prevented incumbents to invest in the type of products, services, platforms, technology and distribution channels required to meet customer needs and expectations.

The number of distribution channels and partners is expected to increase, and insurers will have to align distribution channels to target customer segments offering "do-it-for-you, do-it-with-you, and do-it-yourself" products instead of "do-it-for-all" products. Customers want to receive from insurance the same levels of choice, convenience, transparency and value for money they enjoy across other industries, particularly (i) mobile solutions, (ii) connectedness at points of sale, (iii) data-driven personalization (target segmentation), (iv) on-demand services. New generations are strongly driven by price considerations. As a result, insurance products are likely to be sold more directly and in competitive markets at a lower price, reducing the share of distribution- and marketing-related expenses.

Distribution- and marketing-related activities can directly and indirectly pose significant financial risks to an insurer and other distribution channel participants, as well as to its customers. Risks caused by actions of the distribution channel (e.g., mis-selling, poor underwriting practices, reductions in the volume and quality of business, policyholder churn behaviour, partners risk), deficient management of an insurer's distribution channel and agents (e.g., sales force qualifications, reputational risks due to inappropriate or fraudulent sales practices) have the potential to undermine an insurer's income-generating capacity, long-term sustainability and brand value. In addition, supervisors are particularly vigilant with regards to inappropriate sales and service, which require consumer protection and consequential action.[1]

The new legal framework regulating insurance distribution in EU Member States brought forward by the introduction of the Insurance Distribution Directive (IDD) in October 2018 raised the benchmark of minimum standards of insurance distribution and expanded the scope of regulation to include (re)insurers as well as (re)insurance intermediaries. In line with MiFID and PRIIPs, IDD aims at increasing consumer protection regardless of the distribution channel. IDD covers the entire distribution chain, including reinsurers, aggregators and price comparison websites from which individuals can buy insurance and distributors for whom insurance provides only ancillary services.

Key provisions included in the IDD include: (i) proper product oversight and governance, (ii) demands and needs analysis, suitability and appropriateness assessment; (iii) appropriate information to customers (PID—Insurance Product Information Document); (iv) more strict professional requirements, (v) Transparency on the existence of conflicts of interest (intermediaries must clearly state whether they are acting on behalf of the customer or the insurer), and (vi) Remuneration and incentive mechanisms (intermediaries must disclose the type and origin, the nature and basis of the compensation they receive in relation to a given contract of insurance).

[1]Gutterman (2016), p. 9.

In this chapter we identify and discuss the implications of the introduction of the IDD in the management of distribution risks in insurance companies. We revisit current insurance approaches to this risk and adopt a framework for the analysis covering both risks to the distribution channel, the impact of new underwriting practices caused by the distribution channel on the size and quality of insured portfolios, the impact of management decisions and poor management governance practices relating to the distribution channel and the way insurance companies address inappropriate market conduct risks and consumer protection. The design and implementation of sound distribution risk management guidelines and policies is expected to be within the scope of an insurer's Enterprise Risk Management (ERM). Appropriate distribution risk management demands precise identification, measurement and management practices, along with the adoption of fair business conduct, fair and responsible pricing, and claims management.

The remainder of this chapter is organized as follows. In Sect. 2 we discuss the impact of digital transformation on insurance value chain primary activities, particularly on insurance distribution. In Section we catalogue and discuss the three main forms of distribution risk in insurance and their potential impact on the quality and volume of the insured portfolio or the insurer's income-generating capacity and long-term financial sustainability and brand value. In Sect. 4 we critically examine the implications of the introduction of the Insurance Distribution Directive on distribution risk management and on firm's entire value chain. Finally, Sect. 5 concludes.

2 Digital Transformation and the Changing Landscape for Insurer's Distribution and Value Chain

Distribution is a key aspect of insurers' business models. Insurance companies use a wide range of distribution methods to target their customers. The traditional model of insurance distribution involves direct sales employing own sales personnel (e.g., insurance agents, call centers, appointed representatives) and indirect sales using a captive and/or an independent network of agents, brokers and independent financial advisers (IFAs). In recent years technological innovation, digital transformation, increasing connectivity, data access, advances in predictive analytics, changing customer preferences and customer empowerment have broadened the distribution channels from the traditional paradigm to a wide range of direct and indirect channels between insurers and current and potential customers. The modern insurance distribution model is multi-channel and multi touch-point, includes the traditional intermediaries but incorporates new direct sales channels (e.g., internet, mobile devices) and new intermediaries such as banks, retailers, post office, affinity groups (e.g., members of a car club, sports organisations, union members), price comparison websites, managing general agents (MGA), broker networks and Peer-to-peer (P2P) groups. The increasing diversity of distribution channels follows

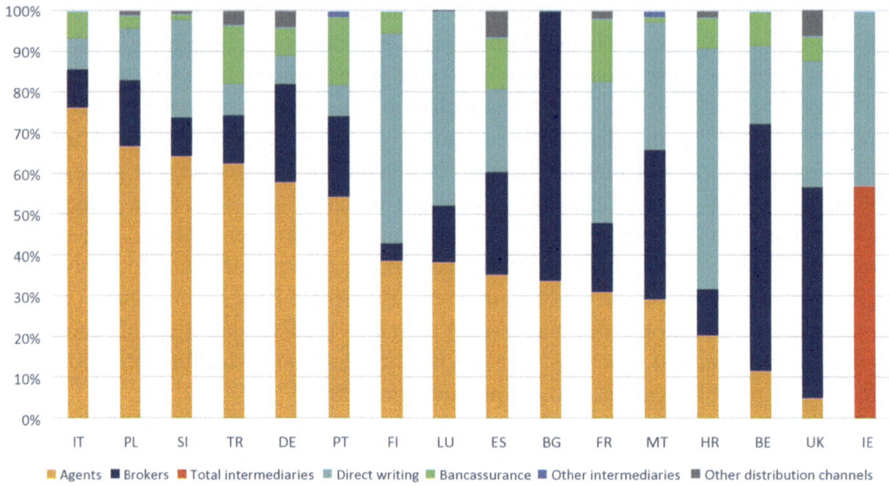

Fig. 1 Non-life distribution channels (% of GWP)—2017. Source: Insurance Europe Data. Notes: Market share computed in terms of gross written premiums (GWP). For NL, health is excluded. Also, "Other" , for 2013 and 2014, represents all non-direct distribution channels For SI, data is from SZZ members only. Branches of companies from EU/EEA countries and FOS are excluded

consumers' needs and preferences and varies across different countries, cultures, markets and even age groups. The number of distribution channels used by insurers and the channel selection process involves a cost/benefit analysis considering the types of products, services and customer segments they want to target, channel requirements by segment, an assessment of the existing business's capabilities to meet customer requirements, a benchmark analysis against competitors, and an evaluation of the channel options.[2] The financial cost of using intermediaries include commission, training, monitoring and administration costs.

In Figs. 1 and 2 we plot the 2017 market share (computed in terms of gross written premiums) of the main distribution channels in Europe in the non-life and life insurance business, respectively.

We can observe that the relative importance of distribution channels varies significantly across countries and Lines of Business (LOB). For non-life products, direct sales through employees or distance-selling are predominant in some countries (e.g., Croatia, Luxembourg, Finland) but for most European countries reported intermediaries (agents and, to a lesser extent, brokers) are the largest distribution channels, particularly in countries like Italy, Poland, Portugal and Turkey. Bancassurance has a more modest share in non-life business in most countries. Contrarily, bancassurance is the main life distribution channel in many European markets, with notable exceptions in the United Kingdom, Slovenia, Greece, Poland

[2]Hutt and Speh (2012), p. 18.

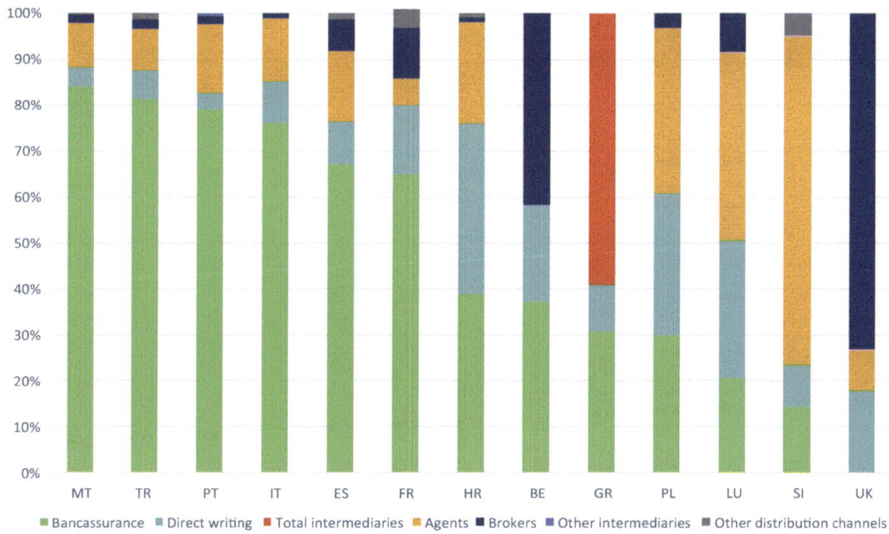

Fig. 2 Life distribution channels in Europe (% of GWP)—2017). Source: Insurance Europe. Notes: Market share computed in terms of gross written premiums (GWP). For DE, employees are included under the category of Agents. For DE, SE and the UK, data is for new business only. For GR, there is no distinction between intermediaries. For NL, "Other" in 2013 and 2014 represents all non-direct distribution channels. For SI, data is from SZZ members only. Branches of companies from EU/EEA countries and FOS are excluded. For BE, bancassurance includes agents

and Luxembourg in which intermediaries are predominant and direct selling is also relevant in some countries.

Contrary to direct sales through employees, mobile technology and telematics do not constraint the location and timing of interactions between insurers and their customers. They will eventually enable customers to arrange most of their insurance needs through remote digital channels and are already affecting customer buying behaviour, from pre-sales activity such as soliciting advice and obtaining personalised quotes, to policy issuance and post-sales services for the policyholder.[3]

The technology adoption trends observed in insurance in recent years include: (i) new tools for data acquisition and analysis such as Artificial Intelligence (AI), Big Data, the Internet of Things (IoT) (sensors and networks), Hyperscale computing, Enterprise Business Process Management (BPM), software that automates underwriting and claims or, (ii) technology for data storage, transaction and security such as Cloud computing, BockChain (mutual distribution ledgers) and digital security and (iii) technology for communication and sales such as mobile devices with apps, chatbots, robot-advisors, social networks, websites, video calls and video platforms. These technologies will first significantly change the way insurers and customers

[3]Swiss Re, 2014, *Digital distribution in insurance: a quiet revolution*. Sigma No 2 /2014, pp. 1–36.

Product design	Channel management & productivity	Risk assessment	Premium collection	Claims first reporting	Investment strategy	Help desk
Actuarial risk management	Compensation management	Rating and quoting	Contract management	Claims handling and settlement	Asset allocation & ALM	Customer relations
Regulatory compliance	Lead management	Reinsurance	Customer service	Fraud management	Risk management	Legal department
Rate making	Marketing	Customer segmentation	Policy renewal	Service	Regulatory reporting	Customer retention
Research	Cross-selling & Up-selling	Expense allocation	Prevention and mitigation			

Fig. 3 Insurance value chain primary activities. Source: Author's preparation

interact (e.g. chatbots, robot-advisors, social networks, video platforms). Second, they are increasingly being used to automatize, standardize and improve the effectiveness and efficiency of insurance business processes (e.g. sales, claims settlement, pricing). Finally, they create opportunities to redesign and customize existing insurance contracts (e.g. telematics insurance, pay-per-use) and to develop new ones.[4]

The disruptive impact of digitalization will not trigger, at least in the short run, the end of insurance intermediaries, but for traditional intermediaries, who fear being replaced by direct sales methods, digital distribution is likely to create a distribution channel conflict, with agents and brokers less keen to remain loyal to a single insurer and more open to a multi-insurer, multi-product line of business. It is not clear how in the future customers will value the personal interaction and expert advice of traditional insurance distribution channels, but it is almost certain that insurance undertakings and distributors will need to alter their business models to meet the more demanding and diversified needs and preferences of customers.

The importance of distribution in insurance goes well beyond the day-to-day activities related to a purchase/sale transaction and spreads out over the entire business value chain. Figure 3 plots the insurance business value chain primary activities, from product development, sales and distribution to customer management. We can observe that the activities in the insurance distribution process include the provision of and access to information on products, services and prices, expert advice, channel management, including productivity and compensation, cross-selling and up-selling activities, but also underwriting tasks, particularly risk assessment, rating and quoting, policy administration, customer service and policy renewal, premium collection and contract management, claims management, risk management and customer management. These activities have been traditionally

[4]See, for instance, Anchen et al. (2015), pp. 1–39 and Eling and Lehmann (2018), pp. 359–396.

developed by intermediaries such as captive or independent agents and brokers, but the enlargement of the distribution channel base is likely to disrupt many of the classical insurance value chain primary activities.

For instance, digitalization is changing the way insurance companies interact with their customers and how they reinvent themselves to meet the customer needs. From a distribution model in which customers typically required personal interaction for product information, demands and needs analysis or suitability and appropriateness assessment, we are moving towards a market in which customers get most information online, compare products and prices via aggregator platforms, purchased and settle contracts online without personal intervention. The buying journey for insurance may involve multiple touchpoints dispersed across different participants in the distribution chain in a more fragmented way. Moreover, in later stages of the value chain, telematics determines how much insurance premium you pay (e.g., pay-as-you-drive auto insurance), and online tools and apps assist in claims reporting and management. Help desks and chatbots assist in customer management. Moreover, digitalization is gradually automatizing business processes and decisions along the value chain, particularly in LOB such as motor insurance, health insurance and home insurance.

New technology has generated innovative personal Peer-to-Peer insurance (P2P) schemes (e.g., Friendsurance) and mutualising insurance, for instance, pooled annuity funds, modern tontines, risk-sharing contracts.[5] The new way of doing business in insurance demands new skills and capacities to extract economic value from the Big Datasets which are generated on a permanent basis by telematics devices, social networks and other sources. In a scenario in which insurers can use the additional information on individuals collected from multiple sources, they will be able to reinvent the underwriting process to structure smaller homogenous risk pools, with an important impact on the traditional implicit tax/subsidy embedded in pooling risks.[6]

3 The Multiple Faces of Distribution Risk in Insurance

Insurance companies use multiple distribution channels to sell its products and the relationships they establish with distributors, partners and existing and potential customers (individuals, commercial companies, non-profit organizations, public entities) are one of their most important intangible assets. Insurance companies sell both short-term life insurance, motor, property, and other casualty insurance

[5]See, for instance, Bravo et al. (2009), pp. 2–20; Alho et al. (2013), pp. 395–436; Milevsky and Salisbury (2015), pp. 91–105; Chen et al. (2017), pp. 5–30; Bravo and El Mekkaoui de Freitas (2018), pp. 212–229; Bravo (2019a), pp. 266–289; Ayuso et al. (2020). In Press; Bravo (2019b).

[6]For an exhaustive analysis on the impact of heterogeneity in life expectancy in the fair value of life annuities and other life insurance contracts see, e.g., Ayuso et al. (2017a,b), Herce and Bravo (2015), Bravo (2016, 2019a, 2020), Bravo et al. (2020) and Bravo and Herce (2020).

contracts and longer-duration complex insurance policies (e.g., variable annuities with embedded financial options) that establish a long-term customer relationship. Similar to other businesses, the risks associated with the entire distribution process can cause a tangible impact to an insurer's long-term sustainability, reputation, brand value, and income-generating capacity, and should be part of a robust Enterprise risk management (ERM) framework in which insurers identify, measure, accept, control, report, and monitor all material risks. Distribution risks are ultimately the responsibility of the insurer, irrespective of the distribution channel used.

There are three main forms of distribution risk in insurance:[7]

1. Risks to the quality and volume of the insured portfolio caused by actions of the distribution channel;
2. Risks to the insurer's income-generating capacity, long-term financial sustainability and brand value caused by actions of the distribution channel;
3. Risks to own distribution channels, which ultimately can affect the profitability and sustainability of companies.

The way insurance distribution channels perform in aligning the actual customer base with the insurer target markets, in terms of not only the size but also the quality of the insured pool, and the extent to which the observed frequency and the severity of risks deviates from the risk pricing assumptions and policyholder behaviour assumed at contract inception significantly influences the nature and type of exposure-to-risk the insurer will be subject to. Insurance distributors have often an important and relatively autonomous role in identifying potential customers and in the underwriting process, actively participating in risk selection. They are often more rewarded for the volume of new business created and less for the quality of business, more for bringing in new customers than for retaining existing policyholders. These incentive mechanisms often create conflicts of interest between the distributor profitability goals, the insurer long-term sustainability and customer interest. Frontloading distributors compensation, i.e., paying more at policy origination than at policy renewal has the potential to affect the distribution channel activities and its long-term sustainability. Distributors tend to become too dependent on generating new business for receiving regular cash flows, have little incentive to keep a policy in force and may not be able to maintain a stable and continuous income stream.[8]

A poor risk selection process resulting in a claims experience inconsistent with pricing assumptions due to: (i) pre-contract informational asymmetry between the insurer and the insured and adverse selection (e.g., identifying potential customers with high-risk lifestyles—smokers, people employed in dangerous jobs, less experienced drivers) when compared to the general population, or to (ii) policyholder

[7]Gutterman (2016), pp. 2–5.

[8]Depending on the jurisdiction, taxation considerations may also be relevant to determine the remuneration policies for employees and insurance distributors and influence the type of recommendation they offer to customers and their appetite for the contracts (Bravo 2016; EIOPA 2017).

moral hazard resulting from misleading information provided and/or from an implicit incentive provided to individuals to take more risks than they normally would without insurance once covered by the insurance contract (e.g., engaging in dangerous driving after contracting maximum auto insurance coverage), or to (iii) applicant's fraudulent operations or, finally to (iv) inappropriate underwriting of policies that do not fit the needs of customers, has the potential to significantly deteriorate insurer's profitability. Insurance companies have many ways to mitigate the impact of adverse selection, moral hazard and fraudulent behaviour (e.g., by limiting the coverage, charging premium loadings, by adding exclusions) but the long-term effects of a poor risk selection process persist.

In the insurance market, the customers' purchase process and claims management depends heavily on intermediaries. A poor risk selection process and inappropriate distribution channel activities are thus expected to have consequences on customer satisfaction, policyholder behaviour and abnormal lapse rates. For instance, an increase in premature voluntary policy terminations or the failure to pay insurance premiums relative to the insurer pricing expectations may be the result of insurance distribution intermediaries incentivising policyholders to swap insurance contracts (including moving to another insurer), not because there are acting in the best financial interest of the policyholder but simply because the broker receives larger front-end commissions for new long-term business or for moving blocks of short-term contracts from one company to another. Additionally, mis-selling practices at the distribution channel level are likely to raise discontent among policyholders and generate premature policy termination and low policy continuation, reducing the ability of insurers to recover acquisition expenses and impacting the company's asset and liability management planning.[9] Moral hazard behaviour resulting in an abnormal frequency and severity of claims or fraudulent actions may sometimes have the connivance of the distribution channel. Some brokers may in extreme cases collude with a third party to take advantage of the insurer. In many cases, the insurance policyholder relationship is actually "owned" by brokers and dealers and not by the insurer, offering the distribution channel an increased capacity to influence policy lapse or non-continuation behaviour counter to the best interest of the policyholders, or increase anti-selection against the insurer.[10]

Additionally, the operation of a given distribution channel has the potential to generate risks to the insurer's income-generating capacity, long-term financial sustainability and brand value. For instance, insurance companies that are critically dependent on a single distribution channel (e.g., bank, retail network) or few group insurance contracts (e.g., large companies) and in which distribution tasks have been mostly outsourced to an intermediary or to a partner are highly exposed to the corporate decisions of the distribution channel (e.g., a sudden loss of sales if a distribution channel does not continue the strategic relationship, finishes the distribution agreement or becomes bankrupt, a big customer swapping insurer, or a lack of

[9] See IAA (2004), and Bravo and Silva (2006).

[10] Gutterman (2016), pp. 8–10.

sufficient bargaining power in the relationship). Additionally, they lose much of the control over the business and maybe severely impacted by underwriting decisions, pricing levels, lack of coordination or misaligned incentives and strategy.

Intermediaries and partners may be more concerned with promoting themselves and their business than committed to a long-term successful and profitable relationship with the insurer. For instance, in the bancassurance distribution model the bank may divert bank customers from purchasing life insurance policies with a savings accumulation profile and try to sell them its own deposit or investment products or channel customers to another insurance company that is directly or indirectly controlled by the bank. In distribution arrangements in which the intermediary or partner are responsible for collecting premiums, additional monitoring and enforcement efforts must be put in place to guarantee premium payments are effectively received by the insurer, preventing fraud, loss of coverage situations and expense recovery risks with major litigation and reputational costs for the undertaking.

Finally, there are risks to the own distribution channels themselves that are similar to operational risks, which may produce adverse impact on existing and new business, loss of brand value and represent significant reputation and financial risks to the insurer. In extreme circumstances, they may even trigger regulatory penal action. According to the Basel Committee, operational risk is defined as "a risk of loss resulting from inadequate or failed internal processes, people and systems or from external events". The main risks for distribution channels are disruptive innovation that deteriorates the continuity chances of some intermediaries, poor reputation of brokers/dealers due to, for instance, past inappropriate sales/claim practices, mis-selling by sales personnel, poor sales management (e.g., uncompetitive pricing or services, pushing products for higher commission LOBs), products and services failing to meet the customers' needs (e.g., due to inadequate administration systems, delayed turnaround time, process failure), inability to maintain a strong relationship with the agents/brokers, lack of alignment of incentives, competition and cannibalization of traditional distribution channels by new channels (e.g., mobile/Internet-based), unskilled sales force due to inadequate hiring and training or regulatory and tax changes.

The capability of the agents/brokers network to remain competitive against other distribution channels and the ability of insurance undertakings to maintain a healthy and mutually profitable relationship with is distributors are critical for long-term competitiveness. Insurers compete for intermediaries with a proven track record of developing and delivering a risk-balanced, profitable book of business. To the extent that this competition for the best distribution partners increase and there are consolidation movements in the agents/brokers market, premium, volume and profitability could be negatively affected. To avoid internal friction when insurers use more than one channel to target the same customers, particularly when the implementation of direct distribution channels may adversely impact the brokers market-share, companies should adopt a multi-channel model. Notice that distribution risk may arise as a result of both people, system, process and external causes, with consequences revealed, for instance, through an increase in customer's complaints and dissatisfaction, increase in churn rates, loss of reputation due to negative media coverage, loss of market-share and revenue.

4 The Impact of IDD on Distribution Risk Management

The Insurance Distribution Directive (IDD)[11] came into force in Europe on 23rd February 2016 replacing the Insurance Mediation Directive (IMD), as part of wider project to amend the way in which financial services are regulated in the European Union (EU). The IDD was implemented with a clear objective of increasing the level of harmonization for insurance distribution regulation across the EU member countries, creating a common playing field for all insurance intermediaries and insurance distribution activities, irrespective of the direct or indirect channel used by customers to purchase their products. This includes (re)insurance manufacturers that sell directly to customers and market participants who sell insurance on an ancillary basis. The IDD also aims to improve consumer protection and effective competition in the market. The directive includes multiple provisions whose impact goes well beyond the distribution function in insurance, regarding for instance the type of information that should be made available to consumers before they sign an insurance contract, the business and transparency conduct standards insurance distributors are required to comply, product oversight and governance requirements, procedures and rules for cross-border business, continuous professional requirements, conflicts of interest management, inducements or cross-selling activities. In line with other regulatory changes such as MiFID II and PRIIPS, IDD establishes more prescriptive rules for intermediaries selling insurance products that expose policyholders to financial markets (e.g., unit-linked and with-profit life insurance contracts).

One of the central principles of IDD is that insurance distributors 'must always act honestly, fairly and professionally in accordance with the best interests (demands and needs) of their customers'.[12] This "best interests" duty of trust or confidence is inspired in similar dispositions contained in the European (MiFID)[13] and U. S. (Securities Exchange Act)[14] Regulatory Frameworks for Financial Instruments, applies to both brokers representing an actual or potential policyholder and insurer representatives, and requires them to act in a diligent and professional way to negotiate the terms of a deal on behalf of and to the principals' advantage, including

[11]Directive (EU) 2016/97 of the European Parliament and of the Council of 20 January 2016 on insurance distribution (Insurance Distribution Directive).

[12]See Recital 46 and Article 17 of the IDD.

[13]See Article 18 of Financial Instruments Directive (MiFID I) (Directive 2004/39/EC of the European Parliament and of the Council of 21 April 2004 on markets in financial instruments and Article 23 (Section I) and Article 13c (CHAPTER IIIA) of MiFID II Directive (Directive 2014/65/ EU of the European Parliament and of the Council of 15 May 2014).

[14]See Sec 10b(5) of the Securities Exchange Act.

not using their position of trust to generate unacceptable benefits or profits for themselves without the knowledge and agreement of their represented, managing any conflicts of interest if necessary. It encompasses in some extent both a duty of care and a fiduciary duty.[15] The "customers' best interests" rule requires, among other things, that all distributors (intermediaries or (re)insurance undertakers) in the distribution chain should make a proper suitability assessment of their actual or potential policyholders demands and needs, offering only contracts which are considered suitable, appropriate and deliver fair value instead of exhibiting their full catalogue of products with broad proclamations about the type of needs each product addresses.[16] Distributors must provide customers personalised recommendations detailing why a given insurance product would fit the customer's demands and needs. The exception would be, in some jurisdictions (e.g., the UK), non-advised retail sales for which firms are not expected to carry out a detailed analysis of a customer's circumstances but should, nevertheless, clearly identify the customer's demands and needs and offer contracts that meets them.[17]

This also signifies that, irrespective of the means of interaction with clients (including automated or semi-automated systems used as a client-facing tool such as robo-advice), insurance distributors will have to maintain and trace the whole process of collecting information about a client and the subsequent suitability and appropriateness assessment, informing and explaining their customers clearly about the distributor's role, responsibility and purpose of the suitability assessment, which ultimately should be for the firm to act in the customer's best interest.[18] Insurance companies that provide advice to customers on insurance-based investment products (IBIPs) must encourage customers to provide accurate and sufficient information about their protection and/or investment objectives, needs, knowledge, risk tolerance, time horizon, experience and financial position, including the capacity to bear losses (e.g., in unit-linked life insurance).[19]

---

[15]For a discussion on this topic see, e.g., FCA, *Discussion Paper on a duty of care and potential alternative approaches*, Discussion Paper DP18/5, July 2018.

[16]See, specifically, paragraphs 1 and 2 of Article 30 of the IDD, which state that an assessment of the suitability or appropriateness of an insurance-based investment product (IBIP) for the customer by the insurance intermediary or insurance undertaking is generally required as part of the sale of an IBIP. For a detailed discussion on this topic see Marano and Rokas (2019).

[17]The UK Financial Conduct Authority (FCA) Handbook, Section COBS 10.4, states that a firm is not required to make a suitability assessment if: "... (a) the service only consists of execution and/or the reception and transmission of client orders, with or without ancillary services, it relates to particular financial instruments and is provided at the initiative of the client; (b) the client has been clearly informed (whether the warning is given in a standardised format or not) that in the provision of this service the firm is not required to assess the suitability of the instrument or service provided or offered and that therefore he does not benefit from the protection of the rules on assessing suitability; and (c) the firm complies with its obligations in relation to conflicts of interest".

[18]For a recent detailed discussion on IDD and digital intermediaries of insurance products see, e.g., See Marano (2019a), pp. 294–315.

[19]See Marano and Rokas (2019), for a detailed discussion on the distribution of IBIPs.

Each firm is in principle free to define the precise method they will use to inform their clients about the suitability and appropriateness assessment, but firms are expected to define and implement a robust record keeping suitability framework (e.g., one including knowledge assessment, customer categorization, individual and portfolio risk level classification, risk scoring, suitability and appropriateness result), enabling a systematic internal/external control and validation of the suitability and appropriateness obligation, both at the individual trade level and at portfolio level. The framework should include target market statements for all products including, for instance, the product description, the target market (age, sex, income, social group, literacy capabilities, family background), the product aim, the customer objectives and needs, the degree of complexity, the distribution strategy, the customers for whom the product is considered inappropriate).

If implemented properly, this framework is expected to reduce distribution risk by minimizing mis-selling practices, by better meeting customers' needs, by improving insurer's reputation and by improving sales management. The framework it also likely to contribute positively to the risk selection process. However, the operational risks and costs involved in consistently implementing the framework in all levels of the distribution chain are massive and should not be neglected. Since identifying customer's needs is one of the key requirements for the success of insurance companies, proper adoption of IDD provisions is expected to have a long-term impact on insurer's income-generating capacity and financial sustainability.

The IDD contains, however, precise pre-contract disclosures and provisions, namely the introduction of a detailed standardised Insurance Product Information Document (IPID) for non-life insurance products, and Key Information Documents (KIDs) for those who produce or sell insurance-based investment products, which had been previously introduced under the packaged retail and insurance-based investment products (PRIIPs) Regulation. The IPID is a precontractual and standalone document which aims to provide clearer and transparent information on non-life insurance products so that consumers can make informed decisions, facilitating also competition between insurance distributors. The IPID document should be easy to read, understand and compare, have a common design, structure and format and will have to be communicated at the time of quotation, renewal and any mid-term adjustment in the contract.[20]

One of areas in which the IDD is expected to have more impact on distribution risk management refers to the new regulatory provisions regarding pre-contract disclosure and transparency on both the nature and basis of the remuneration (e.g., commission, bonus, profit share, other financial incentives or non-monetary benefits) distributors and its employees receive in relation to the insurance contract, and on the performance management practices of an insurer's own sales force. Customers are to be provided information on fees, commissions or benefits all participants in the

[20]EC, 2017, Commission Implementing Regulation (EU) 2017/1469 of 11 August laying down a standardised presentation format for the insurance product information document. *Official Journal of the European Union*, L 209/19, 12.8.2017.

distribution chain receive in relation the insurance contract. Special attention is devoted to compensation components which are not guaranteed, or which are contingent on meeting certain business targets (e.g., new sales). The general principle is that the sales channel remuneration and performance management policies must not conflict with the general duty to act in the customer's best interests, nor prevent any participant in the distribution chain from presenting product information in a clear and non-misleading way, nor making a suitable recommendation for a fair deal. This means insurance companies are responsible for defining and implementing actions aiming to prevent the negative effects of any incentive mechanisms on the quality of the relevant service to the customer and on the insurer or intermediary duty to act in accordance with the best interests of their customers.[21] In this regard, EIOPA[22] recommends insurance undertakings and insurance intermediaries to adopt inducements or inducement schemes that include both quantitative commercial criteria and appropriate qualitative criteria, reflecting compliance with the applicable regulations, fair treatment of customers and the quality of services provided to customers, that are proportionate when considered against the value of the product and the services provided, to avid inducements entirely or mainly paid upfront when the product is sold without any appropriate refunding mechanism if the product lapses or is surrendered at an early stage, and to be cautious about inducements that incorporate any form of variable or contingent threshold or value accelerator which is triggered by touching a sales target barrier based on volume or value of sales.

To that end, the IDD includes specific disclosure requirements for intermediaries in relation to conflicts of interest and transparency. The insurance "...distributor should develop, adopt and regularly review policies and procedures relating to conflicts of interest with the aim of avoiding any detrimental impact on the quality of the relevant service to the customer and of ensuring that the customer is adequately informed about fees, commissions or benefits".[23] Prior the conclusion of an insurance contract, the IDD mandates an insurance intermediary to provides the customer with information on, for instance, whether he has a holding representing 10% or more of the voting rights of the capital in a given insurance undertaking or vice versa, whether he provides or not advice about the insurance products sold on the basis of a fair and personal analysis (which should be proceeded by an analysis of a sufficiently large number of similar contracts available on the market), whether he represents the customer or acts on behalf of the insurance undertaking, whether he is or not under a contractual obligation to conduct insurance distribution business exclusively with one or more insurance undertakings, the nature of the remuneration

[21]See Delloite (2018), pp. 2–10.

[22]EIOPA, 2017, *Technical Advice on possible delegated acts concerning the Insurance Distribution Directive*. EIOPA 17/048, February, pp. 1–150.

[23]See, e.g., Recital 57 of the IDD.

received in relation to the insurance contract and, particularly, the amount of the fee that is paid directly by the customer.[24]

The new pre-contract disclosure and transparency provisions on the nature and basis of the remuneration and in relation to conflicts of interest reinforce a more client-centric approach embedded in the IDD and will force insurers to rethink their pricing, remuneration and distribution business strategies and product governance requirements to be better aligned with customers' interests and to face a more competitive environment, with the corresponding price and margin pressures. In theory, this should contribute to improve the risk selection process and thus the quality of the insured portfolio, reducing distribution risk caused by the actions of the distribution channel. In practice, it is still too soon to confirm how the new disclosure requirements impact on distribution channel strategies, on insurance coverage, on the price of insurance contracts or on the long-term income generating capacity of firms. Guaranteed is that the IDD brings a substantial increase in the obligations relating to information, advisory services, documentation and business conduct.

Another IDD provision with relevant impact on distribution channels and risk management refers to cross-selling activities. When, as part of a package, a non-insurance ancillary product or service is offered together with an insurance product, the distributor must inform the customer about the components, costs, charges, and risks of each component and the customer must be given the chance to buy them separately.[25] This requirement does not prohibit the distribution of insurance products which provide coverage for various types of risks (e.g., multi-risk insurance policies), just requires distributors to unbundle packages detaching the pricing and risk characteristics of each coverage. Offering insurance and claims services on an unbundled basis is particularly useful for large policyholders (e.g., workers compensation insurance, general liability insurance and auto insurance) looking for more flexible, fitted to their specific needs and, potentially, cheaper risk management solutions. For insurers and distributors, this is however likely to reduce risk pooling mechanisms, to pressure revenues and profit margins and to challenge classical distribution infrastructures. Traditionally, to justify the manufacturing and distribution costs of insurance products and services and to be offered at an affordable competitive price, coverages had to be sufficiently broad to address the needs of a large reachable customer base, pooling risks efficiently, resulting in standardized products with complementary coverages. As the advent of digital intermediaries in insurance shows, new technologies such as digitization and aggregation platforms, new processes and methods have reduced the costs of manufacturing and distributing insurance, reducing the primary motive for packing coverages.

Similar to MiFID II, the IDD also introduces product oversight and governance (POG) requirements for all insurance products (except for insurance of large risks).

[24]See, e.g., Article 19 of the IDD.

[25]See, e.g., Article 24 of the IDD.

The approval process for each insurance product should be defined as proportionate to the nature of the insurance products that are about to be sold to customers, it should specify the target market, the risk assessment and assure that the distribution strategy is aligned with the identified market. Regular reviews must also be conducted to verify that products remain effectively distributed and consistent with the objective of the respective target markets.[26] This will require insurers to select the distribution channel that is appropriate for the target market, distributors to define a distribution strategy that does not conflict with the strategy defined by the insurance undertaking and regular monitoring and implementation of corrective actions to better align the product with the needs and objectives of the target market.[27] Most insurance companies manufacture their products based essentially on the sales force feedback, fitting everyone with the same products, with little room for market research. POG requirements demand, together with needs analysis, a greater role for investing in market research and in alternative mechanisms for understanding customers preferences, trends and trust on the brand value.

In theory, the POG requirements have a relevant impact on the whole product value chain, from the process of designing and manufacturing insurance products, making them available to customers (distribution) and monitoring them once distributed. The provisions are aligned with governance requirements established by Solvency II arrangements which demand insurers to prudently manage the business under a risk-based approach. They are expected to contribute to better align the business strategy and interests of insurers and distributors, and thus positively impact on distribution risk. However, the substantial increase in the obligations relating to information, advisory services, documentation and business conduct is likely to reduce the business margins.[28]

The IDD mandates relevant persons within the management structure of (re)-insurance companies or intermediaries involved in the distribution of (re)insurance products, as well as the relevant employees of an (re)insurance distributor directly involved in (re)insurance distribution to be of good repute, have a clean criminal record or any other national equivalent in relation to serious criminal offences linked to crimes against property or other crimes related to financial activities and possess an appropriate level of knowledge and competence in relation to the distribution activity. The appropriateness of the level of knowledge and competence should be proportional to the complexity of the products sold, the type of distribution channel, the role distributors perform, and the activity carried out within the insurance or reinsurance distributor and must be assured by the application of specific Continuing Professional Development (CPD).

The IDD introduces a minimum 15 h CPD for certain staff who are directly involved in insurance distribution, who supervise such staff or who are responsible for insurance distribution within the firm's management structure (IDD, Chapter IV,

[26]See, e.g., Article 25 of the IDD.

[27]For a detailed discussion of POG requirements under the IDD see Marano (2019b), pp. 60–96.

[28]Köhne and Brömmelmeyer (2018), pp. 704–739.

Article 10), but it is expected that professional bodies establish more demanding standards as good practice rather than a legal minimum. The new provisions regarding CPD aim at enhancing public trust in insurance intermediaries through raising professional standards rather than relying on onsite training and experience. Continuous education should target areas not typically covered by professional training (e.g., anti-money laundering legislation, assessment of consumer needs, insurance legislation and regulation), but also risk analysis skills (e.g. risk tolerance assessment, underwriting and risk-selection process) and ethics and professional standards. To the extent that CPD provisions succeed in raising public trust and in helping professions to act honestly, fairly and professionally in accordance with the best interests of their customers, mitigating fraud and mis-selling practices, the introduction of IDD will impact positively on distribution risk management in insurance. Table 1 summarizes the discussion on the impact of IDD main provisions on insurance value chain, including distribution activities.

The demands and needs analysis, the suitability and appropriateness requirements and the cross-selling provisions are expected to have the greatest impact on sales, distribution, underwriting and customer management practices. The remuneration and incentives provisions are expected to have a major impact on product manufacturing and sales and distribution activities. The product oversight and governance provisions are expected to impact product development and distribution activities within insurers and intermediaries.

The activities of claims handling, complaints handling and policy administration and the provision of after-sales services (e.g., loss adjusters and expert appraisers of claims) are key functions of an insurance undertaking that can be in some cases subcontracted. The managing of claims of an insurer on a professional basis and loss adjusting and expert appraisal of claims are activities which do not constitute insurance distribution under the IDD and, as such, are not directly impacted by the regulation.[29] However, since improper management of claims and complaints typically raises discontent among policyholders, generates premature policy termination and deteriorates the insurers reputation, with a non-negligible impact on the insurer's long-term financial sustainability and brand value, insurance companies are expected to require their service providers to adopt at least some of the IDD provisions (e.g., on CPD).

5 Conclusions

The introduction of IDD in insurance distribution as part of wider legislative agenda to change the way in which financial services are regulated in the EU set common rules for all involved in (re)insurance distribution in Europe, including the new disruptive distribution channels brought forward by digital transformation in

[29]See Article 2(2) of the IDD.

Table 1 Value chain impacts of IDD

	Value chain impacts						
	Product development	Sales & distribution	Underwriting	Policy administration	Claims management	Asset management	Customer management
Demands and needs analysis	L	M	M	L	L	L	M
Suitability and appropriateness	L	M	M	L	L	L	M
Remuneration and incentives	H	H	M	L	L	L	L
Conflict of interest	L	M	L	L	L	L	L
Cross-selling	L	M	L	L	L	L	L
Product oversight and governance	H	M	L	L	L	L	L
Information to customers	L	M	L	L	L	L	M
Continuous professional development	L	L	L	L	L	L	L

Source: Author's preparation. Notes: L = Low; M = Medium; H = High

insurance. The directive includes multiple provisions which impact the whole insurance value chain and that go well beyond distribution activities. In this chapter we critically examined the impact of the introduction of IDD on distribution risk management in insurance undertakings and distribution intermediaries, analysing the consequences of IDD main provisions on the quality and volume of the insured portfolio, on the insurer's income-generating capacity, long-term financial sustainability and brand value. We conclude that provisions related to demands and needs analysis, suitability and appropriateness requirements or cross-selling dispositions are expected to greatly influence insurer's sales, distribution, underwriting and customer management primary activities. Inducements and inducement schemes are likely to have a major impact on product manufacturing, sales and distribution activities, whereas the product oversight and governance provisions will prominently impact insurers and intermediary's business strategy, particularly product development and distribution primary activities. Further research is needed to quantitatively assess the economic impact of the introduction of IDD.

Acknowledgements The author gratefully acknowledges comments and suggestions made by editors and by participants at the 8th AIDA Europe Conference, Lisbon, Portugal, 2019.

References

Alho J, Bravo JM, Palmer E (2013) Annuities and life expectancy in NDC. In: Holzmann R, Palmer E, Robalino D (eds) Non-financial defined contribution pension schemes in a changing pension world, Volume 2: gender, politics and financial stability. World Bank Publications, Washington, DC, pp 395–436

Anchen J, Frey A, Kirova M (2015) Life insurance in the digital age: fundamental transformation ahead. Swiss Re Sigma: 6/2015

Ayuso M, Bravo JM, Holzmann R (2017a) Addressing longevity heterogeneity in pension scheme design. J Financ Econ 6(1):1–21

Ayuso M, Bravo JM, Holzmann R (2017b) On the heterogeneity in longevity among socioeconomic groups: scope, trends, and implications for earnings-related pension schemes. Global J Human Soc Sci Econ 17(1):31–57

Ayuso M, Bravo JM, Holzmann R (2020) Getting life expectancy estimates right for pension policy: period versus cohort approach. J Pension Econ Financ. 1-20. https://doi.org/10.1017/S1474747220000050

Bravo JM (2016) Taxation of pensions in Portugal: a semi-dual income tax system. CESifo DICE Rep J Inst Comp 14(1):14–23

Bravo JM (2019a) Funding for longer lives: retirement wallet and risk-sharing annuities. EKONOMIAZ Basque Econ Rev 96(2): 268–291

Bravo JM (2019b) Pricing participating longevity-linked life annuities: a Bayesian model ensemble approach. Preprint. https://doi.org/10.13140/RG.2.2.10113.61283

Bravo JM (2020) Addressing the pension decumulation phase of employee retirement planning. In: Muenstermann I (ed) Who wants to retire and who can afford to retire? IntechOpen, pp 1–21

Bravo JM, El Mekkaoui de Freitas N (2018) Valuation of longevity-linked life annuities. Insur Math Econ 78:212–229

Bravo JM, Silva C (2006) Immunization using a stochastic process independent multifactor model: the Portuguese experience. J Bank Financ 30(1):133–156

Bravo JM, Corte-Real P, Silva C (2009) Participating life annuities incorporating longevity risk sharing arrangements. Working Paper, available from rdpc.uevora.pt
Bravo, JM Herce, JAH (2020) Career breaks, broken pensions? Long-run effects of early and late-career unemployment spells on pension entitlements. Journal of Pension Economics and Finance:1–27
Bravo JM, Ayuso M, Holzmann R, Palmer E (2020) Addressing life expectancy gap in pension policy. Insurance: Mathematics and Economics, preprint revised & resubmitted.
Chen A, Hieber P, Klein J (2017) Tonuity: a novel individual-oriented retirement plan. ASTIN Bull 49(1):5–30
EIOPA (2017) Technical Advice on possible delegated acts concerning the Insurance Distribution Directive. EIOPA 17/048
Eling M, Lehmann M (2018) The impact of digitalization on the insurance value chain and the insurability of risks. Geneva Pap Risk Insur Issues Pract 43(3):359–396
FCA (2018) Discussion Paper on a duty of care and potential alternative approaches. Discussion Paper DP18/5
Gutterman S (2016) Distribution risks. In: IAA risk book - governance, management and regulation of insurance operations. International Actuarial Association
Herce J, Bravo JM (2015) Las pensiones en España y Portugal: Descripción de los esquemas y evolución reciente comparada. In: ¿Es posible planificar la jubilación? Dos años del Instituto BBVA de Pensiones en España. Instituto BBVA de Pensiones, pp 89–126
Hutt MD, Speh TW (2012) Business marketing management: B2B. Cengage, Delhi
IAA (2004) A Global Framework for Insurer Solvency Assessment. International Actuarial Association. Insurer Solvency Assessment Working Party Report, pp 1–185
Köhne T, Brömmelmeyer C (2018) The new insurance distribution regulation in the EU—a critical assessment from a legal and economic perspective. Geneva Pap Risk Insur Issues Pract 43 (4):704–739
Marano P (2019a) Navigating InsurTech: the digital intermediaries of insurance products and customer protection in the EU. Maastricht J Eur Comp Law 26(2):294–315
Marano P (2019b) The product oversight and governance: standards and liabilities. In: Marano P, Rokas I (eds) Distribution of insurance-based investment products: the EU regulation and the liabilities. Springer, pp 60–96
Marano P, Rokas I (2019) Distribution of insurance-based investment products: the EU regulation and the liabilities. Springer
Milevsky M, Salisbury T (2015) Optimal retirement income tontines. Insur Math Econ 64 (1):91–105

Legislation and Other Documents

Directive (EU) 2016/97 of the European Parliament and of the Council of 20 January 2016 on insurance distribution (Insurance Distribution Directive)
EC (2017) Commission Implementing Regulation (EU) 2017/1469 of 11 August laying down a standardised presentation format for the insurance product information document. *Official Journal of the European Union*, L 209/19, 12.8.2017
Delloite (2018) *Insurance Distribution Directive 2018: A challenging year for the European insurance sector*. Performance magazine issue 25. New York, NY: Deloitte.
Swiss Re (2014) *Digital distribution in insurance: a quiet revolution*. Sigma: 2/2014

Redefining Product Management: IDD's Perspective

Diana Renata Bożek

1 Introduction

It should not come as a surprise that it is only possible after a certain period of time to assess legal acts which revolutionized a given area of law. In order to do so, a practice of application of legal provisions needs to be established, first decisions of national courts and governing authorities have to be made and the legal doctrine needs to be formulated. Although, three quarters have already passed since the date of implementation of Insurance Distribution Directive ('**IDD**'),[1] it is still definitely too short to determine whether or not the desired objectives have been achieved. It is however the right moment to give pause for thought about both the promises that the IDD held and disappointments, which it eventually brought.

This chapter discusses the issue of product governance—one that the IDD has redefined. In particular, the requirements of product oversight and governance introduced in the Article 25 of the IDD and further developed in the Commission Delegated Regulation supplementing Directive (EU) 2016/97[2] with regard to product oversight and governance requirements for insurance undertakings and insurance distributors will be analyzed ('**Delegated Regulation**'). Regarding this, the author

[1]Directive (EU) 2016/97 of the European Parliament and of the Council of 20 January 2016 on insurance distribution (Official Journal of the European Union L 26/19).

[2]Commission Delegated Regulation (EU) 2017/2358 of 21 September 2017 supplementing Directive (EU) 2016/97 of the European Parliament and of the Council with regard to product oversight and governance requirements for insurance undertakings and insurance distributors (Official Journal of the European Union I L 341/1).

D. R. Bożek (✉)
Insurance Law Department, Faculty of Law and Administration – Warsaw University, Warsaw, Poland
e-mail: d.bozek@wpia.uw.edu.pl

P. Marano, K. Noussia (eds.), *Insurance Distribution Directive*, AIDA Europe Research Series on Insurance Law and Regulation 3,
https://doi.org/10.1007/978-3-030-52738-9_15

will focus on three key concerns. Special attention will be drawn to the process of identifying target market with respect to each product, assessment of all relevant risks to such identified target market as well as to the assessment of consistency between the intended distribution strategy and the identified target market. Undoubtedly, a formal recognition of the possibility to manufacture insurance product by the insurance intermediaries and providing them with specific obligations resulting from such possibility is an important breakthrough. So far, even in case of the so-called 'brokerage programs', i.e. products created individually by brokers, obligation and liability have been attributed to the insurance companies offering insurance coverage under the brokerage programs. Against this background, it is worth wondering whether the insurance intermediaries will be interested in being 'manufacturers' and entering contracts stipulating detailed conditions of cooperation with the insurance company in accordance with the requirements for the manufacturers, referred to in the Article 3 sec. 4 of Delegated Regulation. Another issue, which should be addressed, is the admissibility of concluding such contracts between the insurance companies and brokers. This regards specifically those countries where a permanent cooperation between insurance company and broker is not practiced or forbidden. Since the IDD has been implemented into the national legal systems, product governance is no longer subject to the internal arrangements of the insurance company nor European or national soft law. Currently, product governance regulation constitutes part of the binding laws thereby it is possible to impose sanctions in case of its violation. The analysis of the shift in the approach to the product governance and its impact on the insurance companies, intermediaries and insurance market will be presented in the last part of this chapter.

2 IDD as a Response to the Needs of the Market

Not only was the aim of the IDD to adjust the current intermediation regulations to a rapidly changing technological and legal environment, but most importantly it was to ensure high level of customer protection (as a "weak part" of market[3]) among all the distribution channels. The objectives were directly expressed in the IDD's recitals. For instance, according to the recital 6 consumers should benefit from the same level of protection despite the differences between distribution channels, whereas recital 16 indicates that this Directive should ensure that the same level of consumer protection applies and that all consumers can benefit from comparable standards. Application of the uniform standards is believed to be beneficial not only for customers but also for distributors by promoting a level playing field and competition on equal terms between intermediaries, whether or not they are tied to an insurance companies (recital 16). Both insurance companies and intermediaries have been obliged to take on new obligations, which also involve costs. Introduction

[3]Schaeken Willemaers (2014), p. 2.

of uniform obligations for all the distributors is justified with the principle of equal treatment of economic operators.

It is difficult not to agree with the IDD that it is beneficial for customer to have insurance products distributed via different channels and by intermediaries cooperating in various forms with the insurance companies, provided they are obliged to comply with the similar customer protection rules. Nevertheless, it is reasonable to voice a concern of whether it is similarly beneficial for distributors. So far, the obligations related to product governance constituted a regulation of soft law nature and were imposed on the insurance companies. Therefore, insurance intermediaries do not have in place any proceedings standards or qualified staff in this field. It thus remains an open question whether a uniform regulation will translate to its uniform application. It goes without saying that distributors cannot be treated equally with the insurance companies in terms of their financial, personal and economic background. Consequences of the unification of obligations will be further examined in part 6 of this chapter.

3 Definitional Problems

European insurance market faced a bunch of challenges raised by the IDD, among which introduction of new terminology, which is considerably different from the traditional insurance contract approach presented in the civil code. Further to this, a lot of terms used by the European legislator are not defined or are used synonymously, which results in blurring the distinction between their original meanings.

From the author's point of view, lack of the definition of insurance 'product' as well as lack of further explanation of what does it mean to govern such product is particularly harmful.

The way of using term of 'insurance product' within the IDD clearly indicates that it is associated with the insurance contract. This conclusion results from recital 10 of IDD which states as follows: *it is important to take into consideration the specific nature of insurance contracts in comparison to investment products regulated under Directive 2014/65/EU of the European Parliament and of the Council. The distribution of insurance contracts, including insurance-based investment products, should therefore be regulated under this Directive and be aligned with Directive 2014/65/EU.* Based on this, the insurance product should be interpreted through the prism of the insurance contract understood as a general type of contract that can be concluded by the insurance company—not as a specific insurance contract concluded with an individual. Shortly after the adoption of the IDD, a dispute over the meaning of the insurance product raised. Some claimed that it should be understood as a 'contract' offered to an individual client, while others argued that 'product' means 'conditions' on the basis of which the insurer concludes individual contracts. In order to solve this dispute, not only linguistic interpretation (noteworthy is the inconsistent use of terminology by the European legislator), but also systemic interpretation of the regulation should be taken into consideration. The author claims that the most important argument against defining product as a contract offered to an individual client is the requirement to distribute the product to the identified target market (provided for in both IDD and Delegated Regulation)—this term alone refers to the multitude of actors.[4] Following on from this argument, the insurance product should be understood as insurance contract's conditions, which stipulate right and obligations of each of the contracting parties. Thus, identification of the insurance product should be easy, as it would be based on the number of a specific management board's resolution, which adopted the insurance contract's conditions.

However, understanding of the term 'product' should not be limited exclusively to the insurance contract's conditions adopted by the management board's resolution. Rather than formalization, it is the repeatability of application of given provisions, which is of more importance. In the light of the IDD provisions, status of the insurance product should be attributed also to the 'templates', clauses and additional provisions which are or may be applicable as a standard (i.e. they are not subject to negotiations) to a particular type of insurance contract and which comprehensively regulate the insurance relationship or the framework in which it can be shaped.[5] This approach though poses the risk of lack of prior identification of the insurance product by the insurance company. This is because the insurance companies predominantly use framework offers (so-called 'insurance programs' or 'dedicated offers') dedicated for customer groups which are not individually negotiable at the level of the insurance contract, and at the same time they are not adopted by the management board's resolution. Bearing in mind the above, it is out of doubt that the said 'insurance program' should be considered the insurance product.

Since the IDD—and national regulations accordingly—provides for the obligation to undertake certain actions with respect to the products, failure to identify the 'template' or 'program' as product may lead to violation of obligations related to the product governance. This, in turn, could be followed by the sanctions imposed by the relevant supervisory authority.

As in the case of 'product', no definition of 'product governance' has been provided by the IDD. It can be though formulated on the basis of the Article 25 of the IDD. The manufacturer is required to have in place a process, which allows to manufacture products and amend them in a conscious manner. Pursuant to the Article 25 the obligations related to product governance are divided into two groups: (i) obligations that should be fulfilled before the product is marketed ('within the process of approval') and (ii) obligations that arise in the course of the product's life. Governance issues are further developed in the Delegated Regulation which specifies that the manufacturers designating a third party to design products on their behalf shall remain fully responsible for compliance with the product approval process (Article 4 sec. 5).[6]

---

[4]Kwieciński (2018), p. 166.

[5]Nawracała (2019), p. 61.

[6]Marano (2019), pp. 69–70.

The first group of obligations includes specification of an identified target market for each product, ensuring that all relevant risks to such identified target market are assessed and that the intended distribution strategy is consistent with the identified target market. In addition, the manufacturer is obliged to take reasonable steps to ensure that the insurance product is distributed to the identified target market. Therefore, the European legislator expects the manufacturer to take specific actions, instead of mere planning.

Delegated Regulation repeats most of the abovementioned obligations and supplements them by introducing the requirement to test the insurance products before bringing them to the market, including scenario analyses where relevant. Such analyzes include assessment of the imaginary state of the future,[7] while their purpose is to simulate functioning of the product under changed operating conditions, i.e. high inflation, economic crisis, etc. It seems though that the scenario analyses should be applied only to the products of sufficiently high time horizon, e.g. to the investment-based insurance products.

After having brought product to the market, it is crucial for the manufacturer to regularly review that product, taking into consideration all the events that could materially affect potential risk for the identified target market. The insurance product may become no longer consistent with the needs of the identified target market due to the external changes, independent from the product itself. Likewise, the distribution strategy adopted at the time of marketing the product may become no longer appropriate. Lack of consistency may result from e.g. changes to the legal regulations (introduction of new legal acts, changes to court jurisprudence), economic or social situation among the target customer group. The frequency of regular reviews is determined by the manufacturer, however, while taking such decision size, complexity, scale of the reviewed products as well as current developments (legal, economic, technological) should be taken into account.

Another obligation of the manufacturer is to make available to distributors all appropriate information on the insurance product and the product approval process, including the identified target market of the insurance product. Although, the importance of providing information on the insurance product is clear and fully justified (distributor should be aware of the product's functioning in order to not mislead the client), certain doubts raise with respect to the amount of information on the product approval process which distributor should receive. Namely, the product approval process is an internal process of the insurance company, thereby it remains confidential. Therefore, information having a direct impact on the distributor (what is the identified target market and distribution strategy), should been distinguished from the information which is irrelevant to the distributor (who is involved in the process of manufacturing the product, what is the division of competencies). It seems safe to say that the mentioned distinction is somehow reflected in Delegated Regulation. Article 8 of Delegated Regulation indicates types of information to be provided to the distributors as well as the purposes of that provision: understanding

[7] Kwieciński (2018), p. 171.

the insurance products by the distributors, comprehending the identified target market, identifying clients for whom the insurance product is not compatible and carrying out distribution activities in accordance with the best interests of the client.

Furthermore, Delegated Regulation sets out certain obligations which should be fulfilled within the product's life cycle by the distributors who are not manufacturers. Pursuant to the Article 10 of Delegated Regulation, distributors should have in place internal procedures to obtain from the manufacturer all appropriate information on the insurance products and to fully comprehend those insurance products. Any specific distribution strategy set up or applied by distributors should not be in contrary to the distribution strategy set up and the target market identified by the manufacturer. Moreover, it should be ensured that the distributors regularly review their product distribution strategy, particularly by verifying whether the insurance products are distributed to the identified target market. In turn, to support product governance carried out by manufacturers, distributors should upon request provide manufacturers with relevant sales information. However, provision of sales information should not be recognized as an obligation to disclose the results of total sales, client lists, etc. By contrast, sales information may include the assessment of consistency between the product and identified target market (i.e. whether the clients being target group are interested in the product) as well as information on what are the target group clients' needs which are not met by the product. Obviously, the purpose of the exchange of information between manufacturer and distributor is to ensure product's consistency and customer protection against misselling.[8]

The product approval process referred to in the Article 25 of IDD should be proportionate and appropriate to the nature of the insurance product, while product oversight and governance measures should be chosen and applied in a proportionate and appropriate manner. There are also products to which the above describe process does not apply. This exemption pertains to the insurance products which consist of the insurance of large risks (Article 25 sec. 4 of IDD).

Notion of large risks has been introduced by Solvency II Directive[9] and it means risks classified under classes 4, 5, 6, 7, 11 and 12 in Part A of Annex I (i.e. railway rolling stock insurance, aircraft insurance, ships insurance, insurance of goods in transit, including merchandise, baggage, and all other goods, aircraft liability insurance and liability for ships insurance respectively). Large risks status is also attributed to credit insurance and suretyship insurance (classes 14 and 15 in Part A of Annex I respectively), where the policyholder is engaged professionally in an industrial or commercial activity or in one of the liberal professions and the risks relate to such activity. Lastly, risks classified under classes 3, 8, 9, 10, 13 and 16 in Part A of Annex I (land vehicles insurance, except for railway rolling stock, fire and

[8]About misseling see also: Ferran (2012), pp. 247–270; Subashini and Velmurugan (2016), pp. 264–267.

[9]Directive 2009/138/EC of the European Parliament and of the Council of 25 November 2009 on the taking-up and pursuit of the business of Insurance and Reinsurance (Solvency II) (Official Journal of the European Union L 335/1).

natural forces insurance, other damage to property, motor vehicle liability insurance, general liability insurance and miscellaneous financial loss insurance respectively), can be considered large risks, in so far as the policyholder exceeds the limits of at least two of the following criteria: (i) a balance-sheet total of EUR 6,2 million; (ii) a net turnover, within the meaning of Fourth Council Directive 78/660/EEC of 25 July 1978 based on Article 54(3)(g) of the Treaty on the annual accounts of certain types of companies (30), of EUR 12,8 million; (iii) an average number of 250 employees during the financial year.

Certainly, introduction of the category of large risks is of great importance for the risks classified under classes 4, 5, 6, 7, 11 and 12 in Part A of Annex I. With respect to these risks, the IDD exempts not only from the requirement to maintain product governance system, but also from the obligation to prepare documents such as IPID.

In turn, as to the most common property insurance (particularly risks classified under classes 8, 9, 10 and 13), large risks definition is understood through the prism of policyholder. This is, the risk can be classified as a large risk only at the moment of conclusion of individual insurance contract as only at this time it is possible to verify whether the policyholder exceeds the limits of at least two of the three abovementioned criteria. It also means that the insurance company is required to adopt the process referred to in the Article 25 of the IDD and Delegated Regulation with respect to these products, unless it identifies target group clients excluding individuals who do not fulfill the above requirement, which seems unlikely. It is also necessary to prepare standardized insurance product information document. Legal doctrine welcomes and justifies the exemption of the insurance companies from the obligations related to product governance in cases where the insurance contract is negotiated, and insurance conditions serve only as a starting point for the dialog between insurance company and policyholder. However, the same arguments cannot be applied to the risks classified under classes 8, 9, 10 and 13. With respect to these risks, regardless the degree of insurance contract individualization, the insurer will not be exempted from the abovementioned obligations due to the fact that it is possible for the insurer to conclude the insurance contract with an individual or entity which do not exceed the limits of at least two criteria referred to in the Article 13 point 27(c) of Solvency II directive. The author claims that it is not reasonable for the IDD to use the term of large risk as a measure to enhance protection of the policyholder[10] (which also reflects the tendency of the protection regime to embrace entities other than consumers[11]). It is customer protection which should be an overreaching aim of the IDD and delegated regulations rather than protection of entities benefiting of their strong position which allows them to negotiate insurance terms and conditions. Besides, it is hard to specify how would a big construction company benefit from receiving standardized insurance product information

[10]Malinowska (2018), p. 28.

[11]The fact that the IDD uses term of 'client' implies providing the 'enhanced protection' to all of the entities, including entrepreneurs. See: Tarasiuk and Wojno (2018), p. 130; Ziemiak and Marszelewski (2017), pp. 100–116.

document where it refers to the insurance contract conditions which where considerably modified within the course of negotiations.

4 Manufacturer

As it was already mentioned, one of the most significant change introduced by the IDD and other related acts is the possibility to consider the insurance intermediaries as product manufacturers. Namely, it is possible where an overall analysis of their activity shows that they have a decision-making role in designing and developing an insurance product for the market. Delegated Regulation provides for the definition of 'a decision-making role'. According to this definition, the insurance intermediary has a decision-making role in particular, where he or she autonomously determines the essential features and main elements of an insurance product, including its coverage, price, costs, risk, target market and compensation and guarantee rights, which are not substantially modified by the insurance company providing coverage for the insurance product. Although, the IDD explicitly provides for the possibility to manufacture insurance product by intermediaries completely on their own, it is a fair question to ask whether a case in which insurance intermediary would act as exclusive manufacturer will occur in practice.

The author argues that it is not possible to manufacture insurance product without the insurance company's contribution. Although, the insurance contract conditions and insurance premium tariff are initially established by broker, involvement of the insurance company is inevitable as insurance contract conditions and insurance premium tariff have to be formally adopted by the insurance company. From client's point of view, it is the insurance company who decides whether or not to provide insurance coverage, insurance contract conditions and other issues related to compensation payment. When considering insurance product manufacturing without any contribution of insurance company, it is fair to pose a question regarding pursuing insurance activity without permission. Conducting insurance business in the territory of EU member states is reserved for strictly defined entities which meet the whole arena of requirements. It is hard to assume that the intention of the European legislator was to extend the scope of entities entitled to pursue insurance activity by the means of product governance regulation. The above arguments are supported by EIOPA's statement 'Technical Advice on possible delegated acts concerning the insurance Distribution Directive'[12] which states that by accepting a given risk, the insurance company covering the risk under the insurance product becomes its manufacturer.

[12]EIOPA, Technical Advice on possible delegated acts concerning the insurance Distribution Directive, https://eiopa.europa.eu/Publications/Consultations/EIOPA%20Technical%20Advice%20on%20the%20IDD.pdf [visited: 31.08.2019].

A situation in which broker creates so-called insurance program for an individual client and specifies in detail scope of insurance coverage will be now be considered. In such case two options can be discussed. In the first option broker adjusts (i.e. modifies, sometimes considerably) insurance contract conditions to an individual client. Here, pursuant to the Article 3 sec. 3 of Delegated Regulation, broker cannot be considered insurance product manufacturer because adaptation of existing insurance products in the context of insurance distribution activities for individual customers is not considered manufacturing. In the second option broker creates a tailor-made insurance contract under which the insurance company provides insurance coverage on the basis of specific arrangements. Similarly to the first option, broker cannot be considered manufacturer as the design of tailor-made contracts at the request of a single customer is not considered manufacturing (Article 3 sec. 3 of Delegated Regulation). Moreover, the second option raises doubts with respect to insurance product itself. As it is hard to identify any target market within the meaning of Article 3 sec. 3 of Regulation 2017/2358, it can be questioned here whether there is an insurance product at all.[13]

It goes without saying that insurance intermediary and insurance company can co-manufacture insurance products, which is confirmed by the Article 3 sec. 4 of Delegated Regulation. This kind of cooperation existed long before the IDD's implementation. So far, it was assumed that although insurance intermediary contributed to product's manufacturing, all the manufacturer's obligations were attributed to the insurance company. In turn, Delegated Regulation provides for the opposite. In according to Delegated Regulation, if both insurance intermediary and insurance company are recognized as manufacturers within the meaning of Article 2 of Delegated Regulation, they should sign a written agreement which specifies their collaboration to comply with the requirements for manufacturers, the procedures through which they should agree on the identification of the target market and their respective roles in the product approval process.

Construction of the legal provision implies that it is an obligation to conclude such agreement (*shall sign a written agreement*) once a decision-making role is attributed to both insurance intermediary and insurance company. This is, both of them determine the essential features and main elements of an insurance product.

Decision-making role of insurance intermediary can be recognized when insurance intermediary presents the insurance company insurance contract conditions which comprehensively regulate rights and obligations of contracting parties, exclusive distribution of certain product and intermediary's right to remuneration for preparing insurance contract conditions (so-called author's commission).[14] Often, it is a distribution strategy applied by the insurance intermediary that allows to recognize him as a co-manufacturer. For instance, offering insurance product via an

[13]Nawracała (2019), p. 65.

[14]Definition of remuneration referred to in Article 2 sec. 1 point 9 of the IDD is very broad. Hence, the author's commission seems to be admissible. See: Ziemiak (2019), p. 37.

online intermediary's platform with an advertising slogan 'insurance product created by broker X in cooperation with insurer Y'.

Regardless the options stemming from the IDD, the analysis of requirements related to the product governance may lead to the following conclusion: insurance intermediaries may not be interested in acting as a product's manufacturer and concluding the abovementioned agreements because of the additional obligations it would impose on them (e.g. obligation to adopt product governance process, obligation to monitor and review product). The insurance companies had product governance processes, allocation of responsibilities and, most importantly, qualified staff long before the entry into force of the IDD. Given the fact that the intermediaries have never been formally recognized as a product manufacturer, it would be challenging for them to establish product governance process in terms of organization and costs. However, banks acting as insurance intermediaries can be considered an exception to the above assumption. It seems that the possibility of implementing product governance systems in those banks is much higher, due to the fact that they already have sufficient human, financial and organizational resources. Furthermore, noteworthy is the fact that, from the bank's perspective, possibility to act as a product manufacturer (or co-manufacturer) allows to mitigate the risks stemming from the regulation on unfair market practices and possible claims raised in relation to copyright infringements when transferring insurance programs copyrights between insurers.[15]

It is a fair question to ask whether the supervisory authority is entitled to impose sanctions if the abovementioned written agreement regarding joint product governance is not signed. When trying to answer this question, first the purpose of signing such agreement should be deciphered. The author claims that the agreement aims at clear allocation of responsibilities and obligations related to the product governance to avoid the situation in which certain obligation remains unallocated. It is believed that precise allocation of responsibilities ensures protection of client's interests and prevents negative competence disputes between intermediary and insurance company. However, if interests and needs of clients are protected, whilst the agreement has not been signed, there are no grounds to impose sanctions. Namely, conclusion of the agreement between intermediary and insurance company is not an end in itself. It is rather a mean or instrument for achieving the purpose of protection of the best interests of client. If the agreement on product's co-manufacturing is not concluded between intermediary and insurance company, it should be presumed that the insurance company acts as a manufacturer and all the related obligations stemming from the IDD and Delegated Regulation are imposed on the insurance company. This approach seems to be confirmed by the insurance practice, soft law (EIOPA's Technical Advice on possible delegated acts concerning the insurance Distribution Directive) and Delegated Regulation which allows insurance intermediaries to act as product's manufacturer. *A contrario*, it can be assumed that insurance companies are naturally considered manufacturers, therefore, there is no

---

[15]Mrozowska-Bartkiewicz and Wnęk (2018), p. 91.

need to stipulate this fact within the legal provisions. Following on from this argument, the insurance company will always act at least as a co-manufacturer.

Delegated Regulation does not limit types of intermediaries which may be recognized as manufacturer or co- manufacturer of insurance product. In practice, the concept of multiple intermediaries occurs both between intermediaries of one type (e.g. agents) and different types (e.g. agent and broker). This allows to reduce costs and to ensure greater distribution efficiency at various stages.[16] Therefore, it should be assumed that any intermediary mentioned within the IDD is allowed to manufacture or co-manufacture insurance product. It is also possible to have insurance product co-manufactured by several intermediaries and insurance company. In such case, the agreement on joint product governance should be multilateral.

In practice, rarely insurance agents purse activities which allow to recognize them as manufacturer due to the fact that they depend on the insurance companies. It is more common for multiagents, or even more for brokers, to act as manufacturer. However, product's co-manufacturing undertaken by broker and insurance company is an issue of different nature.

Problem of the relationship between insurance broker and insurance company has been discussed within different jurisdictions long before the entry into force of the IDD. On the one hand, it was claimed that broker acts exclusively as a representative of policyholder. On the other hand, Austrian, French and German[17] jurisdictions advocated for the so-called theory of double representation which argued that there are cases in which broker represented the interests of both policyholder and insurance company.

Bearing in mind the above, interesting observations are made with respect to Polish insurance practice. Under the previously binding Polish insurance regulation, possibility of cooperation between broker and insurance company was very limited. Among all the possible agreements, legal doctrine recognized broker's commission agreements, legal clauses allowing broker to represent insurer in front of policyholder in a limited scope (e.g. receiving insurance premiums) and framework agreements regarding technicalities of cooperation between broker and insurance company.[18] What is more, all agreements other than broker's commission agreements were subject to many restrictions.[19] Clauses allowing broker to represent insurer were often questioned as some claimed that they indirectly allow broker to perform activities reserved for insurance agents.

Article 24 sec. 1 point 2 of Polish act of 22 May 2003 on insurance intermediation[20] provided for the prohibition of permanent contractual relationship between broker and insurance company. In turn, Article 30 sec. 1 point 2 of the act of

[16]Orlicki (2019), p. 4.

[17]Pokrzywniak (2005), pp. 157–173.

[18]Pokrzywniak (2005), p. 153.

[19]Malinowska (2012), p. 170.

[20]Act of 22 May 2003 on insurance intermediation (Dz.U. 2017, poz. 2486).

15 December 2017 on insurance distribution,[21] which implements the IDD to Polish legal system, not only repeats the abovementioned prohibition, but it also extends it by stipulating that insurance broker is not allowed to maintain any permanent contractual relationship with insurance company, reinsurance company, insurance agent or insurance agent offering ancillary insurance. Given the fact that the above regulations overlap to some extent, legal doctrine established with respect to the Article 24 of no longer binding act on insurance intermediation are still applicable to currently binding regulation. The purpose of the discussed prohibition is to prevent the situation in which broker depends on the insurance company[22] and it has nothing to do with the financial value of such relationship. Rather than the remuneration which broker would receive on the basis of such relationship, it is a permanence of the relationship that is taken into consideration.[23]

Not only does the agreement on joint product governance regulate technical issues regarding broker's remuneration (e.g. broker's commission), but it also implies a community of obligations imposed on broker and insurance company. The agreement should be naturally considered permanent as it regulates product governance, i.e. a process which is spread over time. Further to this, the agreement cannot be recognized as an exemption from prohibition referred to in the Article 30 sec. 6 due to which the prohibition does not apply to insurance contract where insurance broker acts as a policyholder and/or insured and to the agreement concluded between broker and insurance company regarding the method of mutual settlement for brokerage activities in the field of insurance.

The above discussed prohibition is a national instrument and the IDD does not provide for its equivalent. It is worth considering though whether there are any implications for the agreement on joint product governance. Delegated Regulation which refers to this agreement in the Article 3 sec. 4 constitutes a directly applicable legal act. This is, it is binding without implementation. Thus, the problem of incompliance between national and European regulations arises. In such case, the principles developed in the European Court of Justice could be of help. Notably, the principle of the primacy of Community law formulated in case COSTA vs ENEL which states that the transfer of national rights and obligations to the Community legal system entails a permanent limitation of the sovereign rights of the member states which no subsequent, unilateral act incompliant with the Community law cannot call into question.[24]

Regardless the above, it seems that allowing to conclude the agreement on joint product governance, although it would be contrary to the Article 30 sec. 1 point 2 of the act on insurance distribution, is indispensable to achieve regulatory aim of protecting the best interests of the client. The purpose of the agreement on joint product governance is not to establish a permanent relationship between broker and

[21]Act of 15 December 2017 on insurance distribution (Dz.U. 2003, nr 124, poz. 1154).

[22]E. Wieczorek, [in:] Brodecki et al. (2010), p. 1167.

[23]Ziemba and Machulak (2018), p. 202.

[24]Judgment of the Court of 15 July 196, Flaminio Costa v E.N.E.L., Case 6-64.

insurance company, but it is rather to ensure that all the obligations stemming from the product governance are fulfilled.

Some of the polish scholars claim that the status of co-manufacturer can be attributed also to the insurance companies which act permanently as a co-insurer providing insurance coverage for common risks.[25] Although, neither the IDD nor Delegated Regulation refers to cooperation between the insurers, product's co-manufacturing by the insurers should be assumed admissible. Yet, it can be doubted whether the permanent co-insurance agreement includes product's co-manufacturing. Namely, the essence of co-insurance is its accidentalness, i.e. sharing the risk when it is impossible (e.g. due to some reinsurance restrictions) or undesirable (e.g. due to the risk exposition) for the insurance company to provide insurance coverage to the customer on its own. No co-manufacturing of insurance contract conditions (product) exists in case of these kind of co-insurance. Here, the insurance contract is concluded on the basis of the insurance contract conditions of the risk pool leader, which are subject to negotiations. Co-insurers accepts insurance contract conditions offered by the leader for each individual insurance contract.

5 Identification of Target Market

Previously, identification of target market for each insurance product has been treated as a pure marketing and sale task ensuring proper communication and product's targeting, however, after the IDD's implementation, identification of target market becomes a legal obligation.

According to Delegated Regulation, identification of target market by the manufacturer should be understood as description of a group of clients who share a number of features at the general level in order to adjust product's features to the needs, features and purposes of this group. Thus, identification of target market and assessment of client's demands and needs are two different things and therefore should be distinguished.

Target market should be identified before marketing the product, i.e. at the process of product's design. Not only should the insurer firmly identify target market for a given product, but he should also verify the abstract needs, features and purposes of the group which he considers target market.

Although, Delegated Regulation provides some guidelines on how to identify target market, the instructions are rather of general nature. Delegated Regulation allows to adopt different approaches by stipulating that the level of detail of identified target market and criteria used to identify it should be '*relevant*' and enable to decide which customers belong to identified target market. With respect to simple and more common products, target market should be identified more

[25] Kwieciński (2018), p. 167. The author did not find many similar opinions in non-Polish literature. Hence, it may be assumed the view is specific for Polish insurance market.

precisely, taking into consideration the increased risk of damage suffered by the client. Assessment of the target market should take into account the amount of information available to the target group clients and their financial education background.

Following these quite general guidelines, product's manufacturer should decide which approach to take to identify target market—whether it would be more detailed approach referring to the features and needs of given group or general approach where target market is identified at relatively high level without precising the needs.

When considering identification of target market, it should be borne in mind that target market should be identified not only for consumers products but also for products which are offered to the entrepreneurs (*'for each product'*). It can be though challenging for the manufacturers. The insurance products which are mass offered, such as motor vehicle insurance, house insurance or life insurance, are analyzed in detail and distribution strategies are focused on identified target groups (young drivers, single-family houses owners, single persons up to 35 years old). On the other hand, in case of insurance products offered to the entrepreneurs, target groups are usually identified at high level. Clearly, the insurance company gives preference to certain businesses based on the analysis of their loss history and offers them preferential insurance premiums. However, the author claims that this kind of 'risk appetite' related to certain product or class of insurance does not correspond with target group. The primary purpose of identification of target group is to adjust features of the product to the needs, features and objectives of the group of clients, instead of the needs of insurance company. It can be depicted by the following example. Considering entrepreneur's property insurance, it is not attractive for the insurance company to provide the insurance coverage to a company producing upholstered furniture. It does not mean though the said company is excluded from the target group. Unless production of upholstered furniture is directly excluded in the insurance contract conditions, the needs and objectives of that company with respect to the protection in the event of damage to a third party arising from business operations and property possession are taken into consideration. It shows that the company producing upholstered furniture will constitute target market for entrepreneur's property insurance, although, it is not necessarily interesting for the insurance company ('risk appetite'). Lack of that interest will be reflected in the insurance premium.

Identification of target market for entrepreneurs' insurance is often underestimated. It is mostly because of the fact that entrepreneurs' insurance is exempted from the obligations resulting from product governance as they fall into the category of 'large risks'.

However, as it was mentioned in the paragraph pertaining to definitional problems, the most popular property insurance which are interesting for the entrepreneurs (8, 9, 13) are recognized as large risks only at the moment when the individual insurance contract is concluded. Therefore, the majority of entrepreneurs' insurance is subject to all the obligations stemming from product governance. Identification of target group of entrepreneurs' insurance at high level (e.g. entities conducting business activity in Poland possessing machines up to a certain value) allows to mitigate the risk of distributing insurance product beyond target market.

Each insurance product, even the one for which target market has been precisely identified, may be distributed to the client which does not belong to its target group. Neither the IDD nor Delegated Regulation introduces prohibition of insurance distribution beyond target market. Moreover, recital 9 of Delegated Regulation specifies conditions which have to be met in order to distribute beyond target market. Individual assessment of the demands and needs of the customers should be made to verify whether the product correspond those customers. It may turn out that specific features of the client who does not belong to target market justify the conclusion that the analyzed product corresponds to his demands and needs.[26] Moreover, it should be borne in mind that it is possible to have insurance products which are appropriate for the clients outside target market and do not constitute a separate insurance product at the same time. For instance, if summer houses do not belong to target market of home insurance because they are excluded from the insurance coverage under the home insurance conditions, it is still possible to satisfy the demands and needs of a specific client by deleting the said exclusion from the home insurance conditions (summer house insurance).

Although, insurance distribution beyond target market in individual cases (after having analyzed insurance product and client's features and needs) does not seem to be risky, mass insurance distribution beyond target market should be a matter of serious concern to the manufacturer. According to IOPA's statement,[27] in such case, the manufacturer should assess the possible negative impact on the client using the product. Once such impact is identified, the manufacturer take action in order to ease the situation and prevent further occurrence of the harmful event.[28] When trying to ease the situation, the manufacturer can e.g. provide insurance protection to those clients on the basis of specific arrangements. In turn, preventing further occurrence of the harmful event may consists in introducing a system lock preventing intermediary from distributing outside the target market, and if the problem results from the operation of distributor, cooperation with such a distributor should be put to an end, at least in the scope of this product. Also, the discussed situation raises doubts as to the manufacturer's responsibility for distributor's actions. If distributor is chosen—according to the Preparatory Guidelines—with due caution and he was provided with all the required information on the product, its specifics, target market and planned distribution strategy, the author claims that no additional responsibility for

[26] Noussia and Siri (2019), pp. 53–54.

[27] EIOPA, Answers to (EU) 2017-2358 product oversight and governance requirements for insurance, https://eiopa.europa.eu/Publications/Guidelines/Answrs%20to%20Questions%20on%20%28EU%29%202017-2358%20about%20product%20oversight%20and%20governance.xlsb [visited: 31.08.2019].

[28] Marano (2019), p. 81.

distributor's action can be attributed to the manufacturer, particularly when the distributor enjoys the status of independent intermediary.[29]

It is also recommended, especially with respect to the investment-based insurance products, to identify group of clients for which a given insurance product is not appropriate as it does not correspond with their needs, features and objectives. Identification of the so-called 'anti-target group' can improve quality of distribution to target market by establishing a barrier for access to the product for the clients defined as anti-target group.[30] For instance, considering life insurance, insurance contract conditions may exclude persons aged 60 and more from the possibility of being provided with the insurance coverage. Simultaneously, a relevant automatic blockade could be implemented to the sale IT system in order to prevent further proceeding once the intermediary inserts birth date on the basis of which IT system recognizes client's age as 60 or more.

Obligation to identify target market and other obligations stemming from product governance (particularly obligation to prepare insurance product information document) are questioned with respect to mandatory insurance. In some jurisdictions, e.g. in Poland, the law requires certain objects to be insured as well as it precisely specifies scope of the insurance, its conditions, the guarantee sum and lists of exclusions. Insurance premium tariffs is the only element which can be designed here by the insurance company. However, neither the IDD nor the national regulation (Polish) provides for any legal grounds for the possibility to exclude the insurance company from the obligations stemming from product governance. Although, identification of target market should not be difficult (the author proposes to assume that target market consists of the persons who are obliged to insure), preparation of standardized insurance product information document may be challenging. Namely, the law regulating mandatory insurance does not specifies all the issues which are required by the IPID regulation.[31] Thus, there is a risk that some issues would be incompliant with intention of the legislator.

6 Impact of the IDD on Insurance Market's Participants

The IDD constitutes the first legal act which addresses product governance issues. So far, product governance was mentioned in some soft law acts (European and national recommendations), however, it was mostly left to the insurance companies.

---

[29]Financial Conduct Authority, *Insurance Distribution Directive implementation – Feedback to CP17/23 and near-final rules,* https://www.fca.org.uk/publication/policy/ps17-27.pdf, p. 24 [visited: 31.08.2019].

[30]M. Roguski, [in:] Ziemba and Machulak (2018), p. 111.

[31]Commission Implementing Regulation (EU) 2017/1469 of 11 August 2017 laying down a standardized presentation format for the insurance product information document (Official Journal of the European Union L 209/19).

In consequence, product policies of insurance companies were very different. Some of them consisted of an extensive process of launching a new product, including scenarios related to profitability and customers impact, while others focused on determining the potential profit from launching a specific product.

Establishing certain rules at the statutory level, e.g. obligations stemming from product governance, identification of target market, preparation of product's documentation facilitating comparison between the products or assessment of the client's demands and needs, allows national supervision authorities to carry out inspections and impose relevant sanctions. The level of requirements for product manufacturers and distributors initiated by the IDD is very high. Drawing on the findings of the analysis made by Deloitte in the member states of resilient and developed insurance markets, it results that similar requirements exist only in Germany and Great Britain. Many other countries provide for less strict regulations, while in some jurisdictions there were no regulation of product governance (Spain and France).[32]

Adjustment of the insurance business to the new product governance requirements is considered very expensive due to the following reasons: the need to create product documentation for each product (identification of target market, standardized insurance product information document, anti-target group), changes to the internal processes (product approval process), implementation of permanent product's supervision (product monitoring), selection and controlling of distribution strategy. Moreover, the IDD extends the scope of the entities responsible for product governance by adding insurance intermediaries. As it was mentioned in the paragraph addressing product manufacturer issue, it may be impossible for the intermediaries to meet the above requirements due to the costs, lack of organizational resources and lack of experience. It may further result in intermediaries resigning from being product manufacturer (at least formally) and giving way to insurance companies.

Regardless the industry's criticism, the European legislator did not differentiate obligations stemming from product governance. Clearly, the measures provided for in the IDD aim at harmonizing and improving the level of customer protection to eventually achieve the highest standard of protection regardless of the distribution channel. Undoubtedly, what stands behind these goals is also the desire to rebuild customer confidence in insurance markets.[33]

Nevertheless, a broad approach to the obligations which does not take into consideration the individual risk-taking seems to be contrary to the IDD's objectives.[34] Although the preamble to the IDD mentions principle of proportionality and rationality with respect to the interpretation of the legal provisions, the majority of

---

[32]Deloitte, *Insurance Distribution Directive. 2018: a challenging year for the European insurance sector*, https://www2.deloitte.com/content/dam/Deloitte/lu/Documents/financial-services/Insurance/lu-insurance-distribution-directive-2018-challenging-year-european-insurance-sector-012018.pdf, p. 24 [visited: 31.08.2019].

[33]Więcko-Tułowiecka (2018), p. 78.

[34]Malinowska (2017), p. 15.

member states decided to 'copy-paste' the IDD's provisions to their national legal systems.

In consequence, it can be assumed that the insurance intermediaries will not be pursuing activities which may put them in a position of product manufacturer in order to avoid adjusting their business to the whole set of requirements introduced by the IDD and Delegated Regulation. In turn, the insurance companies will probably focus on main and standard products and will be reluctant to distribute insurance products covering new risks. Each time, creation of new product would mean extreme work consumption at the beginning, regardless of the final results.

7 Conclusions

Upgrading product governance to the statutory level constitutes part of the global trend which emerged as a result of the loss of trust in financial markets after the crisis of 2008.[35] The activity of national legislators is driven by the doubts that arose over markets' resiliency and their ability to meet public interest objectives.[36] However, it should be underlined that excessive regulation can easily result in overregulation. This, in turn, may jeopardize development of markets, market participants activity and natural self-regulation. It can also lead to 'automation' in execution of obligation towards clients (provision of documents, signing forms) which would leave no room for a real assessment of client's needs.

The IDD and implementing acts (particularly Delegated Regulation) are of great importance for the product governance as they changed it into a legal obligation of insurance distributors. It is also necessary to underline the role of transparency (i.e. transparency of products, processes and entities) as a guaranty of protection of client's best interests.[37] So far, processes related to the product's life cycle were subject to the internal arrangements of the insurance company which could result in unequal protection standards offered to the customers.

Nonetheless, the discussed regulation creates a number of problems which have been addresses in this chapter. The European legislator does not seem to pay enough attention to the use of terminology created for the IDD's purposes (client, product, product governance) which makes it difficult to identify objective and subjective scope of the imposed obligations. Furthermore, the author draws the attention to the fact that the differences between the distributors[38] (insurance company vs broker) and types of products (house insurance for customers vs specific property insurance for entrepreneurs) have not been taken into account which resulted in the same regulation governing different situations.

---

[35]See also: Marano (2017), pp. 5–29.

[36]Monkiewicz (2014), p. 86.

[37]Malinowska (2016), p. 90.

[38]Maesschalck (2017), pp. 59–77.

When assessing satisfaction of the IDD implementation, the *ratio* of regulation, i.e. client's best interest, should be borne in mind. Undoubtedly, restrictive requirements related to the product governance are likely to enhance protection of client's best interest. An attention should be now drawn to their proportional application in different situations, taking into account type of the product and distributor. Notably, it is worth to give a second thought to the concept of the distributor acting as a manufacturer and co-manufacturer of the product, especially with respect to the obligations that this role entails. Finally, it is necessary to modify—formally or through soft law instruments—a subjective exemption. This is, the status of 'large risk' which exempts from the product governance obligations should be replaced with a different criterium.

As it was mentioned in the introduction to this chapter, it is still too early to assess the efficiency of the IDD or to formulate any firm conclusions. Nevertheless, it is clear that there are fields in which the IDD's provisions should be implemented wisely and not literally, while the proper interpretation of the implementation should be left to the academia.

References

Brodecki Z, Serwach M, Glicz M (2010) Prawo ubezpieczeń gospodarczych. Komentarz. Tom I. Komentarz do przepisów prawnych o funkcjonowaniu rynku ubezpieczeń. Wolters Kluwer, Warszawa

Ferran E (2012) Regulatory lessons from the payment protection insurance mis-selling scandal in the UK. Eur Bus Org Law Rev 13(2):247–270

Kwieciński T (2018) Approval of insurance product. In: Pokrzywniak J (ed) Nowe zasady dystrybucji ubezpieczeń. Wolters Kluwer Polska, Warsaw

Maesschalck N (2017) The Insurance Distribution Directive: what does it change for intermediaries and for others? In: Marano P, Siri M (eds) Insurance regulation in the European Union. Solvency II and Beyond. Palgrave Macmillan

Malinowska K (2012) Broker and insurance company. In: Serwach M (ed) Broker w świetle prawa i praktyki ubezpieczeniowej. Wydawnictwo Uniwersytetu Łódzkiego, Łódź

Malinowska K (2016) Insurance transparency and protection regime under the Insurance Distribution Directive. Wiadomości Ubezpieczeniowe, No. 4

Malinowska K (2017) Concept of insurance product management in meaning of the Insurance Distribution Directive and Implementing Regulations. Wiadomości Ubezpieczeniowe, No. 1

Malinowska K (2018) Notion of 'Large Risks' – Legal Considerations in the Context of Polish and European Law. Prawo Asekuracyjne, No. 4

Marano P (2017) Sources and tools of the insurance regulation in the European Union. In: Marano P, Siri M (eds) Insurance regulation in the European Union. Solvency II and Beyond. Palgrave Macmillan

Marano P (2019) The product oversight and governance: standards and liabilities. In: Marano P, Rokas I (eds) Distribution of insurance-based investment products. The EU regulation and the liabilities. Springer, Cham

Monkiewicz J (2014) Insurance regulations and supervision. In search of a new paradigm. In: Serwach M (ed) Rynek ubezpieczeniowy – nadregulacja czy niedoregulowanie? Wydawnictwo Uniwersytetu Łódzkiego, Łódź

Mrozowska-Bartkiewicz B, Wnęk A (2018) Concept of insurance product manufacturer in meaning of insurance distribution act. In: Malinowska K, Tarasiuk A (eds) Insurance challenges of Anno Domini, Poltext sp. z o.o., Warsaw

Nawracała J (2019) Standardised insurance product information document. Possible interpretation in the context of "insurance product" term. Wiadomości Ubezpieczeniowe, No. 2

Noussia K, Siri M (2019) The legal regime and the relevant standards. In: Marano P, Rokas I (eds) Distribution of insurance-based investment products. The EU regulation and the liabilities. Springer, Cham

Orlicki M (2019) Division of duties among distributors during the process of concluding an insurance contract. Documenting the fulfillment of statutory obligations related to insurance distribution. Wiadomości Ubezpieczeniowe, No. 2

Pokrzywniak J (2005) Broker ubezpieczeniowy – ubezpieczający – ubezpieczyciel. Stosunki zobowiązaniowe, Oficyna Wydawnicza Branta, Bydgoszcz-Poznań

Schaeken Willemaers G (2014) Client protection on European financial markets – from inform your client to know your product and beyond: an assessment of the PRIIPs Regulation, MiFID II/MiFIR and IMD 2. Revue Trimestrielle de Droit Financier, No. 4

Subashini S, Velmurugan R (2016) Mis selling – A bane on growth of life insurance. International Journal of Scientific Engineering and Technology, No.5

Tarasiuk A, Wojno B (2018) Group insurance distribution – selected comments on the Insurance Distribution Directive and its transposition into polish law. In: Malinowska K, Tarasiuk A (eds) Insurance challenges of Anno Domini 2018. Poltext sp. z o.o., Warsaw

Więcko-Tułowiecka M (2018) EIOPA's preparatory guidelines on product oversight and governance arrangements by insurance undertakings and insurance distributors in the context of polish recommendations on product management. Prawo Asekuracyjne, No. 3

Ziemba J, Machulak P (2018) Ustawa o dystrybucji ubezpieczeń. Komentarz, C.H. Beck, Warsaw

Ziemiak M (2019) Remuneration of insurance intermediary in the context of insurance distribution act. Selected issues. Wiadomości Ubezpieczeniowe, No. 2

Ziemiak M, Marszelewski M (2017) Selected remarks on policyholders protection in the draft of Polish act on insurance distribution. Rozprawy Ubezpieczeniowe, No. 3

Legislative Instruments

Directive (EU) 2016/97 of the European Parliament and of the Council of 20 January 2016 on insurance distribution (Official Journal of the European Union L 26/19)

Directive 2009/138/EC of the European Parliament and of the Council of 25 November 2009 on the taking-up and pursuit of the business of Insurance and Reinsurance (Solvency II) (Official Journal of the European Union L 335/1)

Commission Delegated Regulation (EU) 2017/2358 of 21 September 2017 supplementing Directive (EU) 2016/97 of the European Parliament and of the Council with regard to product oversight and governance requirements for insurance undertakings and insurance distributors (Official Journal of the European Union I L 341/1)

Commission Implementing Regulation (EU) 2017/1469 of 11 August 2017 laying down a standardized presentation format for the insurance product information document (Official Journal of the European Union L 209/19)

Act of 22 May 2003 on insurance intermediation (Dz.U. 2017, poz. 2486)

Act of 15 December 2017 on insurance distribution (Dz.U. 2003, nr 124, poz. 1154)

Documents

Deloitte, *Insurance Distribution Directive. 2018: a challenging year for the European insurance sector*, https://www2.deloitte.com/content/dam/Deloitte/lu/Documents/financial-services/Insurance/lu-insurance-distribution-directive-2018-challenging-year-european-insurance-sector-012018.pdf, p. 24 [visited: 31.08.2019]

EIOPA, Answers to (EU) 2017-2358 product oversight and governance requirements for insurance, https://eiopa.europa.eu/Publications/Guidelines/Answrs%20to%20Questions%20on%20%28EU%29%202017-2358%20about%20product%20oversight%20and%20governance.xlsb [visited: 31.08.2019]

EIOPA, Technical Advice on possible delegated acts concerning the insurance Distribution Directive., https://eiopa.europa.eu/Publications/Consultations/EIOPA%20Technical%20Advice%20on%20the%20IDD.pdf [visited: 31.08.2019]

Financial Conduct Authority, *Insurance Distribution Directive implementation – Feedback to CP17/23 and near-final rules*, https://www.fca.org.uk/publication/policy/ps17-27.pdf, p. 24 [visited: 31.08.2019]

Part IV
An Empirical Analysis of the Standardised Pre-Contractual Information Document

The Reality of the Promised Increase in Customer Protection Under the Insurance Distribution Directive

Insurers' Pre-contractual Obligations Under Article 20 of the IDD: IPIDs

Christian Bo Kolding-Krøger, Regitze Aalykke Hansen, and Amelie Brofeldt

1 Introduction

1.1 Hypothesis and Methodology

The Insurance Mediation Directive[1] ("**IMD**") was revised and replaced by the Insurance Distribution Directive[2] ("**IDD**") in 2018. One of the objectives of the revision was to increase the protection of policyholders ('customers') by, *inter alia*, focusing on customer protection.[3] In order to meet that objective, Article 20 provides rules on the conduct of business that insurance distributers ('insurers') must comply with before entering into an insurance contract with a customer when advice is not given to such customer, including the obligation for an insurer to enable a customer to make an informed decision.

This chapter explores whether Article 20 of the IDD actually makes it easier for customers to compare various insurance products in the pre-contractual phase, and whether, in reality, insurers are able to meet the objectives set out in the IDD based on the rules set out in the IDD and the Implementing Regulation.

[1]Directive 2002/92/EC of the European Parliament and of the Council of 9 December 2002 on insurance mediation. The Directive was implemented into Danish law by the previous Danish Insurance Mediation Act (Consolidated Act no 1065 of 22 August 2013 on Insurance Mediation as amended).

[2]Directive (EU) 2016/97 of the European Parliament and of the Council of 20 January 2016 on insurance distribution (recast).

[3]Proposal for a Directive of the European Parliament and of the Council on Insurance Mediation (recast), COM/2012/0360 final - 2012/0175 (COD), section 1.1.

C. B. Kolding-Krøger (✉) · R. A. Hansen · A. Brofeldt
Poul Schmith, Copenhagen, Denmark
e-mail: cbk@poulschmith.com; reha@poulschmith.com; ambr@poulschmith.com

P. Marano, K. Noussia (eds.), *Insurance Distribution Directive*, AIDA Europe Research Series on Insurance Law and Regulation 3,
https://doi.org/10.1007/978-3-030-52738-9_16

The authors' hypothesis is that the promised increase in customer protection by introducing Insurance Product Information Documents ("**IPID**") under the IDD, has not actually materialised. Rather, it has the potential to leave both customers and insurers confused.

Methodologically, this chapter will analyse different IPIDs: two relating to compulsory insurance products (Workers' Compensation Insurance and Third-Party Motor Liability Insurance) and one relating to a non-compulsory insurance product (Contents Insurance).

The analysis will cover IPIDs and underlying insurance terms for insurance products promulgated by at least five different insurers. The geographical scope of the chapter is restricted to Denmark. However, on the assumption that the IDD has been implemented by insurers on the Danish market in the same way as those on the wider European market, the analysis and conclusions reached are applicable across other European jurisdictions.

As the analysis is dependent on there being both an IPID and underlying insurance terms publicly available for each of the insurance products, the analysis will include five insurers who (1) distributes the analysed insurance product, and (2) has both the IPID and underlying insurance terms for this product available online. Consequently, the analysis will not include IPIDs from the same five insurers for each of the three insurance products. In total eight insurers are included.

It is the authors opinion that the eight chosen insurers represent a relevant picture of the Danish insurance market which is dominated by larger players and with smaller—often regional—alternatives. Even though all but one of the included insurers are among the 20 largest insurers in Denmark when looking at gross premium they cannot all be considered big companies. Thus, the eight insurers in the analysis includes one large Danish insurer that also does business in other Scandinavian countries; one large Danish insurer that is a part of a worldwide insurance group; and one large Scandinavian insurer with physical presence in Denmark and a large market share in both its home country and Denmark. Also, it includes two large Danish insurers that to the authors' knowledge only does business in Denmark and three mid-sized to small Danish insurers that also only does business in Denmark.

The authors did not make any findings related to the size or market share of the insurers, nor was the IPIDs from the foreign insurer or from the insurer that is a member of a worldwide group notably different from the IPIDs of the other included insurers.

All the insurers whose IPIDs and underlying terms of cover have been examined are hereinafter referred to, respectively, as A–H.

Although more insurance companies, jurisdictions and insurance products might have been included in a greater examination, the results of the in-depth examination of the chosen IPIDs, coupled with a high-level examination of other products from other insurers, demonstrates a consistent overall trend amongst all IPIDs. The authors are confident that their in-depth examination of the chosen IPIDs is reflective of the wider market and that the analysis and conclusions reached are applicable across other European jurisdictions.

The authors' analysis has also revealed that IPIDs and insurance terms—especially for commercial insurance products—are not always publicly available, or indeed available at all other than by virtue of a customer directly approaching an insurer to enquire about purchasing cover. As underlying insurance terms are necessary in order to analyse whether IPIDs actually give a fair presentation of the insurance cover, which presentation can facilitate customer comparisons of different insurance products, the authors have chosen only to include products where both the IPIDs and underlying insurance terms were publicly available.

The authors also wish to note a wider issue regarding the effectiveness of IPIDs providing customers with an effective means for comparing insurance products in the pre-contractual phase. The simple point is that, to a large extent, IPIDs are not made available to a customer prior to such customer actually concluding a written or oral contract with an insurer.

The analysis of each insurance product will, as a starting point, follow the structure of the IPID by utilising the relevant individual headings, cf. the Implementing Regulation, Article 6(1)(a)–(j). In the interests of brevity and in order to facilitate comprehension, the examination will not include a complete reproduction of the relevant IPIDs. Instead, it will focus on two points: Those where insurers have adopted a completely uniform approach in their IPIDs; and those where there are discrepancies between the insurers' completion of the different sections under the headlines. Accordingly, it is the points where there is either significant uniformity or discrepancy between IPIDs which provide the best launch-pad from which to discuss whether IPIDs actually contribute to give the customer a useful basis for comparing insurance products.

Having analysed the selected IPIDs, the authors examine the challenges that tend to be presented by the same and explore how such challenges may be resolved.

1.2 Structure

Section 1 sets out a short introduction to the problem analysed in this chapter and the hypothesis, methodology, and structure adopted in carrying out such analysis.

Section 2 sets out the legal landscape for the distribution of insurance for policyholders in the EU after the introduction of the IDD.

Section 3 sets out to prove the hypothesis that the introduction of IPIDs, which was designed to give customers a basis for making informed decisions, has not, in fact, resulted in increased customer protection. The hypothesis will be tested by an examination of selected IPIDs for Third Party Motor Liability Insurance (compulsory in Denmark), Workers' Compensation Insurance (compulsory in Denmark), and Contents Insurance (not compulsory in Denmark).

Finally, Sect. 4 sets out the authors' conclusion regarding whether the rules regarding IPIDs mandated in IDD have, in fact, resulted in increased customer protection. In particular, such conclusion will address the issue of whether, in reality, insurers are able to meet the objective of increasing customer protection based on the assumptions set by the IDD and the Implementing Regulation.

2 Introduction to Customer Protection Under the IDD

Before the commencement of the IDD, the sale of insurance products was regulated by the IMD. As the IMD only concerned insurance agents and brokers, it did not contain rules on the sale of insurance products directly from the insurers to customers, cf. Article 1 of the IMD.

The IMD was revised and replaced by the IDD, which entered into force on 22 February 2016. Originally, the IDD should have been implemented by Member States on 23 February 2018, but the implementation date was, ultimately, delayed until 1 July 2018, with the date of application being 1 October 2018, from which date the IMD was repealed.[4]

It appears, from the proposal for the IDD, that the objective of the revision to the IMD was designed to ensure consistency of terms between all participants involved in the sale of insurance products and to increase customer protection. In the proposal, the general objectives were described as being ensuring a level playing field, protection of customers and market integration.[5]

From the wording of recital 6 it is apparent that, as regards customer protection, the objective of the IDD is to ensure the same level of protection for customer irrespective of a particular customer's identity and irrespective of how such a customer purchases an insurance product (in this regard see also Recital 8).[6]

The rules on conduct of business can be found in Chapter V of the IDD. The general principle underpinning such rules is found in Article 17(1), which provides that insurance distributors must always act honestly, fairly and professionally in accordance with the best interests of their customers.[7]

In order to satisfy this principle, the following articles lay down insurance distributors' obligations prior to concluding any contracts with customers.

[4]See Article 1 of Directive (EU) 2018/411 of the European Parliament and of the Council of 14 March 2018 amending Directive (EU) 2016/97 as regards the date of application of the Member States' transposition measures.

[5]Proposal for a Directive of the European Parliament and of the Council on Insurance Mediation (recast), COM/2012/0360 final - 2012/0175 (COD), section 1.1.

[6](6) Consumers should benefit from the same level of protection despite the differences between distribution channels. In order to guarantee that the same level of protection applies and that the consumer can benefit from comparable standards, in particular in the area of the disclosure of information, a level playing field between distributors is essential. (Recital 6 of the IDD).

[7]1. Member States shall ensure that, when carrying out insurance distribution, insurance distributors always act honestly, fairly and professionally in accordance with the best interests of their customers. (Article 17(1) of the IDD).

Articles 18 and 19 contain the general information that insurers and insurance intermediaries must give their customers before concluding an insurance contract. Article 20(1) then stipulates that:

> Prior to the conclusion of an insurance contract, the insurance distributor shall specify, on the basis of information obtained from the customer, the demands and the needs of that customer and shall provide the customer with objective information about the insurance product in a comprehensible form to allow that customer to make an informed decision.
>
> Any contract proposed shall be consistent with the customer's insurance demands and needs.

Thus, insurance distributors are required to enable the customer to make an informed decision by giving objective and comprehensible information about the insurance product before they can be considered to have met the objective of Article 17(1) and therefore can be said to have acted in accordance with the customer's best interest.[8]

In the following section, the authors analyse whether the rules on IPIDs actually result in increased customer protection, and whether insurers are, in fact, able to comply with these rules in practice.

3 Insurance Product Information Documents (IPIDs)

3.1 The Rules on IPIDs

Article 20(4) of the IDD provides that prior to the conclusion of a contract, the insurance distributor in question must provide the relevant information about the insurance product it is selling in a form comprehensible to a customer in order to allow the customer to make an informed decision, whilst also taking into account the

[8]The benefits for insurance customers and society at large afforded by introducing such advice standards, are set out in the Commission Staff Working Document (Commission Staff Working Document Executive Summary of the Impact Assessment accompanying the document Proposal for a Directive of the European Parliament and of the Council on Insurance Mediation, SWD/2012/0192 final, section 7.1.):

> By introducing improved and harmonised advice standards, consumers will gain benefits through an improved comparability of offers, including across different distribution channels. This is likely to lead to an improved understanding by consumers of the services and products on offer. As a result, consumers will be inclined to compare offers and shop around for products and deals better suited to their needs. This reduces the cost/price paid by the consumer.
>
> The consumer needs to buy insurance policies which fit his needs and financial situation. Otherwise, there is a high risk of an early withdrawal on the unsuitable policy and consumer dissatisfaction.
>
> [...] The benefits to consumers and society as a whole from the introduction of high and harmonised advice standards come through a reduction in early withdrawals (reduction in defaults).

complexity of the insurance product and the particular type of customer. Further, Article 20(5), that the information referred to in paragraph 4 have to be provided by way of a standardised insurance product information document.[9]

Article 20(7) states that the product information document must meet certain formal requirements, including that the words '*standardised insurance product information document'* (IPID) must appear on the face of the document. Further, Article 20(8) specifies the information that the document must contain. The product information documents, or IPIDs, must be drawn up by the manufacturer of the non-life insurance product, cf. Article 20(6). In short, the point is that all customers must be provided with an IPID produced by the manufacturer, irrespective of who is actually distributing the particular insurance product.

The rules on IPIDs are a new feature of the IDD regime as compared to that under the IMD. Indeed, the rules were not actually included in the first proposal for the IDD and such early draft provided only that the information in question *could* be given in standardised format.[10] It was only in a proposed amendment that the current Article 20(5) was introduced.[11]

Only in the supplementary report by the Committee on Economic and Monetary Affairs did the document get its full name and the European Insurance and Occupational Pensions Authority ("EIOPA") was authorised to draft implementing technical standards regarding a standardised presentation format.[12]

The objective of an IPID and the standard by which its effectiveness must be judged is to make the customer able to make an informed decision about insurance products by giving comparable standardised information.[13]

---

[9]In relation to the distribution of non-life insurance products as listed in Annex I to Directive 2009/138/EC, the information referred to in paragraph 4 of this Article shall be provided by way of a standardised insurance product information document on paper or on another durable medium. (Article 20(5) of the IDD).

[10]Proposal for a Directive of the European Parliament and of the Council on Insurance Mediation (recast), COM/2012/0360 final - 2012/0175 (COD), Article 25(4). The proposal was given as recital 4a and Article 18(4) in the Opinion of the Internal Market and Consumer Protection.

[11]In the amended proposal, the following was written in Article 18(4) about the duty of information:

> [. . .] It shall be provided in a standardised information sheet by way of a product information document (PID) in plain language [. . .] (see Opinion of the Internal Market and Consumer Protection (30.4.2013) on the proposal for a directive of the European Parliament and of the Council on insurance mediation (recast) (COM(2012)0360 – C7-0180/2012 – 2012/0175 (COD)), A7-0085/2014.).

[12]Supplementary Report of the Committee on Economic and Monetary Affairs on the proposal for a directive of the European Parliament and of the Council on insurance mediation (recast) (COM (2012)0360 – C7-0180/2012 – 2012/0175(COD)), A8-0315/2015.

[13]See Recital 48 of the IDD which describes the objective of the IPID as follows:

> Prior to the conclusion of a contract, including in the case of non-advised sales, the customer should be given the relevant information about the insurance product to allow the customer to make an informed decision. An insurance product information document should provide standardised information about non-life insurance products.

3.2 EIOPA's Work on the Standardised Presentation Format

EIOPA was given the task of drafting implementing technical standards regarding the standardised presentation format of the IPID which was manded by Article 20 (9) of the IDD.

As part of the development of this draft, EIOPA carried out consumer testing and consulted national authorities. The result of this work was the adoption of the Implementing Regulation for the IDD that contains the rules on the standardised presentation format for IPIDs.[14]

EIOPA's draft provides that the IPIDs'

> [...] objective is to ensure that the customer has the relevant information about a non-life insurance product to allow him to easily compare between different product offers and to make an informed decision about whether or not to purchase the product.[15]

This objective was reiterated in Recital 1 of the Implementing Regulation (as read with Recital 3).

The Implementing Regulation contains a detailed description of the requirements pertaining to the format of the IPID, including its length, headings and icons. The Annex to the Implementing Regulation contains a standardised format which meets the requirements.

However, the Regulation does not contain any rules on or guidelines for the substantive contents of the document. It appears from Recital 2 that Article 20(8) of the IDD stipulates the information that the document must contain. However, Article 20(8) only contains contents which (more or less) correspond to the headings in EIOPA's standardised format. Apart from this, no other rules on completion of the IPIDs have been laid down (whether in the Regulation or otherwise).

EIOPA's draft implementing technical standards provide that IPIDs are supplementary to the underlying insurance policy terms and conditions, and that any tailoring of a product to a particular customer must be achieved through modification of the underlying policy terms and conditions, and not through the IPID.[16] Accordingly, it should, in theory, be possible to draft the IPIDs very generally and without including any add-ons or optional cover.

In this regard, see also Recital 16, which provides that:

> This Directive should ensure that the same level of consumer protection applies and that all consumers can benefit from comparable standards. [...].

[14]Commission Implementing Regulation (EU) 2017/1469 of 11 August 2017 laying down a standardised presentation format for the insurance product information document.

[15]Draft Implementing Technical Standards concerning a standardised presentation format for the Insurance Product Information Document of the Insurance Distribution Directive of 7 February 2017, EIOPA-17/056, page 3, section 1.

[16]Draft Implementing Technical Standards concerning a standardised presentation format for the Insurance Product Information Document of the Insurance Distribution Directive of 7 February 2017, EIOPA-17/056, page 4, section 6.

In response to EIOPA's consultation paper on the draft implementing technical standards, several trade organisations commented on the balance between, on the one hand enabling the customer to make an informed decision, and on the other giving insurance manufacturers the flexibility to include the relevant information on the specific insurance product.[17]

Moreover, doubts were raised in EIOPA's consultations about whether EIOPA's proposed presentation format would meet the objective of ensuring customers were able to make an informed decision. For example, Eurofinas said that it was important to use a template that is clear and straightforward for all parties involved, and that the headings used in the IPID-template left room for interpretation.[18] Eurofinas thus requested guidelines about how the IPIDs were to be completed in practice.

---

[17]As an example, the Danish Insurance Association commented on the level of standardisation of the IPIDs (Comments received by Danish Insurance Association to EIOPA-CP-16-007: Consultation Paper on the proposal for the Implementing Technical Standards on a standardised presentation format of the Insurance Product Information Document (IPID) under the Insurance Distribution Directive (IDD), page 3):

> EIOPA should ensure that the level of standardisation introduced in the final IPID leaves manufacturers the necessary flexibility to make an IPID as meaningful as possible for customers.
>
> In order to achieve a successful IPID, flexibility must be introduced for the insurers to be able to ensure that the IPID provides relevant information for the consumer to make an informed decision, while also taken into account the complexity of the insurance products. Introducing a single standardised format should be balanced with the wide range of products that will be covered by the IPID.

As to the proposed length of the IPID, the Danish Insurance Association said (Comments received by Danish Insurance Association to EIOPA-CP-16-007: Consultation Paper on the proposal for the Implementing Technical Standards on a standardised presentation format of the Insurance Product Information Document (IPID) under the Insurance Distribution Directive (IDD), page 11):

> We agree with EIOPA that the IPID should not be too elaborate and should not result in a de facto duplication of the policy terms and conditions, whilst being accurate and non-misleading.

As such, the objective was, at least from a Danish perspective (which perspective the authors believe was broadly shared across the European Union), to find a balance between providing the flexibility required to enable insurers to give the relevant information, whilst ensuring that the IPIDs did not become a duplicate of the full insurance policy terms and conditions.

[18]See the European Federation of Finance House Association (Eurofinas) in Comments received by Eurofinas to EIOPA-CP-16-007: Consultation Paper on the proposal for the Implementing Technical Standards on a standardised presentation format of the Insurance Product Information Document (IPID) under the Insurance Distribution Directive (IDD), page 3–4:

> In order to fully enable consumers to make such well-informed decisions, it is important to use a template that is clear and straightforward for all parties involved, i.e. easy-to-complete for all non-life insurance manufacturers, easy-to-use by intermediaries within all channels and easy-to-understand for all customers. [. . .]
>
> In addition, we think that the headings, as currently phrased, leave room for interpretation. For example, as an insurance manufacturer, how do you determine what main risks – covered or not covered – you are required to list for your product. It would be helpful if the

Assuralia expressed concerns regarding the specification of add-ons, optional covers etc.[19] Assuralia's concerns were shared by several other respondents to EIOPA's consultation, including AMICE,[20] the Financial Services Consumer Panel (FSCP)[21] and Test Achats.[22]

As such, it was proposed that, in the event a particular insurance product contained a number of different coverage levels, or if an insurance product offered different optional coverage, several different and independent IPIDs were to be drawn up in respect of such insurance product, each of which set out different permutations of coverage. In short, one IPID should only contain one type of cover.

> EIOPA could provide indications on how exhaustive this information should be and what benchmarks should be used.

[19]See the Belgian Insurance Association (Assuralia) in Comments received by Assuralia to EIOPA-CP-16-007: Consultation Paper on the proposal for the Implementing Technical Standards on a standardised presentation format of the Insurance Product Information Document (IPID) under the Insurance Distribution Directive (IDD), page 2:

> We regret that EIOPA's work focuses primarily on the comparability of products through extensive standardization of the IPID rather than providing customers with useful information. The proposed format pays little attention to the presentation of options and the distinction between basic (standard, not optional), and optional covers for example, while such information is key for a customer's understanding of the product and could influence his decision to purchase the product. We therefore call on EIOPA to leave manufacturers sufficient flexibility to explain the main product features they consider relevant for the customer in the IPID.

[20]Association of Mutual Insurers and Insurance Cooperatives in Europe (AMICE).

[21]See the Financial Services Consumer Panel (FSCP) in Comments received by FSCP to EIOPA-CP-16-007: Consultation Paper on the proposal for the Implementing Technical Standards on a standardised presentation format of the Insurance Product Information Document (IPID) under the Insurance Distribution Directive (IDD), page 2:

> The panel believes a single IPID will not be sufficient to cover all aspects of insurance products in cases where such products have more than one type of policy. The panel recommends EIOPA to require additional IPID's be made available to consumers when offered add on policies. This can be the case with legal insurance attached to home insurance for example. A single IPID will not capture all the terms and conditions of such separate policies and be mis-leading to consumers. As such, any separate policy should be subject to a separate IPID.

[22]See the Belgian Consumer Organisation (Association Belge des Consommateurs ASBL, Test Achats) in Comments received by Test Achats to EIOPA-CP-16-007: Consultation Paper on the proposal for the Implementing Technical Standards on a standardised presentation format of the Insurance Product Information Document (IPID) under the Insurance Distribution Directive (IDD), page 2:

> The main features of a cover, mentioned in an IPID, should stay identical regardless of the number of other covers with which it is combined. A single IPID already offers not much space to describe the main features of one cover. A single IPID on two pages of an A4 page becomes a misleading document if it has to summarize the key information of more than one cover of a multi-risk policy.

The Dutch Association of Insurers criticised EIOPA's presentation format, because they thought it limiting existing initiatives providing more radical consumer protection.[23] Consequently, the Association proposed how the IPIDs should be drawn up by referring to the already existing Dutch IPID, and hereby emphasised that they thought it necessary to define which were the main characteristics insurance manufacturers were supposed to describe for a specific insurance product.[24] This was necessary, so the Dutch Association said, in order to make the IPIDs comparable.

Nonetheless, the points of criticism set out above, were not, ultimately, taken into account. Thus, different presentation formats for each insurance product were not developed (as suggested by The Dutch Association of Insurers) and no main characteristics was defined. It has not been made clear whether each IPID should only contain the main features of the product, or whether each IPID should include the various permutations possible with add-ons or optional coverage. The problem regarding add-ons and optional coverage (as mentioned by Test Achats and FSCP amongst others) has not been addressed. Nor was any guidance on the completion of the IPIDs provided (as requested by Eurofinas). However, EIOPA did take into consideration the insurance manufacturers desire for flexibility and autonomy.

The following paragraphs discuss whether the current IPID format actually meets the IDD's objective of enabling customers to make an informed decision based on comparable information on various insurance products, or whether the criticisms and concerns levelled by the consulted organisations are still relevant.

---

[23]See the Dutch Association of Insurers in Comments received by the Dutch Association of Insurers to EIOPA-CP-16-007: Consultation Paper on the proposal for the Implementing Technical Standards on a standardised presentation format of the Insurance Product Information Document (IPID) under the Insurance Distribution Directive (IDD), page 5:

> [. . .] the present EIOPA format limits or even prevents existing initiatives providing more radical consumer protection.

[24]The Association stated the following about the Dutch IPID (see Comments received by the Dutch Association of Insurers to EIOPA-CP-16-007: Consultation Paper on the proposal for the Implementing Technical Standards on a standardised presentation format of the Insurance Product Information Document (IPID) under the Insurance Distribution Directive (IDD), page 5 and 17):

> They are based on a standard, recognizable format, differentiating from each product by showing the various cover elements. Individual insurance companies can indicate whether a certain specific element is covered, optional, or not covered.

and

> Various consumer surveys show that consumers find product information the most important element. This information must be itemized and comparable. The Dutch Association of Insurers consequently determined that it is not sufficient to leave it to the provider to describe what is covered and what is not, but instead decided to define, together with a team of product specialists, the relevant product characteristics for a range of products. In the Dutch IPID the most relevant cover elements have their own icon and corresponding subtitle.

3.3 *IPIDs in Practice*

3.3.1 What Is Comparable Information?

As set out above, the objective of IPIDs is to enable a customer to make an informed decision about insurance products by giving comparable standardised information. The question is whether the IPIDs meet this objective in practice. Therefore, the first question that needs to be addressed is, what can be understood by the concept of "comparable"?

The concept, in its pure form, must mean that if two or more insurance manufacturers produce products that are identical, then such manufacturers should also, in theory, produce IPIDs that are, in substance, identical (apart from details such as the name of the manufacturer and information about the company, which information by its very nature can be important for a customer as it enables the customer to retrieve additional information about the company, e.g. information about customer satisfaction and complaint statistics (to the extent such information is available). The same must apply if the coverage is statutory.

At the same time, if the insurance products are not identical, then the IPIDs will only satisfy the IDD's comparability objective if the insurance manufacturers have a uniform approach to setting out, for example, what are considered to be the "main features" of the coverage, or the extent to which the geographical scope of the coverage provided extends. For example, if one assumes that contents insurance includes, as standard, the right to counselling, then the information relating to counselling will only be comparable as between insurance products if all insurance providers list counselling in their IPID.

In practice, an insurer can treat information about a specific coverage in a number of different ways. For example, continuing with the example of counselling:

1. the insurer states whether counselling is covered in the IPID under either *"What is insured?"* or *"What is not insured?"* (both of which are mandatory headings required to be used in the IPID);
2. the insurer does not cover counselling and does not mention counselling in the IPID; or
3. the insurer covers counselling but does not mention counselling in the IPID.

The problem is obvious. Customers are only provided with an effective basis of comparison if all insurance providers adopt a consistent approach to informing customers whether or not, in this case, counselling is covered.

By way of illustration, take a scenario in which one insurance provider mentions in its IPID that the particular insurance product in question covers counselling, whilst another insurance provider does not mention counselling in its IPID at all. For a customer who considers it vital that counselling is covered, the only course of action open is to read the second insurance provider's underlying policy terms. That is the only way for such a customer to determine whether the failure by the second insurance provider to mention counselling in the IPID arises from the fact that such insurance provider does not actually cover counselling at all, or whether it is simply a case that the insurance provider has chosen not to emphasise counselling in its IPID.

Informing a customer, via an IPID, that one particular insurance provider does not provide particular coverage, in this case counselling, is valueless in terms of facilitating a comparison of products unless all the other insurance providers also state in their IPIDs whether such coverage is provided (regardless of whether, in this case, counselling is actually covered or not).

Such information, i.e. that particular coverage is provided by one insurance provider, is also valueless for comparison purposes if other insurance providers also provide the same coverage but have omitted such information from their IPIDs.

If all the insurance providers who are compared fail to mention anything about a particular coverage, in this case counselling, then a customer will have to read each insurance provider's underlying policy terms to determine whether such coverage is included by any, all or indeed none of the providers. In this scenario, the IPID regime has not assisted the customer in making an informed comparison between insurance products. On the other hand, it is arguable that the IPID regime has further exacerbated the problem of a customer believing that counselling was covered by one insurance provider, but not by others.

The examination in the following section illustrates that, as the IPID regime stands today, there is not necessarily a common understanding amongst insurance providers of what is actually needed for two or more IPIDs to be comparable.

3.3.2 Examination of IPIDs

3.3.2.1 The Application of the Standardised Presentation Format in General

Each of the IPIDs analysed by the authors complies with the requirement that the information presented be restricted to two A4 pages. Moreover, each such IPID has been designed in accordance with EIOPA's standardised presentation format, cf. Articles 1, 3 and 4 of the Implementing Regulation.

Save that insurer D and insurer E do not use a 'shield' in the icon next to the heading "*How do I cancel the contract?*" (as prescribed in Article 7(1)(h) of the Implementing Regulation), all the IPIDs are consistent with the standardised presentation format in the Annex to the Implementing Regulation, cf. Article 7(2) of the Implementing Regulation.

Moreover, in accordance with section 2 of the Implementing Regulation, all of the IPIDs state that the document only gives a general overview of the particular insurance product on offer, and that the customer is referred to the underlying policy terms for the complete pre-contractual and contractual information.

Ignoring the relevantly immaterial error regarding the 'shield', the design of the various IPIDs appears uniform and directly comparable.

3.3.2.2 Examination of Contents Insurance Products

As described in Sect. 1.1, the following analysis and the analysis of the other insurance products in Sect. 3.3.2 is based on products from five different insurers. The analysis does not purport to cover the entirety of each IPID, but instead focusses on relevant similarities and differences. Where relevant to the analysis, the IPIDs are (for the sake of brevity) either quoted or summarised in respect of the most important similarities and differences identified by the authors (Table 1).

The analysis demonstrates that insurance providers often treat the same cover very differently.

For example in "*What is this type of insurance?*" insurer A very briefly mentions that contents insurance covers the property that the customer keeps in their home, whereas insurer B sets out examples of losses covered (fire, theft, etc.) and states that the insurance also includes third party liability insurance with a further option to extend coverage to electronics and bicycles.

An analysis of insurer A's policy terms shows that the contents insurance offered covers the customer's property in connection with for example fire, theft, etc., covers bicycles, includes third party liability insurance, and afford the customer an option to add a cover for electronics.

If a customer looks only at the initial description as set out in the IPIDs, they might suffer the misleading impression that insurer B provides more extensive coverage and offers a wider range of optional coverage as compared to insurer A.

In "*What is insured?*" all the IPIDs state that the customer's furniture and household effects are covered in the event of fire, theft and water damage, and that the insurance includes third party liability insurance and legal expenses insurance. Save for these consistent statements, there are no other overlaps between the particular cover that the various insurers have decided to highlight.

For example, insurers B, D and E state that their insurance covers counselling, whereas insurers A and C do not mention counselling at all. As regards insurer A, such failure is arguable consistent with the underlying policy terms, which do not provide cover for counselling. However, as regards insurer C, such failure is, arguably, inconsistent with the underlying policy terms which, upon analysis, reveal that counselling is within the scope of coverage insofar as it relates to travel. In this regard it is particularly notable that neither insurer A nor insurer C mentions counselling in "*What is not insured?*".

One sees a similar pattern in respect of identity theft, which is covered by insurers A, B, C and D, but not by Insurer E. Insurer E's failure to mention identity theft in "*What is insured?*" is consistent with its underlying policy terms, which do not provide coverage in respect of such risk. However, insurer E does not mention identity theft in "*What is not insured?*".

In its IPID, insurer E states that loss of, and damage to, luggage is covered, whereas insurer B states in its IPID that damage to luggage which occurs abroad is covered. Insurers A, C and D do not mention luggage in their IPIDs (whether as something which is within or without coverage). According to the insurers'

Table 1 The IPIDs analysed in respect of contents insurance products

	Insurer A	Insurer B	Insurer C	Insurer D	Insurer E
What is this type of insurance?[a]	*"Contents insurance covering damage to your property that you keep in your home".*	*"The contents insurance covers your contents, e.g. in case of fire, theft and water damage and it also includes third party liability insurance. You may decide to extend the insurance with for example electronics and bicycle insurance."*	*"This insurance covers yours and your household's contents. The insurance also covers your liability as a private individual/private individuals and it also includes legal expenses insurance."*	*"The contents insurance is a package deal that covers more than just your contents. For example, it also includes legal expenses insurance and third-party liability insurance."*	*"The contents insurance covers theft of or damage to your contents. The insurance also provides cover if you injure a third party or damage a third party's property."*
What is insured?[b]	Fire, theft, water damage, legal expenses, identity theft.	Fire, theft, water damage, trauma counselling, identity theft, luggage.	Fire, theft, water damage, legal expenses, identity theft, luggage.	Fire, theft, water damage, legal expenses, trauma counselling, identity theft.	Fire, theft, water damage, legal expenses, trauma counselling, luggage.
What is not insured?[c]	Motor vehicles, objects kept in storage, lodgers.	Motor vehicles, the means of transport in connection with traffic accidents, lodgers.	Motor vehicles, windsurfers and kite surfers.	Damage caused by sparks, liability for damage while doing someone a favour (for example involvement in association activities).	Motor vehicles, damage caused by sparks, white goods.
Are there any restrictions on cover?[d]	Flooding from the sea, etc., theft—as a result of gross negligence.	Liability for damage caused by drones weighing more than 250 g, identity theft, lodgers, legal expenses in connection with certain cases, damage caused by electricity as a result of incorrect usage or overloading, theft committed by persons who the customer has given access to the dwelling.	Special excess in connection with certain damage.	Restricted cover of outbuildings, etc.	Lodgers, injuries when riding a bicycle and sudden damage to electronics, theft either as a result of gross negligence or if caused by persons who the customer has given access to the dwelling.

Where am I covered?[e]	*"The insurance provides cover in Denmark in and at the insureds' all-year dwelling. And furniture and household effects brought along on trips for up to three months."*	*"The insurance provides cover in Denmark and on trips abroad for up to three months."*	*"The insurance provides cover in Denmark in/at your residence and also covers objects temporarily elsewhere than at your residence. The insurance also provides cover in connection with trips abroad for the first three months."*	*"The insurance covers your own property and property for which you bear the risk in connection with lending and hiring. Special rules apply to property that you keep in storage, keep at sports clubs or temporarily elsewhere than at your home. Luggage is covered for up to three months all over the world."*	*"The insurance provides cover in Denmark and Greenland and on trips abroad (including the Faroe Islands) for up to three months. Special rules apply to furniture and household effects that you bring with you to a seasonal dwelling or keep elsewhere than at your fixed address and when moving."*
What are my obligations?[f]	Answer questions honestly, pay on time, inform the insurer of any changes in the insurance relationship, inform the insurer of any damage, mitigate the loss.	Submit correct information when taking out the insurance, pay on time, inform the insurer of any changes in the insurance relationship, prevent and mitigate the loss, notify the loss immediately, report theft, etc. to the police.	Make sure that the information in the policy is correct, contact the insurer as quickly as possible in case of any damage, inform the insurer of any change in the roofing and basement.	Notify the loss as quickly as possible, inform the insurer of any change in the risk.	Notify the loss as quickly as possible, mitigate the loss, report theft, etc. to the police, inform the insurer of any changes.
When and how do I pay?[g]	Annual or monthly payment by using direct debit (Betalingsservice) or a paying-in slip, payment on the payment date at the latest.	Annual, biannual, quarterly or monthly payment by using direct debit (Betalingsservice) or a paying-in slip. First payment on commencement and later as agreed.	Annual or monthly payment by using direct debit (Betalingsservice) in case of monthly payment otherwise possible by using a paying-in slip. First payment on commencement and later as agreed.	The standard is annual payment on the anniversary of the insurance, but often possible to pay more often. Payment by using direct debit (Betalingsservice) or collection in *e-Boks*.	Annual or monthly payment by using direct debit (Betalingsservice) in case of monthly payment otherwise possible by using a paying-in slip.

(continued)

Table 1 (continued)

	Insurer A	Insurer B	Insurer C	Insurer D	Insurer E
When does the cover start and end?[h]	Starts after the decision has been made and runs until the renewal date when it will automatically be renewed for one year at a time.	Starts as agreed and is renewed automatically by one year at a time.	Starts as agreed and runs until the renewal date when it will automatically be renewed for one year at a time.	Is in force for one year at a time unless the policy stipulates otherwise. The insurance continues unless cancelled.	Is in force for one year at a time unless the policy stipulates otherwise. The insurance continues unless cancelled.
How do I cancel the contract?[i]	Written cancellation by giving one month's notice to expire on the renewal date, by giving 14 days' notice after notifying the insurer of a loss, until 14 days after the pay-out has been made or the claim has been rejected, by giving 30 days' notice to expire on the last day of any month in return for the payment of a fee.	Cancellation by giving one month's notice to expire on the renewal date without paying any fee or during a month in return for paying a fee. Cancellation during the first year triggers a higher fee.	Cancellation by giving one month's notice to expire on the first day of any month or for up to one month after the end of damage by giving 14 days' notice. Cancellation in other months than the renewal date month triggers a fee.	Cancellation with invoice month + one month's notice in return for the payment of a fee. Cancellation on the anniversary of the insurance free of charge. Cancellation during the first year triggers a higher fee.	Cancellation by giving 30 days' notice to expire on the last day of a calendar month without a fee until 20 December 2023 and by giving 14 days' notice after pay-out or rejection of a notified loss.

[a]Article 6(1)(a) of the Implementing Regulation with reference to Article 20(8)(a) of the IDD
[b]Article 6(1)(b) of the Implementing Regulation with reference to Article 20(8)(b) of the IDD
[c]Article 6(1)(e) of the Implementing Regulation with reference to Article 20(8)(b) of the IDD
[d]Article 6(1)(f) of the Implementing Regulation with reference to Article 20(8)(d) of the IDD
[e]Article 6(1)(d) of the Implementing Regulation with reference to Article 20(8)(b) of the IDD
[f]Article 6(1)(g) of the Implementing Regulation with reference to Article 20(8)(e), (f) and (g) of the IDD
[g]Article 6(1)(h) of the Implementing Regulation with reference to Article 20(8)(c) of the IDD
[h]Article 6(1)(i) of the Implementing Regulation with reference to Article 20(8)(h) of the IDD
[i]Article 6(1)(j) of the Implementing Regulation with reference to Article 20(8)(i) of the IDD

underlying policy terms, they all cover both loss of, and damage to, luggage. The scope for prospective customers being misled is obvious.

None of the various IPIDs examined adopt a consistent approach to listing exclusions under "*What is not insured?*".

Insurers A, B, C and E's IPIDs explicitly mention that motor vehicles are not covered. However, notwithstanding that its underlying policy terms state that motor vehicles are excluded from coverage, insurer D fails to explicitly state the same in its IPID. Once again, the scope for confusion is obvious. A prospective customer glancing over the IPID documents may well come to the conclusion that motor vehicle cover is only excluded if there is an explicit statement to that effect and thus be misled as to the extent of coverage under insurer D's policy. This is, of course, an extreme example, but it helps to illustrate the problem posed by inconsistency.

Further, the insurers have decided to emphasise (i.e. state explicitly within their IPID) very different exclusions. For example, insurer C states in its IPID that the insurance product does not cover windsurfers and kite surfers. According to underlying policy terms of the other insurers, insurers B, D and E, do cover windsurfers and kite surfers, whilst insurer A does not. It cannot, therefore, be deduced from the fact that insurer C has explicitly stated the relevant exclusion that the other insurers do actually cover windsurfers and kite surfers. As such, a customer requiring cover for windsurfing and kitesurfing would have to read the insurers' underlying policy terms in order to be able to perform a useful comparison. More problematically, perhaps, is the fact that, even then, one is assuming that the customer in fact realises that, despite the fact that an exclusion is not mentioned explicitly, it may still be present in the underlying policy terms. As with the exclusions as to vehicles set out above, the scope for confusion and for a customer to be potentially misled is plain.

The same applies to the exclusion relating to lodgers stated in insurer A's and insurer B's IPIDs. Lodgers are not explicitly listed under "*What is not insured?*" in the IPIDs produced by insurers C, D and E, but, according to those insurers' underlying policy terms, cover is not provided for lodgers. It should be noted, however, that lodgers are mentioned in insurer E's IPID, but the exclusion of coverage is set out under the heading "*Are there any restrictions on cover?*". Accordingly, customers are not able to simply compare the paragraphs in the IPIDs on a like-for-like basis as it is possible that coverage exclusions are set out either in "*What is not insured?*" or in "*Are there any restrictions on cover?*".

The simple conclusion is that, when comparing IPIDs, it cannot be deduced that an exclusion explicitly set out in one insurance provider's IPID, but not explicitly set out in a second insurance provider's IPID, is or is not applicable to the coverage provided by the second provider. It means that a prospective customer will have to consult the underlying policy terms to establish whether specific cover is in fact covered or excluded. More worryingly, perhaps, as set out above, that assumes that a prospective customer has the wherewithal to realise that just because one IPID explicitly sets out an exclusion and another IPID doesn't, that doesn't necessarily mean that the cover represented by the insurance product does not contain such exclusion.

As demonstrated by the above examples, the insurers provide very different information in their IPIDs. An insurer failing to mention a specific risk as either being covered or not covered cannot be interpreted to mean that such risk is either covered or not covered. The problems presented when a customer reads a number of IPIDs, each of which is prepared with different emphasis and on an inconsistent (albeit compliant) basis are obvious; the customer will simply not have the information necessary to make an informed overall comparison. The customer will only be able to properly perform a comparison if they read further information, for example a detailed product sheet or the underlying policy terms.

There is also a significant difference between what the insurers have decided to mention in "*Are there any restrictions on cover?*". For example, insurer C is the only insurer that explicitly states in its IPID that theft is not covered in cases of gross negligence on the part of the insured. This is, however, an ordinary exclusion which, despite not being explicitly set out in any of the other insurance providers' IPIDs, is present in the underlying policy terms. Likewise, insurer E explicitly sets out in its IPID that the insurance does not cover theft in the customer's own home if the dwelling was not locked. Insurer D does explicitly set out this exclusion, but it is contained in "*What is not insured?*", rather than "*Are there any restrictions on cover?*". Insurers A, B and C do not set out such exclusions explicitly in their IPIDs, despite the fact that it is contained in the underlying policy terms.

Further, insurer A's IPID explicitly sets out the ordinary restriction that damage as a result of war, etc. is not covered. Perhaps unsurprisingly, the same restriction applies in respect of the cover offered by the other insurance providers, but this is only apparent from examining the underlying policy terms, as those providers do not set the restriction out in their IPIDs.

The simple conclusion is that it seems to be (at least from a customer's perspective) entirely a matter of chance as to what risks are or are not explicitly set out as covered, excluded or a subject to a restriction on cover in the IPIDs relating to contents insurance products. The consequence is that a customer is not able to effectively compare the overall cover provided by the contents insurance products by simply analysing the IPIDs, notwithstanding the fact that the insurance underlying policy terms are, to a significant degree, consistent in terms of cover, exclusions and restrictions.

In "*Where am I covered?*" the various insurance providers describe the geographical area of cover using phrases that do not lend themselves to easy comprehension by a prospective customer. As such, there is obvious scope for confusion amongst customers as to whether all the contents insurance products actually have the same geographical area of cover. This is despite the fact that, upon examination of each set of underlying policy terms, it is apparent that all of the insurance products have essentially the same geographical area of cover.

For example, insurer B states very briefly in its IPID that the insurance provides cover in Denmark and on trips abroad for up to three months. Upon examining the underlying policy terms, it is apparent that insurance provides cover in Denmark, with the exception of the Faroe Islands and Greenland, and only if the customer's furniture and household effects are in or at the customer's all-year dwelling, in a safe-deposit box, in a warehouse, removal van or container, or in the customer's spouse's or cohabitee's sheltered dwelling. Special rules also apply in connection with furniture and household effects in a seasonal dwelling, those temporarily kept elsewhere than at the customer's all-year dwelling, and those effects purchased abroad and repatriated to Denmark.

By comparison, insurer E states in its IPID that the insurance provides cover in Denmark and Greenland and during trips of a duration of three months abroad (including trips to the Faroe Islands) and that special rules apply to furniture and household effects that the customer brings with them to their seasonal dwelling. Besides the fact that insurer E' policy provides cover in Greenland on the same terms as in Denmark, it is essentially to insurer B's policy. However, this is difficult to deduce from the relevant IPIDs. Insurer B has dealt only with geographical scope of cover, whereas insurer E has gone a step further and also deals with the difference between an all-year dwelling and a seasonal dwelling. A customer comparing the two IPIDs might therefore be led to believe (incorrectly) that insurer B provides more extensive cover than insurer E.

Under "*What are my obligations?*" all the insurance providers state that the customer must inform the insurer of any changes in the insurance relationship. This is variously stated as providing that the customer must "*[...] notify us*", "*[...] contact us if the information in the policy is incorrect*", "*[...] inform us of any changes*", "*[...] inform us of any changes in your risk*", or "*[...] make sure that the information in your policy is correct*", etc. Notwithstanding the slight variation in language used, the content and extent of the obligation remains clear and is able to be easily comprehended and thus easily comparable.

The same applies to the requirements regarding notification of loss where the customer must contact the insurers either "*as quickly as possible*" (insurers C, D and E), "*immediately*" (insurer B), or simply required to "*inform*" the insurance provider (insurer A).

Some insurance providers also stipulate that the customer must pay on time (insurers A and B), that the customer must mitigate the loss (insurers A, B and E) and that losses relating to criminal acts, for example theft, must be reported to the police (insurers B, D and E). What is notable is that despite the fact that not all of the insurance providers list these various obligations in their IPIDs, each set of underlying policy terms contains all of the various obligations. In short, the customer must comply with essentially the same obligations no matter which insurance policy is taken out, however that fact cannot be directly deduced from a comparison of the insurance providers' various IPIDs.

In "*When and how do I pay*?", "*When does the cover start and end*?" and "*How do I cancel the contract*?", the insurance providers provide the same information. Even though the wording utilised is not always the same, all of the insurance providers state, for example, whether it is possible to pay annually, biannually, quarterly or monthly; when the first payment is to be made; and that it is possible to pay by using direct debit (in Danish: *Betalingsservice*) or a paying-in slip. Such is the case for the remaining two headings analysed. Under both headings, the insurance providers have taken a consistent approach when choosing which information to include.

Accordingly, in this regard at least, the IPIDs act as an effective tool for comparison as the information that the insurance providers have chosen to emphasise in their IPIDs completely overlaps.

3.3.2.3 Examination of Compulsory Third Person Motor Liability Insurance

The Danish Road Traffic Act stipulates that the owner or user of a motor vehicle in Denmark must have insurance.[25] The insurance must provide cover for compensation in respect of damage to property and injuries to persons caused by the vehicle and coverage limits are subject to various fixed amounts laid down by law (Table 2).

As was the case with contents insurance, a comparison of the IPIDs produced for third person motor liability insurance reveals that insurance providers often deal with the same elements differently.

In "*What is this type of insurance?*", the insurance providers set out the contents of third person motor liability insurance with varying degrees of detail. For example, on the one hand insurer A states very briefly that the insurance provides cover if the customer's car is involved in an accident. On the other hand, insurer D states that the insurance covers third party liabilities and loss of, or damage to, the customer's motorcar, which cover can be supplemented by various add-ons. Insurer D also describes the rules for when a customer is able to take out no-claims driver insurance (in Danish: *elitebilistforsikring*) or "*standstill insurance*". Insurers B, C and E all refer to the fact that third party liability insurance is compulsory and, together with insurer D, further mention that it is possible to supplement the compulsory insurance with various add-ons.

As third person motor liability insurance is compulsory in Denmark, the main features are by definition the same. If only the main features were described, the IPIDs should, in principle, be identical. However, in practice, that is not the case. As illustrated above, the majority of the IPIDs analysed state, for example, that the compulsory insurance may be supplemented by add-ons and go on to describe such add-ons. This is, perhaps, unsurprising. Insurance providers are likely to be keen to distinguish their products from their competitors and are thus likely to be reluctant to mention only the bare minimum mandatory cover.

The information provided in the IPIDs under "*What is insured?*" varies significantly. For example, insurer E lists the cover that can be selected, including "*third party liability insurance*" without describing what the insurance actually covers. Insurers A, B and D, on the other hand, state that the third-party liability insurance provides cover for personal injury and damage caused to, respectively, third parties and their property by the customer's car. Insurer C adopts a further alternative approach and sets out the specific limits of cover, including that in respect of damage to the car and its equipment, but without, however, making clear that the cover for

[25] Section 105 of Danish Consolidated Act no 1324 of 21 November 2018, the Road Traffic Act (in Danish: færdselsloven).

Table 2 The IPIDs analysed in respect of third person motor liability insurance products

	Insurer A	Insurer B	Insurer C	Insurer D	Insurer E
What is this type of insurance?[a]	*"Motor insurance that provides cover if your car is involved in an accident."*	*The motor insurance includes the compulsory third party liability insurance. You may decide to combine it with insurance covering the loss of or damage to a motorcar or semi-insurance covering the loss of or damage to a motorcar and extend the insurance by add-ons such as roadside assistance, driver's seat (in Danish: førerplads) and insurance against excess (in Danish: selvrisikosikring).*	*"Motor insurance includes your car and provides cover for the damage that you as a driver of the car may be held liable for. Third party liability insurance is compulsory for registered vehicles. If you have chosen insurance covering the loss of or damage to a motorcar, you are covered against most types of damage to your car."*	*"Motor insurance with third party liability insurance and insurance covering the loss of or damage to a motorcar which you may supplement with for example extended auto glass insurance, driver accident insurance and roadside assistance. Bil Elite is motor insurance where the price does not increase following a loss. You will usually get elite insurance if you are minimum 28 years of age and have not had any accidents for the last five years and have been insured by the same insurer. If you pay a fee, you may change the insurance to "standstill insurance" if you do not use your car for a period."*	*"The motor insurance contains the compulsory third party liability insurance that can be combined with insurance covering the loss of or damage to a motorcar including roadside assistance abroad and legal expenses insurance. If the car is a leased car, it is possible to extend the insurance with leasing cover. It is also possible to extend the insurance with add-ons, for example driver's insurance, roadside assistance, no-claim discount and glass, etc."*
What is insured?[b]	*"Third party liability insurance that covers your liability in damages*	*"The insurance provides cover for you, your passengers and everyone to*	The car, fixed equipment, audio and telecom equipment installed	Damage/injury that you or others cause by using your car that you must	The insurance may include the following cover. The cover that you

(continued)

Table 2 (continued)

	Insurer A	Insurer B	Insurer C	Insurer D	Insurer E
	by the sums fixed by the Danish Road Traffic Act if the car that you insure injures other people, damages their property or vehicle in an accident."	*whom you lend the car. We provide cover by the sums fixed in the Danish Road Traffic Act if your car damages property and injures other people. Also if your passengers get hurt."*	subsequently by up to DKK 20,000 for each damage, standard tools only used for the car, bodily injuries by up to DKK 121 million and property damage by up to DKK 24 million.	compensate, liability in damages for injuries to passengers in your car.	have selected is specified in your insurance contract: Liability, [. . .]
What is not insured?[c]	Damage to the policyholder's, the owner's or the user's property, injury to the driver and damage to the driver's property, damage to hooked up vehicle, etc.	Injuries to drivers, damage to the user's or the driver's property, the actual car and a hitched-up trailer, etc.	Injuries to the driver and damage to the driver's property, hitched up trailer, damage to the mechanical and electrical parts of the car, loss if the car has been lent, wear and tear, damage in connection with racing, damage/injuries while the vehicle has been hired out without a driver.	Damage to the car and injuries to its driver, theft of the car.	Removed parts and equipment for the car, mobile phones, fuel and fluids.
Are there any restrictions on cover?[d]	Insurer A is entitled to subrogation in connection with damage/injury, damage/injury as a result of war, earth quakes or nuclear energy.	Damage/injury in connection with motor racing, hiring out the car without a driver.	Double excess in connection with lending the car to a person under the age of 25.	Only one transport to a garage for each damage.	Damage to the car in connection with hiring out the car if the driver is under the influence of alcohol, etc., if the driver does not have a valid driving licence, damage/injury caused by intention or gross negligence.

Where am I covered?[e]	Europe and in the countries outside Europe that are part of the "green card scheme".	Europe and in the countries that are part of the "green card scheme".	Europe and in the countries that are included in the "green card scheme".	Europe and in several countries outside Europe that are included in the "green card scheme".	Europe and in the countries that are included in the "green card scheme".
What are my obligations?[f]	Answer questions honestly, pay on time, inform the insurer of any changes in the insurance relationship, notify the insurer of any loss, mitigate the loss, inform the insurer if you get another car, the user or the owner changes.	Submit correct information when taking out the insurance, pay on time, inform the insurer of any changes in the insurance relationship, prevent and mitigate the loss, notify the loss immediately.	Make sure that the information in the policy is correct, contact the insurer as quickly as possible in connection with any loss, inform the insurer of any change in the risk, report theft, etc. to the police.	Notify the loss as quickly as possible, inform the insurer of any change in the risk, report theft, etc. to the police.	Notify the loss as quickly as possible, mitigate the loss, report theft, etc. to the police, inform the insurer of any changes, contact the insurer before the car is going in for repairs.
When and how do I pay?[g]	The same as for contents insurance	The same as for contents insurance	The same as for contents insurance	The same as for contents insurance	The same as for contents insurance
When does the cover start and end?[h]	Starts after the decision has been made and runs until the renewal date when it will automatically be renewed for one year at a time.	Starts as agreed or when the car has been registered in *Motorregisteret* (the Danish register of vehicles) and is renewed automatically by one year at a time.	Starts as agreed or when the car has been registered in *Motorregisteret* (the Danish register of vehicles) and runs until the renewal date when it will automatically be renewed for one year at a time.	Is in force for one year at a time unless the policy stipulates otherwise. The insurance continues unless cancelled.	Is in force for one year at a time or when the car has been registered in *Motorregisteret* (the Danish register of vehicles). The insurance continues if not cancelled unless the car is removed from *Motorregisteret* (the Danish register of vehicles).

(continued)

Table 2 (continued)

	Insurer A	Insurer B	Insurer C	Insurer D	Insurer E
How do I cancel the contract?[i]	The same as for contents insurance.	The same as for contents insurance.	The same as for contents insurance.	The same as for contents insurance.	The same as for contents insurance.

[a]Article 6(1)(a) of the Implementing Regulation with reference to Article 20(8)(a) of the IDD
[b]Article 6(1)(b) of the Implementing Regulation with reference to Article 20(8)(b) of the IDD
[c]Article 6(1)(e) of the Implementing Regulation with reference to Article 20(8)(b) of the IDD
[d]Article 6(1)(f) of the Implementing Regulation with reference to Article 20(8)(d) of the IDD
[e]Article 6(1)(d) of the Implementing Regulation with reference to Article 20(8)(b) of the IDD
[f]Article 6(1)(g) of the Implementing Regulation with reference to Article 20(8)(e), (f) and (g) of the IDD
[g]Article 6(1)(h) of the Implementing Regulation with reference to Article 20(8)(c) of the IDD
[h]Article 6(1)(i) of the Implementing Regulation with reference to Article 20(8)(h) of the IDD
[i]Article 6(1)(j) of the Implementing Regulation with reference to Article 20(8)(i) of the IDD

the car and its equipment is conditional on attaching the relevant add-on to the policy (i.e. that add-on covering loss of, or damage to, a motorcar).

However, what is not clear from the IPIDs is the fact that the scope of cover afforded by third party liability insurance is, given its compulsory nature, governed by statute. That lack of clarity arises because a number of the insurance providers set out more information about their insurance covering loss of, or damage to, a motorcar and add-ons than they do about the actual scope of third person motor liability insurance. From an insurance manufacturer's point of view this is understandable; they want to distinguish their products beyond the bare minimum statutorily required cover. However, considering the object of the IPIDs and their current standardised format it is not necessarily appropriate or in line with the regulation.

In "*What is not insured?*" the insurance providers have a tendency to mention exclusions that are relevant to their optional insurance covering, for example, the loss of, or damage to, a motorcar, and various other add-ons instead of the exclusions applicable to the mandatory third-party motor liability insurance. In theory these exclusions also apply to the third party liability insurance, but it is debatable whether it is relevant to a customer (who must take out the compulsory third person motor liability insurance) to know that such insurance does not cover damage to the car in connection with, for example, racing (as mentioned by insurer C) as third party liability insurance generally does not cover any damage to the car at all.

Insurer D is the only insurer that has divided the exclusions into sub-headings. Insurer D states under the sub-heading relating to third party motor liability insurance that damage to the car and injuries to its driver as well as theft of the car are not covered. Insurer A states that the insurance offered does not cover damage to the policyholder's, the owner's, the driver's or the user's property, whereas insurer B states only that the user's and the driver's property is not covered. Insurer C states that the driver's property is not covered, and insurer E does not mention anything about the driver's or the user's property.

Notwithstanding the inconsistent approach of the various insurance providers as set out above, upon examination of the various underlying policy terms, it becomes apparent (perhaps unsurprisingly) that each insurance policy offered in fact has the same exclusions relating to damage to property belonging to the owner, the driver, the user and the policyholder, injuries to the driver and damage to a vehicle being towed.

Even though the cover is for all intents and purposes the same, the IPIDs do not give this impression. Instead, the insurance providers have decided to set out information relevant to their particular add-ons, which allows them to distinguish themselves from the others. Moreover, in some of the IPIDs, it is not entirely clear if the cover or the exclusion relates to the compulsory third party liability insurance or the optional add-ons, something which it is, obviously, important for a prospective customer to know.

There is also some difference between the information that the insurance providers have included in their IPIDs under the heading *"Are there any restrictions on cover?"*. Only insurer A mentions that it has a right of subrogation and that damage in connection with war, etc. is excluded. This is despite the fact that such restrictions are present in all of the insurance providers' underlying policy terms in respect of both the third-party liability insurance and any add-ons. The same applies to use of a car for racing (as mentioned by insurer B) and to damage in connection with hiring out the vehicle (as mentioned by insurers B and E).

Once again, the restrictions on the cover are the same, but they are dealt with and described differently in the insurance providers' IPIDs.

In "*Where am I covered?*" the insurance providers take differing approaches to describing the geographical scope of coverage notwithstanding the fact that, upon examination of the underlying policy terms, such geographical scope is identical across the policies. So, insurers A, D and E state that the insurance provides cover in Europe and in the countries outside Europe that are part of the "*green card scheme*", whereas insurers B and C state that the insurance provides cover in Denmark and in the countries that are part of the "*green card scheme*".

The geographical area of cover is exactly the same in all the policies, each and every European country being part of the "*green card scheme*". However, if the prospective customer does not know which countries are part of the "*green card scheme*" (something well within the realms of possibility), the difference in the wording used in the IPIDs might cause the customer conclude that some countries in Europe are not part of the scheme or that the area of cover of insurers A, D and E is broader than that of insurers B and C.

The content under the headings "*What are my obligations?*", "*When and how do I pay?*", "*When does the cover start and end?*" and "*How do I cancel the contract?*" is essentially the same as the content contained in the contents insurance analysed in Sect. 3.3.2.2.

3.3.2.4 Examination of Compulsory Workers' Compensation Insurance

The Danish Workers' Compensation Act stipulates that employers in Denmark are under an obligation to insure their employees and transfer their risk of accidents to an insurer.[26] The insurance is voluntary for self-employed persons and assisting spouses. The insurance must provide some specified benefits in connection with bodily injuries caused by accidents at work (Table 3).

As workers' compensation insurance is compulsory, all the insurance products include the same basic cover, i.e. the benefits listed in the Danish Workers' Compensation Act, for injuries sustained as a consequence of work. Disregarding any add-ons, the IPIDs should, in theory, be more or less identical.

However, as with contents insurance and third-party motor liability insurance, the analysis of the IPIDs for workers' compensation insurance demonstrates that the insurance providers often deal with the same aspect of the cover differently.

[26]Section 50 of Danish Consolidated Act no 216 of 27 February 2017, Workers' Compensation Act (in Danish: arbejdsskadesikringsloven).

Table 3 The IPIDs analysed in respect of workers' compensation insurance

	Insurer C	Insurer E	Insurer F	Insurer G	Insurer H
What is this type of insurance?[a]	*"The insurance covers compulsory workers' compensation insurance so that your employees are in a better position after an industrial injury."*	*"The insurance is compulsory workers' compensation insurance for your employees. If you own the business, it is also possible for you to take out industrial injury insurance for yourself."*	*[No information]*	*"Workers' compensation insurance is compulsory insurance for all businesses with employees. It is also possible to take out the insurance as voluntary insurance for single proprietorships and associations. The insurance provides cover for compensation for impairment and disability as a result of an accident at work in compliance with the Danish Workers' Compensation Act."*	*"All employees employed to do work for a business in Denmark, paid or unpaid, are covered by the Danish Workers' Compensation Act. This is also the case for persons in private households."*
What is insured?[b]	The liability of the business to its employees who are involved in an accident at work under the Danish Workers' Compensation Act.	The employees of the business if they are injured during working hours.	The liability of the business to its employees under the rules on accidents at work laid down in the Danish Workers' Compensation Act.	The liability of the business to its employees under the rules on accidents at work laid down in the Danish Workers' Compensation Act. In addition to the compulsory cover the insurance includes trauma counselling and counselling to persons involved in an accident and dependents.	The liability of the business to the employee in case of an accident caused by the work or the work conditions. Mandatory extensions of the cover: trauma counselling in connection with accidents at the place of work.
What is not insured?[c]	Industrial injuries caused by occupational disease or accidents not caused by the work.	Injuries sustained to or from work are never covered by the insurance,	Injuries that are not accidents, for example occupational disease, injuries	Injuries that are not accidents, for example occupational disease, injuries not caused by the work.	Events that cannot be described as an accident, occupational disease, injuries in the

(continued)

Table 3 (continued)

	Insurer C	Insurer E	Insurer F	Insurer G	Insurer H
		injuries not caused by the work.	not caused by the work or outside working hours.		employee's spare time or on the way to or from work, association activities.
Are there any restrictions on cover?[d]	The insurance provides cover under the Danish Workers' Compensation Act.	Danish Labour Market Insurance decides whether the sustained injury is covered by the workers' compensation insurance. The insurance does not cover injuries that are not approved by Danish Labour Market Insurance.	[No information provided about the workers' compensation insurance]	The limits of cover, etc. are fixed in the Danish Workers' Compensation Act.	Cover is provided under the statutory rules and is based on the limits of cover and rates determined by the Danish Ministry of Employment.
Where am I covered?[e]	*"The workers' compensation insurance covers work done in Denmark with the exception of secondment and business travels."*	*"The geographical area of cover of the insurance is Denmark. If there are any other areas of cover, they will be specified in your insurance contract. Special rules may apply to the individual types of cover. You find the details in the policy terms."*	*"The insurance covers employees employed in Denmark."*	*"The workers' compensation insurance covers work done in Denmark and secondment and business travels abroad."*	*"You are subject to the Act if you work in Denmark. You are also subject to the Act if you are seconded or on business travels abroad. Udbetaling Danmark deals with the rules."*
What are my obligations?[f]	Make sure that the information in the policy is correct, notify the insurer of the loss as quickly as possible and no later than nine days after the event, inform the insurer of any change in the risk.	Notify the insurer of the loss no later than nine days after the event or 48 h after the death, inform the insurer of any move, etc.	Make sure that the information in the policy is correct, notify the insurer of the loss and of any presumption of loss immediately, notify the insurer of any change in the information provided.	Make sure that the information in the policy is correct, notify the insurer of the loss immediately, notify the insurer of any change in the business.	Pay on time, notify the insurer of the loss as quickly as possible and no later than nine days after the first day of absence, notify the insurer of any change in the business.

When and how do I pay?[g]	*"The insurance must be paid on the date specified on the paying-in slip or in notifications at the latest. Payments are made by using a paying-in slip or a payments agreement. The payment for the insurance can be made monthly, quarterly, biannually or annually."*	*"You can pay for the insurance once or several times a year. You can pay for the insurance by using direct debit (Betalingsservice) or a paying-in slip. Registration with direct debit (Betalingsservice) is required in order to make monthly payments."*	*"The payment date is specified on the payment form. Payment can be made by using a paying-in slip or direct debit (Betalingsservice (BS)). It is possible to pay for the insurance annually, biannually, quarterly or monthly."*	*"You must pay the insurance on the date specified on the paying-in slip. If you register the payment with direct debit (Betalingsservice), the payment will be made automatically. It is possible to pay for the insurance monthly, quarterly, biannually or annually. We recommend that you register the payments with direct debit (Betalingsservice), but it is also possible to receive a paying-in slip."*	*"The first premium must be paid when the insurance enters into force. After that, you have to pay the subsequent premiums on the agreed payment dates. It is possible to pay for the insurance monthly, quarterly, biannually or annually by using a paying-in slip or direct debit (Betalingsservice). Monthly payment is conditional on registration with direct debit (Betalingsservice)."*
When does the cover start and end?[h]	*"The insurance covers injuries in the period of insurance."*	*"The insurance is in force in the period specified in your insurance contract. We extend the insurance automatically unless you cancel the policy before then. If you have a policy period of several years, we extend the insurance by the same period."*	*"The insurance covers injuries established in the period of insurance. If the insurance is cancelled, treatment that has already been agreed on is covered for up to three months after the cancellation of the insurance."*	*"The insurance starts on the date specified in the policy. The insurance is in force for one year at a time and we renew it automatically unless otherwise agreed. It is also possible to take out the insurance for a period of three or five years."*	*"The insurance starts on commencement. The date is specified in the policy. The period of insurance is one year, and the insurance will be renewed every year on the renewal date until it is cancelled to expire at the end of a calendar year. The insurance covers the injuries sustained in the period of insurance."*

(continued)

Table 3 (continued)

	Insurer C	Insurer E	Insurer F	Insurer G	Insurer H
How do I cancel the contract?[i]	*"If the insurance has been taken out as an insurance contract with a term of one year, it is possible to cancel the contract by giving one month's notice to expire on the renewal date. If the insurance has been taken out for a period of several years, the insurance may be cancelled in writing by giving a notice of one month to expire on the last day of the insurance period of several years. The notice may be more than a month. If that is the case, it will be specified in the policy. If the insurance is not cancelled by giving the specified notice, the insurance will continue."*	*"It is possible for you to cancel the policy in writing one month before the policy period expires at the latest. You are entitled to cancel the policy after any insurance claim for up to 14 days after we have either made the pay-out or rejected the claim."*	*"If the insurance has been taken out with an insurance period of one year, it is possible to cancel the insurance in writing by giving one month's notice to expire on the renewal date. If the insurance has been taken out for a period of several years, the insurance may be cancelled in writing by giving a notice of one month to expire on the last day of the period of several years. If the insurance is not cancelled by giving the specified notice, the insurance will continue."*	*"Both you and the insurer may cancel the policy in writing by giving minimum one month's notice to expire on the last day of the policy period. However, if the insurance has been taken out for a period of several years, you may cancel the policy to expire on the renewal date in the year when the period expires. Both you and the insurer may also cancel a policy in connection with a loss. The cancellation must be made one month at the latest after the end of the injury and by giving a notice of 14 days."*	*"It is possible to cancel the policy in writing free of charge by giving minimum one month's notice up to the renewal date of the policy."*

[a]Article 6(1)(a) of the Implementing Regulation with reference to Article 20(8)(a) of the IDD
[b]Article 6(1)(b) of the Implementing Regulation with reference to Article 20(8)(b) of the IDD
[c]Article 6(1)(e) of the Implementing Regulation with reference to Article 20(8)(b) of the IDD
[d]Article 6(1)(f) of the Implementing Regulation with reference to Article 20(8)(d) of the IDD
[e]Article 6(1)(d) of the Implementing Regulation with reference to Article 20(8)(b) of the IDD
[f]Article 6(1)(g) of the Implementing Regulation with reference to Article 20(8)(e), (f) and (g) of the IDD
[g]Article 6(1)(h) of the Implementing Regulation with reference to Article 20(8)(c) of the IDD
[h]Article 6(1)(i) of the Implementing Regulation with reference to Article 20(8)(h) of the IDD
[i]Article 6(1)(j) of the Implementing Regulation with reference to Article 20(8)(i) of the IDD

In "*What is this type of insurance?*" insurers C, E and G state that workers' compensation insurance is compulsory. Insurer F has not included this heading in its IPID. Insurer H (incorrectly) states that all employees are subject to the Danish Workers' Compensation Act without giving any other information about the insurance. Insurers E and G mention various add-ons in the description.

In "*What is insured?*", insurers C, F, G and H refer to the Danish Workers' Compensation Act and all the insurance providers list the benefits covered under the Act, including medical treatment expenses and compensation for the loss of the ability to work. The information about the cover provided by all the insurance providers is all-but identical.

In addition to the compulsory benefits, insurer G states that counselling (which is not a compulsory benefit) is covered. Insurer G, therefore, has decided to highlight the fact that it has extended coverage beyond the compulsory minimum. Insurer H states that counselling is a compulsory extension of its cover.

Overall, the information set out in each IPID under the heading "*What is insured?*" is comparable.

In "*What is not insured?*" insurers C, F, G and H state that occupational disease is excluded from the cover offered. Insurers C, E, F and G state that injury not actually caused by work is excluded just as insurers E and H mention that injury sustained on an employee's journey to or from work is not covered.

The Danish Workers' Compensation Act only provides for an obligation to insure employees in connection with industrial accidents. It does not impose an obligation to insure against occupation disease because, historically, occupational disease has not been considered to be an insurable risk in Denmark. The same applies to injuries not sustained as a result of work, including injuries sustained during the employee's journey to and from work, as such injuries are not within the scope of the Act, not having been a direct result of the employee's work or the conditions under which the work is performed.

However, it is difficult to see, based on the insurance providers' IPIDs, that all of the underlying policies are subject to the same (statutory) exclusions because the insurance providers choose to emphasise different exclusions. As such, the basis of comparison is distorted. If one insurance provider decides to mention that occupational disease is excluded, whereas another insurer does not mention such exclusion, the scope for confusion when one is comparing the IPIDs is obvious.

In "*Are there any restrictions on cover?*" insurer F only sets out the restrictions relating to the add-ons it offers in respect of its cover, whereas insurers C, E, G and H all state simply that the cover is provided under the Danish Workers' Compensation Act. This differing approach is adopted despite the fact that, substantively, there is no difference between the cover offered by the insurance providers.

In "*Where am I covered?*" there is a significant difference between what some of the insurance providers state as the geographical area of cover. Insurer H's wording addresses the employee (even though it is the employer that is under an obligation to take out insurance) and states that "*you*" are covered if the work is performed in Denmark or are seconded or on business travels abroad. Insurer G's description of the area of cover is identical to the description provided by insurer H, whereas insurer F states that the insurance covers employees employed in Denmark. In its IPID, insurer C describes the geographical area of cover as being Denmark, with the exception of secondment and business travels. It is unclear whether insurer C's IPID means that the insurance provides cover in Denmark but not if the employee is on business travels or seconded from abroad to Denmark, or whether the insurance provides cover in Denmark and abroad if you are on a business trip or have been seconded from Denmark. The relevant underlying policy terms simply refer to the rules laid down in the Danish Workers' Compensation Act. It is, of course, not the format of the IPID that has made insurer C's description unclear, but rather the wording that insurer C has adopted. Such example clearly illustrates the insurance provider's differing approaches to providing a piece of information which should, in theory, be identical for all of them (because it should correspond exactly to what is set out in the Danish Workers' Compensation Act and the regulations about the coordination of the social security schemes).

The information set out under the heading "*What are my obligations?*" is essentially the same as that set out in the IPIDs for contents insurance and third person motor liability insurance. However, industrial injury cover is subject to a special deadline for notifying Danish Labour Market Insurance and insurers C, E and H provide information about the deadline. All the insurance providers also mention that the customer (i.e. the employer) must inform the insurer of any changes in the business. Insurer C goes further and states that the customer must inform the insurance provider of any change to the risk of the business, albeit that it does not go on to explain precisely what is meant by this.

Under the headings "*When and how do I pay*?", "*When does the cover start and end*?" and "*How do I cancel the contract*?", the insurance providers set out essentially the same conditions as those set in respect of the IPIDs produced for contents insurance (and third party liability motor insurance), as to which see Sect. 3.3.2.2 above for analysis.

3.4 Discussion

3.4.1 The Application of the Standardised Presentation Format in General

Common to the examined IPIDs is that all of them comply with the requirement that the information presented be restricted to the formal requirements as to the allowed two A4 pages. Moreover, each such IPID has been designed in accordance with EIOPA's standardised presentation format, cf. Articles 1, 3 and 4 of the Implementing Regulation.

As mentioned above, insurers D's and E's icon for "*How do I cancel the contract?*" is not as prescribed in Article 7(1)(h) of the Implementing Regulation. Moreover, insurer F's IPID for the workers' compensation insurance does not include the heading *"What is this type of insurance?"* as prescribed in Article 6(1)(a) of the Implementing Regulation (see also Article 20(8)(a) of the IDD).

Each IPID states at the top of the document that it only gives a general overview of the insurance product, which statement is in compliance with Article 2 of the Implementing Regulation, and the customer is referred to the underlying policy terms for the complete pre-contractual and contractual information.

The design of the IPIDs is, therefore, broadly comparable and the small deviations from the standardised format which could occur, and which do in practice occur, is, in the authors' view, not a significant problem that must be addressed.

3.4.2 The Heading "What Is This Type of Insurance?"

In summary, the information set out by the insurance providers to describe the type of insurance offered is characterised by significant differences in the level of detail provided. Some insurance providers describe only the basic (i.e. minimum statutory) cover very briefly, whereas others use several lines to explain the cover or to mention possible add-ons.

The result is that it is not clear that the insurance products on offer are, in fact, more or less identical. In particular, one would expect that at least the description of the compulsory insurances, i.e. third person motor liability insurance and workers' compensation insurance, would be (on the whole) identical, which is not the case.

3.4.3 The Headings "What Is Insured?", "What Is Not Insured?" and "Are There Any Restrictions on Cover?"

The sections about the cover provided by the various insurance products, and the exclusions and restrictions to which such cover is subject, are not dealt with in the same manner by the various insurance providers. This is especially clear when one looks at the IPIDs for non-compulsory contents insurance, which often make clear that one insurance provider might set out cover that the other providers do not. It seems to be more or less (from the customer's perspective) a matter of chance whether cover is mentioned or not.

Sometimes specific cover is not mentioned in the IPID even though it is actually covered by the insurance. In the context of contents insurance, such is the case in respect of insurers A, C and D, each of which do not mention that luggage is covered, even though, upon examination of the relevant underlying policy terms, it is apparent that it is. Elsewhere in the IPIDs, specific cover is not mentioned but such omission is consistent with the fact that cover is not actually provided by the insurance. This is the case, for example, in respect of insurer E, which does not mention, or indeed cover, identity theft. The same applies to exclusions. For example, insurer C is the only provider which mentions that windsurfers and kite surfers are not covered. An analysis of the other insurers' policy terms shows that windsurfers and kite surfers are covered by insurers B, D and E, but not by insurer A.

The scope for customer confusion is, in the authors' view, obvious. Customers cannot trust the IPIDs to provide an effective basis of general comparison or to provide much more than a very superficial indication of cover, exclusions and restrictions. As such, notwithstanding the fact that a customer might have access to a variety of IPIDs, such customer has to read other detailed documentation or the insurance provider's underlying policy terms to find out whether cover not explicitly mentioned in the IPID is or is not included in the product. In the authors' view, what is perhaps most worrying is not that customers have to undertake this arduous task, but that they might not even realise that they need to do so.

The problem is less severe in respect of the compulsory insurance products, which, in reality, also have more or less identical cover. However, there are examples of the same problem as has been observed with contents insurance. For example, in the context of third-party motor liability insurance, even though the cover offered by the various insurance providers in relation to injuries to the driver is essentially the same, the IPIDs do not give this impression. Instead, the providers often decide to set out information about their add-ons and to emphasise various exclusions.

The authors' analysis shows that insurance providers do not necessarily deal with the specific cover in the same way. The consequence is that where an insurance provider does not explicitly mention specific cover that another provider does, the customer cannot actually use the IPIDs as a basis of comparison, but instead has to read the providers' underlying policy terms in order to be able to make a comparison.

The analysis also shows that the insurance providers tend to emphasise elements that relate to their add-ons. Whereas some insurers clearly specify, by, for example, using sub-headings, if a particular element relates to the basic cover and if something relates to the add-ons (for example insurer D in respect of third person motor insurance), other insurers list elements without making it clear whether such elements relates to the basic cover, or the add-ons. The result is that the IPIDs are not an effective tool for making comparisons even in a pre-contractual phase.

The aforementioned tendency also applies to the information set out regarding restrictions. There seems to be some confusion amongst insurance providers about the information required to be provided in "*What is not insured?*" and in "*Are there any restrictions on cover?*". Some providers set out exclusions in "*What is not insured?*" whilst others set out the same exclusions in "*Are there any restrictions on cover?*" (see for example the contents insurance exclusions regarding lodgers). It could be argued that such a discrepancy does not actually affect the utility of the IPIDs as a basis of comparison, but, all other things being equal, it is not useful if the insurance providers and the customers must use a standardised document where it is possible to describe the same element under different headings, particularly where it would be relatively straightforward to solve the problem by specifying the information to be included in the IPID headings.

It appears from Articles 6(1)(e) and (f) of the Implementing Regulation that insurance providers must set out "*information on a summary of the excluded risks*" in the paragraph "*What is not insured?*", whereas the paragraph "*Are there any restrictions on cover?*" must include "*information on the main exclusions*".

There is no other guidance on the information to be included in the IPIDs. It was pointed out in connection with EIOPA's consultations regarding the presentation format that the distinction could be a problem.[27] At the time of the consultations, the sections were entitled "*Main risks not covered*" and "*Main restrictions and exclusions*".

In the authors' view, the concerns expressed are justified and it does not seem as if EIOPA changing the wording has fixed the problem. There is still an overlap between the sections and the insurance providers sometimes mention the same exclusion in two different sections.

3.4.4 The Heading "Where Am I Covered?"

The insurance products analysed by the authors all have essentially the same geographical area of cover. However, it is not always clear from the IPIDs that this is the case. Insurance providers adopt different approaches: some only mention the basis (in this case Denmark), but others also mention any restrictions that could be perceived as a geographical restriction. However, it might be more appropriate for such restrictions to be included under the headings "*What is not insured?*" or "*Are there any restrictions on cover?*" (for example, information about furniture and household effects in seasonal dwellings not being covered by contents insurance).

Further, the descriptions of the same geographical area of cover vary in such a way that it may not be completely clear to a customer what area the insurance actually covers. For example, customers who are not familiar the "*green card scheme*" would have to find out whether the geographical area "*Denmark and the countries that are part of the "green card scheme"*" is the same geographical area as "*Europe and countries that are part of the "green card scheme"*". The risk is, of course, that customer's will not bother to conduct such independent research but will simply make decisions (which may be ultimately deleterious) based on assumptions.

The same applies in respect of the workers' compensation insurance, where the area of cover is governed by statute and is, consequently, the identical across policies, but where the insurance providers adopt differing approaches to describing the same geographical area.

[27] The Belgian Insurance Association (Assuralia) stated that:

> [...] the information to be given in those sections could be (partially) dublicative as both sections are strongly interlinked, especially from a customer's point of view. In case EIOPA insists on maintaining both sections, more clarification has to be provided on the differences between the information to be presented.

3.4.5 The Headings "What Are My Obligations?", "When and How Do I Pay?", "When Does the Cover Start and End?" and "How Do I Cancel the Contract"

The headings "*What are my obligations?*", "*When and how do I pay?*", "*When does the cover start and end?*" and "*How do I cancel the contract?*", which contain practical information for the customer, are worded differently by the various insurance providers. However, such differences do not, on their face, undermine a customer's ability to use the IPIDs to perform an effective comparison of the products. For example, the fact that one insurance provider explicitly states that the customer must pay on time, whereas the other providers do not, is unlikely to give the customer the impression that some insurance providers do not expect a customer to pay on time. Accordingly, it is the authors' view that, in respect of these headings (reflecting Articles 6(1)(g), (h), (i) and (j) of the Implementing Regulation with reference to Article 20(8)(c), (e)–(i) of the IDD), the IPIDs can form a useful basis for comparison.

3.4.6 The Description of Add-Ons in the IPID

As set out in the preceding section, insurance providers often set out in their IPIDs the add-ons available to the cover offered, rather than focusing on the cover provided as standard. In its draft technical standards EIOPA stated that any customer personalisation should be done via the policy terms and conditions, not in the IPID.[28]

This could be interpreted to mean that any add-ons which go beyond the basic cover should not even be mentioned in the IPID. Indeed, concerns were expressed by the trade organisations in their responses to EIOPA's consultations regarding the possibility of including add-ons in the IPIDs.[29]

---

[28]Draft Implementing Technical Standards concerning a standardised presentation format for the Insurance Product Information Document of the Insurance Distribution Directive of 7 February 2017, EIOPA-17/056, page 4, section 6.

[29]For example, FSCP stated that:

> [...] The panel recommends EIOPA to require additional IPID's be made available to consumers when offered add on policies. This can be the case with legal insurance attached to home insurance for example. A single IPID will not capture all the terms and conditions of such separate policies and be misleading to consumers. As such, any separate policy should be subject to a separate IPID. (see Comments received by FSCP on EIOPA-CP-16-007: Consultation Paper on the proposal for the Implementing Technical Standards on a standardised presentation format of the Insurance Product Information Document (IPID) under the Insurance Distribution Directive (IDD), page 2).

See also Test Achats who expressed a similar point of view and stated that:

> [...] A single IPID on two pages of an A4 page becomes a misleading document if it has to summarize the key information of more than one cover of a multi-risk policy. (see Comments received by Test Achats on EIOPA-CP-16-007: Consultation Paper on the proposal

However, Recital 3 of the Implementing Regulation provides that:

> In order to provide customers with product information which is easy to read, understand and compare, a common design, structure and format should be used when presenting the information referred to in Article 20(8) of Directive (EU) 2016/97 in the standardised insurance product information document referred to in Article 20(5) of that Directive, including by way of the use of icons or symbols. Equally, information about add-ons and optional covers, if any, should not be preceded by ticks, crosses or exclamation marks [...] (emphasis added)

As such, it appears as if the Implementing Regulation expressly contemplates a description of possible add-ons in the IPIDs, even though the possibility of add-ons is not actually mentioned in Article 20(8) of the Directive and even though the most natural understanding—when one must apply the standardised format to all insurance products alike—of a specific insurance product's main features does not include whether or not it is possible to buy extended cover. Accordingly, one can conclude that the concerns expressed by the trade organisations were not taken fully into account.

The conclusion of the authors' analysis is that the description of any add-ons seems to cause significant confusion in practice. Such confusion arises because different insurance providers decide to include the description of possible add-ons under different headings and because the descriptions in some instances take up the same or more space than the description of the basic cover provided by the product.

For example, some insurers describe the add-ons in the paragraph "*What is insured?*" and others describe it in "*What is this type of insurance?*" or "*What is not insured?*". Even in a best-case scenario, i.e. where identical information is provided by different insurers but under different headings, it is yet another instance where confusion might undermine the effectiveness of the IPID as a tool for customers to make informed comparisons between insurance products, which, in turn, undermines the objective the rules were initially designed to achieve.

Furthermore, one might question why insurance providers decide to set out information about add-ons in the paragraph "*What is this type of insurance?*". Following to a literal interpretation of the heading, it is not relevant for the description of the type of insurance that the scope of cover of the insurance can be extended by add-ons. The authors have not interviewed any of the insurance providers or asked them questions about their selection of method in connection with this chapter. However, one explanation might be that some insurance providers want to appear more flexible and when providing information about add-ons. Another explanation might be that insurance providers want to distinguish their insurance product from those offered by other providers. The latter explanation is likely correct when it comes to insurance products where an insurance provider's basic cover is governed by statute, for example third person motor liability insurance and workers'

for the Implementing Technical Standards on a standardised presentation format of the Insurance Product Information Document (IPID) under the Insurance Distribution Directive (IDD), page 2).

compensation insurance. The authors fully acknowledge that the information about add-ons can be an important feature of the insurance product and can help give the customer an actual basis for choosing one insurance provider instead of another. However, when considering the purpose of the IDD and the IPID such considerations seems to come second to customer clarity regarding the basic features of an insurance product.

Another problem with setting out information on add-ons is that it is not always clear when the information about the cover, an exclusion from cover, or a restriction on cover is about the basic insurance offering and when it is a possible add-on. In this respect, there is, in the authors' view, clearly scope to improve the guidance given to insurance providers about not only the information to be included in the IPID, but also the best manner in which to present such information in order that customers actually get an IPID that provides a useful pre-contractual basis of comparison.

The authors wholeheartedly support the idea that insurance providers be afforded the opportunity to not only distinguish their insurance products from those products offered by competitors, but also to customise their insurance products so that the insurance offered matches the customer's demands and needs in the best way possible. However, the authors are also of the view that, based on the analysis carried out, that the IPID, in its current format and without any detailed guidance about how insurance providers should provide the required information, is not well-suited to contain a description of possible add-ons and extensions. In the opinion of the authors the possibility of the insurance providers to detail possible add-ons without this influencing on the clarity of the description of the basic features of an insurance product should be addressed.

3.4.7 The Use of Plain Language in the IPID

When analysing the IPIDs, the authors discovered a tendency for insurance providers to use legal terms such as "*gross negligence*", "*theft other than burglary*", "*intention*", and "*subrogation*". The authors also found references to the "*green card scheme*" in the description of the geographical area of cover of the compulsory third person liability insurance. The tendency to use legalistic language and somewhat technical terminology is, to a degree, understandable. However, the authors would query it might be considered that the IPIDs fail to comply with the requirement to use plain language and not any jargon, as to which see Article 5 of the Implementing Regulation.

It is certainly debatable whether any legalistic language is, on its face, plain language and, if not, whether it should be avoided. On the other hand, it could be argued that if insurance providers are not allowed to use ordinary legal terms such as "*gross negligence*", then they will have to explain what the term means. That would mean that the limited space available to insurance providers would be used for long explanations about what the legal terms mean. This is plainly inexpedient, in conflict with the object of the IPID to contain information about the main features of the insurance product, and not at all useful to customers.

Arguably, as long as there is consistency between the various legal terms used by insurance providers, the use of such terms would seemingly not be a problem when making a comparison between the IPIDs.

3.5 Summary and de lege ferenda

The authors' general conclusion following the analysis of the IPIDs is that insurance providers do, essentially, follow EIOPA's standardised presentation format. Visually, the IPIDs appear to be comparable and in accordance with the general objective of the rules.

However, the various IPIDs differ significantly when it comes to the information set out by insurance providers regarding the particular cover offered in the individual insurance products.

It is, in the authors' view, likely that the reason for such differences is that no rules or guidelines have been established for the information to be included in the IPID. The insurance providers themselves are thus able to decide on the information which they believe is relevant to the customer for each insurance product. As has been demonstrated by the analysis of the IPIDs, such decisions often differ, despite the fact that the insurance products and cover are, in most cases, all-but identical.

As discussed above, EIOPA's consultations emphasises that, in relation to technical standards, the objective of the IDD was to find a balance between providing the required flexibility to enable insurance providers to set out the relevant information, but at the same time ensuring that the IPIDs did not become a duplicate of the full insurance conditions. Several trade organisations stated during EIOPA's consultations that an IPID should only include the main features of a product, as a summary of several areas of cover in the same IPID would be an impossible task which would inevitably result in a misleading document (see for example the responses from Test Achats and FSCP). However, the concerns expressed by the trade organisations did not lead to any change in the format of the IPID and no guidelines for the information to be included in the IPID were issued.

The authors' analysis of the IPIDs demonstrates that the concerns expressed by the trade organisations were born out. In this regard, there are two main problems with the information provided in the IPIDs.

First, the cover, exclusions and restrictions that each insurance provider decides to emphasise in a particular IPID seems, from a customer perspective at least (one must assume the providers have their reasons) to be a matter of mere chance. The result is that customers cannot conclude from the fact that an insurance provider has not mentioned a specific type of cover, which is in fact mentioned by another issuer, that there is actually not a big difference, or even any difference at all, between the products. It means that, in most cases, the customer will have to make a comparison of the insurance products based on other detailed information or the underlying policy terms. That is, of course, assuming that the customer realises that they need to consult such detailed information. There is, in the authors view, the very real risk that the customer will simply make assumptions based on the IPID and may therefore be misled as to which product is best suited to their demands and needs.

Second, many insurance providers set out information relating to potential add-ons as well as the basic cover offered. The inclusion of information about potential add-ons means that the information in the IPID about the basic cover is necessarily more superficial (because, quite simply, there is not enough space). However, it also means that often it is not clear whether specific cover, a specific exclusion or a specific restriction relates to the basic cover or the add-ons.

The requirements as to the information to be provided in the IPIDs appears to be so flexible that, at least for the purposes of comparing near-identical products, they are almost inevitably unsuitable. There is no question that the IPIDs are suitable for comparing a product that has very broad cover with a product that has very restricted cover. However, if the products that the customer is looking for and wants to compare do not differ or only differ slightly, then the result of the aforementioned flexibility is that the IPIDs are not suitable for making an informed or useful comparison and do not fulfil the intended object of the IDD.

In reality, there is a risk that the current IPIDs give distorted information about what the insurance products actually cover and do not cover. This could confuse and mislead a customer when such customer is trying to use the IPIDs to make a comparison between products. It is also a poor outcome for the insurance providers, who have spent time and resources on an instrument which, at best, does not facilitate a useful comparison and, at worst, means that customers can be lost because, unlike one of its competitors, an insurance provider has decided not to mention specifically required (but optional) cover in its IPID. It also leaves the insurance providers in a grey area in which it is uncertain whether or not the provider meets the requirements laid down in Article 20 of the IDD. It should be noted in this regard that Article 33(3) of the IDD prescribes that, in the event of any breach of the rules on the conduct of business, including Article 20, Member States must ensure that, as a minimum, the competent authorities have the power to decide that the responsible natural or legal person must cease the conduct and refrain from repeating such conduct and to withdraw the registration of insurers subject to Article 3 (insurance intermediaries and others). Such drastic consequences illustrate the risks posed by insurance providers being left in a state of confusion regarding their regulatory obligations.

The question is: is it possible to transform the IPIDs into a more useful basis of comparison whilst, at the same time maintaining the current visual design and the manageable 2 A4 pages?

If IPIDs that can actually be used as an effective basis of comparison are to be drawn up, it is the authors' opinion that detailed guidelines for the information to be included in the IPIDs must be established and an industry-wide understanding of how particular terms are used must be in relevant insurance sectors.

In this connection, the authors note that EIOPA's draft implementation standard provided that the IPID must facilitate an easier understanding of an insurance product's main characteristics.[30] The problem is, of course, that it is up to the insurance providers themselves to define what such main characteristics are and the analysis set out above shows that the different providers adopt distinctly different approaches in determining what such main characteristics are.

One solution might be to set out the basic cover of the insurance product in question in the IPIDs in a tick-box list.[31] If, for example, the scope of cover was determined by national trade associations, this would at least mean that, all things being equal, all IPIDs for the same insurance product would include the same cover. As such, customers would be provided with a useful basis of comparison in respect of the most common areas of cover in a Member State, even though it would, arguably, be somewhat superficial.

The problem with such a solution is, arguably, that, in reality, a one-size-fits-all approach would make it very difficult for insurers to distinguish themselves from the others. It would be particularly difficult in respect of the compulsory insurance such as workers' compensation insurance where the cover is governed by statute (although one might also query whether it is of any value at all to have IPIDs for insurance products whose cover is dictated by law). Such difficulty in distinguishing insurance providers would, in turn, arguably make it more difficult for customers to actually make a decision as to which insurance provider to choose. Insurance providers and customers would be left with a situation in which an insurance provider who distinguishes themselves by having specific cover, would only be able to demonstrate this distinction if the specific cover was included in the list of boxes chosen by the national trade association.

Another proposal might be to draw up the IPIDs as proposed by the Dutch Association of Insurers (see Sect. 3.2). One consequence of such an approach would be that the format of the IPIDs would have to be designed specifically for each insurance product. For example, it means that the IPIDs for contents insurance and third person motor liability insurance would have two different formats. Those different formats would then be tailored appropriately to set out what cover is provided, what is excluded and whether something is, or is not, an add-on. For instance, a contents insurance IPID might contain a separate heading for luggage and insurance providers would then be able to specify whether or not luggage is covered.

---

[30]Draft Implementing Technical Standards concerning a standardised presentation format for the Insurance Product Information Document of the Insurance Distribution Directive of 7 February 2017, EIOPA-17/056, page 22.

[31]During the preparatory work for the IDD it was emphasised by the European Conservatives and Reformists (ECR), among others, that it was seen as a positive thing that the Directive was flexible instead of stipulating one-size-fits-all conditions. The ECR also stated that it applauded that the Directive gave the insurers room to make sure that customers got the best outcome instead of using tick-box-style exercises (see Ashley Fox on behalf of the ECR Group in the debate on 24 November 2015 in Strasbourg, CRE 24/11/2015-4 concerning A8-0315/2015; Supplementary report on the proposal for a directive of the European Parliament and of the Council on insurance mediation (recast), COM(2012)0360). A proposal to regulate at EU level will hardly be applauded by the ECR.

Notwithstanding these potential advantages, however, the uniform format of the IPID does have a number of advantages which would, of course, be lost.

None of the proposals mentioned above require that significantly more information would have to be provided than that which is set out in the current IPIDs. As such, a customer demanding more unusual cover, for example for windsurfing and kitesurfing, would consequently still have to read the insurance providers' underlying policy terms in order to get a proper basis for comparing products. The proposed solutions would also result in the risk that the insurance providers offering very complex insurance or package deals would not have sufficient flexibility to show what they are actually offering. However, that may not be a bad thing; after all, given that the IPID's are targeted at consumers, one must endeavour to achieve the objective of keeping the IPIDs simple and customer friendly.

A less intrusive proposal is that EIOPA provides some guidelines that determine the information that is most obvious to include under the various key headings, e.g. "*What is insured?*", "*What is not insured?*" and "*Are there any restrictions on cover?*". As for the IPIDs analysed by the authors, the consequence for the insurance providers would be that the flexibility to adopt differing approaches to the information they set out in the IPID would be maintained (albeit slightly curtailed), but the consequence for the customers would be that it will be easier to compare the IPIDs and make informed decisions. All other things being equal, it would, in the authors' opinion, be particularly advisable for national bodies to issue guidelines for uniform descriptions of insurance where the scope of cover of such insurance is prescribed by law.

It is, of course, difficult to determine where the balance as to what information should or should not be included in the IPIDs should lie. However, the confusion surrounding the specification of add-ons seems to be relatively easy to clear up. One solution might be to add in a heading which deals solely with add-ons to the IPID in its current format. The risk is that it would result in the same problems as the other area of cover if it is left to the insurance providers themselves to decide what add-ons to include under such a heading. However, it would solve the current problem whereby insurance providers inconsistently include add-ons in either "*What is insured?*", "*What is this type of insurance?*" or in "*What is not insured?*". Alternatively, EIOPA could provide guidance on where the description of add-ons belongs most naturally in the IPID and how to inform the customer that the information relates to possible add-ons rather than the basic scope of coverage.

4 Conclusion

The objective of this chapter has been to examine whether the rules on the IPIDs mandated by Article 20(1) of the IDD satisfy the objective of increasing customer protection in connection with the sale of insurance products.

An examination of selected IPIDs has demonstrated a discrepancy between the coverage that the insurers choose to emphasize in their IPID for a specific insurance product. Such discrepancies occur notwithstanding the fact that the products in question often have all-but identical coverage (regardless of which insurance provider is offering the product). It seems reasonable to assume that the discrepancy is due to the lack of guidelines and rules given for the completion of the IPIDs, which in turn means that the insurance providers are, to an extent, groping in the dark when they determine what information is relevant in order to allow a prospective customer to conduct a useful comparison. Consequently, the IPIDs are not, in reality, comparable and customers are thus not able to make an informed decision based on an examination of the same. Moreover, the insurance providers spend time and resources on an instrument which does not fulfil its intended purpose. In order for the IPIDs to meet their objective, it is the authors' considered opinion that it is necessary to establish how the insurers can most effectively complete them and provide guidelines in respect of the same.

In summary, the rules on IPIDs do not seem to have resulted in increased customer protection to a significant extent, or indeed to an extent which corresponds to the amount of extra work the insurance providers have to carry out in order to attempt to comply with the rules. In the authors' view, however, this, is more due to the lack of guidance regarding completion of the IPIDs than it is due to problems with the rules on IPIDs themselves. As such, as things stand, the insurance providers do not seem to have any basis for acting other than the way in which they do. In the authors' opinion, it would be sensible to consider providing guidance on the rules on IPIDs when the review of the Directive takes place in 2021.

Danish Legislation

Danish Consolidated Act no 1324 of 21 November 2018, the Road Traffic Act (in Danish: færdselsloven)

Danish Consolidated Act no 216 of 27 February 2017, Workers' Compensation Act (in Danish: arbejdsskadesikringsloven)

EU Legislation

Directive 2002/92/EC of the European Parliament and of the Council of 9 December 2002 on insurance mediation

Directive (EU) 2016/97 of the European Parliament and of the Council of 20 January 2016 on insurance distribution (recast)

Directive (EU) 2018/411 of the European Parliament and of the Council of 14 March 2018 amending Directive (EU) 2016/97 as regards the date of application of the Member States' transposition measures

EU Preparatory Work

Ashley Fox on behalf of the ECR Group in the debate on 24 November 2015 in Strasbourg, CRE 24/11/2015-4 concerning A8-0315/2015; Supplementary report on the proposal for a directive of the European Parliament and of the Council on insurance mediation (recast), COM(2012)0360)

Comments received by Assuralia to EIOPA-CP-16-007: Consultation Paper on the proposal for the Implementing Technical Standards on a standardised presentation format of the Insurance Product Information Document (IPID) under the Insurance Distribution Directive (IDD)

Comments received by Danish Insurance Association to EIOPA-CP-16-007: Consultation Paper on the proposal for the Implementing Technical Standards on a standardised presentation format of the Insurance Product Information Document (IPID) under the Insurance Distribution Directive (IDD)

Comments received by the Dutch Association of Insurers to EIOPA-CP-16-007: Consultation Paper on the proposal for the Implementing Technical Standards on a standardised presentation format of the Insurance Product Information Document (IPID) under the Insurance Distribution Directive (IDD)

Comments received by Eurofinas to EIOPA-CP-16-007: Consultation Paper on the proposal for the Implementing Technical Standards on a standardised presentation format of the Insurance Product Information Document (IPID) under the Insurance Distribution Directive (IDD)

Comments received by FSCP to EIOPA-CP-16-007: Consultation Paper on the proposal for the Implementing Technical Standards on a standardised presentation format of the Insurance Product Information Document (IPID) under the Insurance Distribution Directive (IDD)

Comments received by Test Achats to EIOPA-CP-16-007: Consultation Paper on the proposal for the Implementing Technical Standards on a standardised presentation format of the Insurance Product Information Document (IPID) under the Insurance Distribution Directive (IDD)

Commission Implementing Regulation (EU) 2017/1469 of 11 August 2017 laying down a standardised presentation format for the insurance product information document

Commission Staff Working Document Executive Summary of the Impact Assessment accompanying the document Proposal for a Directive of the European Parliament and of the Council on Insurance Mediation, SWD/2012/0192 final

Draft Implementing Technical Standards concerning a standardised presentation format for the Insurance Product Information Document of the Insurance Distribution Directive of 7 February 2017, EIOPA-17/056

Opinion of the Internal Market and Consumer Protection (30.4.2013) on the proposal for a directive of the European Parliament and of the Council on insurance mediation (recast) (COM(2012)0360 – C7-0180/2012 – 2012/0175(COD)), A7-0085/2014

Proposal for a Directive of the European Parliament and of the Council on Insurance Mediation (recast), COM/2012/0360 final - 2012/0175 (COD)
Supplementary Report of the Committee on Economic and Monetary Affairs on the proposal for a directive of the European Parliament and of the Council on insurance mediation (recast) (COM(2012)0360 – C7-0180/2012 – 2012/0175 (COD)), A8-0315/2015

Correction to: The IDD and Its Impact on the Life Insurance Industry

Kyriaki Noussia

Correction to: Chapter 4 in: P. Marano, K. Noussia (eds.), *Insurance Distribution Directive*, AIDA Europe Research Series on Insurance Law and Regulation 3, https://doi.org/10.1007/978-3-030-52738-9_4

The author unintentionally referred to parts of the chapter "Enaction of Chapter VII of the Insurance Distribution Directive: What Can Member States Learn from the Enforcement Failures of the United States?" by Kathleen M. Defever in this book without proper citation. These inaccurate identifications have been corrected in the chapter.

The updated online version of this chapter can be found at
https://doi.org/10.1007/978-3-030-52738-9_4

P. Marano, K. Noussia (eds.), *Insurance Distribution Directive*, AIDA Europe Research Series on Insurance Law and Regulation 3,
https://doi.org/10.1007/978-3-030-52738-9_17

The manufacturer's authorised representative in the EU is Springer Nature Customer Service Centre GmbH, Europaplatz 3, 69115 Heidelberg, Germany. If you have any concerns regarding our products, please contact ProductSafety@springernature.com

Printed and bound by CPI Group (UK) Ltd, Croydon, CR0 4YY
23/09/2026
02221532-0006